T0137283

IFIP Advances in Information and Communication Technology 646

Editor-in-Chief

Kai Rannenberg, Goethe University Frankfurt, Germany

Editorial Board Members

IFIP – The International Federation for Information Processing

IFIP was founded in 1960 under the auspices of UNESCO, following the first World Computer Congress held in Paris the previous year. A federation for societies working in information processing, IFIP's aim is two-fold: to support information processing in the countries of its members and to encourage technology transfer to developing nations. As its mission statement clearly states:

IFIP is the global non-profit federation of societies of ICT professionals that aims at achieving a worldwide professional and socially responsible development and application of information and communication technologies.

IFIP is a non-profit-making organization, run almost solely by 2500 volunteers. It operates through a number of technical committees and working groups, which organize events and publications. IFIP's events range from large international open conferences to working conferences and local seminars.

The flagship event is the IFIP World Computer Congress, at which both invited and contributed papers are presented. Contributed papers are rigorously refereed and the rejection rate is high.

As with the Congress, participation in the open conferences is open to all and papers may be invited or submitted. Again, submitted papers are stringently refereed.

The working conferences are structured differently. They are usually run by a working group and attendance is generally smaller and occasionally by invitation only. Their purpose is to create an atmosphere conducive to innovation and development. Refereeing is also rigorous and papers are subjected to extensive group discussion.

Publications arising from IFIP events vary. The papers presented at the IFIP World Computer Congress and at open conferences are published as conference proceedings, while the results of the working conferences are often published as collections of selected and edited papers.

IFIP distinguishes three types of institutional membership: Country Representative Members, Members at Large, and Associate Members. The type of organization that can apply for membership is a wide variety and includes national or international societies of individual computer scientists/ICT professionals, associations or federations of such societies, government institutions/government related organizations, national or international research institutes or consortia, universities, academies of sciences, companies, national or international associations or federations of companies.

More information about this series at https://link.springer.com/bookseries/6102

Ilias Maglogiannis · Lazaros Iliadis ·
John Macintyre · Paulo Cortez (Eds.)

Artificial Intelligence Applications and Innovations

18th IFIP WG 12.5 International Conference, AIAI 2022
Hersonissos, Crete, Greece, June 17–20, 2022
Proceedings, Part I

 Springer

Editors
Ilias Maglogiannis
University of Piraeus
Piraeus, Greece

Lazaros Iliadis
Democritus University of Thrace
Xanthi, Greece

John Macintyre
University of Sunderland
Sunderland, UK

Paulo Cortez
Universidade do Minho
Guimaraes, Portugal

ISSN 1868-4238   ISSN 1868-422X (electronic)
IFIP Advances in Information and Communication Technology
ISBN 978-3-031-08335-8   ISBN 978-3-031-08333-4 (eBook)
https://doi.org/10.1007/978-3-031-08333-4

This Springer imprint is published by the registered company Springer Nature Switzerland AG
The registered company address is: Gewerbestrasse 11, 6330 Cham, Switzerland

Preface

Artificial intelligence (AI) is a relatively new scientific area that emerged from the efforts of a handful of scientists from diverse fields approximately 70 years ago. The achievements of AI in the era of the 4th Industrial Revolution are amazing and the expectations are continuously rising. Today AI applications are found in almost all areas of human activities. Healthcare, finance, industry, security, robotics, molecular biology, and autonomous vehicles are only a small sample of the domains that have been influenced by artificial intelligence. However, serious ethical matters have emerged (e.g., privacy, surveillance, bias-discrimination, elimination of entire job categories) requiring corrective legislative actions.

The 18th International Conference on Artificial Intelligence Applications and Innovations (AIAI 2022) offered insight into all timely challenges related to technical, legal, and ethical aspects of intelligent systems and their applications. New algorithms and potential prototypes employed in diverse domains were also introduced.

AIAI is a mature international scientific conference that has been held all over the world and it is well established in the scientific area of AI. Its history is long and very successful, following and propagating the evolution of intelligent systems.

The first event was organized in Toulouse, France, in 2004. Since then, it has had a continuous and dynamic presence as a major global, but mainly European, scientific event. More specifically, it has been organized in China, Greece, Cyprus, Australia, and France. It has always been technically supported by the International Federation for Information Processing (IFIP) and more specifically by the Working Group 12.5, which is interested in AI applications.

Following a long-standing tradition, this Springer volume belongs to the IFIP AICT series and it contains the papers that were accepted to be presented orally at the AIAI 2022 conference. An additional volume collates the papers that were accepted and presented at the workshops which were held as parallel events. The event was collocated with the 23rd International Conference on Engineering Applications of Neural Networks (EANN 2022) and held during June 17–20, 2022, in Crete, Greece. The diverse nature of papers presented demonstrates the vitality of AI algorithms and approaches. It certainly proves the very wide range of AI applications as well.

The response of the international scientific community to the AIAI 2022 call for papers was more than satisfactory, with 158 papers initially submitted. All papers were peer reviewed by at least two independent academic referees. Where needed, a third referee was consulted to resolve any potential conflicts. A total of 72 papers (45.5%) of the submitted manuscripts were accepted to be published as full papers (12 pages long) in the proceedings. Owing to the high quality of the submissions, the Program Committee also decided to accept 11 manuscripts as short papers (10 pages long). The accepted papers cover the following thematic topics and application areas:

- Adaptive Modeling
- Adversarial Neural Networks

- AI and Energy Modeling
- Anomaly Detection Modeling and AI
- Autonomous Shuttles Modeling and AI
- Classification
- Cloud Data Modeling and AI
- Clustering
- Convolutional Neural Networks
- Cybersecurity and AI
- Deep Learning in Medical Applications
- Deep Learning and Fraud Detection
- Deep Learning Models for Face Mask Detection
- Environmental AI Modeling
- Evolutionary and Genetic Algorithms
- Explainable AI
- Feature Selection
- Financial Applications of AI
- Fuzzy Modeling
- Graph Representation of AI Models
- Intrusion Detection Using AI
- IoT
- Industry 4.0
- Learning
- Machine Learning
- Medical AI Modeling
- Metaheuristics
- Molecular Biology AI Modeling
- Natural Language
- Neural Networks Modeling
- Object Detection-Tracking and AI
- Pruning and AI
- Recommendation Systems
- Recurrent Modeling of the Primary Visual Cortex
- Reinforcement Models for Cryptocurrency
- Sentiment Analysis
- Speech and Emotion Recognition
- Text Mining and AI
- Timeseries AI Modeling
- Trading
- Transfer Learning Modeling
- Unsupervised Modeling

The authors of the accepted papers are based in 28 different countries all over the globe, namely, Austria, Brazil, Cyprus, the Czech Republic, Denmark, France, Germany, Greece, Hungary, India, Ireland, Italy, Japan, Lebanon, the Netherlands, Norway, China, Pakistan, Poland, Portugal, South Africa, Saudi Arabia, Serbia, Singapore, Spain, Turkey, the UK, and the USA.

The following seven scientific workshops on timely AI subjects were organized under the framework of AIAI 2022.

- The 11th Mining Humanistic Data Workshop (MHDW 2022)

MHDW 2022 was organized by the University of Patras and the Ionian University, Greece. It aimed to bring together interdisciplinary approaches that focus on the application of innovative as well as existing artificial intelligence, data matching, fusion and mining, and knowledge discovery and management techniques to data derived from all areas of humanistic sciences.

- The 7th Workshop on 5G-Putting Intelligence to the Network Edge (5G-PINE 2022)

The 7th 5G-PINE workshop was organized by the research team of the Hellenic Telecommunications Organization (OTE) in cooperation with many major partner companies. The 5G-PINE workshop was established to disseminate knowledge obtained from ongoing EU projects, as well as from any other action of EU-funded research, in the wider thematic area of "5G Innovative Activities – Putting Intelligence to the Network Edge" and with the aim of focusing on artificial intelligence in modern 5G telecommunications infrastructures. This is achieved by emphasizing results, methodologies, trials, concepts and/or findings originating from technical reports/deliverables, related pilot actions, and/or any other relevant 5G-based applications intending to enhance intelligence to the network edges.

- The 2nd Workshop on Artificial Intelligence and Ethics (AIETH 2022)

The 2nd AIETH workshop was coordinated and organized by John Macintyre (University of Sunderland, UK). It aimed to emphasize the need for responsible global AI. The respective scientific community must be preparing to act preemptively and ensure that our societies will avoid negative effects of AI and of the 4th Industrial Revolution in general. This workshop offered an extensive discussion on potential major ethical issues that might arise in the near future.

- The 2nd Workshop on Defense Applications of AI (DAAI 2022)

The 2nd DAAI workshop was organized by the European Defense Agency (EDA), a European Union (EU) organization. Defense and security systems are becoming more and more complicated and at the same time equipped with a plethora of sensing devices which collect an enormous amount of information both from their operating environment as well as from their own functioning. Considering the accelerating technology advancements of AI, it is likely that it will have a profound impact on practically every segment of daily life, from the labor market to business and service provision. The security and defense sectors will not remain idle or unaffected by this technological evolution. On the contrary, AI is expected to transform the nature of future defense and security domains, because by definition defense and security forces are highly dependent on (accurate) data and (reliable) information. DAAI 2022 aimed at presenting recent evolutions in artificial intelligence applicable to defense and security applications.

- The 1st Workshop on AI in Energy, Buildings and Micro-Grids (AIBMG 2022)

This workshop was organized by Center for Research and Technology (CERTH), Greece. Sustainable energy is hands down one of the biggest challenges of our times. As the EU sets its focus on reaching its 2030 and 2050 goals, the role of artificial intelligence in the energy domain at the building, district, and micro-grid level becomes more prevalent. The EU and member states are increasingly highlighting the need to complement IoT capacity (e.g., appliances and meters) with artificial intelligence capabilities (e.g., building management systems, proactive optimization, prescriptive maintenance). Moreover, moving away from the centralized production schema of the grid, novel approaches are needed not just for reducing energy consumption but also for the optimal management and/or balancing of local (or remote aggregated net metering) generation and consumptions.

The aim of the AIBMG workshop was to bring together interdisciplinary approaches that focus on the application of AI-driven solutions for increasing and improving energy efficiency of residential and tertiary buildings without compromising the occupants' well-being. Applied directly at either the device, building, or district management system level, the proposed solutions should enable more energy efficient and sustainable operation of devices, buildings, districts, and micro-grids. The workshop also welcomed cross-domain approaches that investigate how to support energy efficiency by exploiting decentralized, proactive, plug-n-play solutions.

- The 2nd Workshop on Artificial Intelligence in Biomedical Engineering and Informatics (AIBEI 2022)

Artificial intelligence (AI) is gradually changing the routine of medical practice, and the level of acceptance by medical personnel is constantly increasing. Recent progress in digital medical data acquisition through advanced biosignal and medical imaging devices, machine learning, and high-performance cloud computing infrastructures push health-related AI applications into areas that were previously thought to be only the province of human experts. Such applications employ a variety of methodologies, including fuzzy logic, evolutionary computing, neural networks, or deep learning, for producing AI-powered models that simulate human physiology.

- The 1st Workshop/Special Session on Machine Learning and Big Data in Health Care (ML@HC 2022)

In the present era, machine learning (ML) has been extensively used for many applications to real-world problems. ML techniques are very suitable for big data mining, to extract new knowledge and build predictive models that, given a new input, can provide in the output a reliable estimate. On the other hand, healthcare is one of the fastest growing data segments of the digital world, with healthcare data increasing at a rate of about 50% per year. There are three primary sources of big data in healthcare: providers and payers (including EMR, imaging, insurance claims, and pharmacy data), -omic data (including genomic, epigenomic, proteomic, and metabolomic data), and patients and non-providers (including data from smart phone and Internet activities, sensors, and monitoring tools).

The growth of big data in oncology, as well as other severe diseases (such as Alzheimer's Disease) can provide unprecedented opportunities to explore the biopsychosocial characteristics of these diseases and for descriptive observation, hypothesis generation, and prediction for clinical, research and business issues. The results of big data analyses can be incorporated into standards and guidelines and will directly impact clinical decision making. Oncologists and professionals from related medical fields can increasingly evaluate the results from research studies and commercial analytical products that are based on big data, based on ML techniques. Furthermore, all these applications can be Web-based, so are very useful for the post-treatment of the patients.

The aim of this workshop/special session was to serve as an interdisciplinary forum for bringing together specialists from the scientific areas of computer and web engineering, data science, semantic computing, and bioinformatics-personalized medicine, along with clinicians and caregivers. The focus of this special session was on current technological advances and challenges regarding the development of big data-driven algorithms, methods, and tools; furthermore, it sought to investigate how ML-aware applications can contribute towards big data analysis on post-treatment follow up.

In addition to the paper presentations and workshops, five invited speakers gave keynotes on timely aspects or state-of-the-art applications of artificial intelligence. The keynote presentations were held jointly with EANN 2022. Hojjat Adeli from Ohio State University, USA, gave a speech on "Machine Learning: A Key Ubiquitous Technology in the 21st Century". Riitta Salmelin from Aalto University, Finland, addressed "What neuroimaging can tell about human brain function". Elisabeth André from the University of Augsburg, Germany, discussed "Socially Interactive Artificial Intelligence: Perception, Synthesis and Learning of Human-like Behaviors". Verena Rieser from Heriot-Watt University, UK, gave a speech on the subject of "Responsible Conversational AI: Trusted, Safe and Bias-free" and John Macintyre from the University of Sunderland, UK, addressed the wider AI and ethics area in his talk "Is Big Tech Becoming the Big Tobacco of AI?".

On behalf of the organizers, we would like to thank everyone involved in AIAI 2022, and we hope that you find the proceedings interesting and insightful.

June 2022

Ilias Maglogiannis
Lazaros Iliadis
John Macintyre
Paulo Cortez

Organization

Executive Committee

General Co-chairs

Ilias Maglogiannis	University of Piraeus, Greece
John Macintyre	University of Sunderland, UK

Program Co-chairs

Lazaros Iliadis	Democritus University of Thrace, Greece
Konstantinos Votis	Information Technologies Institute, Greece
Vangelis Metsis	Texas State University, USA

Steering Committee

Ilias Maglogiannis	University of Piraeus, Greece
Lazaros Iliadis	Democritus University of Thrace, Greece

Advisory Co-chairs

Panagiotis Papapetrou	Stockholm University, Sweden
Paulo Cortez	University of Minho, Portugal

Publication and Publicity Co-chairs

Antonios Papaleonidas	Democritus University of Thrace, Greece
Anastasios Panagiotis Psathas	Democritus University of Thrace, Greece

Liaison Chair

Ioannis Chochliouros	Hellenic Telecommunication Organization (OTE), Greece

Doctoral Consortium Chairs

Antonios Papaleonidas	Democritus University of Thrace, Greece
Harris Papadopoulos	Frederick University, Cyprus

Workshops Co-chairs

Panagiotis Kikiras	European Defense Agency, Belgium
Phivos Mylonas	Ionian Univesity, Greece
Katia Kermanidis	Ionian University, Greece

Special Sessions and Tutorials Co-chairs

Spyros Sioutas   University of Patras, Greece
Christos Makris   University of Patras, Greece

Program Committee

Aiello Salvatore   Politecnico di Torino, Italy
Aldanondo Michel   IMT Mines Albi, France
Alexandridis Georgios   University of the Aegean, Greece
Alexiou Athanasios   Novel Global Community Educational Foundation,
                                    Australia
Aloisio Angelo   University of L'Aquila, Italy
Alonso Serafin   University of León, Spain
Amato Domenico   University of Palermo, Italy
Anagnostopoulos   University of the Aegean, Greece
  Christos-Nikolaos
Badica Costin   University of Craiova, Romania
Bezas Napoleon   Centre for Research and Technology Hellas, Greece
Bobrowski Leon   Bialystok University of Technology, Poland
Bozanis Panayiotis   International Hellenic University, Greece
C. Sousa Joana   NOS Inovação SA, Portugal
Campos Souza Paulo Vitor   Federal Center for Technological Education of Minas
                                    Gerais, Brazil
Caridakis George   National Technical University of Athens, Greece
Cavique Luis   University of Aberta, Portugal
Chamodrakas Ioannis   National and Kapodistrian University of Athens,
                                    Greece
Chochliouros Ioannis   Hellenic Telecommunications Organization S.A.
                                    (OTE), Greece
Delibasis Konstantinos   University of Thessaly, Greece
Demertzis Konstantinos   Democritus University of Thrace, Greece
Dimara Asimina   Centre for Research and Technology Hellas, Greece
Diou Christos Harokopio   University of Athens, Greece
Dominguez Manuel   University of Leon, Spain
Drakopoulos Georgios   Ionian University, Greece
Drousiotis Efthyvoulos   University of Liverpool, UK
Ferreira Luis   Polytechnic of Porto, Portugal
Fiannaca Antonino   National Research Council, Italy
Frittoli Luca   Politecnico di Milano, Italy
Fuertes Juan J.   University of León, Spain
Gaggero Mauro   National Research Council, Italy
Georgopoulos Efstratios   University of Peloponnese, Greece
Giancarlo Raffaele   University of Palermo, Italy
Giarelis Nikolaos   University of Patras, Greece
Giunchiglia Eleonora   University of Oxford, UK

Gonzalez-Deleito Nicolas	Sirris, Belgium
Grivokostopoulou Foteini	University of Patras, Greece
Hága Péter	Ericsson Research, Hungary
Hajek Petr	University of Pardubice, Czech Republic
Haralabopoulos Giannis	University of Nottingham, UK
Hatzilygeroudis Ioannis	University of Patras, Greece
Hichri Bassem	GCL International, Luxembourg
Hristoskova Anna	Sirris, Belgium
Humm Bernhard	Darmstadt University of Applied Sciences, Germany
Iakovidis Dimitris	University of Thessaly, Greece
Iliadis Lazaros	Democritus University of Thrace, Greece
Ishii Naohiro	Aichi Institute of Technology, Japan
Islam Shareeful	University of East London, UK
Ivanovic Mirjana	University of Novi Sad, Serbia
Jeannin-Girardon Anne	University of Strasbourg, France
Kalamaras Ilias	Centre for Research and Technology Hellas/Information Technologies Institute, Greece
Kallipolitis Athanasios	University of Piraeus, Greece
Kanakaris Nikos	University of Patras, Greece
Kanavos Andreas	University of Patras, Greece
Kapetanakis Stelios	University of Brighton, UK
Karacapilidis Nikos	University of Patras, Greece
Karatzas Kostas	Aristotle University of Thessaloniki, Greece
Karpouzis Kostas	National and Kapodistrian University of Athens, Greece
Kassandros Theodosios	Aristotle University of Thessaloniki, Greece
Kefalas Petros	CITY College, Greece
Kermanidis Katia Lida	Ionian University, Greece
Kokkinos Yiannis	University of Macedonia, Greece
Kollia Ilianna	IBM/National Technical University of Athens, Greece
Kontos Yiannis	Aristotle University of Thessaloniki, Greece
Koprinkova-Hristova Petia	Bulgarian Academy of Sciences, Bulgaria
Korkas Christos	Democritus University of Thrace/Centre for Research and Technology, Greece
Kosmopoulos Dimitrios	University of Patras, Greece
Kotis Konstantinos	University of the Aegean, Greece
Kotsiantis Sotiris	University of Patras, Greece
Koukaras Paraskevas	Centre for Research and Technology Hellas, Greece
Koussouris Sotiris	Suite5 Data Intelligence Solutions Ltd., Cyprus
Koutras Athanasios	University of Peloponnese, Greece
Krejcar Ondrej	University of Hradec Kralove, Czech Republic
Krinidis Stelios	Centre for Research and Technology Hellas, Greece
Kyriakides George	University of Macedonia, Greece
La Rosa Massimo	National Research Council, Italy
Lalas Antonios	Centre for Research and Technology Hellas/Information Technologies Institute, Greece

Lazaridis Georgios	Centre for Research and Technology Hellas/Information Technologies Institute, Greece
Lazic Ljubomir	UNION University, Serbia
Lederman Dror	Holon Institute of Technology, Israel
Leon Florin	Technical University of Iasi, Romania
Likas Aristidis	University of Ioannina, Greece
Likothanassis Spiros	University of Patras, Greece
Livieris Ioannis	University of Patras, Greece
Lo Bosco Giosuè	University of Palermo, Italy
Logofatu Doina	Frankfurt University of Applied Sciences, Germany
Longo Luca	Technological University of Dublin, Ireland
Maghool Samira	University of Milan, Italy
Maglogiannis Ilias	University of Piraeus, Greece
Magoulas George	University of London, Birkbeck College, UK
Magri Luca	Politecnico di Milano, Italy
Makris Christos	University of Patras, Greece
Malialis Kleanthis	University of Cyprus, Cyprus
Maragoudakis Manolis	Ionian University, Greece
Marano Giuseppe Carlo	Politecnico di Torino, Italy
Margaritis Konstantinos	University of Macedonia, Greece
Martins Nuno	NOS Inovação SA, Portugal
Melnik Andrew	Bielefeld University, Germany
Menychtas Andreas	University of Piraeus, Greece
Mezaris Vasileios	Centre for Research and Technology Hellas, Greece
Michailidis Iakovos	Centre for Research and Technology Hellas, Greece
Mitianoudis Nikolaos	Democritus University of Thrace, Greece
Morán Antonio	University of León, Spain
Moutselos Konstantinos	University of Piraeus, Greece
Muhr David	Johannes Kepler University Linz, Austria
Müller Wilmuth	Fraunhofer IOSB, Germany
Munk Michal	Constantine the Philosopher University in Nitra, Slovakia
Mylonas Phivos	National Technical University of Athens, Greece
Nikiforos Stefanos	Ionian University, Greece
Ntalampiras Stavros	University of Milan, Italy
Oprea Mihaela	Petroleum-Gas University of Ploiesti, Romania
Papadopoulos Symeon	Centre for Research and Technology Hellas/Information Technologies Institute, Greece
Papadourakis Giorgos	Hellenic Mediterranean University, Greece
Papaioannou Vaios	University of Patras, Greece
Papaleonidas Antonios	Democritus University of Thrace, Greece
Papastergiopoulos Christoforos	Centre for Research and Technology Hellas/Information Technologies Institute, Greece
Papatheodoulou Dimitris	KIOS Research and Innovation Center of Excellence, Cyprus
Passalis Nikolaos	Aristotle University of Thessaloniki, Greece

Paulus Jan	Nuremberg Institute of Technology, Germany
Pérez Daniel	University of León, Spain
Perikos Isidoros	University of Patras, Greece
Pimenidis Elias	University of the West of England, UK
Pintelas Panagiotis	University of Patras, Greece
Prada Miguel Ángel	Universidad de León, Spain
Pradat-Peyre Jean-François	Paris Nanterre University and LIP6, France
Psathas Anastasios	Panagiotis Democritus University of Thrace, Greece
Racz Andras	Ericsson Research, Hungary
Rankovic Dragica	UNION University, Serbia
Reitmann Stefan	TU Bergakademie Freiberg, Germany
Rosso Marco Martino	Politecnico di Torino, Italy
Ryjov Alexander Lomonosov	Moscow State University, Russia
Sarafidis Michail	National Technical University of Athens, Greece
Scheele Stephan	Fraunhofer IIS/University of Bamberg, Germany
Scherrer Alexander	Fraunhofer ITWM, Germany
Seferis Manos	National Technical University of Athens, Greece
Serrano Will	University College London, UK
Shi Lei	Durham University, UK
Siccardi Stefano	University of Milan, Italy
Spyrou Evaggelos	Technological Educational Institute of Sterea Ellada, Greece
Staiano Antonino	University of Naples Parthenope, Italy
Stamate Daniel	Goldsmiths, University of London, UK
Stefanopoulou Aliki	Centre for Research and Technology Hellas, Greece
Stucchi Diego	Politecnico di Milano, Italy
Stylianou Nikolaos	Aristotle University of Thessaloniki, Greece
Theocharides Theo	University of Cyprus, Cyprus
Theodoridis Georgios	Aristotle University of Thessaloniki, Greece
Timplalexis Christos	Centre for Research and Technology Hellas/Information Technologies Institute, Greece
Trakadas Panagiotis	National and Kapodistrian University of Athens, Greece
Treur Jan	VU Amsterdam, The Netherlands
Trovò Francesco	Politecnico di Milano, Italy
Tsadiras Athanasios	Aristotle University of Thessaloniki, Greece
Tsaknakis Christos	Democritus University of Thrace, Greece
Van-Horenbeke Franz Alexander	Free University of Bozen-Bolzano, Italy
Versaci Mario	University of Reggio Calabria, Italy
Vidnerová Petra	Czech Academy of Sciences, Czech Republic
Vilone Giulia	Technological University Dublin, Ireland
Vonitsanos Gerasimos	Ionian University, Greece
Votis Kostas	Centre for Research and Technology Hellas, Greece

Abstracts of Invited Talks

What Neuroimaging Can Tell About Human Brain Function

Riitta Salmelin

Department of Neuroscience and Biomedical Engineering Aalto University,
Finland
riitta.salmelin@aalto.fi

Abstract. Over the past few decades, real-time tracking of cortical current flow (magneto/electroencephalography, MEG/EEG) and accurate localization of blood oxygenation changes (functional magnetic resonance imaging, fMRI) have offered windows to the functional architecture of the human brain. The neuroimaging domain has reached its first level of maturity: we now know how to measure and quantify different types of signals and, phenomenologically, we know what type of group-level functional effects to expect in a large variety of experimental conditions. Specific brain areas, networks and electrophysiological dynamics have been proposed to be linked with various perceptual, motor and cognitive functions and their disorders. To reach the next phase in human neuroscience, we need to advance from group-level descriptions to quantitative model-based individual-level predictions. These developments will be illustrated with focus on language function for which descriptive models, largely based on observations of patients with language disorders, are being supplemented by computationally explicit models of mechanisms and representations. Machine learning approaches are essential tools in this endeavor.

Socially Interactive Artificial Intelligence: Perception, Synthesis and Learning of Human-Like Behaviors

Elisabeth Andre

Human-Centered Artificial Intelligence, Institute for Informatics,
University of Augsburg, Germany
andre@informatik.uni-augsburg.de

Abstract. The automatic analysis and synthesis of social signals conveyed by voice, gestures, mimics, etc., will play a vital role for next-generation interfaces as it paves the way towards a more intuitive and natural human-computer interaction with robots and virtual agents. In my talk, I will present computational methods to implement socially interactive behaviors in artificial agents, focusing on three essential properties of socially interactive interfaces: Social Perception, Socially Aware Behavior Synthesis, and Learning Socially Aware Behaviors. I will highlight opportunities and challenges that arise from deep learning approaches that promise to achieve the next level of human-likeness in virtual agents and social robots. I will illustrate my talk with examples from various applications with socially interactive characters or robots, including art and entertainment, cultural training and social coaching, and personal well-being and health.

Responsible Conversational AI: Trusted, Safe and Bias-Free

Verena Rieser

School of Mathematical and Computer Sciences (MACS) at Heriot Watt University, Edinburgh
V.T.Rieser@hw.ac.uk

Abstract. With recent progress in deep learning, there has been an increased interest in learning dialogue systems from data, also known as "Conversational AI". In this talk, I will focus on the task of response generation, for which I will highlight lessons learnt and ongoing challenges, such as reducing `hallucinations for task-based systems, safety critical issues for open-domain chatbots, and the often-overlooked problem of 'good' persona design. I will argue that we will need to solve these challenges to create trusted, safe and bias-free systems for end-user applications.

Is Big Tech Becoming the Big Tobacco of AI?

John Macintyre

Dean of the Faculty of Applied Sciences and Pro Vice Chancellor at University
of Sunderland
John.Macintyre@sunderland.ac.uk

Abstract. The future of AI is being shaped by many forces – politics, economics, and technology all play their part. Whilst science and academia continue to push forward the boundaries of knowledge, private sector investment in AI is growing exponentially, with commercial revenues from AI expected to exceed $500 billion in the near future. At the forefront of this commercial boom in AI is so-called "Big Tech" – the biggest technology companies driving the commercialization of AI products and systems for profit. These companies have vast R&D budgets, and employ an increasingly large fraction of the AI R&D workforce globally. The question is: are they living up to their responsibilities to develop AI for the good of society, or are they just pursuing profit? Will Big Tech follow the very negative pattern of huge companies prepared to inflict harms on society to boost their profits and shareholder dividends? Professor John MacIntyre's talk will look at the emerging issues in AI and examine what impact the behaviour of Big Tech is having on the whole field of AI.

Contents – Part I

Deep Learning - Convolutional

Deep Learning - Recurrent/Reinforcement

Energy Streams Modeling

Evolutionary/Biologically Inspired Modeling and Brain Modeling

Explainable AI/Graph Representation and Processing Frameworks

Contents – Part II

Machine Learning Modeling /Feature Selection

Social Media, Sentiment Analysis/Natural Language - Text Mining

Time Series Modeling/Transfer Learning

Unsupervised Modeling

Adaptive Modeling/Cloud Data Models

A Second-Order Adaptive Decision Model for Proceeding or Terminating a Pregnancy

Lisa Elderhorst[1], Melissa van den Berge[1], and Jan Treur[2(✉)]

[1] Athena Institute, Vrije Universiteit Amsterdam, Amsterdam, The Netherlands
[2] Department of Computer Science, Social AI Group, Vrije Universiteit Amsterdam, Amsterdam, The Netherlands
j.treur@vu.nl

Abstract. This study introduces a second-level adaptive temporal-causal decision model for deciding whether to keep or not to keep a baby. In this model, different actors and factors that influence the decision-making process have been incorporated based on literature. Hereby, the actors are responsible for the Hebbian learning component and make the model adaptive. Complementary speed factors regulate when learning happens. Three scenarios for the different possible outcomes; keeping the baby, having an abortion and putting the baby up for adoption provide insights into the influences of the actors on making a decision.

1 Introduction

Every second, approximately 4.3 babies are born into this world (Malek 2021). Subsequently, yearly in the Netherlands about 200.000 women become pregnant. When a woman becomes pregnant, she has roughly three options; keeping the baby, having an abortion and putting the baby up for adoption (FIOM 2021). Most of the time, women decide to proceed with their pregnancy and keep their baby. For example, in 2019, 170.000 babies were born in the Netherlands. This indicates that proceeding with pregnancy is indeed the option that is chosen most often (CBS 2021). However, as discussed, there are other options for women whose pregnancy is less planned or wanted. To indicate, in 2019 32.233 women had an abortion and 20 women put their baby up for adoption (Inspectie Gezondheidszorg en Jeugd 2021; Werdmuller et al. 2020).

Making a potentially life-changing decision can be difficult and overwhelming (Somers 2014). Therefore, the FIOM (Dutch specialist in the field of unwanted pregnancy) helps to guide women in their decision-making process. For instance, the FIOM recommends for a woman to gain as much (factual) information regarding her options to help her make a decision. Hereby, the FIOM states that this information can be gathered through four different actors: (i) social network (family and friends), (ii) partner (if applicable), (iii) experts (social workers, general practitioners (GPs)) and (iv) clergyman (pastor, priest, imam etc.) (FIOM n.d.-a, n.d.-b). However, they each have different perspectives, morals, values and experiences, and can therefore influence the women's decision in their own unique way (FIOM n.d.-b; Somers 2014). Besides actors, there are

© IFIP International Federation for Information Processing 2022
Published by Springer Nature Switzerland AG 2022
I. Maglogiannis et al. (Eds.): AIAI 2022, IFIP AICT 646, pp. 3–15, 2022.
https://doi.org/10.1007/978-3-031-08333-4_1

internal and external factors that can further affect the outcome of the decision-making process (see Sect. 2).

For understanding the decision-making process, an adaptive decision model is presented in this study. Hereby, decisions can be made because of learning processes over time (Treur 2020). These learning processes are triggered by a stimulus; input from different actors. Therefore, they are called adaptive due to the adaptation of the influences on the final decision. The modelling approach of this study is based on causal relations. In addition, an adaptive learning principle called (meta)plasticity is used (see Sect. 2) (Treur 2020). Hence, the objective is to understand the influences of various information sources on the decision-making process regarding keeping or not keeping a baby by modelling an adaptive decision model.

2 Background

The adaptive temporal-causal network model regarding proceeding with a pregnancy, having an abortion or putting the baby up for abortion is based on empirical data from various sources. This adaptive decision model is a model in which learning happens during decision making. First, the different actors and factors influencing the decision-making process are elaborated on. Additionally, their influence on other factors and actors are presented. Secondly, the generic learning processes are touched upon.

Partner. The male partner of the woman plays a significant role in the decision-making process. For instance, he helps to contribute to the total income of the household. This income is furthermore influenced by the education of the woman. This is important as usually, the higher the level of education, the higher the total income (OECD 2019). In this context, it is assumed that having a large and stable income typically indicates that there are resources available for supporting a baby. As a result, the pregnancy is more likely to be planned or wanted (Finer et al. 2005; Najman et al. 1990). Moreover, having a stable relationship accounted for one of the main reasons for women to proceed with their pregnancy and keep the baby. Vice versa, being single and becoming a single mother is one of the reasons women opt for the decision to have an abortion or adoption (Medoff 1993; Minkus and Drobnič 2021; Najman et al. 1990) Besides monetary influences, a partner also has his own opinion towards the pregnancy. In the Netherlands, the intra-household gender equality is particularly low compared to other high income European countries such as Denmark or Finland (Malghan and Swaminathan 2021). Therefore, gender inequality portrayed in the opinion of the partner can increase the stigma around topics such as abortion, thereby affecting the decision making process (Gemzell-Danielsson and Cleeve 2017). To note, stigma is also influenced by social network and religion (see below).

Social Network. A supportive social network consisting of close family and friends is beneficial for decision making. Specifically, a social network can help lower the stigma regarding terminating a pregnancy, because a woman receives support and is able to discuss matters with her social network (Najman et al. 1990).

Experts. Speaking with experts is not only recommended by the FIOM, but also by hospitals (Somers 2014). Hereby, experts may include GPs, social workers, doctors and abortion clinics or adoption centres (FIOM n.d.-a). All of these actors are qualified to give factual and personalised information to the woman regarding her options (keeping or not keeping the baby). As a result, a woman's lack of knowledge lowers as she gains more information.

Simultaneously, a lack of knowledge is increased by stigma. To exemplify, if a woman experiences that there is stigma about abortions, she is less likely to explore her options as it is made clear not to be accepted by her community. The lack of knowledge maintained by the stigma thus increases the fear of a woman towards keeping the child (Minkus and Drobnič 2021). This fear comprises amongst other things stress, sadness, doubt and anger towards the decision (Najman et al. 1990; Somers 2014). As a result, fear can affect feelings towards keeping the baby and feelings towards not keeping the baby. Hereby, if the woman has little fear, she will have stronger feelings towards keeping the child. Subsequently, with the stimulus of her partner she will decide to keep the baby. Vice versa, if the woman experiences great fear, she will less likely feel like keeping the baby. Hence, the woman then remains with two options; abortion or adoption. In this case, a woman is more likely to have an abortion over an adoption if she is still obtaining education (Minkus and Drobnič 2021). However, these options are both also influenced by religion.

Religion. As mentioned before, religion influences stigma due to their morals and values regarding sex before marriage and ending a life. Religious people (historically) take in a less accepting stance towards matters such as abortion (FIOM n.d.-a). Therefore, religion increases stigma around pregnancy. Additionally, religion influences the feelings towards abortion and feelings towards adoption. As stated, abortions are perceived to be less accepted. Thus, the feelings towards having an abortion are negatively influenced by religion. Moreover, when a woman does not want to keep the baby, the clergyman is more likely to advise her to put the baby up for adoption. Hence, when a woman has spoken to the clergyman, she has gained advice on the matter.

Plasticity and Metaplasticity. Due to the many described influences it can be difficult to make a decision. The process of learning and decision making, according to neurosciences, happens in response to a stimulus (e.g., information). Subsequently, the responding and predicting connections in the brain, based on which a decision is made, are adaptive; an example of this adaptivity (also called called *plasticity*), is Hebbian learning (Hebb 1949), in a simplified form formulated as:

'Neurons that fire together, wire together' (Shatz 1992)

However, when a person – in this case a pregnant woman – learns about her possible options, she does this at different times and speed. As a form of control the learning speed is also adaptive, which makes the occurrence of the learning process itself dependent on contextual circumstances. This is called *metaplasticity*; e.g., (Abraham and Bear 1996; Robinson et al. 2016). The following is an example of a metaplasticity principle:

'Adaptation accelerates with increasing stimulus exposure' (Robinson et al. 2016)

Principles of plasticity and metaplasticity have been applied in the introduced adaptive decision model regarding proceeding with a pregnancy, having an abortion or putting the baby up for abortion. As a result, such a model can be used to better understand the learning effect of information sources on the decision-making process of a woman.

3   Description of the Second-Order Adaptive Decision Model

For the decision-making process of this model, a second-order adaptive network model was designed. The model describes the influences of different factors and the influence of talking to different actors over time. When being pregnant, different factors influence the decision to proceed with or terminate the pregnancy. By using a Hebbian Learning process, the influences of the (f)actors can be strengthened or weakened and therefore they can influence the decision-making process.

The conceptual representation of the causal network model consists of states and connections between the states. These connections can represent a causal impact. It is assumed that the states have activation levels that vary over time. Adaptation of causal relations and other network characteristics are incorporated in the approach too (Treur 2020). The network structure characteristics used are as follows:

Connectivity of the Network. Connection weights $\omega_{X,Y}$ for each connection from a state (or node) X to a state Y.
Aggregation of Multiple Impacts. A combination function $c_Y(..)$ for each state Y to determine the aggregation of incoming causal impacts.
Timing in the Network. A speed factor η_Y for each state

Moreover, self model states (also called reification states) were added to the network to make some of the network characteristics adaptive. For this model, states $\mathbf{W}_{X,Y}$ and $\mathbf{H}_{X,Y}$ were used. The W-states $\mathbf{W}_{X,Y}$ are first-order self-model states; they represent their complementary connection weight $\omega_{X,Y}$. Additionally, in this model there are five second-order self-model states $\mathbf{H}_{\mathbf{W}_{X,Y}}$ representing the timing (speed factor) characteristic $\eta_{\mathbf{W}_{X,Y}}$ for the mentioned first-order self model states $\mathbf{W}_{X,Y}$. Adding these speed factors allowed for determining the moment when each of the learning activities would take place. In this way, metaplasticity of the model was ensured.

Connection weights normally have values between 0 and 1. However, when the connection has a suppressing effect, it also can be negative. For the model of this study, connection weights with values between -1 and 1 are used. The states with a positive impact in the base level are: education (X_1), partner (X_2), religion (X_4), obtaining education (X_6), total income (X_7), fear (X_9), stigma (X_{11}), lack of knowledge (X_{12}), feelings towards keeping the baby (X_{13}), feelings towards not keeping the baby (X_{15}), feelings towards abortion (X_{16}), and feelings towards adoption (X_{18}). States with negative impact in the base level are: planned or wanted pregnancy (X_8), fear (X_9), decision to keep the baby (X_{14}), decision to have an abortion (X_{17}), and decision to start the adoption process (X_{19}).

The influence of the states social network (X_3) on stigma (X_{11}), expert (X_5) on lack of knowledge (X_{12}), opinion partner (X_{10}) on stigma (X_{11}), religion (X_4) on feelings towards abortion (X_{16}), and religion (X_4) on feelings towards adoption (X_{18}) are adaptive and therefore discussed in the next section. States X_1 until X_6 have no incoming connections as these represent the individual factors of a pregnant woman. They do influence other states in the model. Total income of the woman (X_7) is positively influenced by education (X_1) and partner (X_2). Both connections have positive connection weights $\omega_{X,Y}$ of weight 1, as being highly educated and having a stable relationship have a positive effect on the total income of a woman. In addition, opinion partner (X_{10}) also has a positive incoming connection ($\omega_{X,Y} = 1$) from partner (X_2). To indicate, when there is a stable relationship with a partner, the partner has an opinion about the pregnancy which influences the decision process. Planned or wanted pregnancy (X_8) is positively ($\omega_{X,Y} = 1$) influenced by total income (X_7). For instance, when the total income of a pregnant woman is high, the pregnancy is more likely to be planned.

Stigma (X_{11}) is positively influenced ($\omega_{X,Y} = 1$) by religion (X_4) as religion can cause or enhance stigma around topics such as pre-marital sex and abortion. Stigma (X_{11}) itself has a positive influence ($\omega_{X,Y} = 1$) on the lack of knowledge (X_{11}), as stigma is expected to be a dominant factor compared to knowledge. Hereafter, lack of knowledge (X_{12}) has a positive effect ($\omega_{X,Y} = 1$) on fear (X_9). For example, when there is much stigma around a pregnancy and there is a lack of knowledge about pregnancy options, a woman will develop fear around the pregnancy. However, fear (X_8) is negatively influenced ($\omega_{X,Y} = -0.5$) by planned or wanted pregnancy (X_8). A woman who planned or wants a pregnancy is less likely to have fear regarding the pregnancy and therefore the connection is negative.

Fear (X_9) has a negative influence ($\omega_{X,Y} = -0.5$) on the feelings towards keeping the baby (X_{13}). However, partner (X_2) has a positive influence ($\omega_{X,Y} = -0.5$) on the feelings towards keeping the baby (X_{13}). When having fear for the pregnancy, the women will more likely feel negative towards keeping the baby (and therefore positive towards not keeping the baby (X_{15})). Therefore, this influence is negative. Based on literature, having a partner is the biggest reason to keep the baby during a pregnancy (see Sect. 2). Therefore, this influence is positive. As mentioned in the above paragraph, fear (X_9) has a positive impact on the feelings towards not keeping the baby (X_{15}). Subsequently, the feelings towards not keeping the baby (X_{15}) have positive influences on the feelings towards abortion (X_{16}) and adoption (X_{18}). Both with a connection weight of 1.

Lastly, all decision states (X_{14}, X_{17}, and X_{19}) are positively influenced ($\omega_{X,Y} = 1$) by the feeling states (X_{13}, X_{16}, and X_{18}). All decision states are mutually exclusive towards each other and therefore there are negative connections ($\omega_{X,Y} = -0.6$) between them. An overview of the states, the names, an explanation and the incoming connections can be found in the Appendix as Linked Data at

https://www.researchgate.net/publication/357372192.

In this model, there are five first-order self-model states that model the learning process. Together, they represent the actor-network which a pregnant woman uses to gain information to help her with the decision-making process. Thus, as she gains the information through interaction, she learns more about the subject by strengthening the connections involved. To start, the influence of a (supportive) social network (X_3) on stigma (X_{11}) is incorporated in the model ($X_{20} = \mathbf{W}_{\text{Social network, Stigma}}$). As described, after a woman speaks with her supportive social network, she is offered support, knowledge and acceptance, which in turn lowers the stigma. Therefore, this **W**-state models adaptivity of the negative effect on the base level state stigma. Secondly, the adaptive negative influence of experts (X_5) on lack of knowledge (X_{12}) is incorporated through X_{21} ($= \mathbf{W}_{\text{Experts, Lack of knowledge}}$). By providing the woman with more expert information, she gains knowledge about the subject (the connection strengthens), thereby decreasing the lack of knowledge. Thirdly, the opinion of the partner (X_{10}) has a positive influence on stigma (X_{11}).

This learning relation is modelled by means of X_{22} ($\mathbf{W}_{\text{Opinion partner, Stigma}}$). Due to the previously described gender-inequality in the Netherlands, the opinion of the partner is believed to enhance the stigma. Lastly, there is a large influencing role of religion (X_4) on the feelings towards abortion (X_{16}) and feelings towards adoption (X_{18}). These respectively negative and positive connections are translated in X_{23} ($= \mathbf{W}_{\text{Religion, Feelings towards abortion}}$) and X_{24} ($= \mathbf{W}_{\text{Religion, Feelings towards adoption}}$). For all described adaptive states in the first level (X_{20}–X_{24}), the influence of the actor becomes clear after the woman has interacted with them and this has activated a learning process for the connection involved.

Complementary to the connection weight self-model states (the **W**-states) are the speed factor self-model states (the $\mathbf{H_W}$-states) in the second self-model level. The five $\mathbf{H_W}$-states (X_{25}–X_{29}) determine the speed and time of the learning from an interaction between each of the actors and the woman. This has been done by a variation on the principle of metaplasticity mentioned in Sect. 2:

'Adaptation accelerates with increasing stimulus exposure' (Robinson et al. 2016).

Such a principle makes the extent of adaptation context-dependent, depending on environmental circumstances. In this case, the social environment is chosen as what triggers the adaptation. This social environment makes that in certain time periods interaction takes place with certain persons. Exactly this is modeled by activation of the $\mathbf{H_W}$-states as a form of activation of such social interactions. This means that the learning occurs, when such periods take place. An overview of the **W**-states and $\mathbf{H_W}$-states of the model and their description can be found in Appendix as Linked Data at https://www.researchgate.net/publication/357372192. Similar to the states of the base level, self-model states can be defined by three network characteristics: connectivity, aggregation and timing. This knowledge can be translated to the network model (Fig. 1). The connectivity, in terms of incoming and outgoing connections of the self-model state has different functions. First, the outgoing downward causal connections (pink arrows in Fig. 1) from the self-model states representing a causal impact from the specific role (also indicated in the name).

This for example means that in the presented model the connection of $\mathbf{H_W}_{X_3,X_{11}}$ is used for the adaptation speed of the weight of the connection from X_3 on X_{11}. Second, the upward causal connections (blue arrows in Fig. 1) towards the self-model states give the self-model states the dynamic characteristic as desired. They specify the adaptation principle that is addressed, together with the combination function and the downward connection.

By the use of *role matrices*, the network characteristics $\omega_{X,Y}$, $\mathbf{c}_Y(..)$, η_Y that define a network model can be specified in a concise and structured way which is also readable by the dedicated software environment. There are five different types of role matrices and each role matrix shows the data of a specific type. Role matrix **mb** for the base connectivity of the network, **mcw** for the specific connection weights, **ms** for the speed factors, **mcfw** for the combination functions used with their weights, and **mcfp** for the parameters of these combination functions (Treur 2020). The complete specified conceptual representation of the network model by role matrices can be found in the Appendix as Linked Data at https://www.researchgate.net/publication/357372192.

For the numerical representation of the model, a standard canonical difference or differential equation is used:

$$Y(t + \Delta t) = Y(t) + \eta_Y[\textbf{aggimpact}_Y(t) - Y(t)]\Delta t \tag{1}$$

$$\textbf{d}Y(t)/\textbf{d}t = \eta_Y[\textbf{aggimpact}_Y(t) - Y(t)]$$

where $X_1,...,X_k$ are the states from which Y gets incoming connections and

$$\textbf{aggimpact}_Y(t) = \textbf{c}_Y(\textbf{impact}_{X_1,Y}(t),...,\textbf{impact}_{X_k,Y}(t))$$
$$\text{with } \textbf{impact}_{X_i,Y}(t) = \omega_{X_i,Y} X_i(t)$$

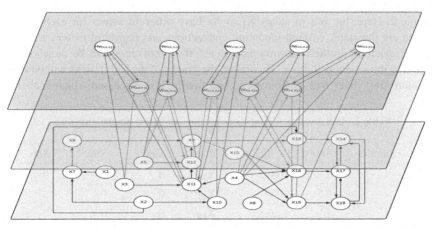

Fig. 1. Overview of the conceptual representation of the model: base level, first self-model level and second self-model level.

By using the combination function $\textbf{c}_Y$, the aggregated causal impact of multiple states X_i on Y at time point t is determined (Treur 2020). The aggregated causal impact on Y, is applied gradually over time by using (and in proportion with) the speed factor η_Y. A dedicated software environment developed in Matlab is available by which the conceptual design representation of a network model is transformed into a numerical design representation. This numerical design description can be used for simulation.

In Matlab, there are different combination functions available in the library. These combination functions can be used to express the desired effect of the impact on the states (Treur 2020). The combination functions, including their description, formula, and parameters, used in the model are shown in Table 1.

Table 1. Overview of the combination functions used for the model

Name	Description	Formula	Parameters	Used for
alogistic $_{\sigma,\tau}(V_1, \ldots, V_k)$	Advanced logistic sum	$[\dfrac{1}{1 + e^{-\sigma(V_1 + \cdots + V_k - \tau)}} - \dfrac{1}{1+e^{\sigma\tau}}](1+e^{-\sigma\tau})$	Steepness σ Threshold τ	X_1 - X_{19}
hebb$_\mu(V_1, V_2, W)$	Hebbian learning: positive weights	$V_1 V_2 (1-W) + \mu W$	Persistence factor μ	X_{22}, X_{24}
hebbneg$_\mu(V_1, V_2, W)$	Hebbian learning: negative weights	$-V_1(1-V_2)(1+W) + \mu W$	Persistence factor μ	X_{20}, X_{21}, X_{23}
steponce$_{\alpha,\beta}(\ldots)$	Activation for period from α to β	1 if $\alpha \leq t \leq \beta$, else 0 (time t)	Start time α End time β	X_{25}- X_{29}

4 Simulation Results

In this section, three different simulations for three different scenarios are shown; keeping the baby, having an abortion and putting the baby up for adoption. For each simulation (and scenario), different combinations of initial values (iv's) are chosen as presented in Table 2. Here, the iv's of states X_1 to X_6 have different values for each scenario as these are the states without incoming connections and represent factors which are scenario specified. In the following paragraphs, the simulations will be shown by first explaining the scenario and iv's. Thereafter, the graphs of the simulations will be shown and interesting states will be discussed. And finally, it is discussed which decision is made.

Table 2. Initial values for the states for three different simulations (Sim).

State	Sim. 1	Sim. 2	Sim. 3	State	Sim. 1	Sim. 2	Sim. 3
X_1	1	1	0.5	X_{16}	0	0	0
X_2	1	0.5	1	X_{17}	0	0	0
X_3	1	1	0.5	X_{18}	0	0	0
X_4	0	0	1	X_{19}	0	0	0
X_5	1	1	0.1	X_{20}	0.5	0.5	0.5
X_6	0.5	1	0.1	X_{21}	0.5	0.5	0.5
X_7	0	0	0	X_{22}	0.5	0.5	0.5
X_8	0	0	0	X_{23}	0.5	0.5	0.5
X_9	0	0	0	X_{24}	0.5	0.5	0.5
X_{10}	0	0	0	X_{25}	0	0	0
X_{11}	0	0	0	X_{26}	0	0	0
X_{12}	1	1	1	X_{27}	0	0	0
X_{13}	0	0	0	X_{28}	0	0	0
X_{14}	0	0	0	X_{29}	0	0	0
X_{15}	0	0	0				

Simulation 1: Keeping the Baby. In simulation Scenario 1, the initial values (iv) as shown in Table 2 were used. They indicate the scenario of a pregnant woman who is highly educated (iv = 1), has a stable relationship with a male partner (iv = 1), has a supportive network of family and friends (iv = 1), does not attend religious services (iv = 0), talks to an expert in the field (iv = 1) and part-time obtains education (iv = 0.5). Figure 2 shows the outcome of the simulation. Note that to improve the clarity and visibility, states X_1–X_6 and X_{20}–X_{24} are not depicted. As can be observed, the decision to keep the baby (X_{14}) is more dominant compared to the decision for having an abortion (X_{17}) or an adoption (X_{19}). Furthermore, the influence of $\mathbf{Hw}_{\text{Opinion partner,Stigma}}$ (X_{27}) via $\mathbf{W}_{\text{Opinion partner,Stigma}}$ on stigma (X_{11}) is slightly positive. The value of stigma (X_{11}) increases after $t = 10$ which may be due to the positive impact of opinion partner (X_{10}) on stigma (X_{11}). However, stigma (X_{11}) lowers again after the influence of $\mathbf{Hw}_{\text{Social network,Stigma}}$ (X_{25}) via $\mathbf{W}_{\text{Social network,Stigma}}$. This leads to the second interesting observation of this simulation: the influence of $\mathbf{Hw}_{\text{Social network,Stigma}}$ (X_{25}) on the base level states. At $t = 30$, the feelings towards abortion (X_{16}) and the decision to have an abortion (X_{17}) were higher compared to the feelings towards keeping the baby (X_{13}) and the decision to keep the baby (X_{14}).

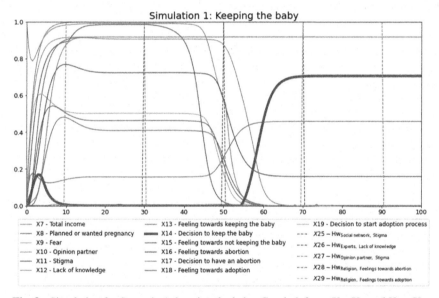

Fig. 2. Simulation for Scenario 1: keeping the baby. Graph: left out X_1–X_6 and X_{20}–X_{24}

However, during the period of $t = 40$ until $t = 50$, stigma (X_{11}), lack of knowledge (X_{12}), and fear (X_9) decreased much. Therefore, the feelings towards abortion (X_{16}) and the decision to have an abortion (X_{17}) decreased and subsequently the feelings to keep the baby (X_{13}) increased. Additionally, due to the influence of $\mathbf{Hw}_{\text{Experts,Lack of knowledge}}$ (X_{26}) at $t = 50$ via $\mathbf{W}_{\text{Experts,Lack of knowledge}}$, the feelings towards abortion (X_{16}), the decision to have an abortion (X_{17}), stigma (X_{11}), lack of knowledge (X_{12}), and fear (X_9) also decreased. Whereas the feelings towards keeping the baby (X_{13}) and the decision to keep the baby (X_{14}) increased. Hereafter, $\mathbf{H_W}_{\text{Religion, Feelings towards abortion}}$ (X_{28}) and $\mathbf{H_W}_{\text{Religion, Feelings towards adoption}}$ (X_{29}) showed limited effect. This can be explained as the initial value of religion (X_4) was set at 0. Hence, the decision to keep the baby (X_{14}) wins.

Simulation 2: Abortion. For Scenario 2, the initial values indicate a pregnant woman who is highly educated (iv $= 1$), in an unstable relationship with a male partner (iv $=$ 0.5), has a supportive network of family and friends (iv $= 1$), not attending religious services (iv $= 0$), talking to an expert in the field (iv $= 1$) and is still obtaining education (iv $= 1$). Figure 3 shows the results of the second simulation, again without the states that hinder visibility. As shown in Fig. 3, the decision to have an abortion (X_{17}) was more dominant compared to the decision for an adoption (X_{19}) or keeping the baby (X_{14}). This can be explained by looking at the different factors and the adaptive influences of the actors over time. Starting with the influences of $\mathbf{H_W}_{\text{Opinion partner,Stigma}}$ (X_{27}) via $\mathbf{W}_{\text{Opinion partner, Stigma}}$ on the base level states, it can be seen that after $t = 10$, stigma (X_{11}) obtained a higher value. This can be explained by the positive effect of the opinion of the partner (X_{10}) on stigma (X_{11}). Second, the influence of $\mathbf{H_W}_{\text{Social network, Stigma}}$ (X_{25}) after $t = 30$ via $\mathbf{W}_{\text{Social network, Stigma}}$ caused stigma (X_{11}) to lower due to the negative effect of the social network (X_3) on stigma (X_{11}).

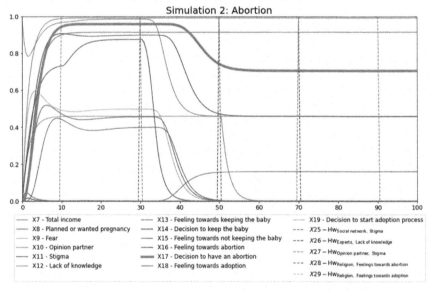

Fig. 3. Simulation for Scenario 2: Abortion. Graph: left out X_1–X_6 and X_{20}–X_{24}.

Furthermore, stigma (X_{11}) had a direct influence on the lack of knowledge (X_{12}) and therefore an indirect influence on fear (X_9). Subsequently, the values of lack of knowledge (X_{12}) and fear (X_9) lowered, which resulted in increased feelings towards not keeping the baby (X_{13}). Thirdly, $\mathbf{H_W}_{\text{Experts, Lack of Knowledge}}$ (X_{26}) between $t = 50$ and $t = 70$ resulted in a decreased lack of knowledge (X_{12}). Hence, the decision to have an abortion (X_{17}) slightly decreased. However, the decision to have an abortion (X_{17}) remained dominant due to the suppression on the decision to keep the baby (X_{14}) and the decision to start the adoption process (X_{19}). Lastly, $\mathbf{Hw}_{\text{Religion, Feelings towards abortion}}$ (X_{28}), and $\mathbf{Hw}_{\text{Religion, Feelings towards adoption}}$ (X_{29}) showed no influence on the states, which can be explained as the initial value of religion (X_4) was set at 0.

Simulation 3: Adoption. In simulation Scenario 3, the initial values indicate the scenario of a pregnant woman who is averagely educated (iv = 0.5), has a stable relationship with a male partner (iv = 1), has a semi-supportive network of family and friends (iv = 0.5), attends religious services (iv = 1), hardly speaks with an expert (iv = 0.1) in the field and not really obtains education (iv = 0.1). Figure 4 shows the results of the last simulation, again without the states that hinder visibility. In the figure it can be seen that $\mathbf{Hw}_{\text{Opinion partner, Stigma}}$ (X_{27}) had a small positive effect on the feelings towards not keeping the baby (X_{15}). Moreover, $\mathbf{Hw}_{\text{Opinion partner, Stigma}}$ (X_{27}) showed a decreasing effect on the feelings towards keeping the child (X_{13}). $\mathbf{Hw}_{\text{Social network, Stigma}}$ (X_{25}) and $\mathbf{Hw}_{\text{experts, Lack of knowledge}}$ (X_{26}) did not have a strong influence on the base-level states, except for lack of knowledge (X_{12}) which lowered at $t = 50$ due to the influence of $\mathbf{Hw}_{\text{experts, Lack of knowledge}}$ (X_{26}).

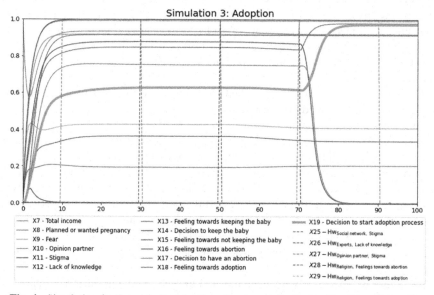

Fig. 4. Simulation for Scenario 3: Adoption. Graph: not displaying X_1–X_6 and X_{20}–X_{24}

However, due to the initial value of religion (X_4) there are some interesting increases and decreases visible between $t = 70$ and $t = 90$. Before $t = 70$, the feelings towards abortion (X_{16}) were higher compared to the feelings towards an adoption (X_{18}) and the feelings towards keeping the child (X_{13}). However, after $t = 70$ the input of state $\mathbf{Hw}_{\text{Religion, Feelings towards abortion}}$ (X_{28}) resulted in a negative impact on feelings towards abortion (X_{16}) and the decision to have an abortion (X_{17}) via

$\mathbf{W}_{\text{Religion, Feelings towards abortion}}$. Moreover, $\mathbf{H}\mathbf{W}_{\text{Religion, Feelings towards adoption}}$ (X_{29}) had a positive influence via $\mathbf{W}_{\text{Religion, Feelings towards adoption}}$ on the feelings towards an adoption (X_{18}) and subsequently on the decision to have an adoption (X_{19}). Hence, due to the influences of $\mathbf{H}\mathbf{W}_{\text{Religion, Feelings towards abortion}}$ (X_{28}) and $\mathbf{H}\mathbf{W}_{\text{Religion, Feelings towards adoption}}$ (X_{29}) the feeling towards abortion (X_{16}) decreased and the feeling towards an adoption (X_{18}) increased. Therefore, the decision to start the adoption process (X_{19}) won.

5 Discussion

The aim of this paper was to understand the influences of various information sources on the decision-making process regarding keeping or not keeping a baby. To accomplish this, a second-order adaptive temporal-causal decision model was created. Hereby, various factors and actors influencing the decision-making process were represented. By including adaptive connections and speed factors, the model was able to simulate dynamic real-life situations. As a result, the model consists of adaptive learning cycles which may influence over a certain period of time the development of the end decision of the pregnant women. For the purpose of this research, three different scenarios were simulated visualising the influence of four actors on the decision-making process. In this way, adaptiveness in terms of both how the model learns (plasticity) and at what speed and time (metaplasticity) for the decision process was modelled. Thus, this model contributed to the current knowledge base by illustrating how the process for a pregnant woman making a decision to either keep or not keep a baby can be influenced over time by different actors.

The model was mathematically verified and validated by means of parameter tuning; see the Appendix as Linked Data at URL

https://www.researchgate.net/publication/357372192.

Additionally, as the context of the model was a logical and real-world process, researcher biases could have influenced the design of the model. What was seen as a logical time span and order, was partly derived from literature, but may also have been influenced by views, interpretations and visions of the researchers themselves. However, the evidence from literature was, to the best of the researchers' knowledge, generalised for this model. Nevertheless, the decision-making process for keeping or not keeping a baby is very personal and context-dependent as with many real world processes. Therefore, it is an open question whether this model will comply with every pregnant woman in the world.

For future research it is thus recommended to seek more empirical data regarding the timing of influences of the different actors to substantiate and improve the model. This can be done by more extensive literature review or by conducting own qualitative or quantitative research regarding the decision-making process. Secondly, as the model makes use of the person dependent factors (X_1–X_6) that may vary for every person, it can be further adapted to fit the context. For example, the model can also be altered to accommodate different cultures or individuals. Lastly, for future research it would be interesting to include more factors by adding more states to the model. In our research we only included 19 factors in the base level, 5 in the first-order, and 5 in the second-order self-model level. However, there are more factors which (possibly) influence the process that can be included in the model for a wider coverage.

References

Abraham, W.C., Bear, M.F.: Metaplasticity: the plasticity of synaptic plasticity. Trends Neurosci. **19**(4), 126–130 (1996)

CBS: Geboorte (2021). https://www.cbs.nl/nl-nl/visualisaties/dashboardbevolking/bevolkingsgr oei/geboren-kinderen

Finer, L., Frohwirth, L., Dauphinee, L., Singh, S., Moore, A.: Reasons Women Have Abortions: Quantitative and Qualitative Perspectives, pp. 1–9 (2005)

FIOM: Hoe kom je tot een besluit? (2021) (n.d.-a)

FIOM: Rol van de omgeving (n.d.-b). https://fiom.nl/ongewenst-zwanger/zwanger-watnu/verder-lezen/rol-omgeving

FIOM: Welke mogelijkheden zijn er? (2021). https://fiom.nl/ongewenst-zwanger/zwanger-watnu/welke-mogelijkheden-zijn

Gemzell-Danielsson, K., Cleeve, A.: Estimating abortion safety: advancements and challenges. Lancet **390**(10110), 2333–2334 (2017)

Hebb, D.O.: The organization of behavior: A neuropsychological theory. John Wiley and Sons, New York (1949)

Inspectie Gezondheidszorg en Jeugd: Jaarrapportage 2019: Wet afbreking zwangerschap (Wafz) (2021)

Malek, P.: Every Second Calculator (2021). https://www.omnicalculator.com/everydaylife/every-second

Malghan, D., Swaminathan, H.: Global trends in intra-household gender inequality. J. Econ. Behav. Organ. **189**(645), 515–546 (2021). https://doi.org/10.1016/j.jebo.2021.07.022

Medoff, M.: An empirical analysis of adoption, vol. XXXI(January), pp. 59–70 (1993)

Minkus, L., Drobnič, S.: Abortion: life-course stages and disruptive life events. Z. Soziol. **50**(3–4), 259–273 (2021). https://doi.org/10.1515/zfsoz-2021-0018

Najman, J.M., Morrison, J., Keeping, J.D., Andenen, M.J., Williams, G.M.: Social factors associated with the decision to relinquish a baby for adoption. Commun. Health Stud. **X**(2), 180–189 (1990)

OECD: Indicator A4. What are the earnings advantages from education? (2019). https://www.oecd-ilibrary.org/sites/ab9c46efen/index.html?itemId=/content/component/ab9c46ef-en#:~:text=Highereducationalattainmentisassociated,peerswithuppersecondaryeducation

Robinson, B.L., Harper, N.S., McAlpine, D.: Meta-adaptation in the auditory midbrain under cortical influence. Nat. Commun. **7**, e13442 (2016)

Shatz, C.J.: The developing brain. Sci. Am. **267**, 60–67 (1992)

Somers, K.: Ongewenst zwanger. Maatwerk **15**(5), 23–24 (2014). https://doi.org/10.1007/s12459-014-0077-9

Treur, J.: Network-Oriented Modeling for Adaptive Networks: Designing Higher-Order Adaptive Biological, Mental and Social Network Models. Springer Nature (2020)

Werdmuller, A., Bolt, S., van Brouwershaven, A.: De landelijke afstand ter adoptie registratie 2019 (2020)

A Self-adaptive Learning Music Composition Algorithm as Virtual Tutor

Michele Della Ventura$^{(\boxtimes)}$

Department of Music Technology, Music Academy "Studio Musica", Treviso, Italy
micheledellaventura.mdv@gmail.com

Abstract. The rapid development of digital technologies has made it possible to enhance teaching and learning spaces even in a complex discipline such as music composition, where however the right attention is still lacking regarding the learning style of students. Existing software, in most cases, propose methods for harmonizing a melody, but they rarely deal with the problems of the harmonization of music bassline. This article presents an intelligent adaptive algorithm to support the learning process of (dyslexic and non-dyslexic) students in the context of the harmonization of music basslines. The algorithm allows students to harmonize a music bassline, giving them advices (Virtual Tutor) in case of mistakes in the concatenation of the chords. Experiments have shown that this form of adaptive learning of the algorithm can improve students' ability to find solutions for the harmonization of music bassline. Future improvements of the method are discussed briefly at the end of the paper.

Keywords: Artificial intelligence · Computer music composition · Dyslexia · e-tutoring · Music education

1 Introduction

The transition to the new millennium highlights the decline of the old industrial society and the emergence of the information society [1, 2] with the new challenges proposed by artificial intelligence (AI). Even music is not immune to this change, on the contrary it was one of the first areas of experimentation and research [3]: from this perspective it is therefore evident the existence of a broad sharing of strategies and methods between musical composition and intelligence artificial. The hardware and software developments, capable of opening new possibilities to musical verifications and experiments, can be seen as multipliers of creativity (for a musician and not only: it is not strange today to find non-musicians who compose music) but at the same time they can lead to an impoverishment of musical skills and musical experience [4]. Musical composition is a complex discipline based on a series of musical grammar rules whose knowledge is essential. The acquisition and mastery of the musical grammar rules represents an obstacle for students in general but especially for dyslexic students who often find themselves in a situation of lack of autonomy and therefore of uncertainty in the carry out an

© IFIP International Federation for Information Processing 2022
Published by Springer Nature Switzerland AG 2022
I. Maglogiannis et al. (Eds.): AIAI 2022, IFIP AICT 646, pp. 16–26, 2022.
https://doi.org/10.1007/978-3-031-08333-4_2

exercise that leads them not to continue with the task. Therefore, the starting point of the challenges related to AI cannot and must not be technology, but a careful analysis and identification of the problems that can be faced with AI. Otherwise, any intelligent system designed without adequate problem analysis becomes useless and ineffective: the ability to carry out procedures without understanding the general concepts and connections is very limiting. There are two main dimensions that can be explored, as regards AI and teaching activity [5]:

1. how AI can improve teaching by helping to solve some problems in the school world,
2. how it is possible to educate people (teachers and students) about AI, so that they can benefit from it.

Starting from these two reflections, this research article intends to present a useful algorithm to support (dyslexic and non-dyslexic) students in the individual study, during the harmonization of a music bassline: this is the first step of the study of music composition, and aims to allow the student to know, learn and consolidate the musical grammar rules. The algorithm, through a training phase, is able to self-learn the fundamental musical grammar rules and therefore provide the student with possible solutions in case of errors made during the harmonization of the chords. The algorithm presents itself as a virtual tutor, to facilitate the learning process: the virtual tutor must support the student [6] in the creation and manipulation of musical objects [7], without replacing it by making the composition.

This paper is organized as follows.

Section 2 provides an overview of earlier automatic music composition researches. Section 3 describes the musical grammar rules as far as chords are concerned. This is followed by a description of the method used to formalize the musical grammar rules. Section 4 shows some experimental tests that illustrate the effectiveness of the proposed method. Finally, in Sect. 5 the paper ends with concluding remarks.

2 Related Works

Computer-assisted musical composition is a synthesis of the evolution of computer-music and computational-musicology. In other words, it is a phenomenon characterized by the existence of software tools that help the composer in the creation and manipulation of musical objects such as a melody, a rhythm or a musical accompaniment. Many algorithms have been designed and developed for these purposes, using different techniques: only those taken into consideration for the development of this research are illustrated below.

A Markov chain is a stochastic process, that is, a random process in which the transition probability that determines the transition to a system state depends only on the immediately preceding system state [8, 9]. Due to this characteristic, Markov chains allow the creation of a musical melody, seen as a sequence of notes [10, 11]. From the point of view of the creative process, Markov chains could create very similar melodies when the order of the chain is very high, but they can provide new combinations of smaller sections (such as a musical motif) that can be reworked with other techniques [12].

A "generative grammar" is a system of explicit and formal rules with an associated lexicon. These rules are formulated in such a way as to be able to generate a set of sentences, that is, combinations of lexical elements, which represent a language [13]. The language defined by a set of rules is made up of all the combinations of the elements that the rules can produce and only those combinations [14]. This approach can be used to chords generation but also to create variation on melodies [15].

A rules-based system uses rules to represent knowledge. Music theory traditionally describes rules that help to guide the compositional process. One way to implement rules in compositional systems is to use Constraint Programming, whose declarative nature is well fit to describe music theory rules [16]. This method can be seen as a guide for the composer and allows you to create new melodies, harmonies and rhythms, but at the same time it represents a limitation because it reduces the variety of the output [17, 18].

Most computer-assisted musical composition systems deal with the generation of a melody or the harmonization of a melody: there are few studies involving the harmonization of a bass line [19, 20].

The focus of the present research is the harmonization of a musical bassline. In this work, we introduce an algorithm able to support the student during the didactic activity in order to enhance the learning process. That's why the primary goal of the algorithm is not to autonomously harmonizing a bassline to obtain an error-free solution, but to support (as a virtual tutor) the student during the harmonization of a bassline giving him/her advices in case of errors in the concatenation of the chords.

3   Designing the Virtual Tutor

The algorithm proposed in this article is inspired by the techniques described in the previous paragraph in order to represent and reason on about the compositional rules. The composition rules are modelled so that the algorithm defines the requirements for an advice to be musically valid. The next paragraphs present an overview of the main musical grammar rules, which are fundamental for the design of the proposed algorithm, and the methods used to formalize them.

3.1   Musical Composition Guidelines

Harmonizing a bass line is an important element of the musical language. It is a traditional system of organizing chords for 4 voices (soprano, alto, tenor and bass) characterized by two aspects [21]:

1) there are 4 voices and each one is singing a melody: this is called melodic movement and represents the horizontal aspect of the harmonization (see Fig. 1, green notes);
2) the 4 voices sing simultaneously producing 4-note chords: this is the harmonic, or "vertical", aspect of the harmonization (see Fig. 1, orange notes). When the three upper voices (Soprano, Alto and Tenor) are within the span of one octave, they are in what is called "close position" (see Fig. 1, red notes). When the tenor and the soprano are further apart than an octave, the chord is in "open position" (see Fig. 1, red notes).

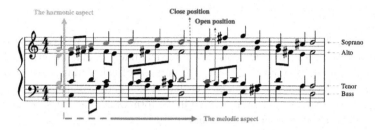

Fig. 1. The harmonic aspect and the melodic aspect of a musical composition.

In harmonizing a bassline, these two aspects must be considered at the same time and therefore two distinct movements can be identified: the melodic motion, when there is a passage from one sound to another in the same voice (see Fig. 1, green notes); the harmonic motion, when two or more melodic motions occur at the same time (see Fig. 1, red notes). In this context it is necessary to respect some fundamental guidelines. In the melodic motion must be avoided (see Fig. 2) [21]:

- augmented intervals (intervals that are one half-step larger than a perfect or major interval),
- diminished intervals (Intervals that are one half-step smaller than a perfect or minor interval),
- the intervals of the seventh,
- intervals larger than an octave.

Fig. 2. Examples of forbidden melodic intervals.

In the harmonic motion it is forbidden to proceed with two same voices at a distance of fifths and octaves (see Fig. 3) [21].

Fig. 3. Examples of parallel fifths and parallel octaves.

3.2 Error Recognition

In order to be able to identify one of the prohibited movements described above, it is necessary to take into account the concept of musical interval, that means, the distance in pitch between any two notes [22]. For the purpose of calculating this distance, the musical score is seen as a list of numbers each of which corresponds to a sound, based on its pitch [23]. The list can be represented in the form of a sequence S_m of N notes n_i indexed according to the order of appearance i:

$$S_m = (n_i)_{i \in [0, N-1]} \tag{1}$$

The pitch of a note can be measured by following two criteria [24]. In the first case (called "real distance"), semitones are used as the unit of measurement (regardless of the key of the piece of music):

C = 0 D = 2 E = 4 F = 5 G = 7 A = 9 B = 11 etc.

In the second case (called ("tonal distance"), the key of the musical piece is considered and the pitch of a sound is measured by referring to the intervals of the musical scale of the key in question, thus measuring it in degrees:

C = 0 D = 1 E = 2 F = 3 G = 4 A = 5 B = 6 etc.

With reference to the first criteria, it is important to consider simultaneously both the distance of the interval and the type of interval (the interval quality).

The distance is calculated by counting how many names of letters of the musical alphabet there are between the two notes. For example, the notes C and E are three letter notes apart and so is an interval of a 3rd.

The type of the interval is defined by the number of tones and semi-tones between the two notes. It may be (see Fig. 4): perfect (P), major (M), minor (m), augmented (A), diminished (d).

Fig. 4. Types of intervals on the C major scale.

If any of the major intervals are reduced by a semitone, then they become minor intervals (see Fig. 5). By flatting any of the major or perfect interval by a semitone, they become augmented intervals (see Fig. 5). By flatting any of the three perfect intervals or a minor interval by a semitone, these become diminished intervals (see Fig. 5).

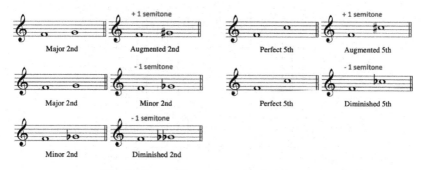

Fig. 5. Types of intervals on the C major scale.

In order to define the interval correctly (thus excluding forbidden intervals), and check a melodic error, it is essential to consider both the tonal distance and the real distance: considering only the number of semitones between two sounds, it is not possible to distinguish between different intervals [23]. In the example of Fig. 6 it is possible to see how between the notes F-G# and F-Ab there is an interval of 3 semitones: in the first case it is an increased interval, while in the second case a smaller interval. Considering the tonal distance first, it is possible to obtain the denomination of the interval (F-G# = second interval; F-Ab = third interval); subsequently, with the real distance the interval can be qualified (F-G# = augmented second; F-Ab = minor third).

Fig. 6. Example of intervals.

In the harmonic motion it is necessary to verify that in the concatenation of two chords, there is no fifth or octave interval between the same pair of voices (see Fig. 3). To do so the *Markov process* [24] is used: the choice was made to describe the passage from one state of the system (number of semitones of the same pair of voices in the first chord) to the next (number of semitones of the same pair of voices in the second chord) uniquely from the immediately preceding state [25, 26].

Figure 7 shows the matrix of transitions, created by the algorithm during the training phase (see paragraph 4), where in column 1 and row 1 the number of semitones between two voices is indicated, while in column 2 and row 2 it is indicated whether it is a new chord (n) or a repeated chord (r). In this way, if two voices repeat the same sounds in two consecutive chords (see Fig. 8), the algorithm does not report an error.

From the analysis of the transition matrix (Fig. 7) it is possible to note how the progressions of perfect fifths (7 semitones) and perfect octaves (12 semitones) have not been identified (orange cells).

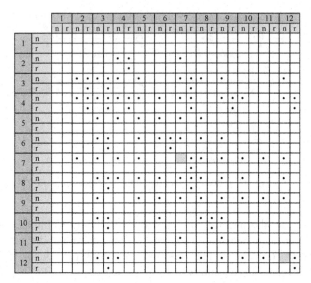

Fig. 7. Transitions matrix related to the harmonic motion.

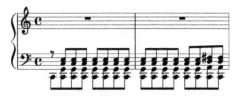

Fig. 8. First 2 bars from Piano Sonata op.53 n.21 by Beethoven: example of repeated fifth (between bass and tenor) and octave (between bas and alto).

4   Obtained Results

The proposed algorithm differs from most of the algorithms already developed for the automatic harmonization of the melody or bass, due to the fact that it takes into account the error as a working tool. Through a self-learning procedure, the prohibited melodic and harmonic motions are formalized, in order to identify any errors made by the student in harmonizing the sounds of the bassline, and suggest possible solutions.

To test the effectiveness of the algorithm, the following steps were followed.

1) Data collection

In order to train and test the algorithm, around 1300 musical pieces (written in choral form) were collected (Dataset): the pieces could be both in close position or in open position. The musical scores were in MIDI format [27] or in XML format [28], and this made it possible to take advantage of the numerous archives of musical pieces (of public domain) written in choral form, present on the web.

2) Data cleaning and preparation
The musical scores were analyzed before the dataset was used for the training phase of the algorithm. The use of incorrect data can produce misleading results. This phase took a long time (due to the fact that every single score was analyzed to identify any transcription errors) but it was essential for the veracity of the results.

3) Training phase of the algorithm
The algorithm read the musical scores in order to create the table representing the correct melodic motions (see Table 1) and the matrix of transitions representing the correct harmonic motions. Both the table representing the correct melodic motions and the matrix of transitions representing the correct harmonic motions were automatically dimensioned on the basis of the characteristics of the musical piece read during this phase.

4) Model test
Two experimental tests were carried out to verify the integrity of the algorithm.

In the first test, 7 music composition teachers used the software to harmonize a musical bassline, first in close positions and then in open positions. This allowed to verify if the algorithm updated the libraries in the case of solutions other than those recognized during the training phase, or in the event of an error if the solutions proposed by the algorithm could satisfy the musical grammar rules. Subsequently, to verify the soundness of the algorithm, teachers were asked to create a choral (8 bars) without having any musical inspiration but using their own personal creativity.

In the second experiment, a group of 40 students (with different levels of preparation and different learning styles) from 2 Music High Schools and 2 Conservatories of music, was asked to harmonize a bassline under the supervision of a Composition teacher who had to note the students' difficulties and errors and the answers of the algorithm.

After this testing phase, 3 teachers (2 from Music High Schools and 1 from Conservatory of music) were asked to permit students the use of the software for a period of 3 months (for their individual study) and to carry out a verification test every month in order to check the learning process.

The results obtained at the end of this period were satisfactory.

On the one hand, the students declared that they found no difficulty in using the software (because it was simple and intuitive), and the advices proposed in the event of an error forced them: to reflect and recognize the type of error; to consult the school book to understand the proposed solution, thus consolidating knowledge.

On the other hand, the teachers expressed their satisfaction: as regards the solutions proposed by the algorithm in the event of an error; regarding the behavior of different students, with particular attention to dyslexic students; as regards the results achieved by the students who, even if the melodic lines obtained by harmonizing the bass were less appreciable, the students had reduced the number of errors in carrying out exercises proposed and carried out independently.

Table 1. Excerpt of the allowed interval identified by the algorithm during the training phase.

Interval	Tonal distance	Real distance
2	1	2
	1	1
3	2	4
	2	3
4	3	5
5	4	7
6	5	9
	5	8
7	6	11
	6	10
8	7	12
...	...	...

5 Discussion and Conclusions

This article presented a self-adaptive learning music composition algorithm, specifically designed to enhance the educational activity, and support the student during the learning process. The algorithm presents itself as a virtual tutor able to support the student during the harmonization of the music bassline, helping him/her to consolidate the musical grammar rules. The experiments conducted show that the use of the algorithm can be beneficial: it can improve the student's ability to recognize which musical grammar rules is necessary to use during the concatenation of the chords and can help him/her to consolidate acquired skills.

An advantage of the algorithm is that there are no control parameters to be set manually. It is based on a self-learning model able to acquire on the one hand the rules relating to the movement of two sounds within the same voice (using the principles of information theory) and on the other hand the rules for the movement of the sounds of the various voices between two consecutive chords (by means of the Markov process).

Artificial intelligence is able to provide teachers with an insightful virtual tutor who is able to help students to solve the challenges and obstacles encountered during their learning path. AI can offer students explanations for a better understanding of disciplinary topics and enrich their knowledge without making them feel inferior. The virtual tutor allows learners, even when they fail, to remedy by trial and error and also to learn from mistakes. Often the fear of making a mistake, for many students (especially dyslexic students), is really limiting. If a virtual tutor is effective, this increases the probability that the student will use an application for self-study more often, improving their skills and competences.

Future research should be oriented towards the implementation of the algorithm to support the student (dyslexic and non-dyslexic) during the harmonization of a bassline in which key changes are present: these are the cause of many harmonization errors due to the change of accidents (sharps, flats).

References

1. Feenberg, A.: Critical Theory of Technology. Oxford University Press, Oxford (1991)

2. Bel, B., Vecchione, B.: Computational musicology. Comput. Hum. **27**, 1–5 (1993). https://doi.org/10.1007/BF01830711
3. Hamman, M.: From technical to technological: the imperative of technology in experimental composition. In: Perspectives in New Music, pp. 40–41 (2002)
4. Coutinho, E., Gimenes, M., Martins, J., Miranda, E.: Computational Musicology: An Artificial Life Approach (2005). https://doi.org/10.1109/EPIA.2005.341270
5. Casini, L., Roccetti, M.: The impact of AI on the musical world: will musicians be obsolete? Mimesis edizioni **4**(3), 119–134 (2018). https://doi.org/10.7413/18258646064
6. Chen, N.S., Cheng, I.L., Chew, S.W.: Evolution is not enough: revolutionizing current learning environments to smart learning environments. Int. J. Artif. Intell. Educ. **26**(2), 561–581 (2016)
7. Collins, A., Halverson, R.: Rethinking Education in the Age of Technology: The Digital Revolution and Schooling in America. Teachers College Press (2018)
8. Brèmaud, P.: Markov Chains: Gibbs Fields, Monte Carlo Simulation, and Queues, vol. 31. Springer Science & Business Media, New York, NY (2013)
9. Della Ventura, M.: The influence of the rhythm with the pitch on melodic segmentation. In: Abraham, A., Jiang, X.H., Snášel, V., Pan, J.-S. (eds.) Intelligent Data Analysis and Applications. AISC, vol. 370, pp. 191–201. Springer, Cham (2015). https://doi.org/10.1007/978-3-319-21206-7_17
10. Pachet, F.: Interacting with a musical learning system: the continuator. In: Anagnostopoulou, C., Ferrand, M., Smaill, A. (eds.) ICMAI 2002. LNCS (LNAI), vol. 2445, pp. 119–132. Springer, Heidelberg (2002). https://doi.org/10.1007/3-540-45722-4_12
11. Shapiro, I., Huber, M.: Markov chains for computer music generation. J. Hum. Math. **11**(2), 167–195 (2021). https://doi.org/10.5642/jhummath.202102.08
12. Papadopoulos, A., Roy, P., Pachet, F.: Avoiding plagiarism in Markov sequence generation. In: Proceedings of the Twenty-Eighth AAAI Conference on Artificial Intelligence, AAAI 2014, pp. 2731–2737. AAAI Press, Quebec City, QC (2014)
13. Chomsky, N.: Syntactic Structures. Janua Linguarum. Mouton & Co, The Hague (1957)
14. Hamanaka, M., Hirata, K., Tojo, S.: Melody morphing method based on GTTM. In: ICMC (Ann Arbor, pp. 155–158. Michigan Publishing), MI (2008)
15. Wiggins, G.: A framework for description, analysis and comparison of creative systems. In: Veale, T., Cardoso, F. (eds) Computational Creativity, pp. 21–47. CSACS. Springer, Cham (2019). https://doi.org/10.1007/978-3-319-43610-4_2
16. Anders, T., Miranda, E.R.: Constraint programming systems for modeling music theories and composition. ACM Comput. Surv. **43**, 1–38 (2011). https://doi.org/10.1145/1978802.1978809
17. Cunha, N.D.S., Subramanian, A., Herremans, D.: Generating guitar solos by integer programming. J. Operat. Res. Soc. **69**, 971–985 (2018). https://doi.org/10.1080/01605682.2017.1390528
18. de Mántaras, R.L.: Making music with AI: some examples. In: Bundy, A., Wilson , S. (eds.) Rob Milne: A Tribute to a Pioneering AI Scientist, Entrepreneur and Mountaineer, pp. 90–100. IOS Press (2006)
19. Rothgeb, J.: Simulating musical skills by digital computer. In: Schwanauer, S.M., Levitt, D.A. (eds.) Reprinted in Machine Models of Music, pp. 157–164. The MIT Press, Cambridge, Mass (1993)
20. Wassermann, G., Glickman, M.: Automated harmonization of bass lines from bach chorales: a hybrid approach. Comput. Music J. **43**(2–3), 142–157 (2020). https://doi.org/10.1162/comj_a_00523
21. Coltro, B.: Lezioni di armonia complementare. Ed. Zanibon (1997)
22. Della Ventura, M.: Analysis of algorithms' implementation for melodical operators in symbolical textual segmentation and connected evaluation of musical entropy. Proc. Int. Conf. Models Methods Appl. Sci. Drobeta Turnu Severin **2011**, 66–73 (2011)

23. Ventura, M.D.: DNA Musicale: matematicamente suono, ABEditore, Milano (2018)
24. Ventura, M.D.: Automatic recognition of key modulations in symbolic musical pieces using information theory. In: Arai, K. (ed.) IntelliSys 2021. LNNS, vol. 294, pp. 823–836. Springer, Cham (2022). https://doi.org/10.1007/978-3-030-82193-7_56
25. Weaver, W., Shannon, C.: The Mathematical Theory of Information. Illinois Press, Urbana (1964)
26. Ventura, M.D.: Voice separation in polyphonic music: information theory approach. In: Iliadis, L., Maglogiannis, I., Plagianakos, V. (eds.) AIAI 2018. IAICT, vol. 519, pp. 638–646. Springer, Cham (2018). https://doi.org/10.1007/978-3-319-92007-8_54
27. Cooper, L.: Mind over MIDI: Information sources and system-exclusive data formats. Keyboard October, pp. 110–111 (1986)
28. DuCharme, B.: XML: The Annotated Specification. Prentice Hall PTR, Upper Saddle River, NJ (1999)

Dynamic Big Data Drift Visualization of CPU and Memory Resource Usage in Cloud Computing

Tajwar Mehmood[(✉)] and Seemab Latif[(✉)]

School of Electrical Engineering and Computer Science (SEECS),
National University of Sciences and Technology (NUST), Islamabad, Pakistan
{tmehmood.phdcs17seecs,seemab.latif}@seecs.edu.pk

Abstract. Drift Visualization gives better insight into the nature of changes in the data distribution. Cloud trace is dynamic and generated at a very high pace, it's a serious problem that needs more deep discussions. Drift in cloud resource usage can cause low resource efficiency. In order to achieve optimal resource utilization, cloud provider needs a prediction model based on the data insights. Efficient drift detection optimizes the model prediction. Changes in data can cause these models to reduce their accuracy over a period of time. The focus of this research is to visualize the drift in the cloud at the cluster level. These visualizations will help cloud providers in understanding major factors contributing to the drift. In this paper, Cluster-based visualization using k-means is used to show the drift in the cloud.

Keywords: Concept drift · Drift detection · CPU usage · Memory usage · Drift visualization

1 Introduction

Cloud resource utilization is an open research area that needs more attention. Multiple types of users are sharing over pay as you go model, each with its own unique demands [8]. Each workload consumes varying resource usage. Cloud resource usage traces are rapidly generated as a stream [19] along with complex changes in the distribution [11]. Cloud provider promises to deliver services to its user with the flexibility of scaling both up and down [6]. User demand can change due to sudden, seasonal, or recurring trends. In order to maintain its reputation and promise in a constantly changing environment, clouds need an adaptive prediction model. A good adaptive model can only be designed if the researcher has deeply analyzed the drift in the respected domain. Visualization provides an easy and effective way to comprehend the drift occurrence.

Static models are designed on the basis of the assumption that no changes are happening in the distribution. They do not have the capability to deal with changes. They are learning from the limited amount of training data. Testing data

© IFIP International Federation for Information Processing 2022
Published by Springer Nature Switzerland AG 2022
I. Maglogiannis et al. (Eds.): AIAI 2022, IFIP AICT 646, pp. 27–36, 2022.
https://doi.org/10.1007/978-3-031-08333-4_3

sets are prone to changes due to many factors. The training set can miss a lot of information about the real scenarios. In such a dynamic environment, we need more than a simple prediction model. Whereas, an adaptive model with constant updating is time-consuming and loss of previous information. Frequent model updates can be prevented by using a drift detector but still do not provide information about the type of changes.

Data distribution changes also referred to as concept drift can fail a predictive model. A change in the distribution of input values can cause a change in the labels mapping. An attribute dependency on label class could have been changed or change can happen within the individual attribute. These changes can occur at a different pace of time. A drift that occurs over a shorter period is a sudden drift. Whereas, a drift that occurs over a longer period of time is the gradual drift. Further, drift can also be categorized as virtual or real. A change in the class label is virtual drift, changes in parameter distribution are referred to as real drift. Concept drift is different from anomalies which can be seen as outliers. Anomalies are caused due to critical data leak or deviating from the normal behavior [3]. Whereas, drift is the changes in distribution that can affect the accuracy of the present prediction model but are still a normal behavior.

Different drift detection techniques can detect the drift type but provide no insight into the pattern. In order to understand patterns from these fluctuating usage traces, we need to understand the reasons that are causing these changes. Visualization is one of the ways to understand the patterns more deeply but also can help in identifying the reasons for the drift. Visualization is an easy and more convenient way to depict the changing pattern that is causing different types of drift. Data Charts and maps can be drawn using different techniques to extract unique information. Statistical analysis can also extract patterns from the data and get detailed insight into the distribution. We needed publicly available resource usage data to continue with this research. There are some cloud trace data publicly available that gives a real insight into the cloud providers' usage traces.

The major contribution of this paper is the visualization of sudden drift in the cloud. This visualization is achieved in three steps. First, the CPU and Memory usage are examined individually. In the next steps, the correlation of both resources that are causing changes in usage is identified. This is further shown using a cluster-based visualization. Lastly, identification of external factors that can indirectly affect the sudden drift in the distribution. This analysis can help researchers design better drift detection techniques for cloud providers.

The paper is organized into three sections. First is the literature review related to the sudden drift in the cloud. In the second section, problem analysis is covered along with the publicly available cloud usage traces. The third section shows the deep analysis of the sudden drift visualization. In the end, the paper is concluded with the future work.

2   Literature Review

Most research in the cloud is done on resource usage prediction rather than searching for the reason for usage changes. Load balancing and other mechanisms are already being used by cloud providers to deal with efficient resource utilization but drift detection is ignored. A usage trace can undergo any type of change in the distribution with respect to time, thus, affecting the prediction. A sudden drift exists nearly in all types of domains. There are many internal and external factors contributing to the causes of the drift. In each domain, different factors are causing these changes in the distribution.

Visualization is an easy way to detect and find the reasons for the changes in the concept. Visualization helps a complicated concept to understand in an easy way. Understanding, analyzing, and identifying patterns is one of the major advantages of visualization. These visualizations can vary from simple to complex techniques. Visualization techniques can be divided into three major categories on the basis of the features i.e. Uni, Bi, and Multi variants. Uni-variant is an analysis of a single feature whereas Bi and Multi Variants are combinations of more than one different feature. A line chart variation is being utilized by [16] and [9] to visualize drift. A simple line plot along with the contribution of each attribute is added. An individual as well as aggregated positive and negative mean is represented above the line plot using dashed lines depicting the drift [9]. The importance of visualizations to study drift using scatter plots is focused on by researchers in the medical informatics domain [13]. Brush's parallel histogram is used by Kelvin et al. [10] to visualize the concept drift. It can represent multi-dimensions of data using parallel coordinates. It can transform multidimensional data relationships in two dimensional understandable form [4]. Marlon et al. [7] and Anton et al. [9] both have done work in the business processes. Initially, [7], worked on sudden and gradual drift visualization using the adaptive window techniques. Later, [9] proposed a visual drift detection mechanism based on drift maps, charts, and graphs. Drift visualization in time series data needs more detail than a single visualization technique. Wang et al. [15] proposed a complete system to visualize drift at individual feature levels as well as the effect of the feature on other features and labels. They combined the effect from three different data sources depicted using heat maps.

3   Problem Analysis

Drift Magnitude is easy to visualize but it only shows the drift at each instance level. Group level visualization helps to show the combined effect of drift. Usage clusters can help to see data in terms of high, medium, and low resource usage and can be referred to as capacity groups. Creating capacity groups allow us to compare two different cloud datasets at the same level. A change in these capacity groups can lead to the detection of drift.

Clustering is a technique that easily divides continuous data into categorical forms. This categorical conversion helps in the visualization of the continuous data in a more understandable way. We have used K-means clustering to find the capacity groups. K-means is the most suitable clustering technique for this visualization. K-means can process large amounts of data efficiently [14]. K-means allows forming of clusters on the basis of Euclidean distance and improves its performance using the Elbow method. Different numbers of clusters are used based on the Elbow method to find the optimum number of clusters [2]. A heuristic is used to select the right value of K. Distortion is the distance from the center of clusters and Inertia is the distance of all points from the center of each cluster. On the basis of distortion and inertia, the optimum value of K is selected. In this paper, each cluster in the chart is represented using a different color.

3.1 Datasets

Two cloud cluster datasets are used to compare utilization and drift patterns. This visualization is performed offline and can be done in real-time as well. Google Cluster Usage [12] and Alibaba [18] Trace are used in this study. Both dataset sets are widely used by the cloud research community. Google Usage Trace can be considered as a benchmark dataset for cloud usage trace understanding. Google usage trace is freely available for research purposes. This is a dataset of a one-month duration. It contains resource usage information of a single cluster. Three main types of resources are monitored i.e. CPU, Memory, and Disk I/O. The values of each resource are normalized from 0 to 1. Zero means low usage and it increases high while moving towards the 1. Alibaba Cluster Usage Trace also released a cluster usage trace to help researchers and students. Alibaba is also the largest Cloud computing platform available. They are also providing data related to CPU and Memory utilization at a task level. All resource usage information is normalized from 0 to 1 in order to compare values with the google usage trace. We have selected a limited number of instances in both datasets to visualize the drift. The current window size of 50000 instances is selected which can be varied to see drift over a short or long time ranges. Both datasets are from different time periods but both follow the non-Gaussian distribution and suffer from drift in distribution. Figures 1 and 2 shows the complete variation in the datasets. Google Data was originally normalized from a 0–1 scale but Alibaba was not normalized. Normalization is necessary in order to compare the two dataset's highest and lowest values at the same scale using the min-max method. Datasets characteristics are summarized in the Table 1.

4 Visualization and Analysis

Alibaba and Google Datasets are compared with respect to CPU and memory resources. A CPU usage of a cloud cluster in Fig. 1 visualizes CPU consumption variance of tasks with respect to time in which we can see prominent spikes in CPU resource usage. CPU usage traces of both datasets have sudden spikes after a certain time. Along with that, there are certain periodic drifts in Google usage

Table 1. Dataset characteristics

Datasets	Alibaba	Google
Selected number of instance	10,48575	10,48575
Normalization range	0 to 1	0 to 1
Duration	2 Months, 1 Cluster	1 Month, 1 Cluster

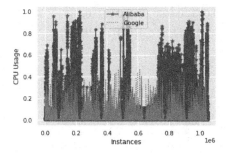

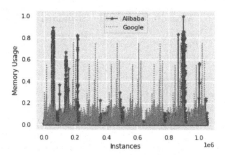

Fig. 1. CPU usage variation   **Fig. 2.** Memory usage variation

data. A cyclic pattern of sudden peak and low usage can is very prominent in the Google CPU usage trace. Whereas, the pattern of Alibaba's CPU usage is very unpredictable. Alibaba resource has higher usage as compared to Google. Google memory usage is given in Fig. 2, a similar recursive pattern to CPU can be visualized because both CPU and Memory usage has a very strong correlation, mentioned at the end of the current section. Sudden decline and peaks of google CPU and Memory are also coordinated in Figs. 1 and 2. Unusual spikes can be seen in Alibaba whereas a recursive pattern can be visualized in Google usage variations. In Figs. 3 and 4, distributions of both datasets are compared. CPU and memory usage distributions of both datasets are similar. Google [12] and Alibaba [18] do not follow the nominal distribution. A right-skewed distribution can be observed as most of the tasks have very low CPU usage. Moving from average towards high usage, there are lesser number of tasks. This distribution can be more understandable using measure of center and measure of spread given in Table 2.

In cloud datasets, distribution is changing over a period of time which can be detected and visualized using a distance measure technique. KS statistical test is to detect changes in distribution. Kolmogorov-Smirnov (KS) test [1] is a non-parametric test suitable for cloud non-Gaussian distribution to confirm the existence of drift in current datasets. It is applied to the dataset and positive results confirmed the existence of drift. Drift magnitude is a property that can give a clear picture of the change. Drift magnitude can be visualized using Hellinger Distance (HD), or Total Variation (TV) [17]. Drift detection follows the following major steps. We can process one or compare two windows to check

Table 2. Measure center and spread of the distribution

DataSet		Alibaba		Google	
Resource type		CPU	Memory	CPU	Memory
Measures of center	Mean	0.029	0.004	0.016	0.021
	Median	0.011	0.001	0.002	0.006
	Mode	0.000	0.000	0.000	0.000
Measure of spread	Standard deviation	0.065	0.025	0.031	0.035
	Range	1	1	0.4736	0.752

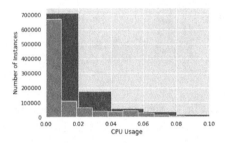

Fig. 3. CPU usage distribution in Google and Alibaba usage

Fig. 4. Memory usage distribution in Google and Alibaba usage

the drift existence. In both cases, there will be a buffer to store some sample data to detect drift in the stream. Buffer data will be divided into required windows. These windows will contain data from equal amounts of data in sequence but from different time periods. HD is the most commonly used to measure distance. In this research, drift magnitude is calculated using the HD method as shown in Fig. 4. Google usage trace shows a recursive pattern but that cannot be observed in the drift magnitude. Higher drift frequency is present in Google as compared to Alibaba as more spikes can be visualized in drift magnitude. Whereas, the Drift Magnitude of Alibaba is high.

In Fig. 6, CPU and memory usage are compared against each other. An increase in CPU Usage has a direct effect on memory usage still there was some unusual presence of instances. As more instances of Google having high CPU and low memory usage. Alibaba also has instances of high memory usage and low CPU usage. To have better insight, the CPU and memory usage correlation is compared and visualized using correlation. We can see it does not follow a normal distribution. To calculate the correlation between CPU and Memory usage, Spearman and Kendalltau measures are used. This correlation test is non-parametric and designed for the non-normal distribution. Two consecutive windows from respected data are used to calculate the correlation. Using Spearman's in Google and Alibaba resources shows a correlation of 0.77 and 0.64.

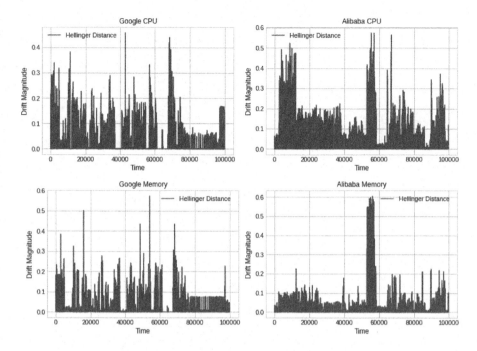

Fig. 5. Alibaba and Google drift magnitude

Kendalltau shows a correlation of 0.54 for Google and 0.45 for Alibaba. These values of both the tests show a strong correlation between the two variables.

Drift detection and visualization need to divide data into sets of windows in order to compare. In this experiment, we have visualized two consecutive windows in clusters. Continuous numerical values of CPU and memory usage are difficult to understand. To compare two different datasets, we need to generalize the usage into clusters. As mentioned earlier, we can see the usage capacity level is defined as high, medium, and low. In Fig. 7, we can see in windows 1 and 2 have nearly the same relation of variables but the cluster formation is different. These changes in formation show the drift at the cluster level. A bigger variation in cluster size can be seen in Alibaba, Fig. 8. Alibaba set is showing a high drift magnitude as compared to google at Cluster Level. In case of more scattered relationships, a cluster level drift visualization is more useful. If data is less scattered than cluster-level this might not capture all the changes in clusters. Thus, simple instance-level drift visualization can do the job. We can see in the Fig. 7 that Alibaba instances are very scattered to google. In the case of Alibaba spread is high thus these changes in clusters can be visualized more clearly as compared to google even though both showed the drift at the cluster level.

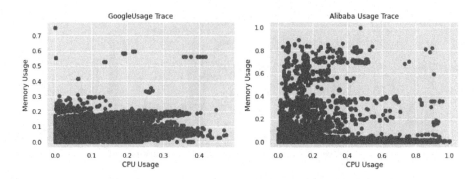

Fig. 6. Google and Alibaba resources correlation

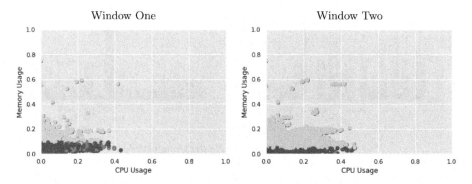

Fig. 7. Cluster visualization of Google resource usage

4.1   External Factors

Multiple and heterogeneous types of users are using the cloud. The facilities cloud provider is claiming is also creating challenges. Cloud allows its users to scale up or down according to their requirements. This rapid elasticity causes more dynamic resource usage. The pay-as-you-go model is also allowing users to reduce costs but creates more variance in the usage. These variations in distribution are not only because of the Cloud providers. There are many external factors that contribute to these changes. Some factors can be personal to users. Epidemic, Seasonal, and Trend peaks can cause a sudden drift. Thus, Cloud has a fluctuating cloud users resource demand [5].

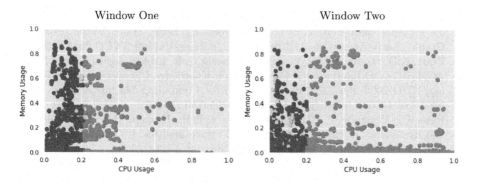

Fig. 8. Cluster visualization of Alibaba resource usage

5   Conclusion and Future Work

Understanding CPU usage is essential for cloud providers. Visualization through most statistical and clustering methods is used to gain more insight and is important for resource prediction. Cloud characteristics, machine, and users heterogeneity, all factors are contributing to the drift. Continuous values are difficult to visualize. Thus, cluster-based visualization helps to see drift at the capacity group level. The above experimentation concludes that more scattered cloud usage data can be visualized more suitably at the cluster level. Alibaba and Google datasets are used to visualize changes in the capacity groups. In the future, this research can be applied in for real-time visualization and drift detection in the dynamic learning environment.

References

1. Berger, V.W., Zhou, Y.: Kolmogorov-Smirnov Test: Overview. Wiley, New York (2014)
2. Bholowalia, P., Kumar, A.: EBK-means: a clustering technique based on elbow method and k-means in WSN. Int. J. Comput. Appl. **105**(9) (2014)
3. Chandola, V., Banerjee, A., Kumar, V.: Anomaly detection: a survey. ACM Comput. Surv. (CSUR) **41**(3), 1–58 (2009)
4. Inselberg, A.: Visualization and data mining of high-dimensional data. Chem. Intell. Lab. Syst. **60**(1–2), 147–159 (2002)
5. Kaur, G., Bala, A., Chana, I.: An intelligent regressive ensemble approach for predicting resource usage in cloud computing. J. Parall. Distrib. Comput. **123**, 1–12 (2019)
6. Kuyoro, S., Ibikunle, F., Awodele, O.: Cloud computing security issues and challenges. Int. J. Comput. Netw. **3**(5), 247–255 (2011)
7. Maaradji, A., Dumas, M., Rosa, M.L., Ostovar, A.: Detecting sudden and gradual drifts in business processes from execution traces. IEEE Trans. Knowl. Data Eng. **29**(10), 2140–2154 (2017). https://doi.org/10.1109/TKDE.2017.2720601
8. Nandgaonkar, S.V., Raut, A.: A comprehensive study on cloud computing. Int. J. Comput. Sci. Mob. Comput. **3**, 733–738 (2014)

9. Yeshchenko, A., Di Ciccio, C., Mendling, J., Polyvyanyy, A.: Visual drift detection for sequence data analysis of business processes. IEEE Trans. Visual. Comput. Graph. (Early Access), 1–1 (2018). https://doi.org/10.1109/TVCG.2021.3050071

10. Pratt, K.B., Tschapek, G.: Visualizing concept drift. In: Proceedings of the Ninth ACM SIGKDD International Conference on Knowledge Discovery and Data Mining, KDD 2003, pp. 735–740. Association for Computing Machinery, New York, NY, USA (2003). https://doi.org/10.1145/956750.956849

11. Reiss, C., Tumanov, A., Ganger, G.R., Katz, R.H., Kozuch, M.A.: Heterogeneity and dynamicity of clouds at scale: Google trace analysis. In: Proceedings of the third ACM Symposium on Cloud Computing, pp. 1–13 (2012)

12. Reiss, C., Tumanov, A., Ganger, G.R., Katz, R.H., Kozuch, M.A.: Heterogeneity and dynamicity of clouds at scale: Google trace analysis. In: Proceedings of the Third ACM Symposium on Cloud Computing. SoCC 2012, Association for Computing Machinery, New York, NY, USA (2012). https://doi.org/10.1145/2391229.2391236

13. Stiglic, G., Kokol, P.: Interpretability of sudden concept drift in medical informatics domain. In: 2011 IEEE 11th International Conference on Data Mining Workshops, pp. 609–613 (2011). https://doi.org/10.1109/ICDMW.2011.104

14. Syakur, M., Khotimah, B., Rochman, E., Satoto, B.D.: Integration k-means clustering method and elbow method for identification of the best customer profile cluster. In: IOP Conference Series: Materials Science and Engineering. vol. 336, p. 012017. IOP Publishing (2018)

15. Wang, X., et al.: Conceptexplorer: visual analysis of concept drifts in multi-source time-series data. In: 2020 IEEE Conference on Visual Analytics Science and Technology (VAST), pp. 1–11. IEEE (2020)

16. Webb, G.I., Lee, L.K., Goethals, B., Petitjean, F.: Analyzing concept drift and shift from sample data. Data Mining Knowl. Discov. **32**(5), 1179–1199 (2018). https://doi.org/10.1007/s10618-018-0554-1

17. Webb, G.I., Lee, L.K., Petitjean, F., Goethals, B.: Understanding concept drift. arXiv preprint arXiv:1704.00362 (2017)

18. Weng, Q., et al.: {MLaaS} in the wild: workload analysis and scheduling in {Large-Scale} heterogeneous {GPU} clusters. In: 19th USENIX Symposium on Networked Systems Design and Implementation (NSDI 22), pp. 945–960 (2022)

19. Yang, C., Huang, Q., Li, Z., Liu, K., Hu, F.: Big data and cloud computing: innovation opportunities and challenges. Int. J. Digit. Earth **10**(1), 13–53 (2017)

On the Interplay of Interpersonal Synchrony, Short-Term Affiliation and Long-Term Bonding: A Second-Order Multi-adaptive Neural Agent Model

Sophie C. F. Hendrikse[1,2], Jan Treur[3(✉)], Tom F. Wilderjans[1,2,4], Suzanne Dikker[1,5], and Sander L. Koole[1]

[1] Amsterdam Emotion Regulation Lab, Department of Clinical Psychology, Vrije Universiteit Amsterdam, Amsterdam, Netherlands
{s.c.f.hendrikse,s.l.koole}@vu.nl, suzanne.dikker@nyu.edu

[2] Methodology and Statistics Research Unit, Institute of Psychology, Leiden University, Leiden, Netherlands
t.f.wilderjans@fsw.leidenuniv.nl

[3] Social AI Group, Department of Computer Science, Vrije Universiteit Amsterdam, Amsterdam, Netherlands
j.treur@vu.nl

[4] Research Group of Quantitative Psychology and Individual Differences, Faculty of Psychology and Educational Sciences, Katholieke Universiteit (KU) Leuven, Leuven, Belgium

[5] NYU – Max Planck Center for Language, Music and Emotion, New York University, New York, USA

Abstract. When people interact, their behaviour tends to become synchronised, a mutual coordination process that fosters short-term adaptations, like increased affiliation, and long-term adaptations, like increased bonding. This paper addresses for the first time how such short-term and long-term adaptivity induced by synchronisation can be modeled computationally by a second-order multi-adaptive neural agent model. This neural agent model addresses movement, affect and verbal modalities and both intrapersonal synchrony and interpersonal synchrony. The behaviour of the introduced neural agent model was evaluated in a simulation paradigm with different stimuli and communication enabling conditions. The outcomes illustrate how synchrony leads to stronger short-term affiliation which in turn leads to more synchrony and stronger long-term bonding, and conversely.

1 Introduction

Whenever people interact, their behaviour tends to become mutually coordinated in time, or synchronized. Interpersonal synchrony has been found to enhance relationship functioning, for example, by inducing greater levels of closeness, concentration, coordination, cooperation, affiliation, alliance, connection, or bonding; e.g., (Accetto et al. 2018; Hove and Risen 2009; Koole and Tschacher 2016; Ramseyer and Tschacher 2011;

© IFIP International Federation for Information Processing 2022
Published by Springer Nature Switzerland AG 2022
I. Maglogiannis et al. (Eds.): AIAI 2022, IFIP AICT 646, pp. 37–57, 2022.
https://doi.org/10.1007/978-3-031-08333-4_4

Tarr et al. 2016; Wiltermuth and Heath 2009). Notably, the benefits of interpersonal synchrony include patterns of mutual adaptation both in the short term and in the long term. For instance, in the context of psychotherapy, a patient and therapist who synchronise their movements (Ramseyer and Tschacher 2011) may experience a stronger sense of sharing the present moment during a therapeutic session (Tschacher et al. 2018). Over multiple sessions, this increased social presence may strengthen the therapeutic bond, which allows the patient and therapist to work together more effectively (Koole and Tschacher 2016). This paper addresses how such different forms of short-term and long-term behavioural adaptivity induced by synchronisation can be modeled computationally by a human-like adaptive neural agent model.

The present model of a neural agent is based on a number of mechanisms in the literatures on cognitive, behavioural, and affective neuroscience. A neural basis for short-term behavioural adaptivity can be found in the recent work on the (nonsynaptic, intrinsic) adaptive excitability of (neural) states; e.g., (Chandra and Barkai 2018; Debanne et al. 2019; Williams et al. 2013; Zhang et al. 2021). By contrast, a neural basis for long-term adaptivity can be found in the classic notion of synaptic plasticity; e.g., (Hebb 1949; Shatz 1992). Together, these two fundamentally different forms of adaptation yield a model of a multi-adaptive neural agent. The two forms of adaptation may also interact with each other, a possibility that we address more fully later on in the present paper.

The amount of adaptation that an agent requires may vary from situation to situation. The capacity to adjust plasticity to the demands of the situation relates to metaplasticity (e.g. Abraham and Bear 1996; Robinson et al. 2016). The present model of a neural agent models metaplasticity as a second-order form of plasticity. The resulting model yields a second-order multi-adaptive neural agent, which is human-like in the sense that it incorporates an interplay of three major mechanisms for adaptivity that according to the neuroscientific literature characterise human agents.

The present model of a neural agent further includes intrapersonal synchrony and interpersonal synchrony and their links to short-term and long-term behavioural adaptivity. To model the pathway from synchrony patterns to this behavioural adaptivity, we included both built-in intrapersonal synchrony and interpersonal synchrony detectors. Here, intrapersonal synchrony means that within an agent actions for the different modalities occur in a coordinated manner. Interpersonal synchrony means that for each modality the actions of the two agents occur in a coordinated manner. The addressed modalities are movement, affect and verbal modalities. We included these three modalities because they have each been shown to be influential in interpersonal behaviour (Koole and Tschacher 2016).

We evaluated the neural agent model in a series of simulation experiments for two agents with a setup in which a number of stochastic circumstances were covered in different (time) episodes. The simulations included not only episodes with a stochastic common stimulus for the two agents, but also episodes with different stochastic stimuli for the agents. Moreover, to analyze the role of communication, stochastic circumstances were also included for episodes when communication was enabled by the environment and episodes when communication was not enabled.

2 Main Assumptions and Background Knowledge

In this section, we present the main assumptions behind the introduced adaptive neural agent model and relate them to the relevant neuroscience literatures. This grounding in neuroscience is based on pathways for a circular interplay of synchrony with both nonsynaptic plasticity (Debanne et al. 2019) and synaptic plasticity (Hebb 1949), thereby covering both short-term time scales and long-term time scales and their interaction. More specifically, the following underlying assumptions are made for the pathways involved.

Interpersonal Synchrony Leads to Adaptation of Joint Behaviour
Interpersonal synchrony is often followed by a behavioural change or adaptation of mutual behaviour; e.g., (Accetto et al. 2018; Fairhurst et al. 2013; Hove and Risen 2009; Kirschner and Tomasello 2010; Koole and Tschacher 2016; Koole et al. 2020; Palumbo et al. 2017; Prince and Brown 2022; Tarr et al. 2016; Valdesolo et al. 2010; Valdesolo and DeSteno 2011; Wiltermuth and Heath 2009). This adaptive shift in mutual behavioural coordination has been observed, for instance, in psychotherapy sessions. Research has shown that therapists were rated more favorably and as more empathic when, beforehand, they were instructed to make their movements more synchronised with the client (Trout and Rosenfeld 1980; Maurer and Tindall 1983; Sharpley et al. 2001, Synofzik et al. 2010). Similarly, Ramseyer and Tschacher (2011) found that initial movement synchrony between client and therapist was predictive of the client's experience of the quality of the alliance at the end of each session. Also Koole and Tschacher (2016) reviewed converging evidence that that movement synchrony has a positive effect on the working alliance between patient and therapist. More generally, synchrony in face-to-face interactions has been found to promote interpersonal affiliation (Feldman 2007; Wiltermuth and Heath 2009).

Behavioural Adaptation After Interpersonal Synchrony Occurs Both in the Form of Short-Term Adaptation and Long-Term Adaptation
Much research on interpersonal synchrony has focused on short-term adaptive changes in interpersonal coordination (Accetto et al. 2018; Hove and Risen 2009; Tarr et al. 2016; Tichelaar and Treur 2018; Wiltermuth and Heath 2009). However, several lines of research have observed effects of interpersonal synchrony on long-term adaptation as well. First, developmental research has observed that movement synchrony between infant and caregivers predict social interaction patterns of the child several years later (Feldman 2007). Second, research on close relationships suggests that early patterns of interpersonal synchrony predict subsequent indicators of relationship functioning, For instance, one study found that spouses' patterns of cortisol variation converged over a period of years, indicating longterm shifts in interpersonal coordination (Laws et al. 2015). Third and last, research on psychotherapy processes has found that markers of interpersonal synchrony in early sessions can predict the development of the therapeutic relationship (e.g., Ramseyer and Tschacher 2011) and therapeutic outcomes (see Koole et al. 2020). Long-term adaptation processes remain less well-studied than short-term

adaptation processes. Nevertheless, the convergence of evidence is sufficient to conclude that interpersonal synchrony is likely to promote both short-term and long-term adaptation in interpersonal relationships.

The Behavioural Adaptation Relies on Different Neural Mechanisms: Synaptic Plasticity of Connections and Nonsynaptic Plasticity of Intrinsic Excitability

In the neuroscientific literature, a distinction is made between synaptic and nonsynaptic (intrinsic) adaptation. The classical notion of synaptic plasticity has been used to explain long-term behavioural adaptation; e.g., (Hebb 1949; Shatz 1992). This addresses how the strength of a connection between different states is adapted over time due to simultaneous activation of the connected states. By contrast, the nonsynaptic adaptation of intrinsic excitability of (neural) states has been addressed in more detail more recently; e.g., (Chandra and Barkai 2018; Debanne et al. 2019; Zhang et al. 2021). The latter form of adaptation has been related, for example, to homeostatic regulation (Williams et al. 2013) and also to how deviant dopamin levels during sleep make that dreams can use more associations due to easier excitable neurons; e.g., (Boot et al. 2017). Moreover, both (synaptic and nonsynaptic) forms of adaptation can easily work together; e.g., (Lisman et al. 2018). In the neural agent model these two adaptation mechanisms and their interaction have been used to model behavioural adaptivity: the former for long-term adaptation and the latter for short-term adaptation. Here an interplay of two types of adaptivity occurs. Synchrony does not only lead to short-term adaptation, but short-term adaptation itself also intensifies interaction which can lead to more synchrony which in turn can strengthen the long-term adaptation. Besides, also long-term adaptivity strengthens interaction which leads to more synchrony and consequently stronger short-term adaptivity. In this way, via multiple circular pathways a dynamic interplay occurs between synchrony, short-term adaptivity and long-term adaptivity.

Plasticity is not a constant feature, it often is highly context-dependent according to what is called metaplasticity; e.g., (Abraham and Bear 1996; Robinson et al. 2016). For example, 'Adaptation accelerates with increasing stimulus exposure' (Robinson et al. 2016). To enable such context-sensitive control of plasticity, second-order adaptation (i.e., adaptation of the adaptation) has been included in the neural agent model, Make which makes the model more realistic.

The Pathways from Synchrony to Behavioural Adaptation Involve Synchrony Detection States

If synchrony occurs for a person and due to this the person adapts the interaction behaviour, this suggests that persons possess a facility to notice or experience synchrony patterns for the different modalities. Indeed, the assumption is made that persons do in some way (perhaps unconsciously) detect synchrony and from there may trigger behavioural adaptation for their interaction behaviour. In the pathway from synchrony patterns to changed interaction behaviour patterns, such synchrony detection states can be considered as specific mediating mental states. In (Treur 2007a, b) such a state p in general is called a mediating state for the effect of a past pattern a on a future pattern b entailed by pattern a; similarly, in (Tse 2013) such a (brain) state is referred to as describing 'informational criteria' for future activation; see also (Treur 2021). In line with previous research described in (Hendrikse et al. 2022c), it is assumed that not only the detected interpersonal synchrony but also the detected intrapersonal synchrony relating to a conscious emotion has a causal effect on the behavioural adaptivity.

3   Self-Modeling Network Modeling

The presented neural agent model is based on network-oriented modeling. Following (Treur 2020a, b), a temporal-causal network model is characterised by (here X and Y denote nodes of the network, also called states):

- *Connectivity characteristics*
  Connections from a state X to a state Y and their weights $\omega_{X,Y}$
- *Aggregation characteristics*
  For any state Y, some combination function $\mathbf{c}_Y(..)$ defines the aggregation that is applied to the impacts $\omega_{X,Y}X(t)$ on Y from its incoming connections from states X
- *Timing characteristics*
  Each state Y has a speed factor η_Y defining how fast it changes for given causal impact

The following difference (or related differential) equations that are used for simulation purposes and also for analysis of temporal-causal networks, incorporate these network characteristics $\omega_{X,Y}$, $\mathbf{c}_Y(..)$ and η_Y in a standard numerical format:

$$Y(t + \Delta t) = Y(t) + \eta_Y[c_Y(\omega_{X_1,Y}X_1(t), \ldots, \omega_{X_k,Y}X_k(t)) - Y(t)]\Delta t \qquad (1)$$

for any state Y and where X_1 to X_k are the states from which Y gets its incoming connections. Note that (1) has a format similar to that of recurrent neural networks. Within the software environment described in (Treur 2020a, Chap. 9), a large number of currently around 60 useful basic combination functions are included in a combination function library. The above concepts enable to design network models and their dynamics in a declarative manner, based on mathematically defined functions and relations. The examples of combination functions that are applied in the model introduced here can be found in Table 1.

Table 1. The combination functions used in the introduced network model

	Notation	Formula	Parameters	Used for
Advanced logistic sum	$\mathbf{alogistic}_{\sigma,\tau}(V_1, \ldots, V_k)$	$[\frac{1}{1+e-\sigma(V_1+\cdots+V_k-\tau)} - \frac{1}{1+e\sigma\tau}](1 + e^{-\sigma\tau})$	Steepness σ Excitability threshold τ	X_4–X_5, X_{10}–X_{16}, X_{24}–X_{26}, X_{31}–X_{38}, X_{45}–X_{47}, X_{54}–X_{59}, X_{63}–X_{71}, X_{75}-X_{93}
Complement-al difference	$\mathbf{compdiff}(V_1, V_2)$	0 if $V_1 = V_2 = 0$ $1 - \frac{|V_1-V_2|}{\max(V_1,V_2)}$ else	–	$X18$–$X23$, $X39$–$X44$ (synchrony detectors)
Random Stepmod	$\mathbf{randstepmod}_{\rho,\delta}(V)$	0 if $0 \leq$ time t mod ρ $\leq \delta$ $aV + (1-a)$rand$(1,1)$ else	Repitition ρ Step time δ	X_3 (common stimulus) X_{60}–X_{62}, X_{72}–X_{74} (communication enablers)

(*continued*)

Table 1. (*continued*)

	Notation	Formula	Parameters	Used for
Random Stepmodopp	**randstepmodopp**$_{\rho,\delta}(V)$	0 if $\delta \leq$ time t mod ρ $\leq \rho$ $aV + (1-a)\text{rand}(1,1)$ else	Repitition ρ Step time δ	X_1–X_2 (individual stimuli)
Euclidean	**eucl**$_{n,\lambda}(V_1, ..., V_k)$	$\sqrt[n]{\dfrac{V_1{}^n+\cdots+V_k{}^n}{\lambda}}$	Order n Scaling factor λ	X_6–X_9, X_{27}–X_{30} (sensing) X_{48}-X_{53} (communication)

Here, for the third and fourth function, rand(1, 1) draws a random number from [0, 1] in a uniform manner and a is a persistence factor (with value 0.5 used in the simulations).

Realistic network models are usually adaptive: often not only their states but also some of their network characteristics change over time. By using a *self-modeling network* (also called a *reified* network), a similar network-oriented conceptualization can also be applied to adaptive networks to obtain a declarative description using mathematically defined functions and relations for them as well; see (Treur 2020a, b). This works through the addition of new states to the network (called *self-model states*) which represent (adaptive) network characteristics. In the graphical 3D-format as shown in Sect. 4, such additional states are depicted at a next level (called *self-model level* or *reification level*), where the original network is at the *base level*.

As an example, the weight $\omega_{X,Y}$ of a connection from state X to state Y can be represented (at a next self-model level) by a self-model state named $\mathbf{W}_{X,Y}$. Similarly, all other network characteristics from $\omega_{X,Y}$, $\mathbf{c}_Y(..)$ and η_Y can be made adaptive by including self-model states for them. For example, an adaptive excitability threshold τ_Y (for a logistic combination function) for state Y can be represented by a self-model state named $\mathbf{T}_Y$ and an adaptive speed factor η_Y can be represented by a self-model state named $\mathbf{H}_Y$.

As the outcome of such a process of network reification is also a temporal-causal network model itself, as has been shown in (Treur 2020a, Chap. 10), this self-modeling network construction can easily be applied iteratively to obtain multiple orders of self-models at multiple (first-order, second-order, …) self-model levels. For example, a second-order self-model may include a second-order self-model state $\mathbf{H}_{\mathbf{W}_{X,Y}}$ representing the speed factor $\eta_{\mathbf{W}_{X,Y}}$ for the dynamics of first-order self-model state $\mathbf{W}_{X,Y}$ which in turn represents the adaptation of connection weight $\omega_{X,Y}$. Similarly, a second-order self-model may include a second-order self-model state $\mathbf{H}_{\mathbf{T}_Y}$ representing the speed factor $\eta_{\mathbf{T}_Y}$ for the dynamics of first-order self-model state $\mathbf{T}_Y$ which in turn represents the adaptation of excitability threshold τ_Y for Y.

In the current paper, this multi-level self-modeling network perspective will be applied to obtain a second-order adaptive network architecture addressing controlled adaptation induced by detected synchrony. In this self-modeling network architecture, the first-order self-model models the adaptation of the base level network, and the second-order self-model level the control over this. As an example, the control level can be used to make the adaptation speed context-sensitive as addressed by metaplasticity literature such as (Abraham and Bear 1996; Robinson et al. 2016). For instance, the metaplasticity principle 'Adaptation accelerates with increasing stimulus exposure' formulated by (Robinson et al. 2016) can easily be modeled by using second-order self-model states; this actually has been done for the introduced model, as will be discussed in Sect. 4.

4   The Adaptive Neural Agent Model

In this section, our adaptive neural agent model is explained in some detail. The controlled adaptive agent design uses a self-modeling network architecture of three levels as discussed in Sect. 3: a base level, a first-order self-model level, and a second-order self-model level. Here the (middle) first-order self-model level models how connections of the base level are adapted over time, and the (upper) second-order self-model level models the control over the adaptation.

4.1   Base level

Figure 1 shows a graphic overview of the base level of the agent model (agents are indicated by the big boxes) and the available Appendix provides explanations for all of its states (see Linked Data at https://www.researchgate.net/publication/359635368).

For each agent, a number of interaction states were modeled: states involved in sensing (indicated by sense) are on the left-hand side of each box, and states involved in execution or expression of actions (move, exp_affect, talk) on the right-hand side. In between these interaction states, within a box are the agent's internal mental states; outside the boxes are the world states. Note that we assume that each agent also senses its own actions, modeled by the arrows from right to left outside the box.

For each agent, we modeled a number of internal mental states such as sensory representation states (rep) and preparation states (prep) for each of the three modalities: movement m, expression of affect b, and verbal action v. Furthermore, each agent has a conscious emotion state for affective response b (cons_emotion). Each of the mentioned states is depicted in Fig. 1 by a light pink circle shape. For each modality, its representation state has an outgoing (response) connection to the corresponding preparation state and it has an incoming (prediction) connection back from the preparation state to model internal mental simulation (Damasio 1999; Hesslow 2002).

Last but not least, there are the six synchrony detector states (depicted in Fig. 2 by the darker pink diamond shapes) which are introduced here. As in (Hendrikse et al. 2022c) we cover three *intrapersonal synchrony detection states* for the three pairs of the three modalities:

movement - emotion (m-b)
movement - verbal action (m-v)
emotion - verbal action (b-v)

These intrapersonal synchrony detection states have incoming connections from the two execution states for the modalities they address. The conscious emotion state is triggered by incoming connections from the preparation state for affective response b

together with the three intrapersonal synchrony detection states, following (Grandjean et al. 2008). In addition, the conscious emotion state has an incoming connection from the verbal action execution state (for noticing the emotion in the verbal utterence) and an outgoing connection to the preparation of the verbal action (for emotion integration in the verbal action preparation).

There are three *interpersonal synchrony detection states* for the three modalities m, b, and v. Each of them has two incoming connections: from the sensing state (representing the action of the other person) and the execution state (representing the own action) of the modality addressed.

For a number of states and connections, their excitability and connection weights are adaptive depending on detected synchrony: detected synchrony leads to becoming more sensitive to sensing a person and expressing to that person (short-tem effect) and to connecting stronger to the person (long-term effect). Here, two different time scales for the adaptations are considered:

- on the short term enhancing the excitability of such internal states, so that they become more responsive or sensitive (a form of instantaneous homeostatic regulation)
- on the long term making the weights of such connections stronger so that propagation between states is strengthened (a form of a more endurable bonding)

This applies to two types of states and four types of connections in particular, all playing an important role in the interaction behaviour of the two agents:

- **Short-term adaptive excitability for internal states**

    - the representation states for each of the three modalities
    - the execution states for each of the three modalities

- **Long-term adaptive internal and external connections**

    - the (representing) connections from sensing to representation states for each of the three modalities
    - the (executing) connections from preparation to execution states for each of the three modalities
    - the (observing) connections from world states to sensing states
    - the (effectuating) connections from execution states to world states

Thus, more synchrony detected will lead to enhanced excitability for these types of states (short-term adaptation) and for these connections to become stronger (long-term adaptation); each type of all these adaptations contributes in its own way (and time scale) to the interaction behaviour of the persons. In the short term, more sensitive states for representations will lead to gaining better images of the modalities of the other person; this will make the sensed signals better available and accessible for the brain. More sensitive states for execution will lead to better expressed own modalities, so that the other person can sense them better.

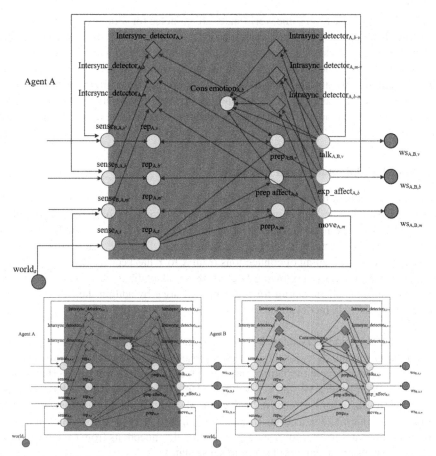

Fig. 1. Base level of (1) the introduced adaptive agent model (upper picture) with three modalities and (in dark pink) six synchrony detection states for intrapersonal and interpersonal synchrony and (2) how the agents interact (lower picture) according to the three modalities (Color figure online)

Over time and repeated interactions, a stronger (external) observing connection will lead to sensing the other person better (e.g., turning sensors in the right direction and bending or getting closer to the other), and a stronger representing connection again (but now in a more endurable manner) will make the sensed signals better available and accessible for the brain. Conversely, a stronger executing connection will also contribute (in an endurable manner) to stronger expression and acting toward the other and a stronger effectuating connection to better availability (for the other) of the action effects in the world (e.g., more visible, better hearable by directing and positioning in the right direction and bending or getting closer to the other). In Sect. 4.2, we discuss in more detail how we modeled these forms of adaptivity and their control using the principle of self-modeling of the network model.

Finally, at the base level some world states are modeled for stimuli *s* that are sensed by the agents. In the simulations, they have stochastic activation levels. In some episodes one common stimulus is observed by both agents (for example when they physically meet and therefore are in the same environment), but in other episodes the agents receive different stimuli. Furthermore, also the world situation's suitability for enabling communication between the two agents is modeled by similar stochastic fluctuations. Moreover, two context states are included to model the conditions to maintain excitability thresholds well.

4.2   Modeling Adaptation and Its Control

We modeled adaptation and its control needed in the neural agent model using a 'self-modeling network'; see Sect. 3 or (Treur 2020a, b). Following what has been described in Sect. 4.1, for a number of states Y adaptive excitability has been modeled via the excitability threshold τ_Y of the logistic function used for these states (see Table 1). Moreover, the strengthening of connections from X to Y has been modeled via adaptive connection weights $\omega_{X,Y}$. Following Sect. 3, these adaptations have been modeled in particular through self-modeling for these τ_Y and $\omega_{X,Y}$ by adding the following first- and second-order self-model states:

- first-order self-model **T**-states $\mathbf{T}_Y$ for short-term adaptation of the adaptive base excitability thresholds τ_Y for the internal representation states and execution states Y for the three considered modalities (movement, affective response and verbal action)
- first-order self-model **W**-states $\mathbf{W}_{X,Y}$ for adaptation of the adaptive base connection weights $\omega_{X,Y}$ for both internal and external connections for the three considered modalities; internal connections from sense states to representation states and from preparation states to execution states, and external connections from execution states to world states and from world states to sense states
- second-order self-model $\mathbf{H_T}$-states for control of the adaptation of the adaptive excitability thresholds τ_Y for the internal representation states and execution states Y
- second-order self-model $\mathbf{H_W}$-states for control of the adaptation of the adaptive base connection weights $\omega_{X,Y}$.

Figure 2 shows the overal design of the network model; here, the first-order self-model states are in the middle (blue) plane and the second-order self-model states in the upper (purple) plane. The first-order states include **T**-states representing the excitability thresholds of representation and execution states and **W**-states representing the weights of the different types of adaptive connections addressed. By changing the activation values of these **T**-states and **W**-states, the corresponding excitability thesholds and connection weights change accordingly. This change occurs due to the influences from the detected synchronies, modeled by the upward (blue) arrows in Fig. 3 from the synchrony detection states in the base plane to the **T**-states and **W**-states in the middle plane.

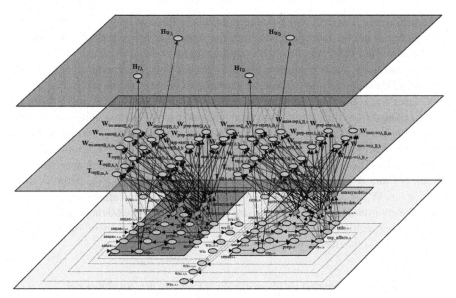

Fig. 2. Overview of the overall second-order adaptive network model (Color figure online)

There are four second-order self-model states to control the adaptation: two second-order self-model states H_{TA} and H_{TB} for excitability adaptation control, one for each agent, and two second-order self-model states H_{WA} and H_{WB} for connection weight adaptation control, also one for each agent. These represent the adaptation speed (learning rate) for the adaptive excitability and connections for the concerning agent. They model the second-order adaptation (or metaplasticity) principle 'Adaptation accelerates with stimulus exposure' (Robinson et al. 2016). To this end they have incoming connections (blue upward arrows from base plane to upper plane) from the stimulus representation states at the base level.

5 Simulation Results

5.1 Design of the Simulation Experiments

In this section, we evaluate our neural agent model in an experimental simulation paradigm. Our paradigm was set up in such a way that we could evaluate the behaviour of our two agents during four different types of consecutive episodes (see Table 2 and Fig. 3) which are explained below. Each of these types of episodes lasted for 30 time units, so that a cycle of four episodes equaled 120 time units. Our total simulation run had a duration of 840 time units and the step size (Δt) was 0.5, resulting in 1680 computational steps in total for each simulation run. This means that each cycle of four episodes was repeated 7 times in each simulation. As it concerns a partly stochastic simulation, we ran 20 repetitions of each simulation with the same episodic paradigm and parameter settings, to get a sense of the robustness of the neural agent model's behaviour. It turned out that general patterns were approximately similar across all independent simulations. Therefore, we selected one simulation to discuss in the upcoming subsections.

Regarding the four different types of episodes in this simulation, they manipulate both whether or not the two agents received the same or a different stochastic stimulus and whether or not they were able to communicate (with some stochastic variations in enabling conditions, due to environmental changes and noise) with each other (Table 2). The specific episodes for the considered example simulation are shown in Fig. 3. The world states $ws_{s,A}$ and $ws_{s,B}$ indicate the different stimuli for agent A and B from the world (activated from time 0 to 60 and then repeated every 120 time units; see the dark solid and dashed blue lines for A, resp. B). Similarly, world state ws_s indicates the common stimulus (activated from time 60 to 120 and then repeated every 120 time units; see the purple line). These three states have values stochastically fluctuating approximately between 0.7 and 0.9. Furthermore, the self-model states $\mathbf{W}_{exec\text{-}wsr,A,B}$ (from A to B) and the states $\mathbf{W}_{exec\text{-}wsr,B,A}$ (from B to A) indicate the communication enabling conditions in the environment. They are activated from time 30 to time 60 thereby fluctuating stochastically roughly between 0.45 and 0.65 and then repeated every 60 time units. All these stochastic activation patterns indeed follow Table 2.

Table 2. Simulation paradigm of each run with the neural agent model

Four different types of episodes: timing and conditions				
Type	Stimulus	Communication enabled	Duration	Time intervals
Episode 1	Different	No	30	0–30 + repetition after each 120
Episode 2	Different	Yes	30	30–60 + repetition after each 120
Episode 3	Common	No	30	60–90 + repetition after each 120
Episode 4	Common	Yes	30	90–120 + repetition after each 120

5.2 Behaviour of the Base States of the Neural Agent Model

For the base states, in the first phase for time 0 to 10 the representations (states $rep_{s,A}$ and $rep_{s,B}$) for the stimulus are activated (the curves fluctuating around 0.8) and preparations (states $prep_{x,A}$) for actions are triggered (curves going to 1); see the upper graph in Fig. 4. This leads, together with the intrapersonal synchrony detection activation (see Fig. 5 and 6), to the conscious emotion around time 10 (red curve going to 1), but this still is only internal processing as no executions of actions take place yet. The action executions (states $move_{m,A}$, $exp\_affect_{b,A}$, and $talk_{A,B,v}$) for both agents start to come up after time 10 (e.g., the purple line); this also depends on the short-term adaptations that will be discussed in Sect. 5.4. The curves immediately under these executions concern the sensing of the other agent's actions (the $sense_{A,x,B}$ and $sense_{B,x,A}$ states); in some periods they are slightly fluctuating due to environmental noise on the communication channels. The actual communication level (the $ws_{x,A,B}$ and $ws_{x,B,A}$ states) is seen below

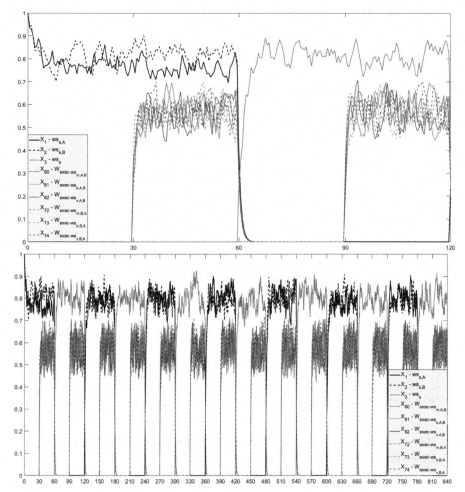

Fig. 3. The stimuli and interaction enabling states in the neural agent model from 0 to 120 time units (upper graph) and from 0 to 840 time units (lower graph). (Color figure online)

it from 30 to 60 and from 90 to 120. For the longer term, the lower graph in Fig. 4 shows that each interval with enabling conditions for communication leads to higher activations of the action executions (the purple line) until values around 0.8 are reached. This is due to a long-term behavioural adaptation that is discussed in Sect. 5.5. Accordingly, the sensing states become higher as well over this longer term, but not as high as the action executions, due to a communication bias incorporated in the model. This overall pattern shows that the enabling conditions for communication have a stronger adaptive effect on the actions than having a common stimulus.

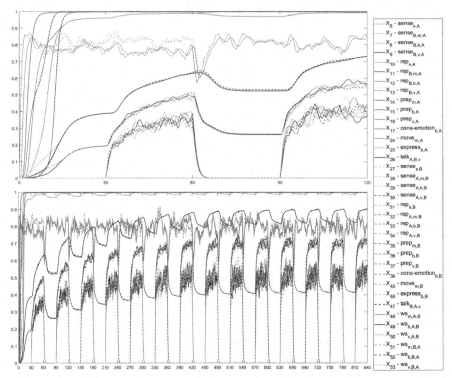

Fig. 4. The base states in the neural agent model from 0 to 120 time units (upper graph) and from 0 to 840 time units (lower graph).

5.3 Behaviour of the Intrapersonal Synchrony and Interpersonal Synchrony Detector States

The curves that the graphs in Fig. 5 and Fig. 6 have in common depict the detected intrapersonal synchrony and interpersonal synchrony. Here:

- the detected intrapersonal synchrony detection is represented by the states intrasyncdet$_{A,x\text{-}y}$ and intrasyncdet$_{B,x\text{-}y}$ shown as the light green and light blue curves going to 1 from time 0 to 15
- the interpersonal synchrony detection is represented by the states intersyncdet$_{A,B,x}$ and intersyncdet$_{B,A,x}$ shown as the red and blue curves going to 0.4 from time 0 to 30 and further to 0.8 from time 30 to 60

Here it can be observed that the detection of intrapersonal synchrony takes place already in the first episode from time 0 to 30, meaning no common stimulus or communication is required. In contrast, the detection of interpersonal synchrony strongly depends on the interaction between the two agents. Note also that the former type of detected synchrony reaches a perfect level of 1, due to the coherent internal makeup of the agents, while the latter type does not get higher than around 0.8. At first sight this may look strange, given that the actual executions of actions of both agents are practically the same, as discussed above (see Sect. 5.2 and Fig. 5). However, this is due to the communication bias that was also noted above in Sect. 5.2. This demonstrates the capability of the model that it is able to distinguish a subjective personally detected interpersonal synchrony from an objective form of interpersonal synchrony detection as might be assigned by an external observer but not by the agent itself.

5.4 The Interplay Between Synchrony and Short-Term Adaptation

In Fig. 5 the synchrony detection states are shown together with the states involved in the short-term adaptation: the first-order self-model T-states that represent the adaptive excitability thresholds for representation and execution states and the second-order self-model H_T-states that represent the T-states' speed factors (adaptive learning rates). Except the synchrony detection states already discussed in Sect. 5.3, the graphs show two light green curves fluctuating around 0.6 for the H_T-states and a blue curve going down to below 0.3 for the T-states.

According to the metaplasticity principle 'Adaptation accelerates with increasing stimulus exposure' (Robinson et al. 2016), the H_T-states indeed fluctuate with the stimuli. Also in accordance with this, when one stimulus period is in transition to another stimulus period, it can be seen that there is a short dip in the values of the H_T-states, as stimuli start from 0, so there is a very short period of a lower level, as can also be seen in Fig. 3. Moreover, it is clear that the T-states (e.g., the blue curve) show an opposite pattern compared to the pattern of the interpersonal synchrony detection states. In particular, in the episodes from 30 to 60 and from 90 to 120 (and so on), where the detected interpersonal synchrony is the highest, the T-states for the excitability thresholds are the lowest. This is a short-term adaptation that makes that these agent states related to the communication with the other agent have a higher excitability due to the detected interpersonal synchrony, which will have an intensifying effect on their communication. Not coincidentally, the mentioned periods are also the periods with good enabling conditions for communication (see also Sect. 5.2). It can also be noted that this tendency is a short-term effect and is reversible: the T-states get higher again when the detected interpersonal synchrony gets lower.

5.5 The Interplay Between Synchrony and Long-Term Adaptation

In Fig. 6 the synchrony detection states are shown together with the states involved in the long-term adaptation: the first-order self-model W-states that represent the adaptive weights for the connections to the representation and execution states and the second-order self-model H_W-states that represent the W-states' speed factors (adaptive learning rates). Here, except the synchrony detection states already discussed in Sect. 5.3, the graphs show the W-states (e.g., a blue curve) slowly and gradually going up to above 0.5 at time 120 and further up to about 0.8 at time 840.

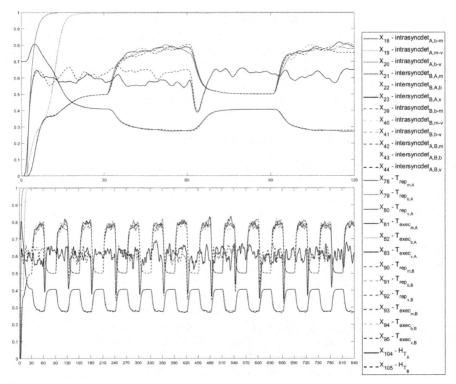

Fig. 5. The detected intrapersonal synchrony, interpersonal synchrony and short-term adaptation T-states in the neural agent model from 0 to 120 time units (upper graph) and from 0 to 840 time units (lower graph). (Color figure online)

Moreover, at a very low level, the curves for the H_W-states can be seen. They also fluctuate according to the metaplasticity principle 'Adaptation accelerates with increasing stimulus exposure' (Robinson et al. 2016), but at a very low level around 0.005 (see the lower graph in Fig. 6). Again, following the same principle, when one stimulus period is in transition to another stimulus period, it can be seen that there is a short dip in the values of the H_W-states. This happens because stimuli start from 0, so there is a very short period of a lower level (see Fig. 3).

The pattern of the **W**-states indeed shows a long-term adaptation effect. It highlights that they get a repeated boost in the time intervals 30–60, 90–120, and so on, and show a form of persistency. These boosts occur specifically in these intervals for a reason. These intervals are when there are communication enabling conditions and as discussed in Sect. 5.4 that induces synchrony and the short-term adaptation via the **T**-states, which in turn add to synchrony. Therefore these two effects are at the basis of these boosts for the long-term adaptation. In this way there is a form of interaction between short-term and long-term adaptation.

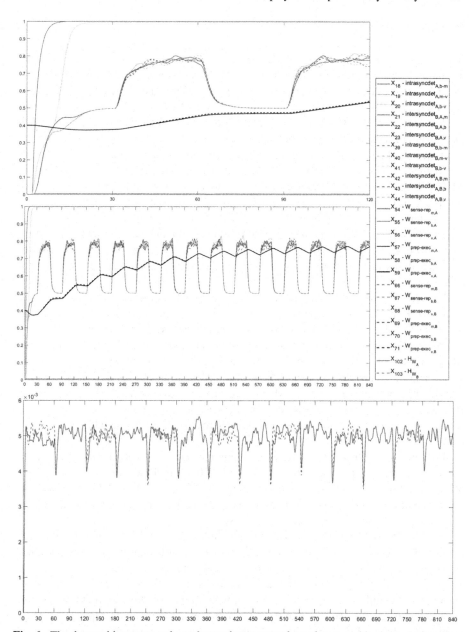

Fig. 6. The detected intrapersonal synchrony, interpersonal synchrony and long-term adaptation **W**-states and $\mathbf{H_W}$-states in the neural agent model from 0 to 120 time units (upper graph) and from 0 to 840 time units (middle graph). The lower graph depicts the $\mathbf{H_W}$-states with a different vertical scale (times 10^{-3}). (Color figure online)

6 Discussion

In this paper, a neural agent model was introduced for the way intrapersonal and interpersonal synchrony induce behavioural adaptivity between the synchronized persons; e.g., (Accetto et al. 2018; Hove and Risen 2009; Kirschner and Tomasello 2010; Koole and Tschacher 2016; Palumbo et al. 2017; Prince and Brown 2022; Tarr et al. 2016; Valdesolo et al. 2010; Wiltermuth and Heath 2009). The model is multi-adaptive in that the behavioral adaptivity covers both short-term and long-term adaptations, reflecting short-term affiliation and long-term bonding. The former type of adaptation was modeled using (nonsynaptic) adaptive excitability (Chandra and Barkai 2018; Debanne et al. 2019; Williams et al. 2013; Zhang et al. 2021), whereas for the latter type a more classical synaptic type of adaptation (Hebb 1949; Shatz 1992) was used. Following the aforementioned literature on synchrony, both types of adaptivity where modeled as driven by the (internally detected) intrapersonal synchrony and interpersonal synchrony for the agent. By also including metaplasticity (Abraham and Bear 1996) in the model to control the adaptations in a context-sensitive manner, the agent model became second-order adaptive.

We already engaged in computational modeling of synchrony between agents in earlier work such as (Hendrikse et al. 2022a, b). However, in the models described there, no (subjective) internal detection of synchrony takes place. Moreover, in (Hendrikse et al. 2022b) no adaptivity was covered, whereas in (Hendrikse et al. 2022a) another type of adaptivity was incorporated, namely of internal connections from representation states to preparation states. As far as we know, (Hendrikse et al. 2022c) describes the only other computational agent model where subjective synchrony detection is addressed. However, by that model no long-term behavioural adaptivity is covered and also no adaptive intrinsic excitability is addressed, whereas both are included in the current model.

Earlier work addressing behavioural adaptation due to coordinated actions can be found in (Accetto et al. 2018; Tichelaar and Treur 2018). In these cases, a dynamic form of the 'bonding based on homophily' principle (McPherson et al. 2001) was used to model the effect of coordination of emotions and actions on behavioural adaptivity but no (subjective) detection of synchrony was used.

Thus a flexible human-like second-order multi-adaptive neural agent model was obtained for the way in which detected synchrony leads to different types of behavioural adaptivity concerning the short-term affiliation and long-term bonding between the two agents. For further work, many more simulation experiments can be designed and conducted, for example to explore the question which types of short-term synchrony are most likely to become translated into long-term benefits for a relationship, or to explore in more detail the roles of intrapersonal synchrony and interpersonal synchrony.

Considered from a wider scientific perspective, the model can provide a basis to develop adaptive virtual agents that are able to concentrate on each other by short-term behavioural adaptivity and bond with each other by long-term behavioural adaptivity in a human-like manner.

References

Abraham, W.C., Bear, M.F.: Metaplasticity: the plasticity of synaptic plasticity. Trends Neurosci. **19**(4), 126–130 (1996)

Accetto, M., Treur, J., Villa, V.: An adaptive cognitive-social model for mirroring and social bonding during synchronous joint action. In: Proceedings of the 9th International Conference on Biologically Inspired Cognitive Architectures, BICA 2018, vol. 2. (Procedia Computer Science, vol. 145, pp. 3–12) (2018). https://doi.org/10.1016/j.procs.2018.11.002

Boot, N., Baas, M., Van Gaal, S., Cools, R., De Dreu, C.K.W.: Creative cognition and dopaminergic modulation of fronto-striatal networks: Integrative review and research agenda. Neurosci. Biobehav. Rev. **78**, 13–23 (2017)

Chandra, N., Barkai, E.: A non-synaptic mechanism of complex learning: modulation of intrinsic neuronal excitability. Neurobiol. Learn. Mem. **154**, 30–36 (2018)

Damasio, A.R.: The Feeling of What Happens: Body and Emotion in the Making of Consciousness. Houghton Mifflin Harcourt (1999)

Debanne, D., Inglebert, Y., Russier, M.: Plasticity of intrinsic neuronal excitability. Curr. Opin. Neurobiol. **54**, 73–82 (2019)

Fairhurst, M.T., Janata, P., Keller, P.E.: Being and feeling in sync with an adaptive virtual partner: brain mechanisms underlying dynamic cooperativity. Cereb. Cortex **23**(11), 2592–2600 (2013). https://doi.org/10.1093/cercor/bhs243

Feldman, R.: Parent–infant synchrony biological foundations and developmental outcomes. Curr. Dir. Psychol. Sci. **16**, 340–345 (2007). https://doi.org/10.1111/j.1467-8721.2007.00532.x

Grandjean, D., Sander, D., Scherer, K.R.: Conscious emotional experience emerges as a function of multilevel, appraisal-driven response synchronization. Conscious. Cogn. **17**(2), 484–495 (2008)

Hebb, D.O.: The Organization of Behavior: A Neuropsychological Theory. John Wiley and Sons, New York (1949)

Hendrikse, S.C.F., Kluiver, S., Treur, J., Wilderjans, T.F., Dikker, S., Koole, S.L.: How Virtual Agents Can Learn to Synchronize: an Adaptive Joint Decision-Making Model of Psychotherapy. Cognitive Systems Research, to appear (2022a)

Hendrikse, S.C.F., Treur, J., Wilderjans, T.F., Dikker, S., Koole, S.L.: On the Same Wavelengths: emergence of multiple synchronies among multiple agents. In: Van Dam, K.H., Verstaevel, N. (eds.) MABS 2021. LNCS (LNAI), vol. 13128, pp. 57–71. Springer, Cham (2022b). https://doi.org/10.1007/978-3-030-94548-0_5

Hendrikse, S.C.F., Treur, J., Wilderjans, T.F., Dikker, S., Koole, S.L.: On Becoming In Sync with Yourself and Others: an Adaptive Agent Model for how Persons Connect by Detecting Intra- and Interpersonal Synchrony, under submission. See also: In Sync With Yourself and With Others: Detection of Intra- and Interpersonal Synchrony Within an Adaptive Agent Model. In: Face2face: Advancing the Science of Social Interaction, Royal Society, London (2022c). https://www.researchgate.net/publication/358964043

Hesslow, G.: Conscious thought as simulation of behaviour and perception. Trends Cogn. Sci. **6**, 242–247 (2002)

Hove, M.J., Risen, J.L.: It's all in the timing: interpersonal synchrony increases affiliation. Soc. Cogn. **27**(6), 949–960 (2009)

Kirschner, S., Tomasello, M.: Joint music making promotes prosocial behavior in 4-year-old children. Evol. Hum. Behav. **31**, 354–364 (2010). https://doi.org/10.1016/j.evolhumbehav.2010.04.004

Koole, S.L., Tschacher, W.: Synchrony in psychotherapy: a review and an integrative framework for the therapeutic alliance. Front. Psychol. **7**, 862 (2016)

Koole, S.L., Tschacher, W., Butler, E., Dikker, S., Wilderjans, T.F.: In sync with your shrink. In: Forgas, J.P., Crano, W.D., Fiedler, K. (eds.) Applications of Social Psychology, pp. 161–184. Taylor and Francis, Milton Park (2020)

Laws, H.B., Sayer, A.G., Pietromonaco, P.R., Powers, S.I.: Longitudinal changes in spouses' HPA responses: convergence in cortisol patterns during the early years of marriage. Health Psychol. **34**(11), 1076 (2015)

Lisman, J., Cooper, K., Sehgal, M., Silva, A.J.: Memory formation depends on both synapse-specific modifications of synaptic strength and cell-specific increases in excitability. Nat. Neurosci. **2018**(21), 309–314 (2018)

Maurer, R.E., Tindall, J.H.: Effect of postural congruence on client's perception of counselor empathy. J. Counseling Psychol. **30**, 158 (1983). https://doi.org/10.1037/0022-0167.30.2.158

McPherson, M., Smith-Lovin, L., Cook, J.M.: Birds of a feather: homophily in social networks. Ann. Rev. Sociol. **27**(1), 415–444 (2001)

Palumbo, R.V., et al.: Interpersonal autonomic physiology: a systematic review of the literature. Pers. Soc. Psychol. Rev. **21**(2), 99–141 (2017)

Prince, K., Brown, S.: Neural correlates of partnered interaction as revealed by cross-domain ALE meta-analysis. Psychol. Neurosc. (2022). https://doi.org/10.1037/pne0000282

Ramseyer, F., Tschacher, W.: Nonverbal synchrony in psychotherapy: coordinated body movement reflects relationship quality and outcome. J. Consult. Clin. Psychol. **79**, 284–295 (2011). https://doi.org/10.1037/a0023419a

Robinson, B.L., Harper, N.S., McAlpine, D.: Meta-adaptation in the auditory midbrain under cortical influence. Nat. Commun. **7**, e13442 (2016)

Shatz, C.J.: The developing brain. Sci. Am. **267**, 60–67 (1992)

Sharpley, C.F., Halat, J., Rabinowicz, T., Weiland, B., Stafford, J.: Standard posture, postural mirroring and client-perceived rapport. Couns. Psychol. Q. **14**, 267–280 (2001). https://doi.org/10.1080/09515070110088843

Synofzik, M., Thier, P., Leube, D.T., Schlotterbeck, P., Lindner, A.: Misattributions of agency in schizophrenia are based on imprecise predictions about the sensory consequences of one's actions. Brain **133**, 262–271 (2010)

Tarr, B., Launay, J., Dunbar, R.I.M.: Silent disco: dancing in synchrony leads to elevated pain thresholds and social closeness. Evol. Hum. Behav. **37**(5), 343–349 (2016)

Tichelaar, C., Treur, J.: Network-oriented modeling of the interaction of adaptive joint decision making, bonding and mirroring. In: Fagan, D., Martín-Vide, C., O'Neill, M., Vega-Rodríguez, M.A. (eds.) TPNC 2018. LNCS, vol. 11324, pp. 328–343. Springer, Cham (2018). https://doi.org/10.1007/978-3-030-04070-3_26

Treur, J.: Temporal factorisation: a unifying principle for dynamics of the world and of mental states. Cogn. Syst. Res. **8**(2), 57–74 (2007)

Treur, J.: Temporal factorisation: realisation of mediating state properties for dynamics. Cogn. Syst. Res. **8**(2), 75–88 (2007)

Treur, J.: Network-Oriented Modeling for Adaptive Networks: Designing Higher-Order Adaptive Biological, Mental and Social Network Models. Springer (2020a)

Treur, J.: Modeling multi-order adaptive processes by self-modeling networks (Keynote Speech). In: Tallón-Ballesteros, A.J., Chen, C.-H. (eds.) Proceedings of the 2nd International Conference on Machine Learning and Intelligent Systems, MLIS 2020. Frontiers in Artificial Intelligence and Applications, vol. 332, p. 206–217. IOS Press (2020b)

Treur, J.: Modeling the emergence of informational content by adaptive networks for temporal factorisation and criterial causation. Cogn. Syst. Res. **68**, 34–52 (2021)

Trout, D.L., Rosenfeld, H.M.: The effect of postural lean and body congruence on the judgment of psychotherapeutic rapport. J. Nonverbal. Behav. **4**, 176–190 (1980)

Tschacher, W., Ramseyer, F., Koole, S.L.: Sharing the now in the social present: duration of nonverbal synchrony is linked with personality. J. Pers. **86**(2), 129–138 (2018)

Tse, P.U.: The Neural Basis of Free Will: Criterial Causation. MIT Press, Cambridge (2013)

Valdesolo, P., DeSteno, D.: Synchrony and the social tuning of compassion. Emotion **11**, 262 (2011). https://doi.org/10.1037/a0021302

Valdesolo, P., Ouyang, J., DeSteno, D.: The rhythm of joint action: synchrony promotes cooperative ability. J. Exp. Soc. Psychol. **46**(4), 693–695 (2010)

Williams, A.H., O'Leary, T., Marder, E.: Homeostatic regulation of neuronal excitability. Scholarpedia **8**, 1656 (2013)

Wiltermuth, S.S., Heath, C.: Synchrony and cooperation. Psychol. Sci. **20**(1), 1–5 (2009)

Zhang, A., Li, X., Gao, Y., Niu, Y.: Event-driven intrinsic plasticity for spiking convolutional neural networks. IEEE Trans. Neural Networks Learn. Syst. (2021). https://doi.org/10.1109/tnnls.2021.3084955

When Domain Adaptation Meets Semi-supervised Learning Through Optimal Transport

Mourad El Hamri[1,2]([✉]), Younès Bennani[1,2], and Issam Falih[2,3]

[1] LIPN - CNRS UMR 7030, Université Sorbonne Paris Nord, Villetaneuse, France
{mourad.elhamri,younes.bennani}@sorbonne-paris-nord.fr
[2] LaMSN - La Maison des Sciences Numériques, Paris, France
[3] LIMOS - CNRS UMR 6158, Université Clermont Auvergne,
Clermont-Ferrand, France
issam.falih@uca.fr

Abstract. This paper deals with the problem of unsupervised domain adaptation that aims to learn a classifier with a slight target risk while labeled samples are only available in the source domain. The proposed approach, called DA-SSL (Domain Adaptation meets Semi-Supervised Learning) attempts to find a joint subspace of the source and target domains using Linear Discriminant Analysis, such that the projections of the data into this latent subspace can be both domain invariant and discriminative. This aim, however, can be rather difficult to accomplish because of the missing labeled data in the target domain. To defeat this challenge, we use an incremental semi-supervised approach based on optimal transport theory, that conducts selective pseudo-labeling for unlabeled target instances. The selected pseudo-labeled target data are then combined with the source data to incrementally learn a robust classifier in a self-training fashion after the subspace alignment. Experiments show the competitiveness of the proposed approach over contemporary state-of-the-art methods on two benchmark domain adaptation datasets. We make our code publicly available (Code is available at: https://github.com/MouradElHamri/DA-SSL).

Keywords: Domain adaptation · Semi-supervised learning · Optimal transport · Self-training · Label propagation

1 Introduction

Deep learning has achieved spectacular performances in a variety of supervised learning applications. Nevertheless, the tremendous performance growth often relies on the assumption that both training and test data are drawn from the same probability distribution. In many real-world applications, drastic degradation can affect the generalization ability of these models when applying to new

© IFIP International Federation for Information Processing 2022
Published by Springer Nature Switzerland AG 2022
I. Maglogiannis et al. (Eds.): AIAI 2022, IFIP AICT 646, pp. 58–69, 2022.
https://doi.org/10.1007/978-3-031-08333-4_5

shifted domains, where the distributions between training and test data are different. This domain shift is due to many factors like environments, acquisition devices, time, locations, etc. Fine-tuning on labeled target data can be considered as a feasible solution, but in numerous practical scenarios, data labeling is tremendously grueling, very expensive and time-consuming. To overcome these issues, domain adaptation transfers knowledge from a relevant well labeled source domain in which the model is trained, to a different yet related unlabeled target domain in which the model is deployed. In particular, domain adaptation seeks to build a robust classifier with a low target risk by leveraging labeled source samples to tackles domain shifts in machine learning applications: healthcare diagnostic systems should be adapted to new physical human variations, industrial quality inspection systems must be accurate for new products, self-driving cars have to be able to adapt to new geographical environments and weather conditions, etc. There are two variants of domain adaptation: unsupervised domain adaptation, where labels are only available in the source domain and all target data are unlabeled and semi-supervised domain adaptation, where few labeled data are available in the target domain. In this work, we focus on unsupervised domain adaptation.

Multiple unsupervised domain adaptation approaches have been suggested, a well-known technique emphasizes aligning the source and target domains by learning a lower-dimensional joint subspace. Nevertheless, the latent subspace may not only push the source and target domains closer, but also confuse instances with different class labels. To enhance the discriminative power in the target domain, further directions were pursued by incorporating additional information contained in the unlabeled target data, such as pseudo-labeling. Pseudo-labeling methods are a form of self-training, which is a common algorithmic paradigm for leveraging unlabeled data in the target domain. Self-training methods train a model to fit pseudo-labels, that is, predictions on unlabeled data made by a previously-learned model. However, the distributional shift between source and target domains makes pseudo-labeling quit difficult, since it is subject to error accumulation. To address the powerlessness of the correctly-pseudo-labeled samples to reduce the bias caused by falsely pseudo-labeled data, selective pseudo-labeling can be an effective way to take into consideration the confidence in the target domain, by selecting a subset of target data to be assigned with pseudo labels using confidence threshold or re-weighting, and only these selected pseudo-labeled target data are jointly combined with source labeled data to train the model.

In this paper, we propose an incremental subspace alignment of the conditional distribution of the target domain with that of the source domain using Linear Discriminant Analysis. Nevertheless, this goal can be rather challenging to reach because of the absence of labeled samples in the target domain. To surmount this obstacle, we use an incremental semi-supervised technique based on optimal transport: Optimal Transport Propagation (OTP) [4], that conducts selective pseudo labeling in the target domain. The selected pseudo-labeled target instances are then used in combination with the source data to incrementally learn the subspace alignment and train the classifier in a self-training manner.

The rest of this paper is organized as follows: Sect. 2 introduces preliminary knowledge on unsupervised domain adaptation settings, self-training for unsupervised domain adaptation and optimal transport theory. Section 3 is devoted to the presentation of our proposed approach. In Sect. 4 a comparative study with state-of-the-art methods is performed on two benchmark datasets. We conclude in Sect. 5.

2   Preliminary Knowledge

2.1   Unsupervised Domain Adaptation

Unsupervised domain adaptation aims to improve the model generalization performance by transferring knowledge from a labeled source domain to an unlabeled target domain. Formally, we have an input space $\mathcal{X} = \mathbb{R}^d$, a discrete label space $\mathcal{Y} = \{c_1, ..., c_k\}$ composed of k classes and two different probability distributions $\mathcal{S}$ and $\mathcal{T}$ over $\mathcal{X} \times \mathcal{Y}$ called respectively the source and target domains. We observe a set $S = \{(x_i, y_i)\}_{i=1}^n$ of n labeled source data drawn i.i.d. from the joint distribution $\mathcal{S}$ and a set $T = \{x_j\}_{j=1}^m$ of m unlabeled target data drawn i.i.d. from the marginal distribution $\mathcal{T}_{\mathcal{X}}$ of $\mathcal{T}$ over $\mathcal{X}$:

$$S = \{(x_i, y_i)\}_{i=1}^n \sim (\mathcal{S})^n, \quad T = \{x_j\}_{j=1}^m \sim (\mathcal{T}_{\mathcal{X}})^m. \tag{1}$$

We assume that the source and target domains share the same label space $\mathcal{Y}$. The objective of unsupervised domain adaptation is to learn a classifier $\eta : \mathcal{X} \to \mathcal{Y}$ with a slight target risk:

$$\mathcal{R}_{\mathcal{T}}(\eta) = \mathbb{P}_{(x,y)\sim\mathcal{T}}(\eta(x) \neq y). \tag{2}$$

In the sequel, we denote by the source domain indifferently the distribution $\mathcal{S}$ and the labeled set S, and by the target domain, the distribution $\mathcal{T}$ and the unlabeled set T.

2.2   Self-training for Unsupervised Domain Adaptation

Self-training is a popular technique that has proven to be very effective for learning with unlabeled data. Self-training algorithms train a model to fit synthetic labels predicted by another previously-learned model.

For unsupervised domain adaptation, pseudo-labeling methods are a form of self-training where the source labels are used to predict pseudo-labels on the unlabeled target data. These methods then train a fresh classifier to fit these pseudo-labels.

The empirical phenomenon that self-training on pseudo-labels often improves over the pseudo-labeler F_{pl} despite no access to true labels has been explained in the work of [15] by Theorem 1. We first need the following definitions and assumptions.

Transformation Set: Let $\mathbf{T}$ be the set of some transformations obtained via data augmentation, the transformation set of x is defined as:

$$\mathcal{B}(x) = \{x' : \exists \, \text{Tr} \in \mathbf{T} \text{ such that } \| x' - \text{Tr}(x) \| \leq r\} \tag{3}$$

$\mathcal{B}(x)$ is the set of points with distance r from some data augmentation of x.

Neighborhood: The neighborhood of x denoted by $\mathcal{N}(x)$ is the set of points whose transformation sets overlap with that of x:

$$\mathcal{N}(x) = \{x' : \mathcal{B}(x) \cap \mathcal{B}(x') \neq \emptyset\} \tag{4}$$

For $S \subset \mathcal{X}$, the neighborhood of S is defined as the union of neighborhoods of its elements: $\mathcal{N}(S) = \underset{x \in S}{\cup} \mathcal{N}(x)$.

Assumption 1 ((a,c)-expansion): Let P be the distribution of unlabeled target data, and P_i for $i \leq k$ be the class-conditional distribution of $x \in \mathcal{X}$ conditioned on the class c_i. We say that the class-conditional distribution P_i satisfies (a, c)-expansion if for all $V \subset \mathcal{X}$ with $P_i(V) \leq a$, the following holds:

$$P_i(\mathcal{N}(V)) \geq \min\{cP_i(V), 1\} \tag{5}$$

If P_i satisfies (a, c)-expansion for all $i \leq k$, then we say P satisfies (a, c)-expansion.

Population Consistency Loss: We define the population consistency loss $R_\mathcal{B}(F)$ as the fraction of examples where a classifier F is not robust to input transformations:

$$R_\mathcal{B}(F) = \mathbb{E}_P[\mathbb{1}(\exists x' \in \mathcal{B}(x) \text{ such that } F(x') \neq F(x))] \tag{6}$$

Assumption 2 (Separation): We assume P is $\mathcal{B}$-separated with probability $1 - \mu$ by ground-truth classifier F^*, as follows: $R_\mathcal{B}(F^*) \leq \mu$.

Assumption 3: Define $\bar{a} = \underset{i \leq k}{max}\{P_i(\mathcal{M}(F_{pl}))\}$ to be the maximum fraction of incorrectly pseudo-labeled examples in any class: $\mathcal{M}(F_{pl})) = \{x : F_{pl}(x) \neq F^*(x)\}$. We assume that $\bar{a} < \frac{1}{3}$ and P satisfies $(\bar{a}, \bar{c})$-expansion for $\bar{c} > 3$.

Theorem 1. *Define $c = \min\{\frac{1}{\bar{a}}, \bar{c}\}$. Suppose Assumptions 3 and 2 hold. Then for any minimizer $\hat{F}$ of $\mathcal{L}(F) = \frac{c+1}{c-1}L_{0-1}(F, F_{pl}) + \frac{2c}{c-1}R_\mathcal{B}(F) - Err(F_{pl})$, we have:*

$$Err(\hat{F}) \leq \frac{2}{c-1}Err(F_{pl}) + \frac{2c}{c-1}\mu. \tag{7}$$

Which explains the perhaps surprising fact that self-training with pseudo-labeling often improves over the pseudo-labeler F_{pl} even though no additional information about true labels is provided.

2.3 Optimal Transport

The birth of optimal transport is dated back to 1781, with the following problem introduced by Gaspard Monge [10]: Let $(\mathcal{X}, \mu)$ and $(\mathcal{Y}, \nu)$ be two probability spaces and $c : \mathcal{X} \times \mathcal{Y} \to \mathbb{R}^+$ a measurable cost function, the problem of Monge aims at finding the transport map $\mathcal{T} : \mathcal{X} \to \mathcal{Y}$, that transport the mass represented by the measure μ to the mass represented by the measure ν and which minimizes the total cost of this transportation, more formally:

$$\inf_{\mathcal{T}} \{ \int_{\mathcal{X}} c(x, \mathcal{T}(x)) d\mu(x) | \mathcal{T} \# \mu = \nu \}, \tag{8}$$

where $\mathcal{T} \# \mu$ denotes the push-forward operator of μ through the map $\mathcal{T}$.

A long period of sleep followed Monge's formulation until the relaxation of Leonid Kantorovitch in 1942 [8]. The relaxed formulation of Kantorovich, known as the Monge-Kantorovich problem, can be formulated in the following way:

$$\inf_{\gamma} \{ \int_{\mathcal{X} \times \mathcal{Y}} c(x, y) \, d\gamma(x, y) \, | \, \gamma \in \Pi(\mu, \nu) \, \}, \tag{9}$$

where $\Pi(\mu, \nu)$ is the set of probability measures over the product space $\mathcal{X} \times \mathcal{Y}$ such that both marginals of γ are μ and ν.

In several real world applications, the access to the measures μ and ν is only available through finite samples $X = (x_1, ..., x_n) \subset \mathcal{X}$ and $Y = (y_1, ..., y_m) \subset \mathcal{Y}$, then, the measures μ and ν can be casted as the following discrete measures, $\mu = \sum_{i=1}^{n} a_i \delta_{x_i}$ and $\nu = \sum_{j=1}^{m} b_j \delta_{y_j}$, where $a \in \sum_n$ and $b \in \sum_m$ are probability vectors of size n and m respectively. The relaxation of Kantorovich becomes then the following linear program [12]:

$$\min_{\gamma \in U(a,b)} \langle \gamma, C_{XY} \rangle_F \tag{10}$$

where $U(a, b) = \{ \gamma \in \mathcal{M}_{n \times m}(\mathbb{R}^+) \, | \, \gamma \mathbb{1}_m = a \text{ and } \gamma^{\mathbf{T}} \mathbb{1}_n = b \}$ is the transportation polytope which acts as a feasible set, C_{XY} is the cost matrix and $\langle \gamma, C_{XY} \rangle_F = trace(\gamma^{\mathbf{T}} C_{XY})$ is the Frobenius dot-product of matrices.

This linear program, can be solved with the simplex algorithm or interior point methods. However, optimal transport problem scales cubically on the sample size, which is often too costly in practice, especially for machine learning applications that involve massive datasets. Entropy-regularization [3] has emerged as a solution to the computational burden of optimal transport. The entropy-regularized discrete optimal transport problem reads:

$$\min_{\gamma \in U(a,b)} \langle \gamma, C_{XY} \rangle_F - \varepsilon \mathcal{H}(\gamma) \tag{11}$$

where $\mathcal{H}(\gamma) = -\sum_{i=1}^{n} \sum_{j=1}^{m} \gamma_{ij} (\log(\gamma_{ij}) - 1)$ is the entropy of γ. This regularized problem can be solved efficiently via an iterative procedure: Sinkhorn-Knopp algorithm.

3   Proposed Approach

The proposed method aims to learn a joint subspace from the source and target domains such that the projected data into the subspace are domain invariant and well separated. To accomplish this aim, linear discriminant analysis (LDA) appears to be a good candidate for many reasons, principally for its capacity to find a linear combination of features, which separates two or more classes of data no matter the domain they come from, providing an appropriate approach for the unsupervised domain adaptation problem, where the source and target data come from different distributions. Nonetheless, LDA needs labeled data to learn the projection matrix. To surmount this challenge, we use pseudo-labels in the target domain produced by a semi-supervised technique (OTP). The reason for choosing OTP is its ability to capture the geometry of data thanks to optimal transport. Furthermore this technique falls into the class of selective pseudo-labeling methods. The benefit of these methods is that they avoid mislabeled target instances from impeding the subspace learning process by spreading the errors to the next iteration which can reduce the robustness of the learned classifier. Thus, we use the labeled source data and the selected pseudo-labeled target data provided by OTP to incrementally learn a robust classifier in a self-training fashion after the subspace alignment.

3.1   Domain Alignment via Linear Discriminant Analysis

To learn a domain-invariant and discriminative subspace $\tilde{\mathcal{X}}$ from $\mathcal{X}$, we employ Linear Discriminant Analysis (LDA), which is a common technique used for dimensionality reduction. LDA can also provides class separability by drawing a decision region between the different classes.

Let $X \in \mathcal{M}_{d,N}(\mathbb{R})$ be a labeled data matrix composed of N samples. Basically, LDA seeks to find a projection matrix W for which the low-dimensional projection of X yields a cloud of points that are close when they are in the same class relative to the overall spread. This projection matrix can be found by maximizing the Rayleigh quotient of the within scatter matrix S_w and between scatter matrix S_b:

$$W = \underset{V}{\operatorname{argmax}} \frac{|V^T S_b V|}{|V^T S_w V|} \tag{12}$$

The maximization problem in Eq. 12 is equivalent to the following generalized eigenvalue problem:

$$S_b w = \lambda S_w w \tag{13}$$

The eigenvectors of Eq. 13 represent the directions of the lower-dimensional feature space learned by LDA, and the corresponding eigenvalues represent the ability of the eigenvectors to discriminate between different classes, i.e. increase the between-class variance, and decreases the within-class variance of each class. The eigenvectors with the d_1 highest eigenvalues give us the LDA projection matrix

$W = [w_1, ..., w_{d_1}] \in \mathcal{M}_{d,d_1}(\mathbb{R})$, from which we can learn the lower-dimensional discriminant representation $\tilde{X} \in \mathcal{M}_{d_1,N}(\mathbb{R})$:

$$\tilde{X} = W^T X \tag{14}$$

3.2 Self-training via Optimal Transport Propagation

To learn a domain-invariant and discriminative subspace $\tilde{\mathcal{X}}$ from $\mathcal{X}$ using the projection matrix W of LDA we need labeled data as stated above. Nevertheless, in unsupervised domain adaptation setting, labeled data in the target domain are unavailable. To address this limitation, we propose to use a semi-supervised learning approach called Optimal Transport Propagation (OTP), able to perform selective pseudo-labeling in the target domain.

3.2.1 Optimal Transport Propagation

Optimal transport propagation (OTP) [4,5] is a transductive semi-supervised method which relies on optimal transport theory to propagate labels between the vertices of a complete bipartite edge-weighted graph in two phases.

Let X_L be a finite ordered set of l labeled samples $\{(x_1, y_1), ..., (x_l, y_l)\}$. Each example (x_i, y_i) of this set consists of a sample x_i from an input space $\mathcal{X}$, and its corresponding label $y_i \in \mathcal{Y} = \{c_1, ..., c_k\}$ where $\mathcal{Y}$ is a discrete label set composed of k classes, and X_U a larger collection of u instances $\{x_{l+1}, ..., x_u\}$, whose labels Y_U are unknown. In the graph construction phase, the first part of the graph $\mathcal{L}$ is composed of labeled data $\mathcal{L} = X_L$ and the second part $\mathcal{U}$ is composed of unlabeled data $\mathcal{U} = X_U$. To compute the edge-weights of the graph, authors suggest to solve the regularized optimal transport problem between the empirical distribution of X_L and X_U:

$$\gamma_\varepsilon^* = \underset{\gamma \in U(a,b)}{\operatorname{argmin}} \ \langle \gamma, C \rangle_F - \varepsilon \mathcal{H}(\gamma), \tag{15}$$

where C denotes the cost matrix defined by: $c_{i,j} = \|x_i - x_j\|^2, \ \forall (x_i, x_j) \in \mathcal{L} \times \mathcal{U}$. The optimal transport plan γ_ε^* can be interpreted as a similarity matrix between the two parts $\mathcal{L}$ and $\mathcal{U}$ of the graph $\mathcal{G}$. To have a class probability interpretation, the matrix γ_ε^*, is normalized to get the affinity matrix $\mathcal{W}$ defined as follows:

$$w_{i,j} = \frac{\gamma_{\varepsilon_{i,j}}^*}{\sum_i \gamma_{\varepsilon_{i,j}}^*}, \ \forall i, j \in \{1, ..., l\} \times \{l+1, ..., l+u\}, \tag{16}$$

where $w_{i,j}, \ \forall i, j \in \{1, ..., l\} \times \{l+1, ..., l+u\}$ is then, the probability of jumping from the vertex $x_i \in \mathcal{L}$ to $x_j \in \mathcal{U}$.

In the second phase, a label matrix U is constructed from the affinity matrix $\mathcal{W}$ to denotes the probability of each unlabeled data x_j to belong to every class c_h. This probability is defined as the sum of the similarity of x_j with the representatives of the class c_h, formally:

$$u_{j,h} = \mathbb{P}(x_j \in c_h) = \sum_{i/x_i \in c_h} w_{i,j}, \forall j, h \in \{l+1, ..., l+u\} \times \{1, ..., k\}, \tag{17}$$

To avoid hard assignment of labels directly from the label matrix U, and the consequent neglect of the different degrees of certainty for each prediction. A certainty score is associated with each pseudo label in the following way:

$$s_j = 1 - \frac{H(U_j)}{log_2(k)}, \quad \forall j \in \{l+1, ..., l+u\}, \tag{18}$$

where U_j is the jth row of the label matrix U, which corresponds to the stochastic vector that encodes the probability of x_j to belong to the different classes, and H is Shannon's entropy.

To endow OTP with the selectivity property during the propagation process, a comparison is made between the certainty score corresponding to each unlabeled instance x_j and a confidence threshold $\alpha \in [0,1]$. If the value of the score s_j is superior to α, x_j is then labeled in the following way:

$$\hat{y}_j = \operatorname*{argmax}_{c_h \in \mathcal{C}} u_{j,h}, \quad \forall j \in \{l+1, ..., l+u\}, \tag{19}$$

Thus, the unlabeled instance x_j will belong to the most likely class c_h. Otherwise, x_j does not receive any label. This process corresponds to one iteration of the incremental approach OTP. In each iteration, the labeled set X_L is enriched with new points from X_U, and the number of samples in X_U is reduced, until convergence, i.e. when all the data initially in X_U are labeled, or, in other words when X_U is reduced to the empty set $\emptyset$.

3.2.2 Domain Adaptation via Optimal Transport Propagation

Once the LDA projection matrix W is learned (at the first iteration, the projection matrix is learned using only the labeled source data), the projection of both source samples S and target samples T in the joint subspace can be obtained as follows:

$$\tilde{S} = W^T S \quad \text{and} \quad \tilde{T} = W^T T \tag{20}$$

Pseudo-labeling in the target domain can then be performed using OTP considering that:

$$X_L = \tilde{S} \quad \text{and} \quad X_U = \tilde{T} \tag{21}$$

The intuition behind the use of OTP as a pseudo-labeling technique is its capability to capture the geometry of the underlying subspace and its selective ability based on the incorporated certainty score which make it closely related to entropy minimization, where the model's predictions are encouraged to be low-entropy (i.e., high-confidence) on unlabeled data. Thus, instead of using all the pseudo-labeled target samples to learn the next projection, we incrementally select a subset $\tilde{T}_p \subset \tilde{T}$ that contains an amount of p pseudo-labeled target samples with the highest certainty score. Nevertheless, this technique has the potential risk to only select instances from particular classes and to overlook the other classes. To prevent this issue, we conduct a class-wise selection in order to ensure that pseudo-labeled target samples of each class have an equal opportunity to be selected. Precisely, for each class c_h, $\forall h \in \{1, ..., k\}$ we select $\frac{p}{k}$ target samples pseudo-labeled as class c_h.

Thereafter, the projected source data is combined with the selected pseudo-labeled target data to form a new augmented source domain, simultaneously, the pseudo-labeled target data must be retired from the target domain in the following way:

$$S \leftarrow \tilde{S} \cup \tilde{T}_p \quad \text{and} \quad T \leftarrow \tilde{T} \setminus \tilde{T}_p \qquad (22)$$

Equations 22 are used to incrementally update the source and target domains. At each iteration, a classifier η is trained on the augmented source samples in a self-training manner. The intuition behind this idea is that at each iteration the classifier becomes more and more robust, since it is trained on both the source data and the selected pseudo-labeled target data, so that in the last iteration, it will be trained on the source samples and the totality of pseudo-labeled target instances, allowing it to improve its accuracy according to Theorem 1.

The overall algorithm called DA-SSL (Domain Adaptation meets Semi-Supervised Learning) is summarized in Algorithm 1.

Algorithm 1: DA-SSL

Parameters: Dimensionality of LDA d_1, sampling rate p
Input   : Labeled source data S, Unlabelled target data T
while *not converged* **do**
> Learn the projection W using source data S
> Get the projected source and target samples $\tilde{S}$ and $\tilde{T}$
> Assign pseudo labels for the projected target data $\tilde{T}$ using OTP
> Select a subset of pseudo-labeled target data $\tilde{T}_p$
> Update the source domain $S \leftarrow \tilde{S} \cup \tilde{T}_p$
> Update the target domain $T \leftarrow \tilde{T} \setminus \tilde{T}_p$
> Learn a classifier η on S

end
return *Predicted labels of the original target data T using η*

---

4   Experiments

In this section, we provide empirical experimentation for the proposed algorithm.

4.1   Datasets

We adopt two datasets that are benchmarks in domain adaptation: ImageCLEF-DA and Office31.

ImageCLEF-DA dataset [2] consists of four domains. We use three of them in our experiments: Caltech-256 (C), ImageNet ILSVRC 2012 (I), and Pascal VOC 2012 (P). There are 12 classes and 50 images for each class in each domain.

Office31 dataset [13] composed of 4110 images. The dataset consists of three domains: Amazon, Webcam and DSLR, 31 common classes from the three domains are used.

4.2 Experimental Protocol

We use ResNet50 [7] features (d = 2048) for ImageCLEF-DA and Office31 datasets. Our proposed approach consists of two hyper-parameters, the dimensionality d_1 of LDA that we set equal to 128 and the sampling rate p that we set equal to 48 for ImageCLEF-DA and 62 for Office31 dataset. We use an SVM with a Gaussian kernel as classifier [1]. The width parameter of the SVM was chosen as $\sigma = \frac{1}{2\mathbb{V}}$, where $\mathbb{V}$ is the variance of the source samples.

Following the standard protocol [6], the comparison is conducted using three deep learning models RTN [9], MADA [11] and iCAN [16], and with a manifold embedded distribution alignment technique based on deep features MEDA [14]. We use the average accuracy as the evaluation metric in all our experiments.

4.3 Results

We use bold and underlined fonts to indicate the best and the second best results respectively. The classification accuracy of our proposed approach and other baseline methods are illustrated in Table 1 and Table 2, from which we can see that our proposed approach achieves the highest average accuracy over the two benchmark datasets. Specifically, DA-SSL achieves an average accuracy of 89.4% on ImageCELF-DA dataset (Table 1), slightly better than MEDA which has an average accuracy of 89.0%. On the Office31 dataset (Table 2), DA-SSL outperforms all other baseline models with an average accuracy of 87.6% against 85.7% by MEDA and 87.2% by iCAN, besides, DA-SSL achieves the best performance in three out of six tasks and the second-best results in two other tasks.

In summary, the proposed approach is highly competitive compared to several state-of-the-art methods, and can outperform competitors on many tasks of the two domain adaptation problems. This results are mainly attributed to the capacity of OTP to capture mush more information than the other methods of pseudo-labeling thanks to the enhanced affinity matrix constructed by optimal transport and to its intrinsic property of selectivity which make it a good candidate for pseudo-labeling target data.

Table 1. Classification accuracy (%) on ImageCELF-DA dataset (ResNet50 features).

Task	RTN	MADA	iCAN	MEDA	DA-SSL
I → P	75.6	75.0	<u>79.5</u>	**79.7**	78.9
P → I	86.8	87.9	89.7	**92.5**	<u>91.8</u>
I → C	95.3	96.0	94.7	<u>95.7</u>	**97.8**
C → I	86.9	88.8	89.9	<u>92.2</u>	**92.6**
C → P	72.7	75.2	**78.5**	**78.5**	<u>78.2</u>
P → C	92.2	92.2	92.0	<u>95.5</u>	**95.8**
Average	84.9	85.8	87.4	<u>89.0</u>	**89.4**

Table 2. Classification accuracy (%) on Office31 dataset (ResNet50 features).

Task	RTN	MADA	iCAN	MEDA	DA-SSL
A → W	84.5	90.0	<u>92.5</u>	86.2	**93.3**
D → W	96.8	97.4	<u>98.8</u>	97.2	**99.0**
W → D	99.4	99.6	**100.0**	99.4	<u>99.6</u>
A → D	77.5	87.8	<u>90.1</u>	85.3	**90.7**
D → A	66.2	70.3	<u>72.1</u>	72.4	71.9
W → A	64.8	66.4	69.9	**74.0**	<u>71.3</u>
Average	81.6	85.2	<u>87.2</u>	85.7	**87.6**

5 Conclusion

In this paper, a novel selective pseudo-labeling approach for unsupervised domain adaptation called DA-SSL is proposed. DA-SSL learn a domain-invariant and discriminative subspace by LDA using labelled source data and pseudo-labeled target data. The pseudo-labeling is performed by OTP, a certainty-aware semi-supervised method that selects samples with high confidence to participate in the next iteration of the incremental learning process. In each iteration of the incremental domain adaptation process, a classifier is learned using the augmented source data composed of the samples in the original source domain and the accumulation of the pseudo-labeled target data in the previous iterations. The proposed approach outperforms several state-of-the-art methods on two benchmark datasets.

References

1. Benabdeslem, K., Bennani, Y.: Dendrogram-based SVM for multi-class classification. J. Comput. Inf. Techno **14**(4), 283–289 (2006)
2. Caputo, B., et al.: ImageCLEF 2014: overview and analysis of the results. In: Kanoulas, E., et al. (eds.) CLEF 2014. LNCS, vol. 8685, pp. 192–211. Springer, Cham (2014). https://doi.org/10.1007/978-3-319-11382-1_18
3. Cuturi, M.: Sinkhorn distances: Lightspeed computation of optimal transport. In: Advances in Neural Information Processing Systems, pp. 2292–2300 (2013)
4. El Hamri, M., Bennani, Y., Falih, I.: Label propagation through optimal transport. In: 2021 International Joint Conference on Neural Networks (2021)
5. El Hamri, M., Bennani, Y., Falih, I.: Inductive semi-supervised learning through optimal transport. In: Mantoro, T., Lee, M., Ayu, M.A., Wong, K.W., Hidayanto, A.N. (eds.) ICONIP 2021. CCIS, vol. 1516, pp. 668–675. Springer, Cham (2021). https://doi.org/10.1007/978-3-030-92307-5_78
6. Gong, B., Shi, Y., Sha, F., Grauman, K.: Geodesic flow kernel for unsupervised domain adaptation. In: 2012 IEEE Conference on Computer Vision and Pattern Recognition, pp. 2066–2073 (2012)
7. He, K., Zhang, X., Ren, S., Sun, J.: Deep residual learning for image recognition. In: Proceedings of the IEEE Conference on Computer Vision and Pattern Recognition, pp. 770–778 (2016)

8. Kantorovich, L.V.: On the translocation of masses. Dokl. Akad. Nauk. USSR (NS) **37**, 199–201 (1942)
9. Long, M., Zhu, H., Wang, J., Jordan, M.I.: Unsupervised domain adaptation with residual transfer networks. In: Advances in Neural Information Processing Systems, vol. 29 (2016)
10. Monge, G.: Mémoire sur la théorie des déblais et des remblais. Histoire de l'Académie Royale des Sciences de Paris (1781)
11. Pei, Z., Cao, Z., Long, M., Wang, J.: Multi-adversarial domain adaptation. In: Thirty-Second AAAI Conference on Artificial Intelligence (2018)
12. Peyré, G., Cuturi, M., et al.: Computational optimal transport: with applications to data science. Found. Trends® Mach. Learn. (2019)
13. Saenko, K., Kulis, B., Fritz, M., Darrell, T.: Adapting visual category models to new domains. In: Daniilidis, K., Maragos, P., Paragios, N. (eds.) ECCV 2010. LNCS, vol. 6314, pp. 213–226. Springer, Heidelberg (2010). https://doi.org/10.1007/978-3-642-15561-1_16
14. Wang, J., Feng, W., Chen, Y., Yu, H., Huang, M., Yu, P.S.: Visual domain adaptation with manifold embedded distribution alignment. In: Proceedings of the 26th ACM International Conference on Multimedia, pp. 402–410 (2018)
15. Wei, C., Shen, K., Chen, Y., Ma, T.: Theoretical analysis of self-training with deep networks on unlabeled data. arXiv preprint arXiv:2010.03622 (2020)
16. Zhang, W., Ouyang, W., Li, W., Xu, D.: Collaborative and adversarial network for unsupervised domain adaptation. In: Proceedings of the IEEE Conference on Computer Vision and Pattern Recognition, pp. 3801–3809 (2018)

Cybersecurity Fraud Intrusion/Anomaly Detection

A Novel GBT-Based Approach for Cross-Channel Fraud Detection on Real-World Banking Transactions

Uğur Dolu[1,2]($^{(\boxtimes)}$) (iD) and Emre Sefer[2] (iD)

[1] Yapi Kredi Technology, Istanbul, Turkey
ugur.dolu@ykteknoloji.com.tr
[2] Ozyegin University, Istanbul, Turkey
ugur.dolu@ozu.edu.tr, emre.sefer@ozyegin.edu.tr

Abstract. The most recent research on hundreds of financial institutions uncovered that only 26% of them have a team assigned to detect cross-channel fraud. Due to the developing technologies, various fraud techniques have emerged and increased in digital environments. Fraud directly affects customer satisfaction. For instance, only in the UK, the total loss of fraud transactions was £1.26 billion in 2020. In this paper, we come up with a Gradient Boosting Tree (GBT)-based approach to efficiently detect cross-channel frauds. As part of our proposed approach, we also figured out a solution to generate training sets from imbalanced data, which also suffers from concept drift problems due to changing customer behaviors. We boost the performance of our GBT model by integrating additional demographic, economic, and behavioral features as a part of feature engineering. We evaluate the performance of our cross-channel fraud detection method on a real banking dataset which is highly imbalanced in terms of frauds which is another challenge in the fraud detection problem. We use our trained model to score real-time cross-channel transactions by a leading private bank in Turkey. As a result, our approach can catch almost 75% of total fraud loss in a month with a low false-positive rate.

Keywords: Gradient boosting tree · Cross channel fraud · Concept drift · Imbalanced data

1 Introduction

Frauds are an inevitable loss for banks and financial institutions. Banks lose reputation and money as a result of fraudulent transactions since customers give importance to reliability when choosing the bank to keep their money. The number of fraudulent transactions and the amount lost due to fraud tend to increase each year. When fraudulent transactions which are taking place all over the world are analyzed, the financial cost of fraud in 2021 is £4.37 trillion [9] which was £3.89 trillion [8] in 2019. The method used by fraudsters also change over time. The most common techniques are phishing, social engineering, verbal

© IFIP International Federation for Information Processing 2022
Published by Springer Nature Switzerland AG 2022
I. Maglogiannis et al. (Eds.): AIAI 2022, IFIP AICT 646, pp. 73–84, 2022.
https://doi.org/10.1007/978-3-031-08333-4_6

persuasion, and computer viruses like Trojan. The total loss of fraud transactions in the UK alone in 2020 is £1.26 billion. Among these fraudulent transactions, 38% of them are performed by remote banking, 45% of them by credit card, whereas 16% of them are performed by social engineering.

For the remote banking, the total amount of fraud loss was £197.3m in 2020. However, when the first six months of 2020 and 2021 are compared, the amount of loss advanced from £79.7m to £133.4m which marks an increase of 67%. Remote banking has three subcategories which are internet banking, mobile banking, and telephone banking. The number of fraudulent transactions in telephone banking has been decreasing over the years. From 2020 to the first six months of 2021, the number of transactions was decreased by 50%. In 2020 the total financial cost of social engineering fraud methods was £479m. However, when the first six months of 2020 are analyzed, the amount is observed as £207.8m, and when the first six months of 2021 are examined, 71% of the increase is detected, which brings the number up to £355.3m [18, 19].

Fraudsters prefer to use remote banking channels with social engineering techniques to persuade victim customers. According to the statistics taken from our real dataset from a private bank in Turkey, more than 40 million transactions take place in each month. However, only around 800 transactions are labeled as fraud. The ratio of fraud transactions is approximately 0.002. Besides that, most academic works used synthetic or static datasets. This kind of work is not applicable to realistic scenarios. In this case, the main dilemma is that fraud methods and customer behaviors are evolving over time, but the model is trained with only synthetic or static data [12].

The concept drift and highly imbalanced data problems are dominant in the detection of channel frauds and need to be targeted with caution. The transactions from accounts and channels form a highly imbalanced dataset, including very few fraud transactions and many more legitimate ones. To solve this problem, various methods were employed, namely undersampling [20] and oversampling [3]. However, these techniques are still problematic because the underlying dataset is exceedingly imbalanced, and instances of the dataset individually carry important information (such as transactions belonging to the same account or customer).

In this study, we have experimented with different equalization techniques; transaction-based, account-based, and customer-based to alleviate the imbalanced data problem. Furthermore, most of the traditional machine learning algorithms may easily be overwhelmed by the majority class in imbalanced data, leading to higher misclassification rates on the minority classes. To overcome this issue, we introduce boosting models such as gradient boosting trees (GBTs). We employ GBT in our study, in which the key idea is to ensemble weak decision trees, is a commonly used machine learning method for binary classification on the imbalanced data. In summary, the contributions of this paper are as follows:

- Our approach supports multiple transaction channels and is capable of detecting frauds between cross-channels.
- Our approach employs feature engineering, concatenating transaction details with customers' demographic and financial information.

– Our approach does not need any additional maintenance, the auto train algorithm will generate the training set from historical data, and will retrain the model. Our method will be applicable in realistic scenarios since: 1 - An automated training mechanism helps to adapt to new behaviors of account holders and fraudsters, 2 - Real data has all fraudsters and customer habits so our approach will not struggle with aging, 3 - We generate training sets according to sampling method, which balances out the data and improves the performance of the model.

This paper is organized as follows: Sect. 2 discusses the related work. Section 3 gives the methodology for generating the training set, feature engineering, and the remaining details of our study. The performance of feature engineering techniques of GBT models for extremely imbalanced data is discussed in Sect. 4 in detail, which is followed by the conclusion section.

2   Related Work

The cross-channel fraud detection systems have to deal with two main issues: binary classification on an imbalanced dataset and handling the concept drift. In this section, in addition to providing a brief overview of the aforementioned problems, we also discuss some of the existing applied approaches to fraud detection for other types of transactions, including credit card.

There are many commercial solutions developed to protect financial organizations and their customers from fraudsters, and many academic works have been developed in this area. FICO is one of the market leaders in this area, with many kinds of software solutions. Most of the products try to catch fraud transactions according to the outputs of the rule-based algorithms. The rule-based algorithms are effective, although they are incapable of capturing the dynamically-changing fraudsters' strategies over time. To provide sustainability, rule-based systems are required to provide a periodic maintenance and detailed analysis to modify the rules and their conditions, which requires a significant amount of human effort. Additionally, the most recent research shows that only 26% of all financial institutions have a team allocated to detect cross-channel frauds [17].

In the literature, only a few number of studies have focused on the concept drift problem in fraud detection task. For example, [5] proposed a method based on a sliding window and an ensemble of classifiers to overcome this problem in the credit card fraud detection. In another study, a fraud detection system based on a concept drift management approach has been presented to retain new concepts on the transaction streams using the cardholder profiles [11]. However, both of these studies have been evaluated on synthetic datasets due to the unavailability of the real benchmark datasets. In this study, we used an approach for the generation of an automatic training set, which will be explained in detail later, to adapt to the drifts on the data as much as possible. The conventional fraud detection systems are developed using the previously known fraud transactions and cannot easily adapt to concept drift.

Moreover, another frequently encountered problem in real-world tasks is learning from imbalanced data for binary- or multi-class classification, where the models are trained on a dataset with an imbalanced distribution of classes [21]. Imbalanced Data, in real-world applications suffer from class imbalance problem. A predictive model trained on imbalanced data tends to correctly predict the majority class samples and to misclassify the samples from minority classes. Therefore, several studies have proposed different approaches to select a subset of training data principally for binary classification in fraud detection. For example, [14] demonstrated how the class distribution in the training set affects the performance of credit card fraud detection. In their experiments, training sets with varying the number of fraudulent transaction distributions from 10% to 90% for each month were utilized to generate a meta-learning model. They obtained the most appropriate performance on the reduction of prediction loss and training time with a 50%–50% class distribution. [2] showed how the performance improves when the majority class is undersampled on the training set. On the other hand, some studies have employed account-based undersampling methods for the construction of the training set [10]. In this work, we also compared transaction- and account-level undersampling strategies by equalizing the counts of fraudulent and legitimate transactions while making sure that all the transactions of both types cover the same time interval in the training sets. Similarly, we use undersampling as a solution to the imbalance problem. However, instead of randomly undersampling data, we generate a training set by equalizing fraudulent and legitimate credit card counts, and transactions of each credit card cover the equal time range [1]. We applied this solution to our problem, instead of credit card count, we instead tried to equalize fraudster and legitimate account counts. Additionally, this structure was tested with different ratios between a swindler and reliable account counts.

Feature Engineering in real-time transactions, customer behaviors are crucial, and their habits can evolve over time. To minimize the error that arises from behaviors [6], the features such as "familiar device", "is account whitelisted or blacklisted", and "is device used for another account before" are integrated to the main transaction dataset. Additionally, to detect more accurate behavioral data, we have also included historical maximum and minimum credit scores, customer age, and financial age [15]. Furthermore, combining transactions with commercial or individual customer-type flags has improved the model's prediction performance in a positive way.

Another cross-channel fraud detection framework [12] proposed a graph analysis extracted from realized transactions in real-time. Their analysis examines the shortest paths between transactions and strongly-connected components in the transaction graph to detect fraudulent transactions. Another work applies a recurrent neural network [13] for cross-channel fraud detection. In the literature, there are not many examples of GBTs for the detection of cross-channel frauds. In this paper, we come up with a GBT model which is capable of generating a prediction score for each transaction that is from internet banking, mobile banking, ATM, and telephone banking. We mainly employ GBTs as they have outperformed the other boosting algorithms.

3 Methodology

In this section, we first give an overview of our study by defining its components. Then, we give details of our generating training set algorithm, feature engineering, encoding mechanism, and training algorithm, which is GBT.

3.1 Overview of the Study

Two main phases are included namely, offline algorithm training, and real-time fraud detection on incoming transactions. During the offline training phase, initially, a training set is composed by the mechanism, which is explained in Sect. 3.2. After building a training set, a GBT model is trained. In the real-time detection phase, transactions and their metadata are fed to apply pre-processing steps, i.e., data sanitization and handling the missing values. Afterwards, it is tried to match the receiver customer identity from the receiver account number if the customer identity is not known. Subsequently, the pipeline will extract demographic, economic, and behavioral features for the sender and receiver and merge them with the main data. The encoder will handle the categorical string values and convert them to the encoded integer to feed the trained GBT model. Finally, the model generates a score for each transaction to classify them as fraud or not. The real-time detection pipeline is illustrated in Fig. 1.

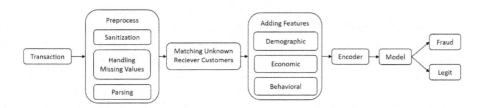

Fig. 1. A flow of a transaction in the study.

3.2 Generating Training Sets

We experimented two types of data balancing mechanisms, which are transaction-level and account-level. In transaction-level balancing, we pick all the fraudulent transactions within a time frame and randomly select the same number of transactions from the legitimate ones. The fraudulent and legitimate transactions are belong to the same customers who has been a sender or receiver of a fraudulent transaction at least once during the time frame of the training set. For the account-level balancing, we employ the technique used by [21]. If at least one transaction is identified as a fraudulent transaction in a given time range, we get all transactions of the receiver and sender of the fraudulent transaction and label them as fraudulent accounts. If any customer has no fraudulent transaction, then we denote the sender and receiver customers as legitimate accounts. We equalize the number of fraudulent and legitimate accounts and create a training set from their transactions. Even though, it still results in a high-class imbalance, it preserves the patterns while decreasing a lot of initial imbalance [21].

For testing, we equalize fraudster and legitimate accounts with different ratios. Because higher sampling of legitimate accounts will increase the diversity of legitimate transactions in the training set, and as a result, it is believed to improve model performance on detecting non-fraud transactions.

The generation of a training set is automated in our study so that it can create new training sets and train new models by itself as time passes. Since the performance of a model decreases over time due to concept drift caused by a change in the behavior of account holders and/or fraudsters, this automation mechanism helps to adapt to new behaviors and prevents a dramatic decrease in prediction performance.

3.3 Feature Engineering

The metadata of any cross-channel transaction contains numerical, categorical, and textual information. All related data is embedded in a feature vector, and this vector is fed to the model to get the prediction for the transaction. The textual fields may contain more than one different value. These fields are parsed to extract features. For instance, a feature, which indicates belonging to a blacklist or white-list of a customer, is fed the model with the value "1" and "0". The parsed fields refer to "1" for blacklist and "0" for white-list. Another example is a field containing "AZ" which means "A" for a device like ATM, and Z for login duration, which indicates more than 29 min. The Model uses numerical fields as they are, but they are encoded as categorical fields. More detail for encoding is given in Sect. 3.4. In addition, demographic, economic, and behavioral features for the receiver and sender of a transaction are added. For instance, features like customers' age and financial age are some of the features which belong to demographic information. Credit scores, client types, and historical payment habits are also included to estimate the fraud probability of a transaction. They are called as behavioral features. After we determine the preliminary model features, the GBT model is trained with behavioral, economic, and demographic features. We also studied the feature importance.

3.4 Encoding

As mentioned above, transaction data has text and numeric values. The model can be fed directly by numeric values, although text values need to be encoded. As an encoding method, we preferred a label encoder. A dictionary, which contains a mapping for text and its corresponding encoded value, is created from the history of each encoded features of the dataset. The encoded list is composed in ascending order of feature values. For the real-time encoding, the value -9999 is added as a response to all unseen values. This provides continuity for a real-time scoring mechanism.

4   Experiments

Our proposed approach is focused on detecting fraudulent transactions on cross-channel operations by using GBT models. Various decision tree algorithms are tested during the research period of our study. However, XGBoost [4] beats Random Forest, and also Decision Tree Classifier. The following section describes the experiments and gives detailed results of our study.

4.1   Experimental Setup

The experiments are performed on a real dataset of a private bank in Turkey. The dataset is divided into two mainframes which are the training set and the test set. The data of the test set includes 6 months of channel transactions from May 2021 to October 2021. During the test set period, out of more than 260 million transactions, around 4000 of them were a fraud. Month by month detailed explanation is given in Table 1.

Table 1. The legitimate and fraudulent transaction counts of test sets used in experiments.

Test set name	Trx CNT	Fraud CNT	Ratio
202105	40013025	644	0.0016%
202106	40867466	670	0.0016%
202107	42121304	690	0.0016%
202108	44368519	951	0.0021%
202109	46337966	826	0.0018%
202110	48144671	863	0.0018%

Table 2. The legitimate and fraudulent transaction counts of training sets used in experiments.

SetID	Trx CNT	Fraud CNT	Ratio	Sender Cust. CNT	Fraud Sender Cust. CNT
A	1634587	10394	0.6359%	20475	10237
B	13339287	10394	0.0779%	204619	10237
C	15532174	11357	0.0731%	223668	11191

For composing the training set, three different strategies are examined. Let's say, the first one is called A, which has an equal number of fraudulent and legitimate accounts in the given time frame. The time range of set A is 16 months and contains data from December 2019 and up to May 2021. Another set, which is B, contains 19 times more legitimate transactions than fraudulent transactions for the same time range as A. The set C is generated with the same algorithm as the B but the time range is from March 2020 to August 2021. Comparison between set A and B indicates the importance of the undersampling method of data. The only difference between sets B and C is the time range difference. The detailed explanation of training sets is given in Table 2.

4.2 Evaluation Metrics

In most regression and classification problems, the error rate is the most commonly preferred success measurement metric to compare the performances of different algorithms. However, the error rate calculation may fail to provide the correct performance measure in such imbalanced datasets. In addition, the minimization of the error rate during learning may not improve Wilcoxon-Mann-Whitney statistics (or AUC scores). Therefore, AUC measures such as the area under the receiver operating characteristics curve (AUROC) is better-suited evaluation metric of binary classification with imbalanced data. Similar to the market leader as FICO, we used Account Detection Rate (ADR), Real-Time Value Detection Rate (RTVDR), and Non-Fraud Transaction Review Rate (NFTR) in our evaluation metrics [7]. The ADR indicates the rate of identified swindler accounts compared to total fraud accounts. The RTVDR refers to the rate of detected fraud amount compared to the total fraud amount. The NFTR is crucial because it directly expresses the rate of non-fraud transactions which are marked as fraud.

4.3 Results

This part includes results and charts from experiments related to generating training sets for extremely imbalanced and dynamically changing data. Furthermore, feature engineering and the combined performance of all studies are described below.

Training Set Ratio. We need to create new dataset by combining fraudster and legitimate accounts with a predefined ratio, because if all the dataset is fed to a training algorithm without any adoption, the model is prone to predict all transactions to non-fraud. Our sampling method contains the ratio between legitimate and swindler accounts. First of all, the equal number of accounts from both sides, which is Set A described in Sect. 4.1 were selected. Set B contains 19 times more legitimate customers during the time interval, which is December 2019 up to May 2021. This optimized ratio was found according to various experiments. The detailed results for test sets are given in Fig. 2. And models trained with those sets tested with the transactions which came to our banks channels during May, June, and July 2021.

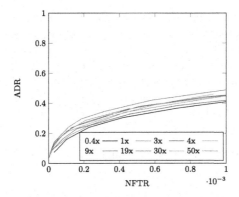

Fig. 2. Containing 19 times more transactions from legitimate customers dramatically increase detection rate.

Concept Drift. As described above, customer behaviors also change over time. As a result of behavioral changes, the performance of the model will decrease slightly over time. In other words model becomes obsolete. To prevent aging of a training model as well as adopting the models performance to changing customer behaviors, training process should be renewed and model should be updated accordingly. In this way, the retrained model will compensate for those performance degradations. While the data between December 2019 and May 2021 is included in set B, the data between March 2020 and August 2021 is included in set C. Both models were tested with transactions of August and September 2021. The proof of concept drift is clearly shown in Fig. 3 and 4. As the result shows clearly, if the older model used in test sets, will have less ADR in the same level of NFTR. The decrease in ADR is dramatically seen in the upcoming months September 2021.

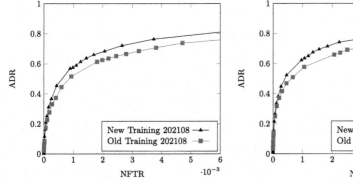
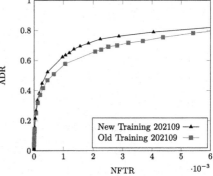

Fig. 3. A detailed result to demonstrate the Concept Drift of August 2021.

Fig. 4. A detailed result to demonstrate the Concept Drift of September 2021.

Demographic, Economic and Behavioral Features. The benefit of demographic, economic, and behavioral features are helpful to characterize customer habits. As an economic feature, we added customers' previous credit scores from the credit bureau of Turkey. Historical credit scores are included as new features up to 12 months from the transaction date. This is a good indicator of senders' and receivers' personal economic situations. The detailed results and proof can be found in Fig. 5. Added features are explained in Table 3.

Table 3. Demographic, and economic features.

Feature name	Description	Category
Account Branch	Branch Location of Account	Demographic
Client Type	Client Type (Commercial/Individual)	Demographic
Customer Age	Customer's Age	Demographic
Financial Age	Customer's Financial Age	Economic
Max & Min Credit Scores	Monthly historical max & min credit scores	Economic

Feature Importance. To optimize features of the model we analyzed integrated feature importance methods of XGBoost. Highly ranked features are chosen according to [4]. This methods contains different approaches for feature importance analysis including cover, gain, total cover, total gain, and weight. All of them are blended and created a finalized optimized feature list for the model. Adding demographic features to the raw attributes of transaction gives us a data set with 172 features. We sorted them by descending order for each feature importance method, and take the union of the first 70 features in each list. The resulted feature list contains 96 features. The performance comparison between models can be inspected in Fig. 6.

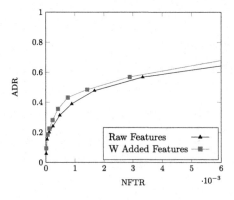

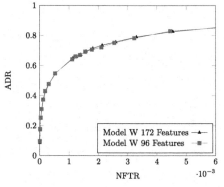

Fig. 5. An in-depth analysis of demographic, economic and behavioral features.

Fig. 6. Exactly the same test performance is investigated both 96 and 172 features for May 2021.

To sum up, when we combine all techniques above, the overall fraud loss amount detection performance of the model with a low false-positive rate is shown in Fig. 7.

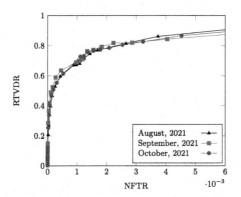

Fig. 7. The model's overall fraud amount detection performance for August, September, and October 2021

5 Conclusion

As a consequence of the emerging technologies, the variety of transaction channels has increased, but only 26% of financial institutions are tracking the frauds in their transaction channels [16]. Our proposed model tracks and scores the monetary transactions to indicate the possibility of fraudulent transactions from the cross channels in real-time. An AI-powered software solution is provided for the outcome of rarely occurred fraudulent transactions, which properly handles the imbalanced class and concept drift problems. Our model detects cross-channel frauds quite accurately over real banking datasets. It can catch almost 75% of total fraud loss with a low false-positive ratio and overcome aging with continuous training. The proposed learning strategy and trained algorithm will be integrated to live system, and our solution will become a good candidate compared to conventional rule-based solutions which require constant maintenance and analysis.

References

1. Bayram, B., Köroğlu, B., Gönen, M.: Improving fraud detection and concept drift adaptation in credit card transactions using incremental gradient boosting trees. In: 2020 19th IEEE International Conference on Machine Learning and Applications (ICMLA), pp. 545–550. IEEE (2020)
2. Bhattacharyya, S., Jha, S., Tharakunnel, K., Westland, J.C.: Data mining for credit card fraud: a comparative study. Decis. Support Syst. **50**(3), 602–613 (2011)
3. Chawla, N.V., Bowyer, K.W., Hall, L.O., Kegelmeyer, W.P.: Smote: synthetic minority over-sampling technique. J. Artif. Intell. Res. **16**, 321–357 (2002)

4. Chen, T., Guestrin, C.: XGBoost: a scalable tree boosting system. In: Proceedings of the 22nd ACM SIGKDD International Conference on Knowledge Discovery and Data Mining, pp. 785–794 (2016)
5. Dal Pozzolo, A., Boracchi, G., Caelen, O., Alippi, C., Bontempi, G.: Credit card fraud detection and concept-drift adaptation with delayed supervised information. In: 2015 International Joint Conference on Neural Networks (IJCNN), pp. 1–8. IEEE (2015)
6. Dheepa, V., Dhanapal, R.: Behavior based credit card fraud detection using support vector machines. ICTACT J. Soft Comput. **2**(4), 391–397 (2012)
7. FICO: Reducing fraud losses with enhanced cnp models on the fico®falcon®platform (2018)
8. Gee, J., Button, M.: The financial cost of fraud 2019: the latest data from around the world (2019)
9. Gee, J., Button, M.: The financial cost of fraud 2021: the latest data from around the world (2021)
10. Jurgovsky, J., et al.: Sequence classification for credit-card fraud detection. Expert Syst. Appl. **100**, 234–245 (2018)
11. Malekian, D., Hashemi, M.R.: An adaptive profile based fraud detection framework for handling concept drift. In: 2013 10th International ISC Conference on Information Security and Cryptology (ISCISC), pp. 1–6. IEEE (2013)
12. Molloy, I., et al.: Graph analytics for real-time scoring of cross-channel transactional fraud. In: Grossklags, J., Preneel, B. (eds.) FC 2016. LNCS, vol. 9603, pp. 22–40. Springer, Heidelberg (2017). https://doi.org/10.1007/978-3-662-54970-4_2
13. Patel, Y., et al.: Cross channel fraud detection framework in financial services using recurrent neural networks. Ph.D. thesis, London Metropolitan University (2019)
14. Philip, K., Chan, S.: Toward scalable learning with non-uniform class and cost distributions: a case study in credit card fraud detection. In: Proceeding of the Fourth International Conference on Knowledge Discovery and Data Mining, pp. 164–168 (1998)
15. Sinayobye, J.O., Kiwanuka, F., Kaawaase Kyanda, S.: A state-of-the-art review of machine learning techniques for fraud detection research. In: 2018 IEEE/ACM Symposium on Software Engineering in Africa (SEiA), pp. 11–19 (2018)
16. Urban, M.: New survey reveals top fraud threats and vulnerabilities. FICO, 11 January 2011. https://www.fico.com/blogs/new-survey-reveals-top-fraud-threats-and-vulnerabilities
17. Urban, M.: Why managing cross-channel fraud is a must. FICO, 22 February 2011. https://www.fico.com/blogs/why-managing-cross-channel-fraud-must
18. Worobec, K.: 2021 fraud - the facts 2021 (2021)
19. Worobec, K.: 2021 half year fraud update (2021)
20. Yen, S.J., Lee, Y.S.: Under-sampling approaches for improving prediction of the minority class in an imbalanced dataset. In: Huang, D.S., Li, K., Irwin, G.W. (eds.) Intelligent Control and Automation, pp. 731–740. Springer, Heidelberg (2006). https://doi.org/10.1007/978-3-540-37256-1_89
21. Yeşilkanat, A., Bayram, B., Köroğlu, B., Arslan, S.: An adaptive approach on credit card fraud detection using transaction aggregation and word embeddings. In: Maglogiannis, I., Iliadis, L., Pimenidis, E. (eds.) AIAI 2020. IAICT, vol. 583, pp. 3–14. Springer, Cham (2020). https://doi.org/10.1007/978-3-030-49161-1_1

An Empirical Study on Anomaly Detection Algorithms for Extremely Imbalanced Datasets

Gonçalo Fontes[2], Luís Miguel Matos[1], Arthur Matta[2], André Pilastri[2(✉)], and Paulo Cortez[1]

[1] ALGORITMI R&D Centre, Department of Information Systems, University of Minho, 4804-533 Guimarães, Portugal
{luis.matos,pcortez}@dsi.uminho.pt
[2] EPMQ - IT CCG ZGDV Institute, 4804-533 Guimarães, Portugal
{goncalo.fontes,arthur.matta,andre.pilastri}@ccg.pt

Abstract. Anomaly detection attempts to identify abnormal events that deviate from normality. Since such events are often rare, data related to this domain is usually imbalanced. In this paper, we compare diverse preprocessing and Machine Learning (ML) state-of-the-art algorithms that can be adopted within this anomaly detection context. These include two unsupervised learning algorithms, namely Isolation Forests (IF) and deep dense AutoEncoders (AE), and two supervised learning approaches, namely Random Forest and an Automated ML (AutoML) method. Several empirical experiments were conducted by adopting seven extremely imbalanced public domain datasets. Overall, the IF and AE unsupervised methods obtained competitive anomaly detection results, which also have the advantage of not requiring labeled data.

Keywords: Autoencoder · Deep learning · Isolation Forest · One-class classification · Random Forest · AutoML · Supervised learning · Unsupervised learning

1 Introduction

Anomaly detection, also known as outlier detection or novelty detection, has been an area of study for several years due to its value in diverse real-world application domains, such as: fraud detection [1], network intrusion [18] and predictive maintenance [14]. Anomaly detection can be defined as the identification of abnormal or anomalous events that deviate from the perceived normal ones [30]. Usually, anomaly detection involves dealing with highly imbalanced data, since anomalous events are often rare [21].

Within this context, Machine Learning (ML) algorithms have been widely applied to anomaly detection. A common approach is to employ supervised learning methods, such as Logistic Regression [29], Decision Trees (DT) [33] and Random Forests [34]. These supervised ML algorithms are often coupled with

© IFIP International Federation for Information Processing 2022
Published by Springer Nature Switzerland AG 2022
I. Maglogiannis et al. (Eds.): AIAI 2022, IFIP AICT 646, pp. 85–95, 2022.
https://doi.org/10.1007/978-3-031-08333-4_7

resampling techniques to balance the training data, such as SMOTE [9] or Gaussian Copula (GC) [32]. Within the supervised learning domain, there has been a stronger focus on the usage of Automated ML (AutoML) [13], which alleviates the modeling effort by automating the ML algorithm and hyperparameter search. Indeed, in a recent study, an AutoML method was compared favorably with other ML algorithms (e.g., DT, RF) when performing an anomaly detection industrial quality inspection task [26]. One disadvantage of the supervised learning approach is that it requires labeled data, which often requires a huge manual effort to create/obtain correct labeled data. An alternative is to employ an unsupervised learning, in particular via a one-class learning approach, where the ML algorithms are only fed with normal examples (the majority class). This includes algorithms such as Isolation Forest (IF) [20] and deep AutoEncoders (AE) [26,34].

In this paper, we attempt to empirically measure the effect of several state-of-the-art ML methods when applied to anomaly detection tasks. The compared methods include: supervised – RF, AutoML; and unsupervised – IF and AE. The four methods were compared by adopting seven extremely imbalanced public domain datasets. The paper is structured as follows. Section 2 describes the related work. Section 3 presents the public domain datasets, preprocessing methods, the compared Machine Learning (ML) algorithms and the evaluation methodology. Then, Sect. 4 presents the obtained results. Lastly, the main conclusions are discussed in Sect. 5.

2   Related Work

Anomaly detection is a key ML task that impacts in several application domains (e.g., Finance, Fraud, Industry, Security). In effect, the early studies addressing this task dates back to the 1960s [15]. In more recent years, a diverse range of algorithms have been proposed for anomaly detection, including based on statistics [17], clustering [1,8], classification [8,26,29,33,34] and graph mining [2]. In particular, supervised classification approaches require labeled data that is often difficult to obtain (e.g., requiring human effort). When labeled data is available, it is often extremely unbalanced, since anomalous events tend to be rare. Thus, some supervised learning studies employ balancing training methods, such as SMOTE [9] or GC [32].

One of the challenges that anomaly detection has to address is that the boundaries between normal and abnormal data are often not clearly defined, typically addressed by using an unsupervised or one-class learning methods [6,36]. Under the one-class learning approach, the training datasets only contain "normal" examples. The assumption is that any anomaly should be more distanced from the training learning space. Examples of one-class ML algorithms include [3,5]: Local Outlier Factor (LOF), One-Class Support Vector Machine (OC-SVM) and Isolation Forest (IF). More recently, Deep learning have been proposed for anomaly detection in diverse applications [7,30]. One popular deep learning model is the AutoEncoder (AE), which when compared with other one-class methods (e.g., LOF, OC-SVM and IF), tends to provide faster training times, thus are capable of handling a larger amount of training data. Another advantage of the AE algorithm is that it can be easily adapted to an online (or continual) learning, thus tackling better the concept drift phenomenon [24,25].

In anomaly detection, there is a recurrent problem, which is the sparseness of anomalous data when applied to a supervised approach. This sparseness makes it quite challenging to model machine learning models, as there are not many examples to feed into the model. In some studies, balancing techniques are used to generate enough minority examples for more robust models to learn (oversampling) or even to reduce the majority class so that the model learns both classes in the same proportion (Undersampling) [23].

Within our knowledge, there is a lack of studies that perform a comparison of both supervised learning and one-class learning ML methods over several anomaly detection tasks, particularly extremely imbalanced ones. This paper fulfills this research gap by comparing the performance of state-of-the-art methods, namely RF, AutoML, IF and AE.

3   Materials and Methods

3.1   Datasets

This work experimented with seven public domain imbalanced datasets that can be tested for anomaly detection, namely:

- The **Predictive Maintenance Modeling Guide Collection (PMMGC)** consists of real-time telemetry readings and failure history acquired over the year of 2015 for 100 machines [28]. The full datasets are related with 876,142 hourly telemetry records (roughly 8,761 records per machine) captured by four sensors installed in each machine that measure tension (voltage), pressure, vibration, and rotation. The measurements were averaged using an hourly time period. In this paper, we selected five datasets from this collection and that are related with machines that contain more failures (the machine identification numbers are shown in Table 1). Each failure indicates the occurrence of a machine component replacement.
- The **PMAI4I** is another Predictive Maintenance dataset that was presented at the Artificial Intelligence for Industries conference (PMAI4I) [27]. It consists of a synthetic dataset that reflects a real predictive industrial maintenance task. The dataset contains 10,000 data points with one input attribute representing the type of product quality (categorical $\in\{$ "low", "medium", "high" $\}$), five numerical inputs (air temperature, process temperature, rotational speed, torque and tool wear) and a target label indicating the occurrence of a machine failure.
- The **Credit Card Fraud Detection (CCFD)** data is related with transactions made by credit cards by European cardholders in September 2013 over two days [10]. The dataset contains a total of 283,726 transactions and 473 frauds. Due to confidentiality issues, the dataset contains only numerical features resulting from a Principal Component Analysis (PCA) transformation.

The only input attributes that have not been transformed with PCA are: *Amount*, which indicates the transaction amount; and *Class*, which indicates whether the transaction was fraudulent or not.

Table 1 characterizes the adopted datasets. The last column (**Failures %**) shows that all datasets are highly imbalanced. In effect, the failure frequency that is lower than 1%, except for dataset PMAI4I (3.39%).

3.2   Data Preprocessing

For the PMMGC datasets, we have first removed all duplicate entries, since several of the selected machine datasets included repetitions of rows for the same anomalies. Moreover, the product quality type attribute of the PMAI4I dataset (the only categorical input feature of all the analyzed datasets) was transformed into a numeric one by using one-hot encoding, as implemented by the `cane`[1] Python module [22,24]. This transformation assumes one binary input per categorical level, namely: "low" → (1,0,0), "medium" → (0,1,0) and "high" → (0,0,1). Regarding the same dataset, in order to increase the imbalanced ratio of the target class to a value that is closer to the percentage of failures of the other datasets, we have performed a random undersampling of the anomaly cases, leading to just 100 anomalies (of a total of 339), thus resulting in a failure rate of 1%.

Table 1. Summary of the adopted anomaly detection datasets.

Source	Dataset	Records	Input features	# Failures	Failures (%)
PMMGC [28]	Machine 17	≈8,761	4	15	0.17
	Machine 22			15	0.17
	Machine 83			14	0.16
	Machine 98			16	0.18
	Machine 99			19	0.22
[27]	PMAI4I	10,000	6	339	3.39
[10]	CCFD	283,726	29	482	0.17

3.3   Anomaly Detection Methods

All ML methods were implemented by using the Python language and the following modules: `scikit-learn`[2] – for IF and RF; `TensorFlow`[3] – for AE; and H2O[4] module for the AutoML.

The IF is a one-class ML algorithm that takes advantage of two significant characteristics of abnormal instances [20]: they are present in fewer quantities

---

[1] https://pypi.org/project/cane/.
[2] https://scikit-learn.org/stable/.
[3] https://www.tensorflow.org/.
[4] https://docs.h2o.ai/.

and are also numerically different to normal instances. The IF adopts this principle, constructing an ensemble of several isolation trees, each containing the abnormal instances closer to the root of the tree (Fig. 1). The `scikit-learn` IF implementation provides a decision score that ranges from $\hat{y}_i = -1$ (highest abnormal score) to $\hat{y}_i = 1$ (highest normal score). In order to obtain an anomaly probability score ($d_i \in [0, 1]$, for an input example i), we rescale the IF scores by computing $d_i = (1 - \hat{y}_i)/2$.

Autoencoders (AE) are unsupervised learning techniques that efficiently compress and encode data into a lower-dimensional representation by assuming a bottleneck layer (with L_b hidden units) [16]. Let $(L_I, L_1, ..., L_H, L_O)$ denote the structure of a dense (fully connected) Deep FeedForward Network (DFFN) with the layer node sizes, where L_I and L_O represent the input and output layer sizes and H is the number of hidden layers. The proposed AE is based on an architecture that previously obtained high quality anomaly detection results in a industrial anomaly detection task [26, 34, 35]. It assumes $L_I = L_O$, a symmetrical encoder and decoder structure (e.g., $L_1 = L_{O-1}$) and the popular ReLu activation function is used by all hidden neural units with the exception of the output layer, which assumes a linear activation function. In the encoder component, the number of hidden layer units decreases by half in each subsequent hidden layer until the bottleneck size (L_b) is reached: $L_1 = L_I/2$, $L_2 = L_1/2$, and vice-versa. Each hidden layer is also attached with a Batch Normalization (BN) layer. Figure 2 represent the base structure used for all datasets in this work.

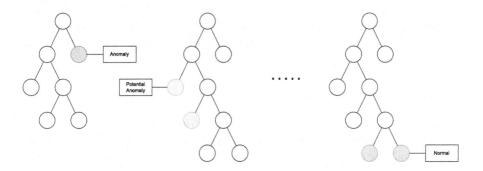

Fig. 1. Exemplification of the IF algorithm.

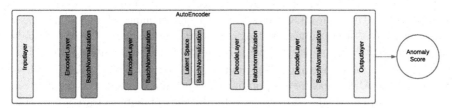

Fig. 2. Exemplification of the adopted base AE structure.

When adapted to anomaly detection, the AE training algorithm is only fed with standard (normal) instances, aiming to generate output values identical to its inputs. In this work, the AE is trained with the Adam optimizer using a batch size of 32, 200 epochs and early stopping (using 10% of the training data as the validation set). The Mean Absolute Error (MAE) is used as the loss function and reconstruction error: $MAE_i = \sum_{k=1}^{n} \frac{|x_{i,k} - \hat{x}_{i,k}|}{n}$, where $x_{i,k}$ and $\hat{x}_{i,k}$ denote the AE input and output value for the i-th data instance and k-th input or output node. The reconstruction MAE error is used as the decision score $d_i = MAE_i$, where higher reconstruction errors should correspond to a higher anomaly probability.

Turning to the supervised learning methods, the RF is a popular method that tends to obtain high quality prediction results when assuming its default hyper-parameter values [11]. The algorithm works as an ensemble of decision trees that form a "forest". Each tree depends on the values of a randomly sampled input vector and a bagging selection of training samples [4]. RF can be used for both regression and classification tasks. In this work, we used RF to output anomaly class probabilities ($\in [0.0, 1.0]$), which are used as the decision score (d_i). As for the AutoML method, we adopt the H2O tool, which performs an automatic training and tuning of several ML algorithms within a user-specified time limit. Under the adopted H2O default configuration, the tool trains four distinct algorithms: RF, Generalized Linear Model (GLM), Gradient Boosting Machine and a default DFFN network. Then, it employs a Stacking Ensemble (SE), which uses all previously trained models to generate inputs for another GLM model. To perform the model selection, we set the tool to optimize the Area Under Curve (AUC) of the Receiver Operating Characteristic (ROC) analysis [12]. The tool was run for a maximum of 10 min, assuming an internal (applied over the training data) 5-fold cross-validation scheme.

3.4   Evaluation

To evaluate the anomaly detection performance, an external (applied over all available data) stratified 5-fold cross-validation scheme. During each of the five iterations, the training data was used to fit the ML model and the test (unseen) data was used to compute the predicted anomaly decision scores and respective ROC analysis [12]. When a model outputs a decision score d_i, the class can be interpreted as positive if $d_i > K$, where K is a fixed decision threshold, otherwise it is considered negative. The ROC curve shows the performance of a two-class classifier across all $K \in [0, 1]$ values, plotting one minus the specificity (x-axis), or False Positive Rate (FPR), versus the sensitivity (y-axis), or True Positive Rate (TPR). The discrimination performance is given by the $AUC = \int_0^1 ROC dK$. It should be noted that the AUC measure is a popular measure that contains two main advantages [34,35]: quality values are not affected by the imbalanced rate of the target class; and quality values are easy to interpret (50% – performance of a random classifier; 70% - good; 80% – very good; 90% - excellent; and 100% - ideal classifier). After executing the 5-fold cross-validation, the AUC results are aggregated by computing the median value (which is less sensitive to outliers when compared withe the average value).

4 Results

In the first set of computational experiments, we executed the external 5-fold cross-validation for the tested seven datasets and four baseline ML algorithms (RF, AutoML, IF) and a generic AE structure. The results are summarized in Table 2. When comparing the supervised learning results (RF and AutoML), the H2O automated method tends to obtain a better anomaly detection performance. For instance, it presents a higher median PMMGC value (66.4% versus 62.5%) and also better median AUC values for the PMAI4I and CCFD tasks. Turning to the one-class methods, both IF and AE obtain the best median AUC values in three cases (IF – Machine 17 and 98, and CCFD; AE – Machine 22 and 99, and PMAI4I). Overall, AE produces a better discrimination accuracy (in terms of median AUC) for PMMGC and PMAI4I, while IF obtains better CCFD results. More importantly, the comparison of supervised versus one-class methods tends to favor the latter ones. In effect, there is only one case (PMMGC Machine 83) where a supervised learning algorithm (RF) obtains the best anomaly detection performance. For all other cases, the IF and AE algorithms tend to outperform the supervised learning methods. This is an important result, since the one-class methods have the advantage of not requiring labeled data during their training procedure that is often more costly given the manual effort required to inspect and tag the examples.

Table 2. Median AUC values for the first comparison experiment (best results are in bold).

Dataset		Supervised		Unsupervised	
		RF	AutoML	IF	AE
PMMGC:	Machine 17	0.5000	0.6664	**0.6830**	0.6459
	Machine 22	0.6667	0.6661	0.7069	**0.7173**
	Machine 83	**0.6667**	0.6638	0.6114	0.4768
	Machine 98	0.6250	0.6250	**0.8155**	0.7979
	Machine 99	0.5000	0.4986	0.6818	**0.7047**
Median PMMGC value:		0.6250	0.6638	0.7069	**0.7173**
PMAI4I		0.5997	0.6732	0.7644	**0.7914**
CCFD		0.8838	0.8979	**0.9554**	0.8813

To further check if a balancing training technique would improve the supervised learning results, we executed a second set of experiments by adopting the five PMMGC datasets, for which the supervised learning anomaly detection performance is weak (e.g., random classification for RF and Machine 17). In these set of experiments, the RF and AutoML training data was first balanced by employing two oversampling techniques, SMOTE and CG, as implemented by the `imblearn` [19] and `sdv` [31] Python modules, using the baseline configurations. We note that in these experiments, the external 5-fold test data is kept without any changes. The obtained results are shown in Table 3.

Rather than improving the performance of supervised learning methods, both resampling techniques tends to diminish the anomaly detection capability. For instance, the median machine AUC value for RF decreased from 62.5% to 49.49% (SMOTE) and 50.0% (GC). Similarly, the AutoML median machine performance decreased from 66.4% to 50% (for both SMOTE and CG). The oversampling poor performance behavior might be explained by the extremely imbalanced nature of the analyzed datasets. Since the percentage of failures is lower than 1%, the SMOTE and GC methods have to generate a substantially high number of false synthetic cases, which creates records of the least representative class with the possibly of containing incorrect information that in turn prejudices the supervised learning.

This further enhances the quality of applying one-class learning instead of balancing the dataset. The one-class learning approach uses the class itself to establish the boundaries that distinguish it from other classes, thus proving to be more useful than balancing extremely unbalanced datasets.

Table 3. Median AUC values for the second comparison experiment using the PMMGC data source (best results are in **bold**).

Machine	SMOTE		Gaussian copula	
	RF	AutoML	RF	AutoML
17	0.4949	0.4991	**0.6667**	0.6641
22	0.6584	**0.6624**	0.5000	0.4991
83	0.4949	0.4986	**0.5000**	**0.5000**
98	0.6561	**0.6621**	0.6250	0.4997
99	0.4874	0.4951	**0.5000**	0.4977
Median machine value:	0.4949	0.4991	**0.5000**	0.4997

5   Conclusions

Due to advances in Information Technology (e.g., Smart Cities, Industry 4.0), anomaly detection is becoming an increasingly relevant task in diverse domains where digital data is in abundance (e.g., industry, finance, security). In this work, we perform an empirical comparison study that considers seven extremely imbalanced public domain datasets and four state-of-the-art Machine Learning (ML) algorithms: one-class – Isolation Forest (IF) and deep AutoEncoders (AE); and supervised – Random Forest (RF) and an Automated ML (AutoML) tool.

Overall, the best anomaly detection results were obtained by the one-class learners (IF and AE), which have the advantage of not requiring labeled data during their training procedure thus proving to be more effective in detecting anomalies than applying dataset augmentation techniques (e.g., SMOTE, GC). In future work, we wish to extend the empirical study by implementing more robust data augmentation techniques, such as using deep Generative Adversarial Networks (GANs), to check if this produces benefits compared with other synthetic data generators (e.g., SMOTE and GC).

Acknowledgments. This work has been supported by the European Regional Development Fund (FEDER) through a grant of the Operational Programme for Competitivity and Internationalization of Portugal 2020 Partnership Agreement (PRODUTECH4S&C, POCI-01-0247-FEDER-046102).

References

1. Ahmed, M., Mahmood, A.N., Islam, M.R.: A survey of anomaly detection techniques in financial domain. Futur. Gener. Comput. Syst. **55**, 278–288 (2016)
2. Akoglu, L., Tong, H., Koutra, D.: Graph based anomaly detection and description: a survey. Data Min. Knowl. Disc. **29**(3), 626–688 (2014). https://doi.org/10.1007/s10618-014-0365-y
3. Alla, S., Adari, S.K.: Beginning Anomaly Detection Using Python-Based Deep Learning. Apress, Berkeley (2019). https://doi.org/10.1007/978-1-4842-5177-5
4. Breiman, L.: Random forests. Mach. Learn. **45**(1), 5–32 (2001). https://doi.org/10.1023/A:1010933404324
5. Breunig, M.M., Kriegel, H., Ng, R.T., Sander, J.: LOF: identifying density-based local outliers. In: Chen, W., Naughton, J.F., Bernstein, P.A. (eds.) Proceedings of the 2000 ACM SIGMOD International Conference on Management of Data, Dallas, Texas, USA, 16–18 May 2000, pp. 93–104. ACM (2000). https://doi.org/10.1145/342009.335388
6. Cao, N., Lin, Y.R., Gotz, D., Du, F.: Z-glyph: visualizing outliers in multivariate data. Inf. Vis. **17**(1), 22–40 (2018). https://doi.org/10.1177/1473871616686635
7. Chalapathy, R., Chawla, S.: Deep learning for anomaly detection: a survey. arXiv preprint arXiv:1901.03407 (2019)
8. Chandola, V., Banerjee, A., Kumar, V.: Anomaly detection: a survey. ACM Comput. Surv. (CSUR) **41**(3), 1–58 (2009)
9. Chawla, N.V., Bowyer, K.W., Hall, L.O., Kegelmeyer, W.P.: SMOTE: synthetic minority over-sampling technique. J. Artif. Intell. Res. **16**, 321–357 (2002). https://doi.org/10.1613/jair.953
10. Credit Card Fraud - Kaggle: Anonymized credit card transactions labeled as fraudulent or genuine (2018). https://www.kaggle.com/mlg-ulb/creditcardfraud
11. Delgado, M.F., Cernadas, E., Barro, S., Amorim, D.G.: Do we need hundreds of classifiers to solve real world classification problems? J. Mach. Learn. Res. **15**(1), 3133–3181 (2014). http://dl.acm.org/citation.cfm?id=2697065
12. Fawcett, T.: An introduction to ROC analysis. Pattern Recognit. Lett. **27**, 861–874 (2006)
13. Ferreira, L., Pilastri, A.L., Martins, C.M., Pires, P.M., Cortez, P.: A comparison of automl tools for machine learning, deep learning and xgboost. In: International Joint Conference on Neural Networks, IJCNN 2021, Shenzhen, China, 18–22 July 2021, pp. 1–8. IEEE (2021). https://doi.org/10.1109/IJCNN52387.2021.9534091

14. Ferreira, L., Pilastri, A., Sousa, V., Romano, F., Cortez, P.: Prediction of maintenance equipment failures using automated machine learning. In: Yin, H., et al. (eds.) IDEAL 2021. LNCS, vol. 13113, pp. 259–267. Springer, Cham (2021). https://doi.org/10.1007/978-3-030-91608-4_26
15. Grubbs, F.E.: Procedures for detecting outlying observations in samples. Technometrics **11**(1), 1–21 (1969)
16. Hinton, G., Salakhutdinov, R.: Reducing the dimensionality of data with neural networks. Science **313**(5786), 504–507 (2006). https://doi.org/10.1126/science.1127647. Cited By 9376
17. Hodge, V., Austin, J.: A survey of outlier detection methodologies. Artif. Intell. Rev. **22**(2), 85–126 (2004)
18. Kumar, V.: Parallel and distributed computing for cybersecurity. IEEE Distrib. Syst. Online **6**(10) (2005)
19. Lemaître, G., Nogueira, F., Aridas, C.K.: Imbalanced-learn: a python toolbox to tackle the curse of imbalanced datasets in machine learning. J. Mach. Learn. Res. **18**(17), 1–5 (2017). http://jmlr.org/papers/v18/16-365
20. Liu, F.T., Ting, K.M., Zhou, Z.: Isolation forest. In: Proceedings of the 8th IEEE International Conference on Data Mining (ICDM), Pisa, Italy, pp. 413–422. IEEE (2008)
21. Longadge, R., Dongre, S.: Class imbalance problem in data mining review. arXiv preprint arXiv:1305.1707 (2013)
22. Matos, L.M., Cortez, P., Mendes, R.: Cane - Categorical Attribute traNsformation Environment (2020). https://pypi.org/project/cane/
23. Matos, L.M., Cortez, P., Mendes, R., Moreau, A.: A comparison of data-driven approaches for mobile marketing user conversion prediction. In: Jardim-Gonçalves, R., Mendonça, J.P., Jotsov, V., Marques, M., Martins, J., Bierwolf, R.E. (eds.) 9th IEEE International Conference on Intelligent Systems, IS 2018, Funchal, Madeira, Portugal, 25–27 September 2018, pp. 140–146. IEEE (2018). https://doi.org/10.1109/IS.2018.8710472
24. Matos, L.M., Cortez, P., Mendes, R., Moreau, A.: Using deep learning for mobile marketing user conversion prediction. In: International Joint Conference on Neural Networks, IJCNN 2019 Budapest, Hungary, 14–19 July 2019, pp. 1–8. IEEE (2019). https://doi.org/10.1109/IJCNN.2019.8851888
25. Matos, L.M., Cortez, P., Mendes, R.C., Moreau, A.: Using deep learning for ordinal classification of mobile marketing user conversion. In: Yin, H., Camacho, D., Tino, P., Tallón-Ballesteros, A.J., Menezes, R., Allmendinger, R. (eds.) IDEAL 2019. LNCS, vol. 11871, pp. 60–67. Springer, Cham (2019). https://doi.org/10.1007/978-3-030-33607-3_7
26. Matos, L.M., Domingues, A., Moreira, G., Cortez, P., Pilastri, A.: A comparison of machine learning approaches for predicting in-car display production quality. In: Yin, H., et al. (eds.) IDEAL 2021. LNCS, vol. 13113, pp. 3–11. Springer, Cham (2021). https://doi.org/10.1007/978-3-030-91608-4_1
27. Matzka, S.: Explainable artificial intelligence for predictive maintenance applications. In: Proceedings - 2020 3rd International Conference on Artificial Intelligence for Industries, AI4I 2020, pp. 69–74 (2020). https://doi.org/10.1109/AI4I49448.2020.00023
28. Microsoft: Predictive maintenance modelling guide (2016). https://gallery.azure.ai/Collection/Predictive-Maintenance-Implementation-Guide-1
29. Muharemi, F., Logofătu, D., Leon, F.: Machine learning approaches for anomaly detection of water quality on a real-world data set. J. Inf. Telecommun. **3**(3), 294–307 (2019)

30. Pang, G., Shen, C., Cao, L., Hengel, A.V.D.: Deep learning for anomaly detection: a review. ACM Comput. Surv. **54**(2), 1–38 (2021). https://doi.org/10.1145/3439950

31. Patki, N., Wedge, R., Veeramachaneni, K.: The synthetic data vault. In: 2016 IEEE International Conference on Data Science and Advanced Analytics (DSAA), pp. 399–410, October 2016. https://doi.org/10.1109/DSAA.2016.49

32. Pereira, P.J., Pereira, A., Cortez, P., Pilastri, A.: A comparison of machine learning methods for extremely unbalanced industrial quality data. In: Marreiros, G., Melo, F.S., Lau, N., Lopes Cardoso, H., Reis, L.P. (eds.) EPIA 2021. LNCS (LNAI), vol. 12981, pp. 561–572. Springer, Cham (2021). https://doi.org/10.1007/978-3-030-86230-5_44

33. Rai, K., Devi, M.S., Guleria, A.: Decision tree based algorithm for intrusion detection. Int. J. Adv. Netw. Appl. **7**(4), 2828 (2016)

34. Ribeiro, D., Matos, L.M., Cortez, P., Moreira, G., Pilastri, A.: A comparison of anomaly detection methods for industrial screw tightening. In: Gervasi, O., et al. (eds.) ICCSA 2021. LNCS, vol. 12950, pp. 485–500. Springer, Cham (2021). https://doi.org/10.1007/978-3-030-86960-1_34

35. Ribeiro, D., Matos, L.M., Moreira, G., Pilastri, A., Cortez, P.: Isolation forests and deep autoencoders for industrial screw tightening anomaly detection. Computers **11**(4), 54 (2022). https://doi.org/10.3390/computers11040054

36. Ruff, L., Görnitz, N., et al.: Deep one-class classification. In: Dy, J.G., Krause, A. (eds.) Proceedings of the 35th International Conference on Machine Learning, ICML 2018, Stockholmsmässan, Stockholm, Sweden, 10–15 July 2018. Proceedings of Machine Learning Research, vol. 80, pp. 4390–4399. PMLR (2018)

Anomaly Detection Using Edge Computing AI on Low Powered Devices

Dragoş-Vasile Bratu$^{(\boxtimes)}$, Rareş Ştefan Tiberius Ilinoiu, Alexandru Cristea, Maria-Alexandra Zolya, and Sorin-Aurel Moraru

Transilvania University of Braşov, 500036 Braşov, Romania
d.v.bratu@gmail.com, smoraru@unitbv.ro

Abstract. In the industrial environment, maintaining a permanent good state of functioning for every piece of equipment has a substantial importance. This, however, is very difficult to attain, due to the mechanical wear, the environment of operation, or improper usage. Predictive maintenance is a practice that is performed to determine the condition of the machinery in service and estimate the time when the maintenance should occur. The challenge of detecting a possible fault in a piece of equipment before it occurs is one of the main tasks of the predictive maintenance process. Reading data from sensors and creating firmware that monitors the equipment can be time and resource-consuming, and not practical if the equipment is changed frequently. Nowadays, the computational power of Artificial Intelligence exceeds that of a computer. As the industrial equipment and the hardware components of a conventional computer are getting increasingly expensive and demanded, more and more entities are running Machine Learning algorithms, which make the data exchange with a server that runs this service a more feasible process. This approach poses several challenges due to latency, privacy, bandwidth, and network connectivity. To solve these limitations, computation should be moved as much as possible towards the Edge, directly on the devices that gather the data. In this article, we propose a compact and low-powered solution that is accurate and small enough to be fitted on a microcontroller or a device that runs on the Edge. This approach ensures that a minimum amount of resources are used. The solution consists of an Unsupervised learning algorithm that can detect anomalies in the vibration patterns of the bearings or the casing of industrial motors. It uses an Autoencoder that takes as input the median absolute deviation of each measurement set provided by an accelerometer, then with the help of a classifier compares the values provided by the output to values that are known to be normal vibration patterns and decides if it deals with an anomaly or not. The low-powered Edge device is an ESP32 board that consumes only 160 mAh on full load but also being powerful enough to maintain WiFi and Bluetooth capabilities when needed. On a more economical operating mode, without WiFi and Bluetooth capabilities it can consume as low as 3 mAh [1]. This feature and the fact that the board is connected directly to the data-gathering sensor makes it preferable to an algorithm hosted on a

© IFIP International Federation for Information Processing 2022
Published by Springer Nature Switzerland AG 2022
I. Maglogiannis et al. (Eds.): AIAI 2022, IFIP AICT 646, pp. 96–107, 2022.
https://doi.org/10.1007/978-3-031-08333-4_8

remote server or a local machine due to low resource consumption and easy maintainability. The Autoencoder is fitted on this board and runs continuously until it encounters an anomaly, which in turn provokes an alert to the user.

Keywords: ESP32 · Autoencoder · Machine learning · Edge computing · Anomaly detection

1 Introduction

In a study performed by Eurostat [1] it was discovered that 41% of EU enterprises used Cloud Computing in 2021 and 73% of those enterprises used sophisticated Cloud services relating to security software applications, hosting enterprise's databases, or computing platforms for application development, testing or deployment. Compared with 2020, the use of Cloud Computing increased by 5 percentage points (Fig. 1). In this paper, a step forward in this direction was made, by proposing a cost-effective IoT solution running on Edge that can perform anomaly detection right on the data-generating device. Generally speaking, anomaly detection [2] is a branch of Artificial Intelligence (AI) that deals with the identification of patterns in a set of data that do not correspond to a normal behavior definition agreed upon beforehand. To detect anomalies, a model that describes the patterns of a normal behavior has to be defined first. Only then, the anomalies can be successfully detected by the model.

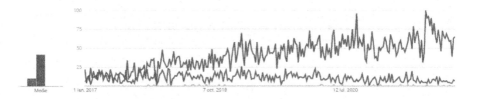

Fig. 1. Comparison between trends of Edge, Fog and Mist computing.

2 Related Work

Anomaly detection in gas turbines described in [7] is achieved with the help of a Deep Autoencoder (DAE) which analyzes the performance state of the turbine, more exactly including DEGT, Exhaust Gas Temperature Margin (EGTM), Delta Fuel Flow (DFF), Delta Core Speed (DN2). Their solution utilizes two traditional DAEs and a k-means clustering model. One DAE together with the k-means clustering model is used for a sample selection mechanism to build the original training set, while another DAE is used to calculate the reconstruction error and high-level feature of each original sample [7]. With the help of the bearing data set an anomaly detection solution using a CNN and GRU was developed as described in [8]. The latter article suggests making use of the temporal component of the data with a novel deep architecture named stacked CNN and GRU combination network (SCG network) to predict the anomaly values. The significant difference between the neural network architecture in this paper and those cited above (esp. those in [5,6]) is the fact that the whole system is built in a robust way, specifically to be fitted into a microcontroller that runs on the Edge with an Autoencoder [4].

2.1 System Model and Overview of Approach

The goal of this project was to develop a Machine Learning algorithm, which can detect abnormalities in the vibration patterns of an AC motor, preventing in this way failures of the equipment and reducing the time necessary for maintenance. Such an algorithm is very important because it supports a predictive [9] approach to device maintenance [10], thus preventing the user or the person responsible for managing the equipment from the undesirable situation of finding that the equipment has sustained severe damage (Fig. 2).

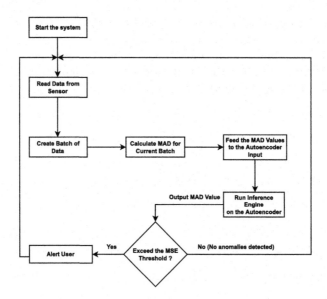

Fig. 2. Workflow diagram of the system

With the support of this method, the user or the person in charge of the equipment will be able to be notified in advance of a possible decay of the health of the motor, and in turn, take actions to prevent such an outcome. The vibration data coming from electric motor bearings was analyzed. Bearings are a key factor in deciding if the system is prone to faulty behavior. Since bearings are moving parts, they are more likely to break down due to heat dilatation, dust particles and wear over time. All these factors can influence the lifespan of the bearings. The Neural Network that was developed in this scope has the task of analyzing the vibration data as it's being produced and determining whether the motor is likely to break in the future. The model was trained with data until the predictions it makes are accurate enough for deployment on the production line. An algorithm for predicting and detecting anomalies can be very demanding from a computational point of view [11]. Making sure that the model is fast, small and reliable enough to run on a microcontroller is crucial.

After the training phase, the model is being compressed until it is small enough to fit on a chip. The goal was to deploy the model on an IoT Edge device that runs alongside the data-producing system.

3   Model Development

As discussed above, the first phase was designing a model that is fitting to the problem of vibration analysis. Vibration data and anomaly detection problems often imply that the data is unlabeled. Another point worth mentioning is that raw data, especially when it comes to vibration, needs to be filtered as, more often than not, it is altered by noise. Simple low-pass filtering is usually enough for most applications, but in order to make an accurate and reliable model, it is necessary to make sure that the network only deals with clean data. To achieve this, an Autoencoder architecture was used, as seen in Fig. 3, for the network, which by construction, also filters out the noise from the data [12,13].

The model was designed to consist of 5 layers, 3 of which are hidden. It also features a regularization layer that prevents the problem of overfitting. Placed after the first hidden layer it features a rate of 0.2 and a (None, 3) shape. The design of this network is relatively simple, the number of inputs being equivalent to the number of outputs. The model has an input size of (8, None) as there are 4 bearings measured on 2 channels each. In contrast, in the hidden layers, the number of neurons decreases considerably to extract only the essential information from the training data, which allows the noise to be eliminated from the information that is being processed. The first hidden layer has an input size of (5, None), whereas the second (middle) has only 3 neurons with an input size of (3, None). This process is called encoding and decoding. The information that is fed into the network is compressed (encoded) inside the hidden layers and then decoded (decompressed) in the output layer. The fidelity with which the output data is reproduced shows the efficiency of the model. In order to determine the number of neurons and layers that would provide reasonable accuracy, we had an experimental approach aimed at training and testing several network architectures and keeping the one that provided the best results. From the repeated reconstruction of the architecture, we concluded that the activation function suited for this project is the rectified linear activation function also known as ReLu. This provided the best results in terms of accuracy, as opposed to a linear one.

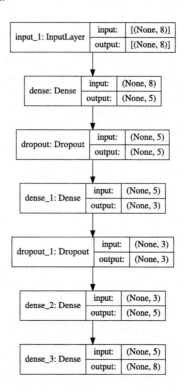

Fig. 3. Model architecture (generated with Graphwiz and pydot)

3.1   Data Preliminary Processing

In order to train the network, a suitable data set is required. The set has to correspond to contain data coming from real devices that are exposed to vibration stress and are prone to malfunction because of it. The "NASA Bearing Data set" was chosen because it contains data recorded from industrial motor bearings that were run until failure. According to [14] four bearings that were installed on a shaft were subjected to a radial load of 6000 lbs (approx. 2721.554 kg) applied to the shaft and bearing while kept on a constant rotation speed of 2000RPM. Each data set consists of individual files that are 1-s vibration signal snapshots recorded at specific intervals. Each file consists of 20,480 points with the sampling rate set at 20 kHz. The development of a reliable model requires, in the beginning, a consistent amount of data. The samples that are being used for the training data set should contain both a normal operating behaviour as well as a visible anomaly. As seen in Fig. 4, this particular data set satisfies the above-mentioned requirements.

The next step was making the feature extraction and the outlier identification. Although sometimes raw data is enough for the training of a model, usually a necessary part of the process is to determine specific features that the Neural Network is going to analyze. This has great implications for the algorithm speed,

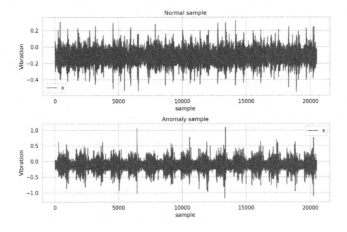

Fig. 4. Comparison between a normal vibration sample and an anomaly one

due to the fact that analyzing raw data is always going to be more computationally expensive than analyzing a filtered version of it. To achieve this, the DC component of the signal was removed by subtracting the mean amplitude. This gives the possibility to visualize the vibration component of the signal and visually identify the outliers as seen in Fig. 5.

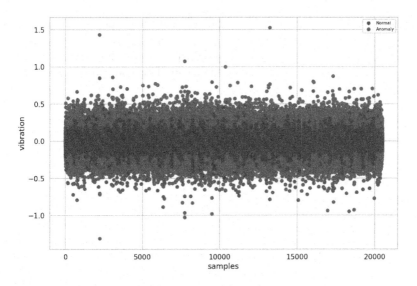

Fig. 5. Healthy and Abnormal vibration data points with DC component removed

It is easy to notice how considerably the anomaly sample in red differs from the normal one colored in blue. The red one is much more spread, whereas the blue one is more compact. Further analysis of the data reveals an even more evident distinction between the two. Further, the Variance, Skew, Kurtosis, and Median Absolute Deviation (MAD) were analyzed. Considering the variance in Fig. 6, average squared differences were measured from the Mean or how far each value from the data set was from the mean. In this way, the data is linearly separable.

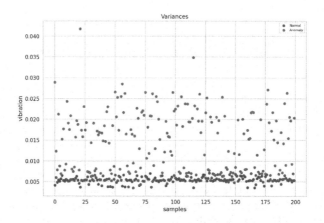

Fig. 6. Comparison between variance of a normal and anomalous vibration samples

High Kurtosis in a data set is an indicator of the existence of outliers and it is used to describe the extreme values relative to a Gaussian distribution. Figure 7 illustrates the above. The mean absolute deviation of a data set is the average distance between each data point and the mean. This confirms the variability in the data set.

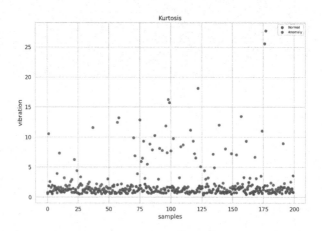

Fig. 7. Comparison between kurtosis of a normal and anomalous vibration samples

While standard deviation (and variance) are exceptional at describing the spread of data in a normal distribution, they can easily be affected by outliers and non-normally distributed data. As a result, MAD offers a more robust way [15] to measure spread for non-normal data as seen in Fig. 8.

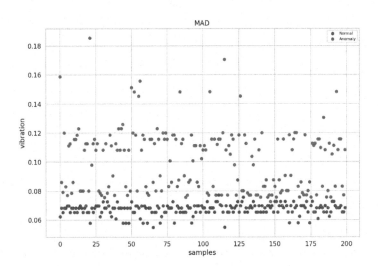

Fig. 8. Comparison between MAD component of a normal and anomalous vibration sample

As can be observed there is a more linear separability between the data that presents an anomaly in the MAD graphic plot. In this way, the algorithm will identify faster and easier the discrepancies between the two types of data.

3.2   Model Training

For training the model, data were split into training (~55%), cross-validation (~10%), and testing sets (~35%). The training set is characterized by the fact that it contains non-anomalous data exclusively. This is because the Autoencoder should train to recognize a normal operation of a motor very well so that everything that does not resemble a normal behavior will be classified as an abnormality.

In our case, the data prior to the bearing failure in the motor is used as a training set. For the validation set, both normal and anomalous data were used. At this step, the network is expected to be able to recognize with good accuracy both normal and anomalous data. The test set consists of random data, similar to what the network would receive from the motors in real-time. Training is done for 50 epochs with a batch size of 55, the optimizer used for this matter being 'Adam' and the loss function being the mean squared error or "MSE". Weights are generated randomly at the beginning of the training process.

Plotting the loss function graph during training for both test and validation sets reveals that the model performed overall with good results, reaching
convergence as seen in Fig. 9.

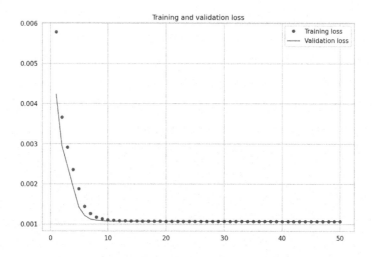

Fig. 9. Comparison between training and validation set learning curve

Plotting the histograms of normal versus anomaly training sets, in Fig. 10,
reveals that there is a clear separation between the Mean Squared Error (MSE)
of the loss function.

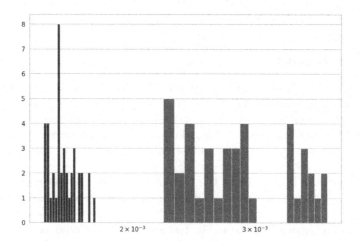

Fig. 10. Comparison between training and validation set Mean Squared Errors

4 Testing the Solution

At this step, constructing a classifier is fairly easy. The last mean squared error value from the validation set was chosen as a threshold. Everything above this will be considered an anomaly. With the help of a confusion matrix, the performance indices of the model can be visualized as can be noticed in Fig. 11. The solution was saved with a .tflite extension (as TensorFlow Lite was used) in order to be flashed on a microcontroller and more concrete on the ESP32 microcontroller (Table 1).

Table 1. Comparison between testing with and without inference.

Phase/Method	No. of samples	No. of samples in each file	Computing time (μs)	Contains anomalies	Error (%)
Testing (only MAD)	200	20 000	2102	No	6.57
Testing (only MAD)	200	20 000	2153	Yes	6.57
Testing (MSE + Inference)	200	20 000	150	No	6.57
Testing (MSE + Inference)	200	20 000	45	Yes	6.57

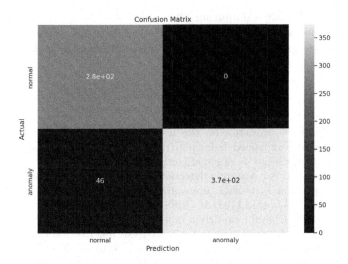

Fig. 11. Confusion matrix (on validation set)

In the testing phase, it was observed that the model flashed on the ESP32 microcontroller is performing remarkably well (~93.42%) in detecting anomalous versus normal data, on data points not seen before by the system. For a normal test sample, that was provided for calibration purposes, the algorithm took 6795 μs to compute the MAD. The inference result for predicting unseen before data was completed in 161 μs. The time for running inference and computing the MAD for an anomaly sample was 106 μs. By comparing the results of what was run in the test environment, in the model design phase, and what was obtained after running the algorithm on target, it was discovered that the error between the predicted values is less than 0.1. This indicates that the algorithm is secure and reliable for deploying and classifying the data in a good manner.

5   Conclusion

Extrapolating on the basis of the article presented, the project has reached a safe phase of operation on the side of anomaly detection and no major problems were found in any of the tests performed. The algorithm performed remarkably well ($\sim$93.42%) in the testing phase. The algorithm is fully developed as described above in the project and is planned to be put into operation on the production line as soon as possible. The Autoencoder can then take the previously computed MAD values as input and try to recreate it as fairly in the output. The classifier then takes the output MAD values of the autoencoder and compares them to a threshold which gives us a signal if we are indeed dealing with an anomalous sample or not. Given that the article addresses a cutting-edge topic in Machine Learning, it may be subject to major transformation and further development in the future from both the platform used (Tensorflow Lite) but also in the overall structure.

The novelty of Edge Computing gives this project a great versatility, the idea being applied in several fields, and the fact that this niche is constantly developing allows updating and optimizing the solution with the latest methods and technologies in the field.

References

1. Cloud computing - statistics on the use by enterprises. https://ec.europa.eu/eurostat/statistics-explained/index.php?title=Cloud_computing_-_statistics_on_the_use_by_enterprises#Use_of_cloud_computing:_highlights
2. Fahim, M., Sillitti, A.: Anomaly detection, analysis and prediction techniques in IoT environment: a systematic literature review. IEEE Access **7**, 81664–81681 (2019). https://doi.org/10.1109/ACCESS.2019.2921912
3. Huang, H., et al.: Digital twin-driven online anomaly detection for an automation system based on edge intelligence. J. Manuf. Syst. **59**, 138–150 (2021)
4. Finke, T., Krämer, M., Morandini, A., et al.: Autoencoders for unsupervised anomaly detection in high energy physics. J. High Energ. Phys. **2021**, 161 (2021). https://doi.org/10.1007/JHEP06(2021)161
5. Gohel, H.A., et al.: Predictive maintenance architecture development for nuclear infrastructure using machine learning. Nucl. Eng. Technol. **52**(7), 1436–1442 (2020)
6. Antonini, M., Vecchio, M., Antonelli, F., Ducange, P., Perera, C.: Smart audio sensors in the internet of things edge for anomaly detection. IEEE Access **6**, 67594–67610 (2018). https://doi.org/10.1109/ACCESS.2018.2877523
7. Fu, S., Zhong, S., Lin, L., Zhao, M.: A re-optimized deep auto-encoder for gas turbine unsupervised anomaly detection. Eng. Appl. Artif. Intell. **101**, 104199 (2021). https://doi.org/10.1016/j.engappai.2021.104199. https://www.sciencedirect.com/science/article/pii/S0952197621000464. ISSN 0952-1976

8. Lee, K., Kim, J.-K., Kim, J., Hur, K., Kim, H.: CNN and GRU combination scheme for bearing anomaly detection in rotating machinery health monitoring. In: 2018 1st IEEE International Conference on Knowledge Innovation and Invention (ICKII), pp. 102–105 (2018). https://doi.org/10.1109/ICKII.2018.8569155

9. Mobley, R.K.: An Introduction to Predictive Maintenance (2002)

10. Mehmeti, Xh., Mehmeti, B., Sejdiu, Rr.: The equipment maintenance management in manufacturing enterprises. IFAC-PapersOnLine **51**(30), 800–802 (2018). https://doi.org/10.1016/j.ifacol.2018.11.192. ISSN 2405-8963

11. Burton, B., Harley, R.G.: Reducing the computational demands of continually online-trained artificial neural networks for system identification and control of fast processes. IEEE Trans. Ind. Appl. **34**(3), 589–596 (1998). https://doi.org/10.1109/28.673730

12. Saad, O.M., Chen, Y.: Deep denoising autoencoder for seismic random noise attenuation. Geophysics **85**(4), V367–V376 (2020). https://doi.org/10.1190/geo2019-0468.1

13. Leite, N.M.N., Pereira, E.T., Gurjão, E.C., Veloso, L.R.: Deep convolutional autoencoder for EEG noise filtering. In: IEEE International Conference on Bioinformatics and Biomedicine (BIBM) 2018, pp. 2605–2612 (2018). https://doi.org/10.1109/BIBM.2018.8621080

14. Lee, J., Qiu, H., Yu, G., Lin, J.: Rexnord Technical Services: IMS, University of Cincinnati. "Bearing Data Set", NASA Ames Prognostics Data Repository. NASA Ames Research Center, Moffett Field, CA (2007). http://ti.arc.nasa.gov/project/prognostic-data-repository

15. Leys, C., Klein, O., Bernard, P., Licata, L.: Detecting outliers: do not use standard deviation around the mean, use absolute deviation around the median. J. Exp. Soc. Psychol. **49**(4), 764–766 (2013). https://doi.org/10.1016/j.jesp.2013.03.013. https://www.sciencedirect.com/science/article/pii/S0022103113000668. ISSN 0022-1031

Enhanced Dependency-Based Feature Selection to Improve Anomaly Network Intrusion Detection

K. Bennaceur[1], Z. Sahraoui[1(✉)], and M. A. Nacer[2]

[1] Computer Science Department, Ecole Militaire Polytechnique, Algiers, Algeria
`zakaria.sahraoui@emp.mdn.dz`
[2] Computer Science Department, Université des Sciences et de la Technologies Houari Boumedienne, Algiers, Algeria
`anacer@mail.cerist.dz`

Abstract. In daily live, online computer systems are becoming more pervasive and integrated. However, the access to the Internet can produce significant issues like cyber-attacks. The network intrusion detection system (NIDS) is a promising security solution that is used to detect attacks. It recently used Deep Learning in the detection process to obtain high performance. The performance of an NIDS depends on the used training dataset and the quality of features, where irrelevant features may decrease the detection performance, oppositely to relevant ones that are able to improve it. Feature selection is a good solution to select only relevant features to participate in the detection process. Chi-square is a supervised feature selection method that select only the most dependent features of the class feature. In this work, an Enhanced Chi-square (EChi2) method is proposed to select and weight features considering its degree of relevance. Experiments results, using the well-known NSLKDD dataset, shows that the proposed method outperforms the Chi-square.

Keywords: Feature selection · Chi-square · Enhanced Chi-square · Anomaly network intrusion detection

1 Introduction

A network intrusion detection system (NIDS) is a security solution that becomes the most common components of every network security infrastructure [1]. It is able to detect all possible attacks. There are two main types of NIDS: 1) Misuse-based NIDS (MNIDS) that detect known attacks using the corresponding signatures, it research the existence of these latter in the traffic payload. 2) Anomaly-based NIDS (ANIDS) that is able to detect unknown or zero-day attacks. It is based on a behavioral approach by classifying traffic sessions into normal or attacks. This supervised classification is applied to a transformed traffic that is composed from a set of featured sessions named training dataset.

© IFIP International Federation for Information Processing 2022
Published by Springer Nature Switzerland AG 2022
I. Maglogiannis et al. (Eds.): AIAI 2022, IFIP AICT 646, pp. 108–115, 2022.
https://doi.org/10.1007/978-3-031-08333-4_9

The anomaly network intrusion detection is a real-time process which needs to be accelerated by reducing the number of the dataset features. On the other hand, classification performance depends strongly on the feature quality [2]. Whereas, a training dataset inevitably contains both relevant and noisy features. Rising these two challenges, feature selection becomes an essential dataset preprocess to improve classification performance, which is used for selecting the most relevant subset of features from the original high-dimensional dataset. It is widely researched in many different domains, such as choosing the causative genes in medical study [3], image segmentation in computer vision [4] and so on.

Authors of [10], have grouped feature selection methods in three groups, namely, wrapper, filter and hybrid. Wrapper methods are based on both a classifier and a classification evaluator (generally, the accuracy) to evaluate the importance of features. Using the classifier they learn different subsets datasets feature, then the classification evaluator indicates witch subset is the best. Whereas, filter methods do not use any classifier to evaluate features which are selected considering some dataset characteristic. The hybrid methods combine both of the wrapper and the filter methods to achieve better classification performance. The advantage of filter methods is that they are scalable and independent from any classifier, they are based on the description of the dataset distribution which is more suitable to study the behavior of the traffic network.

Chi-square is a supervised filter feature selection method that is able to calculate the dependency of each feature on the class feature, then remove any one that have a dependency value less than a threshold. The other ones, that are selected, are deemed to be equivalent in terms of relevance without considering the dependency value. For example, the most dependent feature to the class that is considered as the most relevant feature participate in the classification similarly like the less one feature. In this work, an enhanced Chi-square (EChi2) feature selection method is proposed to weight selected features, where weights express the relevant degree of features. It should improve classification performance as feature space will be compressed in the dimension of features with low relevance and expanded along the dimension of features with high relevance. The proposed method is implemented using useful datasets in anomaly network intrusion detection, namely NSLKDD. Then, a Deep Learning-based binary classification using a full-connected network is applied in order to classify the training dataset and detect attacks. The proposed method's efficiency assessment is based on the classification performance. Experimental results show that the proposed EChi2 outperforms the simple Chi-square.

The remainder of this paper is organized as follows: Sect. 2 reviews the related work. The proposed method is described in Sect. 3. Section 4 presents the experimental results and discussion. Finally, Sect. 5 presents the conclusion.

2   Related Work

This section reviews all recent works that have been interested by weighted feature selection.

In [5], a combination of a Genetic Algorithm (GA) with K-Nearest Neighbor (KNN) classifier has been proposed for weighting features of each class separately from the others. But, it has been found that this separation is unable to match different class accuracies. This indicates that the weighting depends on the entire training dataset. To correct, weights have been averaged, and consequently classification accuracy has been reduced.

In [6], three different weighted feature selection methods are proposed basing on three different classifiers namely, Artificial Neural Network (ANN), Support Vector Machine (SVM), and Decision Tree (DT). The first one learns dataset using one-hidden layer ANN architecture. Since each node in the input layer represents one feature, each feature have been weighted by the sum of all weights of the corresponding node leading to the hidden layer. Selected feature are that having weight greater than a threshold. The second method is based on the Support Vector Machine Recursive Feature Elimination (SVM-RFE) [7]. In each iteration, after training the SVM classifier, features have been weighted and ranked using the guiding coefficient of the hyper-plan, The feature with the smallest weight has been eliminated. The third method has been considered as the strongest one, it has been based on the C4.5 model. A top-down tree has been constructed basing on recursive divide-and-conquer approach [8], where nodes represent features. This method has been began by selecting the top-three level nodes, then different test nodes have been generated in order to update selected feature list.

Authors of [9] have developed a new method to select and weight features, namely AGRM. The method is based on eliminating correlation, i.e. if two features are correlated, it would be better to keep only one and remove the other. Correlation between features, that should be minimized, has been modeled using a mathematical problem, the solution of the latter indicates the weight of each feature.

The weight here represents the level of influence from input feature to the first hidden layer [32]. If the value is small (nearly zero), it means that the feature is not a deciding fac- tor to pick whether a file is a malware or benign file. We will measure the average weight of all features and set a threshold value. We pick all features that have weight value higher than the threshold.

3   Enhanced Chi-square Feature Selection Method

The proposed method selects the most relevant features, then it weight them considering their degree of relevance. The more the feature is relevant the more the feature weight is greater. This way should improve classification performance because it gives more significance to the feature that supports more information. Feature weights are measured statically from the dataset distribution using the Chi-square coefficient. All weights are scaled in the range [0, 1], where the most relevant feature is weighted by 1 and all the other features 'f_i' are weighted by a scaled 'w_i'. There are several steps in this method.

Firstly, the degree of relevance of each feature 'f_i' is evaluated by calculating the dependency 'd_i' of this feature relative to the dataset class, using the Chi-square coefficient given in formula (1).

$$d^2 = \frac{N * (WZ - YX)^2}{(W + X)(W + Z)(Y + X)(Y + Z)}. \tag{1}$$

where,

W is the number of times of the co-occurrence of the feature 'f_i' and the class 'c',
X is the number of times of the appearance of 'f_i' without 'c',
Y is the number of times of the appearance of 'c' without 'f_i',
Z is the number of times of the nonappearance neither 'c' nor 'f_i',
N is the total number of dataset sessions.

This formula shows that the relevance degree measurement is based on the dataset distribution. It increases when the variation of the feature 'f_i' depends on the class 'c'.

Then, all features are ranked based on these coefficient values, where the greatest value is associated with the most relevant feature or the most dependent on the class. Whereas, the less dependent ones that have not any influence on the class are considered as noises, because relevant features cannot be independent of the class [11]. In order to remove these features, an optimal threshold value is empirically set. If the coefficient value is lower than the threshold, the corresponding feature is removed. Features that are not removed are selected to participate in classification.

In the last, each selected features 'f_i' is weighted by a scaled 'w_i' given in formula (2). Weighting is performed by multiplying any selected feature values by the corresponding weight.

$$w_i = \frac{d_i}{d_{max}}. \tag{2}$$

where, d_{max} is the maximum of all the d_i.

4 Results and Discussion

In this section, the experimental dataset for the assessment of the proposed method is described, as well as its preparation. Afterward, it discusses the different performed experiments and the results.

4.1 Experimental Dataset

Reliable and publicly available datasets is one of the fundamentals concerns of researchers and producers in intrusion detection [12]. In this work, tests are performed basing on the NSLKDD dataset [13]. It is the most used in ANID to train and check a lot of Deep Learning-based classifiers [14,15]. It is a new version of the old KDDcup99 dataset, it overcomes its statistical weakness that is duplicating samples in both training and testing datasets. Duplication has been removed from NSLKDD to get high actual accuracy. NSLKDD dataset size becomes reasonable, making it affordable to perform tests on the full dataset without selecting a small subset. One other advantage of NSLKDD is the separation of the testing dataset from the training one. Therefore, prediction steps are performed using the original dataset without any random dividing.

4.2   Dataset Features Preparation

In the NSLKDD dataset, there are two types of features: numeric and nominal. The first type is ready for computation, but nominal features are not. To fix this problem, any nominal features are converted to numeric features by applying the method 1-to-N features proposed in [16]. This method converts each nominal feature, which varies among N values, into N binary features representing only one value. This conversion is performed using WEKA software. In fact, NSLKDD is initially featured by 42 features, but after the 1-to-N transformation, the number of features becomes 122. This is another reason to perform the feature selection.

4.3   Experimental Results and Discussion

The proposed supervised weighted feature selection method is evaluated on a set of experiments. First, it is implemented using the NSLKDD dataset. Several sub-datasets result from varying the number of selected features (NSF). Then, they are classified using a Deep Learning-based full-connected network. Finally, the proposed method is compared with the Chi-square and Pearson feature selection methods considering several classification performance metrics.

Tables 1, 2, 3 and 4 present the comparison between the proposed method and the Chi-square method in terms of classification accuracy, precision, recall, F-score, respectively.

Table 1. Comparison between the proposed EChi2 and other methods in terms of accuracy

NSF	5	10	15	20	30	40	50	60
Pearson	91.2%	91.5%	92.0%	92.8%	**92.9%**	92.3%	91.2%	89.7%
Chi-square	92.9%	94.1%	94.8%	94.9%	**95.0%**	95.0%	94.8%	93.2%
EChi2	93.1%	93.9%	94.2%	95.0%	96.6%	**97.7%**	96.5%	95.7%

The classification performances without any feature selection are: 79.9% of accuracy, 88.2% of precision, 92.1% of recall, and 90.3% of F-score. So, it is noticed that all feature selection methods can boost the classification that is performed by introducing all features, including noisy ones.

Table 2. Comparison between the proposed EChi2 and other methods in terms of precision

NSF	5	10	15	20	30	40	50	60
Pearson	89.5%	91.0%	91.9%	92.2%	**92.9%**	92.6%	92.5%	91.8%
Chi-square	90.5%	92.6%	91.4%	92.5%	**93.8%**	92.3%	92.1%	91.5%
EChi2	91.2%	90.9%	90.7%	91.7%	92.9%	**93.7%**	92.6%	93.3%

Table 3. Comparison between the proposed EChi2 and other methods in terms of recall

NSF	5	10	15	20	30	40	50	60
Pearson	96.6%	97.3%	97.6%	98.2%	98.5%	**98.6%**	98.1%	97.5%
Chi-square	96.9%	96.7%	99.8%	98.7%	98.9%	**99.0%**	98.8%	98.1%
EChi2	96.5%	98.4%	99.4%	97.7%	99.2%	99.2%	**99.5%**	99.2%

Table 4. Comparison between the proposed EChi2 and other methods in terms of F-score

NSF	5	10	15	20	30	40	50	60
Pearson	93.1%	93.8%	94.6%	95.3%	**95.8%**	95.1%	94.6%	94.3%
Chi-square	93.6%	94.6%	95.4%	95.5%	**96.3%**	95.5%	95.2%	95.2%
EChi2	93.7%	94.5%	94.8%	94.6%	95.9%	**96.4%**	95.9%	95.2%

Concerning all classification metrics using Chi-square, Pearson and the proposed method, generally, there is firstly a slight improvement when only a few noisy features are removed (NSF > 40). Then, when NSF gets the optimal value, a maximal enhancement is reached. When more features are removed (NSF < 30), the classification performance starts to decrease because the dataset begins to lose relevant features that help distinguish classes.

Figure 1 presents the comparison between the best results of both Chi-square and EChi2 in terms of the four classification metrics. Regarding the accuracy, the proposed method outperforms the simple Chi-square. This is the strong advantage of this proposed method because the accuracy metric measures the degree of closeness to the perfect classification that does not make any mistakes. Weighting selected features helps the classifier to distinguish more efficiently the classes. Concerning the recall, it is slightly improved to be near to the perfect value, and the precision is not missed.

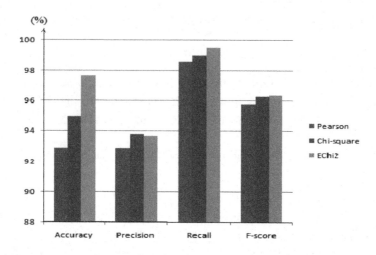

Fig. 1. Comparison between the best results of both Chi-square and the proposed EChi2.

5   Conclusion

This work proposes an enhancement of the Chi-square feature selection method to improve Deep Learning-based anomaly network intrusion detection. The proposed approach weights each selected feature considering the relevant degree. The critical point of our proposal is that it is based on the dataset distribution to improve behavioral-based intrusion detection. Experiments using the useful NSLKDD dataset show that the proposed method outperforms the simple Chi-square and Pearson in terms of accuracy which is the most important classification metric. The other metrics are also considered and the classification performances are not missed. This promising method opens avenues to design a new ANID system based on new and real datasets for potential servers.

References

1. Kolias, C., Kambourakis, G., Maragoudakis, M.: Swarm intelligence in intrusion detection: a survey. J. Comput. Secur. **30**(30), 625–642 (2011)
2. Palmieri, F., Fiore, U., Castiglione, A.: A distributed approach to network anomaly detection based on independent component analysis. Concurr. Comput. Pract. Exp. **26**(5), 1113–1129 (2014)
3. Banerjee, M., Mitra, S., Banka, H.: Evolutionary rough feature selection in gene expression data. IEEE Trans. Syst. Man Cybern. **37**(4), 622–632 (2007)
4. Cheng, M.M., et al.: HFS: hierarchical feature selection for efficient image segmentation. In: Leibe, B., Matas, J., Sebe, N., Welling, M. (eds.) ECCV 2016. LNCS, vol. 9907, pp. 867–882. Springer, Cham (2016). https://doi.org/10.1007/978-3-319-46487-9_53

5. Middlemiss, M.J., Dick, G.: Weighted feature extraction using a genetic algorithm for intrusion detection. In: Congress on Evolutionary Computation, vol. 3, pp. 1669–1675 (2003)
6. Aminanto, M.E., Choi, R., Tanuwidjaja, H.C., Yoo, P.D., Kim, K.: Deep abstraction and weighted feature selection for Wi-Fi impersonation detection. In: IEEE Trans. Inf. Forens. Secur. **13**(3), 621–636 (2017)
7. Guyon, I., Weston, J., Barnhill, S., Vapnik, V.: Gene selection for cancer classification using support vector machines. Mach. Learn. **46**(1), 389–422 (2002)
8. Ratanamahatana, C.A., Gunopulos, D.: Scaling up the Naive Bayesian classifier: using decision trees for feature selection (2002)
9. Nie, F., Yang, S., Zhang, R., Li, X.: A general framework for auto-weighted feature selection via global redundancy minimization. IEEE Trans. Image Process. **28**(5), 2428–2438 (2018)
10. Balasaraswathi, V.R., Sugumaran, M., Hamid, Y.: Feature selection techniques for intrusion detection using non-bio-inspired and bio-inspired optimization algorithms. J. Commun. Inf. Netw. **2**(4), 107–119 (2017)
11. Chandrashekar, G., Sahin, F.: A survey on feature selection methods. Comput. Elect. Eng. **40**(1), 16–28 (2014)
12. Sharafaldin, I., Lashkari, A.H., Ghorbani, A.A.: Toward generating a new intrusion detection dataset and intrusion traffic characterization. In: 4th International Conference on Information Systems Security and Privacy (2018)
13. Tavallaee, M., Bagheri, E., Lu, W., Ghorbani, A.A.: A detailed analysis of the KDD CUP 99 data set. In: IEEE Symposium on Computational Intelligence For Security and Defense Applications, pp. 1–6 (2009)
14. Ferrag, M.A., Maglaras, L., Moschoyiannis, S., Janicke, H.: Deep learning for cyber security intrusion detection: approaches, datasets, and comparative study. J. Inf. Secur. App. **50**, 102419 (2020)
15. Hindy, H., et al.: A taxonomy and survey of intrusion detection system design techniques, network threats and datasets. arXiv preprint (2018)
16. Breiman, L., Friedman, J., Stone, C., Olshen, J., Richard, A.: Classification and Regression Trees. CRC Press, Boca Raton (1984)

HEDL-IDS: A Hybrid Ensemble Deep Learning Approach for Cyber Intrusion Detection

Anastasios Panagiotis Psathas$^{(\boxtimes)}$ (iD), Lazaros Iliadis (iD), Antonios Papaleonidas (iD), and Dimitris Bountas (iD)

Department of Civil Engineering-Lab of Mathematics and Informatics (ISCE), Democritus University of Thrace, 67100 Xanthi, Greece
{anpsatha,liliadis,papaleon,dibounta}@civil.duth.gr

Abstract. The continuously increasing number of activities processed via the internet, often leaves the user vulnerable to cyber-attacks. The goal of the scientific community is to deploy innovative approaches and methodologies, capable to offer protection from potential cyber threats. This research effort aims to contribute to networks' security by introducing the *Hybrid Ensemble Deep Learning* (HEDL) Intrusion Detection System (IDS) that successfully detects nine serious cyber-attacks. Its architecture comprises of three *Deep Neural Networks (DNN)*, three *Convolutional Neural Networks* (CNN) and 3 *Recurrent Neural Networks* (RNN) using *Long-Short Term Memory* (LSTM) layers, running in parallel. The HEDL-IDS was successfully tested against the *UNSW-NB15* dataset, achieving an overall accuracy of 98.35% and 96.25% in the training and testing phases respectively. The performance of the proposed model was evaluated by calculating *Accuracy, Sensitivity, Specificity, Precision and F-1 Score*. The values of all above indices were higher than 0.92, indicating the accurate performance of the developed model. The HEDL-IDS was compared with 20 robust Machine Learning Classification algorithms, sealing its reliability.

Keywords: Hybrid · Ensemble · CNN · DNN · RNN · LSTM · Cyber attacks · Cyber intrusion detection

1 Introduction

Technology keeps evolving rapidly. Nowadays, the vast number of applications used by individuals or groups, for either personal or commercial use, increases. The wide introduction of the *Internet-of-Thing* (IoT) was determinant for the growth of these applications in everyday life [1]. However, the increasing use of computer networks and interconnected systems, paved the way for exploiting their weaknesses. Cyber-attacks cause severe damage and severe financial losses in large-scale networks [2]. Despite the tremendous development in network security, the existing solutions are unable to completely defend computer networks against the malicious threats [3]. The traditional security techniques such as hardware and software firewalls, user authentication and data encryption are not capable enough to fully safeguard networks' security, due to the

© IFIP International Federation for Information Processing 2022
Published by Springer Nature Switzerland AG 2022
I. Maglogiannis et al. (Eds.): AIAI 2022, IFIP AICT 646, pp. 116–131, 2022.
https://doi.org/10.1007/978-3-031-08333-4_10

fast development of intrusion techniques [4]. Thus, the deployment of other approaches and methodologies is imperative.

Intrusion Detection Systems (IDS), a rapidly growing field of study, were suggested in order to facilitate system's security. Using patterns of benign traffic or normal behavior or specific rules that describe a specific attack, IDSs can distinguish between normal and malicious actions [5]. There are two main types of cyber analytics in support of IDSs: misuse-based (sometimes also called signature-based) and anomaly-based [6]. *Signature-based* techniques detect anomalies by matching predefined attack's signatures [7]. Two of the main advantages of these methods are that they are simple to implement and they have low false positive rates. However, it is not feasible for them to detect new cyber threats. *Anomaly-based* (AB) detection techniques rely on the assumption that the intruder's behavior is different from the typical one [8]. They model the network's normal patterns, and they identify anomalies as deviations from them. *Anomaly-based Intrusion Detection Systems* (ABIDSs) can detect zero-day attacks, however they may often result in high *False Alarm Rates* (FARs) due to the fact that several previously unseen (yet legitimate) system behaviors may be classified as anomalies.

This paper introduces a novel *Hybrid Ensemble Deep Learning Approach* for Cyber Intrusion Detection (HEDL-IDS). The architecture of this Hybrid Model comprises of *3 Deep Neural Networks* (DNN), *3 Convolutional Neural Network* (CNN) and *3 Recurrent Neural Network* (RNN) with Long-Short Term Memory (LSTM) layers. The majority vote of these 9 models has been applied for each observation, improving the accuracy and robustness of the results. Additionally, the aforementioned approach searches for the best deep learning structure, as all nine models have different architectures and they are using different parameters. To the best of our knowledge, it is the first time that such a Hybrid Ensemble Deep Learning architecture is employed in the literature, in order to perform Cyber Intrusion Detection (CID). This methodology was tested on a subset of the UNSW-NB15 intrusion detection dataset [9] which comprises of raw network packets, related to several well-known attacks e.g. Denial of Service (DoS), Worms, Fuzzers and Backdoors.

The subset of the UNSW-NB15 that was used in this research, comprises of 2 classes namely: the malicious flow and the benign one.

The rest of the paper is organized as follows: Sect. 2 performs a literature review of IDS based on Machine Learning (ML) and Deep Learning (DL), Sect. 3 describes the dataset and its features. Section 4 provides the architecture of the proposed model. Section 5 presents the experimental results and the evaluation of the model. Finally, Sect. 6 concludes the research.

2 Literature Review

Several ML approaches have been introduced for CID, during the last twenty years. Recently, several DL models have been introduced in the literature, aiming to detect malware, to classify network intrusions and phishing (spam attacks) and to inspect website defacements.

In 2012, Li et al. [10], presented an approach, capable to classify the predefined attack categories such as DoS (Denial of Service), Probe or Scan, U2R (User to Root), R2L (Root to Local), as well as normal traffic. This was achieved by utilizing the most popular KDD'99 cup dataset, by using the hyperplane-based SVM classifier with an RBF kernel. The obtained accuracy was as high as 98.6249%. In 2012, Koc et al. [11], developed a *Hidden Naïve Bayes* (HNB) model, achieving an accuracy equal to 93.72% and an error rate of 0.0628, improving significantly the accuracy of detecting denial-of-services (DoS) attacks. In 2017, Shapoorifard and Shamsinejad, [12] used the NSL-KDD dataset to develop a model, combining the k-Means clustering and the k-Nearest Neighbors (k-NN) algorithms, achieving an accuracy equal to 98%. In 2018, Malik and Khan [13], introduced a hybrid model that combines the *Binary Particle Swarm Optimization* with the Decision Tree Pruning, for network intrusion detection. In 2020, Sarker et al., introduced the *"IntruDTree"* machine-learning security model, which is characterized by low computational complexity and high accuracy, due to the performed feature dimensionality reduction [14].

In 2016, Kim et al. [15], developed a *Long-Short Term Memory* (LSTM) multi class classifier on the KDD Cup 1999 dataset, by considering an input vector of 41 features. In 2018, Zhang et al. [16], employed a convolutional neural network, to model the B2C (Business to Consumer) online transaction dataset of a commercial bank. The model achieved a Precision as high as 91% and a Recall equal to 94%. Convolutional neural networks were also used by Basumallik et al. [17] for packet-data anomaly detection, in phasor measurement units-based state estimator (PHMUB). The IEEE-30 bus and IEEE-118 bus systems, were used as the PHMUB. This research uses a probability of 0.5 with 512 neurons on a fully connected layer. The accuracy reached the value of 98.67%. Thamilarasu and Chawla [18], introduced a *Deep Belief* network to fabricate a feed-forward DNN for an *Internet of Things* (IoT) case. The proposed model was tested against five attacks, namely: The Sinkole, the Wormhole, the Blackhole, the Opportunistic service and the DDoS. The results show a Precision of 96% and a Recall of 98.7% for the case of the DDoS attacks. Khan et al. [19], proposed an intrusion detection system based on the two-stage deep learning model, named TSDL. The KDD99 and the UNSW-NB15 network intrusion public datasets were considered for the TSDL training and testing, with an accuracy equal to 99.996% and 89.134% respectively. In 2020, Demertzis et al. suggested a *Blockchain Security Architecture* that aims to ensure network communication between traded Industrial IoT devices, following the Industry 4.0 standard, based on Deep Learning Smart Contracts. The proposed smart contracts are implementing (via computer programming) a bilateral traffic control agreement to detect anomalies based on a trained Deep Autoencoder Neural Network [20]. In 2021, Psathas et al. [21], presented a hybrid Intrusion Detecting System (IDS) comprising of a 2-Dimensional *Convolutional Neural Network* (2-D CNN), a RNN and a MLP for the detection of nine Cyber Attacks versus normal flow. The timely *Kitsune Network attack* dataset was used in this research. The proposed model achieved an overall accuracy of 92.66%, 90.64% and 90.56% in the train, validation and testing phases respectively.

3   Dataset Description and Pre-processing

This research, has considered the *UNSW-NB15* network intrusion public dataset [9] which contains raw network packets, related to nine different attacks. It was developed in 2015 at the University of New South Wales, of the Australian Defense Force Academy Canberra, Australia [22]. The *IXIA PerfectStorm* tool [23] was utilized to create a hybrid normal and abnormal network traffic. The IXIA tool contains all information about new attacks that are updated continuously from a CVE site [24]. CVE is a list of publicly disclosed cybersecurity vulnerabilities that is free to search, use, and incorporate into products and services, per the terms of use. The simulation period was 16 h of the 22nd of January 2015 and 15 h of the 17th of February 2015. The total volume of captured data is 100 GBs.

The original dataset contains a vast number of network packets, 2,540,044 in total. The malicious traffic is related to nine different *Cyber Attacks* (*Fuzzers, Analysis, Backdoors, DoS, Exploits, Generic, Reconnaissance, Shellcode and Worms*) and comprises of 321,283 packets. The remaining 2,218,761 records correspond to Normal flow. However, due to the fact that there is inhomogeneity in the instances (Cyber Attacks are only 12.5% of the original dataset) a subset of the *UNSW-NB15* dataset was used which was provided by the developers. The subset contains a total of 257,673 records, 164,673 of which corresponds to malicious traffic (nine cyber-attacks) and 93,000 to normal flow (see Table 1). This is a less unbalanced dataset, containing all the traffic of the eight *Cyber Attacks* a part of the *Generic Attack* and a part of the *Normal* flow. Nevertheless, there is still a major issue like *Worms* and *Shellcode* attacks, which correspond to minority classes. Therefore, it was obviously more feasible to perform a binary classification effort. Thus, the records corresponding to normal flow were assigned the value 0, whereas the ones related to the nine cyber-attacks were assigned the value 1 (see Table 1). The 42 features of the subset UNSW-NB15 are listed in the following Table 2.

The features *Proto, State* and *Service* are stored as strings (sequences of characters). Thus, they were transformed by the authors from nominal to numeric. The rest 39 features have numerical (either integer or float) values. The transformations are presented in the following Tables 3 and 4.

Due to the fact that the *Proto* feature has 133 different elements, the table with the correspondence to labels is omitted. For further information about the feature extraction process and the features, refer to [22].

Data handling has been achieved by writing code from scratch in Matlab. After labeling was completed, the dataset had the shape of a 257,673 x 43 *Table* (42 columns contain features' values and 1 contains the respective label). The data *Table* was divided in *Training (75%) 193,256 rows X 43 columns* and *Testing (25%) 64,417 rows X 43 columns.*

Table 1. Type, description and number of subset packets, the number of dataset packets and label of the nine (9) cyber attacks and normal flow considered in this research

Type	Description: the attacker…	# Subset's packets	# Dataset packets	Label
Normal	Natural transaction data	93,000	2,218,761	0
Fuzziers	Attempting to cause a program or network suspended by feeding it the randomly generated data	24,246	24,246	1
Analysis	It contains different attacks of port scan, spam and html files penetrations	2,677	2,677	1
Backdoors	A technique in which a system's security mechanism is bypassed stealthily to access a computer or its data	2,327	2,329	1
DoS	A malicious attempt to make a server or a network's resource unavailable to users, usually by temporarily interrupting or suspending the services of a host connected to the Internet	16,353	16,353	1
Exploits	The attacker knows of a security problem within an operating system or a piece of software and leverages that knowledge by exploiting the vulnerability	44,525	44,525	1
Generic	A technique works against all block ciphers (with a given block and key size), without consideration about the structure of the block-cipher	85,871	215,481	1
Reconnaissance	Contains all Strikes that can simulate attacks that gather information	13,987	13,987	1
Shellcode	A small piece of code used as the payload in the exploitation of software vulnerability	1,511	1,511	1
Worms	Attacker replicates itself in order to spread to other computers. Often, it uses a computer network to spread itself, relying on security failures on the target computer to access it	174	174	1
Total		257,673	2,540,044	

Table 2. Features' abbreviation and respective description in the UNSW-NB15 subset

Feature	Description
proto	Transaction protocol
state	Indicates the state and its dependent protocol
dur	Record of total duration
sbytes	Source to destination transaction bytes
dbytes	Destination to source transaction bytes
sttl	Source to destination time to live value
dttl	Destination to source time to live value
sloss	Source packets retransmitted or dropped
dloss	Destination packets retransmitted or dropped
service	http, ftp, smtp, ssh, dns, ftp-data,irc and (-) if not much used service
Sload	Source bits per second
Dload	Destination bits per second
Spkts	Source to destination packet count
Dpkts	Destination to source packet count
swin	Source TCP window advertisement value
dwin	Destination TCP window advertisement value
stcpb	Source TCP base sequence number
dtcpb	Destination TCP base sequence number
smeansz	Mean of the row packet size transmitted by the src
dmeansz	Mean of the row packet size transmitted by the dst
trans_depth	The pipelined depth into the connection of http request/response transaction
res_bdy_len	Actual uncompressed content size of data transferred from the server http service
Sjit	Source jitter (mSec)
Djit	Destination jitter (mSec)
Sintpkt	Source interpacket arrival time (mSec)
Dintpkt	Destination interpacket arrival time (mSec)
tcprtt	TCP connection setup round-trip time, the sum of 'synack' and 'ackdat'
synack	TCP connection setup time, the time between the SYN and SYN_ACK packets
ackdat	TCP connection setup time, the time between the SYN_ACK and ACK packets

(*continued*)

Table 2. (*continued*)

Feature	Description
is_sm_ips_ports	If the source and destination IP addresses are equal and port numbers are also equal then this variable takes value 1 else 0
ct_state_ttl	No. for each state according to the specific range of values for source/destination time to live
ct_flw_http_mthd	No. of flows that has methods such as Get and Post in http service
rate	No. of packets per Second

Table 3. Service with the corresponding label

Service	-	dhcp	dns	ftp	ftp-data	http	irc	pop3	radius	smtp	snmp	ssh	ssl
Service label	1	2	3	4	5	6	7	8	9	10	11	12	13

Table 4. State with the corresponding label

State	CON	ECO	FIN	INT	PAR	REQ	RST	URN	no	ACC	CLO
State label	1	2	3	4	5	6	7	8	9	10	11

4   The HEDL-IDS Model

It has already been mentioned that the hybrid ensemble modeling approach introduced in this paper, consists of the combination of three ANN with the following architectures: MLP (Fig. 1), CNN (Fig. 2) and RNN (Fig. 3). Thus, the detailed description of their mathematical foundations will be very brief. There is a vast literature review about their structure [25–27].

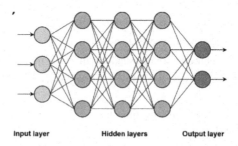

Input layer   Hidden layers   Output layer

Fig. 1. 5-layer DNN model architecture (1 input layer, 1 output layer and 3 hidden layers)

A CNN is defined as a neural network that extracts features at a higher resolution, and then it converts them into more complex features at a coarser resolution, as presented in Fig. 2. Therefore, CNN is based on three types of layers namely: *Convolutional*, *Pooling* and *Fully-Connected*. When these layers are stacked, a CNN architecture has been formed [28]. The feature value at location (x, y) in the kth feature map of Mth layer can be calculated as follows:

$$feature_{x,y,k}^{M} = W_k^{M^T} X_{x,y}^{M} + b_k^{M} \tag{1}$$

where $X_{x,y}^{M}$ is the input patch centered at location (x, y), W_k^{M} is the weight vector of the kth filter, and b_k^{M} is the bias term of the Mth layer. The activation value $activate_{x,y,k}^{M}$ and the pooling value $pool_{x,y,k}^{M}$ of convolution feature $feature_{x,y,k}^{M}$ can be calculated as follow:

$$activate_{x,y,k}^{M} = activation(feature_{x,y,k}^{M}) \tag{2}$$

$$pool_{x,y,k}^{M} = pooling(feature_{a,c,k}^{M}), \quad \forall (a, c) \in N_{x,y} \tag{3}$$

where $N_{x,y}$ is a local neighborhood at location (x, y). The nonlinear activation functions are ReLU, Sigmoid, and Tangent Hyperbolic (Tanh). The Pooling operations are Average and Max Pooling.

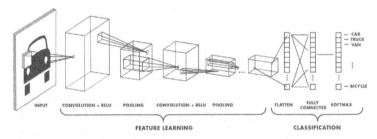

Fig. 2. CNN model architecture with 2 Convolution Layer, 2 Maxpooling Layer, one Flatten and 1 Fully Connected Layer.

The output of the RNNs in each phase, depends on the output computed in the previous state. The same task is recurrently performed for every element of the sequence. In other words, RNNs benefit from their memory that stores previously-calculated information [29]. It is difficult for RNN to remember information for a very long time period, because the backpropagated gradients either grow or they shrink at each time step and they are making the training weights either explode or vanish notably. However, the LSTM has addressed this issue.

A typical LSTM unit is composed of three gates namely: an *input, an output, and a forget gate*. These gates, regulate information into and out of the memory cell. The *Input gate* decides the input ratio and it has an effect on the value of the cell's state. The *forget gate* controls the amount of information that can remain in the memory cell. The *output gate* determines the amount of information in the memory cell that can be used to compute the output activation of the LSTM unit [30]. Figure 3 illustrates the architecture of an LSTM node. X_t is the input, h_t is the output of the LSTM node, h_{t-1} is the output of the previous LSTM node, C_t and C_{t-1} are the cell states at time t and $t-1$ respectively, σ is the sigmoid function (decide what to forget), *tanh* is the tanh function (gives weights), b is the Bias. The notation notation "x" is used where the scaling of information is applied, and the symbol "+" is used where adding information process is performed [31].

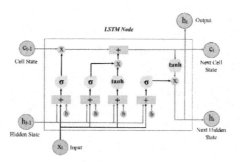

Fig. 3. Structure of an LSTM node

4.1 Architecture of the HEDL-IDS Model

The proposed hybrid approach uses three 2-D CNNs, three RNNs with LSTM layers and three DNNs. The CNN model accepts as input a record of the dimensions 1x42x1, (1 observation, 42 features, and 1 channel). Moreover, the DNN and the RNN models accept as input a record of dimensions 1×42 (1 observation, 42 features). The output of the classification for each model is 0 (corresponding to *benign traffic)* or 1 (corresponding to *malicious traffic)*. The number of filters applied in the CNNs were 2^n, where n = 1, 2… 8. A stride denotes the number of Convolution steps used each time. By default its value is equal to 1. The sizes of the kernel for the testing strides, were 2, 3, 4, and 5. For the LSTMs and the DNNs we have used 50, 100, 150, 200 and 250 nodes. The last layer for all 9 models is a *Dense Layer* with 2 nodes. Furthermore, the penultimate layer of the CNN models (after the *Flatten Layer*) is a Dense Layer with 20 nodes. To avoid overfitting, dropout layers were added after each Flatten, LSTM and Dense Layer. The values tested were 0.2, 0.5 and 0.8. The decision for the layers of the model, as well as for the optimal values of the parameters, was made through a trial and error process. The architecture of the nine models, alongside the used parameters is displayed in the following Table 5. The Dropout Layer's rate is 0.2. The input of each layer is the output of the previous one. Finally, Fig. 4, depicts the architecture of the hybrid approach.

Table 5. Layers and parameters set for the 9 models of HEDL-IDS

NN	Layer	Parameters set
1st CNN	2-D Covolution	(filters, kernel size, strides) = (32, 3, 1)
	2-D Maxpooling	Pool size = (1, 2)
	Flatten	-
2nd CNN	2-D Covolution	(filters, kernel size, strides) = (16, 3, 1)
	2-D Maxpooling	Pool size = (1, 2)
	2-D Covolution	(filters, kernel size, strides) = (64, 3, 1)
	2-D Maxpooling	Pool size = (1, 2)
	Flatten	-
3rd CNN	2-D Covolution	(filters, kernel size, strides) = (8, 3, 1)
	2-D Maxpooling	Pool size = (1, 2)
	2-D Covolution	(filters, kernel size, strides) = (32, 3, 1)
	2-D Maxpooling	Pool size = (1, 2)
	2-D Covolution	(filters, kernel size, strides) = (128, 3, 1)
	2-D Maxpooling	Pool size = (1, 2)
	Flatten	-
1st RNN	LSTM	Nodes = 100
2nd RNN	LSTM	Nodes = 150
	LSTM	Nodes = 50
3nd RNN	LSTM	Nodes = 250
	LSTM	Nodes = 150
	LSTM	Nodes = 50
1st DNN	Dense	Nodes = 100
2nd DNN	Dense	Nodes = 150
	Dense	Nodes = 50
3nd DNN	Dense	Nodes = 250
	Dense	Nodes = 150
	Dense	Nodes = 50

*After each Flatten Layer always a Dense Layer with 20 nodes
**Last Layer of all Models is a Dense Layer with 2 nodes
***Dropout Layer after each Flatten, LSTM and Dense Layer

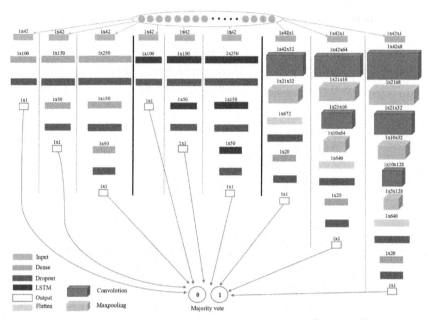

Fig. 4. Architecture of the HEDL-IDS. From left to right 1st DNN, 2nd DNN, 3rd DNN, 1st RNN, 2nd RNN, 3rd RNN, 1st CNN, 2nd CNN and 3rd CNN

All experiments have been performed in Python, using a computer with an Intel Core i9-9900 CPU (3.10 GHz) processor, DDR4 memory (32 GBytes) and GPU NVIDIA GeForce RTX 2070 Super (8GBytes). The Keras [32] and Tensorflow [33] libraries have been employed to build the model's architecture. Based on the literature, in all layers, the *Categorical Crossentropy*, the *Adam Optimizer* and the *ReLU* functions were employed as the *Loss Function*, the *Optimizer* and the *Activation Function* respectively. The *Softmax Activation Function* has been used in the last dense layer of each model.

After training all models, the final prediction was calculated using majority vote. The output space uses majority vote to determine the final y_i. Therefore, y_i is given as follows:

$$y_i = [y_{i1} \dots y_{ij} \dots y_{in}]^T \qquad (4)$$

where n is the model's number, y_{ij} is the prediction of the model's output for the data point i in model j and y_{ij} is defined as follows:

$$y_{i,j} = \arg \max_k [soft \max(y_{i,j}^*)] \qquad (5)$$

where $k \in \{0, 1\}$ for all binary classification.

As it is easily understood from Table 5 and Fig. 4, the complexity of the models increases as their number increases. For example, the 1st RNN has one LSTM layer, the 2nd RNN has two LSTM layers and so on. Thus, if the algorithm consists of four RNNs, the 4th would have 4 LSTM layers. Therefore, for the RNNs, every time a new model is developed, an LSTM layer is added. Respectively, a dense layer is added for the case of the DNNs, and a Convolution and a Maxpool Layers are added for the CNNs. Furthermore, the number of models is also editable. One could choose to deploy 1 DNN, 4 RNN and 2 CNN. In this research, using the specific dataset, number three is the optimal for each algorithm.

5   Evaluation and Experimental Results

The Accuracy is the overall evaluation index of the developed Machine Learning models. However, four additional performance indices have been used to estimate the efficiency of the algorithms. The following Table 6 presents the validation indices used herein.

Table 6. Calculated indices for the evaluation of the binary classification approach

Index	Abbreviation	Calculation
Sensitivity (also known as True Positive Rate or Recall)	SNS, REC, TPR	$SNS = TP/(TP + FN)$
Specificity, (also known as True Negative Rate)	SPC, TNR	$SPC = TN/(TN + FP)$
Accuracy	ACC	$ACC = (TP + TN)/(TP + FP + FN + TN)$
F1 Score	F1	$F1 = 2*(Precision*Sensitivity)/(Precision + Sensitivity)$
Precision (also known as Positive Predictive Value)	PREC, PPV	$PREC = TP/(TP + FP)$

where TP, TN, FP and FN refer to *True Positives, True Negatives, False Positives and False Negatives* respectively. PREC is the measure of the correctly identified positive cases from all the predicted positive cases. Thus, it is useful when the cost of *False Positives* is high. Moreover, SNS is the measure of the correctly identified positive cases from all the actual positive cases. It is important when the cost of *False Negatives* is high. SPC is the true negative rate or the proportion of negatives that are correctly identified. The *F1* score, can be interpreted as the harmonic mean (weighted average) of the Precision and Recall.

The training of the model was performed for 50 epochs for all nine models. The HEDL-IDS performs very well in training, by correctly classifying the majority of the records. The overall accuracy in Training was equal to 98.35%. To be assured that the model can generalize, the authors examined whether the model is efficient in data that has not been used in training (Testing Data). The *Confusion Matrix* and the corresponding indices for the Testing Data are presented in Tables 7 and 8 respectively. The overall accuracy in Testing is as high as 96.25%. Once again, the excellent performance of the algorithm is noticeable. Even for the first time seen data, the number of the misclassification instances is limited. For the intrusion detection problem, the algorithm seems to generalize with high level of success.

Table 7. Confusion matrix for the testing data

	Predicted class		
	Label	0	1
Actual class	0	*22205*	1110
	1	1303	*39799*

Table 8. Evaluation indices for the testing data

Index	SNS	SPC	ACC	F1	PREC
Value	0.9446	0.973	0.962	0.948	0.952

An overall assessment, clearly shows that the performance indices have excellent values and they prove that the model performs a very reliable classification, distinguishing with high accuracy the normal flow from the cyberthreats. Overall, both confusion matrix and indices, indicate a very good performance of the model on the specific data. The algorithm seems to generalize with high level of success, as all indices have values over 0.9 for the intrusion detection problem.

To complete the detailed presentation of the results, HEDL-IDS will be compared with classic (but powerful) Machine Learning classification algorithms. A wide spectrum of ML algorithms were employed on the available dataset, namely: *Fine Tree, Medium Tree, Coarse Tree, Linear SVM, Quadratic SVM, Cubic SVM, Fine Gaussian SVM, Medium Gaussian SVM, Coarse Gaussian SVM, Fine KNN, Medium KNN, Coarse KNN, Cosine KNN, Cubic KNN, weighted KNN, Boosted Trees, Bagged Trees, Subspace Discriminant, RUSBoosted Trees an Subspace KNN*. The results for each algorithm, as well as, the comparison with the proposed model are presented in Table 9.

It is clearly shown in Table 9, that all SVM and KNN algorithms cannot handle the specific dataset efficiently, as there is a problem with the False Positives. The aforementioned algorithms seem to be struggling to identify the Normal class. However, they seem to identify with high accuracy the malicious traffic. The Naïve Bayes approach, seems to have the exact opposite problem. It identifies with high accuracy the Normal traffic but it cannot pinpoint the malicious one. Tree algorithms seem to perform noticeably better. The best performance of all ML algorithms is achieved by the *Ensemble* Methods: *Boosted Trees, Subspace KNN, Subspace Discriminant and RUSBoosted Trees*. This is an indicator that the dataset can be best handled by the ensemble techniques. Overall, it has been shown that the HEDL-IDS is the optimal methodology.

Table 9. Evaluation indices for HEDL-IDS and the machine learning algorithms

Model	SNS	SPC	ACC	F1	PREC
Fine Tree	0.885	0.958	0.930	0.906	0.928
Medium Tree	0.854	0.953	0.915	0.886	0.921
Coarse Tree	0.803	0.937	0.883	0.847	0.896
Linear SVM	**0.961**	0.704	0.729	*0.408*	*0.259*
Quadratic SVM	0.940	0.706	0.730	*0.419*	*0.270*
Cubic SVM	0.229	0.538	0.404	*0.250*	*0.276*
Fine Gaussian SVM	0.868	0.711	0.730	*0.444*	*0.298*
Medium Gaussian SVM	0.912	0.707	0.730	*0.426*	*0.278*
Coarse Gaussian SVM	0.949	0.703	0.727	*0.406*	*0.258*
Fine KNN	0.927	0.710	0.734	*0.436*	*0.285*
Medium KNN	0.918	0.710	0.734	*0.438*	*0.288*
Coarse KNN	0.941	0.707	0.732	*0.424*	*0.274*
Cosine KNN	0.918	0.710	0.734	*0.438*	*0.288*
Weighted KNN	0.934	0.710	0.735	*0.439*	*0.287*
Boosted Trees	0.912	0.939	0.929	0.901	0.890
Subspace Discriminant	0.928	0.855	0.875	0.804	0.709
RUSBoosted Trees	0.842	0.963	0.915	0.888	0.939
Cubic KNN	0.917	0.710	0.733	0.437	0.287
Kernel Naïve Bayes	*0.418*	**0.993**	*0.497*	*0.589*	**0.997**
Subspace KNN	0.804	0.916	0.873	0.829	0.856
HEDL-IDS	**0.945**	**0.973**	**0.962**	**0.948**	**0.952**

6   Conclusions and Future Work

This paper introduces a *Hybrid Ensemble Deep Learning Intrusion Detection* System (HEDL-IDS). The architecture of this hybrid approach comprises of three CNNs, three RNNs and three DNNs running in parallel. For each record, the output space is the majority vote from the nine models. The model was trained and evaluated using the *UNSW-NB15* dataset [9]. It includes records from nine Cyber Attacks and also Normal Netflow. The parameters and the layers of the hybrid model were determined through a trial and error process. The overall accuracy for the training and testing data was as high as 98.35% and 96.525% respectively. The values of the performance indices were above 0.9 for both benign and malicious traffic, for the majority of the cases.

Although the results were very good, there is always room for improvement. There are already plans for future expansion of this research. The first scenario that the authors have to consider is the development of the HEDL-IDS or of a different model to deal with the multi-class classification problem. Another potential scenario is the use of the mathematically based, *Synthetic Minority Over-sampling Technique* (SMOTE) approach [34] for the *Worms* or *Shellcode* attacks. A third scenario is to perform the HEDL-IDS or other approach on the original *UNSW-NB15* dataset. Moreover, the introduced model could be tested on other data sets and finally other Deep Learning techniques, in order to figure out if there is a better approach to classify network traffic. Finally, the authors could test other combinations of layers, with other parameters and maybe a more efficient architecture could emerge. After all, no model is perfect, a model is good when it is practically useful.

References

1. Alqahtani, H., Sarker, I.H., Kalim, A., Hossain, S.M.M., Ikhlaq, S., Hossain, S.: Cyber intrusion detection using machine learning classification techniques. In: Chaubey, N., Parikh, S., Amin, K. (eds.) COMS2 2020. CCIS, vol. 1235, pp. 121–131. Springer, Singapore (2020). https://doi.org/10.1007/978-981-15-6648-6_10
2. Sarker, I.H., Kayes, A.S.M., Badsha, S., Alqahtani, H., Watters, P., Ng, A.: Cybersecurity data science: an overview from machine learning perspective. J. Big Data **7**(1), 1–29 (2020). https://doi.org/10.1186/s40537-020-00318-5
3. Mohammadi, S., Mirvaziri, H., Ghazizadeh-Ahsaee, M., Karimipour, H.: Cyber intrusion detection by combined feature selection algorithm. J. Inf. Secur. Appl. **44**, 80–88 (2019)
4. Tavallaee, M., Stakhanova, N., Ghorbani, A.A.: Toward credible evaluation of anomaly-based intrusion-detection methods. IEEE Trans. Syst. Man Cybern. Part C (Appl. Rev.) **40**(5), 516–524 (2010)
5. Ahmim, A., Maglaras, L., Ferrag, M.A., Derdour, M., Janicke, H.: A novel hierarchical intrusion detection system based on decision tree and rules-based models. In: 2019 15th International Conference on Distributed Computing in Sensor Systems (DCOSS), pp. 228–233. IEEE, May 2019
6. Buczak, A.L., Guven, E.: A survey of data mining and machine learning methods for cyber security intrusion detection. IEEE Commun. Surv. Tutor. **18**(2), 1153–1176 (2015)
7. Kabir, E., Hu, J., Wang, H., Zhuo, G.: A novel statistical technique for intrusion detection systems. Futur. Gener. Comput. Syst. **79**, 303–318 (2018)
8. Hwang, K., Cai, M., Chen, Y., Qin, M.: Hybrid intrusion detection with weighted signature generation over anomalous internet episodes. IEEE Trans. Dependable Secure Comput. **4**(1), 41–55 (2007)
9. The UNSW-NB15 Dataset. https://research.unsw.edu.au/projects/unsw-nb15-dataset
10. Li, Y., Xia, J., Zhang, S., Yan, J., Ai, X., Dai, K.: An efficient intrusion detection system based on support vector machines and gradually feature removal method. Expert Syst. Appl. **39**(1), 424–430 (2012)
11. Koc, L., Mazzuchi, T.A., Sarkani, S.: A network intrusion detection system based on a Hidden Naïve Bayes multiclass classifier. Expert Syst. Appl. **39**(18), 13492–13500 (2012)
12. Shapoorifard, H., Shamsinejad, P.: Intrusion detection using a novel hybrid method incorporating an improved KNN. Int. J. Comput. Appl **173**(1), 5–9 (2017)
13. Malik, A.J., Khan, F.A.: A hybrid technique using binary particle swarm optimization and decision tree pruning for network intrusion detection. Cluster Comput. **21**(1), 667–680 (2018)
14. Sarker, I.H., Abushark, Y.B., Alsolami, F., Khan, A.I.: Intrudtree: a machine learning based cyber security intrusion detection model. Symmetry **12**(5), 754 (2020)
15. Kim, J., Kim, J., Thu, H.L.T., Kim, H.: Long short term memory recurrent neural network classifier for intrusion detection. In: 2016 International Conference on Platform Technology and Service (PlatCon), pp. 1–5. IEEE, February 2016

16. Zhang, Z., Zhou, X., Zhang, X., Wang, L., Wang, P.: A model based on convolutional neural network for online transaction fraud detection. Secur. Commun. Netw. **2018** (2018)

17. Basumallik, S., Ma, R., Eftekharnejad, S.: Packet-data anomaly detection in PMU-based state estimator using convolutional neural network. Int. J. Electr. Power Energy Syst. **107**, 690–702 (2019)

18. Thamilarasu, G., Chawla, S.: Towards deep-learning-driven intrusion detection for the internet of things. Sensors **19**(9), 1977 (2019)

19. Khan, F.A., Gumaei, A., Derhab, A., Hussain, A.: A novel two-stage deep learning model for efficient network intrusion detection. IEEE Access **7**, 30373–30385 (2019)

20. Demertzis, K., Iliadis, L., Tziritas, N., Kikiras, P.: Anomaly detection via blockchained deep learning smart contracts in industry 4.0. Neural Comput. Appl. **32**(23), 17361–17378 (2020). https://doi.org/10.1007/s00521-020-05189-8

21. Psathas, A.P., Iliadis, L., Papaleonidas, A., Bountas, D.: A hybrid deep learning ensemble for cyber intrusion detection. In: Iliadis, L., Macintyre, J., Jayne, C., Pimenidis, E. (eds.) EANN 2021. PINNS, vol. 3, pp. 27–41. Springer, Cham (2021). https://doi.org/10.1007/978-3-030-80568-5_3

22. Moustafa, N., Slay, J.: UNSW-NB15: a comprehensive data set for network intrusion detection systems (UNSW-NB15 network data set). In: 2015 Military Communications and Information Systems Conference (MilCIS), pp. 1–6. IEEE, November 2015

23. The IXIA PerfectStorm tool. http://www.ixiacom.com/products/perfectstorm

24. CVE. https://cve.mitre.org/

25. Yeung, D.S., Li, J.C., Ng, W.W., Chan, P.P.: MLPNN training via a multiobjective optimization of training error and stochastic sensitivity. IEEE Trans. Neural Netw. Learn. Syst. **27**(5), 978–992 (2015)

26. Baek, J., Choi, Y.: Deep neural network for predicting ore production by truck-haulage systems in open-pit mines. Appl. Sci. **10**(5), 1657 (2020)

27. Liu, W., Wang, Z., Liu, X., Zeng, N., Liu, Y., Alsaadi, F.E.: A survey of deep neural network architectures and their applications. Neurocomputing **234**, 11–26 (2017)

28. O'Shea, K., Nash, R.: An introduction to convolutional neural networks. arXiv preprint arXiv: 1511.08458 (2015)

29. Martin, E., Cundy, C.: Parallelizing linear recurrent neural nets over sequence length. arXiv preprint arXiv:1709.04057 (2017)

30. Mahdavifar, S., Ghorbani, A.A.: Application of deep learning to cybersecurity: a survey. Neurocomputing **347**, 149–176 (2019)

31. Le, X.H., Ho, H.V., Lee, G., Jung, S.: Application of long short-term memory (LSTM) neural network for flood forecasting. Water **11**(7), 1387 (2019)

32. Ketkar, N.: Introduction to keras. In: Deep Learning with Python, pp. 97–111. Apress, Berkeley (2017)

33. Dillon, J.V., et al.: Tensorflow distributions. arXiv preprint arXiv:1711.10604 (2017)

34. Chawla, N.V., Bowyer, K.W., Hall, L.O., Kegelmeyer, W.P.: SMOTE: synthetic minority over-sampling technique. J. Artif. Intell. Res. **16**, 321–357 (2002)

Random Forest Based on Federated Learning for Intrusion Detection

Tijana Markovic[1][✉] , Miguel Leon[1] , David Buffoni[2],
and Sasikumar Punnekkat[1]

[1] School of Innovation, Design and Engineering, Malardalen University,
Vasteras, Sweden
{tijana.markovic,miguel.leonortiz,sasikumar.punnekkat}@mdu.se
[2] Tietoevry, Stockholm, Sweden
david.buffoni@tietoevry.com

Abstract. Vulnerability of important data is increasing everyday with the constant evolution and increase of sophisticated cyber security threats that can seriously affect the business processes. Hence, it is important for organizations to define and implement appropriate mechanisms such as intrusion detection systems to protect their valuable data. In recent years, various machine learning approaches were proposed for intrusion detection, where Random Forest (RF) is recognized as one of the most suitable algorithms. Machine learning algorithms are data-oriented and storing data for training on the centralized server can increase the vulnerability of the whole system. In this paper, we are using a federated learning approach that independently trains data subsets on multiple clients and sends only the resulting models for aggregation to a server. This considerably reduces the need for sending all data to a centralised server. Different RF-based federated learning versions were evaluated on four intrusion detection benchmark datasets (KDD, NSL-KDD, UNSW-NB15, and CIC-IDS-2017). In our experiments, the global RF on the server achieved higher accuracy than the maximum achieved with individual RFs on the clients in the case of two out of four datasets, and it was very close to the maximum for the third dataset. Even in the fourth case, the global RF performed better than the average accuracy, although it fell behind the maximum.

Keywords: Intrusion detection · Random Forest · Federated learning

1 Introduction

Expanding use of computer networks has brought many security rules and preventive measures that have to be implemented by every organization whose data must not be compromised. Any malicious activity can seriously affect business processes and allowing unauthorized access to an organization's network can cause irreparable consequences. One of the necessary protective mechanisms is the Intrusion Detection System (IDS), and this research area has received a lot

© IFIP International Federation for Information Processing 2022
Published by Springer Nature Switzerland AG 2022
I. Maglogiannis et al. (Eds.): AIAI 2022, IFIP AICT 646, pp. 132–144, 2022.
https://doi.org/10.1007/978-3-031-08333-4_11

of attention during the past decade [18]. IDS is a software or hardware system that monitors the events occurring in a computer system or network and analyzes those events for signs of intrusion or violations of security polices [5]. IDSs can be divided based on the data sources (network-based NIDS and host-based HIDS), the analysis strategy (signature-based and anomaly-based) and the timing of information sources and analysis (interval-based and real-time) [5,14].

In recent years, artificial intelligence (AI) techniques are becoming widely used in the field of network security. Machine learning (ML) algorithms can learn from data how to distinguish between normal and abnormal activities, and this ability has proved to be very effective for the development of reliable IDSs. Various ML-based solutions were proposed by the researchers to improve the efficiency of IDSs [4]. Different ML algorithms were applied to Intrusion Detection (ID) problems and Random Forest (RF) is recognized as one of the most commonly used [7,22]. Many studies that compared the performances of different ML algorithms on different benchmark datasets concluded that the RF has the highest accuracy [2,9,11,23]. To evaluate the proposed ID techniques, researchers are using different publicly available datasets that are composed of normal traffic and different types of attacks [10]. The most frequently used public datasets are: KDD (24%), NSL-KDD (36%), UNSW-NB15 (18%) and CIC-IDS-2017&CSE-CIC-IDS-2018 (12%) [4].

Since the ML algorithms require a lot of data for training purposes, one of the main obstacles is the security of the provided data. Storing data and performing analysis and predictions on the centralized server can raise various security issues. These obstacles can be solved by the implementation of a collaborative learning approach, without the need of data sharing, and this approach is called federated learning (FL) [13,17]. FL is a decentralized learning technique that trains models locally on clients and transfers the parameters to the centralized server, which fits appropriately to the needs of IDSs [3,8]. Depending on the methodology of data distribution between different clients, FL can be [27]:

- Horizontal (HFL) - datasets have the same features but different instances.
- Vertical (VFL) - datasets have the same instances but different features.
- Transfer (TFL) - datasets are different in both instances and features.

In the literature, most of the models used for IDS in a FL setting are gradient-based, more specifically Deep Learning models. For example, Man et al. [20] proposed a FL mechanism for convolutional neural networks in Internet-of-Things applications. Contrary, we are considering a tree-based model which has been already successfully used in FL (e.g., FL based on Gradient Boosting trees [16]). Thanks to their great parallelism, RF is also a perfect candidate for FL. A federated version of RF has been proposed in [19], and it is proved to be as accurate as the non-federated version. In [25], authors proposed a way to create a decentralized federated forest in a ID scenario.

In this paper, we used a HFL approach to develop an anomaly-based intrusion detection system with a network-based data source (NIDS). The developed IDS is based on RF algorithm and it was evaluated on the most commonly used ID datasets. We summarize the contributions of this paper as follows:

- Comparison of RF hyper-parameters on four different ID benchmark datasets (KDD, NSL-KDD, UNSW-NB15, and CIC-IDS-2017).
- Comparison of different merging methods for aggregating independent RFs.
- Evaluation of RF HFL approach for ID.

This paper is organized as follows: Sect. 2 presents the used methodology, including the details about the used datasets and preprocessing techniques, the explanation of the regular and federated RF algorithm, and the presentation of the experimental setup. In Sect. 3 we present results of the conducted experiments, followed by the conclusion and plans for future work in Sect. 4.

2   Methodology

2.1   Datasets and Preprocessing

The experiments presented in this paper were conducted on four existing ID datasets that are described in this section. For all of those datasets, data about network packets were preprocessed to create the features, and every entry was labeled either as normal activity, or as some type of network attack.

KDD99 [12] was created in a simulated environment, and it contains normal traffic and different types of network attacks. It has 41 features and the full training set contains 4 898 431 entries. In this paper, we used "kddcup.txt" file that contains 10% of data.

NSL-KDD dataset [1] is derived from the KDD99 dataset to solve some of the problems stated in [26]. Total number of entries in NSL-KDD is 148 517 and in this paper we used the data included in "KDDTrain+.txt" file.

UNSW-NB15 dataset [21] contains real normal traffic and simulated attacks. It has 42 features and the whole dataset has 2 540 044 entries. In this paper, we used a partition of data that is configured as a training set, which is included in "UNSW_NB15_ training-set.csv" file.

CIC-IDS-2017 dataset [24] was created in a simulated environment, and it contains normal traffic and different types of network attacks. CIC-IDS-2017 dataset has 78 features and 2 830 743 entries. The data capturing period was 5 days and the entries for each day and attack type are saved in a separate file. In this paper, we used all files except the files for Monday (that contains only normal traffic) and Thursday afternoon (that has an extremely low percentage of attacks –0.01%). Two features from this dataset were removed (flow of bytes and flow of packets per second).

From the selected parts of the datasets, we have removed the instances that belong to classes with less than 800 cases. Additionally, we preprocessed each feature as follows:

- Features with binary values: The values were not changed.
- Features with numerical values: The values were normalized to a range between 0 and 1 using min/max approach.
- Features with categorical values: The values were one-hot encoded.

After applying above-mentioned preprocessing techniques, all datasets were divided with the goal to generate subsets to simulate a HFL setting. For each dataset, we selected a feature to be used as a division criteria, and removed it from the training data used by ML algorithms. We considered only subsets with at least 50 instances of both classes (normal and attack). Datasets were divided based on the value of the following feature:

- KDD99: "protocol" feature, resulting in 3 subsets
- NSL-KDD: "protocol" feature, resulting in 3 subsets
- UNSW-NB15: "service" feature, resulting in 6 subsets
- CIC-IDS-2017: "destination port" feature, resulting in 14 subsets

Table 1 presents a summary for the parts of the datasets that were used in this paper, as well as a summary for all subsets that were generated for federated learning. The number of features in parentheses is the actual number of features used by the ML algorithm after preprocessing.

Table 1. Information and distribution of the used instances for KDD99, NSL-KDD, UNSW-NB15, and CIC-IDS-2017 datasets.

Dataset	No. of instances	No. of features	Feature for subsets	Subsets			
				Feature value	No. of instances	% of instances	% of attacks
KDD99	493 347	40 (115)	Protocol	icmp	283 235	57.41%	99.5%
				tcp	189 786	38.47%	59.5%
				udp	20 326	4.12%	5.7%
NSL-KDD	125 597	40 (119)	Protocol	icmp	8 090	6.44%	83.8%
				tcp	102 517	81.62%	47.7%
				udp	14 990	11.93%	17.1%
UNSW-NB15	79 924	41 (177)	Service	-	45 516	56.95%	39.9%
				dns	21 367	26.73%	85.6%
				ftp	1 550	1.94%	51.1%
				ftp-data	1 396	1.75%	32%
				http	8 244	10.31 %	51.3%
				smtp	1 851	2.32%	65.7%
CIC-IDS-2017	1 543 535	75	Destination port	21	11 781	0.76%	69.4%
				22	13 498	0.87%	45.5%
				53	643 986	41.72%	0.03%
				80	541 594	35.09%	70.6%
				88	3 920	0.25%	4.1%
				135	749	0.05%	21.4%
				139	1 921	0.12%	10.3%
				389	4 477	0.29%	3.6%
				443	312 986	20.28%	0.08%
				445	1 195	0.08%	15%
				465	2 656	0.17%	6%
				1124	259	0.02%	61.8%
				3268	1 903	0.12%	8.4%
				8080	2 610	0.17%	54.4%

2.2   Random Forest

Random Forest (RF) is an ensemble of different versions of the same machine learning algorithm, called Decision Tree (DT) [22].

DT is a predictive model based on constructing a tree that is composed of decision nodes. Beginning at the root node, the input parameters are tested at the decision nodes, with each possible outcome resulting in a branch that can lead either to another decision node or to a terminating leaf [15]. DT classifier employs splitting rules to construct a tree and in this paper we used following [28]:

- *gini* - attempts to find the largest homogeneous class and isolate it from the rest of the data,
- *entropy* - attempts to identify groups by minimizing the within-group diversity.

RF is an aggregation of DTs such that each tree uses a random subset from the examples in the training set. Those subsets are selected independently but with the same distribution for all DTs in the forest [6]. The number DTs that will be used for RF is an important hyper-parameter to achieve a high accuracy and avoid overfitting.

To determine the performance of the individual DT we used the following measures:

- *Accuracy (A)* - accuracy on the validation set
- *Weighed accuracy (WA)* - the weighted accuracy is equal to the accuracy of the DT for the predicted class (on the validation set) multiplied by the average accuracy of that DT for all different classes on the validation set.

In this paper, we used the following ensemble methods to determine the final prediction using the created DTs:

- *Simple Voting (SV)* - takes a majority vote as a predicted class.
- *Weighted Voting (WV)* - takes a majority vote as a predicted class but takes into account the weighted accuracy of the DTs.

2.3   Random Forest Based on Federated Learning

Data distribution for our Federated Learning approach is horizontal, which means that the dataset is divided into a certain number of subsets where each subset has different instances but the same features. A RF model is trained on each client on a specific subset, then, all clients send the RF models to the centralized server, where they are combined in a global RF. Finally, the global RF is sent back to the clients for further usage. Architecture of the proposed approach is presented in Fig. 1.

Since each of the generated RFs is composed of the same number of DTs, different approaches were used to decide which DTs will be merged in the global RF:

- *Sorting DTs per RF based on Accuracy (S_DTs_A)* - DTs per RF are sorted based on the accuracy and the best ones from each RF are selected
- *Sorting DTs per RF based on Weighted Accuracy (S_DTs_WA)* - DTs per RF are sorted based on the weighted accuracy, and the best ones from each RF are selected
- *Sorting All DTs based on Accuracy (S_DTs_A_All)* - all DTs are assembled, sorted based on the accuracy and the best ones are selected
- *Sorting All DTs based on Weighted Accuracy (S_DTs_WA_All)* - all DTs are assembled, sorted based on the weighted accuracy and the best ones are selected

The maximum number of DTs (MaxDTs) that can be used for generating the global RF is the number of DTs per RF multiplied by the number of subsets. The number of the best DTs that will be included in the global RF is a hyper-parameter that may vary from 1 to MaxDTs for S_DTs_A_All and S_DTs_WA_All, and from the number of subsets to MaxDTs for S_DTs_A and S_DTs_WA.

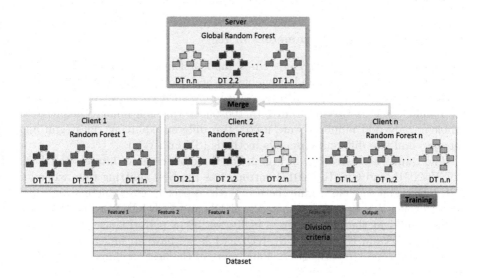

Fig. 1. Architecture of the Random Forest based federated learning

2.4 Experimental Setup

As previously discussed, KDD99, NSL-KDD, UNSW-NB15 and CIC-IDS-2017 datasets have been used for the experiments. Three different experiments have been carried out:

1. *Study of hyper-parameters in RF* - The datasets have been divided into training set, validation set and testing set with a 70%-10%-20% distribution. The validation set was used to find the best combination of hyper-parameters in RF: number of DTs, splitting rule and ensemble method.

2. *Evaluation of RFs on different clients* - The training, validation and testing sets have been divided into subsets using one of the features, as explained in the Sect. 2.1. For each subset a independent RF was trained using the best combination of hyper-parameters from the first experiment.
3. *Federated Learning on the centralized server* - Different RFs were combined into a global one using different merging methods. The global RF is tested on the whole testing set created in the first experiment.

All experiments were performed five times and the mean value was used in all comparisons.

3   Results and Discussion

In this section, we present and discuss the results of our experiments. The best combination of hyper-parameters in RFs is presented in Sect. 3.1. An evaluation of RFs on different clients is shown in Sect. 3.2. Lastly, a study of different merging methods for aggregating independent RFs is presented in Sect. 3.3.

3.1   Study of Hyper-Parameters in RF

As indicated in Sect. 2.2, RFs have three important hyper-parameters: the number of DTs, splitting rule, and ensemble method. To find the best combination of the mentioned hyper-parameters, we conducted a comparative study with the number of DTs varying from 1 to 100 (since this is a binary classification problem, only odd numbers were used), two different splitting rules (gini and entropy) and two different ensemble methods (SV and WV).

The results are presented in Fig. 2. For three of the used datasets (KDD99, UNSW-NB15 and CIC-IDS-2017) entropy was the best splitting rule, while for NSL-KDD, gini was performing better. With respect to ensemble methods, SV outperformed WV in the older datasets (KDD and NSL-KDD), while WV gave better results in the newer ones. Finally, we hit a performance plateau with at least 11 DTs in KDD and NSL-KDD, while we have an increasing trend in UNSW-NB15 and CIC-IDS-2017. A summary of the best combination of hyper-parameters is given in Table 2.

Table 2. Best combination of hyper-parameters in RF, per dataset.

Dataset	KDD99	NSL-KDD	UNSW-NB15	CIC-IDS-2017
Number of trees	65	65	93	77
Splitting rule	entropy	gini	entropy	entropy
Ensemble method	SV	SV	WV	WV

3.2   Evaluation of RFs on Different Clients

Different RFs have been trained and tested on different subsets using the best combination of hyper-parameters found in Sect. 3.1. The number of subsets differs between the datasets: KDD99 and NSL-KDD have 3 subsets each, UNSW-NB15 has 6, while CIC-IDS-2017 has 14 subsets. The results can be found in Fig. 3. Each RF has been trained and tested on the data from its own subset (blue bars in Fig. 3). Additionally, the same RFs have been tested on the entire testing set, independently on which subset the specific RF has been trained on (orange bar in Fig. 3).

As can be observed, the performances are much lower when testing on the entire testing set than on the specific subset. The reason is that the different RFs have not been trained to classify those specific cases. This suggests that the different subsets have some differences between the instances. However, this is not always true, since some RFs manage to get high accuracy compared to the

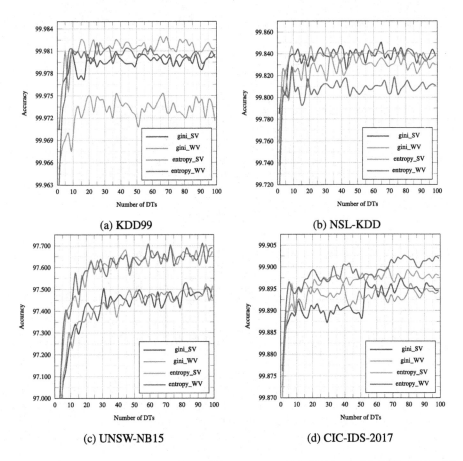

Fig. 2. Performance of RF on the validation set in (a) KDD99, (b) NSL-KDD, (c) UNSW-NB15, and (d) CIC-IDS-2017, for different combinations of hyper-parameters.

percentage of cases that belong to that subset (purple bar in Fig. 3). One good example is the subset with port 3268 in CIC-IDS-2017, where the accuracy of RF is 71.82% and the percentage of instances is 0.12% (Fig. 3d). This means that the RF is capable to correctly classify more instances than a random classifier. On the other hand, there are some RFs that perform much worse than a random classifier (e.g., port 21, 135 or 8080 in CIC-IDS-2017 Fig. 3d).

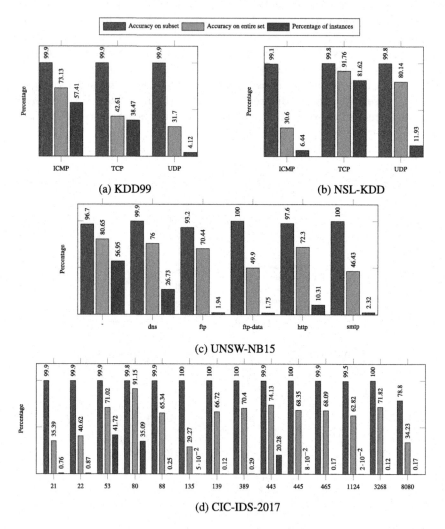

Fig. 3. Performance of independent RFs on different subsets from (a) KDD99, (b) NSL-KDD, (c) UNSW-NB15 and (d) CIC-IDS-2017 dataset.

3.3   Federated Learning on the Centralized Server

As presented in Sect. 2.3 and further explained in Sect. 2.4, four different methods for merging RFs were compared. The best combination of splitting rule and ensemble method per dataset (found in Sect. 3.1) was used during the whole experimentation. The number of DTs for the global RF is studied in this experiment. For the methods S_DTs_A_All and S_DTs_WA_All, we tested all numbers between 1 and MaxDTs, while for the methods S_DTs_A and S_DTs_WA, we tested a multiple of the number of subsets (e.g., for KDD we tested 3,6,9... up to 195 n).

The results are presented in Fig. 4. We can see that combining all DTs and then selecting the best ones is the best option in UNSW-NB15 and CIC-IDS-

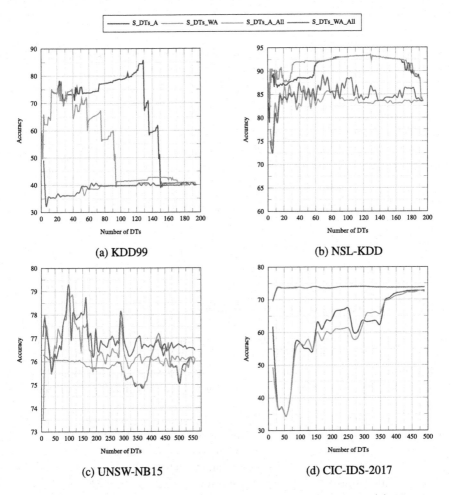

Fig. 4. Performance of the global RF on the testing set of (a) KDD99, (b) NSL-KDD, (c) UNSW-NB15, and (d) CIC-IDS-2017 using four different merging methods.

2017. On the other hand, in KDD99 and NSL-KDD, the option of using the best DTs from each RFs and then combining them is a better option. When the sorting measurement is considered, there is not a big difference between A and WA, except for KDD99, where using A gives a considerable improvement (around 10%).

The best combination of the number of DTs in global RF and the merging method per dataset are given in the upper part of Table 3. The lower part of Table 3 includes the performance of the global RF and the baselines that are used for the comparison. As the baselines, we used the maximum, average, and minimum accuracy of all independent RFs, that are presented in the orange bar of Fig. 3. From Table 3, we can see how the global RF improves the maximum accuracy of individual RFs for KDD99 and NSL-KDD, and it is very close for UNSW-NB15. For CIC-IDS-2017 it fell behind the maximum, but it performed better than the average accuracy.

Table 3. The upper part of the table shows the hyper-parameters needed to obtain the results at the lower part of the table.

Dataset		KDD99	NSL-KDD	UNSW-NB15	CIC-IDS-2017
No. of subsets (RFs)		3	3	6	14
No. of DTs per RF		65	65	93	77
No. of DTs in global RF		129	129	96	308
Merging method		S_DTs_A	S_DTs_A S_DTs_WA	S_DTs_WA_all	S_DTs_A_all S_DTs_WA_all
Accuracy of the global RF		84.77	93.51	79.13	73.26
Baseline	Max accuracy	74	91.76	80.65	91.15
	Avg. accuracy	49.15	67.5	65.95	54.82
	Min accuracy	31.7	30.6	46.43	29.27

4   Conclusion and Future Work

In this paper, a RF-based federated learning approach for ID has been investigated in four different ID benchmark datasets. Different merging methods were evaluated to combine independent RFs, as well as the best combination of RF hyper-parameters including the number of DTs, splitting rule, and ensemble method.

The experiments have shown that combining independent RFs into a global one on the server outperforms the average accuracy of the RFs on the clients. This approach can be used in cases when the data cannot be centralized and in average it will provide a higher performance than using only the local RFs. Although this approach has lower accuracy than applying RF on the entire dataset, this approach is more realistic for real systems due to security restrictions and network overload.

As a part of future work, we plan to evaluate the proposed approach for the attack classification problem, as well as to study different methods for feature selection and reduction.

Acknowledgements. This work has been partially supported by the H2020 ECSEL EU Project Intelligent Secure Trustable Things (InSecTT). InSecTT (www.insectt.eu) has received funding from the ECSEL Joint Undertaking (JU) under grant agreement No 876038. The JU receives support from the European Union's Horizon 2020 research and innovation programme and Austria, Sweden, Spain, Italy, France, Portugal, Ireland, Finland, Slovenia, Poland, Netherlands, Turkey.

The document reflects only the author's view and the Commission is not responsible for any use that may be made of the information it contains.

References

1. NSL-KDD (2009). https://www.unb.ca/cic/datasets/nsl.html
2. Abedin, M., Siddiquee, K.N.E.A., Bhuyan, M., Karim, R., Hossain, M.S., Andersson, K., et al.: Performance analysis of anomaly based network intrusion detection systems. In: 43nd IEEE Conference on Local Computer Networks Workshops (LCN Workshops), Chicago, 1–4 October 2018, pp. 1–7. IEEE Computer Society (2018)
3. Agrawal, S., et al.: Federated learning for intrusion detection system: concepts, challenges and future directions. arXiv preprint arXiv:2106.09527 (2021)
4. Ahmad, Z., Shahid Khan, A., Wai Shiang, C., Abdullah, J., Ahmad, F.: Network intrusion detection system: a systematic study of machine learning and deep learning approaches. Trans. Emerg. Telecommun. Technol. **32**(1), e4150 (2021)
5. Bace, R., Mell, P.: Intrusion detection systems. National Institute of Standards and Technology (NIST), Technical Report 800-31 (2001)
6. Breiman, L.: Random forests. Mach. Learn. **45**(1), 5–32, e4150 (2001)
7. Buczak, A.L., Guven, E.: A survey of data mining and machine learning methods for cyber security intrusion detection. IEEE Commun. Surv. Tutor. **18**(2), 1153–1176 (2015)
8. Campos, E.M., et al.: Evaluating federated learning for intrusion detection in internet of things: review and challenges. Comput. Netw. **203**, 108661 (2022)
9. Farnaaz, N., Jabbar, M.: Random forest modeling for network intrusion detection system. Procedia Comput. Sci. **89**, 213–217 (2016)
10. Ghurab, M., Gaphari, G., Alshami, F., Alshamy, R., Othman, S.: A detailed analysis of benchmark datasets for network intrusion detection system. Asian J. Res. Comput. Sci. **7**(4), 14–33 (2021)
11. Hautsalo, J.: Using supervised learning and data fusion to detect network attacks. [urn:nbn:se:mdh:diva-54957] (2021)
12. Hettich, S., Bay, S.D.: The UCI KDD archive. University of California, Department of Information and Computer Science, Irvine: (1999). http://kdd.ics.uci.edu
13. Kairouz, P., McMahan, H.B., et al.: Advances and open problems in federated learning (2021)
14. Khraisat, A., Gondal, I., Vamplew, P., Kamruzzaman, J.: Survey of intrusion detection systems: techniques, datasets and challenges. Cybersecurity **2**(1), 1–22 (2019)
15. Larose, D.T., Larose, C.D.: Discovering Knowledge in Data: An Introduction to Data Mining, vol. 4. John Wiley & Sons, Hoboken (2014)

16. Li, Q., Wen, Z., He, B.: Practical federated gradient boosting decision trees. In: Proceedings of the AAAI Conference on Artificial Intelligence, vol. 34, pp. 4642–4649, April 2020
17. Li, Q., et al.: A survey on federated learning systems: vision, hype and reality for data privacy and protection. IEEE Trans. Knowl. Data Eng. (Early Access), 1–1 (2021)
18. Liao, H.J., Lin, C.H.R., Lin, Y.C., Tung, K.Y.: Intrusion detection system: a comprehensive review. J. Netw. Comput. Appl. **36**(1), 16–24 (2013)
19. Liu, Y., Liu, Y., Liu, Z., Zhang, J., Meng, C., Zheng, Y.: Federated forest. CoRR abs/1905.10053 (2019). http://arxiv.org/abs/1905.10053
20. Man, D., Zeng, F., Yang, W., Yu, M., Lv, J., Wang, Y.: Intelligent intrusion detection based on federated learning for edge-assisted internet of things. Secur. Commun. Netw. **2021**, 108661 (2021). https://doi.org/10.1155/2021/9361348
21. Moustafa, N., Slay, J.: UNSW-NB15: a comprehensive data set for network intrusion detection systems (UNSW-NB15 network data set). In: 2015 Military Communications and Information Systems Conference (MilCIS), pp. 1–6. IEEE (2015)
22. Resende, P.A.A., Drummond, A.C.: A survey of random forest based methods for intrusion detection systems. ACM Comput. Surv. **51**(3), 1–36, 108661 (2018)
23. Revathi, S., Malathi, A.: A detailed analysis on NSL-KDD dataset using various machine learning techniques for intrusion detection. Int. J. Eng. Res. Technol. **2**(12), 1848–1853 (2013)
24. Sharafaldin, I., Lashkari, A.H., Ghorbani, A.A.: Toward generating a new intrusion detection dataset and intrusion traffic characterization. ICISSp **1**, 108–116 (2018)
25. de Souza, L.A.C., Antonio F. Rebello, G., Camilo, G.F., Guimarães, L.C.B., Duarte, O.C.M.B.: DFedForest: decentralized federated forest. In: 2020 IEEE International Conference on Blockchain (Blockchain), pp. 90–97 (2020)
26. Tavallaee, M., Bagheri, E., Lu, W., Ghorbani, A.A.: A detailed analysis of the KDD CUP 99 data set. In: 2009 IEEE Symposium on Ccomputational Intelligence for Security and Defense Applications, pp. 1–6. IEEE (2009)
27. Yang, Q., Liu, Y., Cheng, Y., Kang, Y., Chen, T., Yu, H.: Federated learning. Synth. Lect. Artif. Intell. Mach. Learn. **13**(3), 1–207 (2019)
28. Zambon, M., Lawrence, R., Bunn, A., Powell, S.: Effect of alternative splitting rules on image processing using classification tree analysis. Photogram. Eng. Remote Sens. **72**(1), 25–30 (2006)

Towards Semantic Modeling and Simulation of Cybersecurity on the Internet of Underwater Things

Stavros Stavrinos, Konstantinos Kotis$^{(\boxtimes)}$ (iD), and Christos Kalloniatis (iD)

Department of Cultural Technology and Communication, University of the Aegean, 83100 Mytilene, Greece
`cti21010@ct.aegean.gr`, {`kotis,chkallon`}`@aegean.gr`

Abstract. As maritime and military missions become more and more complex over the years, there has been a high interest in the research and development of Unmanned Underwater Vehicles (UUVs). Latest efforts concern the modeling and simulation of UUVs collaboration within formations of vehicles (swarms), towards obtaining deeper insights related to critical issues related to cybersecurity and interoperability. The research issues which are constantly emerging in this domain are closely related to the communication, interoperability, and secure operation of trustworthy UUVs, as well as to the volume, velocity, variety, and veracity of data transmitted in low bitrate due to the medium i.e., the water. This paper focuses on such issues in the domain of UUVs, emphasizing interoperability and cybersecurity in swarms of trustworthy UUVs in a military/search-and-rescue (SAR) setting. The aim of this paper is to present preliminary work on a semantic modeling and simulation approach that aims to facilitate commanders of military/search-and-rescue operations to effectively support critical and life-saving decision-making, while handling interoperability and cybersecurity issues on the Internet of Underwater Things (IoUT).

Keywords: IoUT · UUVs · Interoperability · Semantics · Cybersecurity · Simulation

1 Introduction

Semantic modeling (e.g., ontologies) provides the ability to interconnect heterogeneous devices and applications, enabling their communication in a common standardized language. By providing a shared and commonly agreed conceptualization for representing domain knowledge related to entities and relations between them, the efficient and effective interaction between those entities (hardware, software, human) is facilitated [26]. By implementing such a communication ecosystem in a simulated environment, facilitates monitoring and prediction of possible situations in the field of action, eventually supporting efficient decision-making. Specifically, in the domain of IoUT, where there is a need for continuous, reliable, and secure interoperability between various trustworthy

© IFIP International Federation for Information Processing 2022
Published by Springer Nature Switzerland AG 2022
I. Maglogiannis et al. (Eds.): AIAI 2022, IFIP AICT 646, pp. 145–156, 2022.
https://doi.org/10.1007/978-3-031-08333-4_12

underwater assets, the main challenge is to preserve high-level understanding (common semantics) in the communication between them [11]. Especially due to the volume (big data) and veracity (heterogeneous data) of exchanged information, the utilization of suitable semantic models is a key factor.

UUVs are powerful complex assets operating in IoUT environment [31]. Establishing communication between them, as well as between them and other platforms (at sea, air, and surface), is critical. UUVs are self-managed and knowledge-based autonomous agents which can integrate different frameworks and applications, making them effective and versatile assets acting in unknown and hazardous networks, such as in Underwater Wireless Sensor Networks (UWSNs) [12]. The replacement of human factor in autonomous assets operating in such a trustworthy setting (to avoid the cost of human training and loss, as well as to overcome ethical barriers in military operations) is a key reason for their enormous development in the last decade. In addition, collaboration of underwater and aerial unmanned vehicles operating in swarms, unlock many more capabilities and potentials by accomplishing collaborative tasks even more effectively and efficiently. However, due to the complexity of the setting they act, many challenges and key issues are emerging such as interoperability and security issues [24].

To support efficient decision-making of commanders operating in such a complex setting, advanced simulation approaches that are based on the integration of different tools are required, effectively simulating/co-simulating critical situations and possible threats/vulnerabilities of heterogeneous assets 'living' in the underwater environment. The goal is to facilitate standardization of response in such situations towards trustworthy and less risky, decision-making in military and SAR operations.

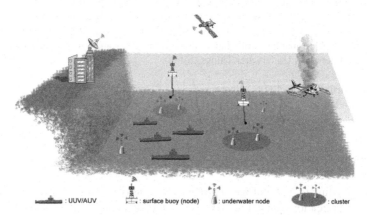

Fig. 1. Topology of UWSN in a SAR scenario involving UUVs, underwater nodes (and clusters), as well as surface nodes.

Let us assume the following SAR scenario (Fig. 1). A swarm of UUVs must travel to an exact location of a plane crash at sea, safely and quickly, while interoperating in an UWSN, while exchanging information/data in real-time, utilizing adaptive path-planning. During the execution of predefined tasks, an unusual delay in communication between them and the underwater nodes is identified, affecting the robustness of the network architecture, resulting in the inability of commander to get the transmitted information. An automated analysis of the incident issues an alert for huge numbers of data packets overwhelming the network, thus, an incoming DoS (Denial of Service) attack is flagged. Consequently, an automated process of various counter-methods and protocols is initiated, such as honeypots, encryption algorithms, security rules etc. Such a scenario must be simulated in order to be possible for commanders to be able to use, validate, and update security protocols, as well as to learn how to effectively antici-pate such critical situations by testing alternative topologies, and so on, minimizing, eventually, handling costs and life losses.

IoUT is a new research and development domain that aims to tackle many of the challenges of UUVs introduced above, such as interoperability, data management, and cybersecurity [25]. The motivation of this research is the exploration of these challenges in order to propose an efficient and effective simulation approach that is necessary for commanders of military/SAR operations to effectively support critical and life-saving decision-making. More specifically, the ultimate goal is to support SAR and military commanders with an efficient UUVs swarm simulation environment that will empha-size interoperability and cybersecurity issues, in order to achieve and establish secure exchange of interoperable data/information. Based on this motivation the contribution of this paper is a) to review existing methods and tools of semantic modeling and simulation for cybersecurity on the IoUT, b) to propose an efficient and effective tool-supported simulation approach that is necessary for commanders of military/SAR operations to effectively support critical and life-saving decision-making.

The remainder of this paper is organized as follows. Section 2 presents related work on semantic modeling and simulation of cybersecurity issues, as well as freely available simulation tools in the domain of IoUT. Section 3 presents our experiments with existing approaches/tools, and introduce the proposed approach. Section 4 discusses identified challenges and issues in the underwater cybersecurity domain. Section 5 concludes the paper.

2 Preliminaries and Related Work

Recently, the utilization of UUVs has been demonstrated, especially in SAR incidents, taking advantage of underwater beacons generated by airplanes, activated in emergency situations (e.g., a crash) [38]. A representative example is the discovery of debris of Air France Flight 447 by a swarm of UUVs (using their side-scan sonar) at a depth of 3,980 m [22].

As presented in related work [6], in order to overcome data heterogeneity between assets, an Ontology-Based Data Access (OBDA) approach is introduced based on the Sensor Observation Sample Actuator (SOSA) ontology [17], providing an interoper-ability layer and a domain-independent generalization of sensor measurements. SOSA ontology provides a formal but lightweight general-purpose specification for modeling interaction of entities in the acts of observation, actuation, and sampling.

To achieve adaptive path-planning and self-management, unmanned underwater assets use, as critical source, the exchanged internal and external data between vari-ous platforms in a UWSN. Hence its robustness, from a cybersecurity aspect, is critical.

Threat modeling and risk analysis are key factors in order to identify the security require-ments of UUVs, as well as to define how adversaries act and achieve their objectives. In related work [23], a holistic approach is proposed, initialized with the identification of threats and vulnerabilities of software and hardware assets that a platform comprises. This process is mandatory in order to prioritize the existing numerous possible attacks. Also, due to the complexity of modern cyber-attacks, authors suggest dividing them into connected sequences of smaller attacks, encounter them as separate vulnerabili-ties. Considering the impact of contemporary sophisticated attacks, they conclude in the necessity of developing fault tolerant and redundant systems in order to survive and counter multiple intrusions.

The successful accomplishment of a task is most often depending on a key factor i.e., its prediction. Simulation tools provide the capability to evaluate a situation and decide following actions quickly and accurately across several domains. In the following para-graphs we present a set of open-source underwater simulation tools, which were chosen with specific requirements in mind: a) capability of heterogenous data integration using ontologies/semantic knowledge, b) support of multiple UUVs (swarms) simulation, c) support of modeling and simulation of sensors and network interfaces, and d) support of simple visualization for realistic scenario representation.

NS-3 (Network Simulator) [29] is a well-known open-source tool that has been used to represent underwater or other types of networks, especially due to its capability to be combined with external software libraries, animators, analysis and visualization tools, in contrast to other simulation tools that provide a single integrated graphical user interface (GUI). It has been developed to support basic networking research and education by providing configuration with numerous Internet protocols. It is compatible to Linux and Windows operating systems. Nevertheless, its operation mainly through command line and C++, may be a barrier for users without coding skills [30].

UWSim is a tool used by researchers for underwater robotic missions' simulation, highly suitable for UWSNs [33]. Users are able to configure their working environ-ment, even with widgets, displaying useful data during an operation. Import of XML data is also possible. A Robot operating system (ROS) can be effectively integrated also via a dedicated interface. Its main advantage is an easily integrated open-source exten-sion, namely UWSim-NET; a network simulator, which gathers the benefits of NS-3 in modeling communication [8]. Finally, playback of the same mission is also available, facilitating the acquired results in a great extent.

Motivated by the need of fast and agile decision-making, and with the aim of inte-grating and dynamically representing knowledge from existing knowledge bases, related work [18] presents a hybrid ontology-based simulation framework for efficiently deriv-ing a simulation model from a knowledge base. By converting use case ontologies into instances in their simulation ontology, using a suitable parser, this related work manages to overcome the time-restriction issue of simulations, even in complex and dynamic environments, also considering the uncertainty of information.

A number of other related processes should be performed by simulation tools. For example, in related work [5], in order to limit energy consumption during data transmis-sion in UWSNs, an Edge-Drone-based software-defined smart IoUT network is proposed and compared to existing approaches, using QualNet simulator. The energy restrictions of underwater sensors, in combination with the continuous process of data analysis, have serious impact in the network. Utilizing this tool, authors managed to perform accurate measurements, and extract useful conclusions for factors such as the packet delivery ratio.

Another active stand-alone open-source tool, namely Gazebo [13, 14], has been included in our survey. Except from its scalability, ease of installation and handling, it is suitable for integration with ROS. This feature allows us to represent swarm of UUVs in an UWSN. Our research plan includes this extension in order to be able to represent packet flows during communications, as well as their protocols and the integration of the Simultaneous Localization and Mapping (SLAM) ontology [10].

Furthermore, simulation tools in the of cybersecurity domain were also investigated. Considering the diversity of each attack strategy and the need for quick response, simplicity of operation, but also facilitation of integrating various data and knowledge from databases, we have examined Nessi2 (Network Security Simulator) [43]. This is network security simulation software providing scalability, fidelity, and extensibility. It has been used for evaluating the security of network architectures [19]. By using MySQL as its main backend database, users can insert any entity, relation or event needed.

HackIt is another tool used for building dynamic cyber-attack scenarios [1]. Providing a realistic approach to a cyber-attack, essentially it provides scanning for vulnerabilities and gaining access. Also, HackIt run various commands used by adversaries, such as *nmap* and *msfconsole,* and is suitable for representing deception method, such as honeypots and honeynets.

Moreover, an effective representation of cyber-attacks must be able to establish the necessary security protocols and confront adversaries or restore the function of the network. In related work [9], an open-source tool chain for modeling and simulating attacks, namely Power-Attack, is utilized. In order to simulate attacks in power systems, but also analyze them, this tool uses a sequence of steps, and PyPower-Dynamics, to provide an extra security layer for dynamic sophisticated attacks. Its major advantage is the fully editable source-code written entirely in Python.

Caldera is an open-source simulation tool for Linux OS, which provides users the ability to create their own adversaries and defenders, as well as their abilities [7, 27]. Thereafter, the process of attack and defend is fully automated. Because of its automated nature, reproducing the same processes is straight forward. Also, the extensibility of this tool is very useful for the cyber domain, due to the heterogeneity of strategies and methods.

Probably one of the most modern open-source penetration testing tools is the Infection Monkey [15]. It has numerous features and configurations e.g., the ability to be executed inside the user's network in order to breach it using methods, tools and strategies from remarkable sources of this domain such as the MITRE ATT&ACK [28] knowledge base. The process is fully automated and can be configured to infect another host to make it a zombie machine. Furthermore, the users can choose specific attack and defense methods, and import their files from external databases.

Finally, with the aim to implement a robotic sensing network to respond adaptively to extreme underwater environmental changes, related work [4] realizes this through a Digital Twin prototype approach. Researchers have managed to reduce cost and time factors drastically by overcoming real-life challenges, such as the replacement of under-water observation system due to software errors and the absence of vessel and crew. Thus, when an adjustment improves measurements in a Digital Twin, it sends a specific message to its Physical Twin in order to inform it, and to make the same adjustment in turn. Authors conclude that Digital Twins prototypes are suitable for simulation in underwater networks.

Although simulation tools support decision-making, the new trend lying above IoT layer is Digital Twins. This technology concerns the bidirectional management of enti-ties and assets of a simulated environment. Tools for representing and managing Digital Twins are neither limited to simulation, nor to the representation of digital prototypes. These tools essentially replicate processes, bridging the digital with the physical infor-mation to model and predict its condition's degradation throughout system's lifecycle and performance [20, 41]. Digital Twins is the future, but this topic is out of the scope of this paper.

Low-bit rate issues, due to the medium (water), have as a consequence latency in exchanging information, which, in combination with the native complexity of UWSN, emerges vulnerabilities in network architecture robustness, affecting the known CIA Triad (Confidentiality, Integrity, Availability of data). In related work [36], the Unified Cybersecurity Ontology (UCO) is presented. UCO, in order to support information integration and cyber situational awareness, maps the most commonly used cybersecurity standards. On the other hand, in Cybersecurity Vulnerability Ontology (CVO) [35], knowledge about known attacks, patterns and strategies of adversaries, as well as possible vulnerabilities exploitation, are included. In related work [35], CVO is utilized in order to develop an accurate and effective cyber intelligence alert system.

Decision-making and adaptive-planning, two main capabilities of UUVs, are depended on a key factor i.e., weather conditions. In related work [37], efforts to over-come sensor-generated Big Data restrictions, as well as to extract accurate informa-tion about weather conditions at exact locations, the Oceanographic Weather Ontol-ogy (OWO) is proposed, supporting data integration in a single platform for analysis, information retrieval, and decision making. The experimental results with the proposed weather data model, data processing, ontology creation, and a query engine, prove the overall importance of the OWO.

3   Experiments and Proposed Approach

Threat modeling automation, distributed simulation, and integration of ontologies in various domains, are necessary to approach the presented problem. The main reason is the heterogeneity and complexity of the UWSN and IoUT domains. So, blending various approaches, tools and methods that originate from those domains is highly promising.

Several related ontologies have been developed or are under development by our team, specifically in the related domains of IoT/IoT-trust[1], drones' semantic trajecto-ries[2], Digital Twins[3], and cybersecurity for communication/network assets. Our aim

---

[1] https://github.com/KotisK/IoTontos.

[2] https://github.com/KotisK/onto4drone.

[3] https://github.com/KotisK/SEC4DigiT.

is to integrate them with existing semantic approaches of cybersecurity and underwater domain ontologies (UCO, CVO and OWO) and utilize them in selected simulation tools. Our previous work in the representation of heterogeneous trustworthy IoT entities to facilitate their semantic data integration in other domains (smart cultural spaces) [42], will be also applied here.

Initially, in order to prove the ease/risk of a cyber-attack and its consequences, we have been experimenting with two different operating systems, a Kali Linux (host machine) as the adversary and a Windows Server 2019 (target machine) as the UUV, or the central platform on surface, or even a surface buoy which communicates with the central platform. We have developed these systems through virtualization using VMware Workstation. The experimentation involves attacker eavesdropped communications using simple tools (Wireshark [3, 40]), extracted vulnerabilities, and the MITM (Man in the Middle) performed ARP Poisoning [39]; a method when attacker tries to associate its IP address with the victim's. The scenario includes adversarial redirection of every command issued by the commander or the leader of a UUV in the adversarial machine. Hence, by "confusing" UUVs, and gaining administrative privileges by taking advantage of vulnerabilities, as well as extracting all necessary information from the knowledge base of the UWSN, the adversary performs a DoS (Denial of Service) attack, by overwhelming the network. Finally, the Security Operations Center (SOC) of the Central Platform imports some new security rules, in order to defend against this type of attack in the future, and implements a honeynet for early alert. Although this approach is the most effective due to the manual attacking method and strategy of the user, it requires knowledge of cyber-security domain commands and tools, and comes in conflict with the required quickness in a critical real-time situation.

Further experimentation was conducted using a semi-automated tool for attack and response, namely Caldera [20]. Process initialized by creating an adversary (agent) with the ability to scan, enumerate, and exploit our network architecture, and then we attacked a given IP address. The responder of the created incident, with its own abilities, was ready to counter these attacks with its own tools, simulating a real-time process. From exported log files we were able to conclude how vulnerable the network is. Ease of handling and configuration of this tool satisfies the need of fast and precise responses, supporting decision-making process of commanders.

Due to its advantage of importing files in XML/RDF format, facilitating the integration of semantic knowledge/ontologies, Nessi2 tool was evaluated. We have achieved the development of semantics in respect to necessary entities and relations between them, such as *attack-type*, *event-type*, etc., as well as *weather conditions* at specific *locations*. Also, we have managed to represent a logical topology of the experimental scenario. Our future goal is the extension of this tool and the realization of a completed scenario.

For our last experiment, a fully automated attack and response process using Infection Monkey [21] has been utilized. The first step was the configuration of attacker machine (in Kali Linux OS). Then, we exploited two target machines (Windows Server 2019 and Ubuntu). To evaluate its functionality, we tried to infect one of the hosts, in order to manipulate it, and unleash our attacks from it. The result was to remain undetected. Finally, from the Security Reports tab, we were able to view critical vulnerabilities about our network architecture.

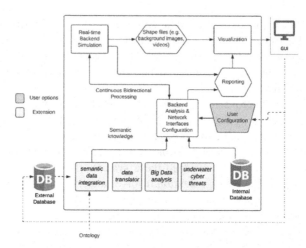

Fig. 2. General high-level architectural design of the proposed cybersecurity simulation tool.

Based on the above-mentioned experimentation and on challenges/issues related to the UWSN and IoUT domains presented in previous sections, we have concluded that it is possible to extend current functionality of existing simulation tools towards supporting the requirements specified in our preliminary work. The high-level architectural design of such an extension is briefly described below (and depicted in Fig. 2):

- Initially, a primary configuration of data found in the internal database of the simulation tool (e.g., plug-ins, user environment, shape files, etc.) is taking place and representation of the initial graphical user interface is displayed. Then, numerous options of the tool can be configured (import templates, network creation, agent configuration, asset creation, etc.), depending on the scenario at hand.
- Thereafter, the Backend Analysis and Network configuration may start, continuously sharing data with the process of Backend Simulation, but also to Reporting.
- When Backend Simulation is prepared, elements from user configuration (background images, etc.) may be also imported.
- Then, Visualization process may start, exporting the graphical content to the user, combined with reporting information (network vulnerabilities, elements of time, statistics, etc.).
- Finally, the whole process can be restarted, either with the same configuration or with a new one.

In order to achieve a robust simulation using an ontological model, capable of a) translating semantic knowledge, b) analyzing huge volumes of heterogeneous data, and c) simulating specific underwater cyber-attacks, we propose the following extensions:

- A *semantic data integration* framework, providing the ability to integrate heterogeneous data in various formats,
- A *data translator framework*, which will convert semantic data in a language understandable by the simulation tool,

- A *Big Data analysis framework*, in order to analyze input data, and extract knowledge and conclusions from them, utilizing the huge amount of data in UWSNs,
- An *underwater cyber threats* framework, which will comprise libraries (tactics, strategies, threats, attacks, etc.) specifically about Internet of Underwater Things, as well as tools to simulate such attacks.

4 Discussion and Future Plans

Based on extensive research in IoUT and cybersecurity domains, we have identified the need to further investigate the key issue of interoperability, standardization, and the lack of common communication protocols. A recent representative approach for tackling this issue is the initiative to define a common language to achieve initial contact and data exchange between nodes, namely, the JANUS by NATO STO CMRE [32, 34]. This is the first underwater digital communications protocol which was promulgated as a NATO standard, enabling interoperability between heterogeneous military and civilian devices. Moreover, in combination with the Software-to-Software Communications protocol [16], the challenge of a required common message encoding and decoding scheme is also delimited.

During further investigation on the topic, we have identified the lack of semantic modeling and simulation tools specifically for the underwater cybersecurity domain. It appears that the communication protocols between traditional operating systems differ from those in underwater communications. Underwater assets include electro-acoustic transducers to receive and transmit sound signals [2]. Thus, adversaries exploit the native vulnerability of water, i.e., latency, but also the inability of inspection of compromised nodes. Hence, the classification of attacks also differs. Node infection, Protocol-Oriented and Repudiation attacks or Jamming DoS are a few examples [37]. On the other hand, countermeasure methods are very similar, making the goal of our research more feasible.

Finally, as the high-level design of the proposed cybersecurity simulation tool is shown in Fig. 2, our future plans include the extension of cybersecurity simulation tools described in Sect. 3. The selection of such tools will be based on availability of source code, license, and developer support, as well as on the requirements that such tool meet in terms of the proposed designed architecture. Gazebo and Nessi2 are two candidates that partially cover requirements in respect to semantic modeling, cybersecurity simulation, simulation of dynamic underwater environments, simulation of swarm of UUVs in IoUT.

5 Conclusion

Although UUVs and their applications are popular in civil and military operations, the establishment of interoperability across various platforms, and the establishment of robust underwater network architectures in IoUT from a cybersecurity perspective, are key challenges. Sharing knowledge between trustworthy IoUT assets in a common machine-understandable language is the key to overcome communication issues emerging due to their heterogeneity and the volume of data they produce. The volume of data, in combination with latency issues in the medium of water, result to numerous vulnerabilities and security issues in UWSNs. Automated threat modeling, semantic knowledge representation, and simulation of the above challenges is required, in order to be able to efficiently predict the impact of fast and trustworthy decision-making in critical situations such as military and SAR ones. Towards this direction, in this paper we have presented related, proposed, and future work towards the semantic modeling and simulation of cybersecurity on the IoUT.

References

1. Aggarwal, P., Gonzalez, C., Dutt, V.: HackIt: a real-time simulation tool for studying real-world cyberattacks in the laboratory. In: Gupta, B.B., Perez, G.M., Agrawal, D.P., Gupta, D. (eds.) Handbook of Computer Networks and Cyber Security, pp. 949–959. Springer, Cham (2020). https://doi.org/10.1007/978-3-030-22277-2_39
2. Ahmad, I., et al.: Analysis of security attacks and taxonomy in underwater wireless sensor networks. Wirel. Commun. Mob. Comput. **2021** (2021). https://doi.org/10.1155/2021/1444024
3. Bagyalakshmi, G., et al.: Network vulnerability analysis on brain signal/image databases using Nmap and Wireshark tools. IEEE Access **6**, 57144–57151 (2018). https://doi.org/10.1109/ACCESS.2018.2872775
4. Barbie, A., et al.: Developing an underwater network of ocean observation systems with digital twin prototypes - a field report from Baltic sea. IEEE Internet Comput. (2021). https://doi.org/10.1109/MIC.2021.3065245
5. Bhattacharjya, K., De, D.: IoUT: modelling and simulation of edge-drone-based software-defined smart internet of underwater things. Simul. Model. Pract. Theory **109**, 102304 (2021). https://doi.org/10.1016/j.simpat.2021.102304
6. Bouter, C., Kruiger, H., Verhoosel, J.: Domain-Independent Data Processing in an Ontology Based Data Access Environment Using the SOSA Ontology (2021). http://ceur-ws.org
7. Caldera Description page. https://www.pwc.co.uk/issues/imitation-game-attacker-emulation.html. Accessed 06 Mar 2022
8. Centelles, D., Soriano-Asensi, A., Martí, J.V., Marín, R., Sanz, P.J.: Underwater wireless communications for cooperative robotics with UWSim-NET. Appl. Sci. **9**(17), 3526 (2019). https://doi.org/10.3390/app9173526
9. Chhokra, A., Barreto, C., Dubey, A., Karsai, G., Koutsoukos, X.: Power-attack: a comprehensive tool-chain for modeling and simulating attacks in power systems (n.d.)
10. Cornejo-Lupa, M.A., Cardinale, Y., Ticona-Herrera, R., Barrios-Aranibar, D., Andrade, M., Diaz-Amado, J.: OntoSLAM: an ontology for representing location and simultaneous mapping information for autonomous robots. Robotics **10**(4), 125 (2021). https://doi.org/10.3390/robotics10040125
11. Domingo, M.C.: An overview of the internet of underwater things. J. Netw. Comput. Appl. **35**(6), 1879–1890 (2012). https://doi.org/10.1016/j.jnca.2012.07.012
12. Fattah, S., Gani, A., Ahmedy, I., Idris, M.Y.I., Hashem, I.A.T.: A survey on underwater wireless sensor networks: requirements, taxonomy, recent advances, and open research challenges. Sensors **20**(18), 1–30 (2020). https://doi.org/10.3390/s20185393
13. Gazebo Github page. https://github.com/osrf/gazebo. Accessed 06 Mar 2022
14. Gazebo Homepage. http://gazebosim.org/. Accessed 06 Mar 2022
15. Infection Monkey. https://github.com/guardicore/monkey. Accessed 06 Mar 2022
16. Braga, J., Martins, R., Petrioli, C., Petroccia, R., Picari, L.: Cooperation and networking in an underwater network composed by heterogeneous assets. In: OCEANS 2016 MTS/IEEE Monterey, pp. 1–9 (2016). https://doi.org/10.1109/OCEANS.2016.7761219

17. Janowicz, K., Haller, A., Cox, S.J.D., le Phuoc, D., Lefrançois, M.: SOSA: a lightweight ontology for sensors, observations, samples, and actuators. J. Web Semant. **56**, 1–10 (2019). https://doi.org/10.1016/j.websem.2018.06.003
18. Jurasky, W., Moder, P., Milde, M., Ehm, H., Reinhart, G.: Transformation of semantic knowledge into simulation-based decision support. Robot. Comput.-Integr. Manuf. **71**, 102174 (2021). https://doi.org/10.1016/j.rcim.2021.102174
19. Kamoun-Abid, F., Rekik, M., Meddeb-Makhlouf, A., Zarai, F.: Secure architecture for Cloud/Fog computing based on firewalls and controllers. Procedia Comput. Sci. **192**, 822–833 (2021). https://doi.org/10.1016/j.procs.2021.08.085
20. Kutzke, D.T., Carter, J.B., Hartman, B.T.: Subsystem selection for digital twin development: a case study on an unmanned underwater vehicle. Ocean Eng. **223**, 108629 (2021). https://doi.org/10.1016/j.oceaneng.2021.108629
21. LHN Infection Monkey page. https://latesthackingnews.com/2022/02/24/__trashed-4/. Accessed 06 Mar 2022
22. LinkedIn page. https://www.linkedin.com/pulse/auv-deepwater-search-rescue-arnt-helge-olsen/. Accessed 06 Mar 2022
23. Madan, B.B., Banik, M., Bein, D.: Securing unmanned autonomous systems from cyber threats. J. Defense Model. Simul. **16**(2), 119–136 (2019). https://doi.org/10.1177/154851291 6628335
24. Mary, D.R.K., Ko, E., Kim, S.-G., Yum, S.-H., Shin, S.-Y., Park, S.-H.: A systematic review on recent trends, challenges, privacy and security issues of underwater internet of things. Sensors **21**(24), 8262 (2021). https://doi.org/10.3390/s21248262
25. Menaka, D., Gauni, S., Manimegalai, C.T., Kalimuthu, K.: Vision of IoUT: advances and future trends in optical wireless communication. J. Opt. **50** (n.d.). https://doi.org/10.1007/s12596
26. Migueláñez, E., Patrón, P., Brown, K.E., Petillot, Y.R., Lane, D.M.: Semantic knowledge-based framework to improve the situation awareness of autonomous underwater vehicles. IEEE Trans. Knowl. Data Eng. **23**(5), 759–773 (2011). https://doi.org/10.1109/TKDE.201 0.46
27. MITRE ATT&CK Description page for Caldera. https://www.mitre.org/research/technology-transfer/open-source-software/caldera%E2%84%A2. Accessed 06 Mar 2022
28. MITRE ATT&CK Homepage. https://attack.mitre.org/. Accessed 06 Mar 2022
29. Nayyar, A., Balas, V.E.: Analysis of simulation tools for underwater sensor networks (UWSNs). In: Bhattacharyya, S., Hassanien, A.E., Gupta, D., Khanna, A., Pan, I. (eds.) International Conference on Innovative Computing and Communications. LNNS, vol. 55, pp. 165–180. Springer, Singapore (2019). https://doi.org/10.1007/978-981-13-2324-9_17
30. NS-3 Introduction page. https://www.nsnam.org/docs/release/3.21/tutorial/html/introduction.html. Accessed 06 Mar 2022
31. Oceanic Engineering Society (U.S.): Autonomous Underwater Vehicles 2016: AUV 2016: 6–9 November 2016, IIS, the University of Tokyo, Tokyo, Japan (n.d.)
32. Potter, J., Alves, J., Green, D., Zappa, G., McCoy, K., Nissen, I.: The JANUS underwater communications standard. In: 2014 Underwater Communications and Networking, UComms 2014 (2014). https://doi.org/10.1109/UComms.2014.7017134
33. Prats, M., Perez, J., Fernandez, J.J., Sanz, P.J.: An open-source tool for simulation and supervision of underwater intervention missions. In: IEEE International Conference on Intelligent Robots and Systems, pp. 2577–2582 (2012). https://doi.org/10.1109/IROS.2012.6385788
34. Public Affairs Office: NATO STO-CMRE Science and Technology Organization Centre for Maritime Research and Experimentation (2020)
35. Syed, R.: Cybersecurity vulnerability management: a conceptual ontology and cyber intelligence alert system. Inf. Manag. **57**(6), 103334 (2020). https://doi.org/10.1016/j.im.2020.103334

36. Syed, Z., Padia, A., Finin, T., Mathews, L., Joshi, A.: UCO: A Unified Cybersecurity Ontology (n.d.). http://tinyurl.com/ptqkzpq
37. Velu, A., Thangavelu, M.: Ontology based ocean knowledge representation for semantic information retrieval. Comput. Mater. Contin. **70**(3), 4707–4724 (2022). https://doi.org/10.32604/cmc.2022.020095
38. Wikipedia page. https://en.wikipedia.org/wiki/Air_France_Flight_447#Underwater_search. Accessed 06 Mar 2022
39. Wikipedia page for ARP spoofing. https://en.wikipedia.org/wiki/ARP_spoofing. Accessed 06 Mar 2022
40. Wireshark Home page. https://www.wireshark.org/docs/. Accessed 06 Mar 2022
41. Wu, J., Yang, Y., Cheng, X.U.N., Zuo, H., Cheng, Z.: The development of digital twin technology review. In: Proceedings - 2020 Chinese Automation Congress, CAC 2020, pp. 4901–4906 (2020). https://doi.org/10.1109/CAC51589.2020.9327756.
42. Zachila, K., Kotis, K., Paparidis, E., Ladikou, S., Spiliotopoulos, D.: Facilitating semantic interoperability of trustworthy IoT entities in cultural spaces: the smart museum ontology. IoT **2**(4), 741–760 (2021). https://doi.org/10.3390/iot2040037
43. Zhao, Y., Wang, Y., Zhang, H., Zhang, C., Yang, C.: Agent-based Network Security Simulator Nessi2 (2015)

Deep Learning - Convolutional

An Efficient Deep Learning Framework for Face Mask Detection in Complex Scenes

Sultan Daud Khan[1], Rafi Ullah[1], Mussadiq Abdul Rahim[1],
Muhammad Rashid[1], Zulfiqar Ali[1], Mohib Ullah[2(✉)], and Habib Ullah[3]

[1] Department of Computer Science, National University of Technology,
Islamabad, Pakistan
[2] Norwegian University of Science and Technology, 2815 Gjøvik, Norway
mohib.ullah@ntnu.no
[3] Faculty of Science and Technology, Norwegian University of Life Sciences,
1430 Ås, Norway

Abstract. COVID-19 has caused a global health crisis that has infected millions of people across the globe. Currently, the fourth wave of COVID-19 is about to be declared as Omicron. The new variant of COVID-19 has caused an unprecedented increase in cases. According to World Health Organization, safety measures must be adopted in public places to prevent the spread of the virus. One effective safety measure is to wear face masks in crowded places. To create a safe environment, government agencies adopt strict rules to ensure adherence to safety measures. However, it is difficult to manually analyze the crowded scenes and identify people violating the safety measures. This paper proposed an automated approach based on a deep learning framework that automatically analyses the complex scenes and identifies people with face masks or without facemasks. The proposed framework consists of two sequential parts. In the first part, we generate scale aware proposal to cover scale variations, and in the second part, the framework classifies each proposal. We evaluate the performance of the proposed framework on a challenging benchmark data set. We demonstrate that the proposed framework achieves high performance and outperforms other reference methods by a considerable margin from experimental results.

Keywords: Face mask detection · Deep learning · Multi-scale object proposals · Fully convolutional neural network

1 Introduction

COVID-19 has been spreading exponentially across the globe, causing more than 5 million deaths now. Due to the lack of proper medical treatment, World Health Organization (WHO) has recommended preventive measures, including wearing masks and maintaining social distance to control the further spread of the

I. Maglogiannis et al. (Eds.): AIAI 2022, IFIP AICT 646, pp. 159–169, 2022.
https://doi.org/10.1007/978-3-031-08333-4_13

disease. For this purpose, government agencies have adopted strict policies to ensure the adoption of preventive measures in public places. However, it is a complicated and tedious job to manually monitor a large number of people in an unconstrained environment. Therefore, in this work, we propose an artificial intelligence-based system that automatically detects and counts the number of people without wearing masks. We believe that the proposed system will support government agencies in predicting the outbreak of COVID-19 by using statistical data obtained by the proposed system.

Face-mask detection is a computer vision problem involving finding faces with masks on in images and videos. Face-mask in images can be easily identified with the human eye. However, the problem of detecting face-mask is challenging for computers due to the complex dynamics of human faces. Due to significant variation in scales [1], poses [2], and appearances of human heads [3], it remains a challenging problem to detect face-mask in complex scenes with high precision and recall rates. Therefore, the goal of the face-masks detector is to detect faces with different orientations, poses, illumination, skin colour, and appearances. Convolutional neural networks (CNN) based deep learning models can easily address the problem of variations in pose and appearance in complex images since these models are inherently transnational invariant. However, CNN based deep learning models can not handle the variations in scales and sizes of objects in natural images, which becomes a challenging problem for the object detectors. Since variation in object scales naturally occurs in natural images, it is essential to address this problem precisely to detect objects of different scales. In this work, we employ a deep learning network and feed the network with a lot of training data to learn the best representative features of face masks. The input to our face-mask detector is an image, and the output is the bounding boxes around the head with a confidence score.

Most traditional methods treat the head detection problem as a particular case of object detection. Generally, the basic architecture of these models follows the pipeline of two-stage detectors, i.e., generation of object proposal followed by classification and regression stage. Object proposal generation network is the pre-processing step and mainly affects the performance of object detectors. The sliding window approach has been adopted by most object detectors that generate object proposals of different sizes and scales for each pixel. This strategy leads to computational cost since it will generate many proposals. This strategy also leads to the accumulation of many bounding boxes around a single object, which lowers the object detector's precision and recall rates. To address these problems, several methods have been reported in the literature to generate the optimum number of object proposals while increasing the precision and recall rates. For example, EdgeBox [4] exploits edge information to generate object proposals that precisely hypothesize an object's location. DeepBox [5] proposed a method that re-ranks the object proposals using a bottom-up strategy to improve the objectness. Deep Proposal [6] builds an inverse cascade network that uses the initial and final layers of the convolutional neural network to hypothesize the promising location of the object. Multi-Box [7] hypothesize the object location by employing bounding box regression.

Usually natural videos and images are complex, where similar objects are different from each other in terms of scales and sizes. For example, the size of objects near the camera appears large, while the size of the same object appears small at a distance. Due to these problems, current two-stage object detectors face challenges detecting an object of various scales. We present a novel strategy for generating object proposals that will capture a wide range of variations in object scales to address this problem. Precisely, we propose a scale-aware object detection framework that follows the traditional pipeline of object detection and consists of the following sequential modules:

1. The first module is the object proposal generation network, which generates multi-scale object proposals to capture the scale distribution of the heads that appeared in an image. Briefly, we train a head/background binary classifier using a fully convolutional network (FCN) [8] on image patches with annotated heads. This network can take an image of arbitrary size and output a dense heat map or objectness map. Each pixel of the heat map shows the probability of the presence of a head and background. For this purpose, we exploit FCN to generate object proposals of different scales and sizes by first generating an image pyramid of multiple levels. Each level of the pyramid corresponds to a copy of the original image of a different resolution. We then feed each pyramid level to FCN and obtain a heat map. The size of the heat map is equal to the size of the corresponding level. After generating heat maps of multiple resolutions, we then resize the feature maps to the same size and employ the non-maximal suppression method to suppress low confidence locations and generate object proposals for the classification stage
2. The second module is the detection module that takes each proposal as an input and provides each proposal to two sibling branches. The first branch classifies each proposal into pre-defined classes, and the second branch is the regression branch that predicts the coordinates of bounding boxes.

We summarize the contribution of proposed framework as follows:

- We exploit a Fully Convolutional Network (FCN) to generate high-quality multi-scale object proposals.
- The proposed object proposal generation strategy reduces the computational cost and increases precision and recall rate compared to traditional approaches.
- We evaluate the performance of the proposed framework on challenging datasets, and from experiment results, we demonstrate the effectiveness of the proposed framework
- We compare the proposed framework with statistical and deep learning models and demonstrate that the proposed framework outperforms other reference methods.

2 Proposed Methodology

In this section, we provide the details of the proposed methodology. As shown in Fig. 1, the input to the framework is an image of arbitrary size, and the output is the set of bounding boxes over the people wearing face-mask. Generally, the proposed framework consists of two sequential networks. The first network is the object proposal generation network. The object proposal generation network is responsible for generating multi-scale proposals of various sizes. The second network is the classification network that classifies each proposal (generated during the first stage) into two classes, i.e., a person with a face mask or without a face mask. We generate multi-scale object proposals by first generating an image pyramid of N number of levels and then providing each level of the pyramid to the object proposal network as an input. The object proposal network generates a heat map that corresponds to each level. We then apply a non-maximum suppression algorithm to suppress the background and obtain the regions belonging to people wearing face masks.

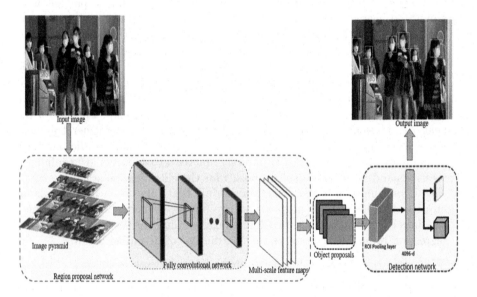

Fig. 1. Pipeline of proposed face-mask detector framework

2.1   Object Proposal Network

The proposed object proposal generation network is based on VGG16 [9], which is a widely adopted model for image classification tasks. The proposed object proposal generation network consists of a stack of five convolutional blocks. The first convolutional block $Block_1$ consists of two convolutional layers, with a filter size of 3×3 and stride 1. The reason behind using the smallest filter size is to capture more delicate details and preserve the spatial resolution of the feature maps. Similarly, the second convolutional block $Block_2$ consists of two convolutional layers with a filter size of 3×3 and a stride of 1. While $Block_3, Block_4, Block_5$ consist of three convolutional layers. The feature map from each convolutional block is passed through the max-pooling layer of filter size 2×2 and stride 2.

Max-pooling layer reduces the resolution of the input feature map and reduces the parameter to increase the training process. The feature maps are then passed through a stack of three fully convolutional layers of size 1×1. We obtain a feature map for each level of the pyramid and then apply the non-maximum suppression method to obtain high confidence object proposals of different sizes. We then apply the ROI-pooling layer to normalize object proposals that will re-size object proposals to make them fit for the detection network.

Difference with Other Networks: Our proposed object proposal generation network is similar to Region Proposal Network (RPN) [10]. However, it differs in the following ways. RPN uses the feature map of the last convolutional layer for generating object proposals. Due to the large receptive field, the last convolutional layer can cover large objects, while the information about the small objects is lost. This is due to the reason that RPN is not able to detect small objects in complex scenes. Furthermore, RPN uses a limited and fixed object scale set $\{128, 256, 512\}$ with limited aspect ratios of $\{1 : 1, 1 : 2, 2 : 1\}$ for detecting multi-scale objects in an image. Such limited scale sets are inadequate for detecting multi-scale objects in complex scenes. Compared to large objects, the size and scale of the human head vary significantly in crowded scenes. However, (RPN) [10] due to limited scale range, can not cover all ranges of scales. Our proposed object proposal network is different from RPN because the proposed network is independent of anchors and generates object proposals specific to the object class.

2.2 Training

For training the object proposal network, we use a patch-wise training scheme. For this purpose, we divide the image into K number of overlapped patches. We then compute Intersection-over-Union (IoU) for each patch. IoU measures the percent of overlap between the given patch and ground truth and computed as $\text{IoU} = \frac{\Omega_p \cap \Omega_g}{\Omega_p \cup \Omega_g}$, where Ω_p is the patch of an image and Ω_g is the ground truth. We select patches as positive samples for which IoU ≥ 0.5 and the rest of the patches are treated as negative samples. Since the background primarily occupies natural images, the number of negative patches will be much larger than positive patches. This creates a data imbalance problem that affects the generalization capability of the network, as the network will be getting more biased towards the negative samples/background. To increase the number of positive samples, we crop several patches around the human head and adopt a data augmentation technique [11] to generate different variants of positive patches.

We use Xavier technique [12] for initializing the weights of the network and use the stochastic gradient descent (SGD) strategy with a learning rate of 0.01 for training the network. We gradually decrease the learning process by using the strategy adopted in [13]. We train the network for 100 epochs on Titan-V GPU with 12 GB RAM and use a batch size of 512 samples.

2.3   Detection Network

After obtaining object proposals using the network discussed in Sect. 2.1, we then employ a detection network that classifies each proposal into pre-defined classes and predicts the bounding boxes. Our detection network re-size multi-scale object proposals by employing an ROI pooling layer and then feeding each object proposal to two different branches. The first is the classification branch, which classifies the object proposals into two categories. The second branch is the regression branch that predicts the bounding boxes of the input proposals.

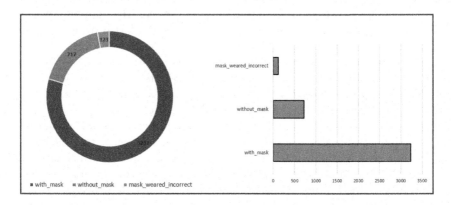

Fig. 2. Distribution of dataset among three classes.

3   Experiment Results

This section provides the details of the dataset used for evaluating and comparing the proposed framework with other related methods. We also discuss the various metrics used for the evaluation.

Mask Dataset: This dataset is collected by MakeML community and is publicly available on the link: https://makeml.app/datasets/mask. The dataset consists of different images captured from different scenes. The images are of different resolutions, and the human head has a wide range of variations in scale, size, orientation, illumination, and appearance. The dataset consists of 4072 images and three classes, i.e., with_mask, without_mask, and mask_weared_incorrect. The distribution of images among these three classes is shown in Fig. 4. From Fig. 4, it is obvious that the dataset contains a large number of images (3232) belonging to the with_mask class, 717 images belong to without_mask and only 123 images to mask_weared_incorrect class. We divide the dataset into two splits, i.e., training and testing. We randomly select 70% images for training and the rest of 30% for testing. Few samples from the dataset are shown in Fig. 3.

To quantitatively evaluate and compare the performance of the proposed framework with other related methods, we use the mean average precision (mAP) metric, which is widely used for evaluating the performance of object detectors.

Fig. 3. Illustrates some random samples of the dataset

Mean average precision (mAP) computes a score and measures how well the detector predicts the object's location by comparing the predicted bounding box and ground truth. Mean average precision is calculated as follows:

$$mAP = \frac{1}{N} \sum_{c=1}^{k=N} AP_c \tag{1}$$

Where N is the total number of classes, and AP_c is the average precision of class c. We now evaluate and compare the proposed framework with other reference methods. For comparisons, we divide the experiment set up into two phases. In the first phase, we compare the proposed framework with hand-crafted feature models, while in the second phase, we perform a comparison with deep learning models. During the first phase of the experiment, we use three different versions of the Viola-Jones algorithm [14] based on the feature selection, namely, VJ-LBP, VJ-HOG, VJ-CRF [15]. We implement these models in MATLAB using built-in functions. In addition to these variants, we use DPM [16] and FFD [17] for comparisons. For DPM, we use the code available on https://github.com/rbgirshick/voc-dpm and for FFD, we use code available on https://github.com/apennisi/fast_face_detector. We use these codes to train the model on the mask dataset, and the obtained results are then compared with the proposed framework. The results of these models are reported in Table 1.

From Table 1, it is evident that the proposed framework beats other reference methods by a significant margin. We observe from experiment results that variants of Viola-Jones face difficulty in detecting heads and faces with different orientations. We observed that these models are very sensitive to noise and

Table 1. Comparison of proposed method with hand-crafted feature models

Methods	mAP @ 0.5	mAP @ 0.7
VJ-LBP	0.39	0.25
VJ-HOG	0.37	0.21
VJ-CRF	0.41	0.32
DPM-Head	0.53	0.47
FFD	0.46	0.39
Proposed	0.75	0.68

illumination, and as a result, these models produce many false positives that further degrade their performance. FFD also utilizes the learning pipeline of Viola-Jones and achieves good performance compared to other variants of Viola-Jones. This is because FFD re-ranks the score of the bounding boxes and adopts a multi-view detection strategy to accumulate channel features. Furthermore, we observe that DPM-Head can detect medium or large heads. However, it faces difficulty detecting small heads of size ($\leq 25 \times 25$ pixels).

We choose Faster R-CNN, R-CNN, SSD, YOLO, and Mask-RCN to compare the proposed framework's performance with other deep learning models. We fine-tunned these models on the mask dataset. To comprehensively analyze the performance of these models on the mask dataset, we use different backbone networks, for example, VGG16, AlexNet, and ZF. Furthermore, we also evaluate the performance of the proposed framework with these backbone networks.

Table 2. Comparison of proposed method with deep learning models

Models	Deep models	mAP @ 0.5
Faster R-CNN [10]	ZF [18]	0.71
	VGG16 [9]	0.72
	AlexNet [19]	0.67
R-CNN [20]	ZF [18]	0.66
	VGG16 [9]	0.68
	AlexNet [19]	0.63
YOLO [21]	13-layered architecture	0.62
SSD [7]	VGG16 [9]	0.58
Proposed	ZF [18]	0.73
	VGG16 [9]	0.75
	AlexNet [19]	0.69

We report the results of these models in Table 2. From Table 2, it is evident that the proposed framework achieves good results compared to other deep learning models. Yolo and SSD achieve relatively low performance. Since these models use the feature map of the last convolutional layer, these models face challenges in detecting small heads that negatively affect the performance. On the other hand, the proposed framework captures significant variation in object scales by generating scale-aware proposals and accurately detecting heads in complex scenes.

Fig. 4. Visualization of results generated by the proposed method. Detected bounding boxes are labeled with the confidence score. (best view is zoomed in)

4   Conclusion

We proposed an efficient detection model to detect people with face masks and without face masks. The proposed framework utilizes a fully convolutional network to generate scale-aware proposals to cover scale variations naturally occurring in images. We perform experiments on challenging benchmark datasets. We evaluate the performance of the proposed framework in both quantitative and qualitative ways. The experiment results demonstrate that the proposed framework beats other reference methods by a significant margin. In future work, we further enhance the performance of the proposed framework and deploy the framework in real-time.

References

1. Khan, S.D., Altamimi, A.B., Ullah, M., Ullah, H., Cheikh, P.A.: TCM: temporal consistency model for head detection in complex videos. J. Sensor. 2020 (2020)
2. Ullah, M., Ullah, H., Alseadonn, I.M.: Human action recognition in videos using stable features (2017)
3. Ullah, M., Kedir, M.A., Cheikh, F.A.: Hand-crafted vs deep features: a quantitative study of pedestrian appearance model. In: 2018 Colour and Visual Computing Symposium (CVCS), pp. 1–6. IEEE (2018)
4. Zitnick, C.L., Dollár, P.: Edge boxes: locating object proposals from edges. In: Fleet, D., Pajdla, T., Schiele, B., Tuytelaars, T. (eds.) ECCV 2014. LNCS, vol. 8693, pp. 391–405. Springer, Cham (2014). https://doi.org/10.1007/978-3-319-10602-1_26
5. Kuo, W., Hariharan, B., Malik, J.: Deepbox: learning objectness with convolutional networks. In: Proceedings of the IEEE International Conference on Computer Vision, pp. 2479–2487 (2015)
6. Ghodrati, A., Diba, A., Pedersoli, M., Tuytelaars, T., Van Gool, L.: Deepproposal: Hunting objects by cascading deep convolutional layers. In: Proceedings of the IEEE International Conference on Computer Vision, pp. 2578–2586 (2015)
7. Liu, W., Anguelov, D., Erhan, D., Szegedy, C., Reed, S., Fu, C.-Y., Berg, A.C.: SSD: single shot MultiBox detector. In: Leibe, B., Matas, J., Sebe, N., Welling, M. (eds.) ECCV 2016. LNCS, vol. 9905, pp. 21–37. Springer, Cham (2016). https://doi.org/10.1007/978-3-319-46448-0_2
8. Long, J., Shelhamer, E., Darrell, T.: Fully convolutional networks for semantic segmentation. In: Proceedings of the IEEE Conference on Computer Vision and Pattern Recognition, pp. 3431–3440 (2015)
9. Simonyan, K., Zisserman, A.: Very deep convolutional networks for large-scale image recognition. arXiv preprint arXiv:1409.1556 (2014)
10. Ren, S., He, K., Girshick, R., Sun, J.: Faster R-CNN: towards real-time object detection with region proposal networks. Adv. Neural Inf. Process. Syst. **28**, 91–99 (2015)
11. Perez, L., Wang, J.: The effectiveness of data augmentation in image classification using deep learning. arXiv preprint arXiv:1712.04621 (2017)
12. Glorot, X., Bengio, Y.: Understanding the difficulty of training deep feedforward neural networks. In: Proceedings of the Thirteenth International Conference on Artificial Intelligence and Statistics, pp. 249–256. JMLR Workshop and Conference Proceedings (2010)

13. Garipov, T., Izmailov, P., Podoprikhin, O., Vetrov, O., Wilson, A.G.: Loss surfaces, mode connectivity, and fast ensembling of DNNs. In: Proceedings of the 32nd International Conference on Neural Information Processing Systems, pp. 8803–8812 (2018)
14. Viola, P., Jones, M.: Rapid object detection using a boosted cascade of simple features. In: Proceedings of the 2001 IEEE Computer Society Conference on Computer Vision and Pattern Recognition. CVPR 2001, vol.1, pp. I–I. IEEE (2001)
15. Ren, X.: Finding people in archive films through tracking. In: 2008 IEEE Conference on Computer Vision and Pattern Recognition, pp. 1–8. IEEE (2008)
16. Felzenszwalb, P.F., Girshick, R.S., McAllester, D., Ramanan, D.: Object detection with discriminatively trained part-based models. IEEE Trans. Pattern Anal. Mach. Intell. **32**(9), 1627–1645 (2009)
17. Yang, B., Yan, J., Lei, Z., Li, Z.:Aggregate channel features for multi-view face detection. In: IEEE International Joint Conference on Biometrics, pp. 1–8. IEEE (2014)
18. Zeiler, M.D., Fergus, R.: Visualizing and understanding convolutional networks. In: Fleet, D., Pajdla, T., Schiele, B., Tuytelaars, T. (eds.) ECCV 2014. LNCS, vol. 8689, pp. 818–833. Springer, Cham (2014). https://doi.org/10.1007/978-3-319-10590-1_53
19. Krizhevsky, A., Sutskever, B., Hinton, G.E.: ImageNet classification with deep convolutional neural networks. Adv. Neural Inf. Processing Systems, **25**, 1097–1105 (2012)
20. Girshick, R., Donahue, J., Darrell, T., Malik, J.: Rich feature hierarchies for accurate object detection and semantic segmentation. In: Proceedings of the IEEE Conference on Computer Vision and Pattern Recognition, pp. 580–587 (2014)
21. Redmon, J., Farhadi, A.: Yolo9000: better, faster, stronger. In: Proceedings of the IEEE Conference on Computer Vision and Pattern Recognition, pp. 7263–7271 (2017)

An Efficient Method for Addressing COVID-19 Proximity Related Issues in Autonomous Shuttles Public Transportation

Dimitris Tsiktsiris[1,2], Antonios Lalas[1]([✉]), Minas Dasygenis[2], Konstantinos Votis[1], and Dimitrios Tzovaras[1]

[1] Information Technologies Institute, Center for Research and Technology Hellas, 6th km Xarilaou - Thermi, 57001 Thessaloniki, Greece
{tsiktsiris,lalas,kvotis,dimitrios.tzovaras}@iti.gr
[2] Department of Electrical and Computer Engineering, University of Western Macedonia, 50100 Kozani, Greece
mdasyg@ieee.org

Abstract. The COVID-19 pandemic has created significant restrictions to passenger mobility through public transportation. Several proximity rules have been applied to ensure sufficient distance between passengers and mitigate contamination. In conventional transportation, abiding by the rules can be ensured by the driver of the vehicle. However, this is not obvious in Autonomous Vehicles (AVs) public transportation systems, since there is no driver to monitor these special circumstances. Since, AVs constitute an emerging mobility infrastructure, it is obvious that creating a system that can provide a sense of safety to the passenger, when the driver is absent, is a challenging task. Several studies employ computer vision and deep learning techniques to increase safety in unsupervised environments. In this work, an image-based approach, supported by novel AI algorithms, is proposed as a service to increase the COVID-19 safety rules adherence of the passengers inside an autonomous shuttle. The proposed real-time service, can detect deviations from proximity rules and notify the authorized personnel, while it is possible to be further extended in other application domains, where automated proximity assessment is critical.

Keywords: Autonomous vehicles · Public transportation · Neural networks · Image processing

1 Introduction

Public transportation systems progressively adopt the concept of autonomous mobility as a service (MaaS) [2]. However, the transition to fully autonomous

Supported by the European Union's Horizon 2020 Research and Innovation Programme Autonomous Vehicles to Evolve to a New Urban Experience (AVENUE) under Grant Agreement No 769033.

I. Maglogiannis et al. (Eds.): AIAI 2022, IFIP AICT 646, pp. 170–179, 2022.
https://doi.org/10.1007/978-3-031-08333-4_14

public vehicles is not seamless and several obstacles arise in the real-world. With the rapid and continuous spreading to this day, COVID-19 is without doubt one of these obstacles. Although urban travel has declined across the globe, public transportation is considered to be the sector that has gotten the hardest hit, as indicated by survey-based data [9]. The phenomenon is caused due to the sometimes-unavoidable closer contact that is observed between people using public transportation vehicles or stations, leading to the impression of public transportation being riskier than any other personal or private means of transport. In addition, the fact that an infected with COVID-19 passenger can contaminate many more before even showing any symptoms [4,7] is especially troublesome for public spaces. Some of the factors that can lead to a high risk of contamination in public vehicles and stations are listed below:

- Limited space for passengers. The risk of contamination increases in proportion to the number of passengers that are confined in the limited space of the vehicle or the station. Since the global pandemic arised, the level of discomfort associated with public transportation has been increased considering the added risk of becoming infected by COVID-19.
- The inability to recognize passengers or workers who may be infected.
- The ease of transferring germs through multiple surfaces, like ticket machines, doors, handrails, or seats.

Nonetheless, there are ways that can mitigate the associated risk to the aforementioned factors. Furthermore, the level of the contamination risk one takes when traveling versus performing activities in public places, for example, is yet to be determined, as several variables determine these levels in different sets of environments. One of the most universally applied measure to prevent the transmission of COVID-19 is physical or social distancing, which started as a recommendation from the World Health Organization (WHO) so as to keep a distance from another individual of at least 1.0 m apart [12]. Although other health organizations recommend keeping a physical proximity of two meters, the original suggestion of WHO has been found to significantly reduce the COVID-19 transmission [1]. Even though conflicting with the concept of public transportation, social distancing is considered, to this day, the most important non-pharmaceutical prevention measure for public transportation services, as physical distancing strongly reduces the level of occupancy in vehicles and stations that serve travellers [10].

Up until now, many technology-based solutions have been proposed across the globe to cope with the COVID-19 [8]. A lot of researchers are looking into the fields of computer vision and deep-learning in order to develop solutions able to reduce virus spread. New, but also existing state-of-the-art technologies are employed for this purpose, tailored in specific applications to reduce COVID-19 propagation.

In this paper, we present an image-based approach, supported by novel AI algorithms, as an end-to-end service to increase the COVID-19 safety rules adherence of the passengers inside an autonomous shuttle. The proposed real-time service, can detect deviations from proximity rules and enable notifications to authorized personnel. Moreover, we implement optimizations tailored to the Autonomous Shuttles for reduced area and power consumption.

The main contributions of this work can be summarized as follows:

- We propose an end-to-end service based on deep learning, for automated distance assessment in Autonomous Shuttles.
- We deploy the service on embedded devices and introduce smart techniques such as adaptive inference to reduce the power consumption.
- We introduce a new dataset for passenger detection from overhead cameras tailored on the environment of the Autonomous Shuttles.

2   Related Work

Various countries track the location data of the suspected and infected individuals using GPS technology. An assortment of different emerging technologies that have a prime role in social distancing scenarios, including Wireless networks, smart devices, Global Positioning System (GPS), computer vision, and deep learning, is proposed by Nguyen et al. [11]. Other studies exploit UAVs and camera sensors for detecting large crowds [5]. So far, several progress has been made in detecting the virus [6]. A study by Prem et al. [14] on the impacts of social distancing upon stopping the virus transmission concluded that it could slowly decrease the peak of the virus attack; however, social distancing remains an unpleasant step for many sectors of the economy. On the other hand, researchers provide effective solutions employing surveillance videos in addition to computer vision, machine learning, and deep learning-based approaches for measuring social distancing. A proposed framework by Punn et al. [15] employs firstly the YOLOv3 model for human detection and then the Deepsort [23] approach for tracking the detected individuals, using both assigned ID information and bounding boxes. As for the dataset, the authors used a frontal view dataset by an open image dataset repository and compared their results with faster-RCNN [18] and SSD [24]. Another approach by Ramadass et al. [16] implemented an autonomous drone-based model for social distance monitoring by using a custom training dataset for the YOLOv3 [17] algorithm, comprised of both front and side perspective frames of people. Opposed to the previous approach by Punn, Ramadass's does monitor face masks too, as the use of a drone camera in conjunction with the YOLOv3 model helps in identifying the physical distance, as well as monitoring individuals with masks in public, from the frontal or side view. Sathyamoorthy et al. [19] implemented their model for detecting people who do not obey social distancing restrictions in crowded situations, using an autonomous robot with an RGB-D sensor and a lidar in order to navigate among crowded places. Lastly, Pouw's et al. [13] proposed framework constitutes a monitoring approach appropriate for social distancing.

Based on the reviewed literature, we have concluded that, even though a considerable progress has been made for monitoring social distancing in public environments, most of the work done is focused on the side or frontal view perspectives of the camera. Moreover, the aforementioned studies do not take into account the impact of power consumption, as energy efficiency is one of the most critical factors for the Autonomous Vehicles. In contrast, we provide an end-to-end solution as a service, tailored to the Autonomous Shuttle environment, with overhead camera perspective and low power consumption.

3 Methodology

Most of the aforementioned works focus on front and side view input for monitor proximity in public outdoor places. In this work, we present a deep learning-based distance assessment service using an overhead perspective, able to function with high accuracy and low power-consumption into the confined space of an autonomous shuttle. To overcome occlusion issues, we employ fisheye wide-angle cameras with a top-down perspective. In this section, we present the datasets used, followed by the network architecture. Finally, we describe the training process and the post-processing steps.

3.1 Dataset

We collected and labelled a new dataset named CERTH - AVenue Overhead Fisheye (C-AVOF). The new dataset contains frames and human objects in a simulated shuttle environment, and also includes challenging scenarios such as crowded rooms, various body poses, and various-light conditions. The camera used for the data capture process is the D-Link DCS-4625 at 1080p resolution output. During the annotation of this dataset, we used Deepsort [22] for tracking the individual passengers in the shuttle across multiple frames and thus our dataset can be also used for additional vision tasks using overhead, fisheye images, such as video-object tracking and human re-identification. Also, for evaluation purposes, some cherry-picked samples from the BOSS dataset [21] were included, especially the scenarios from camera 5 and 7 with the top-down overhead perspective.

3.2 Network Architecture

Inspired by RAPiD [3], the passenger detection network consists of three stages: the backbone network, the feature pyramid network (FPN), and the bounding box regression network. The backbone network works as a feature extractor that takes an image as input and outputs a list of features from different parts of the network. In the next stage, we pass those features into the FPN, in order to extract features related to object detection. Finally, at the last stage, a Convolutional Neural Network (CNN) is applied to each feature vector in order to produce a transformed version of the bounding-box predictions (Fig. 1).

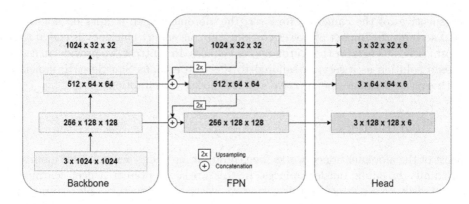

Fig. 1. An illustration of multiple convolutional layers and multi-dimensional matrices such as the feature maps with 1024×1024 input resolution.

3.3 Training

We used the pretrained RAPiD weights on MW-R and HABBOF which we fine-tuned by training on our custom dataset C-AVOF. Rotation, flipping, resizing, and color augmentation are used in the training stage.

3.4 Post-processing

After the detection process, we used the bounding box coordinates in order to compute the centroid. In order to calculate the distance between each bounding box, we used the Euclidean distance formula. Each bounding box is connected with the rest via distance line which represents the real-world distance, when multiplied with a weight factor. The weight value is calculated via the camera calibration process and takes into account various parameters such as the position of the camera and the field of view.

3.5 Experimental Results

The experiments were performed on the Nvidia Jetson AGX Xavier platform that features 512-core Volta GPU with Tensor Cores, 8-core ARM 64bit CPU and 32 GB 256-Bit LPDDR4x RAM. The camera system is the D-Link DCS-4625 panoramic fisheye camera with f/2.0 wide-angle panoramic lens and 5MP (2560×1920 @30 fps) high-resolution video. Results in Table 1 indicate that RAPiD at 608×608 resolution achieved the best performance and the fastest execution speed on our dataset C-AVOF. The averaged FPS value represents the execution speed on the Nvidia Jetson AGX Xavier.

In Fig. 2 and Fig. 3, we can see the visualized results on unseen scenarios from the BOSS dataset. The blue bounding boxes indicate the detections and the numbers represent the confidence of each detection. Red lines denote an unsafe distance while lines in green a sufficient distance.

Table 1. Performance comparison of two state-of-the-art methods on our dataset C-AVOF.

	FPS	MW-R [3]	HABBOF [8]	CEPDOF [3]	C-AVOF (ours)
		AP_{50}	AP_{50}	AP_{50}	AP_{50}
Tamura *et al.* [20] (608)	5.8	77.4	86.1	59.2	77.6
RAPiD (608)	6.5	96.2	97.6	84.3	**97.9**

Handling reflections is still a challenge on certain scenarios, as also happens in similar approaches. Passenger figures might appear to the windows of the shuttle as reflections, especially when the lighting is low. To mitigate this issue, a custom mask is applied on large reflective surfaces.

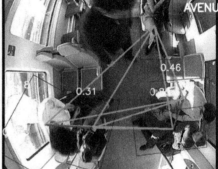

Fig. 2. Results on unseen scenarios from the BOSS dataset. Green lines represent a safe distance while red lines an unsafe. (Color figure online)

3.6   Adaptive Inference

As the service is able to report real-time metrics over the network to the AVENUE dashboard, we exploit this bidirectional communication inside the shuttle ecosystem, to enhance its awareness. By receiving useful data about the vehicle's state, such as the speed, the status of the door and the tires pressure, we can reduce the power consumption and be more energy efficient by decreasing the number of inferences, as Table 2 indicates. Figure 4 illustrates an overview of the dashboard displaying metrics for various services inside the autonomous shuttle ecosystem.

Fig. 3. Results on an unseen crowded scenario from the BOSS dataset, with overlapping detections

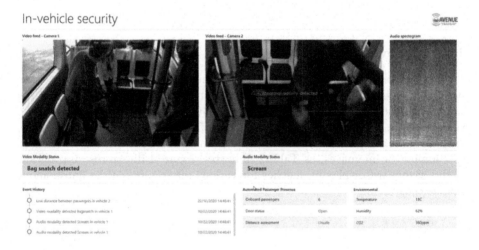

Fig. 4. An overview of the dashboard displaying metrics for various services inside the autonomous shuttle ecosystem.

Table 2. Estimated power consumption between adaptive modes measured on Jetson AGX Xavier using tegrastats utility.

Inference frequency	Power consumption (Wh)
Continuous (real-time)	26.2
Adaptive (crowded-multiple stops)	14.7
Adaptive (average)	11.4

4   Conclusions

In this paper, we present a deep learning approach deployed as a real-time service that can detect deviations from proximity and enable notifications to authorized personnel. As a backend, we are using a pre-trained RAPiD [3] model for human detection and perform fine tuning on our C-AVOF dataset to improve the performance. The model outputs bounding box coordinates that we are using to compute their centroids. By applying the Euclidean distance formula, we are able to compute the pairwise distances for each bounding box. In order to detect proximity violations between passengers, we transform the pixel distance into the real distance by multiplying with a weight value that is defined via camera calibration. Experimental results indicated that the service efficiently identifies passengers with unsafe proximity. The end-to-end service was deployed on the Jetson AGX Xavier with DCS-4625 fisheye camera and the results were visualised via the AVENUE platform. The overhead camera perspective mitigates occlusion issues leading to more robust detections compared to similar approaches with different perspectives. Moreover, as energy efficiency is a critical factor in Autonomous Vehicles, smart techniques based on data deriving from the shuttle ecosystem enabled us to further reduce power consumption by 56%. Finally, we introduce a new dataset for passenger detection from overhead camera perspective. In the future, experiments with an attention-based approach will be conducted to further enhance the accuracy of the model. In addition, an extended version of this approach could be applied in order to calculate the occupancy and weight distribution of the passengers in the shuttle. We believe that our research will be a stepping stone towards increased security in the autonomous public transport and will contribute positively in trust of the passengers to a human driverless transport system during the pandemic, but also beyond with further application-tailored adaptations.

References

1. Chu, H.Y., et al.: Early detection of COVID-19 through a citywide pandemic surveillance platform. N. Engl. J. Med. **383**(2), 185–187 (2020)
2. Cruz, C.O., Sarmento, J.M.: "mobility as a service" platforms: a critical path towards increasing the sustainability of transportation systems. Sustainability **12**(16), 6368 (2020)

3. Duan, Z., Tezcan, O., Nakamura, H., Ishwar, P., Konrad, J.: Rapid: rotation-aware people detection in overhead fisheye images. In: Proceedings of the IEEE/CVF Conference on Computer Vision and Pattern Recognition Workshops, pp. 636–637 (2020)
4. Ferretti, L., et al.: Quantifying SARS-COV-2 transmission suggests epidemic control with digital contact tracing. Science **368**(6491), eabb6936 (2020)
5. Harvey, A., LaPlace, J.: Megapixels: origins, ethics, and privacy implications of publicly available face recognition image datasets. Megapixels **1**(2), 6 (2019)
6. Iqbal, M.S., Ahmad, I., Bin, L., Khan, S., Rodrigues, J.J.: Deep learning recognition of diseased and normal cell representation. Trans. Emerg. Telecommun. Technol. **32**(7), e4017 (2021)
7. Javid, B., Weekes, M.P., Matheson, N.J.: COVID-19: should the public wear face masks? (2020)
8. Li, S., Tezcan, M.O., Ishwar, P., Konrad, J.: Supervised people counting using an overhead fisheye camera. In: 2019 16th IEEE International Conference on Advanced Video and Signal Based Surveillance (AVSS), pp. 1–8. IEEE (2019)
9. Molloy, E.J., Bearer, C.F.: COVID-19 in children and altered inflammatory responses (2020)
10. Musselwhite, C., Avineri, E., Susilo, Y.: Editorial jth 16-the coronavirus disease COVID-19 and implications for transport and health. J. Transport Health **16**, 100853 (2020)
11. Nguyen, T.T., Nguyen, Q.V.H., Nguyen, D.T., Hsu, E.B., Yang, S., Eklund, P.: Artificial intelligence in the battle against coronavirus (COVID-19): a survey and future research directions. arXiv preprint arXiv:2008.07343 (2020)
12. Olivera-La Rosa, A., Chuquichambi, E.G., Ingram, G.P.: Keep your (social) distance: pathogen concerns and social perception in the time of COVID-19. Personality Individ. Differ. **166**, 110200 (2020)
13. Pouw, C.A., Toschi, F., van Schadewijk, F., Corbetta, A.: Monitoring physical distancing for crowd management: real-time trajectory and group analysis. PLoS ONE **15**(10), e0240963 (2020)
14. Prem, K., et al.: The effect of control strategies to reduce social mixing on outcomes of the COVID-19 epidemic in Wuhan, China: a modelling study. Lancet Public Health **5**(5), e261–e270 (2020)
15. Punn, N.S., Sonbhadra, S.K., Agarwal, S.: COVID-19 epidemic analysis using machine learning and deep learning algorithms. MedRxiv (2020)
16. Ramadass, L., Arunachalam, S., Sagayasree, Z.: Applying deep learning algorithm to maintain social distance in public place through drone technology. Int. J. Pervasive Comput. Commun. (2020)
17. Redmon, J., Farhadi, A.: Yolov3: an incremental improvement. arXiv preprint arXiv:1804.02767 (2018)
18. Ren, S., He, K., Girshick, R., Sun, J.: Faster R-CNN: towards real-time object detection with region proposal networks. In: Advances in Neural Information Processing Systems 28 (2015)
19. Sathyamoorthy, A.J., Patel, U., Savle, Y.A., Paul, M., Manocha, D.: COVID-robot: monitoring social distancing constraints in crowded scenarios. arXiv preprint arXiv:2008.06585 (2020)
20. Tamura, M., Horiguchi, S., Murakami, T.: Omnidirectional pedestrian detection by rotation invariant training. In: 2019 IEEE Winter Conference on Applications of Computer Vision (WACV), pp. 1989–1998. IEEE (2019)

21. Velastin, S.A., Gómez-Lira, D.A.: People detection and pose classification inside a moving train using computer vision. In: Zaman, H.B., et al. (eds.) International Visual Informatics Conference, pp. 319–330. Springer, Cham (2017). https://doi.org/10.1007/978-3-319-70010-6_30

22. Wojke, N., Bewley, A.: Deep cosine metric learning for person re-identification. In: 2018 IEEE Winter Conference on Applications of Computer Vision (WACV), pp. 748–756. IEEE (2018)

23. Wojke, N., Bewley, A., Paulus, D.: Simple online and realtime tracking with a deep association metric. In: 2017 IEEE International Conference on Image Processing (ICIP), pp. 3645–3649. IEEE (2017)

24. Zhang, S., Wen, L., Bian, X., Lei, Z., Li, S.Z.: Single-shot refinement neural network for object detection. In: Proceedings of the IEEE Conference on Computer Vision and Pattern Recognition, pp. 4203–4212 (2018)

Automatic Semi-quantitative Histological Assessment of Tissue Traits Using a Smart Web Application

Olympia Giannou[1]([✉]), Dimitra E. Zazara[2,3]([✉]), Anastasios D. Giannou[4,5], Petra Clara Arck[2], and Georgios Pavlidis[1]

[1] Computer Engineering and Informatics Department, Polytechnic School, University of Patras, Patras, Greece
ogiannou@ceid.upatras.gr
[2] Division for Experimental Feto-Maternal Medicine, Department of Obstetrics and Fetal Medicine, University Medical Center Hamburg-Eppendorf (UKE), Hamburg, Germany
di.zazara@uke.de
[3] University Children's Hospital, UKE, Hamburg, Germany
[4] Department of Medicine, UKE, Hamburg, Germany
[5] Department of General, Visceral and Thoracic Surgery, UKE, Hamburg, Germany

Abstract. A smart web application suitable for classifying goblet cell hyperplasia and level of mucus production in stained lung tissues from mice with experimentally induced allergic asthma. Multiple trainer-model approaches are investigated and proposed in this manuscript, based on machine learning techniques, which provide a technological evolution in the analysis of traits of biomedical imaging. Several schemes, which consist of pre-trained image classifiers on ImageNet, are analyzed and compared each other. Lung tissue images of mice with allergic asthma, depicting mucus-containing periodic acid-Schiff (PAS) positive bronchial cells, are fed as input datasets. The performance of each model is evaluated, based on a variety of metrics: accuracy, recall, precision, cross entropy, f1-score, confusion matrix. Such a web tool could contribute to biomedical research by providing an automated standardized way to determine phenotypic severity of histological traits based on a semi-quantitative scoring scale.

Keywords: Lung · Asthma · Tissue · Machine learning · Classification · CNN · Web application

1 Introduction

Asthma is one of the most common chronic respiratory diseases worldwide [1]. The main hallmarks of asthma include chronic airway inflammation, increased mucus production and airway remodeling thereby resulting in narrowing of the airways and recurring episodes of respiratory symptoms such as wheezing, coughing and dyspnea. The

O. Giannou and D. E. Zazara—Equal co-first authors.

I. Maglogiannis et al. (Eds.): AIAI 2022, IFIP AICT 646, pp. 180–191, 2022.
https://doi.org/10.1007/978-3-031-08333-4_15

causes, pathogenesis and treatment strategies of asthma comprise a key focus of biomedical research with animal models for experimental asthma induction being an essential tool for this purpose. Typical endpoints in experimental approaches focusing on the phenotypic traits of asthma are the severity of airway inflammation, mucus production and related goblet cell hyperplasia, as well as peribronchial fibrosis. The assessment of these parameters usually relies on the semi-quantitative evaluation of respectively stained lung tissue sections by more than one independent and blinded observers, based on an empirically defined scoring scale. Thus, to avoid a potential bias and reduce the time required for such a task, an automated, relatively unbiased and easily reproducible semi-quantitative evaluation of such histological phenotypic features is required. In this study, based on images from stained lung tissues isolated from mice suffering from experimental asthma, Machine Learning (ML) and Convolutional Neural Networks (CNN) were employed to develop a smart application, which could automatically evaluate the phenotypic severity of the induced disease based on the provided histological image.

In this way, features of the tissue images are uncovered and automatically extracted based on previous available knowledge during training on different data (transfer learning approach [2]), patterns are recognized and classification of them is elaborated through ML models, so that human visual interpretation, commonly used until now, is avoided. This automated way of disease severity estimation decreases the possibility of human bias and offers a more accurate objective evaluation, independent on the disagreement of different researchers.

Our objective in this work is to present an automated diagnostic tool to efficiently classify the phenotypic severity of an experimentally-induced condition, such as asthma, on a scale from 0 to 4, based on stained tissue sections. The feature of interest examined in this study was mucus production and the abundance of mucus-containing bronchial epithelial cells in the mouse airways. A similar approach may also be followed in other similar histological staining and related semi-quantitative assessments, focusing on e.g. the severity of tissue inflammation, the extent of tissue infiltration etc. The proposed CNN model is selected following a comparison of its performance with this of several different pre-trained model architectures (Table 3) on our dataset of mouse lung tissue sections, using a variety of metrics (accuracy, recall, precision, cross entropy, f1-score, confusion matrix). The advantages and disadvantages of each architecture are also discussed and compared in Sect. 4. The structure of this manuscript is as follows: Sect. 2 describes the related work; the materials and methods are presented in Sect. 3; results and comparisons are given in Sect. 4; conclusions are discussed in Sect. 5.

2   Related Work

Image classification can be efficiently achieved using the approach of transfer learning (TL) and pre-trained image classifier models [3], since the learned features are stored in weighted network structures, freezing a tensor graph [4]. Mainly, the final layer is trained on the new dataset, using less high computing resources and training time. Several studies have used TL on CNNs to achieve image trait classification following different model architectures, pre-trained on the ILSVRC, CIFAR or MNIST image dataset [5].

Tissue image classification using CNNs is generally employed in many biomedical applications. Tumor tissue classification was done with ELM, SVM and DCNN, reaching 97.91% accuracy obtained by DCNN-5 and 97.39% by DCNN-7 [6]. M4-CNN-MaxFeat-based RF achieved 97.1% accuracy in classifying whole lung tissue cancer [7]. Patterns such as emphysema, ground glass, fibrosis, micronodules and healthy lung tissue were classified with an accuracy of 92.2%, 100%, 86.7%, 93.8% and 92.9% respectively [8]. Same classes were detected using PASA, kNN and SVM architectures [9], showing a poorer performance. Multiple classifiers were applied to lung tissue categorization in [10] while SVM classifier was able to correctly classify 88.3% of the instances and 96.4% when detecting healthy tissue versus all other pathological classes. Covid-19 automatic lung tissue images were classified and segmented in [11]. Covid-19 pneumonia was detected using lung ultrasound and severity was classified in scores 0 to 3 using CNN [12]. Histology image classification using ResNet in celiac disease, lung adenocarcinoma and renal cell carcinoma datasets had an accuracy of 87.06%, 94.51% and 90.16%, respectively [13]. Classification of lung adenocarcinoma, squamous cell carcinoma and benign tissue was achieved using CAD with an accuracy of approximately 99% [14]. Colorectal tissue image classification was achieved with a 93–98% throughput using VGG16 and CapsNet architectures [15].

Previous studies resulted in the classification of various diseases, such as pneumonia and cancer, of organs such as lung or liver, focusing on severity scoring in several cases. To our knowledge, our study is the first to present an automated general-purpose biomedical research tool, able to estimate the severity of histological phenotypic traits, based on the analysis of whole histopathology tissue images (WHTI). Additionally, the objective of this study is to present and compare the performance of several image classifiers, using all known available metrics for their evaluation.

3 Material and Methods

3.1 Dataset – Data Collection

The dataset contained images of periodic-acid-Schiff (PAS)-stained lung tissue sections from mice with experimentally-induced allergic asthma. For experimental asthma induction, mice were initially sensitized and subsequently challenged with ovalbumin, as described previously. Tissue collection and PAS-staining were performed as described previously [16]. The abundance of mucus-containing bronchial epithelial cells was evaluated in twenty airways in the lung parenchyma of each mouse, based on the severity scoring scale described in Table 1, following published protocols [17], and a mean score for mucus production for each mouse was calculated.

3.2 Methodology

Input: Our dataset in Sect. 3.1 was fed as input in a variety of CNN architectures for image pattern classification. Images were split into 3 subsets in all experiments: training (80%), validation (10%) and testing (10%). Rescaling, cropping and data augmentation techniques were applied to provide well-defined image patterns in the training model

Table 1. Description of severity score scale.

Severity score	Description
0	*<0.5% PAS-positive cells*
1	*5–25%*
2	*25–50%*
3	*50–75%*
4	*>75%*

architectures. The performance was evaluated on two images at a time (batch size) and the learning rate was equivalent to 0.01. The dataset consisted of five scoring classes, namely 0–4 according to published protocols [17] and each class contained 40 images. The tissue images are fed to the classifier as whole tissue images as they are displayed in Figs. 1 and 3, in which the main tissue area of interest has been isolated.

Convolutional Base (Convolutional Layers, Hidden Layers, Pooling, Fully Connected Layers): Deep learning architectures and pre-trained image classifier models [3] following TL were used to preserve the learned features and the final layer was trained on our dataset, building a scheme which could accurately predict the severity score of an input-tissue-image of mucus-containing PAS-positive bronchial cells. During the training procedure, memorization of patterns of each image was done and corresponding bottlenecks were calculated to help the classifier to detect the different classes before resulting in the predicted score through the final CNN layer. The following open-source image classifier models were used [3]: InceptionV1-4, Inception-ResNet-V2, VGGNet-16 and -19 (descendants of AlexNet), MobileNetV1-2, NASNet and PNASNet (mobile and large version), pre-trained on the ILSVRC, CIFAR or MNIST dataset [5]. All models were implemented in Python 3.8 and Tensorflow 2.1. The tissue images of our dataset were rescaled to fit each pre-trained model image size architecture (Table 3). In the pre-trained model architectures, used and compared in this study, the final regression layer was trained on our dataset, following the transfer learning method. Our experiments were elaborated in a standard-performance computer (32 GB RAM, Intel i7@3.6 GHz).

Output: The described scheme is able to classify input images and determine the severity score to which each image belongs. The score values fluctuate from 0 to 4 according to the Table 1. More specifically, the abundance of mucus-containing bronchial epithelial cells on each tissue image is detected, a score is assigned to it and reported to the scientist via the web application 'Automatic Tissue Severity Detection' (ATSD), designed for the purpose of this study. Our web application ATSD allows researchers to upload the tissue image of mice with allergic asthma, depicting mucus-containing periodic acid-Schiff (PAS) positive bronchial cells and to request the corresponding severity score in scale 0–4 (Sect. 3.1). Firstly, this image is sent as an HTTP request to the REST API server (Django framework [18]). The server feeds this request to the back-end CNN VGG16. VGG16 was identified as the best performing one on our dataset (Sect. 4) based on all required representative metrics (Sect. 3.3). This model predicts the score and sends this diagnosis result through the REST API server to the front-end graphical user interface of the web application ATSD (Fig. 3) for the user (researchers). The REST API server and the CNN model are implemented in Python 3.8. The graphical interfaces of the web application in Fig. 3 are implemented in html (Fig. 2).

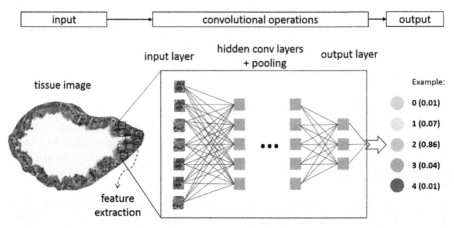

Fig. 1. The proposed overall concept to determine the severity score of our input lung tissue image dataset.

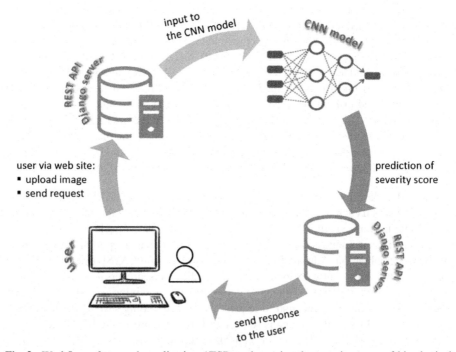

Fig. 2. Workflow of our web application ATSD to determine the severity score of histological phenotypic traits demonstrated on tissue images through a Django REST API.

Through our user-friendly web application ATSD, the user can upload a whole tissue image and then request prediction of its severity score. Finally, the input tissue image accompanied with the predicted score are displayed.

Fig. 3. Graphical User Interface (GUI) of our web application ATSD.

3.3 Metrics

The performance of all different architectures, reported in Sect. 3.2, was evaluated by calculating a variety of metrics: accuracy, f1-score, recall, cross-entropy (loss), precision and confusion matrixes [19], as shown in Table 2.

Table 2. Interpretation of metrics.

Metrics	Best value	Worst value	Description
Confusion matrix	*1 in diagonal axis*	*0 in diagonal axis*	*Diagonal axis: if the predicted positive and predicted negative labels are true*
Accuracy	*1*	*0*	*Fraction of images correctly judged as true*
Cross entropy	*0*	*>0*	*Difference/dissimilarities between two probability distributions*
Precision	*1*	*0*	*Ability to return only relevant objects*
Recall	*1*	*0*	*Ability to identify all relevant objects*
f1-score	1	0	Harmonic mean of precision and recall

4   Results and Comparisons

The performance of accurately determining the severity score of histological phenotypic traits demonstrated on lung tissue images has been evaluated for all reported architectures in Sect. 3.2.

The Inception network is complex, consisting of many techniques to increase performance and its evolutions and improvements lead to many different versions: V1 [20], V2 and V3 [21], V4 and ResNet [22]. V1 is used when salient parts (objects of interest) of an image vary in size. V2 and V3 show more accuracy and less computational complexity with reduced bottlenecks. V4 and Inception-ResNet simplify the previous versions and have different stems. The computational costs between V1 and V3, as well as between V2 and V4 are similar. The differences in the architecture between ResNet-V1 and –V2 [23, 24] are: the addition of a second non-linearity after the addition between x and F(x) on V1 and the removal of the last non-linearity on V2. Additionally, ResNetV2 applies ReLU and batch normalization in a different point compared to ResNetV1. The number

Table 3. Performance of the applied image classifier architectures in determining the severity of airway mucus production in our lung tissue image dataset. (300 training steps)

Architecture [3]	Input image size (pixels)	Accuracy %	Cross entropy	Precision	Recall	F1-score
Inception V1	224 × 224	76.9	1.14	0.65	0.51	0.58
Inception V2	299 × 299	76.2	1.15	0.62	0.50	0.56
Inception V3	299 × 299	69.2	1.14	0.64	0.51	0.57
Inception V4	299 × 299	77.0	1.13	0.65	0.50	0.57
Inception-ResNet-v2	299 × 299	76.7	1.15	0.67	0.52	0.59
ResNetV1 50	224 × 224	84.6	1.14	0.67	0.52	0.59
ResNetV1 101	224 × 224	77.0	1.13	0.63	0.51	0.57
ResNetV1 152	224 × 224	69.0	1.11	0.61	0.50	0.55
ResNetV2 50	224 × 224	76.1	1.12	0.68	0.49	0.59
ResNetV2 101	224 × 224	76.9	1.14	0.64	0.51	0.57
ResNetV2 152	224 × 224	76.8	1.14	0.68	0.55	0.61
VGG 16	**224 × 224**	**89.1**	**0.82**	**0.72**	**0.62**	**0.67**
VGG 19	224 × 224	69.3	1.14	0.61	0.50	0.55
MobileNet_v1_1.0_224	224 × 224	59.9	3.7	0.39	0.41	0.40
MobileNet_v2_1.0_224	224 × 224	60.5	2.4	0.44	0.47	0.45
NASNet-A_Mobile_224	224 × 224	61.5	1.22	0.55	0.43	0.49
NASNet-A_Large_331	331 × 331	67.8	1.17	0.57	0.45	0.51
PNASNet-5_Mobile_224	224 × 224	74.2	1.31	0.61	0.45	0.53
PNASNet-5_Large_331	331 × 331	76.6	1.37	0.63	0.47	0.55

accuracy

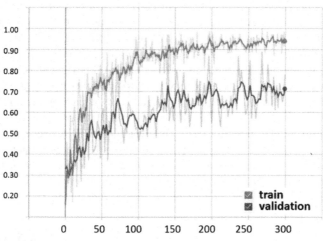

cross-entropy

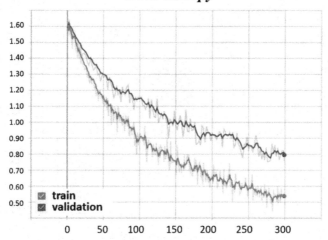

Fig. 4. Based on all metrics, VGG16 was identified as the best architecture in accurately determining the severity score of the examined tissue traits. Accuracy (top), cross-entropy (bottom) over the period in steps (300). Training period in orange, validation period in blue. The values are smoothened by the margin of 0.7, real values are shadowed in fainter color. X-axis: steps in steps; Y-axis: accuracy (up), cross-entropy (down). (Color figure online)

of layers used at each case are shown in Table 3. VGGNet, and specifically VGG16 and VGG19, [25] have an increased depth compared to the other classifier CNNs in order to achieve a better performance. However, the increase in layers fails to significantly increase the performance of VGGNet, as in the case of ResNet, since the weights are updated through back-propagation, which finally only slightly changes each weight.

ResNet achieves a higher performance while the number of layers increases, avoiding the gradient exploding. MobilenetV1 (2 layers in total) [26] is less complex and has a smaller size than any other classifier. For this reason, it is more frequently introduced for mobile devices. MobileNetV2 (2 layers in total) [27] uses inverted residual structure and the non-linearities are removed in narrow layers. Therefore, in general, the performance of MobileNetV2 is slightly better than this of MobilenetV1. PNASNet-5 [28] has a slightly better performance on ILSVRC than NASNet-A [29] and both surpass MobileNetV1 and InceptionV1. In NASNet-A, the blocks are searched by a learning method and are not predefined, while, in PNASNet-5, the search is elaborated in a progressive order, starting firstly from simple cell structures. The mobile versions of PNASNet and NASNet use 224×224 pixel- instead of 331×331 pixel-images in their large versions.

Experiments demonstrated that VGG16 fits better to our dataset in terms of all metrics, as depicted in Table 3. The metric values among all model architectures are not profoundly different. However, VGG16 outperfomed (Figs. 4 and 5).

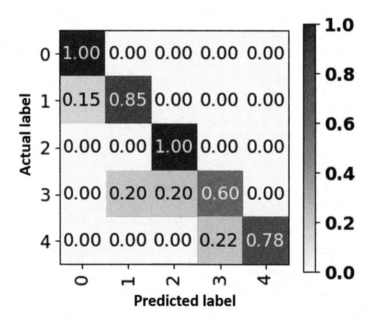

Fig. 5. VGG16 was identified as the best architecture in accurately determining the severity score of the examined tissue traits. Confusion matrix. The scale of probability in which the predicted severity score is closer to the actual one is fluctuated from 1 (dark green) to 0 (white-grey). (Color figure online).

It is observed that it is more difficult for our classifier to correctly predict the severity score 3 (probability = 0.6).

5   Conclusions

Using a machine learning approach, we were here able to develop an accurate scheme based on the architecture VGG16 that can be used as an efficient automatic research tool for the semi-quantitative assessment of the extent of histological phenotypic traits based on whole tissue images. A variety of published open-source pre-trained image classifiers were tested on our tissue images and the model VGG16 was identified as the best performing one based on all required representative metrics. This scheme achieves 89.1% accuracy with 0.82 loss and a good f1-score of 0.67, close to 1, which is the harmonic mean between precision and recall. Thus, the here presented web application can efficiently determine the abundance of mucus-containing bronchial cells in asthmatic mouse lungs and serves as an example for addressing similar histological assessments based on the same principles. Overall, such applications may be used as a general-purpose tool in biomedical research, allowing an automated, standardized, fast and highly accurate image analysis.

6   Future Work

Future work aims to investigate the universality of the developed scheme in a variety of images and histological assays. Specifically, we seek to examine whether the severity score assigned by our web ATSD application each time agrees with the actual score according to standard histological features and the experience of the observer. Optimization of the process will also result in a faster and more efficient outcome.

Acknowledgement. The authors thank Thomas Andreas for excellent technical assistance. We are also grateful to the Microscopy Imaging Facility of the University Medical Center Hamburg-Eppendorf. This work was supported in part by the German Research Foundation to DEZ and PCA (AR232/25-2 and SO1413/1-2) and State Research Funding - FV45, Authority for Science, Research and Equality, Hanseatic City of Hamburg, Germany to PCA. DEZ is also supported by a clinician scientist scholarship awarded by the Medical Faculty of the University of Hamburg. ADG is supported by an Else Kröner Memorial fellowship, the Werner Otto and the "Hamburger Krebsgesellschaft" foundation.

References

1. Reddel, H.K., Bateman, E.D., Becker, A., Boulet, L.-P., Cruz, A.A., Drazen, J.M., et al.: A summary of the new GINA strategy: a roadmap to asthma control. Eur. Respir. J. **46**, 622–639 (2015)
2. Hussain, M., Bird, J.J., Faria, D.R.: A study on CNN transfer learning for image classification. In: Lotfi, A., Bouchachia, H., Gegov, A., Langensiepen, C., McGinnity, M. (eds.) UKCI 2018. AISC, vol. 840, pp. 191–202. Springer, Cham (2019). https://doi.org/10.1007/978-3-319-97982-3_16
3. Classifiers: https://github.com/tensorflow/models/tree/master/re-search/slim#pre-trained-models
4. Convolutional Neural Networks. https://www.tensorflow.org/tutorials/

5. ILSVRC. https://image-net.org/challenges/LSVRC/2012/. CIFAR. https://www.cs.toronto. edu/~kriz/cifar.html. MNIST. http://yann.lecun.com/exdb/mnist/
6. Yang, X., et al.: A deep learning approach for tumor tissue image classification. IASTED Biomed. Eng. (2016)
7. Wang, X., Chen, H., Gan, C., Lin, H., Dou, Q., et al.: Weakly supervised learning for whole slide lung cancer image classification (2018)
8. Depeursinge, A., et al.: Lung tissue classification using wavelet frames. In: 2007 29th Annual International Conference of the IEEE Engineering in Medicine and Biology Society, pp. 6259–6262. IEEE (2007)
9. Song, Y., Cai, W., Zhou, Y., Feng, D.D.: Feature-based image patch approximation for lung tissue classification. IEEE Trans. Med. Imaging 32(4), 797–808 (2013)
10. Depeursinge, A., et al.: Comparative performance analysis of state-of-the-art classification algorithms applied to lung tissue categorization. J. Digit. Imaging 23(1), 18–30 (2010)
11. Zaffino, P., Marzullo, A., et al.: An open-source covid-19 ct dataset with automatic lung tissue classification for radiomics. Bioengineering 8(2), 26 (2021)
12. La Salvia, M., et al.: Deep learning and lung ultrasound for Covid-19 pneumonia detection and severity classification. Comput. Biol. Med. 136, 104742 (2021)
13. DiPalma, J., Suriawinata, A.A., Tafe, L.J., Torresani, L., Hassanpour, S.: Resolution-based distillation for efficient histology image classification. Artif. Intell. Med. 119, 102136 (2021)
14. Nishio, M., Nishio, M., Jimbo, N., Nakane, K.: Homology-based image processing for automatic classification of histopathological images of lung tissue. Cancers 13(6), 1192 (2021)
15. Nguyen, H.-G., Blank, A., Dawson, H.E., Lugli, A., Zlobec, I.: Classification of colorectal tissue images from high throughput tissue microarrays by ensemble deep learning methods. Sci. Rep. 11(1), 1–11 (2021)
16. Zazara, D.E., et al.: A prenatally disrupted airway epithelium orchestrates the fetal origin of asthma in mice. J. Allergy Clin. Immunol. 145(6), 1641–1654 (2020)
17. Myou, S., Leff, A.R., Myo, S., Boetticher, E., Tong, J., Meliton, A.Y., et al.: Blockade of inflammation and airway hyperresponsiveness in immune-sensitized mice by dominant-negative phosphoinositide 3-kinase-TAT. J. Exp. Med. 198(10), 1573–1582 (2003)
18. Django framework. https://www.djangoproject.com/
19. Metrics. https://en.wikipedia.org/wiki/Evaluation_of_binary_classifiers. https://en.wikipe dia.org/wiki/Confusion_matrix. https://en.wikipedia.org/wiki/Precision_and_recall
20. Szegedy, C., Liu, W., Jia, Y., Sermanet, P., Reed, S., Anguelov, D., et al.: Going deeper with convolutions. In: Proceedings of the IEEE Conference on Computer Vision and Pattern Recognition, pp. 1–9 (2015)
21. Szegedy, C., Vanhoucke, V., Ioffe, S., Shlens, J., Wojna, Z.: Rethinking the inception architecture for computer vision. In: Proceedings of the IEEE Conference on Computer Vision and Pattern Recognition, pp. 2818–2826 (2016)
22. Szegedy, C., Ioffe, S., Vanhoucke, V., Alemi, A.A.: Inception-v4, inception-resnet and the impact of residual connections on learning. In: Thirty-First AAAI Conference on Artificial Intelligence (2017)
23. He, K., Zhang, X., Ren, S., Sun, J.: Deep residual learning for image recognition. In: Proceedings of the IEEE Conference on Computer Vision and Pattern Recognition, pp. 770–778 (2016)
24. He, K., Zhang, X., Ren, S., Sun, J.: Identity mappings in deep residual networks. In: Leibe, B., Matas, J., Sebe, N., Welling, M. (eds.) ECCV 2016. LNCS, vol. 9908, pp. 630–645. Springer, Cham (2016). https://doi.org/10.1007/978-3-319-46493-0_38
25. Simonyan, K., Zisserman, A.: Very deep convolutional networks for large-scale image recognition. arXiv preprint arXiv:1409.1556 (2014)
26. Howard, A.G., et al.: Mobilenets: efficient convolutional neural networks for mobile vision applications. arXiv preprint arXiv:1704.04861 (2017)

27. Sandler, M., Howard, A., Zhu, M., Zhmoginov, A., Chen, L.-C.: Mobilenetv2: inverted residuals and linear bottlenecks. In: Proceedings of the IEEE Conference on Computer Vision and Pattern Recognition, pp. 4510–4520 (2018)
28. Liu, C., et al.: Progressive neural architecture search. In: Ferrari, V., Hebert, M., Sminchisescu, C., Weiss, Y. (eds.) ECCV 2018. LNCS, vol. 11205, pp. 19–35. Springer, Cham (2018). https://doi.org/10.1007/978-3-030-01246-5_2
29. Zoph, B., Vasudevan, V., Shlens, J., Le, Q.V.: Learning transferable architectures for scalable image recognition. In: Proceedings of the IEEE Conference on Computer Vision and Pattern Recognition, pp. 8697–8710 (2018)

MERLIN: Identifying Inaccuracies in Multiple Sequence Alignments Using Object Detection

Hiba Khodji[✉][ID], Lucille Herbay[ID], Pierre Collet[ID], Julie Thompson[ID], and Anne Jeannin-Girardon[ID]

University of Strasbourg, ICube Laboratory UMR7357, 1 Rue Eugène Boeckel, 67000 Strasbourg, France
{khodji,collet,thompson,jeanningirardon}@unistra.fr,
lucille.herbay@etu.unistra.fr

Abstract. Multiple Sequence Alignments set the basis for many biological sequence analysis methods. However, they are susceptible to irregularities that result either from the predicted sequences or from natural biological events. In this paper, we propose MERLIN (Msa ERror Localization and IdentificatioN), an object detector that consists in identifying such irregularities using visual representations of MSAs. Our model is developed using a state-of-the-art deep learning object detector, YOLOv4, and trained on a set of MSA images from an in-house built dataset with automatically annotated errors. Our object detector exhibits a mean Average Precision of 71.18% in predicting different types of errors within MSAs. We conducted a thorough examination of the obtained results which showed that our method correctly identifies certain inconsistencies that were missed by the automatic annotation algorithm.

Keywords: Multiple Sequence Alignment · Error detection · Deep neural networks · Object detection

1 Introduction

Multiple Sequence Alignment (MSA) is a fundamental task in bioinformatics that consists in arranging a set of biological sequences (DNA, RNA or proteins) in order to identify regions of similarity that reflect their biological relationships. However, MSAs are prone to errors which can originate either from natural biological variants or from MSA-generating algorithms. Algorithms used to predict protein-coding genes in DNA sequences, for instance, are not always accurate, and often lead to sequence prediction errors. Consequently, today's protein databases are riddled with inconsistencies [15].

Identifying inaccuracies in multiple sequence alignments is not a trivial task, but accurate MSAs are instrumental in developing solutions to address problems spanning different biology related areas of study [3], such as evolutionary studies,

© IFIP International Federation for Information Processing 2022
Published by Springer Nature Switzerland AG 2022
I. Maglogiannis et al. (Eds.): AIAI 2022, IFIP AICT 646, pp. 192–203, 2022.
https://doi.org/10.1007/978-3-031-08333-4_16

protein structure, analysis of effects of genetic mutations, *etc.* Numerous alignment methods have been developed to tackle the MSA dilemma, including, but not limited to, dynamic programming, progressive multiple alignment, iterative alignment, Hidden Markov Models, and Genetic Algorithms [22]. Several other techniques have been proposed in order to evaluate and identify inconsistencies within MSAs [6,12,24]. However, one unprecedented approach to solving this issue consists in using a deep learning *object detector.* Object Detection aims to identify and locate one or several objects in an image or video. This challenging task has been the center of increasing attention in the field of computer vision with applications across a wide and diverse spectrum of fields including traffic monitoring [13], medical image analysis [8], and biology [10]. MSAs can be visually represented in the form of a colored alignment of sequences; we thus hypothesize that the structural information encoded in MSAs can be exploited by deep learning object detection algorithms, which are praised for their ability to capture increasing scale of information and extract contextual information from data.

In this paper, we propose an approach to identify inconsistencies within MSAs of protein sequences. Our method, MERLIN (Msa ERror Localization and IdentificatioN), consists in applying a state-of-the-art deep learning object detector, YOLOv4 [2], to detect and localize different types of errors (deletions, insertions/extension, and mismatches) using visual representations of multiple sequence alignments.

This paper is organized as follows: Sect. 2 introduces related works. Our dataset is presented in Sect. 3. Section 4 describes the experimental protocol used for the proposed approach. Section 5 presents and discusses the experiment results. Finally, Sect. 6 summarizes the conducted work and concludes this paper.

2   Related Works

Constructing an optimal multiple alignment of a set of sequences is a computationally expensive task, which led to the development of heuristic algorithms that sometimes introduce errors into the alignments. These errors can result either from inaccurate alignment algorithms or badly predicted sequences, and consist in the presence of unusual deletions, insertions/extensions, or mismatches that are inconsistent with their local context. A deletion error refers to the absence of one or more amino acids from a sequence. An insertion is the inclusion of an additional sequence segment between two amino acids, while an extension refers to an additional sequence segment which is added on either end (N- or C-terminal) of a sequence. Finally, a mismatch is represented by non-homologous amino acids in one or more columns of the alignment.

As an attempt to investigate the errors introduced into MSAs, the authors in [4] developed EvalMSA, a software tool that allows the detection of divergent sequences and "outliers" in MSAs. The basic idea behind this technique is to evaluate the contribution of each sequence to cause gaps in the alignment using a *gappiness* value (gpp); the sequence with the highest gpp value is deemed strongly divergent and is more likely to introduce gaps in the remaining sequences. EvalMSA was benchmarked with six different alignments derived from the Pfam database [7]. Artificial outliers were added and the sequences were realigned using different alignment algorithms (MUSCLE and ClustalW [21], as well as Expresso algorithm [1]). EvalMSA was able to correctly identify outliers regardless of the algorithm used to generate the MSAs. The method was compared to a similar outlier detection tool, called OD-Seq, introduced in [11]. This approach utilizes a gap metric to measure the similarity of gap placement between pairs of sequences and identify sequences with missing parts compared to the rest of the alignment. In another line of research, Khenoussi et al. [12] set out to identify inaccuracies in protein sequences using MSAs. The authors developed a Bayesien model called SIBIS, which takes an MSA as input and outputs an XML file where all identified inconsistencies are highlighted. The proposed algorithm was compared to MisPred [16] and a profile-based method [23] on a set of MSAs. The obtained results showed a higher sensitivity for SIBIS (81%) compared to 27% for MisPred and 62% for the profile-based approach. In terms of specificity, SIBIS suffered a slight loss (92%) compared to the profile-based method (96%). However, the loss in specificity was considered statistically insignificant.

In this paper we attempt to examine the possibility of using a deep-learning object detector to identify inconsistencies in MSAs. Object detection algorithms are primarily divided into two categories: *two-stage* and *one-stage* detectors. As the name suggests, a two-stage detector is carried out in two stages; in the first stage, the algorithm selects Regions Of Interests (ROIs) (*i.e.* regions with a high probability of containing an object). In the second stage, the region proposals are processed for object classification and bounding box regression. One-stage detectors, on the other hand, require only a *single* pass through the network to localize and classify objects. Although two-stage detectors exhibit a good detection accuracy, they come with a large cost in terms of time and computational power. As an attempt to overcome this limitation, Redmon et al. [19] proposed YOLO (You Only Look Once), a novel deep learning detection paradigm. YOLO owes its name to its ability to process and detect objects in an image/frame in a *single* pass of the network. Therefore, YOLO is a *one-stage detector* that waives the need for a region proposal technique, thereby increasing detection speed.

Here, we are interested in YOLOv4 [2], which is an advanced version of YOLO. YOLOv4 is a one-stage detector that improves upon earlier versions by introducing new techniques that enhance the training process and detection accuracy.

3   Dataset

In order to train and evaluate our object detector, we used multiple sequence alignments from an in-house built dataset [15]. These MSAs are extracted from the Uniprot reference proteomes [5] and RefSeq [17] databases, and were automatically annotated using SIBIS algorithm [12]. As described in Sect. 2, three types of errors can be found in an MSA: deletions, insertions/extensions, and mismatches. It is important to note that, since the original MSAs were not manually annotated, some alignments may contain certain errors that the annotation program failed to detect[1]. The original MSAs were converted into images using ADOMA (Alternative Display Of Multiple Alignment) [28] which is a graphical interface that offers a colored alignment output where amino acids with similar physico-chemical properties share the same color. Figure 1 shows protein sequences in the color format as produced by ADOMA. We then removed the characters from the colored alignments and modified their color code to make the sequences more contrasted. The obtained HTML files were then converted into images using an open source command line tool [27].

Fig. 1. Example of protein sequences shown in the ADOMA [28] colored format.

Once we obtained the MSA images, we designed a simple program to automatically generate the corresponding annotations. To this end, we used a parser that takes an MSA in XML format (output by SIBIS [12]) as input and outputs all existing errors and their corresponding positions. The information provided by the parser is then used to produce annotations in YOLO format.

4   Experimental Setup

The architecture in YOLOv4 consists of a backbone, neck, and head. The backbone is based on CSPDarknet53 [25]; the neck includes a Spatial Pyramid Pooling (SPP) block [9] in order to increase the receptive field and separate out the most significant context features from the backbone; the feature aggregation in the neck is carried out using PANet [14]. The head is in charge of the final detection and implements YOLOv3 [20]. The implementation of YOLOv4 uses the Darknet framework [18]. For our experiment, we split the data (12 229 images) into 80% for training, 10% for validation, and 10% for testing. Since our MSA images are of a large rectangular shape, we set the network size[2] to 1024×512. For training, we used a batch size of 64; an initial learning rate of 0.001; momentum and weight decay are set to 0.9 and 0.0005, respectively. The training was processed for 14 000 iterations[3]. The distribution of classes in the training data is as follows: Internal deletions (32.7%), N-terminal deletions (31.4%), C-terminal deletions (9.57%), Internal insertions (9.07%), N-terminal extensions (7.10%), Mismatches (6.76%), C-terminal extensions (3.40%). This distribution corresponds to the actual proportions of these error types across MSAs in the primate proteomes databank [15]: Internal deletions (36.9%), N-terminal deletions

---

[1] Since SIBIS sensitivity is "only" 81% (v.s. 92% specificity) it means that it is more prone to False Negatives.

[2] Images are resized to the network size during training and detection.

[3] Also known as max batches. It is defined as the number of classes * 2000 by Bochkovskiy et al. in [2].

(29.34%), C-terminal deletions (8.87%), Internal insertions (8.82%), N-terminal extensions (6.43%), Mismatches (6.63%), C-terminal extensions (3.01%).

5   Results and Discussion

The performance of our object detector was evaluated using a set of different metrics as shown in Table 1. The mAP refers to the mean Average Precision, and it is a commonly used evaluation metric for object detection which measures model performance in terms of both classification and localization ability. In order to understand the mAP, we first need to define the Intersection over Union (IoU) and Average Precision (AP). The IoU is an evaluation metric that measures the overlap between a predicted bounding box and the ground truth box in an image; the larger the area of overlap the higher the IoU score. Given an IoU threshold $\alpha = 0.5$, the model determines whether a detection is a True Positive (IoU $\geq \alpha$), or a False Positive (IoU $< \alpha$); a False Negative is when the model fails to detect an object in the image. Based on these elements, the model computes the precision and recall. Precision quantifies the number of true positives over all positive predictions, while recall measures the number of true positives among all correct predictions. The Average Precision (AP) is then computed by finding the area under the precision-recall curve. While AP is calculated for each class, the mAP is defined as the mean of APs across all classes.

Table 1. Evaluation results on the test set (containing a total of 1 223 MSAs). MERLIN achieved an accuracy of 71.18% on the test data.

Metric	Value	Average precision (per class)
mAP	71.18%	Internal deletion, AP = 75.85%
Recall	78%	N-terminal deletion, AP = 93.91%
Precision	72%	C-terminal deletion, AP = 85.83%
F1-score	75%	Internal insertion, AP = 76.57%
Average IoU	67.73%	N-terminal extension, AP = 88.02%
True positives	2 667	C-terminal extension, AP = 66.80%
False positives	1 014	Internal mismatch, AP = 11.32%
False negatives	748	

Every 1000 iterations, the mAP is calculated on the validation set and the corresponding weights are saved in order to find the *best* weights with maximum accuracy. The optimal model weights yielded a validation mAP of 72.89%. We evaluated the performance of our object detector on the test set and reported the results in Table 1. With a default IoU threshold of 50%, our model reached a test accuracy of 71.18% with an average IoU of 67.73%. The results also show that the model correctly identified 78% of all actual positives with a precision of 72%. In Table 1, the average precision (AP) evaluates the performance of the model for each class. To better interpret the obtained results, we compared the number of all annotated errors (*i.e.* errors identified by the Bayesian model SIBIS [12]) in the test set to the number of detected errors by our object detector for each error type. The results are reported in Table 2. Internal deletions are the most present in the test set with a total of 1 132 (representing 33.15% of the test set). The model detected 84.45% of correct internal deletions with an average precision of 75.85%. C-terminal extension errors are the least present in the test set with 92 occurrences (representing only 2.7% of the test set): 66% of these errors were correctly predicted with an AP of 66.80%. N-terminal deletions are the most accurately predicted errors with an AP of 93.91%, while internal mismatches were found to be the most difficult to detect with a low AP of 11.32%. This could be intuitively explained by the following: while deletions, insertions, and extensions alter the structural shape of an MSA, by introducing gaps or additional sequence segments, mismatches are represented by a succession of odd residues (colors) introduced into one or more columns, which makes this particular sequence inconsistency relatively more subtle and difficult to discern. This could also be due to the scarcity of training samples for this class which makes it difficult for the model to learn underlying characteristics of mismatch errors.

Table 2. Comparison results. We compared the number of all annotated errors by SIBIS [12] in the test set to the number of errors detected by our proposed object detector.

	Number of identified errors by SIBIS [12]	Number of identified errors by YOLOv4 [2]
Internal deletion	1 132	1 305 (TP = 956, FP = 349)
N-terminal deletion	1 033	1 139 (TP = 953, FP = 186)
C-terminal deletion	320	342 (TP = 260, FP = 82)
Internal insertion	282	325 (TP = 211, FP = 114)
N-terminal extension	203	253 (TP = 178, FP = 75)
C-terminal extension	92	96 (TP = 61, FP = 35)
Internal mismatch segment	224	221 (TP = 48, FP = 173)
Total	3 415	3 681

5.1 Detecting Inconsistencies in MSAs: Qualitative Analysis

We examined the extent to which our model, MERLIN, is able to make good predictions on randomly selected MSAs from the test set: these MSAs contain different types and number of errors. MERLIN was also tested on MSAs that were annotated as error-free by SIBIS. Table 3 shows error detection results of our detector on randomly selected MSAs. The MSA identified as Q9UEE5 contains three different errors: N-terminal deletion, N-terminal extension, and internal deletion. All three errors were correctly detected by the model with high confidence scores[4]: 99%, 98%, and 93%, respectively. The second example, MSA Q9UHL4, contains an internal insertion error and a mismatch. While the model correctly identified both errors, the mismatch error has a low confidence score (40%) compared to the internal insertion (92%).

Table 3. Examples of prediction results on the test set. Sample MSAs with different inconsistencies correctly predicted by MERLIN.

MSA identifier	Prediction: confidence score %
Q9UEE5	N-terminal deletion: 99%
	N-terminal extension: 98%
	Internal deletion: 93%
Q9UHL4	Internal insertion: 92%
	Internal mismatch: 40%

As stated in Sect. 3, the Bayesian model, SIBIS, used for data annotation is not 100% accurate; in terms of error detection, SIBIS exhibited a higher specificity of 92% with a sensitivity of 81%. Taking this statement into account, it is possible that certain MSAs contain at least one error that SIBIS has failed to detect. Moreover, it is important to note that MSAs may contain certain gaps as well as sequence segments that are structurally similar to deletions, extensions or insertion errors; however, these segments are simple shape variations in the MSA and do not constitute inconsistencies. In order to assess the ability of our object detector to distinguish between these variations and erroneous segments we used our model to identify errors on randomly selected examples amongst MSAs containing such characteristics. Detection results are shown in Fig. 2: Q9NZI2 is an MSA with two N-terminal deletions correctly identified by the model. While the first deletion is a true positive with a high confidence score (98%), the second is a false positive with a lower confidence of 46%; however, a thorough manual examination of the MSA confirmed the presence of the second deletion, which was overlooked by SIBIS. We also observe that the MSA contains inserted sequence segments that were not misidentified by the model as inconsistencies. In Fig. 2b, we present an MSA with a deletion error and two extended sequence segments. While our object detector successfully predicts the error with a confidence of 67%, it does not misidentify the extensions as erroneous. This particular MSA was manually found to contain a mismatch error that was overlooked by both SIBIS and our object detector.

More detection results on randomly selected MSAs are shown in Table 4. MSA Q9UBP4 has one extension error and three deletions. All detected errors are true

---

[4] Class-specific scores which encode the probability of a class appearing in the predicted box and how well the box fits the object.

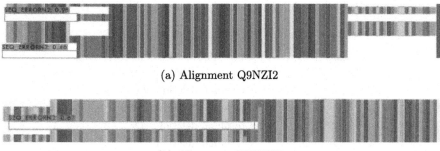

(a) Alignment Q9NZI2

(b) Alignment Q9P2W7

Fig. 2. Alignment Q9NZI2

positives identified by the object detector with high confidence scores (98%–100%). It should be noted that the MSA contains two insertions that were not annotated as errors by SIBIS nor detected by our method. To determine whether these sequence segments constitute sequence inconsistencies, more information about the corresponding genomic sequences and the exon/intron structure is required. Three N-terminal deletions were found in the second example (MSA Q9UK12). While the first deletion is the only true positive prediction with a high confidence of 86%, a close inspection of the MSA revealed that the remaining deletions are true errors that the annotation tool has failed to identify. We also note that the alignment includes two deletions that were left undetected. The model made two correct predictions on MSA Q9UBK7: an extension error with a confidence score of 94%, and an internal insertion error with an equally high detection score of 95%. The third prediction corresponds to an internal deletion with a confidence of 39% that was not annotated by SIBIS, however a manual examination of the MSA suggested that this may be a correct positive prediction. The same observation can be made for MSA Q9Y664, where the model correctly identified three different inconsistencies: a deletion with a score of 48%, an extension with a score of 93%, and an insertion with a score of 34%. However, while the deletion and extension errors are true positives, the internal insertion is a manually confirmed error that was missed by SIBIS. In the last alignment, Q9NYB5, two mismatches were incorrectly detected by our model with low confidence scores.

As mentioned above, SIBIS is an automatic algorithm that sometimes fails to identify errors within MSAs. Therefore, it is reasonable to assume that some MSAs, containing at least one error, were dismissed as error-free. In order to validate this claim, we used MERLIN on three randomly selected alignments from a set of MSAs initially dismissed as containing no known inconsistencies by SIBIS. Prediction results are reported in Table 5. In the first example, MSA Q8WTV1, the model identified a deletion error with a high confidence (84%), while in the second MSA, an extension error was detected with a relatively low confidence of 48%. In the third example, the model identified an insertion with

Table 4. Additional detection results on the test set.

MSA identifier	Prediction: confidence score %
Q9UBP4	N-terminal extension: 99%
	N-terminal deletion: 100%
	N-terminal deletion: 98%
	N-terminal deletion: 100%
Q9UK12	N-terminal deletion: 86%
	N-terminal deletion: 78%
	N-terminal deletion: 78%
Q9UBK7	N-terminal extension: 94%
	Internal insertion: 95%
	Internal deletion: 39%
Q9Y664	C-terminal deletion: 48%
	C-terminal extension: 93%
	Internal insertion: 34%
Q9NYB5	Internal mismatch: 27%
	Internal mismatch: 33%

an even lower confidence of 26%. All the identified inaccuracies were manually confirmed by human expertise.

Table 5. Prediction results on MSAs initially annotated as error-free. MERLIN successfully identifies different types of errors that were overlooked by SIBIS [12]. These predictions were manually confirmed by human expertise.

MSA identifier	Prediction: confidence score %
Q8WTV1	N-terminal deletion: 84%
Q8TEV8	C-terminal extension: 48%
Q9GZW5	Internal insertion: 26%

It is important to note that, regardless of the detection confidence scores, the false positive predictions obtained by the detector warranted a manual re-evaluation of the MSAs which confirmed the accuracy of these predictions. These inconsistencies were not identified by SIBIS [12] in the original alignments [15], and therefore not annotated in our dataset. Thus, it is safe to assume that the number of true positives identified by our object detector is probably higher than 78.10%. Considering all of the above, our trained object detector is a promising tool for the quality assessment of multiple sequence alignments.

5.2   Performance Comparison

We evaluated the performance of our object detector against OD-Seq [11] and EvalMSA [4] on the test set. As described in Sect. 2, these tools rely on a gap metric to identify outlier sequences in a given MSA; that is, divergent sequences that could harm the accuracy of an alignment. Our proposed approach, on the other hand, is designed to detect different inconsistencies within each individual sequence in an MSA. We conducted our comparison based on the number of outlier sequences identified by OD-Seq and EvalMSA, and all erroneous sequences found by MERLIN. Our detector yielded a precision of 83% compared to 77% by OD-Seq and 64% by EvalMSA; in terms of recall, our approach achieved 89% on the test set, outperforming both OD-Seq (29%) and EvalMSA (51%).

5.3   Interpretable Predictions

Our proposed object detector proved effective in identifying inconsistencies within MSAs to assess their accuracy. However, the obtained predictions by the model, while valuable, are limited to the visual representation of the MSAs and cannot be directly exploited by bioinformaticians. To this end, we designed a program to parse all predicted errors for a given MSA into a more accessible format. The program takes YOLO predictions as input and outputs a text file which contains all identified inconsistencies with their corresponding position coordinates (*i.e.* the affected sequence, and start and end columns of the detected error). This information allows researchers to analyze an MSA with commonly used MSA visualization tools such as Jalview [26].

6   Conclusion

In this paper, we investigated a new approach by using a state-of-the-art object detector [2] to identify inconsistencies on visual representations of Multiple Sequence Alignments. We proposed MERLIN (Msa ERror Localization and IdentificatioN), an object detection model to detect and localize different types of errors (deletions, insertions/extensions, mismatches) within MSAs. Our model yielded an accuracy of 71.18% in error detection and achieved better precision (83%) and recall (89%), compared to gap penalty-based techniques, in identifying outlier sequences in MSAs. A qualitative analysis showed that MERLIN can also differentiate between sequence segments structurally similar to alignment errors and actual inconsistencies, and that it can identify and localize errors that were dismissed by annotation tools.

These encouraging results suggest that such an approach is suitable to localize and identify different types of errors in MSAs and, overall, evaluate their quality. This could prompt further research in this field in an effort to provide automated assistance to bioinformaticians working with Multiple Sequence Alignments.

Acknowledgements. The authors would like to thank the BiGEst bioinformatics platform for technical support. This work was supported by the French Infrastructure

Institut Français de Bioinformatique (IFB) ANR-11-INBS-0013, ANR ArtIC ANR-20-THIA-0006 and Institute funds from the French Centre National de la Recherche Scientifique and the University of Strasbourg.

References

1. Armougom, F., et al.: Expresso: automatic incorporation of structural information in multiple sequence alignments using 3D-coffee. Nucleic Acids Res. **34**, W604–W608 (2006). https://doi.org/10.1093/nar/gkl092
2. Bochkovskiy, A., Wang, C., Liao, H.M.: YOLOv4: Optimal Speed and Accuracy of Object Detection. CoRR abs/2004.10934 (2020). https://arxiv.org/abs/2004.10934
3. Chatzou, M., et al.: Multiple sequence alignment modeling: methods and applications. Brief. Bioinform. **17**(6), 1009–1023 (2015). https://doi.org/10.1093/bib/bbv099
4. Chiner-Oms, A., González-Candelas, F.: Evalmsa: a program to evaluate multiple sequence alignments and detect outliers. Evol. Bioinform. **12**, EBO.S40583 (2016). https://doi.org/10.4137/EBO.S40583. pMID: 27920488
5. Consortium, T.U.: UniProt: a worldwide hub of protein knowledge. Nucleic Acids Res. **47**(D1), D506–D515 (2018). https://doi.org/10.1093/nar/gky1049
6. Dragan, M.A., Moghul, I., Priyam, A., Bustos, C., Wurm, Y.: Genevalidator: identify problems with protein-coding gene predictions. Bioinformatics **32**, 1559–1561 (2016). https://doi.org/10.1093/bioinformatics/btw015
7. Finn, R.D., et al.: Pfam: the protein families database. Nucleic Acids Res. **42**(D1), D222–D230 (2014). https://doi.org/10.1093/nar/gkt1223
8. Gao, Y., et al.: Deep neural network-assisted computed tomography diagnosis of metastatic lymph nodes from gastric cancer. Chin. Med. J. **132**, 2804–2811 (2019). https://doi.org/10.1097/CM9.0000000000000532
9. He, K., Zhang, X., Ren, S., Sun, J.: Spatial pyramid pooling in deep convolutional networks for visual recognition. IEEE Trans. Pattern Anal. Mach. Intell. **37**(9), 1904–16 (2015)
10. Hung, J., et al.: Keras R-CNN: library for cell detection in biological images using deep neural networks. BMC Bioinform. **21**, 1–7 (2020). https://doi.org/10.1186/s12859-020-03635-x
11. Jehl, P., Sievers, F., Higgins, D.: OD-SEQ: outlier detection in multiple sequence alignments. BMC Bioinform. **16**, 269 (2015). https://doi.org/10.1186/s12859-015-0702-1
12. Khenoussi, W., Vanhoutreve, R., Poch, O., Thompson, J.: SIBIS: a Bayesian model for inconsistent protein sequence estimation. Bioinformatics **30**, 2432–2439 (2014). https://doi.org/10.1093/bioinformatics/btu329
13. Komasilovs, V., Zacepins, A., Kviesis, A., Estevez, C.: Traffic monitoring using an object detection framework with limited dataset. In: VEHITS (2019)
14. Liu, S., Qi, L., Qin, H., Shi, J., Jia, J.: Path aggregation network for instance segmentation. In: 2018 IEEE/CVF Conference on Computer Vision and Pattern Recognition, pp. 8759–8768 (2018)

15. Meyer, C., Scalzitti, N., Jeannin-Girardon, A., Collet, P., Poch, O., Thompson, J.D.: Understanding the causes of errors in eukaryotic protein-coding gene prediction: a case study of primate proteomes. BMC Bioinform. **21**, 1–16 (2020)
16. Nagy, A., Patthy, L.: Mispred: a resource for identification of erroneous protein sequences in public databases. Database J. Biol. Databases Curation **2013**, bat053 (2013). https://doi.org/10.1093/database/bat053
17. O'Leary, N.A., et al.: Reference sequence (RefSeq) database at NCBI: current status, taxonomic expansion, and functional annotation. Nucleic Acids Res. **44**(D1), D733–D745 (2015). https://doi.org/10.1093/nar/gkv1189
18. Redmon, J.: Darknet: open source neural networks in C (2013-2016). http://pjreddie.com/darknet/
19. Redmon, J., Divvala, S., Girshick, R., Farhadi, A.: You only look once: unified, real-time object detection. In: 2016 IEEE Conference on Computer Vision and Pattern Recognition (CVPR), pp. 779–788 (2016). https://doi.org/10.1109/CVPR.2016.91
20. Redmon, J., Farhadi, A.: Yolov3: an incremental improvement. CoRR abs/1804.02767 (2018). http://arxiv.org/abs/1804.02767
21. Tamura, K., Stecher, G., Peterson, D., Filipski, A., Kumar, S.: MEGA6: molecular evolutionary genetics analysis version 6.0. Mol. Biol. Evol. **30**, 2725–2729 (2013). https://doi.org/10.1093/molbev/mst197
22. Thompson, J.D.: Statistics for Bioinformatics: Methods for Multiple Sequence Alignment. iSTE Press (2016)
23. Thompson, J.D., Linard, B., Lecompte, O., Poch, O.: A comprehensive benchmark study of multiple sequence alignment methods: current challenges and future perspectives. PLoS ONE **6**, e18093 (2011)
24. Vanhoutreve, R., Kress, A., Legrand, B., Gass, H., Poch, O., Thompson, J.: LEON-BIS: multiple alignment evaluation of sequence neighbours using a Bayesian inference system. BMC Bioinform. **17**, 1–10 (2016). https://doi.org/10.1186/s12859-016-1146-y
25. Wang, C.Y., Liao, H.Y.M., Yeh, I.H., Wu, Y.H., Chen, P.Y., Hsieh, J.W.: CSPNet: a new backbone that can enhance learning capability of CNN. In: 2020 IEEE/CVF Conference on Computer Vision and Pattern Recognition Workshops (CVPRW), pp. 1571–1580 (2020)
26. Waterhouse, A.M., Procter, J.B., Martin, D.M.A., Clamp, M., Barton, G.J.: Jalview Version 2-a multiple sequence alignment editor and analysis workbench. Bioinformatics **25**(9), 1189–1191 (2009). https://doi.org/10.1093/bioinformatics/btp033
27. wkhtmltopdf. https://wkhtmltopdf.org
28. Zaal, D., Nota, B.: ADOMA: a command line tool to modify ClustalW multiple alignment output. Mol. Inform. **35**, 42–44 (2015). https://doi.org/10.1002/minf.201500083

PigPose: A Realtime Framework for Farm Animal Pose Estimation and Tracking

Milan Kresovic[1], Thong Nguyen[1], Mohib Ullah[1(✉)], Hina Afridi[1,2],
and Faouzi Alaya Cheikh[1]

[1] Norwegian University of Science and Technology, 2815 Gjøvik, Norway
mohib.ullah@ntnu.no
[2] Geno SA, Hamar, Norway

Abstract. In industrial farming, livestock well-being is becoming increasingly more important. Animal breeding companies are interested in enhancing the total merit index used in breeding programs. Pigs tracking and behaviour analysis plays a crucial role in breeding programs. To this end, we proposed a tracking-by-detection approach for detecting and tracking indoor farm animals for an extended period. We exploited a modified OpenPose model for the detection where the features from the input frames are extracted through EfficientNet, and the detected Keypoints are associated through a greedy optimization mechanism. Additionally, the attention mechanism is incorporated in the pose estimation framework to refine the input frames' features maps. A bipartite graph is created for every two frames to track the animals over an extended period. The edge cost is defined by the spatial distance between the detected Keypoints of the animals in the temporal domain. We collected and annotated the customized dataset from the pig farm to train the model. The dataset and annotation will be made publicly available to help promote research in the farming industry. The proposed method is evaluated on AP^{OKS} and AR^{OKS}, and promising results are achieved.

Keywords: Attention mechanism · Pose estimation · Tracking · Greedy optimization · Bipartite graph

1 Introduction

The welfare of livestock is becoming increasingly more important in industrial farming. Besides altruistic and humane reasons, good animal welfare also contributes to the better food quality of animal products [1]. Even though many regulations have been introduced to manage industrial farming, the current industrial practices do not address sustainability issues [2]. To improve farm products and comply with the animal welfare regulations, breeding companies can leverage vision-based solutions to monitor the animal living and conceive novel animal traits that can enhance the breeding programs [3]. Compared to manual monitoring of animals, computer vision provides a non-invasive solution.

I. Maglogiannis et al. (Eds.): AIAI 2022, IFIP AICT 646, pp. 204–215, 2022.
https://doi.org/10.1007/978-3-031-08333-4_17

Especially, tracking multiple pigs in a pen for an extended period of time provide invaluable information about animal behavior that could be used in the breed programs to enhance the total merit indexes (TMI) [4]. Multi-target tracking is a difficult technical topic that has received a lot of attention in recent decades [5]. A wide range of applications to deal with the problem of multiple object tracking in a scene has been invented such as surveillance of common places [6], sports [7], crowd flow management [8], home robotics [9], and tracking in MRI-guided radiotherapy for various disease diagnosis [10]. Nevertheless, regarding farming industry, such approaches are not prevalent.

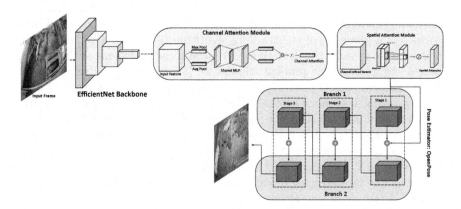

Fig. 1. First, EfficientNet extracts the image features that generate feature maps. The feature maps are refined through channel and spatial attention module. The refined feature maps are given as input to the first stage of Pose estimator. Here the network predicts the PAFs, which presents a degree of association between different animal parts. Later, in stage 2, the network predicts the confidence maps of the animal organs like the nose, left ear, right ear, neck, back, and tail. Finally, the network associate the corresponding organic key points through a greedy optimization.

Thanks to the rapid advancement in video analysis, research on vision-based pig industrial farming has shown a steady increase over the few years. Jaewon et al. [11] proposed an approach for reliable pig detection under various illumination conditions. In addition to RGB, they use additional information like depth maps and infrared images to make detections as trust-worthy as possible. Using non-visual information helps in optimizing the execution and allows for bypassing computationally heavy deep learning models. On the other hand, to obtain this type of information additional hardware is needed to be installed in the pens where the pigs are habituating, which increases the cost of the overall system. Liu et al. [12] used two linear SVM to obtain the candidate regions of pigs on the input image. These candidate regions are then forwarded to the CNN which uses them to classify and identify true pig detection. Furthermore, Ju et al. [13] proposed a hybrid system for segmenting touching-pigs. First, the input data is obtained using the Kinect depth sensor. Afterward, YOLO [14] is used for pig detection.

If the boundary generated by this network is not satisfactory, a more heuristic approach is used where a possible boundary is suggested by analyzing the shape of the pigs. An approach that is addressing the similar problem of pig segmentations is presented by Brunger et al. [15] where instead of using bounding boxes or keypoints location estimation, they focused more on tracing the contours of the pig and obtain the panoptic segmentation. A pipeline for pig tracking-by-detection approach in pig farms has been presented in [16]. Intrinsically, the pipeline uses a CNN based detector and Bayesian filters for tracking. Additionally, after a pig has been detected, the tracking algorithm uses features extracted from detected tag-boxes from the previous step. In a similar line of work, Cowton et al. [17] adapted Faster Region-based CNN for pigs with two real-time multi-object tracking algorithms. The caveats of both these approaches are something that is called frame loss which is a tendency of the tracking algorithm to lose some of the tracking frames because usually, the detection part faced some occlusions of the tracking instances. To address this problem, Sun et al. [18] used Faster-Region-CNN to attain bounding boxes of pigs, where these bounding boxes are forwarded to the SURF algorithm. Together with the background difference method, this algorithm attempts to determine whether the pig will be partially obscured in the next frame and avoid tracking frame loss in that way. As the striving goal of all these methods is to be used for the behavioral analysis of pigs. Methods like [19] try to detect specific behavioral patterns from the input data. Specifically, Li et al. [19] proposed a pipeline for detecting mounting behavior. They used Mask R-CNN [20] is used for detecting pigs in frames and the detected regions of interest are then used to calculate eigenvectors, which are in the end classified with kernel extreme learning machine (KELM) to see if the mounting behavior has happened. The most common tracking paradigm is known as tracking-by-detection [21–24]. In a nutshell, the problem is divided into two parts. The first part is obtaining the

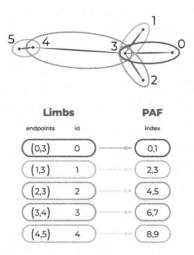

Fig. 2. Description of pig limbs and the corresponding index of PAF.

location of the instances that need to be tracked. While the second part is essentially based on optimization and it aims to associate the corresponding instances for obtaining smooth trajectories in the temporal domain. Historically, the localization of instances in every frame is achieved through a generative [25] or a discriminative [26] model. Different geometric shapes like rectangle, ellipse, circle are used to encapsulate object instances. More recently, methods that localize Keypoints of object instance are getting more popular as it gives the flexibility of detection even in partial occlusion. The detected Keypoints can be reassembled to get a unified skeleton of the target and helped tracked the target for an extended period. This paper focuses on conceiving a multi-target tracking framework for indoor pig tracking. In general, the contribution of the work is three-fold:

- We proposed an attention based pose estimation framework for pigs. We explored the state-of-the-art CNN model for extracting the features from the input frames.
- We collected the data at pig farm, and did the annotation to training and validating our proposed model.
- We tested the proposed pose estimation framework in tracking multiple pigs and achieved promising results.

The paper is organized as follows. Section 2 elaborate the proposed method. The training strategy and loss function is elaborated in Sect. 3. Tracking module is explained in Sect. 4 while Sect. 5 gives the details of the dataset, annotation, implementation, and limitation of the work. Section 6 concludes the paper and gives the future direction.

2   Proposed Method

The pig Keypoint detection pipeline is demonstrated in Fig. 1. At input, it takes the RGB image and extracts the deep features through EfficientNet [27]. By exploiting EfficientNet, the spatial resolution is saved by reusing the backbone weights through dilating convolution, which essentially removes the layer $conv4_2/dw$ of the original model [28]. The extracted feature maps are refined through channel and spatial attention module. We used convolution block attention module (CBAM) [29] for refining the features maps. In the next step, a multiple stages CNN pipeline is applied to extract part confidence maps and part affinity field from the extracted deep features. The confidence map is defined as a two-dimensional representation of the probability that a specific pig body part can be found in the given location. Mathematically, it is represented as:

$$S = (S_1, S_2, ..., S_J) \qquad S_J \in R^{w*h} \qquad (1)$$

where S represents the confidence map and J the number of the pig body part that is assumed to be six in this work. Similarly, the part affinity field is defined as the collection of 2D vectors representing the position and orientation of limbs of the pigs in the image. It essentially represents the form of pairwise connections between the body parts. Graphically, it is represented in Fig. 2. Mathematically, it can be written as:

$$L = (L_1, L_2, ..., L_C) \qquad L_c \in R^{w*h*c} \tag{2}$$

where L L is the part affinity field and C represents the limb index that is five in the case of pigs. After extracted two pieces of information from the deep features, the parsing between confidence maps and PAFs is conducted to assemble all 2D Keypoints locations into individual body poses for every pig in the input. It is essentially an optimization process and solved through the Hungarian algorithm.

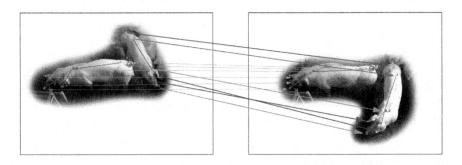

Fig. 3. Temporal association of the detecting keypoints in frame f_{t-1} and f_t.

3   Loss Functions

At each time step, after calculating the confidence map and part affinity field, an L2-loss is computed between the predicted confidence maps and Part Affinity fields to the ground truth maps and fields. Mathematically, the loss function component related to the confidence map is computed as:

$$f_S^{t_k} = \sum_{j=1}^{J} \sum_p W(p).||S_j^{t_k}(p) - S_j^*(p)||_2^2 \tag{3}$$

where S_j^* is the groundtruth confidence map and $S_j^{t_k}$ is the predicted confidence map by the model. Similarly, the loss function component related to affinity field is computed as:

$$f_L^{t_i} = \sum_{c=1}^{C} \sum_p W(p).||L_c^{t_i}(p) - L_c^*(p)||_2^2 \tag{4}$$

where L_c^* is the groundtruth and $L_c^{t_i}$ is the predicted affinity field, respectively. In addition, we have the parameter W that is used to commentate the loss when the Keypoint is not visible in the training sample. By combining the two components, we can write the overall loss of the network as:

$$f = \sum_{t=1}^{TP} f_L^t + \sum_{t=T_P+1}^{T_P+T_C} f_S^t \tag{5}$$

where f_S represented the loss related to the confidence map and f_L is the loss related to the part affinity. To improve the model generalization, data augmentations like rotation, scaling, cropping, and Gaussian noise has been applied to the training set.

4   Tracking

After detecting the Keypoints of individual pigs, we use our tracking approach to track the pigs for extended period of time. We followed the tracking-by-detection paradigm [30] and used spatial distance to associate the corresponding pigs. The illustration of pigs association is depicted in Fig. 3. The edge cost $c_{i,j}$ between the Keypoints of two pigs is measured by the statistical similarity metric [31] as follows:

$$c_{i,j} = \frac{1}{2}(D_{KL}(\varphi_i||M) + D_{KL}(\varphi_j||M)) \tag{6}$$

φ_i and φ_j are the spatial position of pig i and j, respectively. M is the average distance of the two pigs while D_{KL} is the Kullback-Leibler divergence. $c_{i,j}$ is the edge cost that shows the affinity between two pigs in the consecutive frames (Fig. 4).

Fig. 4. (a) Correction detection and tracking, (b) Scenario with Occlusion and overlapping, (c) Wrong detection and tracking, limb liked to a wall, (d) Wrong PAFs among pigs

5   Experiments

In this section, we presented a brief overview of the implementation, parameter selection, the dataset and annotation, and the limitation of the proposed framework.

5.1   Dataset and Annotation

The main contributor of the data is Norsvin that is the largest pig breeding company in Norway. They provided 26 GB of different video recordings of pigs in the pens. The camera position is fixed and the lighting is mostly uniform. The frame size is 2688×1520 with 15 fps. For the purpose of the videos, two different types of pigs were recorded. The dataset was developed in the standard MS-COCO format. We annotated each pig in every frame for six keypoints i.e. nose, left and right ear, neck, back, and tail. In addition to Keypoints, a binary mask of each pig is generated which assists in model training. An annotated sample can be seen in Fig. 5.

Fig. 5. Annotated sample frame

5.2   Implementation

Models were trained with 4 GPUs NVIDIA Tesla V100 16 Gb, with 870 training and 217 validation annotated images. The training PCM and PAF loss for the last training test for different tested models can be seen in Fig. 6. Models were trained in three steps. First, we train the model using the pretrained backbone weights - initialization. The second step was to train the one-stage model with the re-learned backbone weights from the previous step - finetuning the one-stage network. In the last step, we increased the number of stages to 3 and train the model using re-learned weights from the second step - training the three-stage network. The same process was done for all tested networks. On average, each frame is annotated in 12 min. A fully annotated sample frame is shown in Fig. 5. The details of training parameters are listed in Table 1. The empirical parameters PAF threshold (σ) and success ration (τ) are similar to [28].

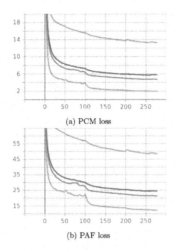

(a) PCM loss

(b) PAF loss

Fig. 6. Training curves of different backbone architectures: Top gray - MobileNet V1, green - EfficientNet-B3-a, blue - EfficientNeet-B3, bottom gray - EfficientNet-B6

Table 1. Empirical parameters, training and inference time

Learning rate	4e−5
Number of epochs	279
Training time	126 min
Batch size	32
Inference time	0.8 s
PAF threshold σ	0.05 s
Success ratio τ	0.8 s

5.3   Results of Pose Estimation

For pose estimation, to calculate the average precision score, instead of using intersection over union, a new similarity called object keypoint similarity (OKS) is created. OKS between the predicted pig pose $\hat{\theta}p$ and the ground truth annotation θp of the pig p is calculated as follows: Simply put, OKS between predicted

$$ks(\hat{\theta}_i^{(p)}, \theta_i^{(p)}) = e^{-\dfrac{\left\|\hat{\theta}_i^{(p)} - \theta_i^{(p)}\right\|_2^{2}}{2s^2 k_i^2}}$$

$$OKS(\hat{\theta}^{(p)}, \theta^{(p)}) = \dfrac{\sum_i ks(\hat{\theta}_i^{(p)}, \theta_i^{(p)})\delta(W_i > 0)}{\sum_i \delta(W_i > 0)}$$

and true pig pose represents averaged keypoint similarity ks measure over all visible keypoints ($W_i > 0$) in a predicted pose with the corresponding true pose keypoints. To calculate ks similarity for predicted keypoint position, we are using an unnormalized Gaussian function that has a center in true keypoint location. The spread of this Gaussian is determined by a standard deviation k_i specific to a keypoint type. Scale s is related to a pig pose bounding box area so that k_s is size-sensitive. It's important to note that k_i is experimentally determined. To do so, multiple observers are needed to annotate the same set of images, and for each keypoint type i a standard deviation σ_i^2 is calculated. k_i is then calculated as:

$$k_i = 2\sigma_i \tag{7}$$

As we couldn't redundantly annotate single images multiple times, we have chosen a constant k_i value of 0.107 for all keypoints (Fig. 7).

	AP^{OKS} (m.p.p. = 20)			AR^{OKS} (m.p.p. = 20)		
OKS	0.5 : 0.05 : 0.95	0.5	0.75	0.5 : 0.05 : 0.95	0.5	0.75
MobileNet V1	0.374	0.675	0.375	0.43	0.704	0.445
EfficientNet-B3a	0.395	0.715	0.393	0.465	0.751	0.476
EfficientNet-B3	0.41	0.723	0.418	0.484	0.770	0.505
EfficientNet-B6	0.448	0.768	0.456	0.519	0.796	0.546

Fig. 7. AP^{OKS} and AR^{OKS} values for different models and different OKS thresholds.

5.4   Results and Discussion

From the values of AP^{OKS} and AR^{OKS}, we can see that the EfficientNet-B6 is performing the best. This is not surprising if we compare the number of parameters for each model. EfficientNet-B6 as such has almost 4 times more parameters than the next best models, EfficientNet-B3 and EfficientNet-B3a, thus increasing the training and inference time. On the other hand, if we compare EfficientNet-B3 with EfficientNet-B3a (a version with the spatial attention proposed by us), we can see that the EfficientNet-B3 is performing a little bit better. Therefore, we can conclude that our modification has not produced any improvements. This could be explained by the fact that the weights for the spatial attention layer have not been initialized by the training on the bigger datasets as all of the EfficientNet original models have been. Overall, the backbone with larger number of parameters and different architecture has yielded much better results than the framework with MobileNet V1 backbone. If we have to optimize for the model size and its performance, we could choose the EfficientNet-B3 model as it best balances gains and losses. We believed that a very small training set was used by expanding the training set with more scenarios, the performance could be improved. Additionally, an ablation study and comparison with the state-of-the-art will highlight the strengthens of the proposed method and will be included in future work.

6   Conclusion

In this paper, we have proposed an improved and optimized Pig Pose framework and tested different backbone CNN models. We have found that by using EfficientNet architecture instead of traditional CNN models, we can acquire significant improvement in the performance. We also showed that adding the attention mechanism didn't provide better results. Additionally, by using a bigger and more diverse dataset, we can managed to create a more robust model. Furthermore, we conducted a more thorough evaluation in terms of AP^{OKS} and AR^{OKS} scores for different models. Future work should include the evaluation of more diverse feature-extractor networks. The pig pose estimation doesn't have to be in realtime, thus, by using bigger models we could improve the prediction. We tested a basic tracker on the proposed model and found a robust pose estimator can yield good tracking results.

Acknowledgment. We would like to thank Norsvin SA for sharing data and the Research Council of Norway for funding this study, within the BIONÆR program, project numbers 282252 and 321409. In special, we would also like to thank Rune Sagevik, Norsvin SA for the image acquisition.

References

1. Quddus Khan, A., Khan, S., Ullah, M., Cheikh, F.A.: A bottom-up approach for pig skeleton extraction using RGB data. In: El Moataz, A., Mammass, D., Mansouri, A., Nouboud, F. (eds.) ICISP 2020. LNCS, vol. 12119, pp. 54–61. Springer, Cham (2020). https://doi.org/10.1007/978-3-030-51935-3_6
2. Post, M.J., et al.: Scientific, sustainability and regulatory challenges of cultured meat. Nature Food **1**(7), 403–415 (2020)
3. Herlin, A., Brunberg, E., Hultgren, J., Högberg, N., Rydberg, A., Skarin, A.: Animal welfare implications of digital tools for monitoring and management of cattle and sheep on pasture. Animals **11**(3), 829 (2021)
4. Weishaar, R., Wellmann, R., Camarinha-Silva, A., Rodehutscord, M., Bennewitz, J.: Selecting the hologenome to breed for an improved feed efficiency in pigs? A novel selection index. J. Anim. Breed. Genet. **137**(1), 14–22 (2020)
5. Ullah, M., Cheikh, F.A.: Deep feature based end-to-end transportation network for multi-target tracking. In: 2018 25th IEEE International Conference on Image Processing (ICIP), pp. 3738–3742. IEEE (2018)
6. Beard, M., Vo, B.T., Vo, B.N.: A solution for large-scale multi-object tracking. IEEE Trans. Signal Process. **68**, 2754–2769 (2020)
7. Wang, T., Shi, C.: Basketball motion video target tracking algorithm based on improved gray neural network. Neural Comput. Appl. 1–16 (2022). https://doi.org/10.1007/s00521-022-07026-6
8. Ullah, M., Ullah, H., Conci, N., De Natale, G.B.: Crowd behavior identification. In: IEEE International Conference on Image Processing, pp. 1195–1199 (2016)
9. Erol, B.A., Majumdar, A., Lwowski, J., Benavidez, P., Rad, P., Jamshidi, M.: Improved deep neural network object tracking system for applications in home robotics. In: Pedrycz, W., Chen, S.-M. (eds.) Computational Intelligence for Pattern Recognition. SCI, vol. 777, pp. 369–395. Springer, Cham (2018). https://doi.org/10.1007/978-3-319-89629-8_14

10. Dhont, J., et al.: Multi-object tracking in MRI-guided radiotherapy using the tracking-learning-detection framework. Radiother. Oncol. **138**, 25–29 (2019)
11. Sa, J., Choi, Y., Lee, H., Chung, Y., Park, D., Cho, J.: Fast pig detection with a top-view camera under various illumination conditions. Symmetry **11**(2), 266 (2019)
12. Liu, Y., Sun, L., Luo, B., Chen, S., Li, Y.: Multi-target pigs detection algorithm based on improved CNN. Trans. Chin. Soc. Agric. Mach. S1 (2019)
13. Miso, J., et al.: A kinect-based segmentation of touching-pigs for real-time monitoring. Sensors **18**(6), 1746 (2018)
14. Redmon, J., Divvala, S., Girshick, R., Farhadi, A.: You only look once: unified, real-time object detection. In: Proceedings of the IEEE Conference on Computer Vision and Pattern Recognition, pp. 779–788 (2016)
15. Brünger, J., Gentz, M., Traulsen, I., Koch, R.: Panoptic segmentation of individual pigs for posture recognition. Sensors **20**(13), 3710 (2020)
16. Zhang, L., Gray, H., Ye, X., Collins, L., Allinson, N.: Automatic individual pig detection and tracking in pig farms. Sensors **19**(5), 1188 (2019)
17. Cowton, J., Kyriazakis, I., Bacardit, J.: Automated individual pig localisation, tracking and behaviour metric extraction using deep learning. IEEE Access **7**, 108049–108060 (2019)
18. Sun, L., et al.: Multi target pigs tracking loss correction algorithm based on faster R-CNN. Int. J. Agric. Biol. Eng. **11**(5), 192–197 (2018)
19. Li, D., Chen, Y., Zhang, K., Li, Z.: Mounting behaviour recognition for pigs based on deep learning. Sensors **19**(22), 4924 (2019)
20. He, K., Gkioxari, G., Dollár, P., Girshick, R.: Mask R-CNN. In: Proceedings of the IEEE International Conference on Computer Vision, pp. 2961–2969 (2017)
21. Meinhardt, T., Kirillov, A., Leal-Taixe, L., Feichtenhofer, C.: Trackformer: multi-object tracking with transformers. arXiv preprint arXiv:2101.02702 (2021)
22. Ullah, M., Cheikh, F.A., Imran, A.S.: Hog based real-time multi-target tracking in Bayesian framework. In: IEEE International Conference on Advanced Video and Signal Based Surveillance, pp. 416–422 (2016)
23. Hung, W.-C., et al.: Soda: multi-object tracking with soft data association. arXiv preprint arXiv:2008.07725 (2020)
24. Ullah, M., Mohammed, A.K., Cheikh, F.A., Wang, Z.: A hierarchical feature model for multi-target tracking. In: IEEE International Conference on Image Processing, pp. 2612–2616 (2017)
25. Bai, Y., Zhang, Y., Ding, M., Ghanem, B.: Sod-mtgan: small object detection via multi-task generative adversarial network. In: Proceedings of the European Conference on Computer Vision (ECCV), pp. 206–221 (2018)
26. Tan, M., Pang, R., Le, Q.V.: Efficientdet: scalable and efficient object detection. In: Proceedings of the IEEE/CVF Conference on Computer Vision and Pattern Recognition, pp. 10781–10790 (2020)
27. Tan, M., Le, Q.: Efficientnet: rethinking model scaling for convolutional neural networks. In: International Conference on Machine Learning, pp. 6105–6114. PMLR (2019)
28. Cao, Z., Hidalgo, G., Simon, T., Wei, S.-E., Sheikh, Y.: Openpose: realtime multi-person 2D pose estimation using part affinity fields. IEEE Trans. Pattern Anal. Mach. Intell. **43**(1), 172–186 (2019)
29. Woo, S., Park, J., Lee, J.Y., Kweon, I.S.: CBAM: convolutional block attention module. In: Proceedings of the European Conference on Computer Vision (ECCV), pp. 3–19 (2018)

30. Ullah, M., Cheikh, F.A.: A directed sparse graphical model for multi-target tracking. In: Proceedings of the IEEE Conference on Computer Vision and Pattern Recognition Workshops, pp. 1816–1823 (2018)
31. Lin, J.: Divergence measures based on the shannon entropy. IEEE Trans. Inf. Theory **37**(1), 145–151 (1991)

Speech Emotion Recognition from Earnings Conference Calls in Predicting Corporate Financial Distress

Petr Hajek[(✉)] [iD]

Science and Research Centre, Faculty of Economics and Administration,
University of Pardubice, Studentska 84, Pardubice, Czech Republic
petr.hajek@upce.cz

Abstract. Sentiment and emotion analysis is attracting considerable interest from researchers in the field of finance due to its capacity to provide additional insight into opinions and intentions of investors and managers. A remarkable improvement in predicting corporate financial performance has been achieved by considering textual sentiments. However, little is known about whether managerial affective states influence changes in overall corporate financial performance. To overcome this problem, we propose a deep learning architecture that uses vocal cues extracted from earnings conference calls to detect managerial emotional states and exploits these states to identify firms that could be financially distressed. Our findings provide evidence on the role of managerial emotional states in the early detection of corporate financial distress. We also show that the proposed deep learning-based prediction model outperforms state-of-the-art financial distress prediction models based solely on financial indicators.

Keywords: Speech emotion recognition · Financial distress · Deep learning · Earnings conference calls

1 Introduction

Financial distress prediction models are widely regarded as some of the most important models in finance due to their capacity to provide early warnings to stakeholders about a firm's impending business failure. Stakeholders have suffered significant losses during recent financial crises. Their plight increases the need to reduce information asymmetries between corporate managers and other stakeholders and provide predictive models of financial distress.

Most models to date tended to focus on corporate financial indicators when predicting financial distress [1]. However, in recent years, there has been an

---

Supported by the scientific research project of the Czech Sciences Foundation Grant No: 19-15498S.

I. Maglogiannis et al. (Eds.): AIAI 2022, IFIP AICT 646, pp. 216–228, 2022.
https://doi.org/10.1007/978-3-031-08333-4_18

increasing amount of literature on the role of sentiment and emotion analysis in a firm's textual documents. Indeed, the additional insights gained about investor and managerial opinions proved to be significant predictors of corporate financial performance. Previous research in this regard has focused on identifying sentiment in managerial communications in annual reports [2–5]. However, the linguistic tone of conference calls also turned out to be a significant predictor of abnormal financial returns [6]. It has been shown that the significance of emotional information can outweigh that of factual financial information disclosed by managers and thus indicate financial risks to a company [7]. Recent evidence also shows that nonverbal managerial communication is incrementally useful when combined with quantitative indicators in predicting corporate financial performance [8,9]. This is explained by the dissonance (cognitive conflict) between a manager's emotional state and a firm's actual financial performance, dissonance that can indicate potential financial distress.

With the above thoughts as a basis, we assert that certain emotions detected in earnings conference calls may indicate corporate financial distress. To the best of our knowledge, this is the first work incorporating speech emotion recognition (SER) in financial distress prediction models. To address this issue, we here propose a hybrid deep learning model that exploits state-of-the-art convolutional neural network (CNN)-based SER to leverage financial distress prediction using a long short-term memory (LSTM) neural network. By combining nonverbal vocal attributes obtained from audio recordings of earnings conference calls and financial indicators from financial statements, we hypothesize that the proposed prediction model will outperform traditional models of financial distress, which are based purely on financial data. In addition, we aim to greatly increase the understanding of the role specific emotions might play in predicting corporate financial distress.

The remainder of this paper is organized as follows. Section 2 presents related literature on the use of managerial vocal cues in finance. Section 3 outlines the conceptual framework proposed for early detection of corporate financial distress. Section 4 presents the vocal and financial variables and describes our data. Section 5 describes the setting of the proposed deep learning architecture. Section 6 shows the experimental results of the proposed SER-based financial distress prediction model, and compares the model with existing approaches based on financial variables. Section 7 provides conclusions and outlines future research directions.

2   Related Literature on Using Vocal Cues in Finance

Previous studies have shown that the accuracy of financial prediction models can be significantly increased by exploiting vocal cues from earnings conference calls. A list of those studies is given in Table 1 and shows the data and vocal features used, the methods used, and the prediction problem addressed in terms of predicted variable.

Regarding the vocal cues used, previous studies mostly analyzed audio recordings from earnings conference calls using two tools, layered voice analysis (LVA) [8,10] and Praat voice analysis [11,12]. LVA allows the user to extract the level of affective states from audio recordings, including different categories of cognitive states and emotional reactions. More precisely, four essential features can be obtained, namely the cognitive level, emotional level, thinking level, and global stress level. The cognitive level captures the cognitive dissonance, and the level of excitement is captured by the emotional level. Mental efforts and physical arousal are approximated using the thinking level and stress level features, respectively. Notably, abnormally high emotional levels indicate a positive affect. Mayew [8] and Price [9] reported that positive and negative affects are significant determinants of cumulative abnormal stock returns. Vocal dissonance markers proved to be useful for identifying financial misreporting [10].

Table 1. Summary of data and methods used in previous studies

Study	Method	Features	Prediction task
[8]	LVA+MLR	Positive affect, negative affect	Cumulative abnormal return
[10]	LVA+MLR	Cognitive dissonance	Financial misreporting
[13]	Praat+GLRT	Fundamental frequency, small-scale perturbations, variations of amplitude maxima, mean harmonics-to-noise ratio, proportion of voiced speech	Financial fraud detection
[14]	SPLCE+ MANOVA	Pitch and voice quality, vocal intensity, response latency, pitch slope	Identifying potentially fraudulent utterances
[9]	LVA+MLR	Emotional activity level, cognitive activity level	Cumulative abnormal return
[11]	Praat+HTML	27 vocal features including pitch, intensity, jitter, and the harmonics-to-noise ratio	Stock price volatility forecasting
[12]	Praat+LSTM	26 vocal features including pitch, intensity, jitter, and the harmonics-to-noise ratio	Stock price volatility forecasting
[15]	Praat+SVM	26 vocal features including pitch, intensity, voice, and harmonicity	Stock price volatility and price forecasting
[16]	Praat+DNN	26 vocal features including pitch, intensity, voice, and harmonicity	Stock price volatility forecasting
[18]	pyAudioAnalysis	Emotion valence, emotion arousal	Artificial intelligence readership
[17]	Praat+MDRM	26 vocal features including pitch, intensity, voice, and harmonicity	Stock price volatility forecasting
This study	CNN-based SER+LSTM	180 spectral features used to detect 8 emotional states	Corporate financial distress prediction

Legend: DNN - deep neural network, GLRT - generalized likelihood ratio test, HMTL - hierarchical transformer-based multi-task learning, LVA - layered voice analysis, MANOVA - multivariate analysis of variance, MDRM - multi-modal deep regression model, MLR - multivariate linear regression, SPLCE - structured programming for linguistic cue extraction, SVM - support vector machine.

From a different perspective, the Praat software allows researchers to quantify a wide range of acoustic features, such as pitch, intensity, jitter, shimmer, and excitation patterns. Throckmorton [13] showed that combining features across linguistic and vocal categories provided better fraud detection than those using financial indicators but only if feature selection was performed. Similarly, statements covering up fraud were reportedly higher pitched and lower in voice quality than legitimate statements [14]. Vocal features extracted using Praat also improved the prediction of stock volatility [11]. A semi-supervised multi-modal learning model was shown to be effective for stock volatility prediction [12], and a neural attentive alignment model effectively captured interdependencies across vocal and verbal modalities in another stock price volatility forecasting model [15]. In a similar manner, cross-model and inter-modal attention for deep verbal-vocal coherence was used for modelling stock price interdependence [16]. Most recent works found that gender bias exists in multi-modal volatility prediction [17] and that company representatives adjust the way they talk when they know machines are listening [18].

To summarize the above findings, until now vocal cues have only been applied to financial fraud detection, cumulative abnormal return forecasting, and stock price volatility forecasting. Recent developments in deep learning-based SER allow us to identify the managerial emotional state in earnings conference calls with high accuracy.

3   Conceptual Framework for Predicting Financial Distress

The conceptual framework proposed in this study is depicted in Fig. 1. As reported above, earlier related studies have only considered managers' vocal features rather than the direct detection of managers' emotions expressed in earnings conference calls. To overcome this limitation, inspired by [19], we first employed a CNN-based SER model, which provided the state-of-the-art performance for the RAVDESS (Ryerson Audio-Visual Database of Emotional Speech and Song) benchmark dataset [20]. The dataset comprises 1,440 recordings classified into eight emotional states: neutral, calm, happy, sad, angry, fearful, disgust, and surprised. This allowed us to recognize eight different emotions. Then, audio recordings of earnings conference calls were fed to the trained SER model to obtain emotional state labels. In the next step, the extracted eight emotional features were combined with 20 financial indicators calculated from financial statement data. Finally, data for the previous four quarters were used in the LSTM model for the 1-year-ahead prediction of financial distress. The LSTM recurrent neural network was used to effectively capture high-level temporal features from sequential quarterly data to accurately predict financial distress. We discuss the proposed deep learning-based architecture in detail in Sect. 5.

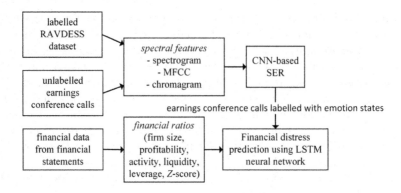

Fig. 1. Conceptual framework for financial distress prediction.

4 Data and Features

The audio file dataset consisted of 1,278 earnings conference calls collected on a quarterly basis from Q1 2010 to Q3 2021 from the EarningsCast database at https://earningscast.com/. The audio data are freely available to the public. For our sample, we considered 40 companies in the United States listed on the New York Stock Exchange (NYSE) with the largest market capitalizations. The reason we chose the earnings conference calls is because they feature business executives discussing their companies' financial information in public, thus conveying financial and voice signals simultaneously [13]. The downloaded audio files were converted to .wav files. It is worth noting that the audio recordings are provided without any segmentation or labels for speakers.

To extract features for SER, we used the Librosa audio library [21]. Specifically, we used 180 spectral features grouped into three different categories, namely, mel-frequency cepstral coefficients (MFCCs) (40 features), mel-scaled spectrograms (128 features), and chromagrams (12 features). These features simulate the way humans receive sound frequencies, with MFCCs forming a mel-frequency cepstrum and the mel scale representing the nonlinear mapping (Fourier transform) of the frequency scale. To represent pitch classes and harmony, chromagrams were obtained using short-time Fourier transform [21]. Overall, our intention was to get a rich representation of the audio recordings, which allowed us to achieve high accuracy in the CNN-based SER model. To illustrate the obtained features, Fig. 2 shows the spectral features for Adobe in Q4 2019.

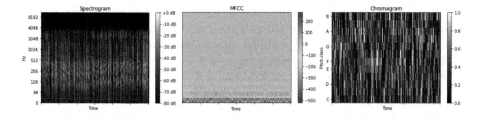

Fig. 2. Illustration of spectral features for Adobe in Q4 2019.

To obtain the matching financial features, we utilized financial statement data collected from the freely available Macrotrends database (www.macrotrends. net). In agreement with related studies on financial distress prediction [22,23], the following financial features were included: (1) firm size (total assets, sales, cash flow, equity), (2) profitability ratios (retained earnings to total assets, return on total assets, return on equity, gross margin, operating margin), (3) activity ratios (asset turnover, inventory turnover, receivable turnover), (4) liquidity ratios (current ratio, cash ratio, working capital to total assets, operating cash flow per share, free cash flow per share), (5) leverage ratios (equity to book value of total liabilities, total debt), and (6) overall financial performance indicator (Altman's Z-score).

Corporate financial distress is defined as a firm's inability to meet its payment obligations on debt. The Altman's model (Altman's Z-score) [24] is the most widely used model for early detection of corporate financial distress. We chose this model to categorize the companies into three classes, namely, safe, grey, and distress zones, because the model was specifically designed for companies listed on U.S. public capital markets. In addition, the model has been shown to be valid for developed markets [24]. The model is able to predict the bankruptcy of a company with high accuracy up to 2 years in advance. The Z-score model for companies with shares publicly tradeable on stock markets is given as follows:

$$Z-score = 1.2x_1 + 1.4x_2 + 3.3x_3 + 0.6x_4 + 1.0x_5, \qquad (1)$$

where x_1 denotes working capital to total assets, x_2 is retained earnings to total assets, x_3 is return on total assets, x_4 is equity to book value of total liabilities, and x_5 is asset turnover. A Z-score of 3 or higher indicates the safe zone (a company with high probability to survive), of 1.80 to 2.99 denotes the grey zone (a company with certain financial difficulties), and of less than 1.80 indicates the distress zone (a high risk for financial distress).

Based on the above groupings for the Z-score, the companies were put into three classes, with 59 samples in the safe zone (4.6%), 329 in the grey zone (25.7%), and 890 in the distress zone (69.7%), indicating a class imbalance problem. Notably, according to [24], the high proportion of companies in the distress zone may indicate a coming financial crisis. The classes were always assigned with a 1-year lag in order to predict financial distress classes 1 year in advance. For the next set of experiments, we additionally categorized the samples into two classes based on whether there was an increase or decrease in the Z-score during the following year. According to the trend of the Z-score, 615 samples were put into the upward class and 663 samples into the downward class. Data for 2010 to 2016 were used as training data, and data for 2017 to 2020 were used to test the performance of the prediction model.

5   Deep Learning Model for Predicting Financial Distress

The deep learning architecture we proposed is depicted in Fig. 3. In it, we used the CNN model for the classification of 8 emotions based on 180 spectral features. As shown in Fig. 3, the model includes one-dimensional convolutional layers. The proposed CNN model is inspired by the architecture developed by [19] and modified for eight emotion classes. Based on the work of [19], the first and second convolutional layers comprised 256 and 128 filters, respectively, with a kernel size of $k = 5$ and a stride step of 1. Next, the max-pooling layer was included with a window size set to 8, followed by another convolutional layer with 128 filters ($k = 5$ and stride $= 1$). Flattening allowed us to continue with the connection of a fully connected layer, followed by a dropout layer (with a dropout rate of 0.2) and a softmax layer with the number of neurons corresponding to the number of predicted emotional classes. Training was performed using the Adam optimizer with a learning rate of 0.0001 and cross-entropy loss as the fitness function. Five-fold cross-validation was used for model evaluation. After the SER model was trained on the RAVDESS dataset, it was possible to use it to label the audio recordings of earnings conference calls based on the 180 spectral features.

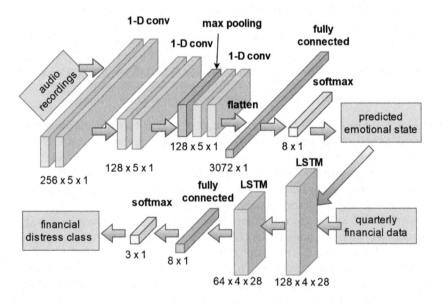

Fig. 3. Deep learning architecture for predicting financial distress.

In the next step, the output emotional state data from the SER module (8 emotional features) were merged with the financial data (20 features) collected from corporate financial statements to produce inputs for two LSTM layers with 128 and 64 neurons, respectively. To make the 1-year-ahead predictions of financial distress, four time steps (quarters) were used. Again, one fully connected dense layer was used to consolidate the output for the forecasted financial distress class (three classes were considered, namely, the safe zone, grey zone, and distress zone). Unlike the CNN architecture, we experimented with different LSTM architectures (one or two LSTM layers with 2^3, 2^4 to 2^9 neurons and one or two dense layers with 2^3, 2^4 to 2^8 neurons) to achieve the best classification performance. The learning configuration for the Adam optimizer was as follows: the learning rate of 0.0001, 100 epochs, and cross-entropy loss used as the fitness function. To conduct the experiments with the proposed deep learning architecture, we used the Keras library on a Jetson AGX Xavier Developer Kit equipped with 512-core Volta GPU with Tensor Cores and 32 GB memory.

6   Results

Using the CNN-based SER system, we were able to achieve 69.8% accuracy on the RAVDESS dataset (using five-fold cross-validation), a result close to that achieved in [19]. The trained CNN-based SER system allowed us to assign emotional state labels to the audio recordings. A calm emotional state prevailed in 67% of the earnings conference calls, happiness followed with 10%, whereas emotional states of surprise or disgust were rarely found ($< 1\%$).

In the next step, we used two separate sets of experiments to predict the financial distress of companies. First, we tested the proposed model on a 1-year-ahead prediction of the three classes of financial distress (safe, grey, or distress). In the second set of experiments, we applied the model to the 1-year-ahead prediction of the trend of financial distress (upward or downward). To evaluate the contribution of the proposed CNN+LSTM prediction model, we compared the prediction results with a baseline model that did not take into account the emotional states of managers during their earnings conference calls. This baseline model is hereafter referred to as the LSTM model. To validate the model, we used several existing models that had been used in previous studies to predict financial distress. We used the values of the above 20 financial ratios 1 year in advance as input variables for all the models compared. Specifically, we used the following models for comparison:

- SMOTE+ADASVM [25] (the combination of the synthetic minority over-sampling technique (SMOTE) with the AdaBoost SVM (ADASVM) ensemble). Since the learning parameters are not presented in the original study, we tested both the linear and polynomial kernel functions for SVM base learners with different values of the regularization parameter $C = \{2^{-1}, 2^0, 2^1, \ldots, 2^5\}$.
- XGBoost [26]. As in [26], the learning rate was set to 0.1, the maximum tree depth for base learners was set to 10, and the subsample ratio was set to 0.7.

- Multilayer Perceptron (MLP) [27] with one hidden layer of 20 ReLUs, trained using the Adam optimizer with the learning rate of 0.001, the maximum number of epochs of 200, and the L2 penalty parameter of 0.0001.
- CUS+GBDT [28] (clustering-based under-sampling (CUS) combined with the gradient boosting decision tree (GBDT)). The number of clusters for CUS was set to 3, 100 estimators were used for GBDT, and the maximum depth of the individual regression estimators was 3.
- Stacking SVM [29]. In agreement with [29], the SVM with linear kernel functions was used to construct the base and meta classifiers. Again, different values of the regularization parameter C were examined.

The Imbalanced-learn library and Scikit-learn library were used for the experiments with the compared methods. To evaluate the performance of the models on the testing data, we used three standard measures of classification performance, that is accuracy (Acc), area under the receiver operating characteristic curve (AUC), and F1 measure (the weighted harmonic mean of precision and recall).

The results in Table 2 show that the existing prediction models provided a high accuracy in predicting financial distress 1 year ahead. Among these models, the best results were obtained by the XGBoost method, despite the fact that, unlike the SMOTE+ADASVM and CUS+GBDT methods, it does not address the problem of data imbalance in the financial distress classes. The high accuracy of our baseline model implied the benefit of a larger window size (time steps) in the proposed LSTM model. We were also able to slightly improve the accuracy by including managerial emotional states, suggesting that while emotional features may be valuable for predicting financial distress, financial ratios are crucial for this prediction. Moreover, the high AUC value indicates that the model performed well on all classes of financial distress. Finally, a balanced performance between precision (0.944 for class and 0.733 for trend prediction) and recall (0.943 and 0.733) was achieved for both prediction tasks.

Table 2. Results of 1-year-ahead financial distress prediction.

Prediction model	Class prediction			Trend prediction		
	Acc	AUC	F1 measure	Acc	AUC	F1 measure
SMOTE+ADASVM	92.04	0.967	0.920	60.30	0.653	0.603
XGBoost	94.15	0.988	0.942	70.02	0.766	0.700
MLP	92.59	0.975	0.926	60.55	0.634	0.605
CUS+GBDT	93.35	0.982	0.934	66.06	0.710	0.660
Stacking SVM	91.96	0.925	0.919	61.89	0.618	0.617
Our baseline LSTM model	94.27	0.990	0.943	72.80	0.789	0.728
Our CNN+LSTM model	**94.36**	**0.991**	**0.944**	**73.26**	**0.801**	**0.733**

Note: the best classification results are in bold.

The inclusion of emotional states had an even greater effect on increasing the classification accuracy when predicting the trend of financial distress. The results for trend prediction are generally consistent with those for financial distress class prediction. However, trend prediction seems to be a more complex task than predicting classes of financial distress. The results again confirmed the validity of the established model for predicting financial distress compared with existing models based on financial ratios only.

To better understand the effect of emotional states on prediction results, we used SHAP (SHapley Additive exPlanations) values, a game theoretic approach used to explain the output of deep learning models [30]. Among the greatest advantages of SHAP values is that they offer both global explainability (the overall decision structure of the model) and local explainability (how a decision is made in the case of individual samples). Here we focused on the global explainability of the model to demonstrate the impact of individual emotional states on the prediction of financial distress. We used the SHAP library to produce the SHAP values. In Fig. 4, we show the SHAP values of the eight emotional states compared with the most important financial indicator (the Z-score 1 year ago). The results show that the emotions of happiness and sadness were the most important emotions for predicting the financial distress class, while the emotions of calm and anger were the most important emotions for predicting the financial distress trend. The emotion of happiness indicated a good financial situation, and the emotion of sadness indicated financial difficulty. For the trend prediction, the effect of emotions was not so clear. Nevertheless, the calm and happy emotions were indicative of an improved financial condition, whereas the angry and sad emotions were more likely to imply deterioration.

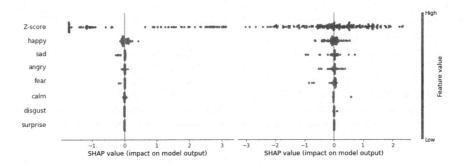

Fig. 4. SHAP values illustrating how emotional states contribute to the prediction of financial distress (class prediction on the left, trend prediction on the right).

7   Conclusion

The present study was designed to determine the effect of emotions in earnings conference calls on the prediction of corporate financial distress. The results of this study imply that state-of-the-art SER systems provide valuable information for financial distress prediction models. It was shown that by incorporating emotional states into the prediction model, the prediction performance can be improved within an appropriate deep learning-based architecture. Consistent with previous literature focused on sentiment analysis in text-based managerial communications [3–5], we observed that positive emotions (e.g., happiness) in audio recordings of earnings conference calls suggested a good financial situation of a company, whereas negative emotions (e.g., sadness and anger) indicated financial difficulties.

The main limitation of this study is that only one overall emotion was considered for the entire audio recording. The emotional states of speakers may change during a conference call, for example, when different topics are discussed. Therefore, in future research, we plan to analyze the content of the transcripts of the earnings conference calls to be able to determine the topic being discussed. Incorporating emotions from the text of transcripts into a multi-modal prediction model is another interesting direction. In a future extension, fuzzy sets can also be used to represent the Z-score, and the prediction horizon can be extended to better account for dynamic business environment.

References

1. Alaka, H.A., et al.: Systematic review of bankruptcy prediction models: towards a framework for tool selection. Expert Syst. Appl. **94**, 164–184 (2018)
2. Hájek, P., Olej, V.: Evaluating sentiment in annual reports for financial distress prediction using neural networks and support vector machines. In: Iliadis, L., Papadopoulos, H., Jayne, C. (eds.) EANN 2013. CCIS, vol. 384, pp. 1–10. Springer, Heidelberg (2013). https://doi.org/10.1007/978-3-642-41016-1_1
3. Hajek, P., Olej, V., Myskova, R.: Forecasting corporate financial performance using sentiment in annual reports for stakeholders' decision-making. Technol. Econ. Dev. Econ. **20**(4), 721–738 (2014)
4. Mai, F., Tian, S., Lee, C., Ma, L.: Deep learning models for bankruptcy prediction using textual disclosures. Eur. J. Oper. Res. **274**(2), 743–758 (2019)
5. Nguyen, B.H., Huynh, V.N.: Textual analysis and corporate bankruptcy: a financial dictionary-based sentiment approach. J. Oper. Res. Soc. **73**, 1–20 (2022)
6. Price, S.M., Doran, J.S., Peterson, D.R., Bliss, B.A.: Earnings conference calls and stock returns: the incremental informativeness of textual tone. J. Bank. Financ. **36**(4), 992–1011 (2012)
7. Myskova, R., Hajek, P.: Mining risk-related sentiment in corporate annual reports and its effect on financial performance. Technol. Econ. Dev. Econ. **26**(6), 1422–1443 (2020)
8. Mayew, W.J., Venkatachalam, M.: The power of voice: managerial affective states and future firm performance. J. Financ. **67**(1), 1–43 (2012)
9. Price, S.M., Seiler, M.J., Shen, J.: Do investors infer vocal cues from CEOs during quarterly REIT conference calls? J. Real Estate Financ. Econ. **54**(4), 515–557 (2017)
10. Hobson, J.L., Mayew, W.J., Venkatachalam, M.: Analyzing speech to detect financial misreporting. J. Account. Res. **50**(2), 349–392 (2012)
11. Yang, L., Ng, T.L.J., Smyth, B., Dong, R.: HTML: hierarchical transformer-based multi-task learning for volatility prediction. In: Proceedings of the Web Conference 2020, pp. 441–451 (2020)

12. Sawhney, R., Khanna, P., Aggarwal, A., Jain, T., Mathur, P., Shah, R.: VolTAGE: volatility forecasting via text-audio fusion with graph convolution networks for earnings calls. In: Proceedings of the 2020 Conference on Empirical Methods in Natural Language Processing (EMNLP), pp. 8001–8013 (2020)
13. Throckmorton, C.S., Mayew, W.J., Venkatachalam, M., Collins, L.M.: Financial fraud detection using vocal, linguistic and financial cues. Decis. Support Syst. **74**, 78–87 (2015)
14. Burgoon, J., et al.: Which spoken language markers identify deception in high-stakes settings? Evidence from earnings conference calls. J. Lang. Soc. Psychol. **35**(2), 123–157 (2016)
15. Sawhney, R., Mathur, P., Mangal, A., Khanna, P., Shah, R.R., Zimmermann, R.: Multi-modal multi-task financial risk forecasting. In: Proceedings of the 28th ACM International Conference on Multimedia, pp. 456–465 (2020)
16. Sawhney, R., Aggarwal, A., Khanna, P., Mathur, P., Jain, T., Shah, R.R.: Risk forecasting from earnings calls acoustics and network correlations. In: INTER-SPEECH, pp. 2307–2311 (2020)
17. Sawhney, R., Aggarwal, A., Shah, R.: An empirical investigation of bias in the multimodal analysis of financial earnings calls. In: Proceedings of the 2021 Conference of the North American Chapter of the Association for Computational Linguistics: Human Language Technologies, pp. 3751–3757 (2021)
18. Cao, S., Jiang, W., Yang, B., Zhang, A.L.: How to talk when a machine is listening: corporate disclosure in the age of AI. National Bureau of Economic Research, no. w27950 (2020)
19. Issa, D., Demirci, M.F., Yazici, A.: Speech emotion recognition with deep convolutional neural networks. Biomed. Signal Process. Control **59**, 101894 (2020)
20. Livingstone, S.R., Russo, F.A.: The Ryerson audio-visual database of emotional speech and song (RAVDESS): a dynamic, multimodal set of facial and vocal expressions in North American English. PLoS ONE **13**(5), e0196391 (2018)
21. McFee, B., et al.: Librosa: audio and music signal analysis in python. In: Proceedings of the 14th Python in Science Conference, vol. 8, pp. 18–25 (2015)
22. Hajek, P., Michalak, K.: Feature selection in corporate credit rating prediction. Knowl.-Based Syst. **51**, 72–84 (2013)
23. Son, H., Hyun, C., Phan, D., Hwang, H.J.: Data analytic approach for bankruptcy prediction. Expert Syst. Appl. **138**, 112816 (2019)
24. Altman, E.I., Iwanicz-Drozdowska, M., Laitinen, E.K., Suvas, A.: Financial distress prediction in an international context: a review and empirical analysis of Altman's Z-score model. J. Int. Financ. Manag. Account. **28**(2), 131–171 (2017)
25. Sun, J., Li, H., Fujita, H., Fu, B., Ai, W.: Class-imbalanced dynamic financial distress prediction based on Adaboost-SVM ensemble combined with SMOTE and time weighting. Inf. Fusion **54**, 128–144 (2020)
26. Huang, Y.P., Yen, M.F.: A new perspective of performance comparison among machine learning algorithms for financial distress prediction. Appl. Soft Comput. **83**, 105663 (2019)
27. Alaminos, D., Fernández, M.Á.: Why do football clubs fail financially? A financial distress prediction model for European professional football industry. PLoS ONE **14**(12), e0225989 (2019)
28. Du, X., Li, W., Ruan, S., Li, L.: CUS-heterogeneous ensemble-based financial distress prediction for imbalanced dataset with ensemble feature selection. Appl. Soft Comput. **97**, 106758 (2020)

29. Liang, D., Tsai, C.F., Lu, H.Y.R., Chang, L.S.: Combining corporate governance indicators with stacking ensembles for financial distress prediction. J. Bus. Res. **120**, 137–146 (2020)
30. Lundberg, S.M., Lee, S.I.: A unified approach to interpreting model predictions. In: Proceedings of the 31st International Conference on Neural Information Processing Systems, pp. 4768–4777 (2017)

The Bonsai Hypothesis: An Efficient Network Pruning Technique

Yasuaki Ito[1(⊠)], Koji Nakano[1], and Akihiko Kasagi[2]

[1] Graduate School of Advanced Science and Engineering, Hiroshima University, Higashihiroshima, Japan
{yasuaki,nakano}@cs.hiroshima-u.ac.jp
[2] Fujitsu Ltd., Tokyo, Japan
kasagi.akihiko@fujitsu.com

Abstract. Machine learning technology has made it possible to solve a variety of previously unfeasible problems. Accordingly, the size of network models has been increasing. Thus, research on model compression by network pruning has been conducted. Network pruning is usually performed on already-trained network models. However, it is often difficult to remove a large number of weights from a network while maintaining accuracy. We suppose that the reason for this is that well-trained networks have many weight parameters with complicated correlations among them, and such parameters make pruning difficult. Based on this supposition, in this paper, we state *the bonsai hypothesis*: pruning can be more effective when starting from untrained models than already trained models. To support the hypothesis, we present a simple and efficient channel pruning algorithm. We performed pruning of untrained and trained models using the proposed algorithm for VGG16 on CIFAR-10 and CIFAR-100. As a result, we found that the untrained models tend to reduce more channels than the already-trained models.

Keywords: Model compression · Channel pruning · Machine learning · Convolutional neural network

1 Introduction

Over the past decade, the development of machine learning technologies, starting with deep learning, has led to rapid progress in AI capabilities. At the same time, the demand for computational power and memory usage is getting higher as networks have become larger and more complicated to adopt practical applications. This high demand often impedes the execution of such applications in computing environments that do not have high performance processors and/or high memory capacities, such as smartphones and IoT devices. As a solution to this problem, a method called *pruning* has been proposed to reduce the number of parameters and the amount of computation by removing some of the weights of the network [1,10,17].

Many pruning methods are derived from [5], in which removing weights is performed as follows.

© IFIP International Federation for Information Processing 2022
Published by Springer Nature Switzerland AG 2022
I. Maglogiannis et al. (Eds.): AIAI 2022, IFIP AICT 646, pp. 229–241, 2022.
https://doi.org/10.1007/978-3-031-08333-4_19

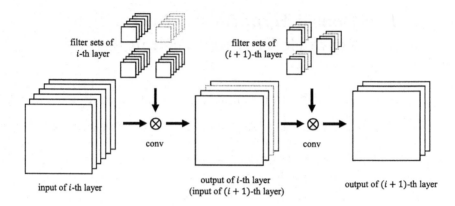

Fig. 1. Channel pruning for a convolutional layer

Step 1: Training the network model to be pruned
Step 2: Pruning unimportant weights of the network
Step 3: Re-training the pruned network
Step 4: Repeat Steps 2 and 3

In Step 1, the network model to be pruned is trained. However, in practice, this step is not necessary to perform when pruning since the target network model has already been trained. For the trained model, in Step 2, we perform the pruning. According to the granularity of pruning, pruning is mainly classified as weight pruning, kernel pruning, channel pruning, and layer pruning. In weight pruning and kernel pruning, since pruning is performed at fine granularity, a large number of weights can be removed, maintaining the accuracy [9,12]. However, the data structure storing weights becomes irregular weight matrices that prevent efficient parallel computation. Therefore, GPU implementations to accelerate the computation for such models have been proposed [4,18]. On the other hand, in channel pruning and layer pruning, models obtained by pruning have a regular structure that can be efficiently computed in parallel [13]. Hence, in this paper, we adopt channel pruning [6,9,11,19] for efficient computation on the GPU. In channel pruning for a convolutional neural network, output channels of a layer and filters related to the channels are removed as illustrated in Fig. 1. For example, when pruning the k-th output channel of the i-th layer, the k-th filter set of the i-th layer and the k-th filter in each filter set of the $(i+1)$-th layer are removed together. After pruning, in Step 3, since the accuracy drops significantly, we retrain the model to recover it. We repeat Steps 2 and 3 until a sufficient number of weight parameters are eliminated and/or a certain number of iterations are performed.

Typically, network pruning is performed on already trained network models as shown above. However, it is often difficult to remove a large number of weights from a network while maintaining accuracy. We suppose that the reason for this is that well-trained networks have many weight parameters with complicated correlations among them, and such parameters make pruning difficult.

In other words, network pruning should be performed before the network has been sufficiently trained. Based on this idea, in this paper, we state *the bonsai hypothesis*.

The Bonsai Hypothesis. *Pruning can be more effective when starting from untrained models than already trained models.*

This hypothesis is analogous to *bonsai*, which is the art of producing a small tree in a small pot that mimics the shape of a real tree. We correspond network models to bonsai trees, untrained networks to saplings, network training to tree growth, and network pruning to tree pruning. Also, well-pruned networks as the goal of network pruning correspond to well-shaped trees called *ideal bonsai trees*. Applying the above hypothesis to the bonsai making process, we can say that it is difficult to make an ideal bonsai by pruning from a fully grown tree, while it is easy to get close to an ideal bonsai by pruning during the growth process from a sapling.

Based on the bonsai hypothesis, the proposed channel pruning is performed from an untrained network initialized randomly. In addition, we propose a simple and efficient network channel pruning technique. Our new idea of the technique includes (i) *early growing of acceptance accuracy*, (ii) *pruning channels using the exponential search*, and (iii) *slightly shaking*. The details are described as follows.

Early Growing of Acceptance Accuracy: In the pruning process of a trained network, retraining is generally performed to recover the accuracy decreased by pruning to the target accuracy. However, in the initial stage of training, since the accuracy of the network is not sufficient compared to the target accuracy, it is not easy to directly use the target accuracy in retraining. Therefore, in the proposed method, the target accuracy at the initial stage of training is obtained from the pre-training. More specifically, we train the network without pruning and record the change in the accuracy during the training. When pruning from an untrained network, we use this history as the target accuracy at the early stage of training and pruning. In terms of bonsai, we observe how a tree grows when it is grown from a sapling without pruning. This corresponds to using the growth process to raise the tree while pruning it again from a sapling to make it an ideal bonsai. While it is not possible to turn a mature tree back into a sapling in actual bonsai, we use the fact that it is possible in network training.

Pruning Channels Using the Exponential Search: In the general pruning approach, channels to be pruned are determined according to some metric, and then the channels are removed. For example, the L_1-norm of weights for each channel is computed, and a certain number or percentage of smaller channels are pruned. However, it is not easy to prune the appropriate number of channels. In this study, to determine the number of pruning channels, we adopt *the exponential search*, which is a method to efficiently find the number of nodes in radio networks with a small number of trials when the unknown number of nodes [14]. This method is employed to obtain the channels to be pruned efficiently. More specifically, by doubling the number of pruned channels while the acceptance threshold is satisfied, a large number of channels are removed in a small number of epochs.

Slightly Shaking: Channel pruning generally involves deleting channels layer by layer and terminating when no more channels can be deleted in any layer. However, in many cases, the pruning is finished before enough channels are removed. Therefore, in the proposed technique, when no more channels in any layer can be removed, the network is trained for a certain number of epochs without pruning. This causes a slight change in the value of the weight parameters at random, which may allow for further pruning. In addition, the proposed method combines dropout [16] to facilitate pruning.

In order to evaluate the performance of the above proposed method, we have performed channel pruning. We have evaluated the proposed approach for image classification by applying to VGG-16 [15] on CIFAR-10 and CIFAR-100 data sets [7]. We performed pruning of untrained and trained models using the proposed method. As a result, for CIFAR-10, we successfully reduced the size of the untrained and trained models to 2.1% and 3.1% of the original model, respectively. On the other hand, for CIFAR-100, we reduced the models to 16.0% and 89.0%, respectively. Also, starting the pruning from an untrained model tends to reduce more weights in the early stages of the iterative pruning, which indicates that the computation time of the pruning decreases more. This result well-relates to the lottery ticket hypothesis [2] and its subsequent results [3,8]. In these studies, pruning is used to find essential sub-structures in the network to achieve good performance, called winning tickets. More specifically, the same initial values as before are assigned to the network compacted by pruning, and further pruning is performed. By repeating this process, the model is pruned while looking for a winning lottery ticket. On the other hand, the proposed approach based on the bonsai hypothesis shows that the pruning depends largely on the initial weights, not on the structure of the network model.

This paper is organized as follows. In Sect. 2, we propose a channel pruning approach based on the bonsai hypothesis. Section 3 shows the results of the channel pruning by the proposed approach. We evaluated the models with untrained models and already-trained models. Section 4 concludes our work.

2   Channel Pruning on the Bonsai Hypothesis

In this section, we propose the channel pruning algorithm on the bonsai hypothesis. For an input network model already trained, called *a target model*, this algorithm prunes the weights of the model. In the algorithm, the transition of the accuracy during the training of the target model is used to determine the acceptance threshold. More specifically, we record the value of the test accuracy at each epoch in the pre-training as shown in Fig. 2. After that, the prefix-maximums of the test accuracy p_i $(i = 1, 2, \ldots)$ at epoch i are computed such that $p_i = \max_{1 \le j \le i} a_j$, where a_j denotes the test accuracy at epoch j obtained in the pre-training of the non-pruning model. In the following pruning algorithm, we use rp_i as the acceptance threshold values that are the lower limits of the test

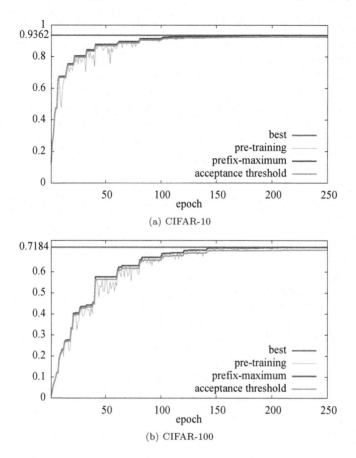

(a) CIFAR-10

(b) CIFAR-100

Fig. 2. The test accuracy in pre-training with no pruning

accuracy at epoch i in training, where r $(r > 0)$ is the acceptance coefficient. The algorithm prunes the model so that the test accuracy of the pruning model maintains at least rp_i. The proposed algorithm performs the following steps.

Step 1: Initialize weights of the model
Step 2: Prune channels by the exponential search for each layer
Step 3: If no channel is pruned in Step 2, retrain the model with no pruning
Step 4: Repeat Steps 2 and 3

The detail of each step is explained as follows.

According to our experiments, the pruning results depend on the initial values of weights. Therefore, it is necessary to run this algorithm several times to remove a sufficient number of weights. Hence, in Step 1, weights are initialized to have different initial values for each execution of this algorithm.

In Step 2, we perform training and pruning on the model for each layer. Algorithm 1 shows the details of this step. To determine the number of pruning channels, we adopt *the exponential search*, which is a method to efficiently find the number of nodes in radio networks with a small number of trials when the unknown number of nodes [14]. This method is employed to obtain the channels to be pruned efficiently. Specifically, while the test accuracy of the pruned model satisfies the threshold, we repeat pruning by doubling the number of removed channels. After each pruning, since the test accuracy drops significantly, we retrain the model for a specific epoch to recover it. If the test accuracy fails to satisfy the threshold after retraining, the pruning is discarded and the model is restored to that before pruning.

Algorithm 1. Channel pruning using the exponential search for layer l

---
1: $pruned \leftarrow 0$
2: $pruning \leftarrow 1$
3: **loop**
4:     Backup the model
5:     $k \leftarrow pruning - pruned$
6:     Prune k channels with small L_1-norm in layer l
7:     Retrain the pruned model for a certain epochs
8:     **if** the test accuracy can be accepted **then**
9:         $pruned \leftarrow pruning$
10:         $pruning \leftarrow pruning \times 2$
11:     **else**
12:         Restore the model to discard the last pruning
13:         **return**
14:     **end if**
15: **end loop**

Step 3 retrains the model with no pruning for several epochs if no channel is pruned in Step 2. The aim of this step is to improve the accuracy of the model and to allow the model to be pruned by slightly changing the values of the parameters. We repeat Steps 2 and 3 until a certain amount of time elapses or a certain number of epochs of training is performed.

3   Experimental Results

In this section, we show the experimental results to evaluate the proposed channel pruning approach for VGG-16 [15]. VGG-16 is one of the popular deep convolutional neural networks that is mainly used image classification problems. The structure of VGG-16 consists of 13 convolutional layers and 3 fully-connected layers. This network is widely used as a benchmark model for machine learning because it has the typical structure of a convolutional neural network. We have trained models using two image classification problems, the CIFAR-10 and CIFAR-100 datasets [7]. The CIFAR-10 dataset consists of 60000 32×32 color images in 10 classes, with 6000 images per class. There are 50000 training images and 10000 test images. On the other hand, the CIFAR-100 dataset consists of 100 classes containing 600 images each. There are 500 training images and 100 testing images per class.

We have trained the VGG-16 models on CIFAR-10 and CIFAR-100 without pruning as pre-training to obtain the transition of the test accuracy. The networks have been trained for a sufficient number of epochs until no improvement in test accuracy is observed. In our experiment, we have trained the models for 250 epochs. Figure 2 shows the transition of the test accuracy in the pretraining. From the results, the test accuracy of the models on CIFAR-10 and CIFAR-100 achieves 0.936 and 0.718, respectively. In our experiments, for the first 250 epochs, we used 0.99 and 0.98 times of the prefix-maximums of test accuracy shown in Fig. 2 as the threshold of acceptable accuracy for pruning. After 250 epochs, we also used the same values at 250 epochs as a threshold. The network models have been trained using momentum-accelerated mini-batch SGD with a batch size of 128 and momentum set to 0.9. Also, the learning rate has been set to 0.1 and decayed to 1/2 every 20 epochs.

For the purpose of confirming the bonsai hypothesis, we have pruned untrained models and already-trained models, called *scratch models* and *trained models*, respectively. Scratch models are initialized randomly and trained models are obtained by training in the above pre-training. For each execution, pruning is performed until the models have trained 2000 epochs. Note that if the test accuracy does not exceed the threshold in Step 2 and the pruning is discarded, the number of epochs at that time is not counted in the above 2000 epochs. For both models, we perform the proposed channel pruning, shown in Sect. 2, 10 times each. The settings for training are basically the same as for the pre-training above, except that the learning rate is fixed after 250 epochs. For the trained models, we start pruning after the pre-training. Specifically, the pruning is performed for a total of 2000 epochs from the 251st epoch to the 2250th epoch. For the recovery of the test accuracy after pruning a channel in Step 2, we have trained the models for 5 epochs. Also, in Step 3, we have performed the training with no pruning for 5 epochs when no layer is pruned in Step 2.

Figures 3 and 4 shows graphs of the total weights over time for 2000 epoch pruning on CIFAR-10 and CIFAR-100, respectively. From the graph of CIFAR-10, we can see that the scratch models can be pruned faster than the trained models, with less fluctuation and more stability. On CIFAR-100, the weights could not be pruned much for the trained models. On the other hand, for the scratch models, a large number of weights were pruned compared to the trained models, including some cases where the weights could not be reduced much. From the curves for successful pruning, a small number of weights are removed in the early stages of pruning. After that, each graph has a sudden exponential downward curve. This is due to the exponential search, which doubles the number of channels to be removed in the case of successful pruning. Since no such curve is observed in the graph where pruning was not successful, we can say that pruning is not successful without this exponential downward curve. Furthermore, in the scratch models, such a rapid descent starts at a small number of epochs. Thus,

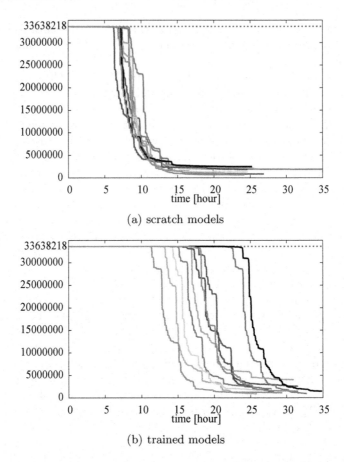

Fig. 3. The total number of weights of the model pruned from scratch and trained models for CIFAR-10

by starting pruning from the scratch model, the pruning is more successful and more effective in fewer epochs. Table 1 shows the total number of weights for the ten executions. According to this table, pruning from the scratch models is more efficient than that from the trained models both on CIFAR-10 and CIFAR-100. In addition, for CIFAR-100, it can be seen that when pruning is successfully performed, more weights can be reduced by pruning from the scratch models. Thus, these results support the bonsai hypothesis, i.e., model pruning should start from scratch models rather than trained models.

Tables 2 and 3 show the resulting number of channels and weights for each layer of VGG16 on CIFAR-10 and CIFAR-100, respectively. These tables show the results of the model with the most weights reduced when pruned from the scratch models. From the tables, we can see that for both CIFAR-10 and CIFAR-100, we can reduce more channels in the layer close to the output. In

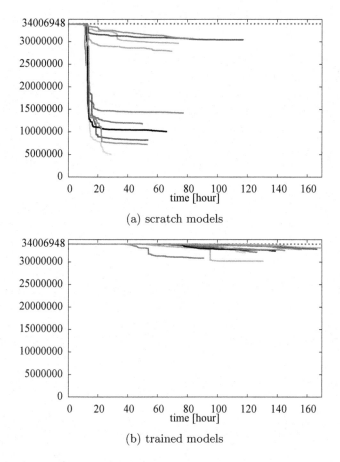

(a) scratch models

(b) trained models

Fig. 4. The total number of weights of the model pruned from scratch and trained models for CIFAR-100

particular, more channels in the second layer of the fully-connected layers are pruned.

Next, we evaluate the computation time of the pruned models. Since the computation time depends on the execution environment, in this paper, the computation time is estimated by evaluating the number of multiplications required to evaluate the model. More specifically, we count the number of multiplications necessary to compute the convolutional layers and the fully-connected layers, not including operations except for multiplications and memory latency. From the pruned results in Tables 2 and 3, the number of multiplications is reduced 3.32×10^8 to 7.13×10^7 for CIFAR-10, while 3.32×10^8 to 1.80×10^8 for CIFAR-100. Thus, we can estimate that by the proposed method, the computing time of evaluating the pruned models is reduced to 21.1% and 54.1%, respectively.

Table 1. The resulting total number of weights of the pruned models for VGG-16 on CIFAR-10 and CIFAR-100

Dataset	Initial model	Minimum	Average	Maximum
CIFAR-10	Scratch	700,967 (2.1%)	1,738,962 (5.2%)	2,990,007 (8.9%)
	Trained	1,033,042 (3.1%)	2,238,188 (6.7%)	5,951,868 (17.7%)
CIFAR-100	Scratch	5,445,432 (16.0%)	17,896,110 (52.6%)	30,994,145 (91.1%)
	Trained	30,260,638 (89.0%)	32,280,803 (95.0%)	33,203,464 (97.6%)

Table 2. The detailed results of the pruning on VGG16 for CIFAR-10

Layer type	Size of feature map	Baseline model		Pruned model	
		#channels	#weights	#channels	#weights
conv 1	32×32	64	1.8×10^3	41	1.1×10^3 (64.06%)
conv 2	32×32	64	3.7×10^4	45	1.7×10^4 (45.09%)
conv 3	16×16	128	7.4×10^4	79	3.2×10^4 (43.43%)
conv 4	16×16	128	1.5×10^5	97	6.9×10^4 (46.80%)
conv 5	8×8	256	3.0×10^5	148	1.3×10^5 (43.82%)
conv 6	8×8	256	5.9×10^5	133	1.8×10^5 (30.04%)
conv 7	8×8	256	5.9×10^5	81	9.7×10^4 (16.44%)
conv 8	4×4	512	1.2×10^6	42	3.1×10^4 (2.60%)
conv 9	4×4	512	2.4×10^6	42	1.6×10^4 (0.67%)
conv 10	4×4	512	2.4×10^6	54	2.0×10^4 (0.87%)
conv 11	2×2	512	2.4×10^6	52	2.5×10^4 (1.07%)
conv 12	2×2	512	2.4×10^6	72	3.4×10^4 (1.43%)
conv 13	2×2	512	2.4×10^6	57	3.7×10^4 (1.57%)
linear 1	1	4096	2.1×10^6	22	1.1×10^4 (0.54%)
linear 2	1	4096	1.7×10^7	119	2.7×10^3 (0.02%)
linear 3	1	10	4.1×10^4	10	1.2×10^3 (2.93%)
Total	—	—	3.4×10^7	—	7.0×10^5 (2.08%)

Thus far, several studies of channel pruning have been devoted. Table 4 shows the performance comparison between our work and the existing approaches [6, 9, 11, 19]. Unfortunately, since the parameter settings of the training and pruning differ, we cannot directly compare the performance with them. From the table, however, the proposed method achieves high compression with almost the same test accuracy. Thus, the bonsai hypothesis, pruning from scratch models, may be applied to existing methods to achieve further pruning.

Table 3. The detailed results of the pruning on VGG16 for CIFAR-100

Layer type	Size of feature map	Baseline model		Pruned model	
		#channels	#weights	#channels	#weights
conv 1	32×32	64	1.8×10^3	59	1.7×10^3 (92.19%)
conv 2	32×32	64	3.7×10^4	59	3.1×10^4 (85.00%)
conv 3	16×16	128	7.4×10^4	113	6.0×10^4 (81.40%)
conv 4	16×16	128	1.5×10^5	113	1.2×10^5 (77.94%)
conv 5	8×8	256	3.0×10^5	216	2.2×10^5 (74.50%)
conv 6	8×8	256	5.9×10^5	184	3.6×10^5 (60.65%)
conv 7	8×8	256	5.9×10^5	195	3.2×10^5 (54.76%)
conv 8	4×4	512	1.2×10^6	368	6.5×10^5 (54.76%)
conv 9	4×4	512	2.4×10^6	331	1.1×10^6 (46.47%)
conv 10	4×4	512	2.4×10^6	228	6.8×10^5 (28.79%)
conv 11	2×2	512	2.4×10^6	275	5.6×10^5 (23.92%)
conv 12	2×2	512	2.4×10^6	177	4.4×10^5 (18.57%)
conv 13	2×2	512	2.4×10^6	93	1.5×10^5 (6.28%)
linear 1	1	4096	2.1×10^6	1003	5.1×10^5 (24.49%)
linear 2	1	4096	1.7×10^7	225	2.3×10^5 (1.35%)
linear 3	1	100	4.1×10^5	100	2.3×10^4 (5.52%)
Total	—	—	3.4×10^7	—	5.4×10^6 (16.01%)

Table 4. Performance comparison of different channel pruning methods to prune the VGG16 models

	CIFAR-10		CIFAR-100	
	Test accuracy	Remaining weights	Test accuracy	Remaining weights
Ref. [6]	92.7%	16.0%	72.0%	35.2%
Ref. [9]	93.1%	11.5%	71.6%	24.0%
Ref. [11]	93.8%	11.5%	73.5%	24.9%
Ref. [19]	93.8%	26.6%	73.3%	62.1%
This work	92.6%	2.1%	70.3%	16.0%

4 Conclusions

In this paper, we have stated *the bonsai hypothesis* which is a hypothesis about network pruning that is analogous to bonsai: pruning can be more effective when starting from untrained models than already trained models. To support the hypothesis, we have presented a simple and efficient channel pruning algorithm. We performed pruning of untrained and trained models using the proposed algorithm for VGG16 on CIFAR-10 and CIFAR-100. As a result, we found that the untrained models tend to reduce more channels than the already-trained models.

References

1. Dhouibi, M., Ben Salem, A.K., Saidi, A., Ben Saoud, S.: Accelerating deep neural networks implementation: a survey. IET Comput. Digit. Tech. **15**(2), 79–96 (2021). https://doi.org/10.1049/cdt2.12016
2. Frankle, J., Carbin, M.: The lottery ticket hypothesis: finding sparse, trainable neural networks. In: Proceedings of International Conference on Learning Representations (2019)
3. Frankle, J., Dziugaite, G.K., Roy, D.M., Carbin, M.: Stabilizing the lottery ticket hypothesis. arXiv preprint arXiv:1903.01611 (2019)
4. Gale, T., Zaharia, M., Young, C., Elsen, E.: Sparse GPU kernels for deep learning. In: Proceedings of the International Conference for High Performance Computing, Networking, Storage and Analysis (2020)
5. Han, S., Pool, J., Tran, J., Dally, W.J.: Learning both weights and connections for efficient neural networks. In: Proceedings of the 28th International Conference on Neural Information Processing Systems, vol. 1, pp. 1135–1143 (2015)
6. Hu, Y., Sun, S., Li, J., Wang, X., Gu, Q.: A novel channel pruning method for deep neural network compression. arXiv abs/1805.11394 (2018)
7. Krizhevsky, A.: Learning multiple layers of features from tiny images. Technical report (2009)
8. Lange, R.T.: The lottery ticket hypothesis: a survey (2020). https://roberttlange. github.io/posts/2020/06/lottery-ticket-hypothesis/
9. Li, H., Kadav, A., Durdanovic, I., Samet, H., Graf, H.P.: Pruning filters for efficient ConvNets. In: 5th International Conference on Learning Representations. OpenReview.net (2017). https://openreview.net/forum?id=rJqFGTslg
10. Liang, T., Glossner, J., Wang, L., Shi, S.: Pruning and quantization for deep neural network acceleration: a survey. CoRR abs/2101.09671 (2021). https://arxiv.org/abs/2101.09671
11. Liu, Z., Li, J., Shen, Z., Huang, G., Yan, S., Zhang, C.: Learning efficient convolutional networks through network slimming. In: Proceedings of the IEEE International Conference on Computer Vision, pp. 2736–2744 (2017)
12. Luo, J.H., Wu, J., Lin, W.: ThiNet: a filter level pruning method for deep neural network compression. In: Proceedings of the IEEE International Conference on Computer Vision, pp. 5058–5066 (2017)
13. Matsumura, N., Ito, Y., Nakano, K., Kasagi, A., Tabaru, T.: A novel structured sparse fully connected layer in convolutional neural networks. Concurr. Comput. Pract. Exp. e6213 (2021). https://doi.org/10.1002/cpe.6213
14. Nakano, K., Olariu, S.: Uniform leader election protocols for radio networks. IEEE Trans. Parallel Distrib. Syst. **13**(5), 516–526 (2002). https://doi.org/10.1109/TPDS.2002.1003864
15. Simonyan, K., Zisserman, A.: Very deep convolutional networks for large-scale image recognition. In: 3rd International Conference on Learning Representations (2015). http://arxiv.org/abs/1409.1556
16. Srivastava, N., Hinton, G., Krizhevsky, A., Sutskever, I., Salakhutdinov, R.: Dropout: a simple way to prevent neural networks from overfitting. J. Mach. Learn. Res. **15**(1), 1929–1958 (2014)
17. Sze, V., Chen, Y.H., Yang, T.J., Emer, J.S.: Efficient processing of deep neural networks: a tutorial and survey. Proc. IEEE **105**(12), 2295–2329 (2017). https://doi.org/10.1109/JPROC.2017.2761740

18. Wang, Z.: SparseRT: accelerating unstructured sparsity on GPUs for deep learning inference. In: Proceedings of the ACM International Conference on Parallel Architectures and Compilation Techniques, pp. 31–42 (2020)
19. Zhao, C., Ni, B., Zhang, J., Zhao, Q., Zhang, W., Tian, Q.: Variational convolutional neural network pruning. In: Proceedings of the IEEE/CVF Conference on Computer Vision and Pattern Recognition, pp. 2780–2789 (2019)

Deep Learning - Recurrent/Reinforcement

Deep Recurrent Neural Networks for OYO Hotels Recommendation

Anshul Rankawat[✉], Rahul Kumar, and Arun Kumar

OYO Hotels and Homes Pvt Ltd., Gurgaon, India
{anshul.rankawat,rahul.kumar26,arun.kumar12}@oyorooms.com

Abstract. Recommendation Systems at OYO solve a complex personalization problem with scale and sophistication. The authors have focused on the development of the best-in-class recommendation system in the hospitality industry using a deep learning based model. The objective of the work is to develop a recommendation model which uses sequences of user interactions with contents derived from user interactions. The hybrid model described in the paper is a deep recurrent neural network based architecture split into two components: first, an embedding generation model and then a deep prediction and ranking model. The models have shown significant performance improvement both online and offline over existing collaborative filtering based models across geographies irrespective of traffic density and hotel supply density. The success of the deep learning based hybrid recommendation model at OYO across different geographies indicates immense potential of such recommender systems in industries such as travel, hospitality etc.

Keywords: Neural network · Deep learning · RNN · GRU · LSTM · BiLSTM · Graph-based model · CTR · Conversion · Realization · CxR · Embeddings · Hit Ratio · Mean reciprocal rank

1 Introduction

While owning a large inventory is a great benefit for OYO's customers as it allows OYO to offer plenty of opportunities for finding a perfect place to stay, this presents a great challenge for customers by overburdening them with choices. Search and Ranking system at OYO partially solves the problem by listing properties for searched locations along with filters available but it still lacks in serving the most relevant and personalized properties to the users which results in significant drop-offs in the funnel.

Recommendation system is one of the most important traffic driving widgets at OYO App which drives traffic on the home page directly to the detail pages of the most relevant properties, customers may be the most interested in and thereby reducing friction points significantly by short-circuiting the funnel (Fig. 1).

There are various algorithms used in the development of recommender systems each with certain advantages over others. The authors in this paper have explored numerous

Published by Springer Nature Switzerland AG 2022
I. Maglogiannis et al. (Eds.): AIAI 2022, IFIP AICT 646, pp. 245–256, 2022.
https://doi.org/10.1007/978-3-031-08333-4_20

Fig. 1. Recommendation widget displayed on OYO mobile App home page

variants of deep learning based models which use hybrid methods of content and collaborative filtering. The approach, implemented on the OYO App now, uses deep learning models on huge amounts of data of customer & property interactions to generate implicit embedding of properties and user interests.

2 Literature Review

Recommendation models are predominantly categorized into collaborative filtering recommender systems, content-based recommender systems and hybrid recommender systems based on the different types of input data [1]. Collaborative filtering generates personalized recommendations about a user's preference based upon the collective preferences of many other users by learning from past user-item interactions. Among numerous collaborative filtering methods, Matrix Factorization is widely used across industries, which projects users and items into a common vector space and tries to capture a user's preference on an item by the inner product between their vectors [13–15]. Content-based recommendations work by creating the user-item profiles using explicit (e.g. user's previous ratings) or implicit data (e.g. browsing history). The content here refers to the attributes of the item in which a user has shown interest in the past. Content-based recommendation systems do not take into account the behavior of the other users in the system. Hybrid recommendation systems appropriately make use of both of the above types of recommendations [11]. Recently, a number of findings in traditional recommender systems have been presented. For example, Su et al. [7] showcased a systematic review on collaborative filtering techniques; Burke et al. [8] demonstrate a comprehensive survey on hybrid recommender system; Fernandez-Tobias et al. [9] and Khan et al. [10] reviewed the cross-domain recommendation models. However, researchers have started using deep learning for recommendation systems since 2015, which seems pretty recent but it's a long time in the purview of current AI development.

The demand and acceptance of deep learning models have been increasing exponentially in the online industry due to their ability to solve complex problems with state-of-the-art results on a high volume of real-time data [2]. Contrary to linear models, a deep learning model based recommendation model can capture the non-linear user-item relationships and can generate high quality recommendations for users. Conventional methods such as matrix factorization models the user-item interaction based on the linear combination of user and item latent factors [12]. Another advantage of deep learning based recommendation systems is that it significantly reduces the efforts in creating explicit tailor-made features by automated feature learning from raw data in an unsupervised or supervised approach. Furthermore, deep learning models like RNN also facilitate the mining of temporal behavior of user-item interactions which plays an vital role in generating session based sequential recommendation in the hospitality industry. Unfortunately, none of the conventional methods are for sequential recommendation since they do not tend to capture the inherent order in a user's browsing behavior.

There are many recent examples which substantiate the pervasiveness of recommendation systems in improving user experience and promoting sales for many websites and mobile applications. Researchers have shown that 80% of movies watched on Netflix came from recommendations [3] and 60% of video clicks on Youtube came from homepage recommendations [4]. Recently, RNN and its variants, Long Short-Term Memory (LSTM) [16] and Gated Recurrent Unit (GRU) [17] have revolutionized the recommender systems by modeling the user behavior sequences [18–24]. The basic purpose of these methods is to represent the user's temporal interactions as a vector with multiple recurrent architectures. By doing that, it can pass the relevant information down to the deep chain of sequences to generate predictions. Cheng et al. [5] presented an App recommender system for Google Play with a deep and wide model. Shumpei et al. [6] proposed a RNN based news recommender system for Yahoo News. All of these models have been passed through successful experimentation and have outperformed the traditional recommendation models which corroborates the ubiquity of deep learning based recommender systems as industrial applications. In the hospitality industry, Garboviv et al. [26] used the skip gram model to learn embedding for vacation rental properties which captures the aspects of user interest, hotel geographic information, hotel attributes, and so on, as latent variables. However, their model does not use any information apart from the click data. To address this shortcoming, we proposed adding more explicit information about the hotel which is derived from aggregated customer behavior towards the hotel in terms of the hotel average monthly rating and the hotel realization values.

3 Methodology

A recommendation system starts with some relevant information about every user, their interactions with our App and uses the information to identify his/her interests. Then it merges this information with the collective behavior of all other consumers who have similar preferences to recommend stuff that the consumer may like.

OYO App has been serving personalized recommendations to its visitors through a collaborative filtering based robust recommendation system which is optimized on browsing data as user's feedback. However, the newly developed model is a hybrid model which uses sequences of user interactions with contents derived from user interactions. Hence, the modeling framework is divided into two major components - i) Embedding Generation Model, ii) Prediction and Ranking Model. Figure 2 illustrates this hybrid architecture of the Embedding Generation Model, and the Prediction and Ranking Model. For every user who had visited the OYO app, the sequence of their browsed hotels and embeddings (generated by Embedding Generation Model) along with the rating tokens and the realization tokens for those hotels are passed into the Prediction and Ranking Model to identify top N hotel recommendations which are subsequently, shown on the OYO app for the users who are viewing the recommendation widget.

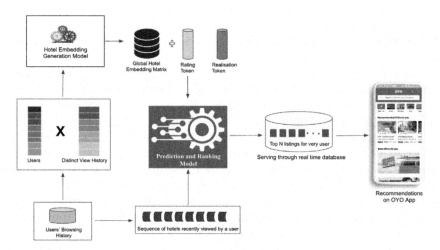

Fig. 2. Recommendation Model Schema demonstrating generation of personalized ranking for every user on OYO App

3.1 Embedding Generation Model

The content can be derived either in the form of explicit feedback (e.g. users' previous ratings) or implicit feedback (e.g. browsing history). The explicit feedback is generated by explicitly asking the consumers about their interest in terms of rating. This feedback is then used to build up a profile of those consumers on various interests. However, the problem with this approach is that it requires extra effort from the consumers. Moreover, not everyone is bothered to leave a rating on everything they see on the platform. Hence this data tends to be very sparse which generally leads to low quality recommendations in conventional methods. Another problem with explicit feedback is that the human perception to rate things differs from individual to individual. The same hotel might be rated differently because customers' preference of parameters differs. If a customer is very particular about cleanliness, a hotel not so clean but very good at other parameters like locations, other amenities etc will still be rated low.

On the other hand, the implicit feedback is generated directly by capturing consumers' behavior through browsing data and/or purchases history. It tends to be more robust because one need not rely on consumers' interaction with the platform for a voluntarily given explicit rating. The predecessor to the recommendation model described in this work was a graph-based model which is optimized on browsing data as user's feedback. Browsing data solves the problem of data sparsity as it contains plenty of information about the consumers but they aren't always reliable in terms of consumers interests because consumers can often click on platforms by accident. Browsing data is also highly susceptible to fraud because there are a lot of bots present on the internet to perform redundant clicks and hamper the quality of data. Hence,using purchases as the implicit positive feedback can be more effective in generating higher quality recommendations for a consumer.

In this work, we derived implicit features using the Embedding Generation Model which is an unsupervised recurrent neural network type of deep learning model. These latent features, along with the hotel average monthly rating and the hotel realization values, act as a precursor to the hotel prediction and ranking model as shown in Fig. 3.

3.2 Prediction and Ranking Model

To understand customers' interactions based on the collective preference of customers, we used hotels in the sequence of visits by a user along with embeddings i.e. implicit features of those hotels. The predecessor model implemented at OYO was a graph-based collaborative filtering model optimized for Click-Through-Rate (CTR) whereas the proposed recommendation model is optimized for realized bookings (Conversion along with Realization of bookings).

We implemented four sequential deep learning architectures (akin to collaborative filtering) i) basic RNN, ii) GRU, iii) LSTM and iv) BiLSTM to identify the most effective model and compare with the predecessor model. Recurrent Neural Networks (RNN) are the type of neural networks that were designed to work with sequential data. In the hospitality industry, the sequential data can be in the form of user reviews, image sequences, browsing history etc. However, during back propagation, RNNs can suffer from having a short-term memory due to vanishing gradient problems. Gradients are values that are used to update weights of the layers within a neural network. The vanishing gradient problem signifies that the gradient value shrinks as it back-propagates through time. If a gradient value becomes extremely small, it does not help in too much learning. Hence, the layers that get a small gradient update tend to stop learning and the model forgets the information on the longer sequences. Researchers have developed GRUs [17], LSTMs [16] and BiLSTMs [25] as the solution to short-term memory. These networks have internal mechanisms called gates that can regulate the flow of information. These gates can learn which data in a sequence is important to keep or throw away. By doing that, it allows relevant information to pass through the long chain of sequences to generate predictions. The layers in GRUs and LSTMs try to preserve the information of the past because the only inputs they have seen are from the past whereas the layers in bidirectional LSTMs (BiLSTM) set up use the the two hidden states combined in any point of time and preserves the information from both past and future.

To train the model, we created a training set of one million users where the sequence of their browsed hotels within a click session acts as an input. Formally, a click session is defined as a sequence of hotels clicked on by a user during a defined window of time or visit. The input sequence is then padded and limited to 15 hotels because the weights in the sequential models can blow up quickly if larger numbers of hotels are taken. Since the neural network has to back propagate through time, an upper bound is required on how many time steps it needs to back propagate to. In this way, we truncate our backpropagation through time, which helps in reducing the time complexity of the model significantly. Our aim was to identify the affinity of a user towards realized booking at high rated hotels in the form of probability which we get as an output from the model. We identified the top N hotels as a list of recommendations for the user based on their probability of realized booking for high rated hotels.

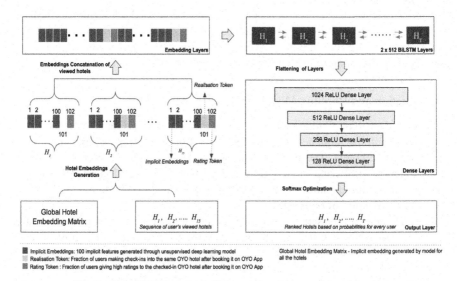

Fig. 3. Deep RNN based prediction and ranking model architecture

Figure 3 illustrates the proposed architecture for an enriched prediction and ranking model. As we can see, each aspect of the hotel is embedded separately, and these representations are later concatenated and further compressed through BiLSTM layers followed by four dense layers before being used for hotel predictions.

4   Performance Evaluation

We first attempted to evaluate performance of embeddings generated from unsupervised learning and then evaluated the ranking list of hotels as our final output generated from supervised learning.

4.1 Embedding Generation Model Evaluation

There is no direct quantitative method to evaluate embeddings holistically. The embedding generation model here provides the vector of length 100 as implicit features for each hotel. We used a cosine similarity index across parameters to measure similarity between hotels and identified the list of top 10 similar hotels corresponding to every hotel in the modeling dataset. Once the list of top 10 similar hotels is generated, we employ four accuracy metrics based on parameters such as location, distance, price and ratings of hotel to evaluate the performance of the embeddings quantitatively. Location, distance, price and ratings are the most important selection criteria for hotel bookings. The four custom metrics are generalized as follows:

$$\text{Sim\_Index}@x = \frac{\sum_{i=1}^{H}(\text{Sim}_{x,i})}{H}$$

where x = Price, Location, Ratings and Distance; H = Total number of hotels; $\text{Sim}_{x,i}$ = fraction of top 10 hotels similar to the target hotel which fulfill criteria of similarity across parameters x. For example - $\text{Sim}_{\text{Price},2}$ means a fraction of the top 10 similar hotels identified for the second target hotel which are within $\pm15\%$ of the price of that target hotel. The criteria for other parameters are as follows: For Distance, it is less than 20 km from the target hotel; for Ratings, it is ±1 rating from the target hotel's rating; and for location, the hotels should be in the same city of the target hotel.

Table 1. Parameter based similarity indices for embedding generation models.

Embedding models	Epochs	Learning rate	Number of embeddings	Sim_Index@ Ratings	Sim_Index@ Price	Sim_Index@ Distance	Sim_Index@ Location
Embedding_v1	50	0.01	50	7.78	7.34	7.50	8.25
Embedding_v2	100	0.005	100	7.83	7.43	7.55	8.23
Embedding_v3	50	0.01	100	7.84	7.47	7.56	8.25
Embedding_v4	150	0.01	100	7.87	7.47	7.60	8.30
Embedding_v5	100	0.01	100	7.87	7.48	7.59	8.28
Embedding_v6	100	0.01	50	7.08	7.49	6.81	7.60
Embedding_v7	100	0.005	100	7.20	6.67	6.91	7.66
Embedding_v8	100	0.01	100	7.26	6.69	6.97	7.72

Based on these similarity indices, we compared the quality of eight variants of the embedding generation models and identified the best model with a sim index for ratings, price, distance and location standing at 7.87, 7.48, 7.59 and 8.28 respectively as shown in Table 1.

Furthermore, we visually evaluated top 10 similar hotels for random 30 hotels selected and observed explicit features like price, locations, ratings, brands etc. The embedding models successfully listed top 10 similar hotels in most of the cases. For example - In Fig. 4, similar hotels generated for hotel A (in extreme left) have similar prices, locations, brands and ratings.

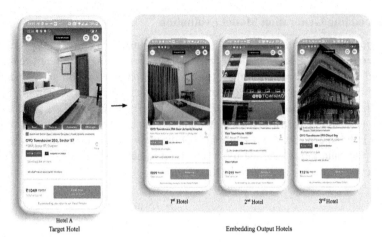

Fig. 4. Visual evaluation of top 3 similar hotels identified for a target hotel using embeddings

4.2 Prediction and Ranking Model Evaluation

Recommendation model provides output in the form of a ranking list of hotels regardless of different modeling frameworks. We thoroughly evaluated the output offline as well as in real-time production setup.

4.2.1 Offline Evaluation

To evaluate the ranking list of hotels, it is always a better approach to directly evaluate the ranking quality instead of the other proxy metrics like mean squared error, etc. In this work, we report two accuracy metrics to evaluate our Prediction and Ranking Model performance.

4.2.1.1 Precision@k or Hit Ratio

In our recommendation setting, precision or hit ratio is defined as the fraction of users for which the booked hotel is included in the list of ordered recommendations having length k.

$$\text{Precision@k} = \frac{U_{hit}^{k}}{U_{all}}$$

where U_{hit}^{k} is the number of users for which the booked hotel is included in the top k recommendation list, U_{all} is the total number of users who booked a hotel in the test dataset.

4.2.1.2 Mean Reciprocal Rank (MRR)

For a given user, the Reciprocal Rank (RR) is defined as the reciprocal of the rank at which the first booked hotel is identified in the list of ordered recommendations. RR is 1 if a relevant hotel is identified at first position, it is 0.5 if the relevant hotel is identified at rank 2 and so on. When the average is determined across all the users, the measure is called the Mean Reciprocal Rank (MRR).

$$RR(u) = \sum_{i<k} \frac{relevance_i}{rank_i}$$

$$MRR = \frac{\sum_{U=1}^{U} (RR(u))}{U}$$

where RR is the reciprocal rank of user u which is the sum of the relevance score of top k hotels weighted by reciprocal rank and MRR is the mean of RR for all the users.

Table 2. Accuracy metrics for hotel prediction and ranking model variants

Models	Batch size	Embedding training	#Dense layers	Nodes per ReLu Dense Layers	Epochs	Precision@20	MRR
Basic RNN v1	64	FALSE	2	512:: 256	80	85.6%	72.0%
Basic RNN v2	128	TRUE	3	512:: 256:: 128	100	87.0%	72.4%
Basic RNN v3	256	TRUE	4	1024:: 512:: 256:: 128	100	88.2%	72.8%
GRU v1	128	FALSE	2	256:: 128	80	89.2%	72.4%
GRU v2	256	TRUE	2	512:: 256	100	82.9%	75.2%
GRU v3	256	FALSE	3	512:: 256:: 128	60	71.6%	69.8%
GRU v4	512	TRUE	4	1024:: 512:: 256:: 128	60	75.8%	73.9%
LSTM v1	128	FALSE	2	256:: 128	80	68.0%	74.5%
LSTM v2	256	TRUE	2	512:: 256	100	82.4%	75.1%
LSTM v3	256	TRUE	3	512:: 256:: 128	80	89.9%	74.6%
LSTM v4	512	TRUE	4	1024:: 512:: 256:: 128	80	84.5%	75.7%
BiLSTM v1	128	FALSE	2	256:: 128	80	84.9%	75.7%
BiLSTM v2	256	TRUE	2	512:: 256	100	85.3%	75.7%
BiLSTM v3	256	TRUE	3	512:: 256:: 128	80	86.6%	75.0%

(continued)

Table 2. (*continued*)

Models	Batch size	Embedding training	#Dense layers	Nodes per ReLu Dense Layers	Epochs	Precision@20	MRR
BiLSTM v4	512	TRUE	4	1024:: 512:: 256:: 128	100	88.0%	75.8%

Based on Precision@20 and MRR, we compared variants of four sequential neural network architectures for sequential models as shown in Table 2 and identified the best model from each category i.e. basic RNN v3, GRU v1, LSTM v3 and BiLSTM v4. Further, we performed the out of time validation with precision@2, 5, 10, 20 and MRR as evaluation metrics for these four best in category models along with the predecessor model, i.e. a graph-based model, to evaluate their robustness on a dataset that is more closely aligned with the real-time environment. The results suggested that the variant of BiLSTM model i.e. BiLSTM v4 has outperformed all the other models with a precision of 62.5%, 55.4%, 48.8%, 41.5% at top 20, 10, 5 and 2 positions of recommendation respectively and with a MRR of 43.1% as shown in Table 3.

Table 3. Out of time model validation for top 4 model variants

Models	Precision@20	Precision@10	Precision@5	Precision@2	MRR
Graph based model	46.6%	41.2%	35.4%	27.4%	30.5%
Basic RNN v3	60.4%	53.0%	46.4%	39.8%	42.0%
GRU v1	59.7%	52.4%	45.9%	39.4%	41.7%
LSTM v3	62.6%	55.4%	48.6%	41.2%	43.1%
BiLSTM v4	62.5%	55.4%	48.8%	41.5%	43.1%

4.2.2 Online Evaluation

During the development phase, we made extensive use of offline metrics (precision@k, MRR etc) to improve the efficacy of our algorithm iteratively. However, for the final vetting of the effectiveness of an algorithm, we relied on real-time experiments via A/B testing because these results are not always correlated with offline evaluation. In a real time experiment, we can measure subtle differences in metrics like conversion, realization etc. that measure user affinity and satisfaction towards the hotel. In our experiment, OYO hotels were selected in a manner that ensured no other experiments were live on those properties during the same time period. User behavior was measured in terms of realized bookings or CxR (CxR is multiplication of booking conversion and realization of bookings) at high rated hotels. Lifts of 3% to 6% were observed in different geographies when compared with existing graph-based collaborative filtering models tested in A/B set ups.

5   Conclusion

With paradigm shift in machine learning algorithms, huge customer interactions on OYO App and improvement in computing power of machines, the recommendation systems on OYO App needed a change of approach for recommendation systems. The authors have tried multiple variants of deep learning based hybrid models to make the recommendation system more effective.

The hybrid model described in the paper is a deep recurrent neural network based architecture split into two components: i) Embedding Generation Model and ii) Hotel Prediction and Ranking Model. Evaluated in A/B testing and offline simulations, the deep learning based hybrid models have shown significant performance improvement in realized bookings and revenue over then implemented graph based collaborative filtering models. The consistent lifts of 3% to 6% in realized hotel bookings compared with previous recommendation models across geographies with different daily active users and hotel density shows robustness of the approach with hybrid deep learning based models.

The intermediate outputs like global hotel embedding matrix can be used in many other personalization solutions like similar hotels widgets on hotel details page, personalized campaign for similar hotels for the hotels viewed but not booked, personalized campaign for similar hotels for the hotels viewed but were sold out etc. The success of the deep learning based hybrid recommendation algorithms across different geographies with different traffic density and supply density demonstrate a great promise to be used in many other industries like Travel, Restaurant and other ecommerce industries.

References

1. Adomavicius, G., Tuzhilin, : Toward the next generation of recommender systems: a survey of the state-of-the-art and possible extensions. IEEE Trans. Knowl. Data Eng. **17**(6), 734–749 (2005)
2. Covington, P., Adams, J., Sargin, E.: Deep neural networks for youtube recommendations. In: Recsys, pp. 191–198 (2016)
3. Gomez-Uribe, C.A., Hunt, N.: The Netflix recommender system: algorithms, business value, and innovation. TMIS **6**(4), 13 (2016)
4. James Davidson, Benjamin Liebald, Junning Liu, Palash Nandy, Taylor Van Vleet, Ullas Gargi, Sujoy Gupta, Yu He, Mike Lambert, Blake Livingston, and Dasarathi Sampath. 2010. The YouTube Video Recommendation System. In Recsys
5. Cheng, H.-T., et al.: Wide & deep learning for recommender systems. In: Recsys, pp. 7–10 (2016)
6. Okura, S., Tagami, Y., Ono, S., Tajima, A.: Embedding-based news recommendation for millions of users. In: SIGKDD (2017)
7. Xiaoyuan, S., Khoshgoaar, T.M.: A survey of collaborative filtering techniques. Adv. Artif. Intell. **2009**, 4 (2009)
8. Burke, R.: Hybrid recommender systems: survey and experiments. User Model. User-Adapt. Interact. **12**(4), 331–370 (2002)
9. Fernandez-Tobias, I., Cantador, I., Kaminskas, M., Ricci, F.: Cross-domain recommender systems: a survey of the state of the art. In: Spanish Conference on Information Retrieval, 24 (2012)

10. Khan, M.M., Ibrahim, R., Ghani, I.: Cross domain recommender systems: a systematic literature review. ACM Comput. Surv. **50**, 3 (2017)
11. Jannach, D., Zanker, M., Felfernig, A., Friedrich, G.: Recommender systems: An Introduction (2010)
12. He, X., Liao, L., Zhang, H., Nie, L., Hu, X., Chua, T.-S.: Neural collaborative filtering. In: WWW, pp. 173–182 (2017)
13. Koren, Y., Bell, R.: Advances in collaborative filtering. In: Ricci, F., Rokach, L., Shapira, B. (eds.) Recommender Systems Handbook, pp. 77–118. Springer, Boston, MA (2015). https://doi.org/10.1007/978-1-4899-7637-6_3
14. Koren, Y., Bell, R., Volinsky, C.: Matrix factorization techniques for recommender systems. Computer **42**(8), 30–37 (2009)
15. Salakhutdinov, R., Mnih, A.: Probabilistic matrix factorization. In: Proceedings of NIPS, pp. 1257–1264. Curran Associates Inc., USA (2007)
16. Sepp Hochreiter and Jürgen Schmidhuber. 1997. Long Short-Term Memory. Neural Computation 9, 8 (Nov. 1997), 1735–1780
17. Cho, K., et al.: Learning phrase representations using RNN encoder–decoder for statistical machine translation. In: Proceedings of EMNLP. Association for Computational Linguistics, pp. 1724–1734 (2014)
18. Donkers, B.L., Ziegler, J.: Sequential user-based recurrent neural network recommendations. In: Proceedings of RecSys, pp. 152–160. ACM, New York, NY, USA (2017)
19. Hidasi, B., Karatzoglou, A.: Recurrent neural networks with top-k gains for session-based recommendations. In: Proceedings of CIKM, pp. 843–852. ACM, New York, NY, USA (2018)
20. Hidasi, B., Karatzoglou, A., Baltrunas, L., Tikk, D.: Session-based recommendations with recurrent neural networks. In: Proceedings of ICLR (2016)
21. Li, J., Ren, P., Chen, Z., Ren, Z., Lian, T., Ma, J.: Neural attentive session-based recommendation. In: Proceedings of CIKM, pp. 1419–1428. ACM, New York, NY, USA (2017)
22. Quadrana, M., Karatzoglou, A., Hidasi, B., Cremonesi, P.: Personalizing session-based recommendations with hierarchical recurrent neural networks. In: Proceedings of RecSys, pp. 130–137. ACM, New York, NY, USA (2017)
23. Wu, C.-Y., Ahmed, A., Beutel, A., Smola, A.J. Jing, H.: recurrent recommender networks. In: Proceedings of WSDM, pp. 495–503. ACM, New York, NY, USA (2017)
24. Yu, F., Liu, Q., Wu, S., Wang, L., Tan, T.: A dynamic recurrent model for next basket recommendation. In: Proceedings of SIGIR, pp. 729–732. ACM, New York, NY, USA (2016)
25. Schuster, M., Paliwal, K.K.: Bidirectional recurrent neural networks. IEEE Trans. Signal Process. **45**(11), 2673–2681 (1997)
26. Grbovic, C.: Real-time personalization using embeddings for search ranking at airbnb. In: Proceedings of the 24th ACM SIGKDD International Conference on Knowledge Discovery and Data Mining, pp. 311–320. KDD (2018)

Fine-Grained Double-View Link Prediction Within the Dynamic Interaction Network

Jianye Pang and Wei Ke[✉]

Xi'an Jiaotong University, Xi'an, Shaanxi, People's Republic of China
`wei.ke@mail.xjtu.edu.cn`

Abstract. Trend prediction in financial trading markets is crucial in decision-making support, normally realized via mining trading patterns or analyzing technique indicators. However, cryptocurrency decentralized exchange (DEX) markets are growing rapidly recently and draw much attention. Different from the centralized market, DEX allows users to observe the whole market data at the order-level, where identity information associated with orders is also available. Moreover, trading pairs in DEX are often manipulated by bots, and user ordering behavior may be affected by these algorithm-controlled bots. These provide us with a novel human-bot game scenario to investigate the predictability of human ordering behavior. In this paper, we model the trading market of the cryptocurrency DEX at each timestamp as a user-order bipartite graph and propose a double-view dynamic network for fine-grained user ordering prediction in a human-bot mixed DEX market. Given the ordering information of the humans and bots, we learn current latent representations of humans and bots using graph neural networks and recurrent neural networks respectively for user ordering prediction. We conduct experiments on real cryptocurrency data from Binance Dex. The experimental results of link prediction demonstrate that our proposed method outperforms the state-of-the-art models.

Keywords: Cryptocurrency decentralized exchange · User-order link prediction · Bot market manipulation · Dynamic network

1 Introduction

Market trend prediction is to predict the price fluctuations in the financial market for financial analysis. It is of great significance for reducing investment risk and making financial decisions. Despite the successful machine learning techniques [2,9,10,26] in predicting traditional market price trends, these methods tried to represent the market performance only from a macro-level, either with indicators describing aggregated behavior from users [9,10] or methods modeling markets across time periods [2,26]. However, most existing studies are designed for centralized exchanges (e.g., stock), where public-available orders cannot be

© IFIP International Federation for Information Processing 2022
Published by Springer Nature Switzerland AG 2022
I. Maglogiannis et al. (Eds.): AIAI 2022, IFIP AICT 646, pp. 257–269, 2022.
https://doi.org/10.1007/978-3-031-08333-4_21

associated with a specific user. This prevents studies on market prediction from the perspective of fine-grained user ordering behavior.

In this study, we are the first to investigate the market trend prediction in decentralized exchanges, i.e., the prediction of which users will place orders at what price in the very near future of a trading pair. Benefiting from the openness, transparency, and credibility of blockchain technology [20,21], decentralized exchanges [12] (DEX) can overcome the problem of opaque trading data [20,21]. Moreover, the fine-grained ordering information with user identity can be directly obtained from DEX OrderBooks [20].

However, there are some unique challenges in DEX market prediction. Firstly, the ordering information with user identity allows us to associate specific orders with their users. It needs to explore the representation of user-order dynamic interactions in the cryptocurrency market. Secondly, in order to improve their rankings and prominence, exchanges support using bots to manipulate markets [1,15]. In this new type of bot-human game market, bot behavior misleads the user's ordering intentions and trading decisions, so as to influence the market trend. Therefore, properly modeling how bots influence user behavior is critical to making accurate predictions.

To address the challenges mentioned above, in this paper, we develop a novel double-view dynamic network framework at the fine-grained timestamp for user ordering prediction in a human-bot mixed DEX market. Specifically, given the real data from Binance DEX[1], at each timestamp, we model the trading market of the current cryptocurrency DEX as a user-order bipartite graph and propose a dynamic network using graph neural network (GNN) and recurrent neural network (RNN) models to represent users, placed orders, and temporal user-order links, where the GNN is designed to model long-term user ordering characteristics in the past time, and the RNN is used to model the instantaneous user attribute variation and ordering information at the current timestamp. Besides, we design a joint training strategy for the dynamic network to acquire final user ordering predictions. The experimental results of link prediction demonstrate our model surpasses other state-of-the-art methods by a large margin. We also conduct extensive ablation results to verify the robustness of our model in market trend prediction.

The paper is organized as follows: Sect. 2 summarizes related work on the traditional stock market and dynamic network. Section 3 details the formulation of a user-order bipartite graph, the process of double-view dynamic network framework at fine-grained timestamps and the joint training strategy. Section 4 presents experimental results and analysis of link prediction. Lastly, the final conclusions are discussed in Sect. 5.

2   Related Work

Traditional Stock Market Analysis. Traditional stock market researches require a thorough understanding of the market and a clear investment strategy [6,18]. Based on the assumption [4] that stock investors seek profit

---

[1] https://www.binance.org/en.

maximization strategies by trying to discover the potential trading patterns to predict the future price trend, it mainly focuses on the trading patterns and the trend prediction of price fluctuations. The SFM [26] model proposed by Zhang et al. aims to clearly discover and distinguish different frequencies of potential trading patterns to predict the stock price using the unit gate of RNN. Li et al. [10] designs a framework of technical trading index optimization, which optimized the original technical index leveraging stock attributes. The RNN-MRF [9] model based on multi-task learning achieves the prediction of price rise or decline by introducing technical indicators.

Continuous Dynamic Network Representation. At present, there are two major paradigms used for network modeling in continuous dynamic network research: dynamic graph neural network (DGNN) and time series [7,22]. DGNN-based network representations mainly introduce timing rules to node aggregation so as to obtain dynamic graph embedding. CTDNE [14] and TDGNN [17] use the time-dependent aggregation method to aggregate the features of adjacent nodes and the time information of the edges to obtain the representation of the target node. Although there are other methods of dynamic graph neural networks, such as EvolveGCN [16] and WD-GCN [13], these methods believe that network changes are discrete time points in the form of the snapshot, which is not suitable for networks with continuous timestamps. Time series-based network representations include RNN and time point process (TPP). In the RNN-based approach, node embeddings are maintained by an RNN-based architecture. Once an event occurs or the network changes, the embedding of interactive nodes will be updated, which enables the embedding to be continuously kept up to date, e.g. the JODIE model [8]. The TPP-based approach, such as the Dyrep [25] and Know-Evolve [24], both use a TPP parameterized by an RNN cyclic architecture.

3 Method

3.1 Preliminaries

Dynamic Network Construction. To formulate the user ordering prediction as a link prediction task, we first construct the dynamic network $\mathcal{G} = \{\mathcal{V}, \mathcal{E}\}$. To determine the nodes and links in the dynamic network, the same account address is recorded as the same user, which is the user node; We sort the order by price and divide the price at equal intervals after excluding the abnormal extreme price. Prices in the same interval are considered to be in the same order, which is regarded as the order node. The user node and order node make up all the nodes $\mathcal{V}$ in the network. Therefore, we construct the dynamic network as a user-order bipartite graph, where each link in $\mathcal{E}$ is a user ordering action at a timestamp.

Problem Definition. Given a dynamic network $\mathcal{G}_t = \{\mathcal{V}_t, \mathcal{E}_t\}$ at the current timestamp t which involves a set of observed user-order links $\mathcal{E}_t = \{(u, v) \mid u, v \in \mathcal{V}_\tau\}$ which happened before the next timestamp $t + 1$, our goal is to predict those unobserved user-order links in $\mathcal{G}$ at timestamp $t + 1$. We treat this task as binary classification, that is, given a pair of nodes (u, v), we predict if there is a user-order link between them at the next timestamp $t + 1$.

3.2   Fine-Grained Double-View Framework

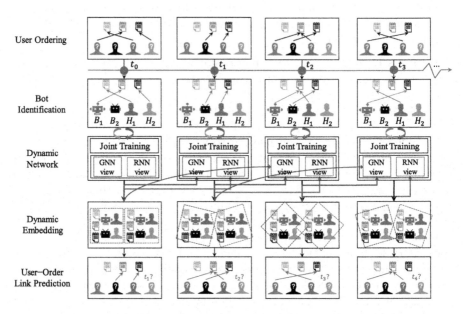

Fig. 1. The overview of our proposed fine-grained double-view framework. B denotes the bot and H denotes the human.

To predict user ordering, we propose a novel fine-grained double-view framework to predict user-order links in a dynamic network. Figure 1 is an illustration of our proposed framework. At each timestamp, firstly, we follow three strong guidelines detailed in the financial research [3] to filter and identify bot addresses as a rough pre-processing. Secondly, we develop a hybrid GNN-RNN-based dynamic network representation method for the user and order embedding at the current timestamp. The GNN is designed to capture network topology changes by considering long-term user ordering information in the global, and the RNN is used to model the instantaneous user drifting and ordering information in the local by the user-order interactions at the current timestamp. The whole framework is trained jointly. Finally, given the updated user and order embedding results in the current network, we predict potential user-order links at the next timestamp with the fully connected network.

3.3 Dynamic Network Representation

Multi-view Dynamic Embedding. We adopt the dynamic embedding of GNN and RNN, which is multi-view and goes into detail as below.

GNN View Dynamic Embedding: Our GNN branch consists of continuous-time candidate neighbors selection, temporal context windows and exponential time-dependent aggregation to obtain GNN's dynamic embedding.

When we update the current node u using neighbor nodes that have historical interactions, we are biased against different neighbor nodes. Here we express the bias in the selection of neighbor nodes when the human node is updated. We suppose the current ordering is more affected by the market price at recent timestamps. For the order occurring at a very early time, we think it causes negative interference, thus we only need to decide the neighbor nodes $N(u) = \{w_\tau\}$, τ is a timestamp t^- near the current timestamp t.

Continuous-Time Candidate Neighbors Selection. We use an exponential function to calculate sampling probability and decide whether neighbor nodes are sampled in this update. Given a target node u at timestamp t, each candidate neighbor $w \in N_t(u)$ has the following probability $p(w)$ of being selected:

$$p(w) = 1 - \frac{e^{t-\tau(w)}}{\sum_{w' \in N_t(u)} e^{t-\tau(w')}} \tag{1}$$

We suppose that the neighbors at the nearer timestamp interacting with the current target node are more likely to be selected as candidate neighbors. Because at the nearer timestamp, the more likely the buying and selling order price will be repeated soon. The longer the time span is, the less likely it is. After we get all probabilities of candidates, we choose n nodes with the highest probabilities as the neighbors.

Temporal Context Windows. Since we need an expected reasonable minimum number of candidates to update the dynamic network, we set a temporal context window for restriction. We suppose the window size can maintain the ordering interest shifts and also obtain sufficient information about the deformation structure of the graph. Therefore, we set the fixed window H to limit the scope of candidates and use the neighbor selection strategy to capture valid neighbors appearing inside the window. Therefore, the first optional time point t_0 is chosen as $t_0 = t - H + 1$.

Exponential Time-Dependent Aggregation. We adopt an exponential time aggregator in the GNN branch to encourage the GNN model to concentrate on local context information. For simplicity, we describe it in a single-layer forward aggregator and it can be easily generalized to multi-layer networks. Assuming the initial target node representation is $\vec{h}_u^0$, the new node representation at time t can be calculated as follows:

$$\vec{h}_u^k = \sigma \left(\sum_{w \in N_t(u) \cup u} \alpha_{uw}^t W \vec{h}_w^{k-1} \right) \tag{2}$$

where k represents the k-th layer of the time aggregator, σ is a nonlinear activation function such as ReLU, W is the learnable shared weight matrix and the neighbor nodes aggregating weights α_{uw}^t at time t can be calculated as follows:

$$\alpha_{uw}^t = 1 - \frac{e^{t-t_{u,w}}}{\sum_{w \in N_t(u) \cup u} e^{t-t_{u,w}}} \tag{3}$$

where $t_{u,w}$ denotes the timestamp nearest to t at which link (u, w) interacts.

RNN View Dynamic Embedding: Inspired by JODIE [8], our RNN branch consists of embedding update, projection and predicting next order embedding to obtain RNN's dynamic embedding.

Embedding Update. RNN branch uses a coupled RNN to update both human and bot links. RNN_U updates dynamic user embedding and RNN_O updates dynamic order embedding which are parameter shared among all users and orders respectively.

When user u interacts with order o, RNN_U updates user embedding $u(t)$ using the order embedding $o(t^-)$ near time t. In the same way, RNN_O updates order embedding $o(t)$ using the user embedding $u(t^-)$. Both embedding updates are represented as follows:

$$
\begin{aligned}
u(t) &= \sigma \left(W_1^u u\left(t^-\right) + W_2^u o\left(t^-\right) + W_3^u f + W_4^u (t - t_o^-) \right) \\
o(t) &= \sigma \left(W_1^o o\left(t^-\right) + W_2^o u\left(t^-\right) + W_3^o f + W_4^o (t - t_u^-) \right)
\end{aligned}
\tag{4}
$$

where f is the feature of user-order interaction links and W_i is the learnable matrix. Note that for the user-order link, we set the feature f to extract according to the actual semantics of the user ordering action. The feature consists of the actual price of the order, the quantity of the order, the current market price, order types (buy or sell), other valuable numerical data from OrderBook and one-hot encoding of categorical information at this timestamp, etc.

Embedding Projection. To predict the future embedding at timestamp t^+, we project the user embedding after the time t of the last user interaction. The projection embedding is the product of a scaled linear factor W_s and the previous user embedding $u(t)$ as $\tilde{u}(t^+) = W_s u(t)$. The greater value of t^+ is, the greater drifting of the projected embedding vector is over time. As t^+ increases, mapped embedding drifts more severely.

Predicting Next Order Embedding. Following JODIE's setting, we train the RNN branch to minimize the L_2 difference between the predicted order embedding $\tilde{o}(t^+)$ computed by using $\tilde{u}(t^+)$ and the real order embedding $\bar{o}(t^+)$ as $\|\tilde{o}(t^+) - \bar{o}(t^+)\|_2$. Therefore, for a given user, we can retrieve the order most likely to interact with at the current timestamp. Since the query is $O(1)$, we can easily query all users to find their potential user-order links where we achieve the "double-end" link prediction leveraging the "single-end" prediction.

Joint Training Strategy. We fuse and rerank the double-view results of GNN and RNN branches at each timestamp to get the final user-order link prediction results at the current timestamp. Specifically, from the GNN view, for the potential link pair (u, v) in the graph, we use the weighted-L1 link aggregation function to obtain the link representation as $|h_v - h_u|$. From the RNN View, for each potential link pair (u, v) in user and order embedding matrices, the link representation is computed as the concatenation $[h_v, h_u]$ of their corresponding embeddings.

For every branch, we train a fully connected network separately and send their user-order link representations respectively to compute the prediction of whether they happen at this timestamp in each view which is regarded as binary classification. Firstly, we rank the Top-k links of each individual multilayer perceptron (MLP) as a preliminary prediction from the GNN view and RNN view according to probabilities from high to low, where k denotes the preset number of candidate links. Secondly, considering both GNN and RNN, the rerank strategy is to combine the total 2k prediction results and sort them by inference probabilities again. If a link appears more than once, the maximum probability of this link is retained.

The GNN branch is trained to minimize the cross-entropy whether the link pair happens at this timestamp as binary classification . The loss of the GNN branch is as follows:

$$\mathcal{L}^{\mathcal{G}} = \sum -(y \log(p) + (1 - y) \log(1 - p)) \tag{5}$$

The RNN branch is trained to minimize the L_2 distance between the predicted order embedding and the ground truth at every interaction, with the same regard to user embeddings and order embeddings. The loss of the RNN branch is as follows:

$$\mathcal{L}^{\mathcal{R}} = \sum (\|\tilde{o}(t) - \bar{o}\left(t^-\right)\|_2 + \|u(t) - u\left(t^-\right)\|_2 + \|o(t) - o\left(t^-\right)\|_2) \tag{6}$$

Hence, we calculate the sum of these two losses in a prediction as follows:

$$\mathcal{L}^{\mathcal{S}} = \mathcal{L}^{\mathcal{G}} + \mathcal{L}^{\mathcal{R}} \tag{7}$$

Due to each timestamp, we need to predict links of the real human and the bot altogether. Here we use a hyperparameter β to balance the modeling power of their ordering behavior. We suppose it is more difficult to learn the prediction of human beings [1, 15], and we need to force the model to better represent real humans. Hence, we re-formulate the total loss as follows to force the distinction between the two objects:

$$\mathcal{L}^{\mathcal{S}} = \mathcal{L}_b^{\mathcal{S}} + \beta \mathcal{L}_h^{\mathcal{S}} \tag{8}$$

4 Experiments

4.1 Datasets

For user-order link prediction, we collect the real data on Binance DEX including the time series of every millisecond OrderBooks and OrderUpdates.

Our previous observation of real DEX data shows that when the market price fluctuates fiercely, the number of human traders participating in the market activity increases dramatically. At this time, a large number of real users flood in and place their strategy lists, which is also consistent with our intuition. Therefore, in order to ensure the fairness of the experiment and to prevent the particularity caused by weekends, we select five days in early June 2020, from June 1 to June 5, from 10 am to 4 pm for 6 h each day, as our experimental data. For market trading pairs, we choose two representative trading pairs Travala-Binance Coin (AVA-BNB) and Atomic Wallet Coin-Binance Coin (AWC-BNB) in Binance DEX to analyze since they are long term active and closely related to Binance native token BNB.

To determine nodes and links in the dynamic network for user-order link prediction, the same wallet address is recorded as the same user node. We determine a reasonable minimum interval of prices based on real OrderBooks and past research [23], and each price interval is considered to be the same order node. Starting at 10 a.m. each day, we split the data into half-hourly portions in a non-overlapping sliding window manner. For user-order link prediction, the links that occur in the first 20 min of every half-hour are set as the training set, the 20 to 25 min as the validation set, and the 25 to 30 min as the test set. Therefore, we test models specific on the interactions that occurred in the last one-third of the time for each data portion. Each model is continuously updated within 6 h of daily data to alleviate potential serious effects caused by remaining missing hours between days.

4.2   Baseline Methods

We compare our method against the following baselines:

- **DynGEM** [5]. This method divides the timeline into discrete time points and learns embedding for the graph snapshots at these time points, which incrementally learns graph autoencoders of varying layer sizes.
- **DySAT** [19]. This method constructs node representations which incorporate the self-attention mechanism into structural neighbors and temporal dynamics to obtain dynamic self-attention network embedding.
- **HTNE** [27]. This method integrates the Hawkes process into deep neural embedding on the neighborhood formation sequence to capture the influence of historical neighbors on the current neighbors.
- **M²DNE** [11]. This method incorporates mutual evolution of micro-dynamics using a temporal attention point process and macro-dynamics using a dynamics equation in a temporal network to model the network structure and alternately affect the process of learning node embedding.
- **JODIE** [8]. This method explicitly models the future trajectory of the nodes in the embedding space for a dynamic recommendation, which defines a projection to predict the dynamic embedding trajectory.

It is worth mentioning that the baselines are all based on network embedding, which includes discrete and continuous network representation of GNN-based and time series-based methods.

4.3   Experimental Settings

Evaluation Metrics. We treat user-order link prediction as a binary classification task. Specifically, with a pair of nodes (u, v) as input, we predict whether user u will place order v at the next timestamp. Following commonly used settings [8,16], we leverage two widely-used classification and ranking metrics, namely Mean Reciprocal Rank (MRR) and Recall.

Parameter Settings. For AVA-BNB, there are approximately 20 user nodes, 200 order nodes, and 400 user-order links every half an hour; For AWC-BNB, there are approximately 40 user nodes, 200 order nodes, and 300 links every half an hour. In the parameter setting of the dynamic network model, we set the embedding size of GNN for user and order nodes to 128, and the number of network layer size to 1. The window size is set to 12 and n in neighbor selection is set to 6. We set the dynamic embedding size in RNN to 128. We set β to 1.0 in AVA-BNB and 2.5 in AWC-BNB. For the k in top-k of joint training and N in Recall@N evaluation metric, we record the top 10. The training epoch is generally set to 60.

4.4   Performance on User-Order Link Prediction

In this section, we evaluate all models' performance on user-order link prediction on Binance DEX with the AVA-BNB market trading pair. We report mean reciprocal rank (MRR) and Recall@10 in Table 1. We draw the following observations.

Table 1. User-order link prediction results of trading pairs AVA-BNB and AWC-BNB. The subscript denotes how the performance of our method compared with the second-best performance.

Model	AVA-BNB		AWC-BNB	
	MRR (%)	Recall@10 (%)	MRR (%)	Recall@10 (%)
DyGEM	51.2	62.5	43.9	57.7
DySAT	55.7	67.3	50.6	65.0
HTNE	35.2	43.8	27.4	38.1
M^{2}DNE	56.1	67.5	50.3	63.6
JODIE	56.6	69.4	51.2	65.3
Ours	$\mathbf{62.4^{+5.8}}$	$\mathbf{74.9^{+5.5}}$	$\mathbf{55.4^{+4.2}}$	$\mathbf{70.7^{+5.4}}$

In terms of all evaluation metrics, our method has consistently and significantly outperformed all the baselines on both two representative trading pairs AVA-BNB and AWC-BNB. Specifically, our model achieves a great improvement of 5.8% and 5.5% respectively on MRR and Recall for AVA-BNB, and 4.2%

and 5.4% respectively on MRR and Recall for AWC-BNB. On the one hand, the GNN view incorporates temporal context information from continuous-time candidate neighbors and time-dependent aggregation, which better captures the global information and topology information of the network. On the other hand, the RNN view learns fine-grained changes and interest drifting in node representation over time and absorbed the characteristics of user ordering at every moment. Therefore, it's suitable to model the rapid change of graph structure and the situation of high-frequency transactions in the fine-grained time.

4.5   Analysis on Model Robustness

To test the robustness of our model, we analyze how the model performance changes as the length of the time duration that needs to be inferred in the future increases. To be specific, we vary the duration time to 5, 10, 15 and 20 min to infer the user-order links. We choose DySAT, JODIE and M^{2}DNE as the baselines since they have relatively competitive performance.

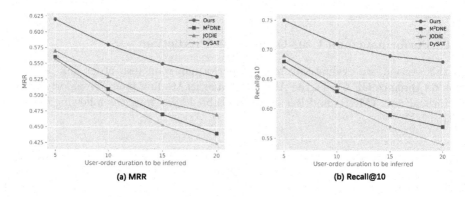

Fig. 2. Performance w.r.t. user-order duration on AVA-BNB.

Our goal is to infer the user-order link at the next timestamp, that is, to keep the model continuously updated over time. This is also in line with the application of trading tools in real scenarios such as the stock market. Due to the dynamic time-varying nature of the cryptocurrency market, with the extension of the duration time, even if the model is always updated, the accumulation of randomness of user behavior at different timestamps will degrade the average inference performance to a certain extent. We report the average performance on different user-order durations to be inferred in Fig. 2, where we can see that even as the duration increases, our method still performs the best compared with other baselines, and it has the slowest performance decline, which highlights the robustness of our model in the user-order link prediction task.

4.6   Impact of β Constrained Parameter

To showcase the impact of constrained hyperparameter β used for training, we set β to 1.0, 1.5 and 2.5, where 1.0 means the weights of the bot loss and of the human loss are set by default 1:1, and 2.5 means that we impose a greater penalty on the weight of human ordering prediction. We report the performance with different β values on AVA-BNB and AWC-BNB in Fig. 3.

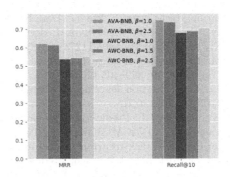

Fig. 3. Performance w.r.t. β constrained parameter.

It is obvious that on AVA-BNB, the performance of β=1.0 is slightly better than 2.5. On AWC-BNB, the performance gets better as the β value increases. One of the most potential reasons is the difference in market trading pairs. Our purpose of β is to balance the learning ability to place orders from humans and bots respectively, and our hypothesis is that it is more difficult to predict orders of real humans, so we add penalty terms on human loss to force the model to focus on human ordering prediction. As a bot-dominated trading market (AVA-BNB), with β increasing, it reduces the modeling power of bot ordering to some extent and slightly lowers the final average performance. As a human-dominated trading market (AWC-BNB), β boosts real human ordering and thus improves the overall performance. We think these are very unique and interesting phenomena in the human-bot mixed cryptocurrency market.

5   Conclusion

This paper formulates user ordering prediction in cryptocurrency DEX as a link prediction task within the dynamic interaction network and proposes a double-view framework at fine-grained timestamps to solve the problem. Compared with baselines, our method shows the proposed framework combines and absorbs the advantages of two graph representations, achieving higher user-order link prediction performance. In addition, our method demonstrates strong robustness through user-order duration experiments. Moreover, compared with multiple market trading pairs, the bot effect on the ordering intentions of real human traders in the human-bot mixed cryptocurrency market is further confirmed.

References

1. Aloosh, A., Li, J.: Direct evidence of bitcoin wash trading. SSRN 3362153 (2019)
2. Chen, C., Zhao, L., Bian, J., Xing, C., Liu, T.Y.: Investment behaviors can tell what inside: exploring stock intrinsic properties for stock trend prediction. In: ACM SIGKDD (2019)
3. Cong, L.W., Li, X., Tang, K., Yang, Y.: Crypto wash trading. SSRN 3530220 (2020)
4. Dash, R., Dash, P.K.: A hybrid stock trading framework integrating technical analysis with machine learning techniques. J. Financ. Data Sci. **2**(1), 42–57 (2016)
5. Goyal, P., Kamra, N., He, X., Liu, Y.: DynGEM: deep embedding method for dynamic graphs. arXiv preprint arXiv:1805.11273 (2018)
6. Habib, A., Hasan, M.M.: Business strategy, overvalued equities, and stock price crash risk. Res. Int. Bus. Fin. **39**, 389–405 (2017)
7. Kazemi, S.M., et al.: Representation learning for dynamic graphs: a survey. J. Mach. Learn. Res. **21**(70), 1–73 (2020)
8. Kumar, S., Zhang, X., Leskovec, J.: Predicting dynamic embedding trajectory in temporal interaction networks. In: ACM SIGKDD (2019)
9. Li, C., Song, D., Tao, D.: Multi-task recurrent neural networks and higher-order Markov random fields for stock price movement prediction: multi-task RNN and higher-order MRFs for stock price classification. In: ACM SIGKDD (2019)
10. Li, Z., Yang, D., Zhao, L., Bian, J., Qin, T., Liu, T.Y.: Individualized indicator for all: stock-wise technical indicator optimization with stock embedding. In: ACM SIGKDD, pp. 894–902 (2019)
11. Lu, Y., Wang, X., Shi, C., Yu, P.S., Ye, Y.: Temporal network embedding with micro-and macro-dynamics. In: CIKM (2019)
12. Malamud, S., Rostek, M.: Decentralized exchange. Am. Econ. Rev. **107**(11), 3320–62 (2017)
13. Manessi, F., Rozza, A., Manzo, M.: Dynamic graph convolutional networks. Pattern Recogn. **97**, 107000 (2020)
14. Nguyen, G.H., Lee, J.B., Rossi, R.A., Ahmed, N.K., Koh, E., Kim, S.: Continuous-time dynamic network embeddings. In: Companion Proceedings of the The Web Conference (2018)
15. O'Leary, D.E.: Open information enterprise transactions: business intelligence and wash and spoof transactions in blockchain and social commerce. Intell. Syst. Account. Financ. Manage. **25**(3), 148–158 (2018)
16. Pareja, A., et al.: EvolveGCN: evolving graph convolutional networks for dynamic graphs. In: AAAI (2020)
17. Qu, L., Zhu, H., Duan, Q., Shi, Y.: Continuous-time link prediction via temporal dependent graph neural network. In: Proceedings of The Web Conference (2020)
18. Sabri, S.R.M., Sarsour, W.M.: Modelling on stock investment valuation for long-term strategy. J. Invest. Manage. **8**(3), 60–66 (2019)
19. Sankar, A., Wu, Y., Gou, L., Zhang, W., Yang, H.: DySAT: deep neural representation learning on dynamic graphs via self-attention networks. In: WSDM (2020)
20. Schär, F.: Decentralized finance: on blockchain-and smart contract-based financial markets. SSRN 3571335 (2020)
21. Shapiro, D.C.: Taxation and regulation in decentralized exchanges. J. Tax. Invest. **36**(1), 4 (2018)
22. Skarding, J., Gabrys, B., Musial, K.: Foundations and modelling of dynamic networks using dynamic graph neural networks: a survey. arXiv preprint arXiv:2005.07496 (2020)

23. Sun, X., Liu, M., Sima, Z.: A novel cryptocurrency price trend forecasting model based on LightGBM. Financ. Res. Lett. **32**, 101084 (2020)
24. Trivedi, R., Dai, H., Wang, Y., Song, L.: Know-evolve: deep temporal reasoning for dynamic knowledge graphs. In: ICML (2017)
25. Trivedi, R., Farajtabar, M., Biswal, P., Zha, H.: DyREP: learning representations over dynamic graphs. In: ICLR (2019)
26. Zhang, L., Aggarwal, C., Qi, G.J.: Stock price prediction via discovering multi-frequency trading patterns. In: ACM SIGKDD (2017)
27. Zuo, Y., Liu, G., Lin, H., Guo, J., Hu, X., Wu, J.: Embedding temporal network via neighborhood formation. In: ACM SIGKDD (2018)

MTMA-DDPG: A Deep Deterministic Policy Gradient Reinforcement Learning for Multi-task Multi-agent Environments

Karim Hamadeh, Julia El Zini, Joudi Hajar, and Mariette Awad[✉]

Department of Electrical and Computer Engineering, American University of Beirut,
Beirut, Lebanon
{ksh17,jwe04,jbh03}@mail.aub.edu, mariette.awad@aub.edu.lb

Abstract. Beyond Multi-Task or Multi-Agent learning, we develop in this work a multi-agent reinforcement learning algorithm to handle a multi-task environments. Our proposed algorithm, Multi-Task Multi-Agent Deep Deterministic Policy gradient, (MTMA-DDPG) (Code available at https://gitlab.com/awadailab/mtmaddpg), extends its single task counterpart by running multiple tasks on distributed nodes and communicating parameters via pre-determined coefficients across the nodes. Parameter sharing is modulated through temporal decay of the communication coefficients. Training across nodes is parallelized without any centralized controller for different tasks, which opens horizons for flexible leveraging and parallel processing to improve MA learning.

Empirically, we design different MA particle environments, where tasks are similar or heterogeneous. We study the performance of MTMA-DDPG in terms of reward, convergence, variance, and communication overhead. We demonstrate the improvement of our algorithm over its single-task counterpart, as well as the importance of a versatile technique to take advantage of parallel computing resources.

1 Introduction

Several techniques have allowed the adaptation of Reinforcement Learning (RL) algorithms for the challenges of the Multi-Agent (MA) arena through the use of centralized [13] and decentralized [7,18] modes of communications. Learning multiple tasks simultaneously, a situation common in the real world presents one way to improve the algorithm's outcomes. Classically achieved through parameter sharing, there are several methods designed to accelerate and improve outcomes over multiple related tasks.

This paper targets the Multi-Task (MT), multi-agent reinforcement learning problem (MTMA-RL), where algorithms simultaneously account for the existence of more than one agent, while taking advantage of the similarity of tasks to accelerate and improve learning. Our work is the first to demonstrate the

---

J. El Zini and J. Hajar—Equal contribution.

© IFIP International Federation for Information Processing 2022
Published by Springer Nature Switzerland AG 2022
I. Maglogiannis et al. (Eds.): AIAI 2022, IFIP AICT 646, pp. 270–281, 2022.
https://doi.org/10.1007/978-3-031-08333-4_22

utilization of simultaneous MT training across separate, but parameter-sharing nodes to enhance an MA algorithm. We show the potentially vast applicability of adapting MA-RL to a parallelized situation, across different tasks. Lowe et al. [7] introduce a multi-agent deep deterministic policy gradient algorithm or MADDPG. We adopt MADDPG as our baseline and we develop MTMA-DDPG, an MT augmentation that takes advantage of task similarity by communicating parameters across nodes training different tasks simultaneously. Communication gradually decreases which is shown to have several potential applications.

To assess different task-sharing properties, we design four different systems, based on the particle environment. We study the effect of parameter sharing and the impact of specifying decay and observe that the decayed version thereof is conducive to better reward and less variance. Furthermore, MTMA-DDPG is capable of being adjusted to accommodate asynchronous learning even across fairly different tasks. It is capable of emulating, with proper design, a pseudo-hierarchical setup; thus broadening the applicability of the algorithm.

MTMA-DDPG evaluation against its "vanilla" MADDPG counterpart across 4 systems shows a consistent outperformance. Our contribution is in providing:

(1) A parallelizable and easily implementable MT version of MADDPG that leverages concurrent task training to boost individual task performance, with the ability to modulate communication via temporal decay.

(2) A robust modification to MTMA-DDPG that generalizes to situations with less restrictive task conditions and that reflects more real-life situations.

We present next the background for MTMA-DDPG and describe its formulation in Sects. 2 and 3 respectively. We then show the experimental setup and results in Sects. 4 and 5 before concluding with final remarks in Sect. 6.

2 Background

2.1 Multi-task Reinforcement Learning (MTRL)

MTRL aims to improve RL performance over a group of related tasks, often by reapplying or sharing knowledge gained across the tasks, such as in [11]. In [8], a distributed actor-critic approach is followed to solve the MT deep RL problem. An agent runs different tasks on different nodes, and shares parameters based on predetermined weights to obtain an average policy. [19] also employs node parameter sharing, mediated by an SVM solver, whereas [20] and [12] use entropy to regulate MT learning.

[1] and [16] show that sharing parameters amongst tasks might negatively impact tasks sometimes. In order to mitigate this problem, [14] and [6] introduce a distilled central policy that combines the common behaviors of the agents on different tasks. However, the inclusion of an additional centralized policy network acts as a single point of failure. Other recent approaches are [2] and [3].

Our MT approach draws from the decentralization presented in [8] and utilizes communicating nodes rather than a centralized mediator. We also use temporal decay to modulate parameter sharing, as it boasts asynchronous capability as well as enables an easier implementation.

2.2   Multi-agent Reinforcement Learning

In MA systems, maximizing the total rewards requires an agent to consider the actions of all the other agents, which increases the difficulty of learning. We focus our attention on centralized training and decentralized execution methods, which are more compatible with the decentralized MT aspect we wish to impart.

One such algorithm is the MADDPG by [7] which is based on the deep deterministic gradient algorithm (DDPG) [5]. MADDPG uses the actor-critic method, both parametric, adapted for a MA setting. In execution, independent policies using local observations are used to learn policies that apply in competitive as well as in cooperative settings in an environment where no specific assumptions are made. To reduce variance among agents, each critic is augmented with information about other agents' policies during training. The target networks in MADDPG are a time-delayed copy of the original network that improves the stability and leads to convergence. A replay buffer is used to sample experience so that the data is independently distributed. Due to its simplicity, ease of implementation, decentralized nature, as well as popularity, MADDPG is suitable to be augmented flexibly for an MT setting and will be adopted as a baseline for our MT approach.

2.3   Multi-task Multi-agent Reinforcement Learning

Only few research work in the literature addressed MTMA-RL. [9] consider a partially observable environment with multiple tasks and multiple agents. Their approach is composed of two stages, an MA specialization stage, conducted using decentralized hysteric deep q-networks, where agents learn individual policies for each task, in a single task setting. This is followed by an MT stage where the learned policies are distilled to obtain a single generalized policy per agent. Both learning and execution are decentralized. While the work of [9] aims to obtain a single generalized policy per agent to handle multiple tasks, ours allows agents to have multiple policies for different tasks. Our objective will be to primarily harness task similarity on different nodes to boost training outcomes.

3   MTMA-DDPG Algorithm

We define a system to be composed of m tasks, running on independent nodes, and n agents. The environment is considered to be partially observable. At time step t, agent i in task l receives an observation $o_{i,l}^t$ from state s_l^t, and outputs an action $a_{i,l}^t$. The environment in l uses the actions of the n agents to determine the rewards $r_{i,l}^t$ and produce s_l^{t+1}. An agent i has the same observation and action space across m tasks, but uses a different parameters for each task.

To address the MTMA nature of the target, we devise MTMA-DDPG, an MT extension for MADDPG [7]. MADDPG uses the actor-critic approach, with a centralized critic during training, and decentralized agents during execution. A separate MADDPG instance is running on each of the m tasks as separate nodes, in a similar fashion to [15] and [8]. Thus, we have $m \times n$ action parameter sets $\theta_{i,l}$ and critic parameter sets $\phi_{i,l}$. We transfer knowledge from the related tasks by allowing the instance running on the lth node (task) to periodically receive the parameters from other tasks while controlling the sharing level.

Formally, at every step t after agent i, l updates $\theta_{i,l}$ and $\phi_{i,l}$ according to MADDPG and sets $\theta_{i,l}$ to be a weighted sum of all $\theta_{i,p}$, where $p \in \{1, 2, ..m\}$. The same is performed for $\phi_{i,l}$. The weights are represented as a 3 dimensional tensor c, where $c_{i,l,p}$ denotes the weights that correspond to the ith agent in the lth task receiving parameters from the pth task. The intuition behind this is that it allows an agent to accelerate the exploration of parameter spaces in the different tasks through the propagation of the parameters as it is learning. Note that the communication occurs on the target networks, which are distinguished with apostrophes in the algorithm code itself.

In order to allow the agent on task l to specialize for each task, we introduce a decay parameter d, which exponentially reduces the coefficients of the other tasks during inter-node communication. Additionally, MTMA-DDPG has been designed to enable asynchronous running of the different tasks on separate nodes. This justifies the temporal modulation of the parameter sharing coefficient rather than using shared network layers. Hence, a full parallel and asynchronous ability of the algorithm is maintained throughout learning.

The pseudocode of MTMA-DDPG is presented in Algorithm 1. This application trains the MA and MT aspects in a joint framework and this breathes new flexibility into the MADDPG algorithm and allows for effective ways to leverage similarity between entire systems.

4 Experimental Setup

The purpose of our experiment is to investigate the properties achieved by different components of the proposed MTMA-DDPG with respect to MADDPG, and to obtain empirical evidence of its effectiveness in terms of convergence, reward, and communication costs. We adopt the MA Particle Environment (MPE) that was developed and optimized for MADDPG-like techniques [10,17]. The existing MPE environment has been extended for this work in MT settings. A custom Pytorch 1.8.0 implementation [4] based on MADDPG defined in [7], is developed in a multithreaded setting to simulate the different nodes (tasks). Experiments are run on a 16-GB RAM device with an Intel i7 processor and no GPU support.

4.1 Environment Setup

We define 4 systems consisting of 2 tasks running on 2 separate nodes. To further validate our system, we create another contrived scheme consisting of 3 tasks. The observation and action spaces remain the same in the different tasks within the same system. The distributed training method for similar tasks is analogous to different machines training MA systems on similar tasks and propagating parameters. We describe our systems below, and we illustrate them in Fig. 1.

Algorithm 1: MTMA-DPPG running in parallel at every processing node $l = 1...m$ where each node solves a task

---

forall the *episodes* **do**

    Initialize a random process W for action exploration;

    Receive initial state s_0;

    for $t = 1 \mapsto$ *max-episode-length* **do**

        for *agent* $i = 1 \mapsto n$ **do**

            $a_{i,l}^{(t)} \leftarrow \mu_{\theta_{i,l}}(o_{i,l}^{(t)}) + W_t$

        Execute $a_l^{(t)} = (a_{1,l}^{(t)}, ..., a_{n,l}^{(t)})$ and observe reward $r^{(t)} = (r_{1,l}^{(t)}...r_{n,l}^{(t)})$ and new state $s_l^{(t+1)}$;

        Store $(s_l^{(t)}, a_l^t, r_l^t, s_l^{(t+1)})$ in replay buffer D_l;

        $s_l^{(t)} \leftarrow s_l^{(t+1)}$;

        for *agent* $i = 1 \mapsto n$ **do**

            $(s_l^j, a_l^j, r_l^j, s_l^{j+1}) \sim D$;

            $y_l^j v \leftarrow r_{i,l}^j + \gamma Q_{\phi_{i,l}'}'(s_l^{j+1}, a_{1,l}', ...a_{n,l}')$ with $a_{k,l}' = \mu_{\theta_{k,l}'}'(o_{k,l}^j)$;

            Update critic by minimizing the loss

            $L_{\phi_{i,l}} = \frac{1}{S} \times \sum_j (y_l^j - Q_{\phi_{i,l}}(x_l^j, a_{1,l}^j, ...a_{n,l}^j))^2$;

            Update critic using sampled gradient

            $\nabla_{\theta_{i,l}} J \leftarrow \frac{1}{S} \sum_j \nabla_{\theta_{i,l}} \mu_{\theta_{i,l}}(o_{i,l}^j) \times \nabla_{a_{i,l}} Q_{\phi_{i,l}}(x_l^j, a_{1,l}^j, ..., a_{i,l}^j, a_{n,l}^j)|$ with $a_{i,l} = \mu_{\theta_{i,l}}(o_{i,l}^j)$;

            $\hat{\phi_{i,l}}' \leftarrow \tau\phi_{i,l} + (1 - \tau)\phi_{i,l}'$;

            $\phi_{i,l}' \leftarrow \sum c_{(i,l,p)} \hat{\phi_{i,p}}'$;

            $\hat{\theta_{i,l}}' \leftarrow \tau\theta_{i,l} + (1 - \tau)\theta_{i,l}'$;

            $\theta_{i,l}' = \sum c_{(i,l,p)} \hat{\theta_{i,p}}'$;

    $c \leftarrow d \times c$;

(S1) The Speaker-Listener System uses cooperative communication from MPE which consists of 2 agents, a stationary speaker, and a mobile listener, as well as 3 colored landmarks. The agents are rewarded if the listener finds its way to the landmark of its color. However, the listener does not know its color, and can only see the landmarks. The speaker can see the listener and should learn to output the listener's color to help it navigate to the target. We define T1 and T2 to be only nominally distinct: in T1, the reward is computed based on the Euclidean distance, whereas in T2, it is based on the Manhattan distance.

(S2) The Spread System is based on cooperative navigation from MPE, where 3 mobile agents share an environment with 3 landmarks. S2 defines the tasks to be fairly dissimilar: In T1, the 3 agents have to cover 3 landmarks and are penalized for colliding with one another, necessitating spreading out. In T2, the agents are also penalized for the collision but are encouraged to minimize the sum of distances between themselves and the landmarks. Consequently, they must go all to the center of the triangle formed by the landmarks, rather than away from each other like in T1.

(S3) The Predator-Prey System that uses predator-prey from MPE, where 3 slow agents (the red circles in Fig. 1) cooperate to chase a faster prey (the green circle). In T1, predators are rewarded for colliding with the prey, whereas the prey is rewarded for maintaining distance from the predators. In T2, predators are rewarded for decreasing the distance between them and the prey but they are penalized for actual collisions. The expected learned behavior is thus hovering around the prey, keeping it between the predators, but not explicitly attacking it, unlike in T1 where a more aggressive approach is learned.

(S4) The Hybrid System is a combination of the S2 T1 and S1 T1. In S2 T1, there are three mobile agents, and in S1 T1, there is one.

(S5) The Contrived 3 Tasks System is a perturbation of S1. S5 T1 is the same as S1 T1, consisting of minimizing the Euclidean distance of the mobile agent from its color. However, S5 T2 and S5 T3 are the minimization of the x-axis distance and y-axis distance to the target respectively.

4.2 Hyper-Parameter Selection

The neural network hyperparameters for the 3 tasks are used as reported in [7]. It remains to determine the decay factor d and the communication tensor c sized $n \times m \times m$. For c, different communication rates can be set within the same system for different agents. However, for simplicity, we set $c_{i,j,k} = x \forall i, j, k, j \neq$

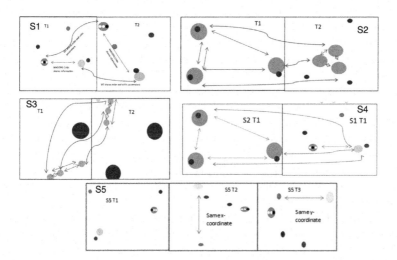

Fig. 1. Illustration of systems S1-5. The landmarks are the small circles, the mobile agents are large and colored, and the speakers are grey. The red arrows indicate communication across tasks and the blue ones across critics within the same task. In S3, the red circles are the predators, and the small green ones are the prey. In S4, the large circles are agents and the black ones are the landmarks. (Color figure online)

k and $c_{i,j,j} = 0 \forall i, j$. Self-communication updates do not actually take place, hence the 0 in these places is strictly a notational choice. Therefore, we use the shorthand $c = x$ to set the non-zero values of the tensor to x. We adopt $c = 0.2$ in our experiments allowing 20% of parameters to be determined jointly. In S1 exclusively, we adopt a $c = 0$ for the speaker communication, as its output is one of 3 discrete values, incompatible with the notion of parameter sharing. For c in MTMA-DDPG, the initial value of c matters less in theory, because different initial settings will decay, in effect producing time-shifted versions of one another. The decay parameter d is standardized for each system according to $0.01 \approx \times d^{\#episodes/2}$ indicating that by the time half the algorithm is done training, c has been decayed to approximately 1% of its strength. Our testing has shown that the value of c does not have a predictable or strong influence on the outcome of training.

Finally, each system is trained until convergence which is equivalent to $10,000$ episodes for S1, S3, and S5 and $15,000$ for S2. S4 is composed of tasks from both S1 and S2, so we train each task for its corresponding number of episodes.

5   Experimental Results

5.1   Emergent Properties of MTMA-DDPG

In order to obtain an intuition about the different components of MTMA-DDPG, we perform an ablation study on S1 as a baseline. The tasks in S1 are similar ruling out the tasks' non-compatibility. For this purpose, MTMA-DDPG is trained with and without decay with different sharing configurations: no communication (akin to vanilla MADDPG re-implemented from [7]), unilateral communication from T1 to T2, or the reverse, and bilateral sharing of information. Table 1 reports the mean episode and final episode rewards averaged over 100 episodes from 4 training seeds for each configuration with their standard deviations, the per-episode number of parameter broadcast as the communication cost factor for each configuration. The latter (per agent) is the number of parameters broadcast which is $m \times (m - 1)$, where m is the number of tasks in the system.) It is worth mentioning that larger systems may require configurations where not all tasks communicate, due to quadratically growing costs of doing so. Finally, we compute the correlation of the smoothed discrete derivative (difference array) for the tasks across different setups and we report it as the correlation of the first difference array (CFDA).

As shown in Table 1, MTMA-DDPG reports a higher mean episode reward and a lower standard deviation than the original MADDPG. For the correlation of the first difference array, a near-zero correlation is found, which does not differ notably between different models. Low correlation between tasks that are sharing parameters is desirable, as that guarantees a level of independence in their performance.

Table 1. Mean Episode Reward (MER), Final Episode Reward (FER), communication cost factor (Comm) and correlation of first difference array CFDA on T1 and T2 for different configurations of S1. Best results are in bold. Note that [7] does not run MADDPG on T2; the environment is defined in this paper.

Setup	MER T1	FER T1	MER T2	FER T2	Comm	CFDA
No sharing (MADDPG)	−0.42 (±0.10)	−0.20	−0.53 (±0.11)	−0.23	0	0.039
No sharing (MADDPG) in [7]	−0.52	−0.13	-	-	0	
Share 2 ↦ 1	−0.42 (±0.11)	−0.21	−0.53 (±0.11)	−0.23	1	0.037
Share 2 ↦ 1 with decay	**−0.30** (±0.02)	−0.12	−0.53 (±0.11)	−0.23	1	0.063
Share 1 ↦ 2	−0.42 (±0.10)	−0.20	−0.59 (±0.10)	−0.32	1	0.051
Share 1 ↦ 2 with decay	−0.42 (±0.10)	−0.20	−0.50 (±0.02)	−0.19	1	0.053
Bilateral sharing (decayless MTMA-DDPG)	−0.35 (±0.12)	−0.25	−0.49 (±0.14)	−0.28	2	0.040
Bilateral sharing with decay (MTMA-DDPG)	−0.31 (±0.03)	**−0.11**	**−0.41** (±0.03)	**−0.13**	2	0.037

Unilateral Sharing: Table 1 shows that 1-way communication without decay is associated with no improvement in the mean reward or final reward in the case of unilateral sharing from T2 to T1, and a decline in performance in the case of T1 to T2. The asymmetry is interesting despite the tasks being visually indistinguishable, meaning that the optimization criterion matters when sharing parameters. Adding decay to unilateral sharing improves both T1 to T2 and T2 to T1 situations, where T1 to T2 goes from being inferior to MADDPG to being roughly on the same level equal and T2 to T1 shows some improvement from MADDPG. More importantly, both unilateral decay setups show up to 5× lower standard deviation when they are receiving decayed parameters, which stabilizes the model in addition to the gain in mean reward. We note that the transmitting agent does not report a different mean or standard deviation in the unilateral situation as it is simply running MADDPG and is not receiving parameters.

Bilateral Sharing: Table 1 shows that Decayless MTMA-DDPG reports improved mean episode rewards for T1 over MADDPG, similar mean episode rewards for T2, and similar final episode rewards for both. However, decayless MTMA-DDPG resulted in a very high model variance. For instance, a visualization of the runs shows some unsuccessful decayless MTMA-DDPG models where agents would even head to the wrong colors. Interestingly, a few converged to extremely strong policies that achieved approximately 0.02 final reward, and a 100% collision rate, which is significantly better than any of the final rewards of the other models presented in this paper or in [7]. The MTMA-DDPG models show mean and final episode rewards that exceed both MADDPG, the unilateral sharing cases in Table 1, as well as decayless MTMA-DDPG. The use of decay results in low variances similar to those reported in unilateral communication with decay for both agents rather than only the recipient. This shows that the decay and runs a lower risk of converging to some locally undesirable joint optimum.

As a summary, bilateral MTMA-DDPG offers improved rewards for both systems regardless of their convergence, (as opposed to unilateral sharing), and the decay is a critical stabilizing factor to reduce variance.

5.2   MTMA-DDPG Performance on Different Systems

We train MTMA-DDPG on S1, S2, and S3 separately and we compare its performance to MADDPG and its counterpart decayless MTMA-DDPG. Figure 2 shows the mean episode reward and its standard deviation averaged over 4 random seeds over different nodes.

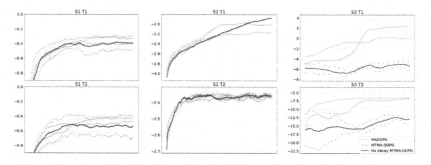

Fig. 2. Average episode reward over training as a function of episodes. Dashed lines indicate 1 standard deviation bounds.

The graphs for S1 show consistency with the results reported in Table 1. Once again, we note that while the decayless MTMA-DDPG provides an average convergence, it is plagued by high variance. In S1, the MTMA-DDPG had a significantly more marked performance increase over MADDPG, where the tasks are similar. This can be explained by a joint broader exploration during the optimization of different tasks. More surprising is that the best model was decayless MTMA-DDPG. Here we note that all 3 models have low variance in the system, in contrast to S1, and decayless MTMA-DDPG was most affected by variance in S1. Still, we see gains in MTMA-DDPG over MADDPG. In T2, the results are more balanced, hinting that T1 is benefiting more from the communication with T2.

In contrast to S2, S3 exhibited high variance in training, likely due to the many agents and the adversarial nature of the task. Decayless MTMA-MADDPG failed to match MADDPG, and the models trained using it converged to lower rewards over the 2 nodes, likely due to the complexity of the task which made learning an average policy more difficult. MTMA-DDPG gained a clear advantage over MADDPG in T1, and both algorithms perform similarly in T2.

This set of experiments shows that MTMA-DDPG generally increases the mean reward over MADDPG, while reducing standard deviation. We also note that the systems with different tasks seemed to benefit more from the MTMA-DDPG. Finally, the benefit is unilateral, as shown in S1, S2, and S3.

5.3   Extension of MTMA-DDPG to Handle Real-Life Tasks (S4)

The goal of this experiment is to demonstrate the algorithm's robustness without strict conditions of similarity, which is important for real-life use. In S4, the agents have different observation spaces: the immobile speaker in S1 T1 neither receives nor propagates any parameters to the agents from S2 T1, and the listener broadcasts and receives parameters from the 3 agents in S2 T1. Since the input space is not the same, we modify the algorithm to only share the hidden layer of the network, as the others were of different shapes.

Exploration of 3 Tasks in a Contrived Hierarchical Setup in S5. The objective of this experiment is two-fold: showing that MTMA-DDPG is capable of accommodating more than 2 tasks and investigating the performance of MTMA-DDPG in accelerating learning when a task can be likened to simpler tasks, and parallel computational resources are available. Faster convergence is obtained with no notable improvement in the quality of the final solution. In fact, the results show a 40% reduction of convergence time from approximately 10,000 to 6,000 episodes.

Figure 3 reports the reward of hybrid MTMA-DDPG in comparison to MAD-DPG and MTMA-DDPG for S1 T1 and S2 T1. Despite the asynchronous nature of the training, and the marked difference in the nature of the systems, we observe solid reward gains.

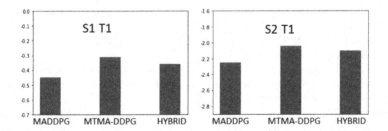

Fig. 3. Average episode reward for MADDPG, MTMA-DDPG (tasks being trained within their default systems), and Hybrid MTMA-DDPG (joint training in the hybrid system).

6   Conclusion

In this work, we presented a parallel task communication augmentation for an MA algorithm within MT settings. We extended the MADDPG algorithm to introduce MTMA-DDPG with temporal decay as a way of tempering sharing and encouraging task specialization. Furthermore, we designed 4 MTMA systems to test our algorithm. We have demonstrated that node communication leads to up to 20% improvement in reward, even and especially when the tasks are dissimilar. Moreover, variance in some tasks saw up to a three-fold decrease.

MTMA-DDPG is an easy-to-implement, efficient and flexible MTMA algorithm. The ability to modify it to generate improvements even among different tasks that do not share the same agents increases the scope of its utility, especially in real applications where systems are not designed in silos. The limitations of our approach are inherited from MADDPG, which is restricted to the particle system and cannot compete with other state-of-the-art methods on some tasks. Finally, the temporally modulated asynchronous parameter sharing between independent nodes can also be used to develop further MT algorithms from parametrized multi-agent algorithms, including the many derivatives of MADDPG itself.

Acknowledgment. This work was supported by the University Research Board (URB) and the Maroun Semaan Faculty of Engineering and Architecture (MSFEA) at the American University of Beirut.

References

1. Bram, T., Brunner, G., Richter, O., Wattenhofer, R.: Attentive multi-task deep reinforcement learning. arXiv preprint arXiv:1907.02874 (2019)
2. Crawshaw, M.: Multi-task learning with deep neural networks: a survey. arXiv preprint arXiv:2009.09796 (2020)
3. El Bsat, S., Ammar, H.B., Taylor, M.E.: Scalable multitask policy gradient reinforcement learning. In: Thirty-First AAAI Conference on Artificial Intelligence (2017)
4. Iqbal, S.: Maddpg-pytorch. https://github.com/shariqiqbal2810/maddpg-pytorch (2017)
5. Lillicrap, T.P., et al.: Continuous control with deep reinforcement learning. arXiv preprint arXiv:1509.02971 (2015)
6. Liu, X., Li, L., Hsieh, P.C., Xie, M., Ge, Y., Chen, R.: Developing multi-task recommendations with long-term rewards via policy distilled reinforcement learning. arXiv preprint arXiv:2001.09595 (2020)
7. Lowe, R., Wu, Y., Tamar, A., Harb, J., Abbeel, P., Mordatch, I.: Multi-agent actor-critic for mixed cooperative-competitive environments. arXiv preprint arXiv:1706.02275 (2017)
8. Macua, S.V., Tukiainen, A., Hernández, D.G.O., Baldazo, D., de Cote, E.M., Zazo, S.: Diff-dac: Distributed actor-critic for average multitask deep reinforcement learning. arXiv preprint arXiv:1710.10363 (2017)
9. Omidshafiei, S., Pazis, J., Amato, C., How, J.P., Vian, J.: Deep decentralized multi-task multi-agent reinforcement learning under partial observability. In: International Conference on Machine Learning, pp. 2681–2690. PMLR (2017)
10. Papoudakis, G., Christianos, F., Schäfer, L., Albrecht, S.V.: Benchmarking multi-agent deep reinforcement learning algorithms in cooperative tasks (2021)

11. Pinto, L., Gupta, A.: Learning to push by grasping: Using multiple tasks for effective learning. In: 2017 IEEE international conference on robotics and automation (ICRA), pp. 2161–2168. IEEE (2017)
12. Pitis, S., Chan, H., Zhao, S., Stadie, B., Ba, J.: Maximum entropy gain exploration for long horizon multi-goal reinforcement learning. In: International Conference on Machine Learning, pp. 7750–7761. PMLR (2020)
13. Sunehag, P., et al.: Value-decomposition networks for cooperative multi-agent learning. arXiv preprint arXiv:1706.05296 (2017)
14. Teh, Y.W., et al.: Distral: robust multitask reinforcement learning. arXiv preprint arXiv:1707.04175 (2017)
15. Tutunov, R., Kim, D., Bou Ammar, H.: Distributed multitask reinforcement learning with quadratic convergence. Adv. Neural Inf. Process. Syst. **31**, 8907–8916 (2018)
16. Vithayathil Varghese, N., Mahmoud, Q.H.: A survey of multi-task deep reinforcement learning. Electronics **9**(9), 1363 (2020)
17. Wang, R.E., Everett, M., How, J.P.: R-MADDPG for partially observable environments and limited communication. arXiv preprint arXiv:2002.06684 (2020)
18. Yu, C., Velu, A., Vinitsky, E., Wang, Y., Bayen, A., Wu, Y.: The surprising effectiveness of mappo in cooperative, multi-agent games. arXiv preprint arXiv:2103.01955 (2021)
19. Zhang, R., Zhu, Q.: Consensus-based transfer linear support vector machines for decentralized multi-task multi-agent learning. In: 2018 52nd Annual Conference on Information Sciences and Systems (CISS), pp. 1–6. IEEE (2018)
20. Zhao, R., Sun, X., Tresp, V.: Maximum entropy-regularized multi-goal reinforcement learning. In: International Conference on Machine Learning, pp. 7553–7562. PMLR (2019)

Reinforcement Learning Approach for Multi-period Inventory with Stochastic Demand

Manoj Shakya[1]($\boxtimes$) , Huey Yuen Ng[2] , Darrell Joshua Ong[2],
and Bu-Sung Lee[1]

[1] Nanyang Technological University, Singapore, Singapore
{manoj013,ebslee}@ntu.edu.sg
[2] Singapore Institute of Manufacturing Technology, Singapore, Singapore
nghy@simtech.a-star.edu.sg

Abstract. Finding an optimal solution to multi-period inventory ordering decision problems with uncertain demand is important for any manufacturing organization. Moreover, these problems are NP-hard as there are many factors to consider including customer demand and lead time which are stochastic in nature. This paper describes a reinforcement learning (RL) approach, Q-learning in particular, to decide on ordering policies. We formulated the finite horizon single-product multi-period problem into a reinforcement learning model in the form of Markov decision processes (MDP) and solve it to obtain the near-optimal solutions. Mixed integer linear programming (MILP) technique is still common in solving these problems; but they usually lack simplicity and may not optimized near to optimal. We formulated the same problem using the mixed integer linear programming model as the baseline algorithm so that we can compare it with RL approach. In comparison to MILP, the reinforcement learning agent performed better in making ordering decisions over the finite horizon. Obtaining better performance in multi-period problem would help the business in taking appropriate inventory decisions and reduce the total inventory costs.

Keywords: Reinforcement learning · Multi-period inventory management · Q-learning

1 Introduction

Optimal solution to inventory control and management problems is the crucial part of business solutions. On top of it, the stochastic inventory models have been the major focus of extensive research because the stochastic nature of variables make problem more challenging and complex. With the evolution of Industry 4.0, machine learning is playing important role in addressing such inventory control problems by optimizing the inventory costs [9].

© IFIP International Federation for Information Processing 2022
Published by Springer Nature Switzerland AG 2022
I. Maglogiannis et al. (Eds.): AIAI 2022, IFIP AICT 646, pp. 282–291, 2022.
https://doi.org/10.1007/978-3-031-08333-4_23

Reinforcement learning is one of the techniques of machine learning (ML). There are generally three different threads in RL. The first one is *optimal control*; the second one is *trial and error*; and the third one is *temporal difference*. These three concepts form the basis of Reinforcement Learning (RL) [14]. Unlike supervised learning and unsupervised learning, the learner (agent) in reinforcement learning is not explicitly told to perform any particular action. In fact, in each time stamp, an agent closely observes the current state and takes an action so that returns it receives is maximum. Using the information of return, also called reward, an agent keeps on updating the knowledge of environment and selects the next possible action. It is a way to map situations to actions so that the environment maximizes a reward value.

In 2002, reinforcement learning was used in solving inventory optimization [3]. Later in 2008, RL techniques were used to solve the beer game problem [2]. Beer game problem is a popular simulation tool for the study of supply chain management that depicts a bullwhip effect. In that study, the Q-learning algorithm [14] and the genetic algorithm (GA) based algorithm were compared. In 2015, a deep-Q-network algorithm was developed making deep RL strong enough to solve many sequential decision making problems [8]. In 2017, deep RL was also introduced to solve beer game problem in supply chain management [9].

In recent years, RL has evolved to handle various supply chain management problems. It was used in addressing the coordination problem of global supply chain management [12]. The model called SMART (Semi Markov Average Reward Technique) was proposed. Considering a general supply chain, the coordination of inventory policies adopted by different agents, such as suppliers, retailers, manufacturers is a major issue. All these agents need to coordinate to minimize the total inventory costs while meeting the customer demand. In [3], RL approach was used to determine and manage the inventory decisions at all stages aiming at optimizing the performance of supply chain. [6] uses approximate SARSA (State Action Reward State Action) and REINFORCE algorithms to solve a supply chain optimization problem which is very much similar to the problem we've considered.

In [2], Q-learning algorithm was proposed to optimize inventory order decisions of four-stage supply chain. Similarly, a research work [5] has used Q-learning and State-action-reward-state-action (SARSA) algorithms and managed to minimize total cost of a retailer when dealing with the inventory management system of perishable products under the random demand and deterministic lead time. The research work by Oroojlooyjadid et al. [9] proposed an RL approach based on Deep Q-Network (DQN) and a transfer learning to calculate the optimal ordering policy. Limited research [4,9–11] have applied deep reinforcement learning models to inventory management problems (for example beer distribution game and newsvendor problems). A paper by Bharti S. et al. [1] applied Q-learning algorithm to solve single agent supply chain problem that is related to ordering decision problem. It is found that Q-learning approach is better than Order-Up-To (OUT) policy and 1-1 policy [1].

Although many studies deal with bullwhip effect and examine how RL and DRL techniques deal with beer game problem, a few studies are made to

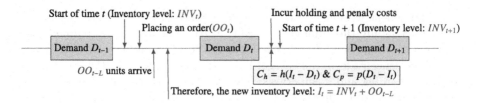

Fig. 1. Timing of the sequential events

understand how RL handle multi-period inventory management problem [13]. This paper contributes on identifying the effectiveness of Q-learning algorithm for the multi-period inventory management problem taking in consideration the stochastic demand and deterministic lead time. In this paper, we have considered the MILP model as baseline as it is one of the popular operation research (OR) approaches and compared the results with that of reinforcement learning approach.

2 Problem Description and Modeling

2.1 Problem Description

We consider a single product and a periodic-review stochastic inventory control system with lost sales and positive lead times.

The event timing of the problem description is depicted in Fig. 1. An inventory manager makes sequential decisions in discrete time steps $t = 1, ..., T$. In the beginning of every time step t, (every month in our case), inventory manager observes the current inventory level INV_t, and open-order level that are unfulfilled orders in the pipeline. Let's denote this open-order as $OO_{t-L}, ..., OO_{t-1}$. Here, $L > 0$ is the lead time which is defined as the duration between placing an order and receiving it. Based on the inventory and order level, inventory manager decides on the amount to be ordered in the current time step t. Note that the order placed is received L time steps later. After placing the order and receiving the items ordered previously, the on-hand inventory at time step t will be $I_t = INV_t + OO_{t-L}$. Now, the inventory manager observes the demand $D_t \geq 0$. If the demand is more than on-hand inventory (i.e. $D_t > I_t$), the lost sales is recorded and penalty cost is incurred. If $I_t > D_t$, a holding cost of $C_h = h(I_t - D_t)$ incurs otherwise a penalty cost of $C_p = p(D_t - I_t)$ is incurred on the part of demand that could not be met due to insufficient on-hand inventory. Therefore, the total cost incurred at the end of time step t can be expressed as $C_t = C_h + C_p = h(I_t - D_t)^+ + p(D_t - I_t)^+$, where $(I_t - D_t)^+ = max(I_t - D_t, 0)$, $(D_t - I_t)^+ = max(D_t - I_t, 0)$, and h, p are pre-specified constants denoting per unit holding cost, and per unit penalty cost respectively.

The Fig. 1 illustrates the sequence of events that is explained above. The next step $t + 1$ begins with the leftover inventory: $INV_{t+1} = (INV_t + OO_{t-L} - D_t)^+$ and the new pipeline of open-order will be: $OO_{t-L+1}, ..., OO_t$.

The objective of inventory control management is to find the policy that an agent should follow so that the total inventory cost of the system consisting of holding cost and penalty cost with lost sales is minimized.

2.2 MDP Formulation

To solve the aforementioned problem, we represent it with Markov decision processes (MDP) [14]. MDP can be expressed as (S, A, Pr, R_a) where S is the set of states, A is the set of actions, Pr is the transition probabilities, and R_a is the reward. Since the Q-learning is model free algorithm, we do not need to consider transitional probabilities.

Decision epochs: In this problem, the length of the timeline is 12 months. $t = \{1, 2, ..., 12\}$.

States: The system state variable provides the important information to the agent so that an agent can make optimal sequential decision in each step. Since the capacity of the store is M, and backlog order is not maintained, a set of states in this problem is the combination of inventory level, lost sales, open-order, and the order received at that time step (we call it shipment received - SR). It can be stated as $S = \{(INV_t, LS_t, OO_{t-L}, SR_t)\}$.

Action: Action set is a set of number that represents the order that can be placed at each time step t. In the beginning of every time step, an action is taken. Based on the assumptions a set of action can be expressed as: $A = 0, 1, 2, ..., M$. Theoretically, the demand can be of any size. If there were no capacity constrains, the set of actions would have been $A = 0, 1, 2, ..., M$. Since we have a limit to capacity of storing items in inventory, the set of action will be $A = \{0, 1, 2, ..., \alpha\}$ where $\alpha = (M - I_t - OO_t)$.

Reward: Since the main objective is to minimize the total inventory cost, the reward can be stated as $r_t(s, a) = h(I_t - D_t)^+ + p(D_t - I_t)^+$. Here, r_t denotes the net reward at time step t, h is unit holding cost, and p is the unit penalty cost.

2.3 Modeling with Q-learning

The state of the environment initially will be (INV, LS, OO, SR) as we initially have zero inventory level, no lost sales, and no any orders in pipeline. The agent (inventory manager) takes an action. i.e. the agent places an order to the supplier. This order OO_t will be appended in transit as an open order because of the lead time. The action/order an agent places follows the exploration and exploitation phenomenon. In exploration process, an agent randomly picks a number OO_t such that $OO_t \in A$. In exploitation process, an agent uses Q-table to get the action so that the reward for that action is maximum. But how does an agent decide which path to follow? Generally an ϵ value (exploration rate) is defined in the environment where $\epsilon \in [0, 1]$. A threshold value is randomly generated. If the threshold value is greater than the ϵ then the agent will exploit the environment and choose the action (i.e. places the order) that has the highest Q-value in the Q-table at time step t. If, on the other hand, the threshold is less than or equal to the ϵ, then the agent will explore the environment, and picks one value (randomly) from the action space.

As the agent performs an action of ordering products from supplier, there incurs costs like ordering cost, purchasing costs and so on. Besides these costs, there are other inventory costs that include holding cost, penalty cost, spoilage cost, and transportation cost etc. But we only consider holding cost and penalty cost in our optimization problem because these are directly related to over-stocking and under-stocking situations. After agent places an order, an environment receives the shipments from supplier. The total inventory level at this moment is $INT_t + OO_{t-L}$. Since we are not serving the backlog order, the new inventory level before serving the demand will be $I_t = (INV_t + OO_{t-L})^+$. We then serve the demand D_t. After the demand D_t is served, the reward is evaluated. By the end of the time step t, in our case a month, a reward can be calculated.

The essence of Bellman equation is to find the optimal policy that can produce the best action at any given state. The basic idea behind the Bellman equation is that the value of a current state is the sum of reward of being in that state and the reward you will be receiving after visiting subsequent states. [13]

$$R_t = r_{t+1} + \gamma r_{t+2} + \gamma^2 r_{t+3} + ... = \sum_{k=0}^{T} \gamma^k r_{t+k+1} \qquad (1)$$

where the discount faction $\gamma \in [0, 1]$. After we observe the reward that we had received taking the action from the previous state, we can update the Q-values for the state-action pair in the Q-table. We use the following Bellman equation to update the Q-value [13]:

$$Q^*(s, a) = Q(s, a) + \alpha\left(- R_t + \gamma \max_{a'} Q(s', a) - Q(s, a)\right) \qquad (2)$$

where $Q^*(s, a)$ represents the action-value function that produces optimal policy, α is the learning rate and γ is the discount factor. The negative reward $(-R_t)$ is used because we want to minimize the cumulative reward value.

2.4   Modeling with MILP

We formulate the same aforementioned problem using MILP. Specifically, MILP is often used for solving optimization problem because it can offer flexible and powerful method to solve some complex problems like inventory management problem [7]. The method that is used here for comparison is a customized inventory planning algorithm that has applications in various industries. Its purpose is to optimize inventory of materials so as to achieve minimal inventory cost, minimal material wastage and maximize customer service level.

The inventory planning algorithm is based on stochastic programming, and the decision variables are the order quantity, and supplier choice over the specified planning horizon. In the model, we optimize the decision variables for multiple materials. There are S suppliers which supply the material m. The model solves an inventory planning problem with a finite planning horizon T which is composed of T planning periods, starting with period $t = 1$ and ending with period $t = T$.

For this experiment, the number of supplies considered is 1, and the number of materials passed to the model is 1. The demand over the planning horizon T is deterministic. The stochastic optimization model considers a finite planning horizon T which is composed of T planning periods, starting with period $t = 1$ and ending with period $t = T$.

3   Experimental Results

Once the training of RL agent was over, we evaluated the performance of the RL model. This section also explains the initial state of the retailer, i.e. the initial inventory level, unit of lost sales, open-order, and shipment received when starting the evaluation.

3.1   Training the Model

In order to train the RL model, we set the parameters as listed in the following Table 1.

Table 1. Parameter values used in training the Q-learning Agent

Parameters	Values
Maximum capacity of a store M	10
Holding cost per unit h	4
Penalty cost per unit p	8
Initial Inventory Level INV	0
Initial Lost Sales $lostsales$	0
Initial open-order $openorder$	0
Initial shipment received SR	0
Lead Time L	2

Table 2. Hyper-parameter values used in training the Q-learning Agent

Parameters	Values
Learning rate α	0.001
Discount factor γ	0.95
Initial exploration rate - ϵ	1.0
Exploration decay rate	0.001
Maximum episode	1e5
Time period T	12

We also set the hyper-parameters for training the RL agent. Table 2 shows the hyper-parameters used during the implementation of Q-learning. These hyper-parameters are selected because it provided the lowest average reward during training phase. After setting the parameters and hyper-parameters, we train the RL agent. The dataset is synthetic and generated using demand distribution. During the training phase, at each time step t, an action is predicted based on exploration value, demand is realised and finally the reward is calculated. This continues till $t = 12$ an then the environment is reset. This is a single rollout also called an episode. An agent was trained with 1e5 episodes.

	a_1	a_2	...	a_m
s_1	$Q(s_1, a_1)$	$Q(s_1, a_2)$	...	$Q(s_1, a_m)$
s_2	$Q(s_2, a_1)$	$Q(s_2, a_2)$	...	$Q(s_2, a_m)$
...	...	...	...	...
s_n	$Q(s_n, a_1)$	$Q(s_n, a\_2)$	...	$Q(s_n, a_m)$

(a) Q-table

	0	1	2	3	4	5
7318	-9648	-9711	-9686	-9371	-5456	-9700
7319	-9656	-9599	-9682	**-4993**	-9703	-9644
7320	-9559	-9580	-9540	-9529	-9578	-9578

(b) Q-values

Fig. 2. Q-table with Q-values

3.2 Agent's Policy

In this experiment, an optimal policy is learned when Q-table is updated subsequently. The value in the cell $Q(s, a)$ represents the value of the action a taken when the state is s. Given a state s, the action a that has highest $Q(s, a)$ is selected. As the iteration during training continues, $Q(s, a)$ for all combination of s, a are calculated with greedy search approach. With this approach, Q-values are converged to the near optimal policy. The Fig. 2a helps us to visualise the Q-function as a simple Q-table.

The state S_t of our environment is the combination of four variables. They are inventory level, backorder, open-order, and shipment received. With the values of these variables, a code (index in this case) is generated using a function. This code represents the row in a Q-table.

Solving a problem using reinforcement learning means finding a policy that provides the maximum reward during the training phase. Hence, the policy of an agent is the corresponding column value of the maximum Q-value in the row i.e. $a = maxQ(s, a)$ where a is the amount to be ordered when state s is reached. Let's take an example of state with inventory level: 2, lost sales: 0, open-order: 9, and shipment received: 4. The state of the environment is $S(2, 0, 9, 4)$ which gives a code/index as 7319. Now, looking at the Q-table, the maximum Q-value in a row 7319 is located at $Q(7319, 3)$. Hence, the policy suggests to place an order of 3 (#column). The Fig. 2b is a snapshot of the Q-table we obtained after training an agent. After placing an order of 3, and the realization of demand is 2, the new state of the environment will be $S(0, 0, 8, 5)$. In the next step, the above procedure is repeated.

3.3 Initial Setting for Evaluation

The demand distribution is shown in Table 3. Let's set that the initial state of the inventory has Inventory $(INV_0) = 10$ units, Lost sales $(LS_0) = 0$, Open order for the first month $(OO_0) = 4$ units, and Open order for the second month $(SR_0) = 5$ units.

We examined the RL agent with 10 different test datasets, each consisting of randomly generated demands with finite planning horizon of $T = 12$ as shown in Table 4. The same test datasets were also being used in MILP model. As shown in Table 4, RL agent performed better than MILP agent in those test datasets. Let's consider the first test dataset out of 10 listed in Table 4 to see

Table 3. Demand distribution

Demand	Cumulative percentile
3	0.25
4	0.75
6	0.95
7	1.00

Table 4. Comparison of inventory cost generated by RL agent and MILP agent from 10 different test datasets.

Test dataset	List of demand	Total cost (RL Agent)	Total cost (MILP)
1	[6 7 6 6 4 3 6 4 4 4 3 3]	**92**	108
2	[6 7 6 6 3 6 4 4 4 4 4 4]	**96**	120
3	[6 6 7 6 3 3 3 7 4 4 3 4]	**88**	116
4	[6 7 6 7 4 4 4 3 3 6 4 6]	**124**	136
5	[6 7 6 6 4 4 6 3 4 3 3 4]	**84**	100
6	[6 6 6 6 3 3 4 3 4 4 6 6]	**96**	128
7	[6 7 6 6 4 4 6 3 3 4 3 4]	**88**	100
8	[6 6 6 6 4 3 3 4 6 3 3 4]	**96**	112
9	[6 7 6 6 4 4 6 3 3 3 3 4]	**84**	96
10	[6 7 6 6 3 6 4 4 4 4 4 6]	**88**	128

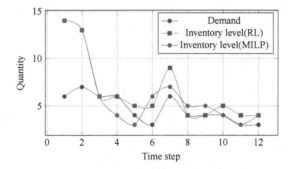

Fig. 3. Inventory level maintained by RL and MILP agents over demand

how inventory levels are maintained. Inventory level is a total stock in hand at a particular time step. Besides total cost, other indicators are also important. Figure 3 shows the inventory level of the first test dataset.

Some of the Key Performance Indicators (KPIs) in inventory management other than total inventory costs are *service level* and *fill rate*. Service level measures the percentage of not getting stock-out i.e. not losing the sales of all customers' demand arriving within a given planning horizon. For example, if the current service level is 80%, it means there are two time steps out of 10 where customers' demand could not be fulfilled. Let D_t be the demand over the time period t and I_t be the current inventory level. Then service level (η_1) is:

$$\eta_1 = \frac{1}{T} \sum_{t=1}^{T} S \tag{3}$$

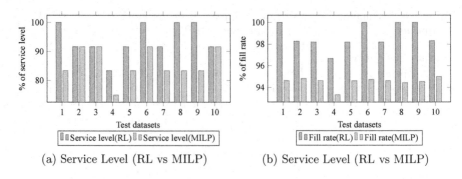

(a) Service Level (RL vs MILP)   (b) Service Level (RL vs MILP)

Fig. 4. Service Level and Fill Rate

where $S = 1$ if stock is available to fulfill the customers' demand, and $S = 0$ otherwise. Unlike service level, fill rate is the percentage of customers' demand that is fulfilled without lost sales. Service level calculates the fraction of replenishment cycle during which customers' demand are fulfilled whereas fill rate calculates the fraction of demand satisfied from available stock. For instance, 98% fill rate means, it fulfilled 98 customers' demand out of 100. The formula to calculate the fill rate (η_2) is:

$$\eta_2 = \frac{\sum_{t=1}^{T} min(D_t, I_t)}{\sum_{t=1}^{T} D_t} \tag{4}$$

Figure 4a and Fig. 4b respectively show the service levels and fill rates maintained by RL and MILP agents in all 10 different test datasets listed in Table 4.

In most of the test datasets, RL agent successfully achieved 100% of service level where as MILP agent struggles to maintain 90% service level. This signifies that RL agent could do better in predicting the future demand and could take an account of supply and demand variance very well. Similarly, most of the time the fill rate obtained by MILP agent is lower than the one obtained by RL agent. The better fill rate obtained by RL agent signifies that the ordering decisions made by RL agent could meet customers' demand very well.

4   Conclusions and Future Work

This paper models the multi-period inventory management problem with stochastic demand into Markov decision processes and solves it using value-based approach of reinforcement learning so called Q-learning. The RL approach of solving the aforementioned problem has shown good result. The RL model in comparison with MILP model shows that it can handle the fluctuation of demand with high service level and good fill rate. In addition, the exploratory results presented in this paper proves that RL can be a good approach for solving multi-period inventory control that adds a great value to smart manufacturing processes. In future, research can be conducted to solve complex multi-period inventory control problems introducing more business and operational constrains.

Acknowledgements. The authors would like to thank the Singapore Institute of Manufacturing Technology (SIMTech), Singapore for its input and support.

References

1. Bharti, S., Kurian, D.S., Pillai, V.M.: Reinforcement learning for inventory management. In: Deepak, B.B.V.L., Parhi, D.R.K., Jena, P.C. (eds.) Innovative Product Design and Intelligent Manufacturing Systems. LNME, pp. 877–885. Springer, Singapore (2020). https://doi.org/10.1007/978-981-15-2696-1_85
2. Chaharsooghi, S.K., Heydari, J., Zegordi, S.H.: A reinforcement learning model for supply chain ordering management: an application to the beer game. Decis. Support Syst. **45**(4), 949–959 (2008)
3. Giannoccaro, I., Pontrandolfo, P.: Inventory management in supply chains: a reinforcement learning approach. Int. J. Prod. Econ. **78**(2), 153–161 (2002)
4. Gijsbrechts, J., Boute, R.N., Van Mieghem, J.A., Zhang, D.: Can deep reinforcement learning improve inventory management? Performance and implementation of dual sourcing-mode problems. SSRN Electron. J .1–26 (2019)
5. Kara, A., Dogan, I.: Reinforcement learning approaches for specifying ordering policies of perishable inventory systems. Expert Syst. Appl. **91**, 150–158 (2018)
6. Kemmer, L., Read, J.: Reinforcement learning for supply chain optimization. In: The 14th European Workshop on Reinforcement Learning, vol. 14 (2018)
7. Küçükyavuz, S.: Mixed-integer optimization approaches for deterministic and stochastic inventory management. In: Transforming Research into Action, pp. 90–105. INFORMS (2011)
8. Mnih, V., et al.: Human-level control through deep reinforcement learning. Nature **518**(7540), 529–533 (2015)
9. Oroojlooyjadid, A., Snyder, L., Takáč, M.: A Deep Q-Network for the Beer Game: an Approach to Solve Inventory Optimization Problems. Deep Reinforcement Learning Symposium, NIPS 2017 (2017)
10. Oroojlooyjadid, A., Snyder, L.V., Takáč, M.: Applying deep learning to the newsvendor problem. IISE Trans. **52**(4), 444–463 (2020)
11. Peng, Z., Zhang, Y., Feng, Y., Zhang, T., Wu, Z., Su, H.: Deep reinforcement learning approach for capacitated supply chain optimization under demand uncertainty. In: Proceedings - Chinese Automation Congress, pp. 3512–3517 (2019)
12. Pontrandolfo, P., Gosavi, A., Okogbaa, O.G., Das, T.K.: Global supply chain management: a reinforcement learning approach. Int. J. Prod. Res. **40**(6), 1299–1317 (2002)
13. Sultana, N.N., Meisheri, H., Baniwal, V., Nath, S., Ravindran, B., Khadilkar, H.: Reinforcement Learning for Multi-Product Multi-Node Inventory Management in Supply Chains. CoRR (2020). http://arxiv.org/abs/2006.04037
14. Sutton, R.S., Barto, A.G.: Reinforcement Learning: An Introduction. The MIT Press, London, England (2018)

The Neocortex-Inspired Locally Recurrent Neural Network (NILRNN) as a Model of the Primary Visual Cortex

Franz A. Van-Horenbeke[✉][ID] and Angelika Peer[ID]

Human-Centered Technologies and Machine Intelligence Lab,
Faculty of Science and Technology, Free University of Bozen-Bolzano, Bolzano, Italy
{fvanhorenbeke,angelika.peer}@unibz.it
https://hct.projects.unibz.it/

Abstract. Our recently introduced Neocortex-Inspired Locally Recurrent Neural Network is a machine learning system that is able to learn feature extraction functions from sequential data in an unsupervised way. While it was designed with the main purpose of feature learning, its structure and desired functioning is highly inspired by models of the feedforward circuits in the neocortex. In this work, we study the behavior of our system when it takes shifting images as input, and we compare it with known behavior of the primary visual cortex. The results show that some of the best-known emerging properties in the primary visual cortex, such as the emergence of simple and complex cells as well as orientation maps, also occur in our system, indicating that also their behaviors can be considered analogous. This validates our system as a potential model of the primary visual cortex that may contribute to further understanding of its functioning. In addition, considering that most areas in the neocortex show similarities in terms of structure and operation, future studies of our system over inputs other than images may also bring new insights about other neocortical areas.

Keywords: Brain-inspired machine learning · Biologically inspired
neural networks · Cognitive architectures · Feature learning ·
Unsupervised learning · Models of the visual cortex

1 Introduction

Within the field of cognitive neuroscience, computational models of different regions of the brain have been extensively used when aiming to understand how these systems work and how the different forms of cognition emerge (e.g., models of the basal ganglia [5], models of the hippocampus [3], etc.). One region that has been intensively studied and that has inspired the development of a series of computational models is the primary visual cortex [14], which is the earliest area in the neocortex processing the incoming visual information. The main

I. Maglogiannis et al. (Eds.): AIAI 2022, IFIP AICT 646, pp. 292–303, 2022.
https://doi.org/10.1007/978-3-031-08333-4_24

advantage of computational models over more descriptive or conceptual models is that they allow us to simulate the system and test different hypotheses. Indeed, they provide full control over the parameters of the system, which allows us to understand how they affect its behavior, and they give the possibility to measure any state variable. Still, not only the models that have been designed with this purpose have been useful in the advancement of our knowledge about the functioning of the different regions of the brain: There are also machine learning systems that, while designed with a complete different purpose, have still drawn inspiration from the structure of regions of the brain. This way, they show analogies with those regions in terms of behavior, and have brought insights about their functioning. A typical example is that of convolutional neural networks (CNNs): These networks have not been designed with the purpose of modeling our visual system, and therefore their design puts performance before being analogous to our brain. Still, they were inspired by the architecture and connections of our visual cortex. This, added to the fact that, due to their great success, they have been extensively and deeply studied, has put them as relevant sources of understanding our visual system [11].

In this sense, our recently proposed Neocortex-Inspired Locally Recurrent Neural Network (NILRNN) [22] is also a machine learning system that mainly seeks performance, but which is strongly inspired by our neocortex. In this study, we compare the behavior of the NILRNN with that of the primary visual cortex, as it is one of the best-known regions of the neocortex. The results show that both systems have analogous behaviors upon all the visual cortex properties for which the NILRNN was evaluated. This, added to the fact that the neocortex seems to be quite homogeneous along its areas in terms of structure and functioning [17], suggests that the use of our system in different applications may bring new insights about the operation of not only the visual cortex, but also other areas of the neocortex.

This article is organized as follows: Sect. 2 introduces concepts about the neocortex and the primary visual cortex, as well as about related computational systems. Section 3 describes the NILRNN architecture. Section 4 presents the results obtained regarding the visual cortex properties for which NILRNN was evaluated. Finally, Sect. 5 discusses on the results obtained and on possible implications.

2   Background

The neocortex is a thin layered region of the brain that is involved in high-level cognitive functions such as sensory perception, rational thought, voluntary motor control or language [13]. It is organized in general in a six-layered structure [18], and it is divided into areas that perform different functions [16]. For example, the primary visual cortex is the first area in the neocortex processing the input visual information. It gets the visual input from the thalamus, processes it and forwards it to the next areas in the visual cortex [21]. Still, the neocortex seems to be quite uniform along most of its areas in terms of structure and operation, and therefore it appears to have a common underlying algorithm along those different areas [17].

The primary visual cortex is one of the better-known areas in the neocortex, and many computational models of it exist. These models usually focus on layers 2, 3 and 4 of the neocortex, and on the feedforward connections, which are the ones in charge of bringing the visual information through the different processing areas to the higher abstraction areas. Neurons in these layers of the primary visual cortex are sensitive to small regions of the input stimuli known as receptive fields, and are typically classified into simple and complex cells: Simple cells, mainly found in layer 4 (L4), tend to fire after edges in their receptive field with a particular orientation and position, while complex cells, mainly found in layers 2 and 3 (L2/3), tend to fire after edges with a particular orientation, but independently of their position (i.e., small shifts in the input affects little their response) [6]. This behavior is typically studied using as visual stimuli sine gratings as those shown in Fig. 1, for which simple cells tend to respond to a specific orientation and phase, while complex cells respond to a specific orientation but are more phase-invariant. In addition, neurons in layers 2, 3 and 4 with similar receptive fields and orientation preferences are found to be located close to each other, forming smooth ordered maps [10]. However, such order does not seem to exist in terms of phase [12].

Fig. 1. Examples of sine gratings of different orientations, spatial frequencies and phases.

In computational models of the primary visual cortex, the behavior of simple cells is typically achieved through Hebbian-like learning techniques, which model how neurons in our brain learn [4]. These learning rules applied over small regions of input images lead the modeled neurons to learn edge patterns of a particular orientation and phase. Regarding complex cells (mainly in L2/3), their expected behavior is often achieved by pooling simple cells (mainly in L4) of similar orientations but different phases, achieving this way a strong response to that orientation in a more phase-invariant way [9]. Considering that neurons in the primary visual cortex with similar orientations but different phases tend to be close to each other, models that satisfy such property can achieve the desired complex cell behavior by just pooling the neurons in a localized region of L4. Antolik et al. [1] proposed a model able to achieve such orientation order and phase disorder in a biologically plausible way by introducing lateral and feedback connections that allow neurons in L4 to contribute to the firing of their neighbors with certain time delay. This makes nearby neurons respond to input patterns that tend to occur close in time, but not to the same input. This way, if the model gets as input shifting images (mimicking the input to our visual system), nearby neurons with similar receptive fields will learn edges with similar orientations but shifted in space, leading to the desired order. Another advantage of this model is that it does not explicitly rely on properties of the input images, and therefore may be also valid for other areas of the neocortex processing different types of data (as most areas have a similar structure).

Computational models of the visual cortex have inspired several machine learning systems, being CNNs a well-known successful example that has also contributed to its understanding [11]. CNNs, however, do not rely on learning a set of patterns that show orientation order but phase disorder to then pool nearby neurons together, but they are explicitly designed (i.e., hardwired) to pool neurons detecting the same pattern at slightly shifted positions of the input image. A key factor to their success seems to be that those shifted versions of the same pattern contribute essentially with the same information to the overall meaning of the input, and by grouping them, the network is losing little relevant information while simplifying the representation. However, this idea is not applicable in general to domains other than vision (e.g., shifting the elements of a generic feature vector may completely change its meaning), and neither seems to correspond to anything occurring in other regions of the neocortex. Our recently proposed NILRNN [22], on the other hand, is indeed designed to achieve orientation order and phase disorder when having shifting images as input. To do so, it relies on the same principle as that of the model by Antolik et al. [1], i.e., it pushes nearby neurons to learn patterns typically occurring close in time, which are then pooled together. This way, it can be argued that NILRNN works because input patterns that tend to occur close in time also have in general a very similar meaning, and can therefore be grouped together. This approach has the added benefit that it applies to almost any domain that deals with sequential data, and is a mechanism that may be also occurring in neocortical regions other than the visual cortex. In fact, considering that, due to such mechanism, the activity in the pooling neurons varies slower in time than the input, this approach is also consistent with the neocortex-related slowness principle, which states that the environment changes in a slower timescale than the sensory input we get from it, and therefore, good representations of the environment should also change in such slower timescale [23]. This makes NILRNN a more accurate model of the visual cortex in terms of structure as well as a potential model of other areas of the neocortex. Still, as we mentioned in Sect. 1, NILRNN was designed as a feature learning system for machine learning applications rather than as a model of the neocortex. In this regard, NILRNN has already shown its effectiveness outperforming other feature learning systems in classification tasks over sequential data domains such as speech recognition or action recognition [22].

3   Materials and Methods

NILRNN is an unsupervised feature learning neural network for sequential data. The NILRNN **feature extraction system**, shown in Fig. 2, consists of three layers: the input layer, the recurrent layer (analogous to L4) and the max pooling layer (analogous to L2/3). Neurons in the recurrent layer are arranged in two dimensions, with neurons close to each other being connected through recurrent connections. This allows neurons to contribute to the firing of their nearby neurons in the next timestep, which, during the training phase, pushes them to learn input patterns that tend to occur successively in time. This way, a form of self-organization mechanism emerges, with a global order appearing due to the local interactions among the components. Since we will work with images as input, the input to this layer will be also partially connected, following a connection pattern that mimics the one observed in the primary visual cortex: Neurons in the recurrent layer are connected to a region of the input (i.e., their receptive field, see Sect. 2), in a way that, when moving along the neurons in the recurrent layer in both directions, the corresponding receptive fields also shift smoothly in both directions, similar to the connection patterns of convolutional layers. This way, neighbor neurons have same or very similar receptive fields. Neurons in the recurrent layer make use of sigmoid activation functions, since their desired behavior consists of just working as detectors of specific patterns in the input. Regarding the max pooling layer, it has a similar input connection pattern, with each neuron pooling neurons from a region of the recurrent layer. All these connection kernels have an approximately circular shape.

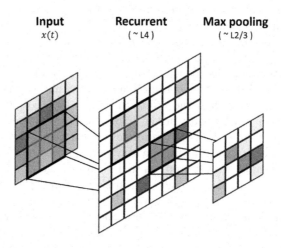

Fig. 2. NILRNN feature extraction system architecture with partially-connected input. The green cells represent input feedforward connections. The blue cells represent local recurrent connections. The red cells represent max pooling connections. (Color figure online)

This feature extraction system can of course be trained as part of a larger neural network and in a supervised way, but in this study we are interested in analyzing its behavior when trained in an unsupervised way, similar to what occurs in the brain. The NILRNN **unsupervised learning system** (see Fig. 3) relies on self-supervised learning techniques similar to those used in autoencoders [7] (Hebbian learning methods are avoided because they typically require complementary mechanisms to lead to the desired results, making the system more complex and harder to design [15]). This way, since the neural network is recurrent, it is trained to reconstruct the input (same as autoencoders) as well as to predict the following inputs. On the other hand, since the max pooling layer does not need to learn any weights nor contributes in a positive way to the desired learning of weights in the recurrent layer, it is not included in the self-supervised learning system. The output layer is formed of several channels with the size and shape of the input layer corresponding to each of the predictions at the different timesteps. Each of these channels are connected to the recurrent layer following a pattern that is symmetric to that defining the connections between the input layer and the recurrent layer. Neurons in the output layer also make use of sigmoid activation functions, which means that the input to the network needs to be in the range $(0, 1)$. Finally, the recurrent layer is designed to have a sparse activity by adding a sparsity term to the cost function, similar to how is done for sparse autoencoders [7]. Sparsity, which consists of allowing only a small percentage of the neurons to be active at a given time, is a behavior that has been observed in the neocortex [8], and it is often very appropriate to represent the observations of the real world because these observations can usually be described through the presence of a limited number of features out of a considerably larger number of possible features (e.g., the presence of certain objects, their location, etc.), besides showing other advantages. This way, the cost function is given by the following equation:

$$J(W, b) = J_{error} + \lambda \cdot J_{regularization} + \beta \cdot J_{sparse} \tag{1}$$

where W and b represent all the variable weights and bias units, J_{error} is the squared-error cost term, $J_{regularization}$ is the L_2 regularization term, J_{sparse} is the sparsity term based on the KL-divergence and applied only to the recurrent layer, and λ and β are cost function weights.

4   Results

To evaluate how the NILRNN has an analogous behavior to that of the neocortex, we have used a network that takes as input an image patch of size 16×16, and has a recurrent layer formed of neurons with a receptive field of size 69 pixels and connected in a recurrent way to 29 neurons of the same layer. Their specific receptive field is defined by a stride of 0.33 neurons (i.e., every three neurons, the receptive field shifts one pixel), leading to a layer size of 46×46. The max pooling layer is defined by a kernel size of 21 neurons and by a stride of 1 neuron, having also a size of 46×46. Regarding the self-supervised learning system, its output is formed of three channels (i.e., it has a size of $16 \times 16 \times 3$, reconstructing the current and next two inputs). The cost function is characterized by weights $\lambda = 1.5 \cdot 10^{-6}$ and $\beta = 0.15$, and by a desired sparsity parameter of 0.04.

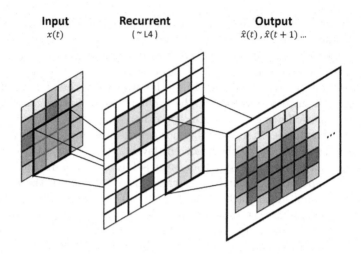

Fig. 3. NILRNN self-supervised feature learning system architecture with partially-connected input and output. The green cells represent input and output feedforward connections. The blue cells represent local recurrent connections. (Color figure online)

For the training, we have used truncated backpropagation through time with a truncation horizon of 4 timesteps, Adam optimization with a stepsize of $2.5 \cdot 10^{-3}$, and a batch size of 1000 samples, and we have trained the system on 400.000 batches. Note that all these hyperparameters have been set manually, and therefore better results may be obtained using other values. Regarding the training input, it consists of sequences of image patches of size 16×16 obtained by moving laterally a 16×16 window along the image at random velocities and directions, and which are taken from whitened natural images [19] normalized to the interval $[0.1, 0.9]$.

Once the system has been trained, we have set images of drifting sinusoidal gratings with different phases, orientations and spatial frequencies as those shown in Fig. 1 as input, and we have analyzed the responses of the neurons in both the recurrent and max pooling layers, similar to how has been done when studying the behavior of the primary visual cortex [2] or of models of it [1]. Figure 4 shows the resultant weights from the training at the input feedforward connections, once normalized (i.e., the input patterns that the neurons at the recurrent layer have learnt to detect). This figure shows that, as expected, the neurons learn to detect edges in the input, with neighbor neurons tending to detect edges with similar orientations but different phases. This can be also observed in the **orientation** and **phase maps** of the recurrent and max pooling layers shown in Fig. 5. These maps are obtained by finding, for each neuron, the orientation and phase of the input pattern that draws the maximum response, for any spatial frequency. As can be seen in this figure, the orientation map for the max pooling layer looks similar and has similar characteristics to those typically obtained from the primary visual cortex (i.e., it has homogeneous regions appearing periodically, pinwheels where many different orientations meet, etc.) [2]. The orientation map for the recurrent layer has similar properties, but with the regions being more scattered, which is something that also occurs in other models of the primary visual cortex, and that, to the best of our knowledge, does not contradict any experimental evidence [1]. In addition, and as expected, regions at similar positions of the two layers have similar orientation preferences. Regarding the phase maps, that of the recurrent layer does not appear to have any order, which is consistent with experimental evidence. On the other hand, some homogeneous regions appear at the phase map of the max pooling layer, but these regions are in general smaller than those at the orientation map, and have the shape of the max pooling kernel (which is a 21 neurons kernel with the shape of a 5×5 square without its 4 corners). This way, they seem to appear simply because the maximum value for a neuron in the max pooling layer corresponds to the maximum of all the maximum values of the neurons it is pooling, so neurons in the recurrent layer having high maximum values will lead most neurons pooling them to have those same maximum values for the same input patterns (i.e., same phases). Other than that, it does not seem to exist any phase order.

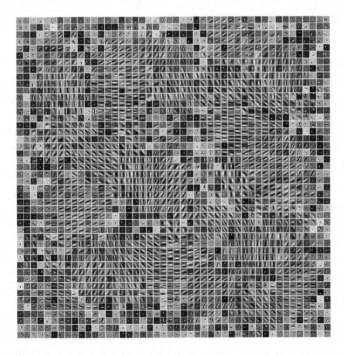

Fig. 4. Normalized weights at the input feedforward connections of an NILRNN trained with shifting images as input.

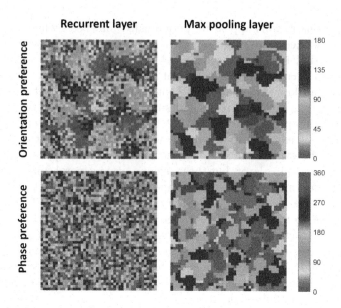

Fig. 5. Orientation and phase maps at the recurrent and max pooling layers of an NILRNN trained with shifting images as input.

In order to evaluate whether the neurons in both layers behave as simple or complex cells, we have calculated their **modulation ratios** [20]. The modulation ratio of a neuron is calculated as the ratio between the first harmonic and the average of the response to a drifting sine of the spatial frequency and orientation for which the maximum response is obtained. Neurons with a more simple-like behavior respond in a strong way to a particular phase with respect to the others, and therefore have a higher modulation ratio, while those with a more complex-like behavior respond more homogeneously, and therefore have a lower modulation ratio. Typically, neurons are classified as complex cells if their modulation ratio is below 1, and as simple cells otherwise. Figure 6 shows the histograms with the modulation ratios of all the neurons of each layer of the NILRNN, as well as a typical distribution obtained when taking a sample of neurons from the primary visual cortex across layers. In this figure we can see how, as expected, most neurons in the recurrent layer behave as simple cells, while most neurons in the max pooling layer behave as complex cells, analogously to what has been observed in the primary visual cortex (see Sect. 2). On the other hand, if we consider the neurons of both layers of our system altogether, the shape of the resultant histogram would be very similar to that obtained for the neurons in the primary visual cortex (except for the relative height of the two peaks, which depends on the size of the sample of neurons at each layer, and therefore should not be considered as a relevant difference).

Finally, Fig. 7 shows the **orientation tuning curves** and **phase responses** of some representative neurons from the inside of the orientation-wise homogeneous regions of both layers of the NILRNN. The orientation tuning curves show

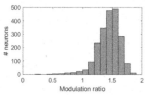 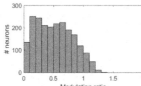 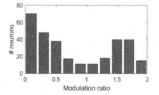

(a) Modulation ratios of the recurrent layer of the NIL-RNN.

(b) Modulation ratios of the max pooling layer of the NILRNN.

(c) Modulation ratios of the primary visual cortex of a macaque monkey [20].

Fig. 6. Modulation ratios of the neurons of each layer of an NILRNN trained with shifting images as input, and of a sample of neurons from several layers of the primary visual cortex of a macaque monkey.

the maximum response value of each neuron as a function of the orientation for any phase and spatial frequency. The phase responses show the response obtained as a function of the phase for the orientation and spatial frequency that give the strongest response. The orientation tuning curves show that all these neurons are indeed finely tuned to a narrow band of spatial frequencies. As expected, and analogously to what has been observed in the primary visual cortex [20], the spatial frequency bands of the neurons in the max pooling layer are broader than those of the neurons in the recurrent layer. Regarding the phase responses, the figure shows how the neurons in the recurrent layer are also finely tuned to a narrow band of phases, while the neurons in the max pooling layer are much more phase-invariant, which corresponds to the behavior of simple and complex cells, respectively, as commented in Sect. 2.

5   Discussion

NILRNN is a neocortex-inspired artificial neural network for the unsupervised learning of features in sequential data. It is strongly inspired by computational models of the primary visual cortex, and it relies on brain-inspired machine learning mechanisms and principles such as sparsity, slowness or self-organization. The results presented in this study show that its behavior is in different ways analogous to that of the primary visual cortex. This means that it can function to some extent as a model of the primary visual cortex, and contribute to obtaining new insights about its principles of functioning, similar to what has ocurred with CNNs. In fact, NILRNN is analogous to the primary visual cortex to a larger extent than CNNs both in terms of structure and of emerging behavior, allowing it for example to develop orientation maps. Furthermore, NILRNN is based on ideas that do not only apply to the visual cortex, but which may also apply to other areas of the neocortex (i.e., it relies on grouping together input patterns that tend to occur close in time, and not on grouping together spatially shifted versions of the same pattern). This allows NILRNN to be applicable to domains

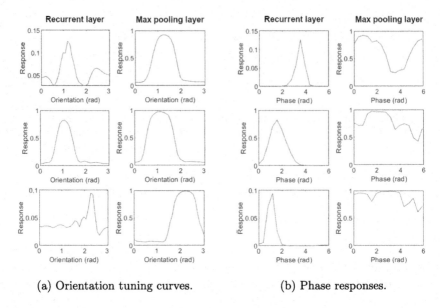

(a) Orientation tuning curves.   (b) Phase responses.

Fig. 7. Orientation tuning curves and phase responses of three representative neurons of each layer of an NILRNN trained with shifting images as input. The positions of the three neurons in both layers are (28,10) (top), (23,38) (middle) and (21,13) (bottom).

with very different properties from those of computer vision, as well as to possibly serve as a model of different areas of the neocortex, and, thus, contribute to the advancement of our knowledge about those areas and the neocortex in general.

Acknowledgements. This research was supported by the Euregio project OLIVER (Open-Ended Learning for Interactive Robots) with grant agreement IPN86, funded by the EGTC Europaregion Tirol-Südtirol-Trentino within the framework of the third call for projects in the field of basic research.

References

1. Antolik, J., Bednar, J.A.: Development of maps of simple and complex cells in the primary visual cortex. Front. Comput. Neurosci. **5**, 17 (2011)
2. Blasdel, G.G.: Orientation selectivity, preference, and continuity in monkey striate cortex. J. Neurosci. **12**(8), 3139–3161 (1992)
3. Burgess, N.: Computational models of the spatial and mnemonic functions of the hippocampus. In: Andersen, P., Morris, R., Amaral, D., Bliss, T., O'Keefe, J. (eds.) The Hippocampus Book, pp. 715–750. Oxford University Press (2007)
4. Choe, Y.: Hebbian learning. In: Jaeger, D., Jung, R. (eds.) Encyclopedia of Computational Neuroscience, pp. 1305–1309. Springer, New York (2015)
5. Cohen, M.X., Frank, M.J.: Neurocomputational models of basal ganglia function in learning, memory and choice. Behav. Brain Res. **199**(1), 141–156 (2009)

6. Gilbert, C.D.: Laminar differences in receptive field properties of cells in cat primary visual cortex. J. Physiol. **268**(2), 391–421 (1977)
7. Goodfellow, I., Bengio, Y., Courville, A.: Deep Learning. MIT Press (2016). http://www.deeplearningbook.org
8. Graham, D.J., Field, D.J.: Sparse coding in the neocortex. Evol. Nervous Syst. **3**, 181–187 (2006)
9. Hubel, D.H., Wiesel, T.N.: Receptive fields, binocular interaction and functional architecture in the cat's visual cortex. J. Physiol. **160**(1), 106–154 (1962)
10. Hubel, D.H., Wiesel, T.N.: Sequence regularity and geometry of orientation columns in the monkey striate cortex. J. Compar. Neurol. **158**(3), 267–293 (1974)
11. Lindsay, G.W.: Convolutional neural networks as a model of the visual system: past, present, and future. J. Cogn. Neurosci. **33**(10), 2017–2031 (2021)
12. Liu, Z., Gaska, J.P., Jacobson, L.D., Pollen, D.A.: Interneuronal interaction between members of quadrature phase and anti-phase pairs in the cat's visual cortex. Vision. Res. **32**(7), 1193–1198 (1992)
13. Lukatela, K., Swadlow, H.A.: Neocortex. The corsini encyclopedia of psychology, pp. 1–2 (2010)
14. Martinez, L.M., Alonso, J.M.: Complex receptive fields in primary visual cortex. Neuroscientist **9**(5), 317–331 (2003)
15. McClelland, J.L.: How far can you go with hebbian learning, and when does it lead you astray. Processes of change in brain and cognitive development: attention and performance xxi, vol. 21, pp. 33–69 (2006)
16. Mesulam, M.M.: From sensation to cognition. Brain J. Neurol. **121**(6), 1013–1052 (1998)
17. Mountcastle, V.B.: The columnar organization of the neocortex. Brain J. Neurol. **120**(4), 701–722 (1997)
18. Narayanan, R.T., Udvary, D., Oberlaender, M.: Cell type-specific structural organization of the six layers in rat barrel cortex. Front. Neuroanat. **11**, 91 (2017)
19. Ng, A.: Deep learning and unsupervised feature learning handouts (2011). https://web.stanford.edu/class/cs294a/handouts.html
20. Ringach, D.L., Shapley, R.M., Hawken, M.J.: Orientation selectivity in macaque v1: diversity and laminar dependence. J. Neurosci. **22**(13), 5639–5651 (2002)
21. Tong, F.: Primary visual cortex and visual awareness. Nat. Rev. Neurosci. **4**(3), 219–229 (2003)
22. Van-Horenbeke, F.A., Peer, A.: Nilrnn: a neocortex-inspired autoencoder-like locally recurrent neural network for unsupervised feature learning in sequential data (2022). (manuscript in preparation)
23. Wiskott, L.: Slow feature analysis: a theoretical analysis of optimal free responses. Neural Comput. **15**(9), 2147–2177 (2003)

TraderNet-CR: Cryptocurrency Trading with Deep Reinforcement Learning

Vasilis Kochliaridis[✉] [ID], Eleftherios Kouloumpris[ID], and Ioannis Vlahavas[ID]

School of Informatics, Aristotle University of Thessaloniki,
54124 Thessaloniki, Greece
vkochlia@csd.auth.gr

Abstract. The predominant method of developing trading strategies is technical analysis on historical market data. Other financial analysts monitor the public activity towards cryptocurrencies, in order to forecast upcoming trends in the market. Until now, the best cryptocurrency trading models rely solely on one of the two methodologies and attempt to maximize their profits, while disregarding the trading risk. In this paper, we present a new machine learning approach, named TraderNet-CR, which is based on deep reinforcement learning. TraderNet-CR combines both methodologies in order to detect profitable round trips in the cryptocurrency market and maximize a trader's profits. Additionally, we have added an extension method, named N-Consecutive Actions, which examines the model's previous actions, before suggesting a new action. This method is complementary to the model's training and can be fruitfully combined, in order to further decrease the trading risk. Our experiments show that our model can properly forecast profitable round trips, despite high market commission fees.

Keywords: Cryptocurreny trading · Deep reinforcement learning · Public activity analysis · Technical analysis · Risk management

1 Introduction

Cryptocurrency tokens have become particularly interesting trading assets, due to their high volatility [12]. Many professional investors and financial analysts are turning to technical analysis, in order to estimate the future prices of cryptocurrencies and spot trading opportunities. Unlike fundamental analysis, which requires a company's financial position, technical analysis merely requires a mathematical formula to be applied to prior market data. Technical analysis provides pattern-based indicators of the momentum, volatility and trend of an asset [14].

Algorithmic trading i.e. the use of computer programs to automate quantitative trading methods, is an essential step towards a more exact specification and implementation of technical analysis. Although algorithmic trading is beneficial due to the speed with which orders are executed, it is primarily reliant on technical indicators, which are prone to producing false buy/sell signals and market

© IFIP International Federation for Information Processing 2022
Published by Springer Nature Switzerland AG 2022
I. Maglogiannis et al. (Eds.): AIAI 2022, IFIP AICT 646, pp. 304–315, 2022.
https://doi.org/10.1007/978-3-031-08333-4_25

trends. To overcome this issue, traders consider combinations of indicators, however it has yet to be determined which combinations are the most effective in each circumstance.

Various studies attempted to apply machine learning techniques to cryptocurrency trading, based on algorithmic trading, as detailed in more depth in the related works Section. The same works prove that especially Deep Reinforcement Learning (DRL), which is a sub-field of machine learning, has the potential to outperform traditional trading strategies. However, our research revealed that past studies have overlooked three critical characteristics of cryptocurrency trading. Firstly, numerous popular and widely used indicators were missing from the training data. They also lack a public activity index which, as we prove later in the paper, contains valuable information about the prices. Finally, several previous models that aim to optimize a portfolio's wealth disregard the trading risk, which is an important aspect of a trading strategy, as also highlighted in Sect. 2.

In this paper we present TraderNet-CR, a DRL agent[1] which relies on both technical analysis and hourly public activity towards cryptocurrency assets. Our agent's actions are intended to exploit potentially beneficial round trips in a market[2] with low risk. The remaining of the paper is structured as follows. Section 2 describes the related work, while Sect. 3 describes the methodological framework in detailed steps. Then, Sect. 4 discusses the empirical results and finally, Sect. 5 concludes this study and presents future research avenues and possible improvements of the algorithm.

2   Related Work

In this Section, we exclusively review works that apply DRL to find optimal trading strategies in a cryptocurrency market. Satarov et al. [16] applied the Deep Q-Learning (DQN) algorithm in order to identify profitable trading points. In this work, their agent was rewarded only during sell actions, with the reward being a subtraction between the current selling price and the most recent buying price. In addition, penalties were given to the same sequential actions. Considering trading fees of 0.15%, the work demonstrated that the Reinforcement Learning (RL) approach performed better than three traditional technical strategies.

Jiang et al. [8] formulated a multi-asset portfolio management problem of high-volumed cryptocurrencies, with a DRL setting that was implemented for both Convolutional Neural Networks (CNNs) and Recurrent Neural Networks (RNNs) and parameter sharing between different assets. The external state is represented as a tensor of historical price ratios for every considered asset. The internal state includes the portfolio weight vector that specifies the current allocation of capital, has length equal to the considered assets and a total sum equal

---

[1] A DRL agent utilizes a deep learning model in order to learn to behave optimally in its environment.

[2] A round trip is a pair of two opposite orders placed one after the other (buy-sell or sell-buy), that aims to take advantage of price differences in order to produce profit.

to 1. The immediate rewards of their agent are expressed as the 1-period logarithmic return of the portfolio. Commission fees of 0.25% are integrated with the introduction of a penalty analogous to the change in the portfolio weights [8].

While the previous work considers a single RL agent to manage the entire portfolio, Lucarreli and Borrotti [11] employed a multi-agent framework by training local RL agents for each financial asset (Bitcoin, Etherium, LiteCoin, Riple). The performance of the each local agent produced a local reward signal, which is combined with the rest signals to formulate a global reward signal. The goal of this multi-agent framework was the maximization of the global reward signal, in order to achieve optimal portfolio management. The state space consisted of closing prices across all assets. Even though they achieved very promising results, they completely disregarded the commissions fees.

To finish with this short related work review, a major problem of the existing literature is that the current state of the art DRL methodologies operate on low commission fees. Additionally, in their works, they prioritized in maximizing the investment profits, rather than minimizing its risk. In our work, we aim to improve upon existing literature by (a) including new features such as technical indicators and public activity indicators, (b) experimenting with a more advanced deep RL algorithm design, (c) adding a trading rule as an extension of our main algorithm, which customizes the agent's trading behavior and further reduces the trading risk.

3   Methodology

Cryptocurrency trading poses several challenges for reinforcement learning for various reasons. First of all, since the cryptocurrency market involves non-stationary and noisy time series data, the prediction of future prices and directional movements becomes a quite difficult task [9]. Additionally, an RL agent will make a sequence of actions in order to maximize its rewards, however it is hard to reward that sequence of actions before the end of the evaluation period, which often leads to the sparse rewards problem[3]. In this Section, we discuss some of the methods that are used to tackle the above challenges in cryptocurrency trading. Additionally, we propose a new method, named N-Consecutive actions method, which is used to further reduce the trading risk.

3.1   Problem Formulation

Unlike prior efforts, we omit the portfolio's wealth from the agent's input state to simplify the complexity of the stochastic nature of trading. Rather than attempting to maximize its initial wealth, the agent is trained to earn profits by spotting profitable round trips and taking the appropriate hourly actions. This is accomplished by utilizing a reward function that compensates the agent's actions based

---

[3] The sparse reward problem happens when an environment rarely produces a reward. This usually slows down the training process of a DRL agent [15].

on the maximum future profit they may generate, as described in more detail later in this Section. There are three available actions to our agent. At each timestep, our agent may either suggest to BUY or SELL a unit or HOLD.

State Space. Our state space is represented with a matrix $s = [c, v, t, g, d]$ of S-dimensional columns, where S denotes a timeframe size, which is used to define the number of previous feature rows that are included in the current state. In our experiments, we found that $S = 20$ is an ideal timeframe size for every cryptocurrency asset. Each row represents the state of a time step (the state in a previous hour) as a vector $s_0, s_1, ..., s_{18}$, with s_{19} as the current state. The state includes the close differences $c \in R$ of consecutive hours, the volume differences $v \in R$, the 24-h time index $t \in [0, 23]$, the google trends score $g \in [0, 100]$, and the technical indicators, based on the past data $d \in R^D$.

Public Activity. Public activity may occasionally foreshadow impending bullish or bearish signals[4]. We define as public activity the time of the day which the trading takes place, as well as the google trends score in that specific hour. Google trends, is a 0 to 100 scale that measures the online traffic of searched terms. The terms that we used in our experiments were the names of the cryptocurrency assets. This indication could be highly valuable in cases where the online presence of influencers causes unexpected spikes or drops of the prices and volumes.

Technical Indicators. At each state, we compute the technical indicators using prior market data. The indicators are listed as follows:

- **Exponential Moving Average** (EMA): a moving average indicator that was serves as a building block for several other indicators [3].
- **Double Exponential Moving Average** ($DEMA$): a moving average indicator that is used to reduce market noise in price charts. Unlike EMA, it contains less lag and it is consider more responsive [13].
- **Moving Average Convergence Divergence** ($MACD$): a trend indicator that compares the the EMAs of two different windows [5].
- **Volume-Weighted Average Pricing** ($VWAP$): a weighted average technical indicator that is computed by adding up the close price for every transaction, mainly used by financial institutions and funds [3].
- **Relative Strength Index** (RSI): a momentum indicator that measures the magnitude of recent price changes to assess overbought or oversold conditions [4].
- **Intraday Momentum Index** (IMI): an alternative indicator to RSI that considers the relationship between the opening and thec losing price over the course of the day [10].
- **Average Directional Index** (ADX): a trend strength indicator that is bounded between 0 and 100, just like RSI and IMI [4].
- **Commodity Channel Index** (CCI): an indicator which can gauge an overvalued or undervalued market. In contrast to other oscillators that range in a bounded interval [1].

---

[4] A signal is called bullish when the close price begins to rise. On the other hand, a signal is called bearish when the close price starts to drop.

- **On-balance volume** (OBV): a momentum indicator that relies on patterns of volume flow to predict changes in price [7].
- **Accumulation/Distribution Indicator** (A/D): an indicator which can estimate if volume flow is adequate for the continuation of a trend, or whether a reversal is about to take place [6].
- **Bollinger Bands** ($BBands$): It is a technical analysis tool that defines a interval specified by adding and subtracting 2 moving standard deviations from a Simple Moving Average (SMA) signal [2].

Architecture. We selected the Proximal Policy Optimization (PPO) algorithm as the agent's architecture, because it is fast, stable and has been proven to achieve state of the art results in many RL environments. For the actor network, we used a convolutional neural network to represent the policy. The convolutional layer with 32 filters, kernel size of 5 and stride of 1, which ends up in a fully connected network. The fully connected network includes two hidden layers of 256 units each and relu activation functions. The same architecture was used for the critic network, which uses the Adam optimizer to update its weights with Learning Rate $Lr = 0.00025$. As in the original paper [17], we set the clipping parameter $\epsilon = 0.3$, without parameter sharing between the two networks. We set each mini-batch of samples to be trained for 40 epochs. The architectures for the general PPO agent and TraderNet-CR actor-critic networks are provided in Figs. 4 and 5 of Appendix A respectively.

Reward Function. In cryptocurrency trading, small increases or drops in the price of a cryptocurrency asset would result in unprofitable investments, due to high commission costs for each transaction. As it is quite improbable that the close price would change drastically during the first few hours of a transaction, the agent would have to wait many steps to determine whether an action that was suggested was correct be rewarded or penalized otherwise. This eventually leads to the sparse rewards problem. In order to detect profitable round trips, within the next k hours.

To address this issue, we designed the reward function in such a manner that the agent is rewarded based on the maximum return that an action can generate within the next K (hours). This eventually trains the internal layers of the agent's architecture to estimate the future price fluctuations within the near future. Given that f is the fee percentage, the reward function can be mathematically modeled as:

$$r_t = \begin{cases} C_{max} - C_t - f(C_{max} + C_t) & BUY \\ C_t - C_{min} - f(C_{min} + C_t) & SELL \\ -max(r_{t(a_i)}) & HOLD \end{cases} \tag{1}$$

with

$$a_i \in \{BUY, SELL, HOLD\}.$$

where

$$C_{max} = max\{C_{t+1}, C_{t+2}, ..., C_{t+k}\} \qquad (2a)$$
$$C_{min} = min\{C_{t+1}, C_{t+2}, ..., C_{t+k}\} \qquad (2b)$$

The above reward function ensures that if the agent anticipates a spectacular increase in the price when buying or a huge drop in the price when selling, then it receives a favourable reward. In cases where an action would lead to unintended losses, then it is penalized, in order to be discouraged of suggesting the same actions in similar states.

In many previous works, no reward was used ($r_t = 0$), during the holding time. However, in our investigation we have found out that the agent could sometimes prefer to converge to holding its position and avoiding any type of transaction, due to early negative returns. We encourage the agent to avoid holding, by penalizing it if it wrongly holds its position.

3.2 N-Consecutive Actions

Small price fluctuations in the market could possible distort the overall trend. Even with the use of technical analysis and public activity, the agent could be tricked by the market noise and suggest unprofitable actions. An indication of generating misleading actions could be in cases where the agent switches between BUY and SELL actions in consecutive timesteps. To avoid such cases, we defined a rule during the exploitation period, in which an action a_t will be accepted only if the N previously suggested actions by the agent are identical ($a_t = a_{t-1} = a_{t-2} = ... = a_{t-N}$). This method increases the probability that a generated action is profitable and thus reduces the trading risk. Furthermore, this method does not interfere with the agent's training and can be used as a safety mechanism that operates alongside with the agent's decision system.

4 Results

In this Section we analyze the importance of public activity and its correlation with the market data. Finally, we review the performance evaluation of the proposed approach. The experimental code supporting the results presented is publicly available and can be found on Github[5]. The training data consist of OHLCV[6] data from the last 5 years of six popular cryptocurrencies (Bitcoin, Ethereum, Solana, Cardano, Monero, Polygon) and were extracted from *Crypto Data Download*[7].

---

[5] https://anonymous.4open.science/r/Finance-AI-08C2.

[6] OHLCV datasets consist of five columns: Open, High, Low, Close, Volume of a market at a specific time.

[7] https://www.cryptodatadownload.com/data/.

4.1   Public Activity Importance

Throughout our research, we discovered that the *close* and *volume* features of our datasets are associated with the public activity. As shown in Plots (a), (b) of Fig. 1, there are distinct hours during the day when the most transactions occur. The plot (1c) also shows that there are considerable fluctuations in the direction of the close price throughout the same hours. Also, it is worth mentioning that the trend scores also seem to be correlated with the time of day, as plotted in (1d). In order to correctly plot these correlations, we first standarized the data using a window of 24 h and calculated the mean values of the features for each hour.

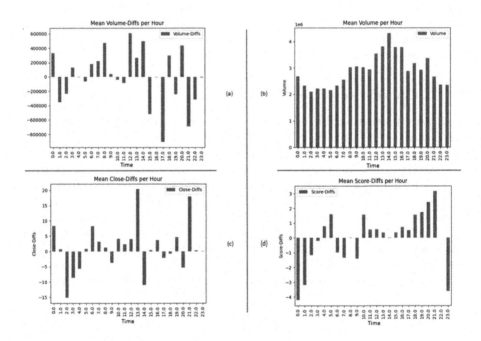

Fig. 1. Correlation analysis between the public activity and Bitcoin data

4.2   TraderNet-CR Evaluation

Our agent was trained separately in each market and was evaluated in the 15 latest successive days of the market dataset. The evaluation performance for each market can be seen in Fig. 2. For each agent, we measured its mean rewards per hour, its theoretical maximum profit or loss (PNL) percentage and its risk at the end of the evaluation. The first metric measures the mean reward that the agent is receiving from the environment. The second metric measures the theoretical maximum profit percentage at the end of the evaluation period, if we always liquidate the shares that are generated by the agent's previous actions at the right time. Finally, the risk is defined as the percentage of the profitable transactions. To measure the agent's performance, we used commission fees of 0.5% and 1.0%. The Table 1 shows the performance of each agent for different commission fees.

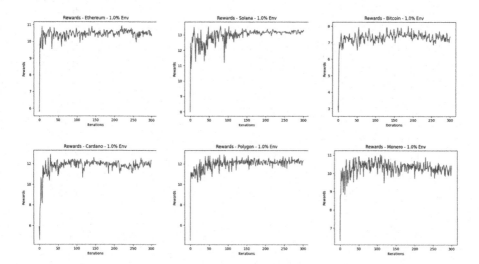

Fig. 2. The mean reward of the agent in each market. Commissions of 1.0% were used in each market.

Even though the Theoretical PNL indicates the maximum possible profit of the agent within a trading period, some traders might also be interested in the profit achievable with an actual trading strategy. In order to compute the profit, we used a trading strategy during the 15-day evaluation period, named Greedy PNL, in which we liquidated all the agent's shares generated by its previous actions, once they become profitable. Even though this strategy doesn't guarantee the maximum possible profit per round trip, it ensures that the agent doesn't miss profitable opportunities. The performance of this strategy can be show in Fig. 3 and Table 1.

From our experiments, it is clear that our approach is profitable in every market that the agent was evaluated. In addition, we observe that the agent performed best in cryptocurrency markets with low trading volumes, such as Solana, Cardano and Polygon markets. To the best of our knowledge, these markets have not been included in previous DRL trading approaches.

Table 1. The metrics of the expertiments for each cryptocurrency asset.

Crypto Env	Mean reward	Theoretical PNL %	Greedy PNL %	Risk %
Bitcoin 0.5%	10.12	248.96	2.6	0.15
Bitcoin 1.0%	7.36	15.84	0.63	0.26
Ethereum 0.5%	12.77	351.28	3.87	0.11
Ethereum 1.0%	9.42	123.91	0.97	0.2
Monero 0.5%	13.46	693.23	5.73	0.06
Monero 1.0%	10.43	339.52	1.24	0.18
Polygon 0.5%	13.46	702.71	7.83	0.06
Polygon 1.0%	10.43	336	2.83	0.18
Cardano 0.5%	15.71	662.63	33.69	0.04
Cardano 1.0%	12.73	229.79	7.47	0.17
Solana 0.5%	16.38	130.51	76.23	0.07
Solana 1.0%	13.27	58.72	19.58	0.16

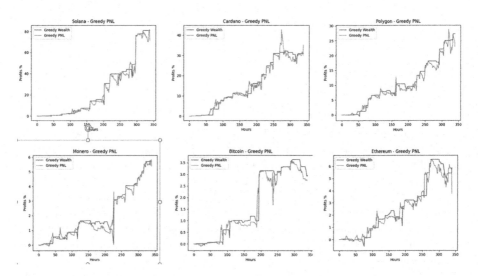

Fig. 3. The greedy PNL measurements for each experiment using the 2-Consecutive Actions rule

4.3   Optimizing Risk with N-Consecutive Actions

Every investor's principal aim is to generate as much profit as possible with the least amount of risk. However, some traders may prefer to trade only in situations where the likelihood of profiting from an investment is quite high. Using the "N-Consecutive Actions" rule, which is described in Sect. 3, we demonstrate how the risk can drop even further. As shown in Table 2, a decent window size of 2, can drastically decrease the trading risk in all markets. However, one should keep in mind that lowering an investment's risk may result in lower profit returns. This implies that the greater the window size, the lower the returns, but also the associated risks.

Table 2. The analytical trading risk for each agent, using window sizes ranging from 0 to 5. Zero length implies that no rule was used.

Window size (N)						
Crypto (1.0%)	$N = 0$	$N = 1$	$N = 2$	$N = 3$	$N = 4$	$N = 5$
Bitcoin	0.26	0.27	0.25	0.26	0.21	0.19
Ethereum	0.2	0.18	0.17	0.14	0.10	0.08
Monero	0.18	0.17	0.15	0.16	0.14	0.16
Polygon	0.18	0.15	0.13	0.14	0.12	0.12
Cardano	0.17	0.16	0.14	0.09	0.13	0.15
Solana	0.16	0.13	0.07	0.09	0.11	0.11

5   Conclusion

In this paper, we adopted a state of the art RL algorithm, named PPO, in order to detect profitable round trips with low trading risk. We used features from OHLCV market data, technical analysis and public activity indicators to represent the states of the environment. Additionally, we designed an intelligent reward function that boosts the agent's learning capability. After the training process, we applied the N-Consecutive Actions method, which increases the quality of the suggested actions. We tested our methodology in six popular cryptocurrencies for 15 successive evaluation days, using fees of 0.5% and 1.0%, in which the agent outputs an action every hour. Even with heavy commission fees and the most greedy liquidating strategy, the agent managed to deliver profits. In continuations of this work, we would like to investigate if portfolio wealth optimization can be improved using our methods, as well as add more rules to create a stronger end-to-end trading agent.

Appendix: A

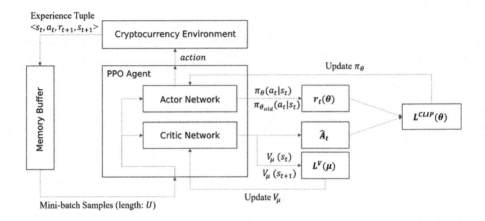

Fig. 4. A typical PPO Agent architecture

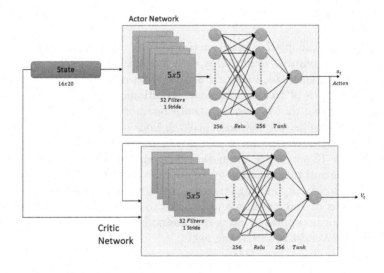

Fig. 5. The TraderNet-CR actor-critic network architecture

References

1. Low, R.K.Y., Tan, E.: The Role of Analyst Forecasts in the Momentum Effect. Wiley Trading (2006)
2. Baiynd, A.M.: The Trading Book: A Complete Solution to Mastering Technical Systems and Trading Psychology. McGraw-Hill (2011)
3. Brown, R.G.: Smoothing, Forecasting and Prediciton of Time Series. Dover Publications (1963)

4. Brown, R.G.: New Concepts in Technical Trading Systems. Trend Research (1978)
5. Brown, R.G.: Technical Analysis Power Tools for Active Investors. Financial Times Prentice Hall (2005)
6. Gerstein, M.: Evaluation of the chaikin power gauge stock rating system. Chaikin Analytics (2013)
7. Granville, J.E.: Granville's New Key to Stock Market Profits. Papamoa Press (2018)
8. Jiang, Z., Xu, D., Liang, J.: A Deep Reinforcement Learning Framework for the Financial Portfolio Management Problem, pp. 1–31 (2017). http://arxiv.org/abs/1706.10059
9. Livieris, I.E., Stavroyiannis, S., Iliadis, L., Pintelas, P.: Smoothing and stationarity enforcement framework for deep learning time-series forecasting. Neural Comput. Appl. **33**(20), 14021–14035 (2021). https://doi.org/10.1007/s00521-021-06043-1
10. Low, R.K.Y., Tan, E.: The role of analyst forecasts in the momentum effect. Int. Rev. Finan. Anal. **9** (2016)
11. Lucarelli, G., Borrotti, M.: A deep q-learning portfolio management framework for the cryptocurrency market. Neural Comput. Appl. **32**(23), 17229–17244 (2020)
12. Mudassir, M., Bennbaia, S. Unal, D.H.M.: Time-series forecasting of bitcoin prices using high-dimensional features: a machine learning approach. Neural Computing and Applications (2020)
13. Mulloy, P.: Technical Analysis of Stocks and Commodities **40**(1) (1982)
14. Murphy, J.J.: Technical analysis of the financial markets: a comprehensive guide to trading methods and applications. Penguin (1999)
15. Noel, A.D., van Hoof, C., Millidge, B.: Online reinforcement learning with sparse rewards through an active inference capsule (2021)
16. Sattarov, O., Muminov, A., Lee, C.W., Kang, H.K., Oh, R., Ahn, J., Oh, H.J., Jeon, H.S.: Recommending cryptocurrency trading points with deep reinforcement learning approach. Appl. Sci. **10**(4), 1506 (2020)
17. Schulman, J., Wolski, F., Dhariwal, P., Radford, A., Klimov, O.: Proximal policy optimization algorithms (2017)

Transformer-Based Zero-Shot Detection via Contrastive Learning

Wei Liu⬤, Hui Chen⬤, Yongqiang Ma⬤, Jianji Wang⬤,
and Nanning Zheng(✉)⬤

Institute of Artificial Intelligence and Robotics, Xi'an Jiaotong University,
Xi'an 710049, Shaanxi, China
{xianjiaodaliuwei,chenhui0622}@stu.xjtu.edu.cn,
{musayq,nnzheng}@xjtu.edu.cn, wangjianji@mail.xjtu.edu.cn

Abstract. Zero-Shot Detection (ZSD) is a challenging computer vision problem that enables simultaneous classification and localization of previously unseen objects via auxiliary information. Most of the existing methods learn a biased visual-semantic mapping function, which prefers predicting seen classes during testing, and they only focus on region of interest and ignore contextual information in an image. To tackle these problems, we propose a novel framework for ZSD named Transformer-based Zero-Shot Detection via Contrastive Learning (TZSDC). The proposed TZSDC contains four components: transformer-based backbone, Foreground-Background (FB) separation module, Instance-Instance Contrastive Learning (IICL) module, and Knowledge-Transfer (KT) module. The transformer backbone encodes long-range contextual information with less inductive bias. The FB module separates foreground and background by scoring objectness from images. The IICL module optimizes the visual structure in embedding space to make it more discriminative and the KT module transfers knowledge from seen classes to unseen classes via category similarity. Benefiting from these modules, the accurate alignment between the contextual visual features and semantic features can be achieved. Experiments on MSCOCO well validate the effectiveness of the proposed method for ZSD and generalized ZSD.

Keywords: Zero-Shot Detection · Transformer · Contrastive learning

1 Introduction

In recent years, deep learning has made great progress in object detection [1,8]. However, these methods strongly rely on large-scale annotated data. When lacking sufficient annotated data, the performance of these methods drops rapidly [12,13]. In reality, it is difficult for detectors to generalize to new target domains where annotated data is scarce or absent. However, it's easier for humans to recognize a new class by analogy with similar objects they know.

© IFIP International Federation for Information Processing 2022
Published by Springer Nature Switzerland AG 2022
I. Maglogiannis et al. (Eds.): AIAI 2022, IFIP AICT 646, pp. 316–327, 2022.
https://doi.org/10.1007/978-3-031-08333-4_26

In order to solve the above problems, Zero-Shot Object detection (ZSD) [7,9, 14,16,17] is proposed to classify and locate unseen classes with only seen classes contained during training. Most ZSD models [9,14,16] usually learn a visual-semantic mapping function using visual data and related semantic information of seen classes. At the testing stage, they use the learned model to map visual features into an embedding space and perform the nearest neighbor search to predict unseen classes. Several studies [7,25] use a generative model to synthesize features of unseen classes, and then retrain a classifier of unseen classes, turning zero-shot learning into supervised learning.

These methods [9,16] learn the model on seen classes while ignoring semantic information available for unseen classes, making the model significantly biased towards the seen classes when testing, which will greatly degrade the performance of ZSD and generalized ZSD (GZSD). Besides, current zero-shot detection networks that are based on one-stage or two-stage detection methods for secondary design, only focus on local information near an object's region of interest and do not explicitly encode long-range dependencies between objects, which are crucial to detect multiple objects in an image.

In this paper, we develop a novel framework for ZSD called Transformer-based Zero-Shot Detection via Contrastive Learning (TZSDC), which consists of four modules: transformer-based detector named Deformable DETR [26], Foreground-Background (FB) separation module, Instance-Instance Contrastive Learning (IICL) module, and Knowledge-Transfer (KT) module. We use the Deformable DETR to encode the input images for contextual features. To alleviate the confusion between unseen classes and backgrounds, the FB module makes full use of the existing visual background to compute an objectness score for the output query embeddings. Meanwhile, in order to make visual features in the embedding space more discriminative, the IICL module performs contrastive learning between instances to optimize the visual manifold structure, so that the intra-class spacing is more compact and the inter-class distances are far away from each other. To alleviate the bias problem that the learned model prefers seen classes, the KT module realizes the knowledge transfer from seen classes to unseen classes via category similarity.

The main contributions of the paper can be summarized as (i) We propose a novel framework TZSDC that integrates the transformer and contrastive learning into zero-shot detection, achieving an accurate visual-semantic alignment. (ii) We design a FB module to alleviate the confusion of unseen classes and the background, and a KT module to realize the knowledge transfer from seen classes to unseen classes through category similarity. (iii) Experiments on MSCOCO verify that the proposed method can effectively improve the performance on ZSD and GZSD tasks.

2   Related Work

Object Detection. In the past few years, object detection has received huge attention and developed rapidly. For traditional object detection frameworks, there are mainly two types, one-stage methods such as SSD [11], YOLO [18], FCOS [21], and two-stage methods such as Faster R-CNN [19], R-FCN [3]. Their general methods are to generate bounding boxes, determine which box contains objects, and then classify high-confidence boxes. However, due to the design of convolution, they only focus on local information near the region of interest. In recent years, Transformer [2,26] is developing rapidly in the field of computer vision, DETR [2] applies the transformer to the field of target detection, and Deformable DETR [26] adopts the idea of deformable convolution [4], which integrates multi-scale information and accelerates the convergence speed of DETR. DETR [2] can encode long-range dependencies at multi-scales to enrich contextual information. In this work, we choose Deformable DETR as our basic detection framework.

Zero-Shot Learning (ZSL). ZSL is a classic task in computer vision. It aims to use seen examples to train networks and reason about unseen classes with the help of semantic information. Zero-shot learning can be divided into embedding models and generative models. The embedding models [5,20] mainly learn a mapping function to convert visual features and semantics into an embedding space and then classify by searching the nearest semantic descriptor in the embedding space. In our work, we adopt a basic visual-semantic embedding model, take the latent space as the embedding space, and exploit the similarity between seen and unseen classes to explicitly transfer knowledge from the source class to the target class, promoting better visual semantic alignment.

Zero-Shot Object Detection (ZSD). ZSD is a recently proposed task that can identify and localize unseen objects. Most of them focus on learning embedding functions from visual space to semantic space. MS-Zero [6] designed an asymmetric mapping method to reduce the impact of new noise on the classifier, which first maps visual features to semantic space respectively, and then maps semantic features to visual space. Polarity Loss [15] was proposed to find a more suitable alignment of visual and semantic information, which is an improvement on the basis of Focal Loss to solve the problem of imbalance between positive and negative samples. BLRPN-ZSD [24] designed a background perceptron to use external annotations to solve the confusion of unseen classes and backgrounds. In our work, we introduce the foreground objectness branch to learn from existing visual background data to better separate unseen classes from the background. At the same time, we introduce a contrastive network in the classification branch to explicitly transfer knowledge from the source class to the target class, which is helpful to alleviate the domain transfer problem and the visual-semantic gap.

3   Method

Problem Settings. In ZSD, we are given S seen classes in $\mathcal{Y}^s$ and U seen classes in $\mathcal{Y}^u$, where seen classes and unseen classes are disjoint. We can denote

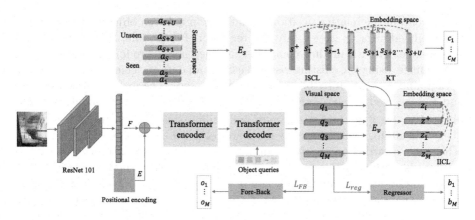

Fig. 1. Illustration of TZSDC. First, TZSDC extracts multi-scale features F from the input image with ResNet101. Next $E + F$ are fed into the transformer encoder and decoder, where E represents the position encoding. After the decoder, a set of query embeddings $\mathcal{Q} = \{q_i\}_{i=1}^{M}, q_i \in \mathbb{R}^D$ are obtained from M learnable object quries and FB module seperates the foreground and background. Next, E_v and E_S are used to map query embeddings $Q = \{q_i\}_{i=1}^{M}$ and semantic embeddings $A = \{a_c\}_{c=1}^{S+U}$ into a common embedding space. IICL and ISCL are performed for better visual-semantic alignment through instance-instance and instance-semantic contrastive learning.

that $\mathcal{Y}^s \cap \mathcal{Y}^u = \emptyset$, $\mathcal{Y}^s \cup \mathcal{Y}^u = \mathcal{Y}$. We use $\mathcal{Y}^s = \{Y_1, Y_2, \cdots, Y_S\}$ to represent the seen classes and $\mathcal{Y}^u = \{Y_{S+1}, Y_{S+2}, \cdots, Y_{S+U}\}$ to represent unseen classes. Let $\mathcal{D}^{tr} = \{(x_i, y_i) \mid x_i \in \mathcal{X}, y_i \in \mathcal{Y}^s\}_{i=1}^{N}$ be the training dataset containing N images. During training and testing, semantic word-vectors $A = \{a_c\}_{c=1}^{S+U}$ are provided for each class $c \in \mathcal{Y}^s \cup \mathcal{Y}^u$ to conduct a knowledge transfer. The task of ZSD is to learn a detector to recognize and localize unseen classes during testing.

3.1 Overall Architecture

The overall framework for zero-shot detection is shown in Fig. 1. It adopts the standard Deformable DETR [26] as a backbone for ZSD by introducing (i) a Foreground-Background (FB) separation module to reduce confusion of unseen classes and backgrounds; (ii) an Instance-Instacne/Instance-Semantic Contrastive Learning (IICL/ISCL) module to optimize the visual manifold structure in the embedding space; (iii) a Knowledge Transfer (KT) module to transfer knowledge from seen to unseen classes via category similarity.

Given an input image $x \in \mathcal{X}$, ResNet 101 extracts multi-scale features F with a sine-cosine position encoding E added to preserve the position information. Then multi-scale features with position encoding are fed into the transformer encoder and decoder which contain deformable convolution [4]. Driven by cross-attention and self-attention mechanism, the decoder converts a set of M learnable object queries into a set of M query embeddings $\mathcal{Q} = \{q_i\}_{i=1}^{M}, q_i \in \mathbb{R}^D$

which contain the relative positional relationship between objects. And then the query embeddings Q are fed into the regressor, FB module, IICL module, and KT module. The FB module computes an objectness score for the output query embeddings, using the existing visual background data to achieve foreground and background separation by binary cross-entropy loss. The mapping functions E_v and E_S are used to map query embeddings $Q = \{q_i\}_{i=1}^{M}$ and semantic embeddings $A = \{a_c\}_{c=1}^{S+U}$ into a common embedding space. Then in IICL module, query embeddings with the same label are regarded as positive samples z^+, the others are regarded as negative samples z^-, and instance-instance contrastive learning is performed to optimize the visual manifold structure. Besides, the ISCL module selects semantic feature s_i corresponding to the class of z_i as the only positive sample, the remaining $S-1$ semantic features as negative samples to perform instance-semantic contrastive learning. Meanwhile, unseen semantic embeddings are used in the KT module to enable knowledge transfer via category similarity between seen and unseen embeddings.

3.2 FB Module

The decoder outputs $Q = \{q_i\}_{i=1}^{M}, q_i \in \mathbb{R}^D$ from M learnable object queries, each of which has a corresponding bounding box and category. And then the classifier recognizes the query embeddings into $S + U + 1$ classes: S seen classes, U unseen classes, and background. However, most query embeddings will be predicted as background due to a lack of supervision from visual images of unseen classes. In order to alleviate the confusion between unseen classes and backgrounds, we introduce $FB : \mathbb{R}^D \rightarrow [0, 1]$ to separate the foreground and background.

Considering M is generally larger than the number of categories $S + U$, for those queries without actual categories, we regard them as backgrounds. FB module computes an objectness score o_i for query embeddings q_i. The objective of the FB module is to assign higher confidence to query embeddings corresponding to foreground objects than to those corresponding to the backgrounds. Therefore, the foreground and background separation loss function is defined as follows:

$$\mathcal{L}_{FB} = -\sum_{i=1}^{M} m_j \log o_i + (1 - m_i) \log (1 - o_i) \tag{1}$$

where:

$$m_{ij} = \begin{cases} 1, & y_i \ is \ the \ foreground \\ 0, & y_i \ is \ the \ background \end{cases} \tag{2}$$

3.3 IICL/ISCL Module and KT Module

Due to the gap between visual and semantic features, using visual space or semantic space as a common embedding space is not ideal. In order to align the two spaces, we use two functions E_v, E_s to map query embeddings $Q = \{q_i\}_{i=1}^{M}$

and semantic embeddings $A = \{a_c\}_{c=1}^{S+U}$ into a common embedding space to optimize the manifold of visual and semantic features.

$$z_i = E_v\left(q_i\right) \tag{3}$$

$$s_j = E_s\left(a_j\right) \tag{4}$$

where q_i represents the query feature of the i-th class, a_j represents the semantic feature of the j-th class.

Instance-Instance Contrastive Learning (IICL). Instances with similar semantic attributes are usually close together in the embedding space, thus leading to misclassifications. To reduce such misclassifications, we need to optimize the manifold structure of visual features in the embedding space. Inspired by the alignment (closeness of features from positive pairs) and uniformity of the feature distribution to contrastive loss [22], we utilize contrastive loss to learn discriminative features. Given an input image, query embeddings with the same label are regarded as positive samples z^+, and the others are regarded as negative samples z^-. We assume that there are P_i positive samples and N_i negative samples for i-th object in the input image. The IICL loss $\mathcal{L}_{II}$ is as follows:

$$\mathcal{L}_{II} = \mathbb{E}\left[-\log \frac{\exp\left(z_i \cdot z^+\right)/\tau_v)}{\sum_{k=1}^{P_i} \exp\left(z_i \cdot z_k^+/\tau_v\right) + \sum_{j=1}^{N_i} \exp\left(z_i \cdot z_j^-/\tau_v\right)}\right] \tag{5}$$

where τ_v is the temperature parameter of $\mathcal{L}_{II}$.

Instance-Semantic Contrastive Learning (ISCL). The above loss drives positive pairs between visual features compact. Besides, in order to achieve an accurate visual-semantic alignment, we use the semantic information of the source class for supervision and select semantic feature s_i corresponding to the class of z_i as the only positive sample, the remaining $S-1$ semantic features as negative samples. The instance-semantic contrastive loss $\mathcal{L}_{IS}$ can be calculated as follows:

$$\mathcal{L}_{IS} = \mathbb{E}\left[-\log \frac{\exp\left(z_i \cdot s^+\right)/\tau_s)}{\exp\left(z_i \cdot s^+/\tau_s\right) + \sum_{j=1}^{S-1} \exp\left(z_i \cdot s_j^-/\tau_s\right)}\right] \tag{6}$$

where τ_s is the temperature parameter of $\mathcal{L}_{IS}$ and S is the number of seen classes.

Knowledge Transfer (KT). The task of ZSD is to recognize and locate unseen classes. If only visual information and semantic embeddings of seen classes are used during training, it is easy to bias the model to seen classes. In order to alleviate the bias problem, we use category similarity between seen classes and unseen classes to transfer knowledge from the source classes to the target classes.

We assume that the semantic attribute of the unseen class can be obtained by the linear combination of the attributes of seen classes, which is also widely adopted in ZSL [23]. For example, "zebra" has a shape like "horse", and the color is black and white like "panda". Inspired by this observation, we use least square regression (LSR) to obtain the reconstruction coefficient of each seen class semantic attribute. The reconstruction coefficient is the category similarity, which is calculated as follows:

$$d_u = \arg\min_{d_u} \left\| a_u - \sum_{k=1}^{S} a_k d_{uk} \right\|_2^2 + \beta \|d_u\|_2 \tag{7}$$

where d_{uk} is the category similarity between the u-th unseen class and k-th seen class, and $a_u \in \{a_c\}_{c=S+1}^{S+U}$, $a_k \in \{a_c\}_{c=1}^{S}$, β is the regularization coefficient. After we get the similarity d_u between unseen classes and seen classes, we can use the images of seen classes to learn the similar unseen classes. The knowledge transfer loss $\mathcal{L}_{KT}$ is defined as:

$$\mathcal{L}_{KT} = -\frac{1}{N} \sum_{i=1}^{N} \sum_{j=S+1}^{S+U} d_{jy_i} \log \widetilde{\zeta_{ij}} + (1 - d_{jy_i}) \log \left(1 - \widetilde{\zeta_{ij}}\right) \tag{8}$$

where $\zeta_{ij} = z_i \cdot s_j$, z_i, s_j are calculated by Eq. (3) and Eq. (4). $\widetilde{\zeta_{ij}}$ is the normalization of ζ_{ij}.

Regression Loss. As with Deformable DETR [26], we use a linear combination of the L1 loss and the IOU loss as our regression loss $\mathcal{L}_{reg}$:

$$\mathcal{L}_{reg} = \lambda_{iou} \mathcal{L}_{iou} \left(b_i, \hat{b}_i\right) + \lambda_{L1} \left\| \left(b_i - \hat{b}_i\right) \right\|_1 \tag{9}$$

3.4   Training and Inference

Training. The proposed method includes FB loss $\mathcal{L}_{FB}$, regression loss $\mathcal{L}_{reg}$, IICL loss $\mathcal{L}_{II}$, ISCL loss $\mathcal{L}_{IS}$, KT loss $\mathcal{L}_{KT}$. The total loss function is as follows:

$$\mathcal{L}_{total} = \mathcal{L}_{reg} + \mathcal{L}_{IS} + \alpha \mathcal{L}_{KT} + \gamma \mathcal{L}_{II} + \lambda \mathcal{L}_{FB}. \tag{10}$$

where α, γ, λ are hyper-parameters to balance each loss term. We train our model using a two-stage training approach. In the first stage, we use all seen classes to train a Deforamble DETR framework that only contains the FB module. In the second stage, we replace the classifier in Deformable DETR with our current IICL module, ISCL module, and KT module. Then the model is finetuned based on first-stage parameters.

Inference. Given a test image I, M object query embeddings $Q = \{q_i\}_{i=1}^{M}$ are computed, and then bounding boxes are obtained with the regressor. Next, object query embeddings are mapped into the common embedding space and are used to predict the class by nearest neighbor search.

4   Experiments

4.1   Experimental Settings

Datasets. We evaluate our method on MSCOCO 2014 [10] which contains 82,783 training images and 40,504 validation images. For MSCOCO 2014 with 80 categories, We follow the 65/15 split [15]. As for semantic embeddings in the classification subnet, we use 300-dimensional vectors from word2vec [15] for MSCOCO 2014.

Evaluation Protocol. For MSCOCO 2014, we choose mAP and Recall@100 as our evaluation metrics. We conduct experiments under both standard and generalized settings and evaluate the Harmonic Mean (HM) to show the performance of GZSD.

Implementation Details. We choose ResNet101 which is pretrained on ImageNet to extract multi-scale features. The transformer encoder-decoder structure is consistent with the standard Deformable DETR. The dimension of object queries is 512 and M is set to 100. The regressor consists of 3 multi-layer perceptrons (MLP), the FB module is one fully-connected layer and the mapping function E_s, E_v are accomplished by one fully-connected layer. Hyperparameters α, γ, λ in Eq. (10) are set as 0.2, 0.3, 0.1. And the temperature parameter τ_v, τ_s in Eq. (5), Eq. (6) and Hyperparameters $\lambda_{iou}, \lambda_{L1}$ in Eq. (9) are set to 0.1, 0.1, 2.0, 5.0, and The TZSDC framework is trained using SGD optimizer with the learning rate of 0.01 and momentum of 0.9 for 50 epochs in the first stage and the learning rate of 0.002 and momentum of 0.999 for 20 epochs in the second stage.

4.2   Comparison with Other Methods

As shown in Table 1, we compare the performance of the proposed model with TL-ZSD [14], PL [15], BLC [24], SU-ZSD [7] on MSCOCO for both ZSD and GZSD. As can be seen, our method achieves the best performance on both mAP and recall for ZSD. Compared with the second-best method SU-ZSD [7], the mAP of our method is improved from 19.00% to 19.58%, and the recall is improved from 54.00% to 56.45%, which indicates that our method improves the discriminatory ability for unseen classes. For GZSD, our method achieves the best performance in the unseen class. The unseen performance is improved without sacrificing the seen accuracy too much, and our HM value is competitive to the generative model SU-ZSD [7]. This shows that our model has learned a good visual-semantic alignment model, which realizes knowledge transfer from seen classes to unseen classes.

As can be seen from Table 2, which shows the class-wise AP performance for ZSD, our method improves the mAP of "mouse", "hotdog", "hairdrier" which are not similar to the seen classes at all, indicating that our model extracts the

Table 1. Comparison with other methods for ZSD/GZSD on MSCOCO dataset. We report both mAP(%) and recall@100. Bold represents the best result.

| Method | S/U split | ZSD | | GZSD | | | | | |
| | | | | Seen | | Unseen | | HM | |
		mAP	Recall	mAP	Recall	mAP	Recall	mAP	Recall
TL-ZSD [14]	65/15	14.57	48.15	28.79	54.14	14.05	37.16	18.89	44.07
PL [15]	65/15	12.40	37.72	34.07	36.38	12.40	37.16	18.89	44.07
BLC [24]	65/15	13.10	51.65	36.00	56.39	13.10	51.65	19.20	53.92
SU-ZSD [7]	65/15	19.00	54.00	**36.90**	**57.70**	19.00	**53.90**	**25.08**	**55.74**
Ours	65/15	**19.58**	**56.45**	32.54	56.76	**19.20**	52.73	24.15	54.67

Table 2. Class-wise AP comparison with other methods on unseen classes of MSCOCO with 65/15 split for ZSD.

	Airplane	Train	Parking	Cat	Bear	Suitcase	Frisbee	Snowboard	Fork	Sandwich	Hotdog	Toilet	Mouse	Toaster	Hairdrier	mAP
TLZSD [14]	19.6	**63.4**	3.7	43.2	3.7	13.8	12.8	24.2	12.6	9.7	6.0	1.5	2.3	**2.0**	0.0	14.6
PL [15]	20	48.2	0.6	28.3	13.8	12.4	**21.8**	15.1	8.9	8.5	0.9	5.7	0.0	1.7	0.0	12.4
SU-ZSD [7]	10.1	48.7	1.2	**64.0**	**64.1**	12.2	0.7	28	**16.4**	**19.4**	0.1	18.7	1.2	0.5	0.2	19.0
Ours	**31.5**	45.0	**12.5**	55.1	42.3	**13.9**	5.5	**29.0**	6.40	15.9	**11.4**	**19.2**	**3.7**	1.2	**0.2**	**19.6**

contextual information of the images and is able to understand the scenario, for example, where there is a computer or keyboard, there is usually a mouse. What's more, our method achieves the best performance in 8 out of 15 categories, further demonstrating the superiority of our method.

4.3   Ablation Studies

To further verify the effectiveness of each component, we conduct ablation studies on the MSCOCO dataset with the 65/15 split. Table 3 shows the mAP of our model for ZSD and GZSD under different combinations of components. $\sqrt{}$ indicates the model with corresponding module loss.

The Effect of FB Module. In order to verify the contribution of the FB module to the model, we remove the FB module during training. It can be observed that the performance of ZSD and the performance of unseen in GZSD drop from 19.58% to 19.25%, and 19.20% to 18.97% respectively, while the performance of seen is only improved by 0.06%. The result shows that after adding the FB module, the model can effectively reduce the confusion between unseen classes and backgrounds.

The Effect of KT Module. During training, we remove the loss function $\mathcal{L}_{KT}$, that is, only visual features and semantic attributes of seen classes are used, while semantic features of unseen classes are not involved. The result in Table 3 shows that the performance of ZSD has dropped by 2.35% and the performance of

Table 3. Effectiveness of each loss term for both ZSD and GZSD, measured by the mAP on MSCOCO 2014 with 65/15 split.

$\mathcal{L}_{reg} + \mathcal{L}_{IS}$	$\mathcal{L}_{FB}$	$\mathcal{L}_{KT}$	$\mathcal{L}_{II}$	ZSD	Seen	Unseen	HM
√	√	√	√	**19.58**	32.54	**19.20**	**24.15**
√		√	√	19.25	32.60	18.97	23.98
√	√		√	17.23	**35.72**	13.91	20.02
√	√	√		18.14	33.17	17.97	23.31

Fig. 2. Qualitative results on 65/15 split of MS COCO for ZSD and GZSD. The bounding boxes of seen classes and unseen classes are remarked as green and red respectively. (Color figure online)

unseen in GZSD has dropped sharply by 5.29%. If we don't explicitly transfer knowledge from seen classes to unseen classes through category similarity, both ZSD and GZSD performance will drop, and GZSD performance drops more sharply. It indicates that knowledge transfer has a greater impact on GZSD and can effectively alleviate the problem that the learned model will bias toward seen classes in GZSD.

The Effect of IICL Module. After removing the IICL Module, ZSD performance and unseen performance in GZSD drop by 1.44% and 1.23%, respectively. The result shows that IICL can optimize the visual feature distribution in embedding space, enabling the model to learn more discriminative features.

4.4   Qualitative Result

In order to qualitatively evaluate our results, we show the detection results of our method on MSCOCO in Fig. 2. For ZSD, the image only contains unseen classes, for GZSD, the image may contain both seen classes and unseen classes. The results show that the proposed model is able to detect seen and unseen classes in different complex scenes, and it can detect multi-scale objects, such as large-scale "train", "bed" and small-scale "traffic light", "suitcase", which verifies the effectiveness of the proposed model.

5   Conclusion

In this paper, we propose a novel framework for ZSD named Transformer-based Zero-Shot Detection via Contrastive Learning (TZSDC), which includes Deformable DETR, FB module, IICL module, and KT module. Deformable DETR extracts multi-scale contextual features, FB module separates the foreground objects from the background to alleviate the confusion of unseen classes and the background, IICL module optimizes the visual manifold structure in the embedding space to make the visual feature more discriminative, and KT module transfers knowledge from seen to unseen classes via category similarity. Experiments on MSCOCO well validate the effectiveness of the proposed method for ZSD and GZSD.

Acknowledgments. This work is supported by the National Science Foundation of China (No. 62088102), China National Postdoctoral Program for Innovative Talents from China Postdoctoral Science Foundation (No. BX2021239).

References

1. Cai, Z., Vasconcelos, N.: Cascade R-CNN: delving into high quality object detection. In: Proceedings of the IEEE Conference on Computer Vision and Pattern Recognition, pp. 6154–6162 (2018)
2. Carion, N., Massa, F., Synnaeve, G., Usunier, N., Kirillov, A., Zagoruyko, S.: End-to-end object detection with transformers. In: Vedaldi, A., Bischof, H., Brox, T., Frahm, J.-M. (eds.) ECCV 2020. LNCS, vol. 12346, pp. 213–229. Springer, Cham (2020). https://doi.org/10.1007/978-3-030-58452-8_13
3. Dai, J., Li, Y., He, K., Sun, J.: R-FCN: object detection via region-based fully convolutional networks. Adv. Neural Inf. Process. Syst. **29** (2016)
4. Dai, J., et al.: Deformable convolutional networks. In: Proceedings of the IEEE International Conference on Computer Vision, pp. 764–773 (2017)
5. Frome, A., Corrado, G., Shlens, J., et al.: A deep visual-semantic embedding model. Proceedings of the Advances in Neural Information Processing Systems pp. 2121–2129 (2013)
6. Gupta, D., Anantharaman, A., Mamgain, N., Balasubramanian, V.N., Jawahar, C., et al.: A multi-space approach to zero-shot object detection. In: Proceedings of the IEEE/CVF Winter Conference on Applications of Computer Vision, pp. 1209–1217 (2020)
7. Hayat, N., Hayat, M., Rahman, S., Khan, S., Zamir, S.W., Khan, F.S.: Synthesizing the unseen for zero-shot object detection. In: Proceedings of the Asian Conference on Computer Vision (2020)
8. He, K., Gkioxari, G., Dollár, P., Girshick, R.: Mask R-CNN. In: Proceedings of the IEEE International Conference on Computer Vision, pp. 2961–2969 (2017)
9. Li, Y., Shao, Y., Wang, D.: Context-guided super-class inference for zero-shot detection. In: Proceedings of the IEEE/CVF Conference on Computer Vision and Pattern Recognition Workshop, pp. 944–945 (2020)

10. Lin, T.-Y., Maire, M., Belongie, S., Hays, J., Perona, P., Ramanan, D., Dollár, P., Zitnick, C.L.: Microsoft COCO: common objects in context. In: Fleet, D., Pajdla, T., Schiele, B., Tuytelaars, T. (eds.) ECCV 2014. LNCS, vol. 8693, pp. 740–755. Springer, Cham (2014). https://doi.org/10.1007/978-3-319-10602-1_48
11. Liu, W., et al.: SSD: single shot MultiBox detector. In: Leibe, B., Matas, J., Sebe, N., Welling, M. (eds.) ECCV 2016. LNCS, vol. 9905, pp. 21–37. Springer, Cham (2016). https://doi.org/10.1007/978-3-319-46448-0_2
12. Liu, X., Liu, X., Zhang, W., Wand, J., Wang, F.: Parallel data: from big data to data intelligence. Pattern Recogn. Artif. Intell. **30**(8), 9 (2017)
13. Pang, J., Chen, K., Shi, J., Feng, H., Ouyang, W., Lin, D.: Libra R-CNN: towards balanced learning for object detection. In: Proceedings of the IEEE/CVF Conference on Computer Vision and Pattern Recognition, pp. 821–830 (2019)
14. Rahman, S., Khan, S., Barnes, N.: Transductive learning for zero-shot object detection. In: Proceedings of the IEEE/CVF International Conference on Computer Vision, pp. 6082–6091 (2019)
15. Rahman, S., Khan, S., Barnes, N.: Improved visual-semantic alignment for zero-shot object detection. In: Proceedings of the AAAI Conference on Artificial Intelligence, vol. 34, pp. 11932–11939 (2020)
16. Rahman, S., Khan, S., Porikli, F.: Zero-shot object detection: learning to simultaneously recognize and localize novel concepts. In: Jawahar, C.V., Li, H., Mori, G., Schindler, K. (eds.) ACCV 2018. LNCS, vol. 11361, pp. 547–563. Springer, Cham (2018). https://doi.org/10.1007/978-3-030-20887-5_34
17. Rahman, S., Khan, S.H., Porikli, F.: Zero-shot object detection: joint recognition and localization of novel concepts. Int. J. Comput. Vis. **128**(12), 2979–2999 (2020)
18. Redmon, J., Farhadi, A.: YOLO9000: better, faster, stronger. In: Proceedings of the IEEE Conference on Computer Vision and Pattern Recognition, pp. 7263–7271 (2017)
19. Ren, S., He, K., Girshick, R., Sun, J.: Faster R-CNN: towards real-time object detection with region proposal networks. Adv. Neural Inf. Process. Syst. **28** (2015)
20. Socher, R., Ganjoo, M., Manning, C.D., Ng, A.: Zero-shot learning through cross-modal transfer. Adv. Neural Inf. Process. Syst. **26** (2013)
21. Tian, Z., Shen, C., Chen, H., He, T.: FCOS: fully convolutional one-stage object detection. In: Proceedings of the IEEE/CVF International Conference on Computer Vision, pp. 9627–9636 (2019)
22. Wang, T., Isola, P.: Understanding contrastive representation learning through alignment and uniformity on the hypersphere. In: International Conference on Machine Learning, pp. 9929–9939. PMLR (2020)
23. Xie, G.S., et al.: Region graph embedding network for zero-shot learning. In: Vedaldi, A., Bischof, H., Brox, T., Frahm, J.-M. (eds.) ECCV 2020. LNCS, vol. 12349, pp. 562–580. Springer, Cham (2020). https://doi.org/10.1007/978-3-030-58548-8_33
24. Zheng, Y., Huang, R., Han, C., Huang, X., Cui, L.: Background learnable cascade for zero-shot object detection. In: Proceedings of the Asian Conference on Computer Vision (2020)
25. Zhu, P., Wang, H., Saligrama, V.: Don't even look once: synthesizing features for zero-shot detection. In: Proceedings of the IEEE/CVF Conference on Computer Vision and Pattern Recognition, pp. 11693–11702 (2020)
26. Zhu, X., Su, W., Lu, L., Li, B., Wang, X., Dai, J.: Deformable DETR: deformable transformers for end-to-end object detection. arXiv preprint arXiv:2010.04159 (2020)

Energy Streams Modeling

Efficient Large-Scale Machine Learning Techniques for Rapid Motif Discovery in Energy Data Streams

K. K. Lykothanasi[1,2], S. Sioutas[1] ⓘ, and K. Tsichlas[1(✉)] ⓘ

[1] Computer Engineering and Informatics Department, University of Patras, Patras, Greece
{sioutas,ktsichlas}@ceid.upatras.gr
[2] Department of Computer Science, KU Leuven, Leuven, Belgium

Abstract. Domestic appliance power consumption measurement was, until recently, a problem without a satisfying solution. It required the use of a measuring device for each appliance to be studied, and thus the spending of a considerable amount of both money and time. The technological advancements made in the past few decades have enabled the engineering of smart devices that connect to the central panel of a building and log the features of the electrical current passing through it. Using Machine Learning algorithms, we can create models that extract individual appliance information ("signature") from the signals recorded by these measuring devices. This process can lead to the production of systems that could be particularly useful for the consumers. They would not only allow individuals to alter their power consumption profile to minimise their spending and environmental impact, but also notify them if an appliance seems to be malfunctioning. In addition, the energy providers could harness the potential of usage statistics collected from their customers to estimate the energy demand for any given moment within a day. This would prevent the production of excess energy or the overloading of the power supply network infrastructure. The objective of this work is the implementation of an efficient Deep Neural Network (DNN) model that will be able to predict the state (On/Off) of a set of electrical appliances during a specific time span, based on the aggregate power signal of the house within which they operate. The contribution of this work concerns the use of a Recurrent Neural Network (RNN) that categorises the behaviour of multiple appliances (multi-label classification). The results are quite promising and pave the way for a more in-depth treatment of the problem.

Keywords: Machine Learning · Energy consumption · Non-intrusive Load Monitoring · Energy disaggregation · Recurrent Neural Networks

1 Introduction

Until recently, it was not feasible for consumers to know their precise home power consumption and more specifically to know exactly the amount of energy used by each appliance. However, the technological advancements of the last few decades enable

© IFIP International Federation for Information Processing 2022
Published by Springer Nature Switzerland AG 2022
I. Maglogiannis et al. (Eds.): AIAI 2022, IFIP AICT 646, pp. 331–342, 2022.
https://doi.org/10.1007/978-3-031-08333-4_27

consumers to discover their power consumption profile with the use of smart meters. With this knowledge, the consumer can adjust their behaviour and their power consumption, in order to profit financially and improve their quality of life.

The term Non-Intrusive Load Monitoring – NILM means "a process that analyses the variations in the features of the electricity of a house and concludes which of the appliances are operating as well as the energy consumption of each one" [1]. Alternatively, it is referred to as energy disaggregation. Formally, the problem is stated as:

Let $T = \{1, 2, ..., T\}$ be a set of time points and $X = \{X_1, X_2, ..., X_T\}$ be the set of measurements of the total energy consumption of N appliances (aggregate signal) that correspond to these points. Then, the objective of NILM is for a given point $t \in T$ to disaggregate the consumption y_t^i of appliance i, so that at every time point $\in T$ it holds that:

$$X_t = \sum_{i=1}^{N} y_t^i + \sigma(t) \tag{1}$$

where $\sigma(t)$ represents the consumption of unknown devices or noise.

The applications of NILM are numerous and significant. Firstly, the average consumer has access to a detailed analysis of their energy consumption, according to which they can adapt their energy consumption habits, with multiple environmental and financial benefits. Additionally, they are warned when an appliance operates anomalously (e.g. because of a malfunction or of excessive use due to negligence). Secondly, the energy provider can predict the energy requirements of their network more accurately using the more detailed consumption data. Thus, they can avoid excess energy production or network overload. In addition, the energy provider can propose flexible programs to the consumer, with cheaper charge per kWh depending on current energy demand, to balance the network load.

The aggregate energy data is collected from a smart meter that is connected to the central switchboard of a house. Various methods have been used for energy disaggregation, mainly [30] Hidden Markov Models, Optimization Methods, Template Matching Methods (e.g., Dynamic Time Warping), Source Separation Methods (e.g., Matrix Factorisation), Shallow Learning (e.g. Random Forests), Deep Learning (e.g. Convolutional Neural Networks), Graph Signal Processing. This work is focused on deep learning methods. These methods dominate the most recent NILM literature due to their superior performance in identifying appliances using the aggregate signal. The dominant approach in shallow and deep learning is the construction of different models, one for each appliance. This is preferred because each appliance has different consumption characteristics, and a single model can fit to them better than one model can fit to all appliances. However, multi-label classification has been recently [30, 31] introduced to NILM research mainly on the grounds of better efficiency and deployment simplicity, even though it lacks effectiveness in terms of appliance identification when compared to the single-label classification approach. To the best of the authors' knowledge, only Convolutional Neural Networks (CNNs) have been used for multi-label classification [32].

In this work, the objective is the design and training of an RNN that takes as input the aggregate signal, and outputs the operational state (On/Off) of a group of appliances.

The contribution of this extended abstract is the use of an RNN for multi-label energy disaggregation by a single neural network that has high precision and very low classification error in new (unknown) data, that may come from other sources. For the authors, these results are the first step towards an in-depth treatment of energy disaggregation where efficiency is considered of equal importance to effectiveness. This is because, as highlighted in [30], the computational cost of high-performance methods with respect to effectiveness is prohibitive for large-scale deployment.

The paper is structured as follows: Sect. 2 briefly presents the state-of-the-art, while Sect. 3 describes the system design and data pre-processing. Section 4 presents the implementation and the experimental results. Section 5 contains the conclusion, with extensions and future work.

2 Related Work

The concept of NILM was first introduced by G. W. Hart in [2], where he defined the problem, and presented an algorithm based on clustering of the electric measurements that provided encouraging results. Since then, many approaches have been developed. An extensive review of these techniques can be found in [3, 4, 30], while a more detailed analysis is presented in [5]. The rest of this section is only a shallow review of the research done on NILM.

Hidden Markov Models (HMM) were initially used for the NILM problem based on the assumption that the hidden states correspond to the different analysed appliances in the house, and the observations to the features of the aggregated signal that is measured. The authors of [6], developed an HMM where the hidden states are the points of the set that is produced by the Cartesian product of the operating state labels of all the appliances of interest in the house. This state coding involves calculations with sparse matrices. Thus, the derived algorithm is effective for data with low sampling rate. Despite this, the algorithm is not sufficient for modelling all the appliances of a typical house, since the complexity increases exponentially over the number of appliances. In [7], a "Difference Factorial HMM (FHMM)" is described. This model does not need data labels for training, it is computationally effective and not affected by local extrema. Based on FHMMs, the authors of [8] propose an estimation algorithm that achieves good generalisation for different but similar appliances. The disadvantage of this approach is that during the training on a specific appliance, it is assumed that no other appliance changes state.

Recurrent Neural Networks (RNN) [9] are a type of neural network (NN) that do not only use the current input, but also the previous output to produce the new output. They use state vectors that operate as internal "memory units" of the neurons. Thus, RNNs have been utilised in a variety of applications where data sequence processing is needed [10]. A special type of RNNs, the Long Short-Term Memory (LSTM) networks, have a more complex internal structure, that enables them to correlate points of the sequence with larger relative distance between them compared to a conventional RNN. This characteristic resolves the problem of vanishing gradient. Thus, LSTM networks are more effective for time series processing as is the case of NILM. Such applications are presented in [11] and [12], where the networks are provided with the aggregated signal as an input and disaggregate it to a signal of a specific appliance in the output, obtaining very promising results for specific types of appliances. Recently, a new type of RNN was introduced as another solution to the vanishing gradient problem: the Gated Recurrent Unit (GRU) [13]. GRU networks require less calculations, resulting in less training time. Simulation results show that the effectiveness of GRUs is comparable to that of LSTMs [14].

The Convolutional Neural Network (CNN) [15] is a type of Multi-Layer Perceptron (MLP), that performs convolution of the inputs in at least one layer. CNNs have been used for NILM in order to extract the signal of one appliance from the aggregated signal [16].

Another type of NN that has been used for NILM is the Denoising Autoencoder (DAE) [17]. A DAE assumes that the input contains noise, and the output is an attempt to reconstruct the input without this noise (unsupervised learning). A disadvantage of this method is that every network can isolate the signal of only one appliance, thus requiring multiple DAEs for a group of appliances.

Finally, the combination of NNs and Markov Models has been explored. In [18], a CNN is used to extract the features of one appliance, and it is combined with a Hidden Semi-Markov Model (HSMM) that models this appliance.

The evaluation of these techniques is based on various publicly available datasets. These datasets vary widely with respect to sampling rate, number of features and types of appliances. One of the most used public datasets is the Reference Energy Disaggregation Data Set (REDD) [19]. It contains measurements from 6 houses, in a time span that ranges from a few days to a few months, with a sampling rate 15 kHz for the aggregated signal, 0.5 Hz for circuits with a single appliance and 1 Hz for circuits with more than one appliance (each house has 10–24 different appliances). The Almanac of Minutely Power dataset (AMPds) [20] contains samples with a time distance of 1 min (0.0167 Hz), that were being collected for one year from a house with 19 appliances. There is also a second edition, AMPds2, with the data of one more year of observations. UK Domestic Appliance-Level Electricity (UK-DALE) [21] is a dataset that contains measurements of 5 houses in the UK, for a period of 2.5 years. The sampling rates for the aggregate signal and for each appliance are 16 kHz and 0.167 Hz respectively. Finally, ENERTALK [22] is a data set collected from 22 houses in Korea. The aggregate signal, as well as the consumption of the up-to-7 measured appliances, are sampled at 15 Hz for time periods that range between 29 and 122 days.

3   System Design and Data Pre-processing

Due to the sequential nature of the aggregate signal in NILM, an RNN seems to be the most promising approach. Thus, a Deep RNN was used in this study, with two different types of neurons, LSTM and GRU. Preliminary tests with both types of neurons showed that their performance was comparable. Therefore, the GRU type was selected since it is the most computationally efficient. The number of network inputs was equal to the number of features of each dataset. The number of hidden layers was determined by trial and error. In the architectures tested in the majority of the design experiments, the number of hidden neurons decreased from the input to the output layer, while the activation function for all the hidden neurons was the hyperbolic tangent (tanh).

The network outputs were binary class labels, with each label corresponding to exactly one appliance. Consequently, the output layer was a dense layer comprised of a number of neurons equal to the number of appliances used in each dataset. The activation function of the output layer was the sigmoid, thus the output values are in the range [0, 1]. Binary cross-entropy was selected as the loss function, since every sample can either belong or not to each of the more-than-one classes (multi-label classification task) and the objective was to optimize the performance for every class separately. Finally, several optimisers were tested: Stochastic Gradient Descent (SGD), AdaGrad, Adam and RMSprop. The best results were obtained using Adam [24] with learning rate equal to 0.001.

3.1 Datasets

ENERTALK. ENERTALK was the publicly available dataset chosen for the experiments. The second dataset was collected from the DinRail Cerberus Smart Meter of Meazon S.A. [25]. Among the 22 houses that are included in ENERTALK, only houses that has measurements of 3 to 5 appliances were considered (houses 01, 02, 04, 05, 06, 08, 17, 18 and 21). Ultimately, house 02 was selected because of the types of contained appliances: a fridge, a TV, a washing machine, and a rice cooker. The measurements were logged for 31 days and represent the everyday use of all appliances. The recorded features both the aggregated signal and each device were the following:

- **Timestamp:** The time instant of the measurement at Unix milliseconds timestamp format.
- **Active Power:** The real value of the power that is consumed from an AC circuit. It is measured in Watts (W) and given by the formula: $P = V_{RMS} \times I_{RMS} \times \cos\varphi$, where V_{RMS} is the active voltage, I_{RMS} is the active current intensity and φ is the angle between the voltage and current phasors.
- **Reactive Power:** The energy that flows towards the load and in reverse along a wire in an AC circuit. It is measured in Volt-Ampere Reactive (var) and given by the formula: $Q = V_{RMS} \times I_{RMS} \times \sin\varphi$.

MEAZON. The DinRail Cerberus device is installed in the central panel of a house and records the aggregate signal. The sampling rate of the smart meter is 50 Hz, which makes it a precise tool for data collection for NILM. It has the following operation states: power analysis and harmonic analysis for three harmonic frequencies or for all available harmonics. The dataset contains measurements of a house, with 5 sampled devices: AC, oven, press, stove, and vacuum cleaner. There are gaps between the recorded operation of each device. The smart meter records 13 features for each sample out of which 7 were selected for the authors' experiments, in order to compare the results with those of [25]. These features were timestamp, active power, and reactive power as defined above, in addition to.

- **RMS Current:** The active current intensity in Amperes (A), given by: $I_{RMS} = \frac{I_{peak}}{\sqrt{2}}$.
- **Phase Shift:** The angle φ between the voltage and current phasors (phase difference).

- **Apparent Power:** The power that is theoretically consumed by an AC circuit. It is measured in Volt-Amperes (VA), and it is given by the formula: $S = V_{RMS} \times I_{RMS}$.
- **Crest Factor:** It is calculated using the formula: $CF = \frac{I_{peak}}{I_{RMS}}$.

Regarding the ground truth, separate smart meters were not used for each appliance, since during the operation logging of each appliance, no other appliances of interest were in use. Operation labels (On/Off) have been added manually for each appliance. As a result, there are 5 editions of the dataset with the same data and different labels, since in [25], the objective was the construction of one separate classifier for each appliance.

3.2 Data Pre-processing

ENERTALK Dataset. The first 10 overlapping days of measurements for all selected houses were utilised. The dataset is provided in the Parquet format (distributed systems file format). The data for each day is stored in a separate directory, which contains one file with the measurements corresponding to each device. All data except for the timestamp was kept. The first 4 days were used as the training set, the next 4 days as the validation set and the last 2 days as the test set. The labels for every device were binary-encoded, with 0 corresponding the Off state and 1 to the On state. For every sample each appliance was individually assigned the On label if the sampled value of active power was greater than 15 Watts. This threshold is used in [21] to calculate the ratio of On to Off states.

According to [11], NN performance is better if the data is normalised in the range [0, 1]. The authors also tested other methods, such as the transformation to a Gaussian distribution with a mean of 0 and a variance of 1, but the performance was not improved. Thus, [0, 1] normalisation was applied in this work. It should be noted that the normalization step followed the division of the data to the three subsets. Otherwise, there would have been an information leak from the training to the test set and the model would have been biased [26].

DinRail Cerberus Dataset. The data pre-processing had already been performed in [25]. The labels had been divided into different files per appliance. These files were merged by the authors to create the final data set, which included measurements of all appliances. Then, the data was split into training and test sets with a ratio of 85/15 and both sets were normalized separately to the range [0, 1], as was done with ENERTALK.

4 System Implementation and Training

The language of choice for the implementation of the RNN model was Python 3.7, with NumPy (1.19.5), pandas (1.2.4), PyArrow (4.0.0) and scikit-learn (0.22.2.post1) being the packages used for reading, pre-processing, and storing the data. Matplotlib (3.2.1) was used to produce the graphs. The models were created, trained and evaluated using TensorFlow (2.4.1) [27] as the backend and Keras as the high-level interface. The experiments were conducted on the Google Colaboratory platform.

The hidden layers of the RNN were implemented using GRU cells (tensorflow.keras.layers.GRU) with tanh as the activation function, whereas the output layer was a simple densely connected one (tensorflow.keras.layers.Dense) with sigmoid as the activation function. Adam (tensorflow.keras.optimizers.Adam) was chosen as the optimization algorithm for the training process. In the rest of this section, the authors present their experiments to discover the optimal structure of the NN (the number of hidden layers and the number of neurons in each layer, since the number of inputs and outputs are defined by the training set). The network output is represented by a (n × 1) binary vector, where n is the number of the appliances, and each output corresponds to an appliance state. When the appliance is On, then the respective bit is 1, otherwise it is 0. When training the NN on ENERTALK, the additional techniques of validation and early stopping (tensorflow.keras.callbacks.EarlyStopping) were used. More specifically, at the end of every epoch the network was fed the validation samples and the classification error and accuracy values were recorded. If the validation error increased or the accuracy decreased from epoch to epoch then training stopped, in order to achieve better generalization. In the experiments, the training process stopped when the accuracy did not improve more than 0.001 after 20 epochs. This technique was not used for the Meazon dataset, since it is very small. Figure 1 depicts a flowchart that describes the model training and selection process.

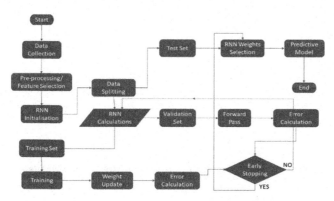

Fig. 1. Experimental process flow chart

As already mentioned, binary cross-entropy was the chosen loss function. Consequently, binary accuracy was chosen as the accuracy function. Additionally, the values of Mean Squared Error (MSE) and Mean Absolute Error (MAE) were calculated for each epoch.

Since the training of a NN is a stochastic process (due to the random initialisation), the results presented below are the mean values of each metric over 10 runs of every experiment. Experiments with more than 10 runs were performed, but there was no significant difference in the results. The presented graphs depict the values obtained from one experiment instance.

4.1   1st Model

The first experiments were focused on a structure with two hidden layers with a decreasing number of cells from the input to the output layer, since they performed better in preliminary tests. The architecture with the best experimental results consisted of 64 cells in the first and 32 cells in the second hidden layer respectively. Table 1 shows the mean values of the metrics in the testing phase for both datasets, while Fig. 2 depicts the evolution of the metrics during training.

Table 1. Test results for 1st model

	Binary cross-entropy (Loss)	Binary accuracy
ENERTALK	0.5059	0.7755
Meazon	0.7338	0.7873

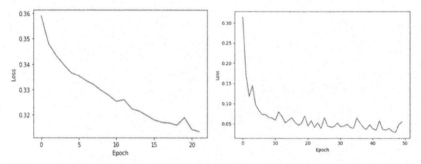

Fig. 2. Training loss for ENERTALK (left) and Meazon (right) datasets – 1st model

During the training of the network for the ENERTALK dataset, it was observed that, while the achieved accuracy was sufficient (over 80% after the 5th epoch) and the error values were relatively small, there was a significant decrease in validation accuracy after very few epochs (usually 5). Thus, the network was overfitting on the data of the training set. This fact was also confirmed by the prediction accuracy on the test set, which was smaller, although the opposite result was expected due to the sufficient amount of the data used and the assumed complexity of this classification task. Overfitting was also observed in the Meazon dataset. In this case it was expected, since every sample corresponds to the operation of one or none of the appliances, and therefore the classification task was "easier".

4.2   2nd Model

The next group of experiments focused on improving generalization for both datasets. Overfitting was reduced via regularization, by applying the Dropout technique [28].

Dropout is a strategy based on the "dropping/deletion" of some randomly selected neurons during training, meaning that their output is ignored. In this way, the capacity of the network is reduced, and the rest of the neurons are forced to learn a more general classification strategy. To apply Dropout to a network layer, a new parameter P_d is introduced, which is the probability of a neuron being dropped. After several experiments with different values of P_d, the results indicated that the best value was $P_d = 0.4$ for every hidden layer of the network. Table 2 shows the mean values of the testing metrics, while Fig. 2 depicts the evolution of the metrics during training.

Table 2. Test results for 2nd model

	Binary cross-entropy (Loss)	Binary accuracy
ENERTALK	0.5345	0.8091
Meazon	0.0198	0.9683

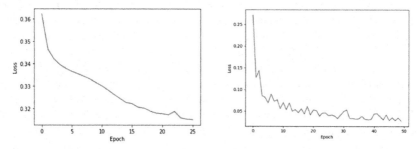

Fig. 3. Training loss for ENERTALK (left) and Meazon (right) datasets – 2nd model

For the ENERTALK dataset there was no significant difference between the two models. The classification accuracy was better by up to 3% but the error metrics slightly increased. These results showed that overfitting had been handled but not to the expected extent: the difference between training and testing accuracy had been reduced, but the improvement in every training epoch was not reflected in the validation (Fig. 3).

In contrast, the training of the 2nd model with the Meazon dataset presented significant improvement with very good results overall. Of course, we must note that the Meazon dataset is "clean", since every device operates separately. Additionally, the test data is a small sample of one relatively small dataset. However, the results were very promising for future work on more data from DinRail Cerberus or other smart meters with sampling rates of around 50 Hz.

It was determined that the 2nd model performed in an almost optimal manner for the Meazon dataset. As a result, the next set of experiments continued to explore models tailored to the ENERTALK dataset. However, in most of the new experiments both datasets were used for the sake of completeness. The first approach to decrease overfitting was the further decrease of the numbers of neurons of the network, considering that a network with lower elasticity (capacity) is more capable to generalize instead of adapting to the data. However, the results of these experiments were the opposite. In most of the runs, all scores were lower, and the test accuracy did not even come close to the training accuracy. Similar results were obtained when the dropout technique was used.

Subsequently, some of the more basic hyperparameters of the network were reconsidered. Firstly, the Rectified Linear Unit (ReLU) activation function was used, as it has proved to be very effective in DNN training while avoiding the vanishing gradient problem [29]. Finally, additional experiments with different values of the learning rate were performed, in order to confirm that the overfitting was not caused by the granularity of the weight updates. Unfortunately, all these attempts were not successful at eliminating, or even decreasing overfitting.

5   Conclusions and Future Work

In this work, a deep RNN was designed, implemented, trained, and evaluated that receives as input the instant aggregated signal from the central electricity switchboard of a house and predicts the operational state of a group of appliances. In other words, it decides whether each of the appliances of interest is functioning or not (On/Off) in each time point. The final model was extracted via extensive experimentation, using several architectures as well as many combinations of different values of the hyperparameters. The final model was tested on two datasets with high sampling rate: the publicly available ENERTALK (4 appliances) and the dataset in [25] with data recorded by the Meazon smart meter (5 appliances). The Meazon dataset is simpler since it contains 6 features and at every time step only one device was in operation. The ENERTALK dataset has two features and simultaneous operation of more than one device at every time step. The classification performance was adequate for both datasets but, as expected, the highest performance was achieved for the easier problem of the Meazon dataset. However, in the case of the ENERTALK dataset, the phenomenon of overfitting was observed, which meant that the classification capability of the network was lower than expected.

The proposed model can be improved in several ways. First, for the Meazon dataset, it would be very interesting to test the trained model with a new dataset containing measurements when 2 or more of the 5 appliances are operating concurrently. Note that the sampling rate of the Meazon smart meter is 50 Hz, while it also generates a set of features that may make the classification task more efficient when compared to the ENERTALK dataset. The ENERTALK dataset is perhaps a more challenging problem due to the lower sampling rate and the small number of features. A way to face the problem is to use data from more than one house, and for testing to use data from houses that have not been used in training.

Acknowledgments. This research has been co-financed by the European Regional Development Fund of the European Union and Greek national funds through the Operational Program Competitiveness, Entrepreneurship and Innovation, under the call RESEARCH – CREATE – INNOVATE (project code:T2EDK-00127)».

References

1. Nonintrusive load monitoring (2020). https://en.wikipedia.org/w/index.php?title=Nonintrus ive_load_monitoring&oldid=993516814
2. Hart, G.W.: Nonintrusive appliance load monitoring. Proc. IEEE **80**, 1870–1891 (1992). https://doi.org/10.1109/5.192069
3. Verma, A., Anwar, A.: A Comprehensive Review on the NILM Algorithms for Energy Disaggregation. arXiv:2102.12578 [cs, eess] (2021)
4. Faustine, A., Mvungi, N.H., Kaijage, S., Michael, K.: A Survey on Non-Intrusive Load Monitoring Methodies and Techniques for Energy Disaggregation Problem. arXiv:1703.00785 [cs]. (2017)
5. Liu, H.: Non-intrusive Load Monitoring: Theory, Technologies and Applications. Springer, Singapore (2020). https://doi.org/10.1007/978-981-15-1860-7
6. Makonin, S. et al.: Exploiting HMM Sparsity to Perform Online Real-Time Nonintrusive Load Monitoring (NILM). IEEE Trans. Smart Grid, 1–11 (2015). https://doi.org/10.1109/TSG.2015.2494592. (in press)
7. Kolter, J.Z., Jaakkola, T.: Approximate inference in additive factorial HMMs with application to energy disaggregation. In: Artificial Intelligence and Statistics, pp. 1472–1482 PMLR (2012)
8. Parson, O. et al.: Non-intrusive load monitoring using prior models of general appliance types. In: Twenty-Sixth Conference on Artificial Intelligence (AAAI-2012) (26/07/12), 24 July 2012
9. Haykin, S.S.: Neural Networks and Learning Machines. Prentice Hall, Hoboken (2009)
10. Recurrent neural network (2021). https://en.wikipedia.org/w/index.php?title=Recurrent_neu ral_network&oldid=1027494214
11. Kelly, J., Knottenbelt, W.: Neural NILM: deep neural networks applied to energy disaggregation. In: Proceedings of the 2nd ACM International Conference on Embedded Systems for Energy-Efficient Built Environments, pp. 55–64 (2015). https://doi.org/10.1145/2821650.282 1672
12. He, W., Chai, Y.: An empirical study on energy disaggregation via deep learning. In: 2016 2nd International Conference on Artificial Intelligence and Industrial Engineering (AIIE 2016) November (2016). https://doi.org/10.2991/aiie-16.2016.77
13. Cho, K. et al.: Learning Phrase Representations using RNN Encoder-Decoder for Statistical Machine Translation. arXiv:1406.1078 [cs, stat] (2014)
14. Gated recurrent unit (2020). https://en.wikipedia.org/w/index.php?title=Gated_recurrent_ unit&oldid=997015931
15. Fukushima, K.: Neocognitron: a self-organizing neural network model for a mechanism of pattern recognition unaffected by shift in position. Biol. Cybern. **36**(4), 193–202 (1980). https://doi.org/10.1007/BF00344251
16. Shin, C. et al.: Data Requirements for Applying Machine Learning to Energy Disaggregation. Energies. 12, 9, 1696 (2019). https://doi.org/10.3390/en12091696
17. Kramer, M.A.: Nonlinear principal component analysis using autoassociative neural networks. AIChE J. **37**(2), 233–243 (1991). https://doi.org/10.1002/aic.690370209
18. Huss, A.: Hybrid model approach to appliance load disaggregation : expressive appliance modelling by combining convolutional neural networks and hidden semi Markov models (2015)
19. Kolter, J., Johnson, M.: REDD: a public data set for energy disaggregation research. Artif. Intell. **25**, 59–62 (2011)
20. Makonin, S., et al.: AMPds: a public dataset for load disaggregation and eco-feedback research. In: 2013 IEEE Electrical Power Energy Conference, pp. 1–6 (2013). https://doi.org/10.1109/EPEC.2013.6802949

21. Kelly, J., Knottenbelt, W.: The UK-DALE dataset, domestic appliance-level electricity demand and whole-house demand from five UK homes. Sci. Data. **2**(1), 150007 (2015). https://doi.org/10.1038/sdata.2015.7

22. Shin, C. et al.: The ENERTALK dataset, 15 Hz electricity consumption data from 22 houses in Korea. Sci. Data. **6**(1), 193 (2019). https://doi.org/10.1038/s41597-019-0212-5

23. Batra, N. et al.: NILMTK: an open source toolkit for non-intrusive load monitoring. In: Proceedings of the 5th International Conference on Future Energy Systems, pp. 265–276 (2014). https://doi.org/10.1145/2602044.2602051

24. Kingma, D.P., Ba, J.: Adam: a method for stochastic optimization. arXiv:1412.6980 [cs] (2014)

25. Koutroumpina, C.: Intelligent way of managing energy data flow. University of Patras (2020)

26. sklearn.preprocessing.minmax_scale — scikit-learn 0.24.2 documentation. https://scikit-learn.org/stable/modules/generated/sklearn.preprocessing.minmax_scale.html. Accessed 22 June 2021

27. Google, Inc.: tensorflow: TensorFlow is an open source machine learning framework for everyone

28. Hinton, G.E., et al.: Improving neural networks by preventing co-adaptation of feature detectors. arXiv:1207.0580 [cs] (2012)

29. Glorot, X. et al.: Deep sparse rectifier neural networks. In: Proceedings of the Fourteenth International Conference on Artificial Intelligence and Statistics, pp. 315–323. JMLR Workshop and Conference Proceedings (2011)

30. Angelis, G.F., et al.: NILM applications: literature review of learning approaches, recent developments and challenges. Energy Build. **261**, 111951 (2022)

31. Tabatabaei, S.M., et al.: Toward non-intrusive load monitoring via multi-label classification. IEEE Trans. Smart Grid. **8**(1), 26–40 (2017). https://doi.org/10.1109/TSG.2016.2584581

32. Ayub M., El-Alfy, E.S.M.: Multi-target energy disaggregation using convolutional neural networks. Int. J. Adv. Comput. Sci. App. **11**(10), 684–693 (2020)

Energy Load Forecasting: Investigating Mid-Term Predictions with Ensemble Learners

Charalampos M. Liapis$^{(\boxtimes)}$, Aikaterini Karanikola, and Sotiris Kotsiantis

Department of Mathematics, University of Patras, 265 04 Patras, Rion, Greece
c.liapis@upnet.gr, karanikola@upatras.gr, sotos@math.upatras.gr

Abstract. In the structure of the modern world, energy and especially electricity is a prerequisite for regularity. Thus, the requirement for accurate forecasts regarding power system loads seems self-evident. In machine learning, a time series forecasting endeavor can be treated as a regression problem. In such scenarios, ensemble methods are often used for robustness and increased accuracy of the generated predictions. This work is a comparative investigation of the use of ensemble schemes for medium-term forecasting of energy system load. The use of over 300 regression schemes is investigated, in a total of 8 different modifications of the input data, over 5 different time-frames, that is, one day, 7-day, 14-day, 21-day, and 30-day horizons, resulting in a loop of 12000 experiments. Summary tables with representative results from the corresponding Friedman rankings are presented.

Keywords: Energy system load · Power load forecasting · Ensemble learning · Regression forecasting · Medium-term forecasting

1 Introduction

Energy management, from the production stage to storage, sharing and consumption, is a multifactorial issue in which huge interests of diverse parties coexist, from individuals and production or distribution companies to states and geopolitical formations.

With regard to electricity, and since production and consumption are linked by a synchronicity condition, continuous load monitoring is necessary to regulate the operation of power stations in such a way as to generate the amounts of energy required. Thus, failures in relevant decisions could lead to a variety of problems. Producing more energy than needed may lead to environmental, storing, or supply issues. Less available energy than required may result in sharp increases in production expenditures, given emerging requirements for immediate use of higher-cost units [1]. In addition, black-outs in large areas can have significant consequences on the well-being and well-functioning of society [2]. It is, therefore, imperative that the best possible forecasts of electricity load are

© IFIP International Federation for Information Processing 2022
Published by Springer Nature Switzerland AG 2022
I. Maglogiannis et al. (Eds.): AIAI 2022, IFIP AICT 646, pp. 343–355, 2022.
https://doi.org/10.1007/978-3-031-08333-4_28

available, as such predictions will help to optimize the power management plan and to make as many sound decisions as possible [3]. Thus, through forecasting, it is possible to ensure the robustness of the entire system.

Predicting energy load, however, is not an easy process. For example, fluctuations in consumer needs depend on many factors. And there is a multitude of such factors than can cause demand to diversify. Meteorological conditions, seasonal and calendar regularities, regional economic standards, the use of new technologies, or the level of industrialization, all tend to alter the energy requirements [2, 4]. There are also random factors that are impossible to foresee. Understandably, the problem of predicting energy system load has been of particular concern to the scientific community with a wealth of relevant research output. On this basis, a variety of methods, ranging from statistical or machine learning to hybrid, have been used in different scenarios with various time horizons and range of applications.

This work aims to apply an extensive comparison of regression models for predicting energy load, investigate whether regression-based ensembles exhibit better performance compared to individual learners and, if so, identify the timeframes where these improvements occur. The work has the following structure: after this short introduction, an indicative part of the literature so far is presented. Next, the methodology and the experimental setup and procedure are introduced. Then, results of the comparison of 24 regression methods for predicting the energy load in 5 different time horizons follow, in contrast with a presentation of outputs of a variety of potential ensemble regressors. Finally, an evaluation of the findings of the work along with a brief report of its possible future extensions are outlined.

2   Related Work

In the contemporary social context, the demand for accurate forecasts on energy system load seems more relevant than ever. The growing interest in the subject from the scientific community has led to the publication of numerous papers. This chapter is an attempt to present some of the recent research output. However, this multitude of works, together with the fact that the space is - justifiably - limited make this report just an indicative starting point for the reader.

Regarding regression methods, *multiple linear regression* (MLR) has been used in big data to predict energy load over a 7-day horizon using three-year historical data [5]. The use of *support vector regression* (SVR) in energy problems is also relatively common, mainly due to the fact that these methods identify global minimums rather than local ones, and so, in certain tasks, they appear superior to many, even state-of-the-art, machine learning methods, such as *artificial neural networks* (ANNs) [6]. In [7], the SVR is used for peak load prediction using both historical load values and the corresponding meteorological data. A combination of SVR and *empirical mode decomposition* (EMD) is used in [8] to predict energy load, both in terms of extensive geographic coverage and individual buildings, while in [9], the method is utilized in conjunction with *feature selection*, exploiting the national energy load data of Great Britain and France. Deep learning techniques are also quite popular. In [10], *sequence-to-sequence recurrent neural networks* with *attention mechanism* are used to predict the energy load at different time horizons, while in [11], *metaheuristic-search-based* algorithms are used to find the optimal or relatively optimal values for tuning the hyperparameters of *long short-term memory* architectures (LSTMs). *Feedforward deep neural networks* (FF-DNNs) and *recurrent deep neural networks* (R-DNNs) architectures are compared in [12] on short-term scenarios, while *deep neural network (DNN)* - based load forecasting models are proposed for short-term forecasts in [13]. A combination of *convolutional* and *recurrent neural networks* is presented in [14], comparing it with *linear regression* and SVR in one-day horizon forecasts, using historical and meteorological inputs. LSTM and *gated recurrent unit* (GRU) networks are used with different configurations in [15] for a two-month horizon forecast. Also, a comparison of LSTMs with the classic *auto-regressive integrated moving average* and *exponential smoothing* methods in a small-scale residential scenario of 12 households is presented in [16].

Works comparing classic machine learning methods in terms of their performance in the problem of predicting energy load are presented in [17], in [18], and in [19]. In [20], the *auto-regressive integrated moving average* (ARIMA), SVR and *tree-based* regression, are compared in a household load prediction scenario, while in [21], an LSTM model using *feature selection* and *genetic* algorithm is compared with 7 well-known machine learning algorithms in scenarios of a number of different time horizons. In addition, [22] presents a comparison of eight neural network-based methods in a short-term load forecasting scenario.

Regarding ensemble methods, such schemes combine a finite number of models in order to formulate the final output. They are used due to their robustness and increased accuracy [23], despite the difficulty of their production and the increase in computational costs. Ensembles, given accurate and diverse constituents [24], and bearing in mind the inevitable trade-offs [25], tend to generalize better than individual learners [26]. Thus, the use of ensembles has been suggested for various forecast scenarios, such as pandemic [27], stock market [28], and weather forecasts [29]. In [30], a review of the relevant literature regarding ensemble methods in regression problems is presented. Regarding the use of ensemble methods for energy load forecasting, one can likewise mention a number of related works. Some of them exploit the use of LSTMs in combination with other modern techniques, such as *fully connected cascade* (FCC) networks [31], ARIMA [32] and MLR [33]. SVR-based ensembles using a *sub-sampling* strategy that ensures the diversity of the base learners are presented in [34], while a modified version of *passive aggressive regression* (PAR) for online load forecasting is presented in [35]. Regarding regression tree methods, a scheme based on *multiple regression trees* (CART) is presented in [36], while *gradient boosting* regression tree ensembles are examined in contrast to statistical methods in [37].

In summary, all of the above show that both a thorough comparison of a large number of regression models over the energy load forecasting problem and the creation of ensembles based on such schemes are both useful and complement the existing literature.

3   Experimental Setup

We proceed to sketch the experimental process. Below, the raw input as well as the construction of the final data set used, the base learners tested, the formalization according to which the ensembles were formed and the evaluation metrics will be presented.

3.1   Data

The raw data contains Greek hourly energy system load records ranging from 30 November 2020 to 13 November 2021 [38]. A 24-h rolling average was applied to the initial time series, and then a weighted value was exported as representative of each day. Thus, a new normalized daily time series was created, a component

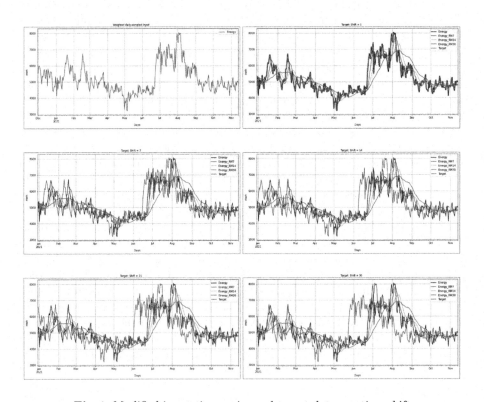

Fig. 1. Modified input time series and target data per time-shift

on which the experiments were performed. Then, on the newly formed time series, a rolling mean procedure was applied again for 7-day, 14-day, and 30-day windows.

From the variants of these 4 extracted time series, a variety of input data was created, which consisted of the univariate version and 7 additional multivariate combinations of the individual aforementioned time series. The experiments were performed over 5 time horizons: one-day, 7-day, 14-day, 21-day, and 30-day forecast frames. Based on the prediction time step, works can be characterized as short-term, medium-term or long-term. Thus, the present work is about medium-term predictions. Figure 1 depicts the processed time series used in terms of the corresponding prediction time-shifts.

3.2 Algorithms

It has already been mentioned that - in this work - the forecast scenario has been standardized and treated as a regression problem. So, at first, comparisons were made between the individual regression methods and their possible per-2 groupings, the results of which were then used to investigate possible ensembles that exploit triads of the best-performing algorithms. In terms of individual models and base learners, a total of 24 regression methods were utilized. Table 1 contains both the names of the algorithms used together with their respective abbreviations, as well as the reference papers, since it is practically impossible to present them within the limits of the present work.

Table 1. Algorithms

	Abbr	Algorithm		Abbr	Algorithm
1	ada	AdaBoostRegressor [39]	13	las	LassoRegression [51]
2	ard	AutoRelevanceDetermination [40]	14	lar	LeastAngleRegression [50]
3	cat	CatBoostRegressor [41]	15	lgbm	LightGradientBoost [52]
4	dt	DecisionTreeRegressor [42]	16	lr	LinearRegression [53]
5	en	ElasticNet [43]	17	mlp	MultiLevelPerceptron [54]
6	et	ExtraTreesRegressor [44]	18	omp	OrthogonalMatchingPursuit [55]
7	xgb	ExtremeGradientBoosting [45]	19	par	PassiveAggressiveRegressor [56]
8	gbr	GradientBoostingRegressor [46]	20	rf	RandomForestRegressor [57]
9	hub	HuberRegressor [47]	21	rsc	RandomSampleConsensus [58]
10	knn	KNeighborsRegressor [48]	22	rid	RidgeRegression [59]
11	kr	KernelRidge [49]	23	svr	SupportVectorRegression [60]
12	llar	LassoLeastAngleRegression [50]	24	tr	TheilSenRegressor [61]

The *pycaret* python library [62] was utilized to conduct the experiments. All examined ensembles were formed under a simple low-cost scheme that produces the final prediction by averaging the outputs of base regressors fit on the training set.

3.3   Metrics

The results were evaluated according to the following 6 metrics: *mean squared error* (MSE), *root mean square error* (RMSE), *root mean squared logarithmic error* (RMSLE), arithmetic *mean of the absolute errors* (MAE), *mean absolute percentage error* (MAPE) and the coefficient of determination R^2. The formalizations could not be presented here due to space constraints. A more detailed description of the structure of the metrics used and how to interpret them can be found in [63].

4   Results

In total, more than 8 *data setups* × 300 *algorithmic setups* × 5 *time-shifts* = 12000 *experimental loops* were performed over different data set splits. Due to the size of the results, only a very small part of them was chosen to be presented. Specifically, the results will contain the 5 algorithm schemes with the best performances per metric, regardless of whether they are individual or ensemble methods. This arrangement was formulated after Friedman [64,65] ranking tests produced over the metric data of each method. Tables 2, 3, 4, 5 and 6 contain the results grouped by prediction time-frame. A much larger portion of the results can be found at shorturl.at/fvOP9. It should be noted that, in the results presented, the values of the metrics refer to the corresponding scores of their Friedman rankings.

Table 2. Friedman rankings (shift = 1)

	Method	MAE	Method	MAPE	Method	MSE
1st	tr	7.625	tr	7.25	tr	7
2nd	tr+gbr+omp	12	tr+gbr+omp	12.25	tr+gbr+omp	14.375
3rd	tr+lgbm+omp	18.125	tr+lgbm+omp	17.75	tr+lgbm+omp	16.625
4th	hub+rsc+gbr	22.125	tr+rsc+gbr	21.75	tr+par	21.625
5th	tr+rsc+gbr	22.375	hub+rsc+gbr	22	par+gbr+omp	24.75
	Method	R2	Method	RMSE	Method	RMSLE
1st	tr	123	tr	7	tr	6.375
2nd	tr+gbr+omp	115.625	tr+gbr+omp	14.375	tr+gbr+omp	14.25
3rd	tr+lgbm+omp	113.375	tr+lgbm+omp	16.625	tr+lgbm+omp	16.125
4th	tr+par	108.375	tr+par	21.625	tr+par	22.25
5th	par+gbr+omp	105.25	par+gbr+omp	24.75	tr+hub	24.5

From the Friedman ranking tables, in each of the time horizons examined, the relative efficiency of the ensemble methods can be observed. Overall they appear to occupy the top positions in the rankings, losing only to *Theil-Sen Regressor* in

Table 3. Friedman rankings (shift = 7)

	Method	MAE	Method	MAPE	Method	MSE
1st	tr	4.5	tr	4.375	tr	4.75
2nd	tr+hub	8.375	tr+hub	8.875	tr+hub	7
3rd	tr+par	9.5	tr+hub+rsc	9.125	tr+par	8.125
4th	tr+hub+rsc	10.5	tr+par	9.75	tr+par+hub	9.125
5th	tr+par+hub	11.125	tr+par+hub	11.375	tr+hub+rsc	11.75
	Method	R2	Method	RMSE	Method	RMSLE
1st	tr	125.25	tr	4.75	tr	4.875
2nd	tr+hub	123	tr+hub	7	tr+hub	6.875
3rd	tr+par	121.875	tr+par	8.125	tr+par	8.5
4th	tr+par+hub	120.875	tr+par+hub	9.125	tr+par+hub	9.25
5th	tr+hub+rsc	118.25	tr+hub+rsc	11.75	tr+hub+rsc	11.25

Table 4. Friedman rankings (shift = 14)

	Method	MAE	Method	MAPE	Method	MSE
1st	tr+rsc+gbr	22.125	tr+rsc+gbr	20.625	rsc+omp	23
2nd	rsc+omp	22.625	rsc+omp	22.75	tr+rsc+lgbm	25.125
3rd	tr	26	tr	24	tr+rsc+omp	26.875
4th	tr+rsc+lgbm	26.375	tr+rsc+lgbm	24.5	tr+rsc+gbr	27.25
5th	tr+hub+rsc	28.5	tr+hub+rsc	25.875	hub+rsc+omp	28.5
	Method	R2	Method	RMSE	Method	RMSLE
1st	rsc+omp	107	rsc+omp	23	rsc+omp	22.125
2nd	tr+rsc+lgbm	104.875	tr+rsc+lgbm	25.125	tr+rsc+lgbm	23.75
3rd	tr+rsc+omp	103.125	tr+rsc+omp	26.875	tr+rsc+gbr	26.125
4th	tr+rsc+gbr	102.75	tr+rsc+gbr	27.25	tr+rsc+omp	26.25
5th	hub+rsc+omp	101.5	hub+rsc+omp	28.5	tr	26.75

Table 5. Friedman rankings (shift = 21)

	Method	MAE	Method	MAPE	Method	MSE
1st	tr+par+gbr	18.625	tr+par+gbr	19	tr+par+gbr	20.5
2nd	par+hub+gbr	18.875	par+hub+gbr	20.125	tr+rsc+omp	20.625
3rd	tr+hub+gbr	20.5	tr+hub+gbr	21.25	par+hub+gbr	22.25
4th	tr+rsc+omp	25.25	tr+rsc+omp	25	tr+hub+gbr	23.875
5th	tr+par	27.625	tr+par	25.875	tr	26.125
	Method	R2	Method	RMSE	Method	RMSLE
1st	tr+par+gbr	109.5	tr+par+gbr	20.5	tr+rsc+omp	20
2nd	tr+rsc+omp	109.375	tr+rsc+omp	20.625	tr+par+gbr	21.625
3rd	par+hub+gbr	107.75	par+hub+gbr	22.25	tr	22.75
4th	tr+hub+gbr	106.125	tr+hub+gbr	23.875	par+hub+gbr	23.625
5th	tr	103.875	tr	26.125	tr+par	24.625

Table 6. Friedman rankings (shift $= 30$)

	Method	MAE	Method	MAPE	Method	MSE
1st	tr+rsc+omp	19	tr+rsc+omp	18.75	tr+rsc+omp	20.25
2nd	hub+rsc+lgbm	22.75	hub+rsc+lgbm	21.75	hub+rsc+lgbm	24.375
3rd	tr+par+rsc	24.5	tr+par+rsc	23.625	tr+rsc+llar	25.625
4th	rsc+omp	25.125	tr+rsc	23.75	tr+par+lgbm	26.625
5th	tr+rsc	26.5	tr+par+gbr	25.125	rsc+omp	27.25
	Method	R2	Method	RMSE	Method	RMSLE
1st	tr+rsc+omp	109.75	tr+rsc+omp	20.25	tr+rsc+omp	20.5
2nd	hub+rsc+lgbm	105.625	hub+rsc+lgbm	24.375	hub+rsc+lgbm	23.25
3rd	tr+rsc+llar	104.375	tr+rsc+llar	25.625	tr+rsc+llar	26.25
4th	tr+par+lgbm	103.375	tr+par+lgbm	26.625	tr+par+lgbm	26.375
5th	rsc+omp	102.75	rsc+omp	27.25	tr	27

the first two time-shifts investigated. Regarding longer prediction steps, ensembles prevail. This apparent superiority in scenarios involving longer time-frames has come after an extensive comparison, first, of individual algorithms and, subsequently, of their possible groupings. Although there are ensembles that seem to dominate some of the scenarios, there is still no general predominance of a particular one. However, further investigation of the efficient formations seems to point to a prospect of clear conclusions regarding the proposal of a specific methodology.

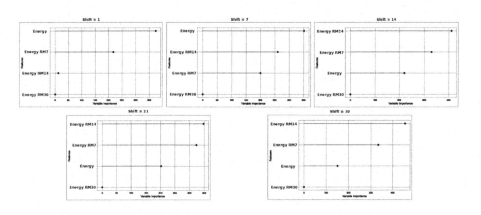

Fig. 2. Feature importance per time-shift - data setup No8

Finally, Fig. 2 shows indicative representations of the feature importance for each time-frame, regarding the *Theil-Sen* method and over the eighth setup of the ones used, that is, the one that contained as input, in a multivariate layout, all the versions of the modified time series produced. It can be observed that in longer-range forecasts, the predictive importance of the smoothed input time series created by the use of wider rolling averages increases. This indicates that during the forecasting methodology set up, the creation of possible variations of the data set given, with such appropriate preprocessing, may increase efficiency in the long run.

5 Discussion and Future Work

Concluding, in this work, the use of regression ensembles to forecast the Greek energy system load was investigated. Ensembles consisting of 2 or 3 base learners were implemented, forming combinations from a total of 24 regression methods, regarding 5 prediction time-frames. Weighted versions of the raw data were used as input in both univariate and multivariate configurations. Results show that, as the time horizon grows, ensemble methods seem to dominate, implying that, in longer prediction time steps, their use can be beneficial.

The exported results suggest that future extensions of the present work could relate to the use of more complex grouping schemes over even longer forecast time horizons and larger data sets. In addition, the continuation of the experiments towards an extensive presentation of the results creates the possibility of formalizing specific ensemble schemes. Lastly, additional information such as meteorological factors or season regularities could be used in such weighted multivariate settings to improve the predictive effectiveness of the models.

References

1. Bianchi, F.M., De Santis, E., Rizzi, A., Sadeghian, A.: Short-term electric load forecasting using echo state networks and PCA decomposition. IEEE Access. **3**, 1931–1943 (2015). https://doi.org/10.1109/ACCESS.2015.2485943
2. Zhang, J.: Research on power load forecasting based on the improved Elman neural network. Chem. Eng. Trans. **51**, 589–594 (2016). https://doi.org/10.3303/CET1651099
3. Filatova, E.S., Filatov, D.M., Stotckaia, A.D., Dubrovskiy, G.: Time series dynamics representation model of power consumption in electric load forecasting system. In: Proceedings of the 2015 North West Russia Section Young Researchers in Electrical and Electronic Engineering Conference ElConRusNW 2015, pp. 175–179 (2015). https://doi.org/10.1109/EIConRusNW.2015.7102256
4. Khamaira, M.Y., Krzma, A.S., Alnass, A.M.: Long term peak load forecasting for the Libyan Network. In: First Conference for Engineering Sciences and Technology (CEST-2018), pp. 185–193 (2018). https://doi.org/10.21467/proceedings.2.23
5. Saber, A.Y., Alam, A.K.M.R.: Short term load forecasting using multiple linear regression for big data. In: 2017 IEEE Symposium Series on Computational Intelligence (SSCI), Janua, pp. 1–6 (2018). https://doi.org/10.1109/SSCI.2017.8285261
6. Clarke, S.M., Griebsch, J.H., Simpson, T.W.: Analysis of support vector regression for approximation of complex engineering analyses. J. Mech. Des. Trans. ASME. **127**, 1077–1087 (2005). https://doi.org/10.1115/1.1897403

7. Azad, M.K., Uddin, S., Takruri, M.: Support vector regression based electricity peak load forecasting. 11th International Symposium on Mechatronics and its Applications, ISMA 2018. January 2018, pp. 1–5 (2018). https://doi.org/10.1109/ISMA.2018.8330143

8. Ghelardoni, L., Ghio, A., Anguita, D.: Energy load forecasting using empirical mode decomposition and support vector regression. IEEE Trans. Smart Grid. **4**, 549–556 (2013). https://doi.org/10.1109/TSG.2012.2235089

9. Maldonado, S., González, A., Crone, S.: Automatic time series analysis for electric load forecasting via support vector regression. Appl. Soft Comput. J. **83**, 105616 (2019). https://doi.org/10.1016/j.asoc.2019.105616

10. Sehovac, L., Grolinger, K.: Deep learning for load forecasting: sequence to sequence recurrent neural networks with attention. IEEE Access. **8**, 36411–36426 (2020). https://doi.org/10.1109/ACCESS.2020.2975738

11. Bouktif, S., Fiaz, A., Ouni, A., Serhani, M.A.: Multi-Sequence LSTM-RNN Deep Learning and Metaheuristics for Electric Load Forecasting. Energies. **3**, 1–21 (2020)

12. Din, G.M.U., Marnerides, A.K.: Short term power load forecasting using Deep Neural Networks. 2017 26th International Conference on Networks Communication, ICNC 2017, pp. 594–598 (2017). https://doi.org/10.1109/ICCNC.2017.7876196

13. Ryu, S., Noh, J., Kim, H.: Deep neural network based demand side short term load forecasting. Energies. **10**, 1–20 (2017). https://doi.org/10.3390/en10010003

14. He, W.: Load forecasting via deep neural networks. Procedia Comput. Sci. **122**, 308–314 (2017). https://doi.org/10.1016/j.procs.2017.11.374

15. Kumar, S., Hussain, L., Banarjee, S., Reza, M.: Energy load forecasting using deep learning approach-LSTM and GRU in spark cluster. In: Proceedings of 5th International Conference on Emerging Applications of Information Technology, EAIT 2018, pp. 1–4 (2018). https://doi.org/10.1109/EAIT.2018.8470406

16. Mubashar, R., Javed Awan, M., Ahsan, M., Yasin, A., Partab Singh, V.: Efficient residential load forecasting using deep learning approach. Int. J. Comput. Appl, Technol (2021)

17. Almalaq, A., Edwards, G.: A review of deep learning methods applied on load forecasting. In: Proceedings of the 16th IEEE International Conference on Machine Learning and Applications, ICMLA 2017, pp. 511–516, December, 2017. https://doi.org/10.1109/ICMLA.2017.0-110

18. Aslam, S., Herodotou, H., Mohsin, S.M., Javaid, N., Ashraf, N., Aslam, S.: A survey on deep learning methods for power load and renewable energy forecasting in smart microgrids. Renew. Sustain. Energy Rev. **144**, 110992 (2021). https://doi.org/10.1016/j.rser.2021.110992

19. Hammad, M.A., Jereb, B., Rosi, B., Dragan, D.: Methods and models for electric load forecasting: a comprehensive review. Logist. Sustain. Transp. **11**, 51–76 (2020). https://doi.org/10.2478/jlst-2020-0004

20. Shabbir, N., Ahmadiahangar, R., Kutt, L., Rosin, A.: Comparison of machine learning based methods for residential load forecasting. In: 2019 Electric Power Quality and Supply Reliability Conference (PQ) & 2019 Symposium on Electrical Engineering and Mechatronics, PQ SEEM 2019, pp. 1–4 (2019). https://doi.org/10.1109/PQ.2019.8818267

21. Bouktif, S., Fiaz, A., Ouni, A., Serhani, M.A.: Optimal deep learning LSTM model for electric load forecasting using feature selection and genetic algorithm: comparison with machine learning approaches. Energies **11** (2018). https://doi.org/10.3390/en11071636

22. Dudek, G.: Neural networks for pattern-based short-term load forecasting: a comparative study. Neurocomputing. **205**, 64–74 (2016). https://doi.org/10.1016/j. neucom.2016.04.021
23. García-pedrajas, N., Hervás-Martínez, C., Ortiz-boyer, D.: Cooperative Coevolution of Artificial Neural Network Ensembles for Pattern Classification. IEEE Trans. Neural Netw. Publ. IEEE Neural Netw. Councilt. **9**, 271–302 (2005)
24. Cuncheva, L., Whitaker, C.: Measures of diversity in classifier ensembles. Mach. Learn. **51**, 181–207 (2003). https://doi.org/10.1049/ic:20010105
25. Chandra, A., Chen, H., Yao, X.: Trade-off between diversity and accuracy in ensemble generation. In: Jin, Y. (eds.) Multi-Objective Machine Learning. Studies in Computational Intelligence, vol 16, pp. 429–464. Springer, Heidelberg (2019). https://doi.org/10.1007/3-540-33019-4_19
26. Tumer, K., Ghosh, J.: Analysis on decision boundaries in linearly combined neural classifiers. Pattern Recognit. **29**, 341–348 (1996)
27. Liapis, C.M., Karanikola, A., Kotsiantis, S.: An ensemble forecasting method using univariate time series COVID-19 data. In: ACM International Conference Proceeding, vol. S, pp. 50–52 (2020). https://doi.org/10.1145/3437120.3437273
28. Nti, I.K., Adekoya, A.F., Weyori, B.A.: A comprehensive evaluation of ensemble learning for stock-market prediction. J. Big Data **7**(1), 1–40 (2020). https://doi.org/10.1186/s40537-020-00299-5
29. Kankanala, P., Member, S., Das, S., Pahwa, A.: ADABOOST+: an ensemble learning approach for estimating weather-related outages in distribution systems. IEEE Trans. Power Syst. **29**, 359–367 (2014)
30. Mendes-Moreira, J., Soares, C., Alipio, M.J., De Sousa, J.F.: Ensemble approaches for regression: a survey. ACM Comput. Surv. **45**, (2012). https://doi.org/10.1145/2379776.2379786
31. Wang, L., Mao, S., Wilamowski, B.M., Nelms, R.M.: Ensemble learning for load forecasting. IEEE Trans. Green Commun. Netw. **4**, 616–628 (2020). https://doi.org/10.1109/TGCN.2020.2987304
32. Tang, L., Yi, Y., Peng, Y.: An ensemble deep learning model for short-term load forecasting based on ARIMA and LSTM. 2019 IEEE International Conference on Communications, Control, and Computing Technologies for Smart Grids, SmartGridComm 2019, pp. 1–6 (2019). https://doi.org/10.1109/SmartGridComm.2019.8909756
33. Li, J., et al.: A novel hybrid short-term load forecasting method of smart grid using MLR and LSTM neural network. IEEE Trans. Ind. Informat. **17**, 2443–2452 (2021). https://doi.org/10.1109/TII.2020.3000184
34. Li, Y., Che, J., Yang, Y.: Subsampled support vector regression ensemble for short term electric load forecasting. Energy. **164**, 160–170 (2018). https://doi.org/10.1016/j.energy.2018.08.169
35. Von Krannichfeldt, L., Wang, Y., Hug, G.: Online ensemble learning for load forecasting. IEEE Trans. Power Syst. **36**, 545–548 (2021). https://doi.org/10.1109/TPWRS.2020.3036230
36. Dudek, G.: Short-term load forecasting using random forests. Adv. Intell. Syst. Comput. **323**, 821–828 (2015). https://doi.org/10.1007/978-3-319-11310-4_71
37. Papadopoulos, S., Karakatsanis, I.: Short-term electricity load forecasting using time series and ensemble learning methods. In: 2015 IEEE Power Energy Conference Illinois, PECI 2015. 1–6 (2015). https://doi.org/10.1109/PECI.2015.7064913
38. IPTT Energy System Load. https://www.data.gov.gr/datasets/admie_realtimescadasystemload/

39. Drucker, H.: Improving regressors using boosting techniques. In: Proceedings of the Fourteenth International Conference on Machine Learning, pp. 107–115 (1997)

40. Wipf, D., Nagarajan, S.: A new view of automatic relevance determination. In: Platt, J., Koller, D., Singer, Y., Roweis, S. (eds.) Advances in Neural Information Processing Systems. Curran Associates, Inc., Red Hook(2008)

41. Prokhorenkova, L., Gusev, G., Vorobev, A., Dorogush, A.V., Gulin, A.: CatBoost: unbiased boosting with categorical features arXiv: 1706. 09516v5 [cs. LG], 1–23. 20 Jan 2019

42. Breiman, L., Friedman, J.H., Olshen, R.A., Stone, C.J.: Classification and Regression trees. Routledge, New York (2017)

43. Zou, H., Hastie, T.: Regularization and variable selection via the elastic net. J. R. Stat. Soc. Ser. B Stat. Methodol. **67**, 301–320 (2005). https://doi.org/10.1111/j.1467-9868.2005.00503.x

44. Geurts, P., Ernst, D., Wehenkel, L.: Extremely randomized trees. Mach. Learn. **63**, 3–42(2006). https://doi.org/10.1007/s10994-006-6226-1

45. Chen, T., He, T., Benesty, M., Khotilovich, V., Tang, Y., Cho, H., et al.: Xgboost: extreme gradient boosting. R Packag. version 0.4-2. 1, 1–4 (2015)

46. Friedman, J.H.: Greedy function approximation: a gradient boosting machine. Ann. Stat. **29**, 1189–1232 (2001). https://doi.org/10.1214/aos/1013203451

47. Hampel, F.R., Ronchetti, E.M., Rousseeuw, P.J., Stahel, W.A.: Robust Statistics: The Approach Based on Influence functions. John Wiley & Sons, New York (2011)

48. Devroye, L., Gyorfi, L., Krzyzak, A., Lugosi, G.: On the strong universal consistency of nearest neighbor regression function estimates. Ann. Stat. **22**, (2007). https://doi.org/10.1214/aos/1176325633

49. Vovk, V.: Kernel Ridge Regression. In: Schölkopf, B., Luo, Z., Vovk, V. (eds.) Empirical Inference: Festschrift in Honor of Vladimir N. Vapnik, pp. 105–116. Springer, Berlin (2013). https://doi.org/10.1007/978-3-642-41136-6

50. Efron, B., Hastie, T., Johnstone, I., Tibshirani, R.: Least angle regression. Ann. Stat. **32**, 407–499 (2004). https://doi.org/10.1214/009053604000000067

51. Tibshirani, R.: Regression shrinkage and selection via the Lasso. J. R. Stat. Soc. Ser. B. **58**, 267–288 (1996). https://doi.org/10.1111/j.2517-6161.1996.tb02080.x

52. Fan, J., Ma, X., Wu, L., Zhang, F., Yu, X., Zeng, W.: Light gradient boosting machine: an efficient soft computing model for estimating daily reference evapotranspiration with local and external meteorological data. Agric. Water Manag. **225**, 105758 (2019). https://doi.org/10.1016/j.agwat.2019.105758

53. Seber, G.A.F., Lee, A.J.: Linear Regression Analysis. John Wiley & Sons, New York (2012)

54. Murtagh, F.: Multilayer perceptrons for classification and regression. Neurocomputing **2**, 183–197 (1991). https://doi.org/10.1016/0925-2312(91)90023-5

55. Rubinstein, R., Zibulevsky, M., Elad, M.: Efficient implementation of the K-SVD algorithm using batch orthogonal matching pursuit. CS Tech. 1–15 (2008)

56. Crammer, K., Dekel, O., Keshet, J., Shalev-Shwartz, S., Singer, Y.: Online passive-aggressive algorithms. J. Mach. Learn. Res. **7**, 551–585 (2006)

57. Breiman, L.: Random Forests. Mach. Learn. **45**, 5–32 (2001). https://doi.org/10.1017/CBO9781107415324.004

58. Choi, S., Kim, T., Yu, W.: Performance evaluation of RANSAC family. In: Proceedings of the British Machine Vision Conference, BMVC 2009, 7–10 September 2009, pp. 1–12 (2009)

59. Marquardt, D.W., Snee, R.D.: Ridge regression in practice. Am. Stat. **29**, 3–20 (1975). https://doi.org/10.1080/00031305.1975.10479105

60. Smola, A. j., Schölkopf, B.: A tutorial on support vector regression. Stat. Comput. **14**, 199–222 (2004)
61. Dang, X., Peng, H., Wang, X., Zhang, H.: The Theil-Sen Estimators in a Multiple Linear Regression Model. Manuscript, pp. 1–30 (2009)
62. Ali, M.: PyCaret: An open source, low-code machine learning library in Python. https://pycaret.org/
63. Liapis, C.M., Karanikola, A., Kotsiantis, S.: A multi-method survey on the use of sentiment analysis in multivariate financial time series forecasting. Entropy. **23**, 1603 (2021)
64. Friedman, M.: The use of ranks to avoid the assumption of normality implicit in the analysis of variance. J. Am. Stat. Assoc. **32**, 675–701 (1937). https://doi.org/10.1080/01621459.1937.10503522
65. Dunn, O.J.: Multiple Comparisons Among Means. J. Am. Stat. Assoc. **56**, 52 (1961). https://doi.org/10.2307/2282330

Machine Learning Techniques for Regression in Energy Disaggregation

Christos Konstantopoulos$^{(\boxtimes)}$, Spyros Sioutas, and Konstantinos Tsichlas

Department of Computer Engineering and Informatics, University of Patras,
Patras, Greece
chris.konstanto@upatras.gr, {sioutas,ktsichlas}@ceid.upatras.gr

Abstract. Non-Intrusive Load Monitoring (NILM) or Energy disaggregation may be the holy grail of energy efficiency. The impact of energy disaggregation at the commercial level of home customers is the increased utility customer engagement and the reduced energy usage. The goal at this level is to itemize the consumer's energy bill, analyze the energy usage and cost per household appliance and make personalized and prioritized energy savings recommendations. All these should be viable through a single sensor per household that monitors the total energy consumption and other related quantities. Energy disaggregation is a set of computational approaches for extracting end-use appliance level data from an aggregate energy signal without any plug-level sensors. In the present work, we used a smart meter designed by Meazon S.A. to monitor the energy consumption of a house for 70 days and use basic machine learning methods for regression. To this end, we use an extensive set of features to train our models apart from using only active power. Furthermore, we make comparisons with respect to accuracy and training time between Decision Tree, Random Forest and k-NN machine learning methods.

Keywords: NILM · Energy disaggregation · Supervised machine learning · Decision Tree · Random Forest · k-NN

1 Introduction

Non-Intrusive Load Monitoring (NILM), also referred to as Energy Disaggregation, was firstly introduced by George W.Hart, Ed Kern and Fred Schweppe in the early 1980s. Household energy consumption signals are analyzed and decomposed into various sub-signals, which correspond to the energy consumption of individual appliances. The difficulties arising in this problem involve the existence of multiple sources of uncertainty, such as "noise" present in the background, multiple devices with almost the same energy consumption and similar behavior as well as appliances with complex energy profiles (e.g., multiple states).

The problem of energy disaggregation can be formulated as follows [1]:

$$X_t = \sum_{i=1}^{N} y_t^i + \sigma(t)$$

© IFIP International Federation for Information Processing 2022
Published by Springer Nature Switzerland AG 2022
I. Maglogiannis et al. (Eds.): AIAI 2022, IFIP AICT 646, pp. 356–366, 2022.
https://doi.org/10.1007/978-3-031-08333-4_29

The term $\sigma(t)$ represents devices which contribute to the total consumption at time t but are not taken into account as well as the background noise. The set $X = \{X_1, X_2, ..., X_T\}$ includes the central consumption of N total devices at different time instances $t = \{1, 2, ..., T\}$. Therefore, the objective is to find the contribution y_t^i of the i-th device separately, where $i \in \{1, 2, ..., T\}$.

NILM is constantly gaining attention due to the development of smart grids as well as the development of cheap smart meters with enhanced capabilities. This is also due to the undeniable advantages of NILM allowing us to face certain challenges. Among them the following can be distinguished [15,16]:

- **Detailed information about consumption:** the main advantage for customers is that the analytical energy consumption will allow them to adopt an energy saving behavior. In addition, real-time information on running devices could be a useful tool, i.e., provide reminders to turn off certain devices before consumers leave home, especially those that are likely to cause serious damage or those that require excessive energy.
- **Separate device power consumption:** This allows the consumers to identify the devices that consume the most energy in their home and in general the contribution of each device in the total energy consumption. In fact, [17] estimates savings of 9% to 20% by implementing an energy consumption strategy based on these power analytics.
- **Detection of dysfunctional devices:** a precise device usage archive is useful for checking device status and detecting faulty devices.
- **Illegal load detection:** detection of abnormal loads in households is more accurate and can be used to report potential energy theft in public and private buildings.
- **Environmental intelligence**: allows for other detection approaches without the need to apply new sensors. Instead of turning all devices into smart devices, which is very expensive and not environment-friendly, a single smart meter can provide the necessary information to implement various policies.

1.1   Impact of NILM

Many studies demonstrate the impact of NILM on consumption behavior [2]. This research has shown a potential saving (theoretically) of 15% in energy consumption. However, a later analysis of 36 studies over 15 years [3] shows that it is possible to influence people's decision to reduce their consumption by up to 12%, providing real-time information or even daily or weekly information as depicted in Fig. 1.

Even though the first commercialization of a NILM system was done in 1996 by the company Enetics Inc, the generalized use of the NILM system remains low, as the process is time-consuming, costly due to the difficulties in installation but also highly inaccurate on a larger scale. For these reasons, NILM is still considered unreliable, which prevents its widespread adoption. Nevertheless, there are many start-ups and companies that try to commercialize NILM.

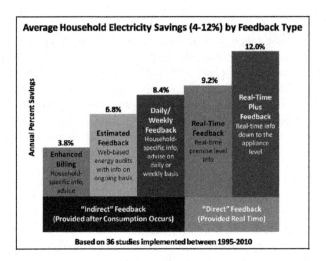

Fig. 1. Analysis of the impact of different feedback methods on behavior change [3]

1.2 Our Contributions

In this paper, we process the data generated by a smart meter (designed by Meazon S.A.) that was installed in the central electricity switchboard of a house. Our goal is to identify the appliances that operate in each time instance and compute the total energy consumed by each appliance. To this end, experiments are carried out using three different machine learning techniques for energy disaggregation from the aggregate signal, which are detailed in Sect. 4. Our contribution lies in the use of a set of features to train our models rather than using only active power. This set contains "Active Power", "Angle between V and I", "Reactive Power" and "Crest Factor". Our goal is to measure and compare the accuracy of the predictions of the methods as well as their performance. After the evaluation of the above experiments with the usual metrics in the Regression field (MSE, MAE, RMSE), an attempt was made to compare these methods in terms of their effectiveness and efficiency.

2   Related Work

Many different algorithmic approaches have been used for NILM that contain among others machine learning, signal processing and deep learning methods with artificial neural networks. The latter are increasingly being used as they have proven their effectiveness in various settings. Initially, one of the most used techniques are different variants of Hidden Markov models (HMMs) such as [4,17,18,20], presenting clearly satisfactory results. Other approaches include signal processing techniques (Dynamic Time Warping) [5,5,21], and Graph Signal Processing [6,7].

Machine learning techniques have been extensively used, such as Decision Trees [21], Random Forests [8,22] or even genetic algorithms like [9,19,23–25]. In addition, Support Vector Machines have been used in [11,26] and in [10]. In [11], the authors experimented with k-NN and Naive-Bayes [10]. Convolutional Neural Networks (CNN) and Recurrent Neural Networks (RNN) have also been used as in [12–14].

Our paper is structured as follows. In Sect. 3 we discuss the dataset and in Sect. 4 we discuss our experimental setup and our methodology with respect to the experimental evaluation. In Sect. 5, we provide our experimental findings while we conclude in Sect. 6.

3   Data Preprocessing

The sampling rate of the smart meter is at 1Hz. In Fig. 2, we observe a sample of the energy consumption (60 min) of all the appliances in the house as well as of the energy consumption of the boiler and the oven separately.

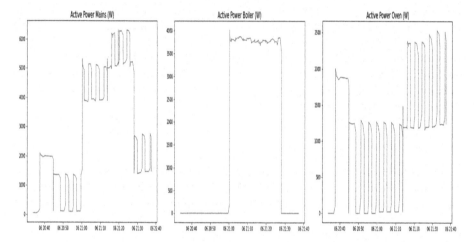

Fig. 2. Energy consumption of appliances from 06/06/21 20:40 to 06/06/21 21:40

The data set includes NaN (Not a Number) values at many positions. In order for the models to be able process the data, it's necessary to solve this missing values problem. We tried three different approaches, at first by replacing NaN with zero values, then with the mean value of each column and at last with the median of each column. The results of the algorithms were almost the same in all three cases so we adopted the median approach. The reason that all methods had the same effect was that the NaN values were existent for very small time intervals, and thus their impact on the effectiveness was non-observable.

The dataset has 2.539.386 measurements (rows) that correspond to 70 days, and dimension of 12 (columns) that correspond to the 3 appliances (mains, oven and boiler) with 4 features each. We manually split the dataset into training, test and validation. The training set has 1.523.632 measurements, the validation set has 507.877 and the test data has 507.877 measurements.

4   Experimental Results

The experiments were performed on a 64-bit operating system with an Intel Core i7-10700 processor and with 16 GB RAM.

We are setting the values of the main consumption on the X variable and the data from the boiler (or oven) on the Y. In order to improve the effectiveness of the algorithms and select the best possible classifiers, some tuning experiments were performed in order to achieve the maximum possible performance. The behavior of each machine learning method is determined by certain parameters.

The tuning experiments aim at selecting the most appropriate values for these parameters, which are evaluated on the basis of evaluation metrics and aim to extract the best prediction model of each algorithm. In addition, to avoid overfitting, the cross-fold validation method is used, which is a sampling process used to evaluate machine learning models in a limited data sample. The basic parameter tested in the DT and RF methods is minimum samples split, which specifies the minimum number of samples needed to separate a node. A range with different values for this parameter was initialized for each method. We execute a repeated procedure and as result we have a unique classifier for each different value of minimum sample split. The best classifier is the one with the lowest value of the evaluation metrics.

4.1   Decision Tree

For DT, the range of values for minimum samples split was between 2 and 400 with step 5. Afterwards, we use the best estimator in order to make predictions and the results are shown in Fig. 3. The performance of the model is observed through graphs, comparing the actual values of the oven consumption (blue line) with those predicted by the model (red line).

In general, the model's predictions are successful and for long time intervals they match the actual consumption, but in some other time intervals the model does not perform well. This may be the result of the complicated behavior of the specific device.

In the next experiment the same model is far more accurate for the boiler as it is confirmed by Fig. 4. As we notice, the model's predictions are quite successful and they match the actual consumption. The first diagram of Fig. 4 depicts the predicted consumption for a complete operation cycle of the appliance (from ON state until OFF state). In the second diagram we can observe in more detail the predicted consumption versus the real consumption during the operation of the boiler (this is why we use a different scale on the y axis). The model is highly accurate and generally follows the changes of the real consumption.

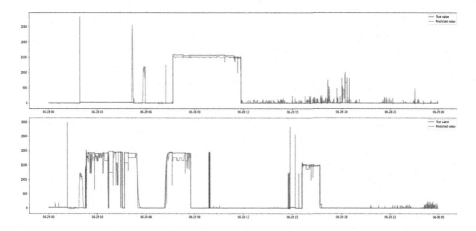

Fig. 3. Real vs Predicted consumption of Decision Trees for the oven.

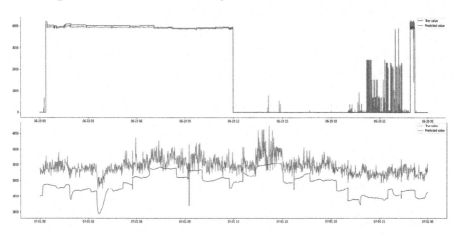

Fig. 4. Real vs Predicted consumption of Decision Trees for the boiler.

4.2   Random Forest

The same set of experiments were also conducted for a Random Forest-based regressor. The only difference is the chosen range of the minimum sample split variable. It is set between 2 and 30 with step 2 for efficiency reasons.

Figure 5 depicts the results of regression with the RF model for the oven. The model's predictions are successful in general and match the actual consumption in many cases. The results are almost the same with the DT model, although we set a lower value for minimum samples split.

Figure 6 presents the experimental results for the boiler. The model's predictions are quite successful and they match to a great extent the actual consumption. The first diagram of Fig. 6, depicts the predictions for the whole operation cycle of the boiler (from the ON state until OFF state). In the second diagram

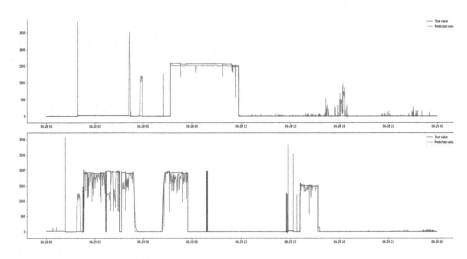

Fig. 5. Real vs Predicted consumption of Random Forest for the oven.

it is depicted in greater detail the predicted versus the actual consumption when the boiler is operating.

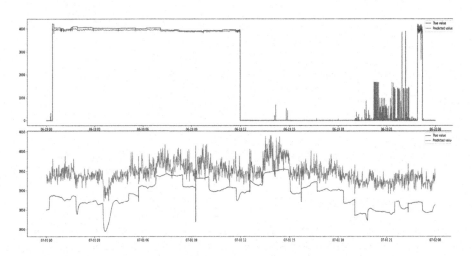

Fig. 6. Real vs Predicted consumption of Random Forest for the boiler.

4.3 k-NN

The tuning of the k-NN regressor is related to the number of neighbors. The range of k value is ranging between 2 and 30. Each value returns a different classifier/estimator and we keep the best one by calculating their RMSE value. The best value for the oven is $k = 29$. The results of this model for the oven are depicted in Fig. 7 and for the boiler in Fig. 8. The k-NN model performs similarly to the previously two models. The results for the boiler are better as expected, although the best results were achieved by using $k = 20$ neighbors.

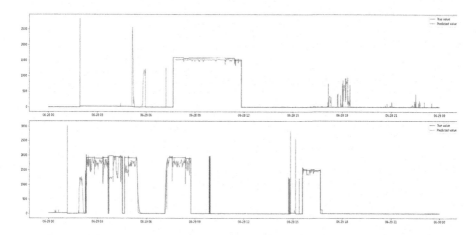

Fig. 7. Real vs Predicted consumption of k-NN for the oven.

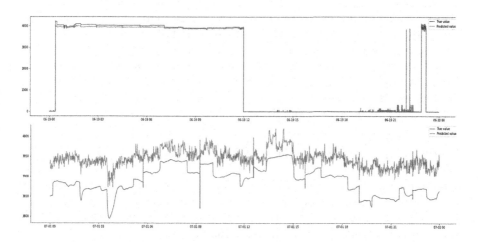

Fig. 8. Real vs Predicted consumption of k-NN for the boiler.

5   Results and Performance

In this section we present the performance of our models in terms of the Mean-Square-Error (MSE), Mean-Average-Error (MAE) and Rooted-Mean-Square-Error (RMSE). In addition, the execution time of tuning, training and regression are reported. In Table 1 we provide the error measures for the oven while in Table 2 we provide the error measures for the boiler.

Table 1. Performance: Decision Tree vs Random Forest vs *k*-NN (Oven)

Oven application			
Metrics	DT	RF	k-NN
MSE	878.13	882.89	1860.53
MAE	3.25	2.88	3.91
RMSE	29.63	29.71	43.13

Table 2. Performance: Decision Tree vs Random Forest vs *k*-NN (Boiler)

Boiler application			
Metrics	DT	RF	k-NN
MSE	184.03	179.42	202.8
MAE	1.44	1.43	1.12
RMSE	13.57	13.39	14.24

DT and RF are superior to *k*-NN, concerning the case of the oven as it can be seen from Table 1. The differences between DT and RF is almost insignificant with respect to accuracy. In the case of the boiler, all three models have the almost the same behavior with the RF marginally outperforming the others. With respect to execution time, DT is significantly faster than RF and *k*-NN for both appliances. In the case of the oven, DT requires 18 min and 7 s to train in contrast to RF, which needs 1 h, 16 min and 46 s, and *k*-NN, which is the slowest method, requiring 28 h and 15 min. The same holds for the case of the boiler where DT requires 21 min and 10 s, RF requires 1 h, 39 min and 34 s, and the *k*-NN requires 28 h and 6 min.

6   Conclusions and Future Work

In the present work, we study the regression problem for energy disaggregation in a real-world dataset. More precisely, we used a smart meter to collect measurements related to the aggregate consumption of a household. Three different supervised machine learning methods are applied: 1) Decision Tree, 2) Random Forest and 3) *k*-NN. Our main goal and the significant difference to the existing literature, is that we take advantage of a set of automatically (by the smart meter) generated features to train our models. In particular, we do not only use active power data, but our models are also trained with "Angle between *V* and *I*", "Reactive Power" and "Crest Factor" features. Our findings indicate that regression in energy disaggregation is possible and these features enhance the accuracy of our models. The experimental comparison shows that DT and RF are far more accurate than *k*-NN, although the differences between them seems to be insignificant. Concerning the training time, DT is the superior method, outperforming RF and *k*-NN.

This research constitutes a first step towards a more profound understanding of regression in energy disaggregation. In the future, we intend to focus on extensive experimental evaluation for deep learning methods and more specifically with Neural Networks. Our main focus is to make use of CNNs and RNNs.

Acknowledgements. This research has been co-financed by the European Regional Development Fund of the European Union and Greek national funds through the Operational Program Competitiveness, Entrepreneurship and Innovation, under the call RESEARCH - CREATE - INNOVATE (project code:T2E DK-00127)».

References

1. Anthony, F., et al.: A Survey on Non-Intrusive Load Monitoring Methodies and Techniques for Energy Disaggregation Problem. arXiv:abs/1703.00785 (2017)
2. Fischer, C.: Feedback on household electricity consumption: a tool for saving energy? Energy Effi. **1**, 79–104 (2008). https://doi.org/10.1007/s12053-008-9009-7
3. Karen, E.-M., Kat, D., John, L.: Advanced metering initiatives and residential feedback programs: a meta-review for household electricity-saving opportunities. American Council for an Energy-Efficient Economy (2010)
4. Kolter, J., Johnson, M.: REDD: A Public Data Set for Energy Disaggregation Research. Artificial Intelligence, p. 25 (2011)
5. Liu, B., Luan, W., Yu, Y.: Dynamic time warping based non-intrusive load transient identification. Appl. Energy **195**, 634–645 (2017). https://doi.org/10.1016/j.apenergy.2017.03.010
6. Zhao, B., Stankovic, L., Stankovic, V.: On a training-less solution for non-intrusive appliance load monitoring using graph signal processing. IEEE Access **4**, 1784–1799 (2016). https://doi.org/10.1109/ACCESS.2016.2557460
7. He, K., Stankovic, L., Liao, J., Stankovic, V.: Non-intrusive load disaggregation using graph signal processing. IEEE Trans. Smart Grid **9**(3), 1739–1747 (2018). https://doi.org/10.1109/TSG.2016.2598872
8. Schirmer, P.A., Mporas, I.: Statistical and electrical features evaluation for electrical appliances energy disaggregation. Sustainability **11**, 3222 (2019). https://doi.org/10.3390/su11113222
9. Hock, D., Kappes, M., Ghita, B.V.: Non-intrusive appliance load monitoring using genetic algorithms. IOP Conf. Ser. Mater. Sci. Eng. **366**, 012003 (2018). https://doi.org/10.1088/1757-899X/366/1/012003
10. Yang, C.C., Soh, C.S., Yap, V.V.: A systematic approach in appliance disaggregation using k-nearest neighbours and native Bayes classifiers for energy efficiency. Energ. Effi. **11**(1), 239–259, 012003 (2017). https://doi.org/10.1007/s12053-017-9561-0
11. Altrabalsi, H., Stankovic, V., Liao, J., Stankovic, L.: Low-complexity energy disaggregation using appliance load modelling. AIMS Energy **4**(1), 1–21, 012003 (2016). https://doi.org/10.3934/energy.2016.1.1
12. Jack, K., William, K.: Neural NILM: Deep Neural Networks Applied to Energy Disaggregation (2015). https://doi.org/10.1145/2821650.2821672

13. Xia, M., Liu, W., Wang, K., Xu, Z., Xu, Y.: Non-intrusive load disaggregation based on deep dilated residual network. Electric Power Syst. Res. **170**, 277–285, 012003 (2019). https://doi.org/10.1016/j.epsr.2019.01.034
14. Kim, J., Le, T.-T.-H., Kim, H.: Nonintrusive load monitoring based on advanced deep learning and novel signature. Comput. Intell. Neurosci. **2017**, 1–22, 012003 (2017). https://doi.org/10.1155/2017/4216281
15. Revuelta, H.J., et al.: Non Intrusive Load Monitoring (NILM): A State of the Art. PAAMS (2017)
16. Behzad, N., Sadaf, M., Fabio, R.: Data Analytics for Energy Disaggregation: Methods and Applications (2018). https://doi.org/10.1016/B978-0-12-811968-6.00017-6
17. Kim, H., Marwah, M., Arlitt, M., Lyon, G., Han, J.: Unsupervised disaggregation of low frequency power measurements. Proc. SIAM Conf. Data Mining. **11**, 747–758, 012003 (2011). https://doi.org/10.1137/1.9781611972818.64
18. Mingjun, Z., Nigel, G., Charles, S.: Signal Aggregate Constraints in Additive Factorial HMMs, with Application to Energy Disaggregation. Advances in Neural Information Processing Systems, vol. 4 (2014)
19. Zhang, G., Wang, G., Farhangi, H., Palizban, A.: Residential electric load disaggregation for low-frequency utility applications. In: 2015 IEEE Power and Energy Society General Meeting, pp. 1–5 (2015). https://doi.org/10.1109/PESGM.2015.7286502
20. Parson, O., Ghosh, S., Weal, M., Rogers, A.: Using hidden Markov models for iterative non-intrusive appliance monitoring. Neural Information Processing Systems workshop on Machine Learning for Sustainability, Sierra Nevada, Spain (2011)
21. Georgia, E., Lina, S., Vladimir, S.: Power disaggregation of domestic smart meter readings using dynamic time warping. In: ISCCSP 2014–2014 6th International Symposium on Communications, Control and Signal Processing, Proceedings, pp. 36–39 (2014). https://doi.org/10.1109/ISCCSP.2014.6877810
22. Gong, F., Liu, C., Jiang, L., Li, H., Lin, J.Y., Yin, B.: Load disaggregation in non-intrusive load monitoring based on random forest optimized by particle swarm optimization. In: 2017 IEEE Conference on Energy Internet and Energy System Integration (EI2), pp. 1–6 (2017). https://doi.org/10.1109/EI2.2017.8245609
23. Dominik, E., Anita, S., Wilfried, E.: Evolving Non-Intrusive Load Monitoring (2013). https://doi.org/10.1007/978-3-642-37192-9_19
24. Baranski, M., Voss, J.: Genetic algorithm for pattern detection in NIALM systems. In: 2004 IEEE International Conference on Systems, Man and Cybernetics (IEEE Cat. No.04CH37583), vol. 4, pp. 3462–3468 (2004). https://doi.org/10.1109/ICSMC.2004.1400878
25. Dominik, E., Wilfried, E.: EvoNILM -evolutionary appliance detection for miscellaneous household appliances. In: GECCO 2013 - Proceedings of the 2013 Genetic and Evolutionary Computation Conference Companion (2013). https://doi.org/10.1145/2464576.2482733
26. Kenneth, B.S.: Model-Driven Analytics of Energy Meter Data in Smart Homes (2014)

Evolutionary/Biologically Inspired Modeling and Brain Modeling

Biologically Plausible Complex-Valued Neural Networks and Model Optimization

Ryan Yu[1]([envelope]), Andrew Wood[1], Sarel Cohen[3], Moshick Hershcovitch[2], Daniel Waddington[2], and Peter Chin[1]

[1] Boston University, Boston, MA 02215, USA
{ryu1,aewood,spchin}@bu.edu
[2] IBM Research, Cambridge, USA
moshikh@il.ibm.com, daniel.waddington@ibm.com
[3] The Academic College of Tel Aviv-Yaffo, Tel Aviv, Israel
sarelco@mta.ac.il

Abstract. Artificial Neural Networks (ANNs) are thinly based on biological neural pathways. In an ANN, each node computes its activation by applying a non-linearity to a weighted sum of its inputs. While this formulation has been wildly successful for a variety of tasks, it is still a far cry from its biological counterpart, largely due to ANNs lack of phase information during computation. In this paper, we adapt ANNs to operate on complex values which naturally allows the inclusion of phase information during the forward pass. We demonstrate that our complex-valued architecture generally performs better compared to real-valued and other complex-valued networks in similar conditions. Additionally, we couple our model with a biologically inspired form of dimensionality reduction and present our findings on the MNIST and MusicNet data sets.

1 Introduction

Inspired by the brain, the first Artificial Neural Network (ANN), called the *Perceptron* was developed in 1961 [14]. The Perceptron, like a real neuron, computes its output as a function of its input. By studying real neurons, Rosenblatt designed the Perceptron to compute its output (called its *activation*) as a weighted sum of its inputs passed through a step function. Perceptrons were then trained by fitting the coefficients of the weighted sum as well as the bias to data. While Perceptrons performed well on simple tasks, they could not be stacked together which limited their usefulness for more complex tasks.

Through relaxing the step function with differentiable counterparts, the first modern ANN was created. The major benefit of using a differentiable nonlinearity was that ANN nodes were stack-able; solving the previous limitation of the Perceptrion. In general, ANNs are formulated as a graph of nodes with the weights and bias of each node as free parameters. The graph (often called a *computation graph*) is traditionally organized into layers: the nodes of a layer process the activations from nodes at the previous layer, while the first layer processes the input data.

I. Maglogiannis et al. (Eds.): AIAI 2022, IFIP AICT 646, pp. 369–382, 2022.
https://doi.org/10.1007/978-3-031-08333-4_30

ANNs have since risen in popularity and have produced state of the art results for several problems [2,12,18,25,26]. However, while new ANN architectures have been developed since the Perceptron, all architectures are still fundamentally based on the original 1960s s biological approximation. While there has been work on updating ANNs with a more modern understanding of biology, one important observation from biological neurons that does not see explicit representation in their artificial counterparts is neural synchrony. Neural synchrony is a biological phenomenon where neurons learn to fire near-simultaneously. Different degrees of synchronization affect the output of the receiving neuron; highly synchronized input neurons will elicit a stronger response in their target compared to the same number of non-synchronized input neurons. Synchronization of artificial neurons can be represented and trained using complex-valued neural networks.

In this paper we extend the work of [13] and [20] and present a novel complex-valued ANN architecture inspired by neural synchrony. We demonstrate that our model performs better on two data sets, MNIST and MusicNet, compared to real-valued ANNs. Furthermore, we combine our model with a cortical-stem inspired preprocessing technique called Geometric Multi-Scale Resolution Analysis (GMRA) to improve performance by giving our model the underlying representation of data. We evaluate our performance on the MNIST [6] and MusicNet [19] data sets.

2   Background and Motivation

2.1   Neural Synchrony and Biological Neural Networks

Timing plays a crucial role in Biological Neural Networks (BNNs). A biological neuron accumulates positive charge in its body until it reaches an activation threshold, at which point it will produce an output. The amount of positive charge accumulated is a direct result of the input signals it receives from input neurons. The charge of a neuron will always approach its negative value resting potential; if weak positive stimuli is received, but not enough to cross the activation threshold, this positive charge is "leaked" out of the neuron over a short time period. Therefore the output of the neuron does not only depend on the intensity of the inputs, but also the degree of time-synchronization between the inputs. Different degrees of synchronization in the input will illicit different responses in the neuron [15]. An example can be seen in Fig. 1.

The notion that groups of neurons fire together with respect to time, known as *neural synchrony*, is not a novel concept [15,16,21]. The phenomenon is posited to play a key role in biological information processing. Horn *et al.* provides evidence that without neural synchrony, the brain creates less stable representation of audio stimulus. These fluctuations in representation may contribute to deficits in auditory brain-stem function by negatively impacting how neurons represent complex acoustic sounds. Furthermore, multiple studies found that the cells of certain brain regions were more likely to produce an output if the inputs to it were time synchronized rather than time dispersed [7,17].

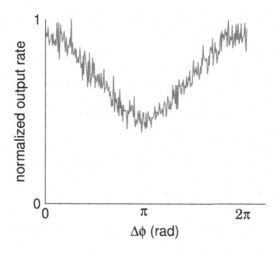

Fig. 1. Taken from [13] displays the normalized output rate of a biological neuron that is stimulated with two rhythmic spike trains as a function of the phase difference between the two stimuli.

2.2   Complex-Valued Neural Networks

Current ANNs operating on real values have no method of internally representing time. Time can be introduced to ANNs via complex numbers. A complex value z, can be defined in two forms. First, $F = x + iy$ where $x, y \in \mathbb{R}$ is the Cartesian form. In the Cartesian form, the real component of z is x, and the imaginary component of z is y. The polar form can be described as $F = (r, \phi)$ where $r, \phi \in \mathbb{R}$. In the polar form, r is known as the magnitude and ϕ is referred to as the phase offset. By treating r as the output strength of the activation and ϕ as the phase difference between neurons, Reichert *et al.* created complex-valued artificial neurons that can process timing information of their inputs similar to biological cells. A visualization of the desired behavior which they were able to mimic via an ANN can be seen in Fig. 1.

Complex-valued neural networks replace some or all of the (originally real-valued) model parameters with complex-valued ones. Fortunately, while there are special considerations that need to be taken with regards to initialization and normalization Trabelsi *et al.* has shown that, with slight modifications, the same learning algorithms can be used to train and test complex-valued networks.

Several studies have already demonstrated the effectiveness of complex-valued neural networks [3,4,9,20]. Gao *et al.* demonstrate that complex-valued neural networks performed better than the rest of the strategies implemented for enhancing radar imaging [4]. Reichert *et al.* proposed a biologically plausible deep network that constructs better data representations through complex values [13].

2.3   Geometric Multi-scale Resolution Analysis (GMRA)

GMRA is a dimensionality reduction technique that is inspired by the cortex. At the microscale, neurons in the cell fire, which induces neural synchrony. Neural synchrony at the macroscale produces patterns, which, when combined with other firings, have been long believed to be the intermediary representation of data [5,15,16,21]. These patterns are described by not only which neurons are firing (a subset of the population), but the activity of the firings as well, meaning that macroscale neural synchrony is a lower-dimensional representation of the data processed at the microscale. Therefore, it is believed that the cortex finds a lower-dimensional representation of data by producing increasingly abstract representations as a function of scale. GMRA mimics this behavior by processing a point cloud at different scales to produce increasingly fine-grained manifolds.

The GMRA algorithm contains three steps to compute manifolds at different scales:

1. It computes a leveled tree decomposition of the manifold into dyadic cells. Dyadic cells have the following properties:
   (a) Each dyadic cell contains a subset of the points that exist within a sphere of fixed radius.
   (b) The children of a dyadic cell contain disjoint subsets of the points contained inside the parent.
   (c) The children of a dyadic cell cover the points inside the parent.
2. It computes a d-dimensional affine approximation (i.e. linear approximations) for each dyadic cell. This approximation represents the basis of each dyadic cell and is a linear piecewise approximation (i.e. the SVD decomposition of the cell's covariance).
3. It computes a sequence of low-dimensional affine difference operators that encode the difference between subsequent levels of the tree (i.e. scales). These difference operators allow efficient querying of the points by scale as well as projection of new points.

As seen in Fig. 2, the linear approximation, called the *scaling function* fit to each group can be queried by starting at scale 0 (the roughest scale), getting the approximation for the query at that scale, and then applying the difference operator (*wavelet correction*) to get the approximation at the next scale (finer scale). Since each level of the tree represents the decomposition of the point cloud at a scale, by walking from the root to the child at the appropriate level, GMRA produces low-dimensional embeddings for each point at arbitrary scales.

By using GMRA as a preprocessing technique, we provide our complex-valued ANNs with low-dimensional representations of the data which are tailored to the embedded manifold.

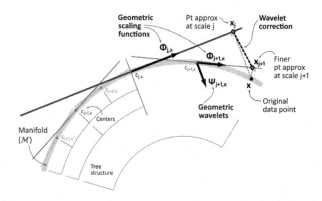

Fig. 2. A visualization of the linear approximation of a point using a basis function at scale j, the approximation at a finer scale $j+1$ and difference operator (geometric wavelet) from scale j to scale $j+1$. This image was taken from [1].

3 Methodology

3.1 Complex-Valued Model

Our model builds on the work from Reichert *et al.*; they define the forward pass of their complex-valued ANN layer using the following equations [13]:

$$t_1 = (|X| \times W) \tag{1}$$
$$t_2 = |X \times W| \tag{2}$$
$$O = \mathcal{F}(r_1 * t_1 + r_2 * t_2) \tag{3}$$

where $X \in \mathbb{C}^{N \times M}$, $W \in \mathbb{R}^{M \times P}$, N is the batch size, M is the dimensionality of the data, and P is the dimensionality of the output of the layer. O is a $N \times P$ output of the layer and is derived via a weighted combination (with coefficients r_1, r_2 typically set to 0.5 each) passed through non-linearity $\mathcal{F}$.

The order of the operations in Expression (1) produces values which are invariant to any phase offsets between inputs and their respective weights; the magnitude of values with opposing phase values are not cancelled, but summed. Expression (2) is the opposite: by performing $X \times W$, any vectors with opposing phases conflict with each other in the multiplication, meaning that t_2 contains the timing information between inputs while t_1 contains the magnitude of the transformed inputs. By sharing weight matrices between the two operations, Reichert *et al.*'s model learns how to process the timing between input firings as well as the magnitude of the inputs firings. With this formulation, Reichert *et al.* were able to reproduce the observations in Fig. 1 using their ANN.

Our model attempts to improve this idea. While Reichert *et al.* define their input to be complex-valued and their free parameters to be real-valued, we define the opposite: $X \in \mathbb{R}^{N \times M}$, $W \in \mathbb{C}^{M \times P}$, and a bias term $b \in \mathbb{R}^{P \times 1}$. Our forward pass, while different, follows the same spirit:

$$t_1 = (X \times |W|) \tag{4}$$

$$t_2 = |X \times W| \tag{5}$$

$$O = \mathcal{F}(r_1 * t_1 + r_2 * t_2 + b) \tag{6}$$

In Reichert *et al.*'s model, each artificial neuron had a unique phase value which is shared amongst all its connections. This models a biological setting where a neuron sends a signal, and it is received by all recipients at the same time. However, a stimulus from a neuron sent to multiple destination neurons simultaneously may not trigger simultaneous responses from the destination neurons. This discrepancy can be caused by a variety of subtle differences, such as difference in distance the signal must traverse or differences in connection strength between sender and receiver. In our formulation, each edge is given the potential for a unique phase value. We believe that this model more accurately captures biology where synaptic processing is nontrivial. Our model is able to express these realistic discrepancies while Reichert *et al.*'s mode cannot. The individual phase values for each artificial synapse is learnt separately via gradient descent.

Additionally, we incorporated layer regularization in our complex-valued models. Regularization is the synthetic counterpart to the biological trait of thresholding. After the neuron fires, it enters a refractory period, which makes it extremely difficult for the neuron to fire again for a short duration, thus limiting the maximum number of times a neuron is able to fire over a period of time. Both of these features can be replicated in an artificial setting by increasing the threshold value of the activation function, and by using bounded activation functions or activity regularizers. We tested with two forms of regularization: batch normalization, and layer regularization. We found that while layer normalization has a net positive effect on our complex ANN, batch normalization destabilizes the model by almost certainly pushing the ANN into a state of either vanishing or exploding gradient. Therefore, our models used layer normalization between every feed forward layer in both complex and real-valued variants.

Lastly, by using real-valued layer outputs and complex-valued weights, we can bypass some of the uncertainties when applying our model to naturally real-valued data. Most complex-valued network studies find success on naturally complex-valued data [2,20], or mixed results on transforming naturally real-valued data into the complex plane [8,10].

3.2 Data Sets

We used two data sets, MNIST [6] and MusicNet [19]. A breakdown of the data sets (preprocessed and in original form) is shown Table 1.

Interestingly, we were able to reduce MNIST into a 11-dimensional representation using GMRA. This is encouraging since there are only 10 labels in MNIST. The 11-dimensional representation was chosen from the roughest scale, which we selected after comparing recovered images against the original representation, which we found to be subjectively adequate. MNIST served as our first proof of concept data set for both high dimensional input (MNIST) and low dimensional input (GMRA-MNIST).

Table 1. A breakdown of the data sets, preprocessed (GMRA-*) and no tag to represent the original data sets.

Name	# examples	Dimensionality	# labels
MNIST	70k	784	10
GMRA-MNIST	70k	11	10
MusicNet	>6000000	4096	84
GMRA-MusicNet	327887	163	84

MusicNet is a data set created by [19]. The data set is composed of recordings of classical music from a variety of instruments, such as piano and violin, and a varying number of performers per recording (e.g. solo, duet, quartet, etc.). There are 330 musical excerpts each ranging from one to three minutes in length. All audio files were re-sampled to 11 KHz. Three music files, with IDs ['2303', '2383', '1819'] were reserved as the test subset, and all other files were randomly split for training and validation during each experiment.

The task associated with this data set is automatic music transcription: the transcription of audio to musical score. To accomplish this, the learning model does not process the entire audio file at once, but instead processes overlapping windows of size 4096. The output of the model is a binary vector of length 84, where a 1 indicates at index k indicates that note k was present at the midpoint of the 4096 length audio clip.

To obtain the GMRA coefficients of MusicNet, we converted the MusicNet data set into a point cloud using the approach mentioned above; however we had trouble deciding an appropriate setting for the stride. With a stride of 1 we generated over 6 million 4096 floating point vectors and quickly ran into a hardware bottleneck. We therefore used the technique of Wood et al. who implemented the GMRA algorithm with a new python package called PyMM [23,24]. PyMM, short for Python Micro MCAS is a python wrapper for a larger library called MCAS (Memory Centric Active Storage) [22]; middleware that provides an interface between applications and Non-Volatile Memory. Non-Volatile Memory is new hardware which occupies memory slots (instead of RAM) and boasts orders of magnitude higher capacity than RAM while running at a third of the speed. As explained by Wood et al., by combining GMRA with PyMM, we can process point clouds significantly larger than with ordinary machines at the cost of run time. For this reason, we settled on a stride of 4096 and generated 327,887 non-overlapping points. These 327,887 points represent approximately a 5% subset of the original data.

In total, the GMRA algorithm took 8 days to process this point cloud and consumed in excess of 500 GB of Non-Volatile Memory. GMRA produced representations at 36 different scales, of which we used the roughest scale as it produced an acceptable reconstruction error, and was also one of the only scales which all the points share the same dimensionality (i.e. different dyadic cells can have different dimensionalities). At the roughest scale, the MusicNet data was reduced from 4096 dimensions to 163 dimensions, a 25× reduction.

3.3 Experiments

Our experiments consisted of training real-valued and complex-valued ANNs on each data set using a cross validation training scheme, and compared their performance averaged over the cross validation splitting. The data set is randomly shuffled and split between training, testing, and validation with percentages of 80%, 10%, and 10% respectively. For MNIST our uniform shuffling procedure roughly preserves the class balancing of the splits, we measured the performance of each model via its accuracy. For MusicNet there were predetermined data points deliberately set aside for validation and testing, as was done in [19,20]. When training a model, we used the Early Stopping [11] mechanism. Our early stopping window was set to three.

MNIST. In our experiments on MNIST, we varied the number of nodes inside a hidden layer. For the MNIST data set, we trained fully connected shallow real-valued ANNs in parallel with complex-valued network counterparts. Our MNIST experiments serve as a proof of concept for both high dimensional data (MNIST) and very low dimensional data (GMRA-MNIST). The data set was selected due to its accessibility, and training speed.

From these experiments we discovered the following limitation of our model: not all operations with complex values are yet supported on the GPU during back propagation. As a result, the training time increases drastically as you scale the network in terms of depth and size per layer. While the limits on the size of our network prevent it from being used in lieu of deep real-valued neural networks, we wanted to compare the performance of our architecture to real-valued architectures of the same size in the context of smaller networks and dimensionality reduction.

MusicNet. There are three main goals for our experiments in MusicNet. First is to explore the performance of our complex-valued layers compared to real-valued layers in a setting that is not single class classification. In MusicNet, multiple notes may be played at the same time, compared to MNIST in which every image belongs only to one class. Second, to explore performance on an inputs other than images. Lastly, to assess our models in conjunction with a dimensionality reduction technique (GMRA) applied to a challenging data set.

To these ends, two sets of experiments were repeated. The first set of experiments used the original MusicNet data points with each input point as a length 4096 vector. Four networks were trained on the original MusicNet files. A complex-valued, shallow classifier with a single hidden layer of dimension 2048 and a real-valued shallow classifier of the same dimensions were trained in parallel and assessed. Then, a network with a single real-valued convolutional layer and complex-valued classifier was trained in parallel with a completely real-valued network of the same specifications.

Our second set of experiments looked at very small shallow networks in conjunction with GMRA reduction on MusicNet. Each network, real-valued and complex-valued, was comprised of a single hidden layer of only 200 nodes. These experiments used a 5% subset of the MusicNet that was converted into GMRA coefficients. As previously stated, the decision to use a small fraction of the original data set was made in order to accommodate for the time constraint associated with GMRA processing.

4   Results and Discussion

4.1   MNIST

Two conclusions can be drawn from our experiments on MNIST. First, our complex-valued model has the potential to out perform real-valued models of the same size. As can be seen in Fig. 3, our complex ANN significantly outperformed its real-valued counterpart for every configuration of a three-layer ANN on both MNIST data sets.

Second, GMRA in conjunction with shallow models can lead to very strong performance with the added benefit of a significantly smaller number of parameters, and a significantly faster training speed. As was stated in Table 1, GMRA-MNIST reduced each point from a 784 length vector, to an 11 point vector. Despite this, both real and complex-valued networks are still able to perform at a high level, as shown in Fig. 3.

Note that performance on GMRA-MNIST is around 10% worse than that of MNIST. We believe that this is an artifact of using the roughest scale embeddings from GMRA. While these embeddings, when recovered into the original image space, were satisfactory to our subjective evaluation, GMRA does induce signal degradation. By using the roughest scale, we invite the accompanying signal loss to influence model performance. Despite using the roughest scale, both models are able to achieve around 90% accuracy with a short early stopping window. On MNIST, our model is statistically better than the corresponding real-valued ANN with 99.9% confidence, and overlaps significantly with its real-valued counterpart on GMRA-MNIST.

4.2   MusicNet

Original MusicNet. We began our experiments for the original MusicNet data set by first training two shallow classifiers using the same training methods (including data split) laid out by [20] and [19]. We found that for the original data set, our shallow complex-valued classifier achieved a significantly higher AP over repeated trials (Table 2).

In order to compare our method with previous shallow networks on MusicNet [19,20], we added a single real-valued convolutional layer to our model. We found that the addition of a single convolutional layer improved Average Precision (AP) for both real and complex-valued classifiers. It remained consistent that the complex-valued classifier out performed the real-valued classifier with the addition of a single convolutional layer (Table 2).

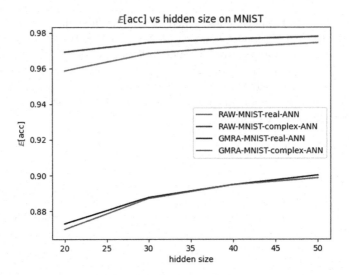

Fig. 3. Expected accuracy averaged over the trials for a given hidden layer size on both MNIST data sets. Note that this image actually includes error bars to show variances, however the variances are on the order of $1e^{-6}$; they cannot be seen without extreme magnification.

We also found that our shallow complex-valued network preformed significantly better than the shallow complex-valued and shallow real-valued network reported in [20]. Our shallow complex-valued classifier with a convolutional layer achieved a 67.5% AP compared to the 66.0 % AP from a complex-valued model of the same dimensions previously reported (Table 2).

A sample reconstruction from our best model ("Shallow Complex w Conv" on Table 2) is presented in Fig. 4 as well as the original ground truth data. By comparing the two figures, we can visually match every note in the ground truth to a counterpart in the reconstruction. The main discrepancies appear to be that

Table 2. The breakdown of our experiments and testing Average Precision (AP) for each network architecture on both original and GMRA MusicNet data sets. All fully connected classifiers had two layers: a hidden layer of size 2048 and an output layer of size 84. The results cited from [20] use the same network dimensions as "Conv + Fully Connected". For GMRA MusicNet experiments, the hidden layer used 200 nodes instead of 2048.

	Real-Valued	Complex-Valued
Original data, fully connected	56 AP %	**64.0 AP %**
Original data, conv + fully connected	65.8 AP %	**67.5 AP %**
Original data, [20]	66.1 AP %	66.0 AP %
GMRA data, fully connected	42.2 AP %	**46.1 AP %**

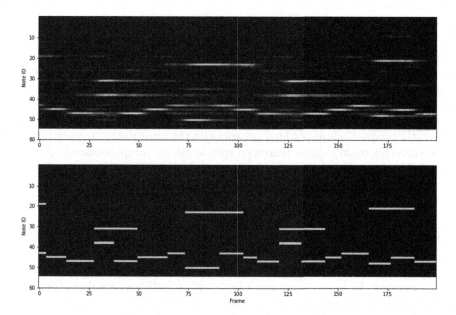

Fig. 4. A sample transcription from our complex-valued shallow model with a convolutional layer compared to the true transcription. (Above) The output of our model for frames 0 to 200, and note IDs 10 to 65. (Below) The actual transcript corresponding to the same frame and notes as above.

the presence of small note artifacts in the reconstruction, where there should be silence, and increased note duration in the reconstruction compared to the truth.

GMRA MusicNet. Our second set of MusicNet experiments use the GMRA coefficients of the subset of MusicNet. For both real-valued and complex-valued classifiers, the AP of real-valued and complex-valued networks decreased by 14 and 18, respectively, when compared to the same architecture trained on the original data points. The decrease in performance can be attributed to two factors. First, using GMRA can result in some information loss; this is seen clearly by the experiments on GMRA-MNIST. The second factor is the difference in training set size. Due to the computational costs of GMRA, this study uses a subset of the MusicNet data set for both raw and GMRA experiments. The subset is comprised of over 327,000 data points and labels. It is approximately 5% of the total number of data points. Despite the large decrease in the number of data points and the dimension reduction of each point from a 4096 length vector to a 163 length vector, both real and complex-valued networks trained on GMRA MusicNet were able to reach over 40 AP%.

Comparing performance between real-valued and complex-valued networks, it remains consistent that complex-valued networks performed significantly better. An interesting observation was found during our experiments: there were multiple instances where the real-valued classifier failed to converge to a meaningful solution. The AP reported in Table 2 for real-valued networks trained on GMRA coefficients was computed for instances where the real-valued network did not fail. Failure to converge was determined by observing the validation AP over several epochs. Instances where validation AP was significantly lower, less than a third, of other experiments, and the validation AP did not improve after 10 epochs, were deemed a failure. Because all validation AP that were categorized as normal did not express high variance, identifying failure experiments was straight-forward. Complex-valued networks on the same data set never failed to converge. This could suggest increased robustness for complex-valued models in terms of their application to dimension reduction problems.

5 Threats to Validity

While our experiments show an improvement between complex and real-valued neural networks, there are a few limiting factors. We recognize that our early stopping window is small, and that with a larger window, real-valued networks might improve. However, there are a few reasons as to why we do not expect a larger window to change the trend.

First, complex ANNs have twice the number of parameters as real-valued ANNs with the same number of nodes. Therefore, we expect that be increasing the window, complex ANNs would benefit more than real-valued networks due to saturating the larger number of parameters. We confirmed this behavior by performing preliminary experiments with a larger window. With an early stopping window size of 10, we observed complex ANNs achieve an expected boost of 5% accuracy on GMRA-MNIST, and 5% on MNIST. On the same data sets with the same increased window, we observed that real-valued ANNs did not improve on average.

Second, since our complex ANNs have twice the number of parameters as real-valued ANNs, our experiments might be viewed as an apples to oranges comparison. However, our complex ANN, despite having twice the number of parameters, first can only express half of the parameter values as its real-valued counterparts, since complex numbers take up the same number of bytes as real values but split those bytes between real and imaginary components. Second, we ran preliminary experiments where we doubled the precision in a real-valued ANN (from 32 to 64 bits per value) and found that this model still performed worse than our complex-valued ANN of the same precision.

6 Conclusion and Future Work

In conclusion, we introduce a novel complex-valued network architecture that has complex-valued weights but has real-valued layer outputs. In order to demonstrate how well our complex-valued models performed, we assessed its metrics on two data sets, MNIST and MusicNet. In addition, we tested the dimension reduction technique, GMRA, used in conjunction with real and complex-valued networks. GMRA was able to greatly reduce the input space, from 784 to 11 in

MNIST and 4096 to 163 in MusicNet. This significantly reduced training time and model size. In both raw and GMRA MNIST and MusicNet, our shallow complex-valued network significantly outperformed a shallow real-valued network of the same parameter count.

Finally, we offer a few extensions to improve our proposed model. The first extension is the application our complex-valued dense architecture to any existing neural network and any data set by replacing the existing network's real-valued classification layer(s). Currently this is not practical for all deep networks. Because certain operations in our implementation lack GPU support, training large networks with the proposed dense layer incurs a large time penalty. An implementation of our architecture which uses multiple real valued weight matrices and GPU supported functions to simulate the behaviour of a complex weight matrix is ideal.

The second extension is to study the results of making complex-valued architecture more similar to our current understanding of biological networks. Biological neurons function in an all-or-nothing manner. If it receives an input above its activation threshold, the neurons fire, otherwise it will not. Artificial neurons will output the sum of its inputs assuming the sum is positive. An implementation of activation thresholding such that a neuron would produce positive output only if it receives multiple strong positive inputs would bring artificial neurons more in line with our current understanding of biology. It would be interesting to observe such an implementation in conjunction with our proposed complex-valued architecture.

References

1. Allard, W.K., Chen, G., Maggioni, M.: Multi-scale geometric methods for data sets II: geometric multi-resolution analysis. Appl. Comput. Harmon. Anal. **32**(3), 435–462 (2012)
2. Cole, E., Cheng, J., Pauly, J., Vasanawala, S.: Analysis of deep complex-valued convolutional neural networks for mri reconstruction and phase-focused applications. Magn. Reson. Med. **86**, 1093–1099 (2021). https://onlinelibrary.wiley.com/doi/10.1002/mrm.28733
3. Dramsch, J., Lüthje, M., Christensen, A.N.: Complex-valued neural networks for machine learning on non-stationary physical data. Comput. Geosci. **146**, 104643 (2021). ISSN 0098–3004. https://doi.org/10.1016/j.cageo.2020.104643
4. Gao, J., Deng, B., Qin, Y., Wang, H., Li, X.: Enhanced radar imaging using a complex-valued convolutional neural network. IEEE Geosci. Remote Sens. Lett. **16**(1), 35–39 (2019). https://doi.org/10.1109/LGRS.2018.2866567
5. Hornickel, J., Kraus, N.: Unstable representation of sound: a biological marker of dyslexia. J. Neurosci. **33**(8), 3500–3504 (2013). ISSN 0270–6474. https://doi.org/10.1523/JNEUROSCI.4205-12.2013, https://www.jneurosci.org/content/33/8/3500
6. LeCun, Y.: The MNIST database of handwritten digits (1998). http://yann.lecun.com/exdb/mnist/

7. Matsumura, M., Chen, D., Sawaguchi, T., Kubota, K., Fetz, E.E.: Synaptic interactions between primate precentral cortex neurons revealed by spike-triggered averaging of intracellular membrane potentials in vivo. J. Neurosci. **16**(23), 7757–7767 (1996). ISSN 0270–6474. https://doi.org/10.1523/JNEUROSCI.16-23-07757.1996, https://www.jneurosci.org/content/16/23/7757

8. Mönning, N., Manandhar, S.: Evaluation of complex-valued neural networks on real-valued classification tasks. CoRR, abs/1811.12351 (2018). http://arxiv.org/abs/1811.12351

9. Mönning, N., Manandhar, S.: Evaluation of complex-valued neural networks on real-valued classification tasks (2018)

10. Popa, C.-A.: Complex-valued convolutional neural networks for real-valued image classification, pp. 816–822 (2017). https://doi.org/10.1109/IJCNN.2017.7965936

11. Prechelt, L.: Early stopping-but when? pp. 55–69 (1998)

12. Purwins, H., Li, B., Virtanen, T., Schlüter, J., Chang, S.-Y., Sainath, T.N.: Deep learning for audio signal processing. CoRR, abs/1905.00078 (2019). http://arxiv.org/abs/1905.00078

13. Reichert, D.P., Serre, T.: Neuronal synchrony in complex-valued deep networks (2014)

14. Rosenblatt, F.: Perceptron simulation experiments. Proc. IRE **48**(3), 301–309 (1960). https://doi.org/10.1109/JRPROC.1960.287598

15. Singer, W.: Neural synchrony: a versatile code for the definition of relations? Neuron **24**, 49–65 (1999)

16. Stanley, G.B.: Reading and writing the neural code. Nat. Neurosci. **16**, 259-263 (2013). https://www.nature.com/articles/nn.3330

17. Stevens, C., Zador, A.: Novel integrate-and-fire-like model of repetitive firing in cortical neurons (1998)

18. Tan, M., Le, Q.V.: Efficientnet: rethinking model scaling for convolutional neural networks. CoRR, abs/1905.11946 (2019). http://arxiv.org/abs/1905.11946

19. Thickstun, J., Harchaoui, Z., Kakade, S.: Learning features of music from scratch (2017)

20. Trabelsi, C., et al.: Deep complex networks, Negar Rostamzadeh (2018)

21. Uhlhaas, P.J., et al.: Neural synchrony in the cortical networks: history, concept and current status. Front. Integr. Neurosci. **3**, 17 (2009)

22. Waddington, D., Dickey, C., Hershcovitch, M., Seshadri, S.: An architecture for memory centric active storage (MCAS). arXiv preprint arXiv:2103.00007 (2021)

23. Waddington, D.G., Hershcovitch, M., Dickey, C.: PYMM: heterogeneous memory programming for python data science. In: PLOS 2021: Proceedings of the 11th Workshop on Programming Languages and Operating Systems, Virtual Event, Germany, 25 October 2021, pp. 31–37. ACM (2021). https://doi.org/10.1145/3477113.3487266

24. Wood, A., et al.: Non-volatile memory accelerated geometric multi-scale resolution analysis. In: 2021 IEEE High Performance Extreme Computing Conference (HPEC), pp. 1–7. IEEE (2021)

25. Wyse, L.: Audio spectrogram representations for processing with convolutional neural networks. In: Workshop on Deep Learning for Music (2017)

26. Xu, Y., Kong, Q., Huang, Q., Wang, W., Plumbley, M.D.: Attention and localization based on a deep convolutional recurrent model for weakly supervised audio tagging. CoRR, abs/1703.06052 (2017). http://arxiv.org/abs/1703.06052

Comparative Study by Using a Greedy Approach and Advanced Bio-Inspired Strategies in the Context of the Traveling Thief Problem

Julia Garbaruk[1]([envelope]) [iD], Doina Logofătu[1]([envelope]) [iD], and Florin Leon[2] [iD]

[1] Frankfurt University of Applied Sciences, Frankfurt am Main, Germany
j.garbaruk@outlook.de, logofatu@fb2.fra-uas.de
[2] Gheorghe Asachi Technical University of Iaşi, Iaşi, Romania
florinleon@tuiasi.ro

Abstract. Traveling Salesman Problem and Knapsack Problem are perhaps the best-known combinatorial optimization problems that researchers have been racking their brains over for many decades. But they can also be combined into a single multi-component optimization problem, the Traveling Thief Problem, where the optimal solution for each single component does not necessarily correspond to an optimal Traveling Thief Problem solution. The aim of this work is to compare two generic algorithms for solving a Traveling Thief Problem independently of the test instance.

Keywords: Traveling Thief Problem · Combinatorial optimization · Evolutionary algorithms

1 Introduction

In real-world economy, we often have to do with different components that influence each other. For example, if we want to reduce transport costs, we can try to avoid empty runs, enter into collaborations with other companies, join transport networks, combine transports or, for example, only arrange removal on certain days of the week in order to purchase larger quantities. This in turn may have negative effects on the availability of the products or on-time delivery to customers. So you can say that different components are always related and that we usually cannot optimize one component without it having a negative impact on others. It is similar with many areas of our everyday life - for example, when we buy food, we usually make sure that it is of high quality on the one hand and that the costs are as low as possible on the other. If we decrease the cost of spending on a product, it is very likely at the expense of quality. Conversely, if we increase our quality standards, the price usually also deteriorates. As you can see, the principles of multi-objective optimization play an important role in our lives.

© IFIP International Federation for Information Processing 2022
Published by Springer Nature Switzerland AG 2022
I. Maglogiannis et al. (Eds.): AIAI 2022, IFIP AICT 646, pp. 383–393, 2022.
https://doi.org/10.1007/978-3-031-08333-4_31

The Traveling Thief Problem (TTP), which was presented by Bonyadi et al. in 2013, is an NP-hard combinatorial optimization problem that combines two well-known subproblems: the Traveling Salesman Problem (TSP) and the Knapsack Problem (KNP). The motivation behind this was to systematically investigate the interactions between two hard component problems and to use this knowledge to solve real-world problems more efficiently [8]. Research over the past few years has shown that there are many ways to resolve a TTP. Most of the publications aimed to solve it by using different types of algorithms: Heuristic Based, Local Search, Coevolution, Evolutionary Algorithm, Ant Colony Optimization etc. But the success of the algorithm used depends very much on the selected test instance. In our work we wanted to introduce two relatively simple, generic algorithms with which one can solve any TTP and produce results relatively quickly.

2   Problem Description

2.1   Traveling Thief Problem

The Traveling Thief Problem [1,2] combines the TSP and the KNP in the following way: The traveling thief can collect items from each city he is visiting. The items are stored in a knapsack carried by him. In more detail, each city π_i provides one item, which could be picked by the thief. z is a binary vector, where each element shows if the item at city j where picked or not.

There is an interaction between the subproblems: The velocity of the traveling thief depends on the current knapsack weight w, which is carried by him. It is calculated by considering all cities, which were visited so far, and summing up the weights of all picked items. The weight at city i given π and z is calculated by:

$$w(i, \pi, z) = \sum_{k=1}^{i} \sum_{j=1}^{m} a_j(\pi_k) w_j z_j \tag{1}$$

The function $a_j(\pi_k)$ is defined for each item j and returns 1 if the item could be stolen at city π_k and 0 otherwise. The current weight of the knapsack has an influence on the velocity. When the thief picks an item, the weight of the knapsack increases and therefore the velocity of the thief decreases. The velocity v is always in a specific range $v = [v_{min}, v_{max}]$ and could not be negative for a feasible solution. Whenever the knapsack is heavier than the maximum weight Q, the capacity constraint is violated. However, to provide also the traveling time for infeasible solutions the velocity is set to v_{min}, if $w > Q$:

$$v(w) = \begin{cases} v_{max} - \frac{w}{Q} \cdot (v_{max} - v_{min}) & \text{if } w \leq Q \\ v_{min} & \text{otherwise} \end{cases} \tag{2}$$

If the knapsack is empty the velocity is equal to v_{max}. Contrarily, if the current knapsack weight is equal to Q the velocity is v_{min}. Furthermore, the traveling time of the thief is calculated by:

$$f(\pi, z) = \sum_{i=1}^{n-1} \frac{d_{\pi_i, \pi_{i+1}}}{v(w(i, \pi, z))} + \frac{d_{\pi_n, \pi_1}}{v(w(n, \pi, z))} \tag{3}$$

The calculation is based on TSP, but the velocity is defined by a function instead of a constant value. This function takes the current weight, which depends on the index i of the tour. The current weight, and therefore also the velocity, will change on the tour by considering the picked items defined by z. In order to calculate the total tour time, the velocity at each city needs to be known. For calculating the velocity at each city the current weight of the knapsack must be given. Since both calculations are based on z and z is part of the knapsack subproblem, it is very challenging to solve the problem to optimality. In fact, such problems are called interwoven systems as the solution of one subproblem highly depends on the solution of the other subproblems.

Here, we leave the profit unchanged to be calculated as in the KNP problem. Finally, the TTP problem is defined by

$$\begin{aligned}
&min\ f(\pi, z) \qquad traveling\ time \\
&max\ g(z) \qquad\qquad profit
\end{aligned}$$

$$f(\pi, z) = \sum_{i=1}^{n-1} \frac{d_{\pi_i, \pi_{i+1}}}{v(w(i, \pi, z))} + \frac{d_{\pi_n, \pi_1}}{v(w(n, \pi, z))}$$

$$g(z) = \sum_{j=1}^{m} z_j b_j \tag{4}$$

$$s.t.\ \pi = (\pi_1, \pi_2, ..., \pi_n) \in P_n$$

$$\pi_1 = 1$$

$$z = (z_1, ..., z_m) \in \mathbb{B}^m$$

$$\sum_{j=1}^{m} z_j w_j \le Q$$

2.2 Test Data (Input)

For our research we have used the test instances of the TTP provided by the organizators of GECCO 2019 (Bi-objective Traveling Thief Competition). They are very versatile and provide all the information needed to construct a Traveling Thief Problem. First, the general parameters such as number of cities or items in the test instance are described. This is followed by a list with the coordinates of all cities as well as a list of profit, weight and the city of each item.

The 9 test instances differ in the following aspects:

- Number of cities (smallest value: 280 cities, highest value: 33810 cities)
- Number of items (smallest value: 279 items, highest value: 338090 items)

- Capacity of Knapsack (smallest value: 25936, highest value: 153960049)
- Knapsack data type (bounded strongly correlated, uncorrelated and similar weights or uncorrelated)

Moreover we have determined that we consider a maximum of 100 solutions in the Pareto front for each test instance.

2.3   Result Format (Output)

For each problem two output files are generated: One file containing the tour and packing plan (*test.x*) and one file containing the time and profit for each solution (*test.f*).

test.x contains for each solution two lines, where the first represents the permutation vector and the second line the packing plan encoded by 0 and 1. The output might look like this:

```
1 2 3 4
0 0 0

1 4 3 2
0 0 0

1 2 3 4
0 0 1

1 4 3 2
1 0 0

1 4 3 2
0 1 0

1 3 2 4
1 0 1

1 2 3 4
0 1 1

1 4 3 2
1 1 0
```

test.f contains the corresponding time and profit separated by space. An example output might look like this:

```
20.0000000000000000  0.0000000000000000
20.0000000000000000  0.0000000000000000
20.9279869067103130  25.0000000000000000
22.0377358490566020  34.0000000000000000
27.3636363636363630  40.0000000000000000
28.5852929784761830  59.0000000000000000
33.1072075335023540  65.0000000000000000
38.9144385026737900  74.0000000000000000
```

3   Algorithms

3.1   Greedy Algorithm

In this approach we solve the two sub-problems separately or independently of each other. First of all, we need a TSP solver. To find the shortest path, we chose the Nearest Neighbor Algorithm, which is a heuristic method from the graph theory. Starting from a node as a starting point, the minimum weighted adjacent edge is selected to the next node. This will be continued successively until all nodes have been combined into a Hamiltonian circle. The result of this is a tour π^*, in our case starting at city 1. As long as the maximum capacity constraint and maximum number of solutions are not violated, items are picked. The $getNextItemGreedily$ method returns the next item which is not picked so far and provides the best $\frac{b_i}{w_i}$ rate. Then the picking decision vector z is combined with π^* and $sym(\pi^*)$ and is added to the set. Finally the resulting Pareto front is returned.

Algorithm 1. Greedy Algorithm

Require: $P \leftarrow$ Traveling Thief Problem
    $\pi^* \leftarrow$ nearestNeighborHeuristic
    $z \leftarrow z^{empty}$
    front $\leftarrow \{F(\pi^*, z), F(sym(\pi^*), z)\}$
    while $\sum_{j=1}^{m} w_j z_j \leq Q$ **and** front.size $<$ max. number of solutions **do**
        $i \leftarrow$ getNextItemGreedily(P, z) ▷ Based on the best profit/weight rate
        $z_i \leftarrow 1$
        add(front, $F(\pi^*, z)$)
        add(front, $F(sym(\pi^*), z)$
    end while
    return front

3.2   Evolutionary Algorithm (NSGA-II)

Evolutionary algorithms are popular approaches to generate Pareto optimal solutions. The main advantage of evolutionary algorithms, when applied to solve

Algorithm 2. Nearest Neighbor Heuristic

$route \leftarrow 1$	▷ route starts at city 1
$j \leftarrow 1$	▷ next city
$l \leftarrow j$	▷ current city

$W \leftarrow \{1, 2, ..., n\} \backslash \{j\}$
while $W \neq \emptyset$ **do**
    Let $j \in W$ such that $c_{lj} = min\{c_{li}|j \in W\}$
    Connect l to j and update the $route$
    $W \leftarrow W \backslash \{j\}$
    $l \leftarrow j$
end while
return route

multi-objective optimization problems, is the fact that they typically generate sets of solutions, allowing computation of an approximation of the entire Pareto front. The algorithm we used for solving the Traveling Thief problem is the NSGA-II.

As usual for evolutionary algorithms all individuals in NSGA-II are factored and added to the population in the beginning. Then each individual gets a rank based on its level of domination and a crowding distance which is used as a density estimation in the objective space. The binary tournament selection compares rank and crowding distance of randomly selected individuals in order to return individuals for the recombination. After executing recombination and mutation the offspring is added to the population. In the end of each generation the population is truncated after sorting it by domination rank and crowding distance.

Non-dominated Sort. The-non dominated sort represents the core component of the whole algorithm. It splits the population into sets of non-dominated solutions and orders them into a hierarchy of non-dominated Pareto fronts. Based on this, the solutions in a Pareto front are assigned a rank. The rank is needed to calculate the fitness of a solution. Solutions with the highest rank (smallest rank number) are considered the fittest.

Crowding Distance. The Crowding Distance provides an estimate of the density of solutions surrounding a solution. The Crowding Distance of a particular solution is the average distance of the two adjacent solutions (along all objective functions (in this case time and profit)). Solutions with higher Crowding Distance are considered good, since it guarantees diversity and spread of solutions.

Tournament Selection. The tournament selection selects randomly two parents from the population. From these two parents, a winner is determined. With the probability p, the parent with the higher fitness will be selected. Accordingly, the worse solution is selected with the probability $1 - p$. It is important to give a worse solution a chance to witness offspring, because otherwise there is a risk of premature convergence because of too strong selective pressure towards best solution.

If the Tournament Selection was done twice, we have two winners, which then produce the offspring.

Recombination. We have to keep in mind that each city in the path may only appear once. This condition applies both to parents and to newly created paths. If a city occurs several times as a result of the recombination and some another city does not occur at all, this must be repaired. We used a simple recombination method that ensures from the outset that each city occurs exactly once. One of the parents ($p1$) inherits a randomly selected area of its path to the child. The rest of the path is populated with the values from the other parent ($p2$). For this, the algorithm iterates through the entire path of $p2$ and check whether the currently viewed city is already included in the child path. If not, it will be added to the next free place in the child path. Of course, the packing plan must also be recombined. To do this, we performed a simple crossover operation at a random point of the packing list. After the recombination of the packing plan, the maximum capacity of the knapsack may have been exceeded. To fix this, randomly selected items are removed from the packing list until the knapsack has reached a permissible weight again.

Mutation. Since each city must be visited exactly once, it makes sense to simply swap two randomly chosen cities. This is possible without any problem, since there is a connection from every city to every other city.

A mutation can also occur in the packing list. We opted for a simple mutation method in which a randomly determined bit that represents an item or rather its status (collected or not collected) is toggled. After the packing plan has been mutated, the maximum capacity of the knapsack may have been exceeded. To fix this, randomly selected items are removed from the packing list until the knapsack has reached a permissible weight again.

4   Experimental Results

We show our test results using the test instance with the following parameters:

- 280 cities
- 279 Items
- Knapsack capacity of 25936

The profit and the weight of the items correlate strongly (the correlation is ignored here because the methods are generic).

Since NSGA-II has more additional parameters, such as mutation rate and population rate, we have also tried various possible combinations of these parameters in order to better compare the results with the greedy approach.

Algorithm 3. Fast Non-dominated Sort

Require: Popualtion P
  for each $p \in P$ **do**
    $S_p = \emptyset$ ▷ S_p: set of solutions that the solution p dominates
    $n_p = 0$ ▷ n_p: nr. of solutions which dominate the solution p
    for each $q \in P$ **do**
      if $p < q$ **then**   ▷ if p dominates q
        $S_p = S_p \cup \{q\}$ ▷ add q to the set of solutions dominated by p
      else if $q < p$ **then**
        $n_p = n_p + 1$ ▷ increment the domination counter of p
      end if
    end for
    if $n_p = 0$ **then**   ▷ p belongs to the first front
      $p_{rank} = 1$
      $F_1 = F_1 \cup \{p\}$
    end if
  end for
  $i = 1$ ▷ initialize the front counter
  while $F_i \neq \emptyset$ **do**
    $Q = \emptyset$ ▷ used to store the members of the next front
    for each $p \in F_i$ **do**
      for each $q \in S_p$ **do**
        $n_q = n_q - 1$
        if $n_q = 0$ **then**   ▷ q belongs to the next front
          $q_{rank} = i + 1$
          $Q = Q \cup \{q\}$
        end if
      end for
    end for
    $i = i + 1$
    $F_i = Q$
  end while
  return $\{F_1, F_2, ...\}$ ▷ return all Pareto fronts in the population

---

Algorithm 4. Crowding Distance Assignment

Require: Front F
  $l \leftarrow |F|$ ▷ number of solutions in the front F
  for each i **do**
    $F[i]_{distance} = 0$ ▷ set the distance to 0 at the beginning
  end for
  for each objective m **do**   ▷ for time and profit
    $F = sort(F, m)$ ▷ sort using each objective value
    $F[0]_{distance} = \infty$ ▷ so that boundary points are always selected
    $F[l - 1]_{distance} = \infty$ ▷ so that boundary points are always selected
    for $i = 1$ **to** $l - 2$ **do**   ▷ for all other points
      $F[i]_{distance} = F[i]_{distance} + (F[i + 1].m - F[i - 1].m)/(f_m^{max} - f_m^{min})$

In our first example we compare the results of the Greedy Algorithm with NSGA-II depending on the population size of the NSGA-II. The appropriate population size is still the subject of discussion. Many different approaches are known: For example, there is the 10x*Dimensions* rule, according to which you get the right number of individuals for the population by multiplying the number of objectve functions by 10. Some others recommend large populations, which should be divided into subpopulations. The population size also does not always have to be static, but could, for example, shrink over time. However, the best way is always to test different population sizes and get a solution tailored to the specific problem and its parameters.

We decided to test different static population sizes, from 20 up to 500. We have set the number of generations to 10,000, since from there the changes take place slower and you can still see the tendency. The mutation rate remained constant at 4%. As you can see in Fig. 1, the results of the NSGA-II increase significantly with increasing population size, but only up to a certain limit. Up to a population size of 100, the rule "the more the better" seems to apply. At a population size of 200, however, it turns out that the results are not getting much better and the range of values is also shrinking as the solutions seem to converge more and more. With a population size of 500, this problem becomes even clearer - the curve that forms the Pareto front is getting very short, which means is that the tours and packing plans are becoming increasingly similar. We therefore consider a population size of ca. 100 to be recommended in this case. Nonetheless, NSGA-II scores significantly worse here than the simple Greedy Algorithm. Not only in relation to the approximation of the Pareto curve to the axes, but also in relation to the range of the solutions. This is noteworthy because Greedy Algorithm only creates a single route using the Nearest Neighbor Algorithm which, as we know, is almost never optimal, while NSGA-II is able to create many different paths. It seems that a single path that has a high probability of getting close to optimum is better than trying to optimize several random paths.

We now consider how the results change when we change the mutation rate of the NSGA-II algorithm. From now on, we use the population size that has been found to be optimal for the respective test case (100).

The present results show that it is definitely advisable to play with the mutation rate. Increasing the mutation rate has an effect similar to increasing the population rate. Above a certain value, however, this has an adverse effect because too many good individuals are rejected, which leads to an overall deterioration in the gene pool. In this test case, the mutation rate should not be more than approx. 30%. We were surprised that such a high mutation rate leads to improved results. Usually a single digit mutation rate is the rule. But here, too, the result of the NSGA-II does not come close to the result of the Greedy Algorithm, which is very astonishing.

In all other test instances, it was also observed that the greedy algorithm delivers better results on balance, regardless of the setting of the population size and the mutation rate (Fig. 2).

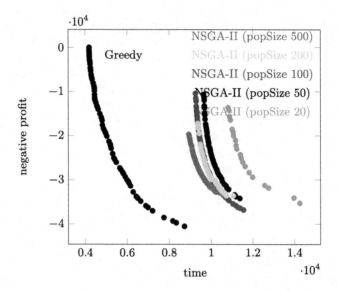

Fig. 1. Results of the NSGA-II for the Traveling Thief Problem depending on the population size after 10,000 generations in contrast to the Greedy Algorithm (test case 1)

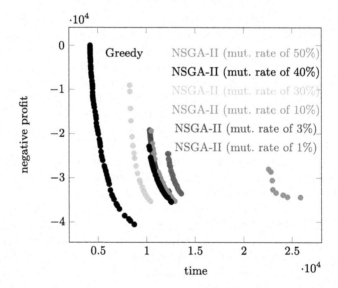

Fig. 2. Results of the NSGA-II for the Traveling Thief Problem depending on the mutation rate after 10,000 generations in contrast to the Greedy Algorithm (test case 1)

5   Conclusion

In this work we compared two different approaches to solving the Traveling Thief Problem - a simple greedy algorithm and an advanced evolutionary algorithm. Surprisingly, the greedy algorithm performed far better, although it can only create a single route for the thief. The advantage of the evolutionary algorithm of creating different paths is likely not to be fully effective because the paths are generated randomly. Given their size, they cannot achieve a satisfactory result, regardless of how the population size and the mutation rate are set.

This is definitely an interesting observation, because it is generally assumed that an evolutionary algorithm can predict the outcome much better than simple heuristic methods. One idea for the future would be to work with an optimized initial population in order to give the algorithm a head start and to take full advantage of its special features. The result of the greedy algorithm could be used for this. In order to generate different routes, one could, for example, choose the second best path from one node to the next at a random point while the path is being created. As result, the following route would change every time and differ from others, but at the same time it would still be much better than a purely randomly generated route.

References

1. Blank, J., Deb, K., Mostaghim, S.: Solving the bi-objective traveling thief problem with multi-objective evolutionary algorithms. In: Trautmann, H., et al. (eds.) EMO 2017. LNCS, vol. 10173, pp. 46–60. Springer, Cham (2017). https://doi.org/10.1007/978-3-319-54157-0_4
2. Bonyadi, M.R., Michalewicz, Z., Barone, L.: The travelling thief problem: the first step in the transition from theoretical problems to realistic problems. In: 2013 IEEE Congress on Evolutionary Computation, pp. 1037–1044. IEEE (2013)
3. Deb, K.: A fast elitist non-dominated sorting genetic algorithm for multi-objective optimization: NSGA-2. IEEE Trans. Evol. Comput. 6(2), 182–197 (2002)
4. Mei, Y., Li, X., Yao, X.: On investigation of interdependence between sub-problems of the travelling thief problem. Soft. Comput. 20(1), 157–172 (2016). https://doi.org/10.1007/s00500-014-1487-2
5. Srinivas, N., Deb, K.: Muiltiobjective optimization using non-dominated sorting in genetic algorithms. Evol. Comput. 2(3), 221–248 (1994)
6. Zamuda, A., Brest, J.: Population reduction differential evolution with multiple mutation strategies in real world industry challenges. In: Rutkowski, L., Korytkowski, M., Scherer, R., Tadeusiewicz, R., Zadeh, L.A., Zurada, J.M. (eds.) EC/-SIDE - 2012. LNCS, vol. 7269, pp. 154–161. Springer, Heidelberg (2012). https://doi.org/10.1007/978-3-642-29353-5_18
7. Garbaruk, J., Logofătu, D.: Convergence behaviour of population size and mutation rate for NSGA-II in the context of the traveling thief problem. In: Nguyen, N.T., Hoang, B.H., Huynh, C.P., Hwang, D., Trawiński, B., Vossen, G. (eds.) ICCCI 2020. LNCS (LNAI), vol. 12496, pp. 164–175. Springer, Cham (2020). https://doi.org/10.1007/978-3-030-63007-2_13
8. Wagner, M., Lindauer, M., Mısır, M., Nallaperuma, S., Hutter, F.: A case study of algorithm selection for the traveling thief problem. J. Heuristics 24(3), 295–320 (2017). https://doi.org/10.1007/s10732-017-9328-y

Exploring the Relationship Between Visual Information and Language Semantic Concept in the Human Brain

Haodong Jing[1,2], Ming Du[1,2], Yongqiang Ma[1,2], and Nanning Zheng[1,2(✉)]

[1] Institute of Artificial Intelligence and Robotics, Xi'an Jiaotong University, Xi'an, Shaanxi, People's Republic of China
{jinghd,x1978626209}@stu.xjtu.edu.cn, musayq@xjtu.edu.cn,
nnzheng@mail.xjtu.edu.cn
[2] National Engineering Laboratory for Visual Information Processing and Applications, Xi'an Jiaotong University, Xi'an, Shaanxi, People's Republic of China

Abstract. Functional magnetic resonance imaging (fMRI) can be used to map patterns of brain activity and understand how information is expressed in the human brain. Using fMRI data to analyses the relationship between visual cortex and language semantic representation is of significance for building a new deep learning model. The cognition of visual semantic concept refers to the behavior that people can distinguish and classify the semantic concept of visual information they see. Many previous research literatures have revealed semantically active brain regions, but lack of modeling the relationship between visual information and language semantic concept in human brain, which is very important to understand the brain mechanism of concept learning. In this paper, we propose a Semantic Concept Cognitive Network (S-ConceptNet) model of brain cortical signals based on fMRI, The model organizes visual and linguistic semantic information into a unified representation framework, which can effectively analyses the generation process of semantic concept, and realize the function of semantic concept cognition. Based on S-ConceptNet, we also use the Dual-learning model to reconstruct the brain signal, judge the corresponding concept category through the S-ConceptNet, compare the reconstructed image with the image of this category. And finally output semantic information corresponding to the brain signal through similarity. We verify the effect of the model and conduct comparative experiments, and the experimental results are better than previous work, and prove the effectiveness of the model proposed in this paper.

Keywords: Brain-inspired computing · Semantic perception · fMRI · Semantic Concept Cognitive Network · Dual-learning

This work was supported by the National Natural Science Foundation of China (NO. 62088102) and China National Postdoctoral Program for Innovative Talents from China Postdoctoral Science Foundation (NO. BX2021239).

I. Maglogiannis et al. (Eds.): AIAI 2022, IFIP AICT 646, pp. 394–406, 2022.
https://doi.org/10.1007/978-3-031-08333-4_32

1 Introduction

In recent years, the research of artificial intelligence has made great progress, but the current artificial intelligence system is still far from the function of the human brain [1]. More and more researchers realize that only by fully understanding the brain can machines be able to think, reason and learn flexibly and quickly [2]. In order to achieve this goal, in recent years, more and more scientists have invested in artificial intelligence research based on neuroscience (especially the research of brain cognitive mechanism and the modeling of brain function), and constructed new artificial intelligence from cognitive processes [3]. AI algorithm framework. The analysis of fMRI brain signals under visual stimuli is a research hotspot in this field [4].

In past, a series of studies have been carried out on fMRI visual brain signals under semantic stimuli using various methods. Initially, people used statistical methods and simple linear models to model fMRI brain signals, and used Bayesian inference [5, 6] to analyze the data. In recent years, deep neural networks (DNNs) [7], VAEs [8], DCCAE [9], semantic attractor networks [10] and other methods [11, 12] have been used to study this issue. In the research on how the brain comprehends semantic textual information, in the past ten years, most researches have focused on the study of "brain signals under single semantic stimulation", or the cognitive process of semantic brain signals in English. However, there is a lack of relevant research and analysis on the cognitive neural basis of Chinese semantic processing and the understanding of semantic concepts, especially the understanding of semantic concepts under visual conditions.

The current research on visual cognition and semantic understanding of the brain includes primary visual cortex and higher visual cortex (HVC), left inferior frontal gyrus (IFG), medial prefrontal cortex (mPFC) [13–15], The information of these brain regions can reveal the internal information flow of the brain in the process of semantic cognition, which can help interpret the operation principle of the human brain [16, 17].

Our team has been committed to exploring brain signal related research. The motivation of our research is that the understanding and classification of semantics is very important in the research of artificial intelligence, which can help machines to reason and understand the world more intuitively, rather than the mechanized and poorly generalized classification generated after a lot of training. model (like some visual recognition tasks), such human brain research and corresponding model building is meaningful for the further development of artificial intelligence.

Previously, we proposed related models such as the brain signal analysis model based on voxel correlation. On the basis of previous work, we consider how to introduce the understanding of semantic concept information in the visual cognitive process of the brain based on the correlation analysis model, so as to improve the understanding of the brain and information reconstruction.

The Semantic Concept Cognitive Network model (S-ConceptNet) proposed in this paper uses the powerful function of recurrent neural network to fit the cognitive function of the brain to classify concepts and semantic feature values in our cognitive experiments. The cognitive function of semantic concepts is then based on the S-ConceptNet model, this paper establishes the image reconstruction and concept classification model of brain signal, so as to verify the validity of the model.

2   An End-to-End Dual-Learning Method

Brain decoding based on fMRI brain signals usually requires the acquisition of a large number of pairs of (Image, fMRI) data. However, in many studies, it is difficult to obtain a large number of pairs of data, and limited data has many limitations in the training process of the model [18].

In recent related research, some scholars have proposed a new idea of Dual-Learning to solve related problems. It can overcome the inherent lack of training data by introducing self-supervision using unlabeled data. The Dual-learning trains two types of networks: Encoder, which encodes the Image to the corresponding fMRI data; Decoder, which decodes the fMRI to the corresponding Image data. Cascading the two networks forward, The En-De network produces a model whose input and output are the same Image, which enables unsupervised training on a large number of images recorded with brainless signals. Then, concatenating the two networks in reverse, De-En, can produce a model whose input and output are fMRI signals and have the same weights as the previously trained network. The encoding and decoding models represent the original bidirectional dual pair and form a closed loop, allowing the application of bidirectional learning and unsupervised training on fMRI data [19–21].

But with further research, we believe that the previous work could be improved:

First, the bidirectional learning model does not have sufficient application of labeled data pairs, and only uses a large number of unpaired fMRI and image data to train the encoding and decoding process. There is room for improvement in data application and loss function definition.

Second, the image restoration model constructed by Dual-Learning only stays on the statistical features of voxel data without further analysis of the internal relationship of voxel information. It is essentially a pixel-based image processing method, which cannot be effectively used. To understand semantic information and classify concepts, The fit to the brain's processing of semantic conceptual information can be improved.

3   Semantic Concept Cognitive Network

One of the most important challenges in semantic concept cognition is how to describe the correspondence between semantic concepts and acquired fMRI data. To characterize hidden associations between two different forms of data, we propose a cross-modal ranking loss for semantic stimulation and reconstructed brain signals. The corresponding schematic ordering in semantic concept stimulus classification is shown in Fig. 1.

In accomplishing such a ranking loss, we consider an LSTM network for fMRI feature ranking: a common LSTM unit is composed of a cell, an input gate, an output gate and a forget gate. The cell remembers values over arbitrary time intervals and the three gates regulate the flow of information into and out of the cell.

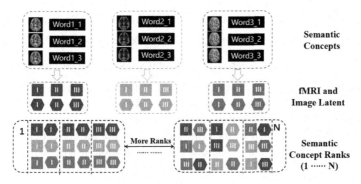

Fig. 1. Ranking loss in semantic concept understanding

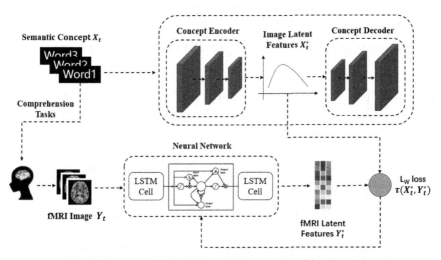

Fig. 2. The framework of Semantic Concept Cognitive Network.

The main components of the semantic concept cognitive model constructed in this paper are shown in the Fig. 2. We respectively construct a network that extracts eigenvalues from the stimulus image and from the fMRI brain signal for the construction of the semantic concept cognitive model.

Starting from the stimulus image, we characterize the feature values of the semantic concept image through the corresponding encoder deep network, and map it into the image latent space z^i. The LSTM network is used to extract the latent eigenvalues of brain signals and map them into the fMRI latent space z^f.

Here, we denote $\left(X_t^*, Y_t^*\right)$ as the semantic image and fMRI brain signal at time point t generated by the stimulus image encoder. We further use $\left(X_t^{*'}, Y_t^{*'}\right)$ to denote non-corresponding samples, where $\left(X_t^{*'}\right)$ denotes stimulus images independent of $Y_t^{*'}$, and $Y_t^{*'}$ indicates brain activity not induced by $X_t^{*'}$. Our model ensures that fMRI combinations with high correlations are in the front and those with low correlations are in the tail. Specifically, for the semantic information of the same concept, it will be given the highest ranking, for a pair of the same concept but not the correct category, it will be set as medium, and for the wrong concept identification, it will be classified as an irrelevant sample, and given The lowest weight for this sample. We give the ranking loss as follows:

$$L_{Loss} = \lambda_W L_W = \frac{1}{T} \sum_{t=1}^{T} L_{Wight}\left(X_t^*, Y_t^*\right) \tag{1}$$

Among them, the ranking loss $L_{Wight}\left(X_t^*, Y_t^*\right)$ of a single paired sample is defined as:

$$L_{Wight} = \sum_{X_t^{*'}} \left[\gamma - \tau\left(X_t^*, Y_t^*\right) + \tau\left(X_t^{*'}, Y_t^*\right)\right]_+ + \sum_{Y_t^{*'}} \left[\gamma - \tau(X_t^*, Y_t^*) + \tau\left(X_t^*, Y_t^{*'}\right)\right]_+ \tag{2}$$

In the formula, γ is the margin, $\tau\left(X_t^*, Y_t^*\right) = -\left\|\left(\max\left(0, X_t^* - Y_t^*\right)\right)\right\|^2$ is used to measure the stimulus image and evoked brain Order violation penalties for similarity between activities. Also, $[x]_+$ means $\max(x, 0)$.

λ_W is a hyperparameter that balances the influence of the loss function on the overall model.

In the network eigenvalue matching training, using the eigenvalue correlation ranking mentioned above, the latent space of the two types of data is mapped into a common space through the sorting loss L_W, and the corresponding eigenvalues of different concepts are carried out. The weights are sorted so that the final trained network can form a corresponding pairing relationship between the semantic images of the same conceptual category and the fMRI brain signals.

In the process of model application, in the testing phase, we input the fMRI brain signals collected by the experiment, the model will label different concept categories, and identify the concept category to which the input brain signal belongs, and our semantic concept category represented by the brain signal, which helps us further understand semantic information.

The algorithm of Semantic Concept Cognitive Network is shown in Algorithm 1.

Algorithm 1 Semantic Concept Model

Require:

Semantic images and fMRI brain signals at n time points t generated by the stimulus image encoder$(X_t^*, Y_t^*) = \{(X_1^*, Y_1^*), (X_2^*, Y_2^*), \cdots, (X_n^*, Y_n^*)\}$, m non-corresponding samples$(X_t^{*'}, Y_t^{*'}) = \{(X_1^{*'}, Y_1^{*'}), (X_2^{*'}, Y_2^{*'}), \cdots, (X_m^{*'}, Y_m^{*'})\}$, where $X_t^{*'}$ represents stimulus images independent of $Y_t^{*'}$, while $Y_t^{*'}$ represents brain activity not evoked by $X_t^{*'}$

Ensure:

min L_{loss} ; **The best sorting result**

1:   **First, The governing equations of LSTM are defined as follows:**

2:   $i_t = \sigma(y_t + U_i h_{t-1} + b_i)$

3:   $f_t = \sigma(y_t + U_f h_{t-1} + b_f)$

4:   $\tilde{c}_t = \tanh(W_c y_t + U_c h_{t-1} + b_c)$

5:   $c_t = i_t * \tilde{c}_t + f_t * c_{t-1}$

6:   $o_t = \sigma(W_o y_t + U_o h_{t-1} + b_o)$

7:   $h_t = o_t * \tanh(c_t)$

8:   **for** $x = 1$ to n **do**

9:     **for** $y = 1$ to m **do**

10:       $L_{Wight} = \sum_{X_t^{*'}} \left[\gamma - \tau(X_t^*, Y_t^*) + \tau(X_t^{*'}, Y_t^*) \right]_+ +$

11:       $\sum_{Y_t^{*'}} \left[\gamma - \tau(X_t^*, Y_t^*) + \tau(X_t^*, Y_t^{*'}) \right]_+$

12:       $\tau(X_t^*, Y_t^*) = -\|(\max(0, X_t^* - Y_t^*))\|^2$

13:       $L_{loss} = \lambda_W L_W$

14:       **update** L_{Wight}

15:     **end for**

16:     $L_W = \frac{1}{T}\sum_{t=1}^{T} L_{Wight}(X_t^*, Y_t^*)$

17:     **update** c_t , h_t

18:   **end for**

---

4   Brain Signal Semantic Understanding Model

The model constructed in this paper is shown in the following Fig. 3.

4.1   Improved Dual-Learning Model

We optimize the bidirectional learning model in the algorithm model, and defines a total of four loss functions to optimize the performance of decoding training.

First, the L^E loss function between the predicted $fMRI_1^*$ data encoded by the real Image and the real brain signal fMRI data to optimize the Decoder; the second is the real brain signal. The L^D loss function between the predicted $Image_2^*$ decoded by fMRI and the real Image optimizes the Decoder. The labeled (Image, fMRI) training set is needed in the calculation and training process of these two loss functions.

Secondly, the Decoder is optimized by applying the L^{DE} loss function between the real Image and the predicted image $Image_1^*$ obtained by encoding and decoding it;

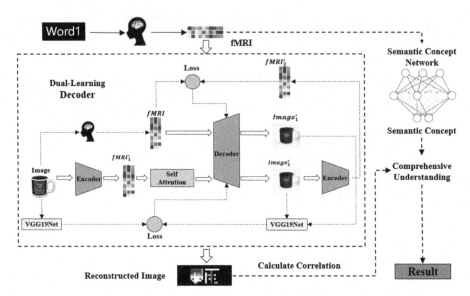

Fig. 3. The framework of brain signal semantic understanding.

Applying the real brain signal fMRI data and decoding and encoding it the L^{DE} loss function between $fMRI_2^*$ data optimizes the Decoder. This method is the Dual-learning.

And we also introduced the self-attention mechanism module in the transformer to the model for further screening of voxels to enhance effective brain signals.

Encoder and decoder are trained as follows:

We first perform supervised training of the encoder to allow it to converge in the first stage, and then provide guidance for the unstable decoding task, thereby performing encoder supervised training:

Let $\hat{f} = E(i)$ denote the fMRI response encoded by the Encoder from image i, we define the functional fMRI loss as the mean squared error and cosine near-convex combination relative to the real fMRI data f, the loss is defined as:

$$L_f\left(\hat{f}, f\right) = \rho \left\| \hat{f} - f \right\|_2 - (1 - \rho) \cos\left(\angle(\hat{f}, f)\right)$$ (3)

ρ is the empirical hyperparameter, and this loss is used to train the Encoder.

After the encoder training is completed, the encoder is fixed for decoder training. The training loss of the decoder in this paper includes four main losses:

$$L^{Model} = L^D + L^E + L^{ED} + L^{DE}$$ (4)

L^D: Decoder supervised training Given a (fMRI, Image) training pair (f, i), a supervised loss L^D is applied to the decoded image, $\hat{i} = D(f)$, and the image reconstruction target L_i is defined by:

$$L^D = L_i\left(\hat{i}, i\right)$$ (5)

L_i includes the loss of image color loss L_{Color} and its features $L_{features}$. We use $\omega(i)$ to express the features of image i, and choose ω as a pretrained feature extractor, the image loss $\hat{i}$ of the reconstructed image is:

$$L_i\left(\hat{i}, i\right) = L_{Color}\left(\hat{i}, i\right) + L_{features}\left(\hat{s}, s\right) + M\left(\hat{s}\right) \tag{6}$$

$$L_{Color}\left(\hat{i}, i\right) \propto \left\|\hat{i} - i\right\|_1, L_{features}\left(\hat{i}, i\right) \propto \left\|\omega\left(\hat{i}\right) - \omega(i)\right\|_2, M\left(\hat{s}\right) \propto SSIM \tag{7}$$

L^E: Encoder supervised training as shown, given a (Image, fMRI) training pair (f, i), apply a supervised loss $L^E, \hat{f} = E(i)$ to the encoded fMRI, and pass the fMRI Rebuild target L_f definition:

$$L^E = L_f\left(\hat{f}, f\right) \tag{8}$$

L^{ED}: We used about 10,000 additional semantic images from the 120-concept data of the semantic image database built by the team, allowing to learn common high-level feature representations for various new concepts. In order to meet the image training without fMRI brain signal, we map the image to itself via the Encoder-Decoder transformation:

$$i \rightarrow \hat{i}_{ED} = D(E(i)) \tag{9}$$

On an unlabeled image i, the unsupervised loss L^{ED} of the loss is:

$$L^{ED} = L_i\left(\hat{i}_{ED}, i\right) \tag{10}$$

L^{DE}: We select a large number of unlabeled fMRI images in the experimental and public datasets for training, so that the network can better decode the fMRI features, we pass the Decoder-Encoder The transformation maps the fMRI response to itself:

$$f \rightarrow \hat{r}_{DE} = E(D(f)) \tag{11}$$

On an unlabeled fMRI f, the unsupervised loss L^{DE} of the loss is:

$$L^{DE} = L_f\left(\hat{f}_{DE}, f\right) \tag{12}$$

It is worth noting that the fMRI signals we use here are from the acquired dataset (which is in line as we have never used nor know their corresponding test images). This allows the decoder to generalize more to fMRI statistics. After training the decoder with these four losses $L^D + L^E + L^{ED} + L^{DE}$, we use it for decoding reconstruction of fMRI data.

The algorithm of improved Dual-learning Network is shown in Algorithm 2.

Algorithm 2 Dual-learning model

Require:

There are three groups of data needed in the training: paired(Image, fMRI) training pair $(f, i) = \{(f_1, i_1), (f_2, i_2), \cdots, (f_n, i_n)\}$, a large number of semantic concept images $i^* = \{i_1^*, i_2^*, \cdots, i_m^*\}$ without corresponding brain signal data selected from our semantic concept data set, and fMRI brain signals $f^* = \{f_1^*, f_2^*, \cdots, f_v^*\}$, without corresponding image data collected from our experiments and a large number of public data sets $L_f(\hat{f}, f)$ Is fMRI loss function, $L_i(\hat{i}, i)$ Is the image loss function, $D(F, I)$ stands for $flag_{f \to i}$, $E(F, I)$ stands for $flag_{i \to f}$, the training step size refers to the data set itself.

Ensure:

min L^{Model} ; The reconstructed image that is most similar to the real image

1:     $L^{Model} = L^D + L^E + L^{ED} + L^{DE}$
2:     $L_f(\hat{f}, f) = \rho \|\hat{f} - f\|_2 - (1 - \rho) \cos(\angle(\hat{f}, f))$
3:     $L_i(\hat{i}, i) = L_{Color}(\hat{i}, i) + L_{features}(\hat{s}, s) + M(\hat{s})$
4:     **for** $a = 1$ to n **do**
5:       $L^D = L_f(\hat{f}, f)$, **update** $D(F, I)$
6:     **end for**
7:     **fixed** $D(F, I)$
8:     **for** $s = 1$ to $n + m + v$ **do**
9:       **for** $x = 1$ to n **do**
10:       $L^D = L_i(\hat{i}, i)$, **update** $E(F, I)$
11:       $L^E = L_f(\hat{f}, f)$, **update** $E(F, I)$
12:      **end for**
13:      **for** $y = 1$ to m **do**
14:        $i \to \hat{i}_{ED} = D(E(i))$
15:        $L^{ED} = L_i(\hat{i}_{ED}, i)$, **update** $E(F, I)$
16:      **end for**
17:      **for** $z = 1$ to v **do**
18:        $f \to \hat{f}_{DE} = E(D(f))$
19:        $L^{DE} = L_f(\hat{f}_{DE}, f)$, **update** $E(F, I)$
20:      **end for**
21:    **end for**

4.2 Brain Semantic Understanding Model

The image reconstruction model based on semantic concepts constructed in this paper is mainly composed of three parts: bidirectional learning reconstruction network, semantic concept cognitive network, and image semantic information discrimination network. The discriminative result of ideal semantic information cognition.

In an image semantic discrimination process, first, the brain signal of the visual brain area generated by the semantic information stimulation is input into the Dual-learning reconstruction network we constructed. The decoder trained by multiple loss functions can be obtained from the brain signal. The semantic image corresponding to the brain signal was reconstructed from the fMRI data, and its similarity with all stimulus sources was calculated.

Secondly, the brain signal of the semantic brain area generated under the stimulation of the same semantic information is input to the semantic concept cognitive network, and the semantic concept cognitive network can make a conceptual judgment on the fMRI brain signal we input, and the semantic concept category corresponding to the output brain signal.

Finally, the image semantic information discrimination network can combine the results obtained in the first two steps for further judgment, and analyze the similarity between the restored and reconstructed image and the semantic image of the determined semantic category. One is the result we need to output - the semantic infor-mation corresponding to the fMRI brain signal.

5 Experiments and Results

In this paper, a task-state fMRI experiment was designed and completed by our team. The visual stimulus images are 18 Chinese semantic text images. At the beginning of the experiment, a preparatory phase was performed first, with a blank space of 24 s, so as to stabilize the state of the instrument and relax the mental state of the subjects. After the preparatory phase is over, the subject of the experiment begins. In 18-s cycles, a 9-s blank was presented in each cycle, followed by a 9-s visual stimulus image before the next cycle was started. The subjects' fMRI brain signals were continuously collected throughout the experiment. Each image is presented 4 times in random order. We chose some of visual stimulus images shown in Fig. 4.

Fig. 4. Some of visual stimulus images.

The experiment was completed in the First Affiliated Hospital of Xi'an Jiaotong University using a 3.0T Ge MR scanner. Six subjects, aged between 20 and 25, were recruited in the experiment. Three male and Three women read and signed the information sheet of magnetic resonance examination before the experiment. All subjects have normal vision or corrected vision, no history of mental illness or neurological disease, no psychological disease, no long-term medication, right-handed.

Before the start of the experiment, the subjects were shown and told the content of the experiment and the tasks that the subjects needed to complete. Before the start of the experiment, the subjects were told to lie on their backs, breathe calmly, keep their heads still, stay awake, and focus on the central fixation point during the experiment.

The data collection process is as follows: First, collect T1 structural image data with the following parameters. Repetition Time (TR): 2250 ms, Echo Time (TE): 3.06 ms, Flip Angle: 90°, Field of view (FOV): 214 mm × 214 mm, Voxel size: 1 mm × 1 mm

× 1 mm. After the acquisition of T1 structural image data, single-image stimulation experiment and double-image stimulation experiment were carried out in turn to collect T2 functional image data. The parameters are as follows. Repetition Time (TR): 3000 ms, Echo Time (TE): 30 ms, Flip angle: 90°, Field of view: 214 mm × 214 mm, Voxel Size: 3 mm × 3 mm × 3 mm. The screen resolution is 800 * 800 and the refresh rate is 24 Hz.

Finally, the experiment obtained 6 sets of fMRI data for 6 subjects, each set of data is a four-dimensional matrix with a size of 61 * 73 * 61 * 200, of which the first three dimensions are the size of the 3D whole-brain fMRI image, and 200 is the time point number.

The data preprocessing of this experiment was done by DPABI software.

The fMRI brain signals of four groups of subjects with complete experimental results and less noise in the subject data were selected for image reconstruction, and compared with the results of the Hcorr-Net [22] and unimproved bidirectional learning model previously proposed by our team. The correct rate of pixel-based image classification is shown in the Table 1.

Table 1. Results of image reconstruction.

Subject	Hcorr-Net	Dual-learning	Ours
Sub1	60.12%	62.13%	67.63%
Sub2	57.56%	58.22%	65.11%
Sub3	59.94%	59.75%	64.36%
Sub4	55.23%	60.09%	70.75%

The histogram of the correct rate of image reconstruction can better show the difference between the three, as shown in the Fig. 5.

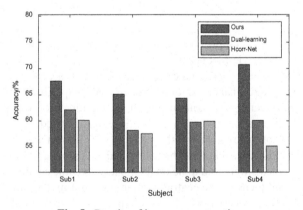

Fig. 5. Results of image reconstruction.

The fMRI brain signals of six groups of subjects were used to judge the correctness of semantic concepts, and a total of 18 groups were carried out. The correct rate of semantic concept understanding is shown in the Table 2.

Table 2. Results of semantic concept understanding.

Subject	Sub1	Sub2	Sub3	Sub4	Sub5	Sub6
Correct rate_1	94.44%	88.88%	100%	94.44%	83.33%	88.88%
Correct rate_2	100%	94.44%	94.44%	83.33%	88.88%	77.77%
Correct rate_3	83.33%	88.88%	72.22%	100%	83.33%	100%
Correct rate_4	88.88%	100%	88.88%	94.44%	77.77%	94.44%

We can clearly see from the results that compared with the previous work, the model we constructed has significantly improved in image reconstruction, and the indicators of image restoration have improved in all aspects. Moreover, our model accomplishes what other work cannot do—understands and classifies semantic concepts, and achieves high accuracy in experimental results across multiple subjects.

6 Conclusion

In this paper, our team proposes a Semantic Concept Cognitive Network (S-ConceptNet), which measures the relationship between images and brain activity data through ranking loss in multi-category learning through neural networks. The semantic concept analogy corresponding to the fMRI brain signal of the input semantic brain area can be accurately judged. Our S-ConceptNet model mainly addresses three problems: how to obtain a cognitive model of brain semantic concepts through experiments, how to fit the process of semantic concept understanding, and how to use this cognitive mechanism to guide the work of coding modeling. The results of collecting experimental data and performing image reconstruction show that S-ConceptNet effectively simulates the process of brain semantic concept understanding and reveals the cognitive mechanism related to semantic tasks. In comparative experiments, the actual effects of our proposed model are compared, and It is found that the image encoding and decoding model applying S-ConceptNet is better than the previously proposed model on the image restoration task, and can accurately output the semantic information corresponding to the brain signal, which proves that the S-ConceptNet is effective in the image restoration task. Performance improvements have been made in the corresponding areas of work.

The work of this paper helps to explain the working mechanism of human semantic cognition process, and reveals the relationship model between visual information and language semantic concepts in the research of brain-like artificial intelligence. Several models proposed in this paper still have room for improvement. In future work, fMRI data sets from other related experiments can be added, and the fMRI data used can be screened for correlation or causality for further improvement. and generalize the S-ConcepetNet model for further research discovery.

References

1. Gazzaniga, M.S., Ivry, R.B., Mangun, G.: Cognitive Neuroscience; The Biology of the Mind, 3rd edn. Norton, New York (2014)
2. Robbins, S.: A misdirected principle with a catch: explicability for AI. Mind. Mach. **29**(4), 495–514 (2019)
3. Zheng, N.-N., et al.: Hybrid-augmented intelligence: collaboration and cognition. Front. Inf. Technol. Electr. Eng. **18**(2), 153–179 (2017). https://doi.org/10.1631/FITEE.1700053
4. Logothetis, N.K., Pauls, J., Augath, M., et al.: Neurophysiological investigation of the basis of the fMRI signal. Nature **412**(6843), 150–157 (2001)
5. Fujiwara, Y., Miyawaki, Y., Kamitani, Y.: Modular encoding and decoding models derived from Bayesian canonical correlation analysis. Neural Comput. **25**(4), 979–1005 (2013)
6. Miyawaki, Y., Uchida, H., Yamashita, O., et al.: Visual image reconstruction from human brain activity: a modular decoding approach. J. Phys. Conf. Ser. **197**(1), 012021 (2009)
7. Shen, G., Dwivedi, K., Majima, K., et al.: End-to-end deep image reconstruction from human brain activity. Front. Comput. Neurosci. **13**, 21 (2019)
8. Horikawa, T., Kamitani, Y.: Generic decoding of seen and imagined objects using hierarchical visual features. Nat. Commun. **8**(1), 1–15 (2017)
9. Rakhimberdina, Z., Jodelet, Q., Liu, X., et al.: Natural image reconstruction from fMRI using deep learning: a survey. Front. Neurosci. 1730 (2021)
10. Mao, Z., Su, Y., Xu, G., et al.: Spatio-temporal deep learning method for ADHD fMRI classification. Inf. Sci. **499**, 1–11 (2019)
11. Qureshi, M.N.I., Oh, J., Lee, B.: 3d-cnn based discrimination of schizophrenia using resting-state fMRI. Artif. Intell. Med. **98**, 10–17 (2019)
12. Lin, Y., Li, J., Wang, H.: DCNN-GAN: reconstructing realistic image from fMRI. In: 16th International Conference on Machine Vision Applications (MVA), pp. 1–6. IEEE (2019)
13. Noonan, K A., Jefferies, E., Visser, M., et al.: Going beyond inferior prefrontal involvement in semantic control: evidence for the additional contribution of dorsal angular gyrus and posterior middle temporal cortex. J. Cogn. Neurosci. **25**(11), 1824–1850 (2013)
14. Binder, J.R., Desai, R.H., Graves, W.W., et al.: Where is the semantic system? A critical review and meta-analysis of 120 functional neuroimaging studies. Cereb. Cortex **19**(12), 2767–2796 (2009)
15. Jefferies, E.: The neural basis of semantic cognition: converging evidence from neuropsychology, neuroimaging and TMS. Cortex **49**(3), 611–625 (2013)
16. Grodniewicz, J.P.: The process of linguistic understanding. Synthese **198**(12), 11463–11481 (2020). https://doi.org/10.1007/s11229-020-02807-9
17. Zhang, Q., Wang, H., Luo, C., et al.: The neural basis of semantic cognition in Mandarin Chinese: a combined fMRI and TMS study. Hum. Brain Mapp. **40**, 5412–5423 (2019)
18. Behrens, T.E.J., et al.: Non-invasive mapping of connections between human thalamus and cortex using diffusion imaging. Nat. Neurosci. **6**(7), 750–757 (2003)
19. Du, C., Li, J., Huang, L., et al.: Brain encoding and decoding in fMRI with bidirectional deep generative models. Engineering **5**(5), 948–953 (2019)
20. Wang, H., Huang, L., Du, C., et al.: Neural encoding for human visual cortex with deep neural networks learning "what" and "where". In: IEEE Transactions on Cognitive and Developmental Systems, pp. 827–840 (2020)
21. Beliy, R., et al.: From voxels to pixels and back: Self-supervision in natural-image reconstruction from fMRI. In: Advances in Neural Information Processing Systems, vol. 32 (2019)
22. Yu, S., Zheng, N., Wu, H., et al.: Exploring brain effective connectivity in visual perception using a hierarchical correlation network. In: Proceedings of the IFIP International Conference on Artificial Intelligence Applications and Innovations 2019, pp. 223–235 (2019)

Hierarchical Causality Network: Find the Effective Connectivity in Visual Cortex

Ming Du[1,2] (ID), Haodong Jing[1,2], Yongqiang Ma[1,2(✉)] (ID), and Nanning Zheng[1,2] (ID)

[1] Institute of Artificial Intelligence and Robotics, Xi'an Jiaotong University, Xi'an, Shaanxi, People's Republic of China
{x1978626209,jinghd}@stu.xjtu.edu.cn, musayq@xjtu.edu.cn, nnzheng@mail.xjtu.edu.cn
[2] National Engineering Laboratory for Visual Information Processing and Applications, Xi'an Jiaotong University, Xi'an, Shaanxi, People's Republic of China

Abstract. Studying the human brain is of great significance to the development of AI. The analysis of fMRI brain signal of visual cortex is a research hotspot in this field. One of key issues in analyzing fMRI brain signals is how to establish effective connectivity model from brain signals. Traditional analysis methods regard voxel correlations as effective connectivity. However, the result obtained by these methods are not effective connectivity but functional connectivity. To achieve real effective connectivity, we need to analyze the causality relationship between voxels. Therefore, we propose a hierarchical causality network model (Hcausal-Net). The model stratifies the voxels of the visual cortex in fMRI brain signals, and analyzes the causality relationship between voxels by Granger Causality Analysis (GCA), and then infer the effective connectivity given by Hcausal-Net. The voxels sensitive to the stimuli are extracted, and the forward encoding process model of visual perception is established. Finally, in the experiment, we also improved the image restoration method based on machine learning and conduct comparative experiments, and the results are better than the previous work, which proves the effectiveness of the model proposed in this paper.

Keywords: Brain-inspired computing · Visual perception · fMRI · Hierarchical Causality Network (Hcausal-Net) · Granger causality analysis

1 Introduction

The neural mechanism of the human brain completing the visual information processing is a very valuable research topic [1]. It is of great significance for the development of a new model of AI and algorithm of intelligent computing such as image recognition, scene understanding, semantic understanding [2]. Blood Oxygen Level-Dependent functional

This work was supported by the National Natural Science Foundation of China (No. 62088102) and China National Postdoctoral Program for Innovative Talents from China Postdoctoral Science Foundation (No. BX2021239).

Magnetic Resonance Imaging (BOLD-fMRI) is an emerging brain signal acquisition technology that can display high-level brain activity in the form of images [3]. The analysis of fMRI brain signals of visual cortex is a research hotspot in this field [4].

In the past decade, a series of studies have been carried out on fMRI brain signals of visual cortex by using various methods. Initially, researchers used statistical methods and Bayesian inference to establish the model of fMRI brain signals [5, 6]. In recent years, Deep Neural Networks (DNNs) [7], Deep Canonically Correlated Auto-Encoders (DCCAE) [8], Variational Auto-Encoder (VAEs) [9], Semantic Attractor Networks [10] and other methods [11, 12] have been used to research this question. Nowadays, analyzing fMRI brain signal of visual cortex has become a hot research field and still has a broad space for development.

In the research of fMRI brain signals, the connectivity between voxels is the focus [13], and the connectivity between voxels can be divided into three categories: structural connectivity is biological connection [14], and functional connectivity is the correlation of responses [15], and effective connectivity is the causality of responses [16]. However, most existing connectivity models ignored the effective connectivity information, which may provide information about the information flow in the brain.

In 2019, the author's team proposedHierarchical Correlation Network (Hcorr-Net), which focus on the correlation relationship in visual cortex, and analyzed the fMRI brain signals of visual cortex and established a hierarchical model of the visual cortex [17]. However, there is a flaw in this model: it doesn't use causality analysis method, which may confuse the effective connectivity with the functional connectivity. To solve this problem, in this paper, we proposed Hierarchical Causality Network (Hcausal-Net), which is a hierarchical causality model based on previous work. The Hcausal-Net model replaces the correlation analysis with Granger Causality Analysis (GCA), so that the result is true effective connectivity rather than functional connectivity. Then, based on the Hcausal-Net, we establish the forward encoding process of visual information and apply it to the image reconstruction model to verify the effectiveness.

The contents of this chapter are arranged as follows. Section 2 introduced the previously proposed Hcorr-Net model. Section 3 proposes the framework of the hierarchical causality model Hcausal-Net. Section 4 describes the process of forward encoding, including data classification and image reconstruction. In Sect. 5, we design experiments and collect fMRI brain signal data, and use those data to verify the performance of the method proposed in this paper. In Sect. 6, conclusions are given.

2 Hierarchical Correlation Network

In 2019, the author's team proposed Hierarchical Correlation Network (Hcorr-Net), which is a hierarchical correlation model for analyzing the brain connectivity in visual perception process [17]. Hcorr-Net models the forward encoding process of visual information in the human brain by analyzing the correlation between voxels in fMRI data, and applies it to the encoding and decoding of visual information, and reconstruct the visual stimulus picture from fMRI brain data.

The Hcorr-Net model treats each brain area in the visual cortex as a layer in the network, and treats each voxel in the brain area as a node in a layer of the network, and established a hierarchical forward coding model from image to low-level visual cortex and then to high-level visual cortex. The correlation between voxels and the correlation between voxel and pixel is determined by calculate the Pearson correlation coefficient. Through the above methods, the receptive fields of pixels in the brain were finally determined, revealing the effective connectivity in visual cognitive tasks.

But with further research, we believe that the previous work could be improved. First, in Hcorr-Net, when we analyze the correlation between voxels, only the Pearson correlation coefficient is calculated. This method is too simple and can be improved. Second, in Hcorr-Net we only analyzed the correlation between voxels, and thought that is causality relationship and that is effective connectivity. However, correlation is not the same as causality [18]. Even if there is a correlation between two voxels, there may not be a causality relationship between two voxels. The causality relationship has not been fully considered in Hcorr-Net model, so it can be improved.

3   Hierarchical Causality Network

In order to solve the problems of Hcorr-Net, we use the method of Granger Causality Analysis (GCA) to rebuild the forward encoding model and propose the Hierarchical Causality Network (Hcausal-Net). The framework of our method is shown in Fig. 1.

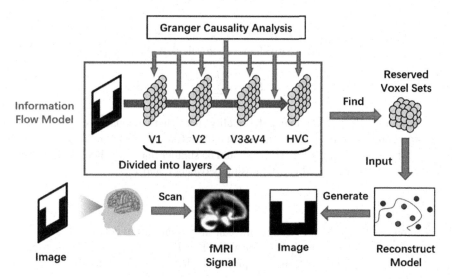

Fig. 1. The framework of our method.

3.1 Granger Causality Analysis

Granger Causality Analysis (GCA) is a method for analyzing the causality between time series [19]. It is based on Vector Autoregressive model (VAR), and by it we can find the causality relationship between two time series without prior knowledges. Nowadays, GCA has become a common method for fMRI brain signal analysis [20].

Suppose there are two time series $X = \{x_1, x_2, \cdots, x_n\}$ and $Y = \{y_1, y_2, \cdots, y_n\}$, and n is the number of time points. Now we want to judge that if Y is a cause of X by GCA. First, we build the Vector Autoregressive equations, predicting the value of X by the history information of X:

$$x_j = \sum_{i=1}^{k} a_i x_{j-i} + \sigma_j, j = k+1, k+2, \cdots, n \tag{1}$$

k is the degree of the model. $a_i(i = 1, 2, \cdots, k)$ are parameters we need to estimate. $\sigma_j(j = k+1, k+2, \cdots, n)$ are residuals. By solving those equations, we can get all those residuals, then calculate residual sum of squares (RSS) Ω_1:

$$\Omega_1 = \sum_{i=k+1}^{n} \sigma_i^2 \tag{2}$$

Then, Add the information of Y to those equations to predict the value of X:

$$x_j = \sum_{i=1}^{k} b_i x_{j-i} + c_i y_{j-i} + \delta_j, j = k+1, k+2, \cdots, n \tag{3}$$

$b_i(i = 1, 2, \cdots, k)$ and $c_i(i = 1, 2, \cdots, k)$ are parameters we need to estimate. $\delta_j(j = k+1, k+2, \cdots, n)$ are residuals. Then calculate the RSS Ω_2:

$$\Omega_2 = \sum_{i=k+1}^{n} \delta_i^2 \tag{4}$$

The smaller RSS is, the better the quality of predictive equations is. If there is a causality relationship between Y and X, then the information contained in Y should be able to help the prediction of X, so Ω_2 should be smaller than Ω_1. Therefore, GCA uses $F_{Y \to X}$ to measure the causality relationship between X and Y:

$$F_{Y \to X} = \ln\left(\frac{\Omega_1}{\Omega_2}\right) \tag{5}$$

The bigger $F_{Y \to X}$ is, the stronger the causality relationship between X and Y is. If there is no causality relationship between X and Y, $n \cdot F_{Y \to X}$ will obey $\chi^2(k)$ distribution. So, we can use hypothesis testing to judge whether there is a causality relationship between X and Y. If

$$F_{\chi^2(k)}(n \cdot F_{Y \to X}) \geq 1 - \alpha \tag{6}$$

there is a causality relationship between X and Y. Otherwise, there is no causality relationship between X and Y. $F_{\chi^2(k)}$ is the distribution function of $\chi^2(k)$ distribution. α is significance level.

3.2 Conditional Granger Causality Analysis

GCA can be used to analyze the causality relationship between two time series, but there are many voxels in fMRI brain signals and they can influence each other. There is a complex causality network in fMRI brain signal.

So, it may lead to a problem to use GCA directly. The problem is confusing causality with correlation. If voxel A can affect voxel B, and voxel A can also affect voxel C, then both the time series of voxel B and the time series of voxel C may contain part of the information of the time series of voxel A. Even if there is no causality relationship between voxel B and C, it may be misjudged that there is a causality relationship between voxel B and C because the information of voxel A is included.

Therefore, the result of GCA may be "fake causality". To solve this problem, John Geweke proposed Conditional Granger Causality Analysis (CGCA) [21].

Suppose there are three time series X, Y, and Z. By GCA, it is judged that there is a causality relationship between Y and X. Now we need to judge whether there is a true causality relationship between Y and X, or that is just a correlation because of Z.

First, add the information of Z to the prediction of X:

$$x_j = \sum_{i=1}^{k} a_i x_{j-i} + b_i z_{j-i} + \sigma_j, j = k+1, k+2, \cdots, n \tag{7}$$

Then get the RSS Ω_1. Then add both the information of Z and Y to the prediction of X:

$$x_j = \sum_{i=1}^{k} c_i x_{j-i} + d_i x_{j-i} + e_i z_{j-i} + \delta_j, j = k+1, k+2, \cdots, n \tag{8}$$

Then get the RSS Ω_2. If there is a causality relationship between Y and X, Y should provide some information that is not contained in Z, which can make the prediction more accurate, so Ω_2 should be smaller than Ω_1. Therefore, CGCA uses $F_{Y \to X|Z}$ to measure the causality relationship between X and Y that is independent of Z:

$$F_{Y \to X|Z} = \ln\left(\frac{\Omega_1}{\Omega_2}\right) \tag{9}$$

The latter process is the same as GCA.

CGCA provides us with a method to remove the interference of external factors to judge whether there is a causality relationship between two time series. When we establish the model of the causality relationship between many factors, we can use GCA to find causality relationship and use CGCA to remove "fake causality", and finally we can find all the causality relationships between all the factors.

3.3   Hierarchical Causality Network

In this paper, we reconstruct the Hcorr-Net model by CGCA method, and the Hierarchical Causality Network (Hcausal-Net) is proposed to establish the model of the effective connectivity between voxels in the visual cortex and solve problems of Hcorr-Net. The framework of Hcausal-Net is shown in the Fig. 2.

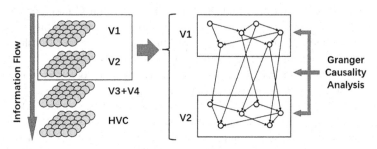

Fig. 2. The framework of Hcausal-Net.

In the Hcausal-Net model, we divide the visual cortex into 4 levels: V1, V2, V3 + V4, and higher visual cortex (HVC), and analyze the voxel causality relationship within a layer (intra-layer causality) and the voxel causality relationship between layers (inter-layer causality). The causality relationship within a layer is the effective connectivity between the voxels in the same layer, and the causality relationship between layers is the effective connectivity between the voxels of two adjacent layers.

The effective connectivity network is established by GCA and CGCA. The essence of effective connectivity is the causality relationship between voxels. Two voxels with a causality relationship must have a correlation relationship. It means correlation is a necessary condition for causality, and causality is a sufficient condition for correlation. Correlation analysis is simpler than causality analysis. Therefore, we can use correlation analysis to help causality analysis.

Firstly, we analyze the correlation of all voxels by calculating the Pearson correlation coefficient and comparing it with a threshold. After the correlation analysis is completed, we use GCA to analyze the causality relationship. Since correlation is a necessary condition for causality, two voxels that don't have a correlation relationship must not have a causality relationship. Therefore, in the analysis, only the voxel pairs with correlation are analyzed, which greatly reduces the computational complexity.

After that, we use CGCA to remove all those "fake causality relationships", and find those true causality relationships in visual cortex. The algorithm of analyzing causality within a layer is shown in the algorithm. 1, and the algorithm of analyzing causality between layers is shown in the algorithm. 2. Algorithm 1 and algorithm 2 are both combination of hierarchical network proposed by authors team and GCA method.

First, find the effective connectivity within a layer. Then, for each pair of adjacent layers, find the effective connectivity between the two layers. Finally, we combine the two results together and get the effective connectivity network of visual cortex. That is the process of Hcausal-Net.

Algorithm 1 Analyzing Causality Within a Layer

Require:

There is a layer of Hcausal-Net L. $V = \{V_1, V_2, \cdots, V_n\}$ is the voxel sets of L, and n is all voxel number of V. Each voxel is a time series, $V_i = \{V_{i1}, V_{i2}, \cdots, V_{im}\}$, and m is the length. Granger Causality Analysis function $GCA(X, Y)$. Conditional Granger Causality Analysis function $CGCA(X, Y, Z)$. Threshold of correlation coefficient R.

Ensure:

Matrix $(C^L)_{n \times n}$. If V_j is a cause of V_i, $C^L_{i,j} = 1$, otherwise $C^L_{i,j} = 0$.

1:   $C^L = 0_{n \times n}$
2:   **for** $i = 1$ to n **do**
3:     **for** $j = 1$ to $i - 1$ **do**
4:      **if** $\dfrac{Cov(V_i, V_j)}{\sqrt{Var(V_i) \cdot Var(V_j)}} > R$ **then**
5:        $C^L_{ij} = GCA(V_i, V_j)$, $C^L_{ji} = GCA(V_j, V_i)$;
6:      **end if**
7:     **end for**
8:   **end for**
9:   **for** $i = 1$ to n **do**
10:    **for** $j = 1$ to n **do**
11:     **if** $C^L_{ij} = 1$ **then**
12:      **for** $k = 1$ to n and $k \neq i, j$ **do**
13:        **if** $C^L_{ik} = 1$ and $CGCA(V_i, V_j, V_k) = 0$ **then**
14:          $C^L_{ik} = 0$;
15:          **break**;
16:        **end if**
17:      **end for**
18:     **end if**
19:    **end for**
20: **end for**

Algorithm 2 Analyzing Causality Between Layers

Require:

   There are two layers of Hcausal-Net, L_1 and L_2. $V^1 = \{V_1^1, V_2^1, \cdots, V_{n_1}^1\}$ and $V^2 = \{V_1^2, V_2^2, \cdots, V_{n_2}^2\}$ are the voxel sets of L_1 and L_2, and n_1 and n_2 are all voxel number of V_1 and V_2. Each voxel is a time series, $V_i = \{V_{i1}, V_{i2}, \cdots, V_{im}\}$, and m is the length. Granger Causality Analysis function $GCA(X, Y)$. Conditional Granger Causality Analysis function $CGCA(X, Y, Z)$. Threshold of correlation coefficient R.

Ensure:

   Matrix $(C^{L_1 L_2})_{n_2 \times n_1}$. If V_j^1 is a cause of V_i^2, $C_{i,j}^{L_1 L_2} = 1$, otherwise $C_{i,j}^{L_1 L_2} = 0$.

1:   $C_{i,j}^{L_1 L_2} = 0_{n_2 \times n_1}$
2:   **for** $i = 1$ to n_2 **do**
3:     **for** $j = 1$ to n_1 **do**
4:       **if** $\dfrac{Cov(V_i^2, V_j^1)}{\sqrt{Var(V_i^2) \cdot Var(V_j^1)}} > R$ **then**
5:         $C_{i,j}^{L_1 L_2} = GCA(V_i^2, V_j^1)$
6:       **end if**
7:     **end for**
8:   **end for**
9:   **for** $i = 1$ to n_2 **do**
10:    **for** $j = 1$ to n_1 **do**
11:      **if** $C_{i,j}^{L_1 L_2} = 1$ **then**
12:        **for** $k = 1$ to n_1 and $k \neq j$ **do**
13:          **if** $C_{i,k}^{L_1 L_2} = 1$ and $CGCA(V_i^2, V_j^1, V_k^1) = 0$ **then**
14:            $C_{i,k}^{L_1 L_2} = 0$;
15:            break;
16:          **end if**
17:        **end for**
18:      **end if**
19:    **end for**
20: **end for**

---

4   Forward Encoding Process

The effective connectivity model proposed in this paper models the effective connectivity between voxels in the visual cortex, and by it we can clarify the transmission process of visual information in the visual cortex. According to the transmission process of the known visual information, the visual stimulation image can be inferred and reconstructed according to the fMRI brain signal.

   The way of image reconstruction in this paper is the same as that of Hcorr-Net, the difference is using Hcausal-Net instead of Hcorr-Net. In Hcorr-Net, first, the image is decomposed into pixels, and the image reconstruction is realized by restoring the pixels one by one, and the problem is transformed into a single-output fitting problem. Adding visual stimulus image information Before the V1 layer, for each pixel, calculate the correlation coefficient between it and each voxel in V1 layer, then set the threshold and select all voxel sets in V1 layer that have correlation with image pixels; then, through the forward propagation model, find all the voxels that are related to the current pixel, and filter out the voxels that are not related to the current pixel by this method, and only keep the voxels related to the current pixel. Get all the voxels related to the current pixel, and then use them as input, and use the machine learning method to train the model to reconstruct the current pixel. Do this for each pixel and merge all those results, we can reconstruct the stimuli image.

In the work of Hcausal-Net, we maintain the advantage of Hcorr-Net that is able to cooperate with various machine learning methods. This paper will combine Hcausal-Net with Support Vector Machine (SVM) for image restoration to verify the effectiveness of Hcausal-Net, and compare the results with that of Hcorr-Net.

5   Experiments and Results

In this paper, a task-state fMRI experiment was designed and completed by us. Visual stimulus images are 8 geometric figures based on a 4 × 4 grid. All visual stimulus images are shown in Fig. 3.

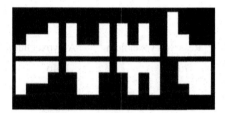

Fig. 3. Visual stimulus images.

At the beginning of the experiment, a preparatory phase was performed first, with a blank screen lasting 24 s. After the preparatory phase is over, the subject of the experiment begins. In 18 s cycles, a 9 s blank was presented and followed by a 9 s visual stimulus image before the next cycle was started. The subjects' fMRI brain signals were continuously collected throughout the experiment. Each image is presented 4 times in random order.

The experiment was completed in the First Affiliated Hospital of Xi'an Jiaotong University by using a 3.0-Tesla GE MR scanner. Five subjects aged between 20 and 25 were recruited in the experiment. Three male and two female read and signed the information sheet of magnetic resonance examination before the experiment. All subjects have normal vision or corrected vision, no history of mental illness or neurological disease, no psychological disease, no long-term medication, right-handed.

Before the start of the experiment, the subjects were shown and told the content of the experiment. Before the start of the experiment, the subjects were told to lie on their backs, breathe calmly, keep their heads still, stay awake, and focus on the central fixation point during the experiment.

The data collection process is as follows: First, collect T1 structural image data with the following parameters. Repetition Time (TR): 2250 ms; Echo Time (TE): 3.06 ms;

Flip Angle: 90°; Field of View (FOV): 214 mm × 214 mm; Voxel Size: 1 mm × 1 mm × 1 mm. After the acquisition of T1 structural image data, the experiment was carried out in turn to collect T2 functional image data. The parameters are as follows. Repetition Time (TR): 3000 ms; Echo Time (TE): 30 ms; Flip angle: 90°; Field of View (FOV): 214 mm × 214 mm; Voxel Size: 3 mm × 3 mm × 3 mm. The screen resolution of the screen to display stimulative image is 800 × 800 and the refresh rate is 24 Hz.

Finally, we obtained 5 sets of fMRI data for 5 subjects, each set of data is a four-dimensional matrix with a size of 61 × 73 × 61 × 200, of which the first three dimensions are the size of the 3D whole-brain fMRI image, and 200 is the time points number.

The data preprocessing of this experiment was done by DPABI software. During the preprocessing, we found that there are two sets of data that the quality of them is too low, so we desert those data. Therefore, finally we got 3 sets of valid fMRI data. We only use the data of visual cortex.

Following the methods described in Chapters 3 and 4, Hcausal-Net is constructed to build an encoding model and we can use it for image reconstruction. The data of each subject were analyzed separately and were not pooled. After the above steps, the results of the reserved voxel set as shown in the Table 1.

Table 1. Reserved voxel num of all layers.

Subject	Layer	Reserved voxel num	All voxel num	Reserved rate
Sub1	V1	470	1146	41.01%
	V2	517	2823	18.35%
	V3&V4	251	3093	8.12%
	HVC	21	3021	0.70%
	All	1259	10083	12.49%
Sub2	V1	394	1146	34.38%
	V2	156	2823	5.53%
	V3&V4	48	3093	1.55%
	HVC	17	3021	0.56%
	All	615	10083	6.09%
Sub3	V1	446	1146	38.92%
	V2	201	2823	7.12%
	V3&V4	78	3093	2.52%
	HVC	25	3021	0.83%
	All	750	10083	7.43%

Then use the model to do the image reconstruction, and compare the result with the result of Hcorr-Net. The correct rate of pixel is shown in the Table 2.

The correct rate of the two-class model should be higher than 50%. Therefore, we drew a histogram with 50% as the baseline, as shown in the Fig. 4.

Table 2. Results of image reconstruction.

Subject	Hcorr-Net	Hcausal-Net
Sub1	65.63%	68.75%
Sub2	67.19%	74.11%
Sub3	60.94%	73.21%

It can be seen from the table and the figure that the accuracy of image reconstruction is improved when the Hcausal-Net model is used compared to the model using Hcorr-Net, which verifies the effectiveness of the Hcausal-Net model proposed in this paper. The higher the accuracy of image reconstruction is, the better the quality of information flow model is. Therefore, we can say that the Hcausal-Net model is better than Hcorr-Net model in the task of establishing model of the information flow in visual cortex.

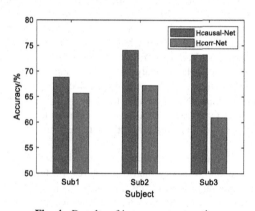

Fig. 4. Results of image reconstruction.

6   Conclusion

In this paper, we proposed Hierarchical Causality Network (Hcausal-Net) to explore effective connectivity in visual perception by establishing the model of the causality relationships between voxels of fMRI signals in the visual cortex. First, we introduced the Hierarchical Correlation Network (Hcorr-Net) proposed by the author's team, analyzed its defects and deficiencies. Next, we used Granger Causality Analysis method (GCA) instead of correlation analysis, and proposed the Hcausal-Net model to solve three problems: finding voxel causality network in visual stimulation tasks, using voxel causality network for encoding modeling. Then, we used fMRI data to restore visual reconstruction, and the results of image reconstruction show that Hcausal-Net has screened out effective fMRI signals and constructed a forward coding model for visual tasks. Finally, we compared the results of image reconstruction of the two models, and it is found that the Hcausal-Net model is better than the Hcorr-Net model in the image restoration task, which proves that the Hcausal-Net solves the inherent defects of the Hcorr-Net to a certain extent. The work of this paper helps to explain the neural mechanism of visual processing and contributes to visual scene understanding in the research of brain-like artificial intelligence. In the future, we will further verify the validity of the proposed model with more data. Furthermore, the eye-tracking data will be added to improve the robustness of the model.

References

1. Gazzaniga, M.S., Ivry, R.B., Mangun, G.: Cognitive Neuroscience; the Biology of the Mind, 3rd edn. Norton, New York (2014)
2. Robbins, S.: A misdirected principle with a catch: explicability for AI. Mind. Mach. **29**(4), 495–514 (2019)
3. Logothetis, N.K., Pauls, J., Augath, M., et al.: Neurophysiological investigation of the basis of the fMRI signal. Nature **412**(6843), 150–157 (2001)
4. Zheng, N.-N., et al.: Hybrid-augmented intelligence: collaboration and cognition. Front. Inf. Technol. Electr. Eng. **18**(2), 153–179 (2017). https://doi.org/10.1631/FITEE.1700053
5. Miyawaki, Y., Uchida, H., Yamashita, O., et al.: Visual image reconstruction from human brain activity: a modular decoding approach. J. Phys. Conf. Ser. **197**(1), 012021 (2009)
6. Fujiwara, Y., Miyawaki, Y., Kamitani, Y.: Modular encoding and decoding models derived from Bayesian canonical correlation analysis. Neural Comput. **25**(4), 979–1005 (2013)
7. Shen, G., Dwivedi, K., Majima, K., et al.: End-to-end deep image reconstruction from human brain activity. Front. Comput. Neurosci. **13**, 21 (2019)
8. Yu, S., Zheng, N., Ma, Y., Wu, H., Chen, B.: A novel brain decoding method: a correlation network framework for revealing brain connections. IEEE Trans. Cogn. Dev. Syst. **11**, 95–106 (2018)
9. Geenjaar, E., White, T., Calhoun, V.: Variational voxelwise rs-fMRI representation learning: evaluation of sex, age, and neuropsychiatric signatures. In: Proceedings of the 2021 IEEE International Conference on Bioinformatics and Biomedicine (BIBM). pp. 1733–1740 (2021)
10. Mao, Z., Su, Y., Xu, G., et al.: Spatio-temporal deep learning method for ADHD fMRI classification. Inf. Sci. **499**, 1–11 (2019)
11. Qureshi, M.N.I., Oh, J., Lee, B.: 3D-CNN based discrimination of schizophrenia using resting-state fMRI. Artif. Intell. Med. **98**, 10–17 (2019)
12. Lin, Y., Li, J., Wang, H.: DCNN-GAN: Reconstructing realistic image from fMRI. In: 16th International Conference on Machine Vision Applications (MVA), pp. 1–6. IEEE (2019)
13. Horikawa, T., Kamitani, Y.: Generic decoding of seen and imagined objects using hierarchical visual features. Nat. Commun. **8**(1), 1–15 (2017)
14. Behrens, T.E.J., et al.: Non-invasive mapping of connections between human thalamus and cortex using diffusion imaging. Nat. Neurosci. **6**(7), 750–757 (2003)
15. Melssen, W.J., Epping, W.J.M.: Detection and estimation of neural connectivity based on cross correlation analysis. Biol. Cybern. **57**(6), 403–414 (1987)
16. Fleischer, V., Muthuraman, M., Anwar, A.R., et al.: Continuous reorganization of cortical information flow in multiple sclerosis: a longitudinal fMRI effective connectivity study. Sci. Rep. **10**(1), 1–11 (2020)
17. Yu, S., Zheng, N., Wu, H., et al.: exploring brain effective connectivity in visual perception using a hierarchical correlation network. In: Proceedings of the IFIP International Conference on Artificial Intelligence Applications and Innovations 2019. pp. 223–235 (2019)
18. Pearl, J., Mackenzie, D.: The Book of Why: The New Science of Cause and Effect, 1st edn. Basic Books (2018)

19. Granger, C.W.J.: Investigating causal relations by econometric models and cross-spectral methods. Econometrica **37**(3), 424–438 (1969)
20. Chuang, K.-C., Ramakrishnapillai, S., Bazzano, L., Carmichael, O.T.: Deep stacking networks for conditional nonlinear granger causal modeling of fMRI data. In: Abdulkadir, A., et al. (eds.) MLCN 2021. LNCS, vol. 13001, pp. 113–124. Springer, Cham (2021). https://doi.org/10.1007/978-3-030-87586-2_12
21. Geweke, J.F.: Measures of conditional linear dependence and feedback between time series. J. Am. Stat. Assoc. **79**(388), 907–915 (1984)

The Generalization of Selection of an Appropriate Artificial Neural Network to Assess the Effort and Costs of Software Projects

Dragica Rankovic[1], Nevena Rankovic[2(✉)], Mirjana Ivanovic[3], and Ljubomir Lazic[4]

[1] Faculty of Applied Sciences Nis, Department of Mathematics, University Union "Nikola Tesla", 18000 Nis, Serbia
[2] School of Computing Belgrade, Department of Computer Science, Union University, 11000 Belgrade, Serbia
nrankovic@raf.rs
[3] Faculty of Sciences, Department of Mathematics and Informatics, University of Novi Sad, 21000 Novi Sad, Serbia
[4] School of Computing Belgrade, Department of Computer Engineering, Union University, 11000 Belgrade, Serbia

Abstract. Estimation of effort and costs is crucial for successfully implementation of software projects. Project development time is an essential factor, both for project clients and project developers. The amount of money needed to invest in a project influences the decision whether to start a project or not or whether it will be completed successfully or not. In practice, the cost of a project is most often compared to the cost of similar projects, which have been successfully completed. The article proposes combining the experimental information of the Taguchi method with ANN ((*Artificial Neural Network*) learning, and constructs a progressive Taguchi neural network model to decrease the number of experimental runs and time required. The main goal of this paper is to make generalization of the conditions and criteria for successful project realization based on a large number of experimental results that authors obtained so far. Furthermore, the most reliable and efficient artificial intelligence model for effort and cost estimation is identified.

Keywords: Software estimation · ANN · Taguchi method · Generalization

1 Introduction

Three approaches have been most commonly used in software project estimations: COCOMO2000 (*Constructive Cost model*), parametric model [1–3], COSMIC FFP (*Function Point Analysis*) model based on functional point analysis [4–6] and the UCP (*Use Case Point Analysis*) method, based on the analysis of users and use cases [7, 8]. For each of these three approaches, which are based on different effort and cost estimation methods, a new, improved model was selected and constructed. Previously used models

© IFIP International Federation for Information Processing 2022
Published by Springer Nature Switzerland AG 2022
I. Maglogiannis et al. (Eds.): AIAI 2022, IFIP AICT 646, pp. 420–431, 2022.
https://doi.org/10.1007/978-3-031-08333-4_34

of the proposed approaches did not give good enough results to improve projects' success significantly. Three new, improved models were constructed using different ANN architectures based on different Taguchi's orthogonal vector plans [9, 10]. ANNs are an excellent artificial intelligence tool for information 2 processing and can significantly contribute to the construction of new, improved soft-ware evaluation models. Due to ANN's ability to learn from different data sets (observations), it is possible to generate accurate and reliable results to avoid unforeseen situations. Different ANN architectures are used to identify the simplest one that meets the additionally set of criteria. Each of these enhanced approaches includes

- constructing and identifying the best model for estimating effort and cost,
- selection of the best ANN architecture whose values converge the fastest to the minimum magnitude relative error,
- use of publicly available real relevant datasets according to the input values of the proposed model [2, 8–10],
- achieving the minimum number of performed experiments, reduced software effort estimation time due to convergence rate.

Additional criteria and constraints are introduced to monitor and execute experiments using a precise algorithm to execute all three new proposed models. In addition to monitoring the convergence rate of each ANN architecture, the influence of the input quantities of each model on the change in the value of the mean magnitude relative error (MMRE) of the model is monitored. The models constructed in this way have been experimentally tested and their positive results have been confirmed several times on different sets of real industrial projects and can be successfully applied in practice. Furthermore, obtained results indicate that the achieved error values are lower than these obtained in the previous models. Therefore, the proposed models in this paper can be reliably applied and used to estimate efforts and costs for software development and the development of projects in other areas of industry and science [11, 12].

The rest of the paper is organized as follows. The second section is devoted to related work. Selection of the appropriate ANN architecture based on Taguchi's orthogonal vector plan is discussed in the third section. The fourth section presents clustering method based on different ANN architectures. The section five is devoted to convergence rate and determination of optimal number of iterations. Selection of activation function and encoding/decoding method are presented in section six while last section concludes the paper.

2 Related Work

Preliminary estimates of efforts can usually lead to delays in project implementation, requests for additional funds, overtime work of experts, and the other problems. Also, they can directly affect the quality of the software. Due to not considering all the necessary parameters for assessing the implementation of software, it often happens that individual activities, such as additional testing, completion of documentation, and additional definition of user requirements, are reduced to a minimum of effort. All this can lead to many failed projects that are currently frequent situation in the software industry. Previous methods of estimating efforts and costs during the implementation of software projects were based on unreliable and inaccurate methods, techniques, and models. The result of such incomplete assessments is many unsuccessful and not completed projects. All research indicates that only about 30% of projects are successfully completed, [13, 14], while the remaining percentage of projects remain unresolved or 3 ultimately fail. The most commonly used methods so far are similarity method, method of analysis and synthesis, assessment based on expert knowledge, and various parametric methods. In addition to various assessment methods, software companies use various auxiliary software tools and services to meet customer requirements. Many re-searchers [1, 4, 5, 6, 11, 12] have proposed different combinations of parametric and non-parametric effort and cost estimation models to construct reliable software of high standards and performance. It is necessary to analyze and experimentally test the most successful methods and models so far in order to adequately improve them and support more successful realization of software projects [15, 16].

3   Selection of the Appropriate ANN Architecture Based on Taguchi's Orthogonal Vector Plan

COCOMO2000 is a parametric model that calculates the size of a system as a combination of mathematical models. Basic input data are three parameters obtained experimentally by measuring actual values during project development. Measurement-based on the number of lines of source code is used to determine the size and complexity of the software project. It is most often used to determine the effort and time needed to implement a project. The new, improved COCOMO2000 model uses four different ANN architectures based on different Taguchi orthogonal vector plans. Artificial neural networks (ANNs) are recognized for their ability to provide good results when dealing with problems where there are complex relationships between inputs and outputs, and where the input data is distorted by high noise levels. The performance of neural networks depends on the architecture of the network and their parameter settings. Determining the architecture of a network (size, structure, connectivity) affects the performance criteria, such as the learning speed, accuracy of learning, noise resistance and generalization ability.

There is no clearly defined theory which allows for the calculation of the ideal parameter settings and as a rule even slight parameter changes can cause major variations in the behavior of almost all networks. This paper describes an innovative application of the Taguchi method for the determination of these parameters to meet the training speed and accuracy requirements. Using the Taguchi method, both the micro-structural and macro-structural aspects of the neural network design parameters can be considered concurrently. The most straightforward architecture, ANN-L9 (Fig. 1), is based on the orthogonal plan L9 on three levels and four weighting factors. More complex ANN-L18 (Fig. 1) is based on the orthogonal plan L18 on two and three levels and eight weighting factors. Slightly more complex ANN-L27 (Fig. 2) is based on the orthogonal plan L27 on three levels with thirteen weighting coefficients. The most complex ANN-L36 (Fig. 2) architecture used in this model is based on the L36 orthogonal plan at two and three levels and twenty-three weighting coefficients [17–19].

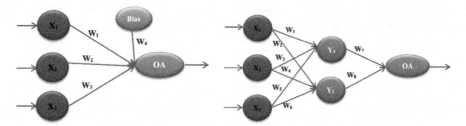

Fig. 1. ANN architecture with none hidden layer (ANN-L9) and one hidden layer (ANN-L18).

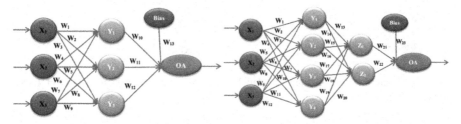

Fig. 2. ANN architecture with one hidden layer (ANN-L27) and two hidden layers (ANN-L36).

Function point analysis is an approach that was created in order to overcome the shortcomings of the previous approach, which is founded on measuring the size of the system based on the number of lines of code. In this approach, the functionality of the system is measured on the basis of quantities, expressed in functional points. Different systems may have similar functionality, but may use different technologies or programming languages, so they differ in the number of source lines of code. A number-based approach has developed a large number of models to most effectively and accurately estimate functional size. This paper will present the recent method from the family of functional points, COSMIC FFP. This method is used in the process of estimating the effort and cost of the functional size of software projects and is based on fourteen parameters that are reduced to four input sizes. In previous functional point methods, five input quantities were used. The new, improved COSMIC FFP model used two different ANN architectures, based on different Taguchi's orthogonal vector plans. The simplest architecture ANN-L12 (Fig. 3), is based on the orthogonal plan L12 on two levels and eleven weighting coefficients. More complex ANN-L36prim, is based on the orthogonal plan L36prim (Fig. 3) at two and three levels and sixteen weighting coefficients [20–22].

UCP is the latest and the most commonly used method for estimating the effort and costs for the realization of software products. Although it is not standardized within ISO standards such as the COCOMO2000 and COSMIC FFP methods, it results in estimation errors between 20% and 35%. The best result achieved with this method is an error value of about 10%. System users and use cases are used to determine the functional size by the UCP method. The new, improved UCP model used two different ANN architectures based on different Taguchi orthogonal vector plans. The most straightforward architecture, ANN-L16 (Fig. 4), is based on the orthogonal plan L16 on two levels and fifteen weighting coefficients. The more complex ANN-L36prim (Fig. 4) is based on the orthogonal plan L36prim at two and three levels and sixteen weighting coefficients [23, 24].

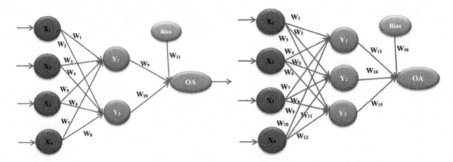

Fig. 3. ANN architecture with one hidden layer (ANN-L12) and one hidden layer (ANN-L36prim).

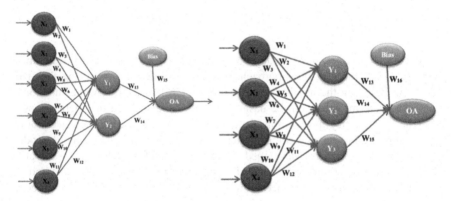

Fig. 4. ANN architecture with one hidden layer (ANN-L16) and one hidden layer (ANN-L36prim).

In addition to different architectures, the clustering method significantly contributes to controlling the different values of actual projects from practice, which aims to realistically estimate and reduce the minimum relative error of the model. The activation function used is the sigmoid function of the hidden and output layers. This function enables additional homogenization of input quantities and contributes to the rate of convergence of each of the listed ANN architectures. Experiments have shown that the number of iterations in each ANN architecture is less than 10, significantly shortening the estimation time. The new proposed models' reliability, accuracy, and efficiency have been repeatedly tested and validated on several different data sets and by verification with statistical analysis methods. Based on the obtained estimated value, various metrics were calculated, such as MAE (Magnitude Absolute Error), MRE (Magnitude Relative Error), MMRE (Mean Magnitude Relative Error) [2, 8–10].

4 Clustering Method Using Different ANN Architectures

One of the main processes in the design of neural networks is to systematically select the design parameters at both the micro-structural and macro-structural levels. Technical experience together with experiments, through computer simulations, are needed to establish the most suitable values for these design parameters. A common approach to establish these values is through the trial and error method. The Taguchi method provides a mathematical tool called the orthogonal arrays which allows the analysis of the relationships between a large number of design parameters within the smallest number of possible experiments. Noise factors including the initial values of connection weights and the values of input data are considered as external to the system and as such they cannot be controlled at all. The Taguchi method provides a means to design a neural network that is insensitive to these noise factors by setting of the design factors, such as the number of hidden layers and hidden neurons, through a set of systematic experiments. Let W be the total number of weights in the network, then in the process of training ANN at least 2W observations in the training data set are required. Depending on the proposed approaches, the training process on different ANN architectures also involves using specific data sets. The choice of appropriate datasets depends on the model and size of the input and publicly available databases. A COCOMO2000 data set was used for the ANN training procedure in the first proposed approach. The same data set was used for the ANN testing process in the other projects, and the validation process used the data sets COCOMO81, NASA60, and Kemerer. The number of projects should be greater than the number of weighting factors of the proposed ANN architecture on each selected data set. For the ANN-L9, ANN-L18, and ANN-L27 architectures, the minimum project requirement is met for all datasets used. In the ANN-L36 architecture, which has 23 weighting coefficients, the number of testing projects was 20, so the required condition was not met (Dataset_2). In the ANN-L36 architecture, which has 23 weighting coefficients, the number of projects for the third validation was 15, so the required condition was not met (Dataset_5). It can be concluded that in all parts of the experiment within the first proposed approach the fulfillment of the conditions is 90% (see Table 1).

Table 1. The number of projects greater than the number of weighting factors (COCOMO2000).

Datasets		No. of projects	Experiment	Weighting factors (coefficients)			
				ANN-L9 (4)	ANN-L18(8)	ANN-L27 (13)	ANN-L36 (23)
Dataset_1	COCOMO 2000	10 0	Training	+	+	+	+
Dataset_2	COCOMO 2000	20	Testing	+	+	+	/
Dataset_3	COCOMO81	51	Validation1	+	+	+	+
Dataset_4	NASA	60	Validation2	+	+	+	+
Dataset_5	Kemerer	15	Validation3	+	+	+	/

The ISBSG dataset divided into five selected clusters was used for the ANN training process for the second proposed approach. The same data set in the five selected clusters were used for the ANN testing procedure. The number of projects in both procedures on each selected cluster is 70:30; 70 projects were used for training and 30 for testing. Desharnais data set and data set combined from different, realistic industrial projects were used for the validation process. The number of projects should be greater than the number of weighting factors of the proposed ANN architecture on each selected data set. In the ANN-L12 architecture, which has 11 weighting coefficients, only the number of testing projects was 7, so the required condition for one data set was not met (Dataset_5). With the ANN-L36prim architecture, which has 16 weighting coefficients, the number of testing projects is 15, so the set condition is not met (Dataset_1). There were 13 testing projects (Dataset_3), so the required condition was not met within the third cluster. The number of training and testing projects (Dataset_5) was 14 and 7 projects, respectively. Within the Desharnais data set (Dataset_6), the number of projects was 14, and the set condition was not met. The number of data sets that met the criteria was 7 out of 12 [3]. It can be concluded that in all parts of the experiment, according to the second proposed approach, the fulfillment of the conditions is 75% (see Table 2).

Table 2. The number of projects greater than the number of weighting factors (COSMIC FFP).

Datasets		Number of project	Experiment	Weighting factors (coefficients)	
				ANN-L12 (11)	ANN-L36prim (16)
Dataset_1	ISBSG (Functional Size < 10)	37	Training	+	+
	ISBSG (Functional Size < 10)	15	Testing	+	/
Dataset_2	ISBSG (10 < Functional Size < 50)	45	Training	+	+
	ISBSG (10 < Functional Size < 50)	17	Testing	+	+
Dataset_3	ISBSG (50 < Functional Size < 100)	30	Training	+	+
	ISBSG (10 < Functional Size < 100)	13	Testing	+	/
Dataset_4	ISBSG (100 < Functional Size < 500)	60	Training	+	+
	ISBSG (10 < Functional Size < 500)	17	Testing	+	+
Datset_5	ISBSG (Functional Size > 500)	14	Training	+	/
	ISBSG (Functional Size > 500)	7	Testing	/	/
Dataset_6	Desharnais	14	Validation1	+	/
Dataset_7	Combined	33	Validation2	+	+

For the ANN training process, the third proposed approach used the Benchmark (Mendeley) data set divided into a 70:30 scale, 70% of the projects for the training process and 30% for the testing process. Combined real, industrial projects (Dataset_3, Dataset_4) were used for the validation procedure. The number of projects should be greater than the number of weighting factors of the proposed ANN architecture on each selected data set. In the ANN-L16 architecture, which has 15 weighting factors, the condition is that the number of projects for all parts of the experiments is greater than the number of weighting factors. With the ANN-L36prim architecture, which has 16 weighting coefficients, the condition is met that the number of projects for all parts of the experiment is greater than the number of weighting coefficients [2]. It can be concluded that in all parts of the experiment within the third proposed approach, the fulfillment of the conditions is 100%, (see Table 3).

Table 3. The number of projects greater than the number of weighting factors (UCP).

Dataset		Number of projects	Experiment	Weighting factors (coefficients)	
				ANN-L16(15)	ANN-L36prim(16)
Dataset_1	UCP Benchmark Dataset	50	Training	+	+
Dataset_2	UCP Benchmark Dataset	21	Testing	+	+
Dataset_3	Combined	18	Validation1	+	+
Dataset_4	Combined Industrial projects	17	Validation2	+	+

5 Convergence Rate and Number of Iterations Performed

One of the goals of the new, improved models is to achieve the minimum number of iterations performed to reduce the time required for estimation. For each of the four listed ANN architectures. Table 4 shows the number of iterations that need to be performed to meet the set value for the GA (Gradient Descent) criterion. The minimum number of iterations required is for ANN-L27 and ANN-L36 architectures for small and medium clusters. The most significant number of iterations should be performed for the ANN-L18 architecture, and it is nine iterations. It can be concluded that the number of iterations required is minimal (equal to nine), which leads to a quick estimate using the COCOMO2000 model.

Table 4. Number of iterations performed for each ANN architecture - COCOMO2000

COCOMO2000 model											
ANN	ANN-L9			ANN-L18			ANN-L27			ANN-L36		
No. of iterations	S	M	L	S	M	L	S	M	L	S	M	L
GA < 0.01	7	6	8	7	6	9	5	5	8	5	5	7

* (S-Small cluster, M-Medium cluster, L-Large cluster)

The number of iterations required in the second COSMIC FFP approach for both proposed architectures is six, except for the ANN-L12 architecture, where there are five for Dataset_1 and Dataset_3. It can be concluded that the number of required iterations is minimal (equal to six), which leads to an even faster estimate using the COSMIC FFP model (see Table 5).

Table 5. Number of iterations performed for each ANN architecture - COSMIC FFP.

COSMIC FFP model										
ANN	ANN-L12					ANN-L36prim				
No. of iteration	D_1	D_2	D_3	D_4	D_5	D_1	D_2	D_3	D_4	D_5
GA < 0.01	5	6	5	6	6	6	6	6	6	6

(D_1-Dataset_1, D_2-Dataset_2, D_3-Dataset_3, D_4-Dataset_4, D_5-Dataset_5)

Four iterations are required to meet the set GA criterion in the first proposed ANN-L16 architecture for the UCP model. For the ANN-L36rpim architecture, the number of iterations is equal to six. It can be concluded that the number of iterations required is the lowest compared to the other two models (equal to six), which leads to an even faster estimate using the UCP model (see Table 6).

Table 6. Number of iterations performed for each ANN architecture - UCP.

UCP model		
No. of iteration	ANN-L16	ANN-L36prim
GA < 0.01	Training	Training
	4	6

In all three proposed approaches, the minimum number of iterations required to meet the GA criteria is 4 in the UCP model for the ANN-L16 architecture. It can be concluded that this architecture converges the fastest to the minimum value of MMRE [2, 8, 9].

6 Selection of Activation Function and Encoding/Decoding Method

During our research, for all experiments of all three proposed approaches, different activation functions in the hidden and output layers were used. The experiments were performed with different functions: sigmoid function, hyperbolic tangent, Gaussian function, and others. The sigmoid function gave the best results in all experiments, i.e., the lowest MMRE value, and was used in all three proposed improved models [1, 6]. Different coding methods were used to homogenize different nature of input values: fusion method, logarithmic method, combined method, etc. The best results were achieved in all experiments with the fuzzification method used in all three proposed models (Fig. 5) [2, 8, 9].

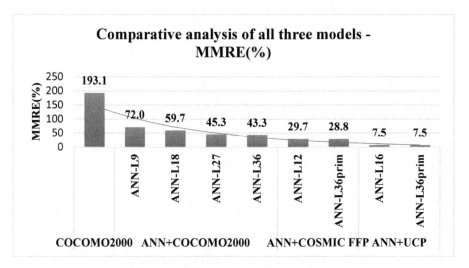

Fig. 5. MMRE values in all approaches.

By comparing the obtained results using all three new proposed improved models, it can be concluded:

- The most enormous value of the error in estimating effort and cost is in the parametric COCOMO2000 methods and goes to 193.1%;
- The best result, the lowest value of MMRE in the first proposed model is 43.3%, which is 4.5 times better result compared to the parametric method;
- In the second proposed model, the error on the ANN-L36prim architecture is 28.8% which is 6.7 times better result compared to the parametric method;
- In the third model, which is the best result in all performed experiments, the MMRE value for both proposed ANN architectures is 7.5%, which is 25.7 times better than parametric methods.

Comparing the models with each other we come to the following conclusions,

- The second proposed model ANN + COSMIC FFP has 1.6 times less error than the first model ANN + COCOMO2000;
- The third proposed ANN + UCP model has a 5.8 times lower error than the first proposed model ANN + COCOMO2000;
- The third proposed ANN + UCP model has a 3.8 times lower MMRE value than the second proposed model ANN + COSMIC FFP [2, 8, 9].

7 Conclusion

Depending on the size of the project for which the effort and costs need to be assessed, the number of inputs, and other specific factors, all three new, improved models can be used. After several rounds of experiments and analysis of the obtained results, it can be concluded that the third proposed model gives the lowest value of relative error, and it is 7.5%. If we consider that the minimum number of iterations required to reach the minimum MMRE is only four, the best ANN architecture can be identified, and that is ANN-L16 within the UCP model. The analysis of effort and cost estimates presented in this paper gives better results than the previous ones and shows that better, more advanced models can be constructed. The presented applied scientific methods can help in improving this area of software engineering. The new methodology does not exclude the possibility of applying a subjective assessment of labor and costs but can help the project team, pointing out potential problems due to discrepancies in different methods. In this way, teams can perform additional analysis to better assess and correct the results in the shortest possible time. Otherwise, project teams would have to share their own risk if only their subjective opinion is taken into account. The results obtained can help project teams, software engineers, and test engineers to make short-term plans with high and long-term reliability. Therefore, teams can with great confidence realize all phases of analysis and design and complete the project on time. If the additional estimation is needed, it is possible to anticipate the effort and costs that each project task is realized in a quality and optimal way.

References

1. Stoica, A., Blosiu, J.: Neural learning using Orthogonal arrays. Adv. Intell. Syst. **41**, 418 (1997)
2. Rankovic, D., et al.: Convergence rate of artificial neural networks in software development projects. Inf. Softw. Technol. J. **138**(10) (2021)
3. Boehm, B.W., et al.: Software Cost Estimation with COCOMO II, 1st edn. Prentice Hall Press, Upper Saddle River (2009)
4. Popović, J.: Enhancing methods for effort estimation in software projects. Doctoral dissertation, University of Belgrade, School of Electrical Engineering,
5. Meli, R., et al.: On the applicability of COSMIC-FFP for measuring software throughout its life cycle. In: Proceedings of the 11th European Software Control and Metrics Conference, pages 18–20, Springer, Cham (2000)

6. Shah, M.A.: Ensembling artificial bee colony with analogy-based estimation to improve software development effort prediction. IEEE Access **8**, 58402–58415 (2020)
7. Kaur, A., Kaur, K.: Effort estimation for mobile applications using use case point (UCP). In: Panigrahi, B.K., Trivedi, M.C., Mishra, K.K., Tiwari, S., Singh, P.K. (eds.) Smart Innovations in Communication and Computational Sciences. AISC, vol. 669, pp. 163–172. Springer, Singapore (2019). https://doi.org/10.1007/978-981-10-8968-8_14
8. Rankovic, N., et al.: Improved effort and cost estimation model using Artificial Neural Networks and Taguchi method with different activation functions. Entropy **23**(7), 854 (2021)
9. Rankovic, N., et al.: A new approach to software effort estimation using different artificial neural network architectures and Taguchi orthogonal arrays. IEEE Access **9,** 26926–26936 (2021)
10. Rankovic, N., Rankovic, D., Ivanovic, M., Lazic, L.: A novel UCP model based on artificial neural networks and orthogonal arrays. Appl. Sci. **11**(19), 8799 (2021)
11. Khaw, J.F., Lim, B., Lim, L.E.: Optimal design of neural networks using the Taguchi method. Neurocomputing **7**(3), 225–245 (1995)
12. BaniMustafa, A.: Predicting software effort estimation using machine learning techniques. In: 8th International Conference on Computer Science and Information Technology (CSIT), pp. 249–256, IEEE (2018)
13. A Guide to the Project Management Body of Knowledge (PMBOK Guide). 3rd edn. Project Management Institute, Inc. (2004). ISBN: 1-930699-45-X
14. Ayat, M., et al.: Current trends analysis and prioritization of success factors: a systematic literature review of ICT projects. Int. J. Manag. Proj. Bus. **14**(3), 652–679 (2021)
15. Kumar, P.S., et al.: Advancement from neural networks to deep learning in software effort estimation: perspective of two decades. Comput. Sci. Rev. **28**(11), 100288 (2020)
16. Suresh Kumar, P., Behera, H.S.: Estimating software effort using neural network: an experimental investigation. In: Das, A.K., Nayak, J., Naik, B., Dutta, S., Pelusi, D. (eds.) Computational Intelligence in Pattern Recognition. AISC, vol. 1120, pp. 165–180. Springer, Singapore (2020). https://doi.org/10.1007/978-981-15-2449-3_14
17. Sazli, M.H.: A brief review of feed-forward neural networks. Commun. Faculty Sci. Univ. Ankara Ser. A2-A3 Phys. Sci. Eng. **50**(01) (2006)
18. Jeang, A., Chang, C.L.: Combined robust parameter and tolerance design using Orthogonal arrays. Int. J. Adv. Manuf. Technol. **19**(6), 442–447 (2002)
19. Kechagias, J.D., et al.: A comparative investigation of Taguchi and full factorial design for machinability prediction in turning of a titanium alloy. Measurement **151**, 107213 (2020)
20. Kassab, M., Neill, C., Laplante, P.: State of practice in requirements engineering: contemporary data. Innov. Syst. Softw. Eng. **10**(4), 235–241 (2014). https://doi.org/10.1007/s11334-014-0232-4
21. Carroll, E.R.: Estimating software based on use case points. In: Companion to the 20th Annual ACM SIGPLAN Conference on Object-Oriented Programming, Systems, Languages, And Applications, pp. 257–265, San Diego, CA, USA (2005)
22. Nassif, A.B., Capretz, L.F., Ho, D.: Enhancing use case points estimation method using soft computing techniques. J. Glob. Res. Comput. Sci. **1**(4), 12–21 (2010)
23. Nassif, A.B.: Software size and effort estimation from use case diagrams using regression and soft computing models. Doctoral dissertation, Western University (2012)
24. Azzeh, M.: Fuzzy model tree for early effort estimation machine learning and applications. In: 12th International Conference on Machine Learning and Applications, pp. 117–121, Miami, Florida, USA, IEEE (2013)

Trade Between Population Size and Mutation Rate for GAAM (Genetic Algorithm with Aggressive Mutation) for Feature Selection

Marc Chevallier$^{(\boxtimes)}$ (ID), Nistor Grozavu, Faouzi Boufarès, Nicoleta Rogovschi, and Charly Clairmont

LIPN Laboratory, Sorbonne Paris Nord University, Villetaneuse, France
{chevallier,nistor.Grozavu,faouzi.boufares,
nicoleta.rogovschi}@lipn.univ-paris13.fr, charly.clairmont@synaltic.fr
https://lipn.univ-paris13.fr/, https://www.synaltic.fr/

Abstract. The "curse of dimensions" is a term that describes the many difficulties that arise in machine learning tasks as the number of features in the dataset increases. One way to solve this problem is to reduce the number of features to be provided to the model during the learning phase. This reduction in the number of dimensions can be done in two ways, either by merging dimensions together or by selecting a subset of dimensions. There are many methods to select the dimensions to be kept. One technique is to use a genetic algorithm to find a subset of dimensions that will maximize the accuracy of the classifier. A genetic algorithm specially created for this purpose is called genetic algorithm with aggressive mutation. This very efficient algorithm has several particularities compared to classical genetic algorithms. The main one is that its population is composed of a small number of individuals that are aggressively mutated. Our contribution consists in a modification of the algorithm. Indeed we propose a different version of the algorithm in which the number of mutated individuals is reduced in favor of a larger population. We have compared our method to the original one on 17 datasets, which allowed us to conclude that our method provides better results than the original algorithm while reducing the computation time.

Keywords: Features selection · Machine learning · Genetic algorithm · Metaheuristic

1 Introduction

In our post-digital transition world, more and more data is accumulated every year in companies. Much of this data is of poor quality [1]. Improving data quality is therefore becoming a task of great importance [2]. There are many

---

Supported by Synaltic: www.synaltic.fr.

methods to improve data quality. A large number of methods are based on the extraction of metadata on data: this field is called data profiling [3]. Our research in this area led us to study the features extracted by the Sherlock algorithm (an automatic semantic data type detection algorithm) [4]. We have reused similar features for several other data profiling tasks [5,6]. However, one obstacle to the industrial use of these methods is the large number of features extracted. Indeed, the time cost of extracting each feature increases with the volume of data. We are therefore confronted with the need to reduce the number of features extracted in order to be able to process larger volumes of data.

This is how we got interested in the possibilities of dimensional reduction. There are two main types of approaches, those which seek to merge the features together to create a smaller number of features (like ACP [7] or Autoencoder [8]). The best subset is the one that will give the best accuracy for a given classifier. And the methods that will try to select the best subset of the present features. Since the first possibility still requires the extraction of the initial set of characteristics, we turned to the second. This area is the field of feature selection [9]. This topic can be divided into two branches. The first one gathers the methods named "filters" which do not use a classifier to select the features, examples of algorithms of this type are: Correlation-based Feature Selection [10], Information Gain, Re-liefF [11]. The advantage of these methods is that they are very fast.

The second grouping includes approaches using a classifier for feature selection. This field of research is itself subdivided into two types of methods, the methods called "Wrapper" and the methods called "Embedded". In Embedded methods the choice of features is done by evaluating the features at each iteration during the learning phase. These methods are not usable with all learning algorithms. An example of this type of algorithm is LASSO [12]. In wrapper methods the selection of features takes place after the classifier has been trained. Algorithms of this type for example: random selection, Recursive feature Elimination [13], genetic algorithms [14]. We have chosen to focus on genetic algorithms because although their computational cost is high, they can obtain excellent results with any classifier.

2 Related Work

2.1 Genetic Algorithm

Genetic algorithms are bioinspired population-based metaheuristic algorithms popularized by J. Holland in the 1970s [15,16]. The goal of these algorithms is to minimize or maximize an objective function called fitness function. The parameters of this function are encoded in the form of a chromosome. Traditionally this encoding is done in a binary way, so a chromosome is a list of genes that can only take the values 0 and 1. The functioning of these algorithms is based on two basic operations. The first is the mutation which consists in altering a chromosome by randomly changing some of its genes. And the second one is the crossing which consists in mixing two chromosomes in order to create two new ones. The classic method to do this is to break the two parent chromosomes into 1 point and then swap the pieces of chromosomes from the two parents to form two children. There are however several other methods to do this more efficiently [16].

Genetic algorithms generally have 5 parameters: the population size, the number of iterations, the chromosome size, the mutation probability and the crossover probability. The overall operation of the algorithm is as follows: a population (group of chromosomes) is randomly generated. Each individual generated in this way is evaluated using the fitness function. Depending on the results of this evaluation and the probability of crossover a daughter population is generated by crossing the initial population. Then a part of the daughter population is mutated according to the selected mutation probability. The daughter population is then evaluated using the fitness function. Finally a selection step takes place among the individuals of both populations (according to the fitness score) and a population of the same size as the initial population is kept. The algorithm then repeats this process of crossover, mutation, evaluation, selection until the number of iterations (generations) is reached. The chromosomes of the best individual of the last generation encode a good solution to the problem we are trying to solve.

For the feature selection problem, the encoding is done in the following way: if a dataset contains 10 features, the chromosomes will be of size 10, a 1 will represent a feature that can be used during the training of the classifier, a 0 an absent feature. The fitness function is the accuracy of the classifier. This method presents two problems. First, it is not possible to choose the number of features that we want to keep. Secondly, genetic algorithms tend to get trapped in local optimums. In the case of feature selection the algorithms tend to keep a number of features slightly less than half of the total number of features. This number can be reduced by modifying the fitness function to penalize the use of too many features. But this only reduces the number of selected features by 20% [17].

2.2   Genetic Algorithm with Aggressive Mutation GAAM

The Genetic Algorithm with Aggressive Mutations (GAAM) is an algorithm that has been specifically designed for feature selection [18]. This algorithm has several major differences from classical genetic algorithms. First of all, the encoding of genes does not use a binary system but integers. If a dataset contains N features, the encoding uses N integers, each number representing 1 feature. In addition, the value 0 represents the absence of characteristics. Then the algorithm allows to choose the maximum number of features that we want to keep, this number corresponds to the size of the chromosome. For example if a dataset has 10 features and we want to keep a maximum of 5, examples of chromosomes would be: [2 7 9 10 8], [3 2 2 10 5] [0 7 8 9 5]. If a gene is present several times as in [3 2 2 10 5] the duplicates are eliminated and replaced by 0.

Then the mutation system is different from that of traditional algorithms, indeed each individual will allow to create a number of mutants equal to its size. Each mutant is a copy of the initial chromosome where only 1 gene has been mutated (by random draw between 0 and the size of the chromosome), for the first mutant individual it is the first gene that is mutated, for the second the second gene and so on. For example if we have gene [2 3 4] the mutants will be for example [4 3 4], [2 0 4] and [2 3 2]. The crossover is a classical 1 point crossover, each individual is crossed in order to generate a daughter population of size equal to the size of the initial population. Thus the algorithm does not require a mutation probability and crossover probability parameter.

The last difference between the GAAM algorithm and the classical genetic algorithms lies in the order in which the operations are performed. Indeed, the randomly generated initial population is not evaluated at the beginning of the algorithm, it is simply used to generate the daughter population and the mutant population. So if we start with N individuals with chromosomes of size T we obtain N individuals in the daughter population and N*T individuals in the mutated population. We have thus 2*N + N*T individuals to evaluate at the end of the first generation. We keep then the N best individuals. GAAM is described in the Algorithm 1.

Algorithm 1 : GAAM, G represents the number of generations, N the number of individuals, T the size of the chromosomes, L the size of the dataset.

INPUT : $G:int, N:int, T:int, L:int$
$g = 0$
Step 1 : Build N individuals with T genes randomly picked in $\{0,1,2..L\}$ in order to produce the initial population Ip
Step 2 : Aggressive mutation : Create Mp the mutate population
for j=1 to N **do**
  for x=1 to T **do**
    pick a random value m in $\{0,1,2..L\}$
    Assign to D a copy of **Ip(j)**
    $D(x)=m$
    add D to Mp
  end for
end for
Step 3 : Crossover : Apply a classical holland crossover on each individuals
Step 4 : Create $Tp=Ip+Mp+Cp$ the total population evaluate each individual with the fitness function and rank them according to their fitness.
Step 5 : Drop the $N+N*T$ individuals with the lowest fitness from Tp and replace Ip by the remaining,$g+=1$
If $g = G$ return $Ip(0)$ else back to step 2

---

3   Modified Genetic Algorithm with Aggressive Mutation mGAAM

The GAAM algorithm is very efficient but the aggressive mutation principle forces to use only a small number of initial individuals in order not to have too many individuals to evaluate after the mutation step. This low number of initial individuals will lead to a low genetic diversity within the population, which may cause the algorithm to remain trapped in a local optimum. We wanted to evaluate the impact of the initial population size on the results of the algorithm. We have therefore defined a version of GAAM, named mGAAM where the size of the initial population can be modified compared to a classical version of the GAAM algorithm. Thus our algorithm takes as parameters the size of a population and the number of iterations of a classical version of GAAM. Our goal is to keep approximately the same number of individuals in the population as the version of GAAM defined with these parameters while proposing a lower or higher number of individuals in the initial population while keeping the same number of crossed individuals as in the initial version. Thus the parameter that will be adjusted is the number of mutant chromosomes generated by a chromosome during the mutation step. If we use a larger population than the original version, for example 20 instead of 10, the number of mutated individuals will be reduced in order to obtain on average the same number of individuals per iteration as the original version of the algorithm.

Our method changes the steps 2 and 3 of the GAAM algorithm. For step 3, we keep only a number of crossed individuals equal to mGAAM_pop_seize. This number corresponds to the size of the population to which we compare ourselves. We cross all the individuals then we draw the desired number. Algorithm 2 replaces the mutation step of the original version. It is enough to add to the original version a parameter GAAM_pop_size which describes the size of the population to which one wishes to compare. Moreover the N corresponds to mGAAM_pop_size in Algorithm 2. When the population size is smaller than the target population size, each gene is mutated several times. The overall mutation process depends on probabilities so the number of individuals generated at each generation is not fixed. However, the average size of the population at each iteration (before the selection step) corresponds to the size of the one of the classical GAAM algorithm (for the parameters we have chosen). In order to maintain this correspondence the mutation rate to be used must be calculated each time the experimental parameters change, this is done using the Algorithm 3.

4   Comparisons Between Gaam and mGaam

Our experimental setup is a Google Colab [23] instance with a Xeon 2.30 GHz 4-core and 25 GB Ram. The classifier used is a naive Bayesian classifier [19], we chose this classifier because it has the advantage of being extremely fast to train. The evaluation of the results is done using the average of the accuracy calculated on 3 cross validation.

The 17 used datasets are present and described in the UCI machine learning repository [20]. We used the versions of these datasets freely available on Open ML [21,22]. The datasets used are described in Table 1. The datasets contain mostly numerical data, the categorical data are encoded.

Algorithm 2 : Mutation mGAAM pop the population, L the number of features in the dataset, mGAAM_pop_size : is the desired population size, GAAM_pop_size is the size of the population being compared to, T is the size of the chromosome

INPUT : *pop:list, L:int, mgaam_pop_size:int, gaam_pop_size:int, T:int*

INIT : tm ← Calc_tm_standard(mgaam_pop_size, gaam_pop_size,T)
offspring ← []

for *j=1 to size(pop)* **do**
    tmp_offspring ← []
    tmp_tm = copy(tm)
    while *tmp_tm>0* **do**
        for *i=1 to T* **do**
            ind *gets* copy(pop[j])
            $rho \leftarrow random\_uniform(0,1)$
            if $rho < tmp\_tm$ **then**
                new_val ← random value between 0 and L

            ind[i]← new_val
            add ind to tmp_offspring
        tmp_tm ← tmp_tm - 1
    offspring ← offspring + tmp_offspring
return offspring

Algorithm 3 : Calc_tm_standard mgaam_pop_size : is the desired population size, GAAM_pop_size is the size of the population being compared to, T is the size of the chromosome

INPUT : *mGAAM_pop_size:int, GAAM_pop_size:int, T:int*

tm ← $\frac{gaam\_pop\_size*(T+1)-mgaam\_pop\_size)}{T*mgaam\_pop\_size}$
return *tm*

Each result presented is calculated from the results of 50 simulations. The mutation rates for mGaam are automatically calculated to keep the number of individuals equal (at each generation) to what would be used by the original Gaam algorithm with 10 individuals (N), and 100 iterations (G). We have chosen to use these parameters because they are always used in the original articles concerning GAAM [17,18]. The number of individuals to be evaluated and the number of characteristics must remain low in order to avoid an explosion of the number of individuals to evaluate at each iteration.

Table 1. Description of the datasets used

Name	Features	No. of classes	Examples	Source
Leaf [24]	15	30	340	openml.org/d/1482
Thoracic-surgery	16	2	470	openml.org/d/4329
Credit-g [27]	20	2	1000	openml.org/d/31
Climate-model [28]	20	2	540	openml.org/d/40994
Dermatology	34	6	358	openml.org/d/35
Ionosphere	34	2	351	openml.org/d/59
Audit [25]	36	2	1552	openml.org/d/42931
SPECTF	44	2	349	openml.org/d/1600
Hill-valley	100	2	1212	openml.org/d/1479
Spectrometer	101	48	531	openml.org/d/313
Musk	167	2	6598	openml.org/d/1116
Semeion	256	10	1593	openml.org/d/1501
Madelon	500	2	2600	openml.org/d/1485
Har [29]	561	6	10299	openml.org/d/1478
Isolet	617	26	7797	openml.org/d/300
Parkinson-speech-uci [26]	753	2	756	openml.org/d/42176
Micro-mass	1300	10	360	openml.org/d/1514

5   Results

The results of our experiments are shown in Table 3 and 4. First of all the column corresponding exactly to the original algorithm is the one where the population size is 10. By observing the results we notice that in the majority of the datasets the results are better when the population size is higher than 10, very often a size of 60 with a low mutation rate gives better results. This is explained by the fact that using a larger starting population allows to obtain on average better individuals at the end of the first iteration. These better initial individuals then allow to obtain mostly better final results at the end of the 100 generations. This effect can be seen in the Fig. 1 which represents the average accuracy results at each iteration for the Credit g dataset. We can also see in the Fig. 1 that it is useless to increase the population indefinitely, the population of size 90 having no advantage over the population of size 60.

We can then see that progressively when the number of features increases in the datasets, the best solutions are found for smaller population sizes. This is explained by the fact that our method tries to have the same number of individuals at each iteration as the initial algorithm. This constraint implies that at each generation when the population is greater than 10 we evaluate less new individuals than the initial GAAM algorithm. Indeed with the initial algorithm and the parameters of the experiment at each iteration (except the first one) 10 individuals from crossing and 100 individuals from mutations are evaluated. Whereas with the method we used in the experiment if the population is 30 there are on average only 90 new individuals evaluated in each generation. This has the effect of making the algorithm faster but also reduces the speed of convergence. But when the number of features becomes important the algorithm does not have time to converge completely because the problem becomes more difficult. This effect can be visualised in Fig. 2 on the Micro-mass dataset. We can thus explain the decrease in performance of the largest populations when the number of features increases.

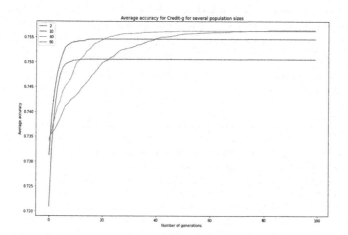

Fig. 1. Average accuracy for Leaf for several population sizes

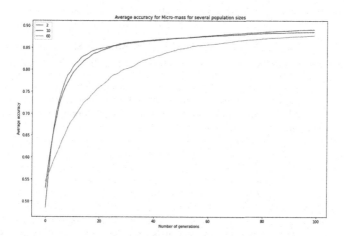

Fig. 2. Average accuracy for Micro-Mass for several population sizes

This problem can be alleviated by replacing the Algorithm 3 with Algorithm 4. The modification in the method of calculation allows to obtain a larger number of individuals evaluated at each iteration (equivalent to what we have with the classical GAAM algorithm). The change of calculation method increases the mutation rate in mGAAM (when the initial population is greater than the size of the population of the GAAM algorithm which is used as a comparison point) to compensate for the deficit of individuals evaluated at each iteration because of the non-evaluation of individuals of the previous generation during a new generation. We have tested (with the same parameters as before) the Algorithm 4 on the micro-mass Dataset, the results are presented in the Table 2. There is a clear improvement in the results for large populations. However, the drawback of this modification is the absence of gain in computation time compared to the original algorithm.

Algorithm 4 : Calc_tm_imp mgaam_pop_size : is the desired population size, gaam_pop_size is the size of the population being compared to, T is the size of the chromosome, G the number of generations

---

INPUT : $mgaam\_pop\_size{:}int, \ gaam\_pop\_size{:}int, \ T{:}int, G{:}int$

$tm \leftarrow \frac{gaam\_pop\_size - mgaam\_pop\_size}{G*T*mgaam\_pop\_size} + \frac{gaam\_pop\_size}{mgaam\_pop\_size}$

return tm

Table 2. Results on Micro-mass using Algorithm 4 to generate the mutation rate

Dataset/Population size		10	20	30	40	60
Micro-mass	Mean	88.588	88.861	**89.216**	89.155	89.155
	Median	88.472	88.888	**89.444**	89.027	89.444
	Max	88.588	91.944	**92.222**	91.666	**92.222**

Table 3. Results of the mGaam algorithm on several datasets defined against a version of gaam using 10 individuals, 10 and 100 iteration size chromosomes, calculated from the results of 50 simulations, part a.

Data/Pop		2	4	6	8	10	20	30	40	60
Leaf	$\overline{m}$	73.227	73.220	73.250	73.392	73.333	73.534	73.504	73.510	**73.552**
	Mdn	73.552	73.552	73.552	73.552	73.552	73.552	73.552	73.552	73.552
	max	73.552	73.552	73.552	73.552	73.552	73.552	73.552	73.552	73.552
Thora	$\overline{m}$	79.590	84.246	83.233	84.766	84.953	85.119	85.217	85.238	**85.285**
	Mdn	84.254	84.257	85.106	85.106	85.106	**85.319**	**85.319**	**85.319**	**85.319**
	max	**85.319**	**85.319**	**85.319**	**85.319**	**85.319**	**85.319**	**85.319**	**85.319**	**85.319**
Credit	$\overline{m}$	75.053	75.383	75.291	75.399	75.461	75.505	75.563	75.555	**75.623**
	Mdn	75.250	**75.599**	**75.599**	**75.599**	**75.599**	**75.599**	**75.599**	**75.599**	**75.599**
	max	**75.899**	**75.899**	**75.899**	**75.899**	**75.899**	**75.899**	**75.899**	**75.899**	**75.899**
Clima	$\overline{m}$	92.107	92.107	92.344	92.388	92.437	92.640	92.725	92.748	**92.862**
	Mdn	91.851	92.037	92.407	92.407	92.592	92.777	**92.962**	**92.962**	**92.962**
	max	**92.962**	**92.962**	**92.962**	**92.962**	**92.962**	**92.962**	**92.962**	**92.962**	**92.962**

(*continued*)

Table 3. (*continued*)

Data/Pop		2	4	6	8	10	20	30	40	60
Derma	$\overline{m}$	96.155	96.704	96.899	96.866	96.844	96.990	97.118	97.083	**97.207**
	Mdn	96.659	96.935	96.935	96.935	96.935	96.935	96.935	96.935	**97.207**
	max	**98.046**	**98.046**	**98.046**	**98.046**	**98.046**	**98.046**	**98.046**	**98.046**	98.046
Ionos	$\overline{m}$	87.054	88.501	88.632	88.689	88.552	88.957	88.991	89.065	**89.105**
	Mdn	88.319	88.603	88.888	88.888	88.603	88.888	88.888	**89.173**	**89.173**
	max	**89.458**	**89.458**	**89.458**	**89.458**	**89.458**	**89.458**	**89.458**	**89.458**	89.458
Audit	$\overline{m}$	87.722	88.307	87.951	88.858	89.664	89.745	89.784	89.802	**89.808**
	Mdn	89.432	89.559	89.496	89.559	89.689	89.818	**89.883**	**89.883**	89.819
	max	90.142	90.142	90.142	90.142	90.142	**90.142**	90.142	**90.142**	90.142
SPEC	$\overline{m}$	81.810	81.896	81.942	82.164	82.131	82.406	82.463	82.423	**82.531**
	Mdn	81.951	81.951	81.951	82.234	82.228	82.517	**82.520**	**82.520**	82.520
	max	**83.092**	**83.092**	**83.092**	**83.092**	**83.092**	**83.092**	83.092	**83.092**	83.092
Hill	$\overline{m}$	52.306	52.369	52.391	52.422	52.420	52.447	52.516	52.514	**52.534**
	Mdn	52.310	52.392	52.392	52.392	52.392	52.433	**52.557**	**52.557**	52.557
	max	**52.640**	**52.640**	**52.640**	**52.640**	**52.640**	**52.640**	52.640	**52.640**	52.640
Spect	$\overline{m}$	57.212	57.370	57.578	57.401	57.589	57.883	57.902	**58.131**	58.037
	Mdn	57.250	57.438	57.532	57.438	57.721	58.003	58.003	**58.192**	58.003
	max	58.568	**58.945**	**58.945**	**58.945**	**58.945**	58.568	**58.945**	**58.945**	**58.945**

Table 4. Results of the mGaam algorithm on several datasets defined against a version of gaam using 10 individuals, 10 and 100 iteration size chromosomes, calculated from the results of 50 simulations, part b.

Data/Pop		2	4	6	8	10	20	30	40	60
Musk	$\overline{m}$	95.060	95.233	95.124	95.267	95.294	95.251	95.290	**95.338**	95.284
	Mdn	95.141	95.217	95.240	95.285	95.308	95.240	95.346	**95.369**	95.270
	max	**95.452**	**95.452**	**95.452**	**95.452**	**95.452**	**95.452**	95.452	**95.452**	**95.452**
Seme	$\overline{m}$	66.367	66.178	66.204	**66.817**	66.726	66.514	66.661	66.572	65.546
	Mdn	66.823	66.478	66.603	66.917	**66.980**	66.698	66.917	66.792	65.599
	max	**68.926**	68.424	68.361	68.738	68.424	**68.926**	68.424	68.361	68.047
Made	$\overline{m}$	63.856	63.833	63.895	64.039	63.963	**64.353**	64.131	63.941	64.078
	Mdn	63.653	63.730	63.692	63.884	63.961	**64.212**	63.961	63.827	63.923
	max	65.038	65.577	65.347	**65.808**	65.731	65.615	65.577	65.308	65.346
Har	$\overline{m}$	90.949	**90.966**	90.957	90.842	90.937	90.853	90.761	90.742	90.411
	Mdn	90.994	90.989	**91.018**	90.965	91.013	90.940	90.756	90.804	90.435
	max	91.270	91.261	**91.280**	91.270	91.261	91.261	91.212	91.203	91.096
Isol	$\overline{m}$	74.846	74.979	4.971	74.805	**75.089**	74.722	74.339	74.296	73.241
	Mdn	74.746	75.073	5.099	74.996	**75.022**	74.868	74.586	74.284	73.252
	max	76.221	76.195	6.016	75.990	**76.208**	75.798	75.926	75.824	75.221
Parkin	$\overline{m}$	85.169	85.185	85.433	85.489	85.544	85.642	85.820	**85.899**	85.396
	Mdn	85.251	85.052	85.582	85.317	85.449	85.582	85.780	**85.978**	85.317
	max	87.301	87.566	87.169	86.904	87.566	87.037	87.301	**87.962**	87.169
Micro	$\overline{m}$	**89.111**	89.183	88.588	88.649	88.588	88.550	88.838	88.544	87.755
	Mdn	89.166	**89.444**	88.611	88.888	88.472	88.611	88.611	88.611	87.777
	max	91.944	**92.222**	91.944	91.944	91.111	91.666	91.666	91.388	90.833

6   Conclusion

In this paper we have presented a modification of the GAAM algorithm. The main modification is to decrease the number of mutations that each individual undergoes while using a larger population. It appears from the experiments that we have performed that our algorithm has two advantages over the original algorithm. First, the features selected by our algorithm lead to better accuracy results. Secondly, using a larger population reduces the computation time, by decreasing the total number of individuals to be re-evaluated at each iteration. In the case of datasets containing a large number of features, we have introduced a second possibility to calculate the mutation rate. This one does not have the advantage of a time saving but allows to maintain better results than the original algorithm at equal computation cost. Future studies should be conducted to combine our method with the techniques implemented in fGAAM [31] to speed up the algorithm. Moreover, we could be interested in combining our new method with seeding techniques of the initial population [30] to try to improve the results. Finally it would also be interesting to compare the method with other advanced feature selection techniques [32,33].

Acknowledgements. I gratefully acknowledge Astrid Balick for her generous support. Supported by organization Synaltic.

References

1. Redman, T.: The impact of poor data quality on the typical enterprise. Commun. ACM **41**, 79–82 (1998)
2. Ilyas, I., Chu, X.: Data Cleaning. Association for Computing Machinery (2019)
3. Abedjan, Z., Golab, L., Naumann, F., Papenbrock, T.: Data profiling. Synth. Lect. Data Manag. **10**, 1–154 (2018). https://doi.org/10.2200/s00878ed1v01y2018 10dtm052
4. Hulsebos, M., et al.: Sherlock: a deep learning approach to semantic data type detection. In: Proceedings of the 25th ACM SIGKDD International Conference on Knowledge Discovery and Data Mining, pp. 1500–1508 (2019). https://doi.org/10.1145/3292500.3330993
5. Chevallier, M., Boufarès, F., Grozavu, N., Rogovschi, N., Clairmont, C.: Near duplicate column identification: a machine learning approach. In: 2021 IEEE Symposium Series on Computational Intelligence (SSCI), pp. 1–7 (2021). https://doi.org/10.1109/SSCI50451.2021.9659897
6. Chevallier, M., Rogovschi, N. Boufarès, F., Grozavu, N., Clairmont, C.: Detecting near duplicate dataset. In: Proceedings of the 13th International Conference on Soft Computing and Pattern Recognition (SoCPaR) 2021. LNNS, vol. 417, pp. 1–10 (2022). https://doi.org/10.1007/978-3-030-96302-6_36
7. Karl Pearson F.R.S.: LIII. On lines and planes of closest fit to systems of points in space. Lond. Edinb. Dublin Philos. Mag. J. Sci. **2**, 559–572 (1901). https://doi.org/10.1080/14786440109462720
8. Wang, Y., Yao, H., Zhao, S.: Auto-encoder based dimensionality reduction. Neurocomputing **184**, 232–242 (2016). https://www.sciencedirect.com/science/article/pii/S0925231215017671. RoLoD: Robust Local Descriptors for Computer Vision 2014

9. Liu, H., Motoda, H.: Feature Selection for Knowledge Discovery and Data Mining. Springer, New York (1998). https://doi.org/10.1007/978-1-4615-5689-3

10. Hall, M.: Correlation-based feature selection of discrete and numeric class machine learning. University of Waikato, Department of Computer Science (2000). https://hdl.handle.net/10289/1024

11. Urbanowicz, R., Meeker, M., La Cava, W., Olson, R., Moore, J.: Relief-based feature selection: introduction and review. J. Biomed. Inform. **85**, 189–203 (2018). https://www.sciencedirect.com/science/article/pii/S1532046418301400

12. Tibshirani, R.: Regression shrinkage and selection via the lasso. J. Roy. Stat. Soc.: Ser. B (Methodol.) **58**, 267–288 (1996). https://rss.onlinelibrary.wiley.com/doi/abs/10.1111/j.2517-6161.1996.tb02080.x

13. Guyon, I., Weston, J., Barnhill, S., Vapnik, V.: Gene selection for cancer classification using support vector machines. Mach. Learn. **46**, 389–422 (2002). https://doi.org/10.1023/A:1012487302797

14. Reeves, C.: Genetic algorithms. In: Handbook of Metaheuristics, pp. 109–139 (2010)

15. Holland, J.: Adaptation in natural and artificial systems. University of Michigan Press (1975)

16. Rimcharoen, S., Leelathakul, N.: Ring-based crossovers in genetic algorithms: characteristic decomposition and their generalization. IEEE Access **9**, 137902–137922 (2021)

17. Rejer, I., Lorenz, K.: Classic genetic algorithm vs. genetic algorithm with aggressive mutation for feature selection for a brain-computer interface. Przeglad Elektrotechniczny **1**(2), 100–104 (2015)

18. Rejer, I.: Genetic algorithm with aggressive mutation for feature selection in BCI feature space. Pattern Anal. Appl. **18**(3), 485–492 (2014). https://doi.org/10.1007/s10044-014-0425-3

19. Zhang, H.: The Optimality of Naive Bayes (2004)

20. Dua, D., Graff, C.: UCI Machine Learning Repository. University of California, Irvine, School of Information (2017). http://archive.ics.uci.edu/ml

21. Vanschoren, J., Rijn, J., Bischl, B., Torgo, L.: OpenML: networked science in machine learning. SIGKDD Explor. **15**, 49–60 (2013). http://doi.acm.org/10.1145/2641190.2641198

22. Matthias Feurer OpenML-Python: an extensible Python API for OpenML. arXiv:1911.0249. https://arxiv.org/pdf/1911.02490.pdf

23. Bisong, E.: Google Colaboratory. Building Machine Learning and Deep Learning Models on Google Cloud Platform: A Comprehensive Guide for Beginners, pp. 59–64 (2019). https://doi.org/10.1007/978-1-4842-4470-8_7

24. Silva, P.F.B., Marçal, A.R.S., da Silva, R.M.A.: Evaluation of features for leaf discrimination. In: Kamel, M., Campilho, A. (eds.) ICIAR 2013. LNCS, vol. 7950, pp. 197–204. Springer, Heidelberg (2013). https://doi.org/10.1007/978-3-642-39094-4_23

25. Hooda, N., Bawa, S., Rana, P.: Fraudulent firm classification: a case study of an external audit. Appl. Artif. Intell. **32**, 48–64 (2018). https://doi.org/10.1080/08839514.2018.1451032

26. Sakar, B., et al.: Collection and analysis of a Parkinson speech dataset with multiple types of sound recordings. IEEE J. Biomed. Health Inform. **17**, 828–834 (2013)

27. Groemping, U.: South German Credit Data: Correcting a Widely Used Data Set. Reports in Mathematics (2019)

28. Lucas, D., et al.: Failure analysis of parameter-induced simulation crashes in climate models. Geosci. Model Dev. **6**, 1157–1171 (2013). https://gmd.copernicus.org/articles/6/1157/2013/

29. Anguita, D., Ghio, A., Oneto, L., Parra, X., Reyes-Ortiz, J.: A Public Domain Dataset for Human Activity Recognition using Smartphones. ESANN (2013)

30. Chevallier, M., Rogovschi, N., Boufarès, F., Grozavu, N., Clairmont, C.: Seeding initial population, in genetic algorithm for features selection. In: Abraham, A., et al. (eds.) SoCPaR 2020. AISC, vol. 1383, pp. 572–582. Springer, Cham (2021). https://doi.org/10.1007/978-3-030-73689-7_55

31. Rejer, I., Jankowski, J.: fGAAM: a fast and resizable genetic algorithm with aggressive mutation for feature selection. Pattern Anal. Appl. (3), 1–17 (2021). https://doi.org/10.1007/s10044-021-01000-z

32. Eid, H., Abraham, A.: Adaptive feature selection and classification using modified whale optimization algorithm. Int. J. Comput. Inf. Syst. Ind. Manag. Appl. **10**, 174–182 (2018)

33. Chotchantarakun, K., Sornil, O.: An adaptive multi-levels sequential feature selection. Int. J. Comput. Inf. Syst. Ind. Manag. Appl. **13**, 10–19 (2021)

Explainable AI/Graph Representation and Processing Frameworks

A Novel Human-Centred Evaluation Approach and an Argument-Based Method for Explainable Artificial Intelligence

Giulia Vilone[(✉)] and Luca Longo

The Artificial Intelligence and Cognitive Load Research Lab,
The Applied Intelligence Research Center, School of Computer Science,
Technological University Dublin, Dublin, Ireland
{giulia.vilone,luca.longo}@tudublin.ie

Abstract. One of the aim of Explainable Artificial Intelligence (XAI) is to equip data-driven, machine-learned models with a high degree of explainability for humans. Understanding and explaining the inferences of a model can be seen as a defeasible reasoning process. This process is likely to be non-monotonic: a conclusion, linked to a set of premises, can be retracted when new information becomes available. In formal logic, computational argumentation is a method, within Artificial Intelligence (AI), focused on modeling defeasible reasoning. This research study focuses on the automatic formation of an argument-based representation for a machine-learned model in order to enhance its degree of explainability, by employing principles and techniques from computational argumentation. It also contributes to the body of knowledge by introducing a novel quantitative human-centred technique to evaluate such a novel representation, and potentially other XAI methods, in the form of a questionnaire for explainability. An experiment have been conducted with two groups of human participants, one interacting with the argument-based representation, and one with a decision trees, a representation deemed naturally transparent and comprehensible. Findings demonstrate that the explainability of the original argument-based representation is statistically similar to that associated to the decision-trees, as reported by humans via the novel questionnaire.

Keywords: Explainable Artificial Intelligence · Argumentation · Human-centred evaluation · Non-monotonic reasoning · Explainability

1 Introduction

Explainable Artificial Intelligence (XAI), an emerging sub-field of Artificial Intelligence (AI), mainly aims to develop a unified approach to learning data-driven models with high prediction accuracy and a high degree of explainability. The explosion of data availability and the success of Machine Learning (ML) have led

© IFIP International Federation for Information Processing 2022
Published by Springer Nature Switzerland AG 2022
I. Maglogiannis et al. (Eds.): AIAI 2022, IFIP AICT 646, pp. 447–460, 2022.
https://doi.org/10.1007/978-3-031-08333-4_36

to the fast development of models that can reach outstanding predictive performances. Unfortunately, most of these 'black-box' models have underlying complex structures that are difficult to comprehend and explain. Researchers have attempted to open up these black-boxes by developing numerous XAI methods that generate different formats of explanations (numerical, rules, textual, visual or mixed) [19,27]. However, the main criticism refers to the fact that these methods do not necessarily capture and describe the actual inference process of an ML model, and they merely report its outputs without attempting to verify if they are consistent with the user's domain knowledge or are instead based on spurious correlations of the data. Instead, we believe that understanding the inferential process of a model should be seen as a reasoning process that discloses the relationships between input and output. ML models are often built to discover "comprehensible, interesting knowledge (or patterns) from data" [11]. This means that a mechanism is necessary to support humans in the comprehension of the inherent learnt inferential process of a model. This mechanism should be aligned to the way human reasons. Argumentation is a multidisciplinary field within AI that focuses on how arguments can be presented, supported or discarded in a defeasible reasoning process, and it investigates formal approaches to assess the validity of the conclusions reached [4,17]. Argumentation Theory (AT) provides the basis for implementing defeasible reasoning computationally, inspired by how humans reason [17]. Our expectation is that argumentation can be a viable solution for XAI methods. This expectation was preliminarily tested via a human-centred study. This included the development of a questionnaire for explainability that was employed for comparing a traditional rule-base decision-tree and a novel argument-based explanation method.

The remainder of this manuscript is organised as follows. Section 2 summarises the strategies used by scholars to generate rule-based explanations of ML models and how to assess the quality of these explanations. Section 3 describes the design of a primary research experiment. Section 4 discusses the findings of this experiment and its limitations. Lastly, Sect. 5 highlights the contribution to the existing body of knowledge and suggests future directions.

2   Related Work

Rule-based explanations represent a structured but intuitive format for conveying information to humans compactly. They can help disclose the logic of a quantitative model into a set of rules that can be read, interpreted and visualised. For this reason, scholars consider rule-based and tree-based models as naturally transparent and intelligible [7,9]. However, current methods from XAI generating rule-based explanations are usually limiting themselves to produce a list of rules mimicking the inferential process of an underlying model and not aggregated together to form a richer reasoning process [16]. Similarly, these methods do not focus on the potential inconsistencies among these rules and, should they arise, do not provide any tool to handle them [26]. Possible solutions to the above issues can be provided by Argumentation Theory (AT). This is a multidisciplinary field, inspired by how humans reason, that focuses on how arguments can be presented, supported or discarded in a defeasible reasoning process. In formal logic, a defeasible concept consists of a set of pieces of information or reasons that can be defeated by additional information or reasons [18]. Technically speaking, AT focuses on modelling non-monotonic reasoning and it investigates formal approaches to assess the validity of the conclusions reached by arguments [4,17]. Arguments are usually designed by domain experts, forming a knowledge-base in single or multi-agent environments [24]. In a single-agent environment, arguments are often built by an autonomous reasoner, and often conflictual information tends to be minimal. In a multi-agent environment, multiple reasoners participate in argument building, and more conflicts among them are usually conceived, enabling in practice non-monotonic reasoning [20]. Defeasible argumentation can provide a sound formalisation for reasoning with uncertain and incomplete information from a defeasible knowledge-base [12]. The process of defeasible argumentation often involves the recursive analysis of conflicting arguments in a dialectical setting to determine which arguments should be accepted or discarded [10]. Abstract Argumentation Theory is the dominant paradigm, whereby arguments are abstractly considered in a dialogical structure, and formal semantics are usually adopted to partition these into conflict-free sets of arguments that can be subsequently used for supporting decision-making, explanations and justification [10,17]. Existing argument-based frameworks have some peculiar features [12,13,22]:

- a knowledge-base in the form of interactive arguments is usually formalised with a first-order logical language;
- *attacks* are modelled whenever two arguments are in conflict;
- a mechanism for conflict resolution implements in practice non-monotonicity, which provides a dialectical status to the arguments in the knowledge-base.

Minimal work exists on automatic argument mining from models generated by ML algorithms, and the integration between AT and ML is still a young field. [6,12,22]. A solution, based on a two-step approach, was proposed in [25]. First, rules were extracted from a given dataset with the Apriori algorithm for association rule mining. In the second step, these rules were interpreted as the input for structured argumentation approaches, such as ASPIC+ [21]. Using their argumentative inferential procedures, a new observation was classified by constructing arguments on top of these rules and determining their justification status. Alternatively, argumentative graphs were exploited to represent the structure of argument-based frameworks [23]. Arguments are treated as nodes connected by directed edges which are the attacks. The status of the arguments is given by a label (accepted or rejected), computed using argumentation semantics [2].

In summary, the literature review conducted showed that minimal work exists at the intersection of ML and AT, how models learnt can be exploited to augment their interpretation via argumentation and, in turn, improve their explainability. In relation to this, the first issue is the automatic extraction of rules and their conflicts from these models. The second issue is their automatic integration into an argumentation framework that can serve as a mechanism for interpreting and explaining the inferential process of such models and, successively, increase their explainability without any explicit human declarative knowledge.

3   Design

The informal research hypothesis is that the rules extracted from data-driven ML models by an XAI method support the automatic formation of an argumentation framework. This framework is expected to possess higher explainability when compared to a decision tree, another interpretable XAI method. Decision trees have been selected as a baseline since they are widely used within Computer Science because considered naturally intelligible and transparent [7,9]. The difference in the degree of explainability of the two methods was tested by considering each question of the survey separately and not by aggregating their answers. In this way, it was possible to determine which characteristics were discriminative. To test the research hypothesis, a set of phases are described in the following paragraphs and depicted in the diagram of Fig. 1.

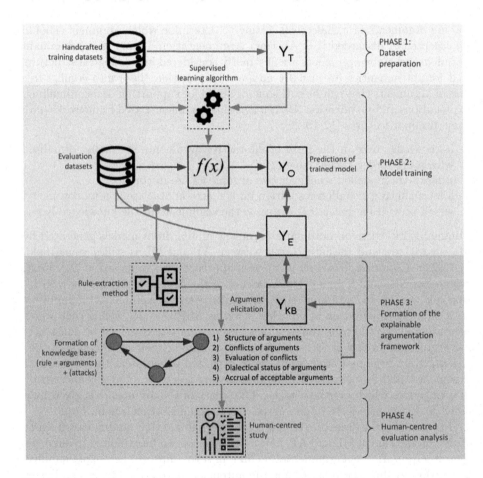

Fig. 1. High-level representation of the process to build the envisioned argument- and rule-based XAI method.

Phase 1: Dataset Preparation. The first step is to select a training dataset containing multi-dimensional data built by domain experts. The dataset must not present issues that can prevent the successful training of a model, such as the course of dimensionality or a significant portion of missing data. The block Y_T in Fig. 1 represents the labeled dependent variable. In this study, the experiment was carried out on the Airline Passenger Satisfaction dataset, publicly available from Kaggle's repository[1], which contains 129,880 records collected from an airline passenger satisfaction survey. The survey was designed to identify which factors lead to customer satisfaction for an airline, such as the quality of food and drinks, the passenger's satisfaction level with the check-in, and on-boarding services. The questionnaire contained 14 Likert-scale questions from 1 (very dissatisfied) to 5 (very satisfied), with a further option 0 meaning 'not-applicable', and four numeric questions related to the passenger's age, flight distance and departure/arrival delay in minutes. The remaining four questions were categorical and recorded the passenger's gender, the customer type (loyal/disloyal), the type of travel (personal/business) and the seating class (business/economy/economy plus). 393 records have missing data points. As they represent 0.3% of the entire dataset, these records were simply removed and not interpolated.

Phase 2: Model Training. Based on a supervised learning algorithm, a data-driven ML model is trained on the dataset to fit Y_T. The block Y_O in Fig. 1 represents the output obtained from the trained model (represented by block $f(x)$) over the evaluation dataset (test data). The block Y_E represents the original labelled dependent variables of the evaluation dataset. It is compared with Y_O to assess the model's evaluation accuracy. The architecture used in this study was a feed-forward neural network with two fully-connected hidden layers. The number of hidden nodes and the value of other hyperparameters, reported in Table 1, were determined by performing a grid search to reach the highest feasible prediction accuracy. An early stopping method was exploited to avoid overfitting during the training process by stopping it when the validation accuracy did not improve for five epochs in a row. In any case, the number of epochs was limited to 1000. The network was trained five times over five training subsets extracted from the Airline Passenger Satisfaction dataset with the five-fold cross-validation technique. The model with the highest validation accuracy was selected.

Phase 3: Formation of the Explainable Argumentation Framework. Once a model has been trained, it has to be translated into an explainable representation. In this study, an argumentation framework is formed, as described in the following five layers [17].

Layer 1: Definition of the Internal Structure of Arguments. In standard logic, an argument consists of a set premises linked to a conclusion. The selected trained model and the evaluation dataset are fed into a bespoke rule-extraction method

---

[1] https://www.kaggle.com/teejmahal20/airline-passenger-satisfaction.

Table 1. Optimal hyperparameters of the neural network obtained through grid search procedure and the resulting prediction accuracy.

Model parameters	Value
Optimizer	Adam
Weight initialisation	Uniform
Activation function	Relu
Batch size	50
Hidden neurons	5
Loss function	Categorical cross-entropy
Accuracy (test set)	92.97% (92.55%)

returning a set of IF-THEN rules by using a three-step algorithm. This method prunes the not relevant input variables by recursively removing one at a time, retraining the model and checking if the prediction accuracy decreases. If this is the case, the pruned variable is removed, otherwise reinstated. Then, the evaluation dataset is split into groups according to the output class predicted by the model. This means that all the instances assigned by the model to the same class are grouped together. Finally, the Ordering Points To Identify the Clustering Structure (OPTICS) [14] algorithm was used to further divide the groups into clusters corresponding to areas of the input space with a high density of samples. Each cluster is translated into a rule by determining the two extreme samples for each relevant variable (thus, the minimum and maximum values that include all the samples in the cluster). The rule's antecedents correspond to these ranges, and the conclusion is the predicted class of the cluster's samples. A typical rule is presented below:

$$IF\ m_1 \leq X_1 \leq M_1\ AND \ldots AND\ m_N \leq X_N \leq M_N\ THEN\ Class_X \qquad (1)$$

where X_i, $i = 1, \ldots, N$ are the N independent relevant variables of the input dataset, m_i and M_i, $i = 1, \ldots, N$ are respectively the minimum and maximum values w.r.t the i-th independent variable of the instances included in the cluster. In this study, an argument coincides with an IF-THEN rule automatically generated by the rule-extraction method previously described. The premises and conclusion of an argument correspond to the rule's antecedents and conclusion.

Layer 2: Definition of the Attacks Between Arguments. Once arguments are formed, their inconsistencies are added via the notion of 'attack'. Usually, attacks are binary relations between two conflicting arguments, and they can be of different kinds. In this study, the following types were considered [17]:

- *rebutting attack* occurs when an argument negates the conclusion of another;
- *undercutting attack* occurs when an argument is attacked by arguing that there is a special case that does not allow its application.

Attacks are often specified by domain experts, and their automatic extraction is still an open research problem [8]. In this study, a novel method for automatically identifying conflicting rules was developed. In this new method, attacks were detected by checking if there were pairs of *overlapping* rules reaching different conclusions. Two rules overlap if there is an intersection area between their *covers*. The cover of a rule is the set of data points whose attribute values satisfy the rule's antecedents [15]. As shown in Fig. 2, two rules can be fully overlapping, with one rule including the second one (part a), partially overlapping (part b) or covering the same portion of the input space (part c). The first case could be seen as an undercutting attack as the first rule represents a particular case of the external rule. Partly and fully overlapping rules could be equivalent to a rebutting attack as two rules start from the same premises, at least in part, but reach different conclusions.

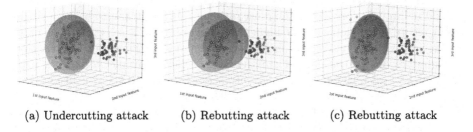

(a) Undercutting attack   (b) Rebutting attack   (c) Rebutting attack

Fig. 2. Relative positions of two conflicting rules that can be a) fully overlapping, with one rule including the other, b) partially overlapping or c) covering the same area of the input space.

Layer 3: Evaluation and Definition of Valid Attacks. Once arguments and attacks have been represented in a dialogical structure, the formalised knowledge-base, an essential aspect of argument-based systems is the ability to determine the success of an attack. Different approaches are presented in the literature to determine a successful, thus valid, attack [17]. For example, these include a) binary attacks, b) strengths of arguments, and c) strengths of attacks. In this study, a binary notion of attack is considered; thus, the attacks that were automatically produced by the method described in layer 2 are all kept in the knowledge-base. However, for each input record, not all the arguments and attacks are activated since not all the premises are applicable. The activated portion of the knowledge-base is considered for the next computations.

Layer 4: Definition of the Dialectal Status of Arguments. Dung-style acceptability semantics investigate the inconsistencies that might emerge from the interaction of arguments [10]. Given a set of arguments where some attack others, a decision must be taken to determine which arguments can be accepted. In Dung's theory, the internal structure of arguments is not considered. This leads to an abstract argumentation framework (AAF) which is a finite set of arguments and attacks. In Dung's terms, usually, an argument defeats another argument if and only if it represents a reason against the second argument. Here, it is also essential to assess whether the defeaters are defeated themselves to determine the acceptability status of an argument. This is known as *acceptability semantics*: given an AAF, it specifies zero or more conflict-free sets of acceptable arguments. However, other semantics have been proposed in the literature, not necessarily based on the notion of acceptability, such as the ranking-based semantics [1]. This study employed the *ranking-base categoriser* semantic, introduced by [3], which consists of a recursive function that rank-orders a set of arguments from the most to the list acceptable. The rank of an argument is inversely proportional to the number of its attacks and the rank of the attacking arguments. This semantic deems as acceptable those argument(s) with the lowest number of attacks and/or attacks coming from the weakest arguments.

Layer 5: Accrual of Acceptable Arguments. The previous layer produces a rank of arguments, those fired out of the entire knowledge-base, and a final conclusion should be brought forward as the most rational conclusion associable to a single input record of the dataset. The highest-ranked argument is selected as the most representative, and its conclusion is deemed the most rationale for representing an input record of the dataset. In the case of ties (multiple arguments with the highest rank), these are grouped into sets according to the conclusion they support. The set with the highest cardinality is deemed the most representative of an input record of the dataset, and the conclusion supported by its argument is deemed the most rationale. In the case of ties with respect to cardinality, the input case is treated as undecided, as not enough information is available to associate a possible conclusion.

Phase 4: Human-Centred Evaluation Analysis. The degree of explainability of the proposed argument-based explanation method was evaluated involving human volunteers. Explainability is an ill-defined construct, and numerous notions underlying the construct of explanations exist [28]. In this study, a questionnaire aimed at measuring the explainability of this novel XAI method was developed by modelling a number of these notions (Table 2). The questionnaire was based on Likert-scales from 1 (strongly disagree) to 5 (strongly agree). Some of the questions were phrased negatively to minimise response and quiescence biases. The mix of positive and negative questions, presented in random order to each participant, should force the respondent to read them carefully and provide meaningful answers, thus reducing these biases [5]. The survey ended with an open-text question to collect suggestions for improving the XAI methods just used by volunteers. Five close demographic questions to collect background information about the respondents preceded the above questionnaire: their highest level of education, age, whether English is their first language, their knowledge of the airline industry and the AI technologies. Two groups of participants were randomly formed: one receiving the argument-based XAI method (Fig. 3, a, top) and another receiving a decision-tree XAI method, treated as a baseline as specified in the research hypothesis (Fig. 3, b, bottom). Both explanations methods contain an interactive table with a subset of the data from the selected Airline Passenger Satisfaction dataset (Fig. 3, bottom). Participants could select an instance from this table to check which rules (and attacks) were fired and the final inference produced by the XAI method. Participants could spend as much time as they wished to familiarise themselves with the XAI method and the other components of the platform. Once satisfied, they could progress with the survey.

Table 2. Questions of the survey designed to assess the degree of explainability of an XAI method according to a set of notions.

#	Question	Assessed notion
1	I have learned something from the XAI method	Actionability
2	The XAI method taught me nothing new	Actionability
3	The relationship between input data & the predictions is clear	Causality
4	The relationship between input data & the predictions is vague	Causality
5	No rules in the XAI method return surprising predictions	Cognitive relief
6	The structure of the XAI method is not clear	Simplicity
7	The XAI method can be understood quickly	Explicitness
8	The XAI method takes a long time to understand	Explicitness
9	The XAI method is understandable	Understandability
10	The XAI method is incomprehensible	Comprehensibility
11	The XAI method provides useful information	Informativeness
12	The XAI method is not informative	Informativeness
13	External support was required to understand the XAI method	Intelligibility
14	The XAI method is engaging	Interestingness
15	The XAI method is not interesting	Interestingness
16	The XAI method allows me understand the ML model's logic	Mental fit
17	The ML model returns accurate predictions for all reasonable inputs	Algorithmic transparency
18	The XAI method makes me mistrust the model	Persuasiveness
19	The XAI method only includes most relevant data variables	Simplification

The final step was aimed at testing the research hypothesis by assessing, with the non-parametric Mann-Whitney U statistical test, if there are statistically significant differences in the degree of explainability of the two proposed XAI methods. The Mann-Whitney U test checks if two samples come from the same distribution. Alternatively, it tests if a cumulative distribution first-order stochastically dominates the other one, meaning that it assigns higher probabilities to the larger values. In this case, this means that the distribution of the responses related to the argumentation graph contains more positive answers ("agree" or "strongly agree") than the distribution related to the decision tree. The Mann-Whitney U test was preferred to the parametric hypothesis tests, such as the t-Student, because of the nature of the data. As they come from Likert-scale questions, it is impossible to assume that they follow the normal statistical distribution required by these parametric tests.

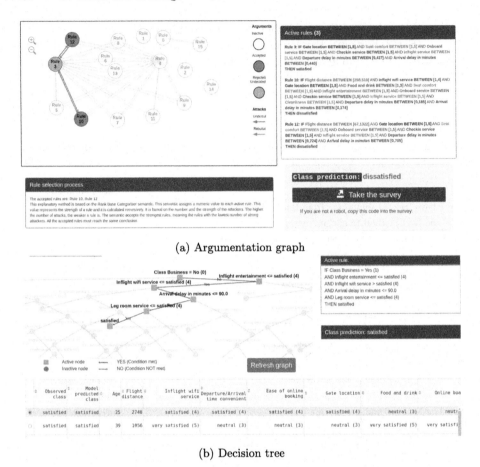

(a) Argumentation graph

(b) Decision tree

Fig. 3. Screenshots of the two alternative XAI methods embedded in the online platform used to carry out the evaluation survey.

4   Results and Discussion

The survey was promoted among authors' acquaintances and colleagues. It was carried out during the end of 2021 and the beginning of 2022 when Ireland was experiencing a surge of COVID-19 cases, so the only way to contact people was via online tools (emails and chats). This harmed the response rate. As a result, only 39 people completed the survey, of which 19 were presented with the decision tree and 20 with the argument graph. The majority of the participants were 25–34 and 35–44 years old with a Master's or Doctorate degree and 4+ years of experience with AI technologies, but with limited knowledge of the airline industry; 23 participants were not native English speakers (see Fig. 4).

First, the Cronbach's Alpha test was exploited to check the reliability of the explainability survey (Table 2) grouped by the two XAI methods. The alpha

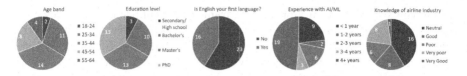

Fig. 4. Distributions of the responses given by participants to the questions related to their demographic and knowledge background.

coefficients were 0.88% for the argumentation graph and 0.9% for the decision tree, suggesting that the two surveys had high reliability. The Spearman-rank correlation coefficients were computed for each pair of the 19 Likert-scale questions to check that two notions of explainability, expected to be theoretically related, are in fact related. In particular, two questions assessing the same notion but worded differently (usually one positively and the other negatively) should be strongly correlated. For example, the first and second questions should be inversely correlated as both were designed to measure the actionability of the two XAI methods, but positively and negatively, respectively. As noticeable from the correlation matrices depicted in Fig. 5, these two questions are indeed inversely correlated in both surveys with Spearman coefficients of -0.57 (argumentation-graph) and -0.7 (decision tree). The same occurs for the other pairs: questions number 3–4, 11–12, and 14–15.

The Mann-Whitney U test returned p-values lower than the typical tolerance level of 5% for two questions: 1) 'the structure of the XAI method is not clear' (q.6) (p-value 2,19%), and 2) 'the XAI method takes a long time to understand' (q.8) (p-value 1,49%). The Mann-Whitney U test did not return any significant pieces of evidence to support the alternative hypothesis for the remaining 17 questions, meaning that there are no statically significant differences in the distributions of the responses given to these questions (see Fig. 6).

Overall, it is not possible to say that the argumentation graph was perceived neither as less nor more explainable than the decision tree, as only two questions out of 19 showed a statistically significant difference in the distribution of their answers. Furthermore, the survey was answered by a limited number of participants, and many of them have at least four years of experience with AI and ML. It is likely that they were familiar more with decision trees rather than with argumentation frameworks. However, the fact that the argumentation framework received the same scores, on average, across questions is indeed a positive outcome for its explainability. In fact, its graph-like visualisation represents the rules in a compact format as each rule is fully contained in a node and is expandable, whereas a rule in the decision tree can be represented as a long chain of nodes and edges. Decision trees always produce a set of conflict-free rules as their ML algorithms perform a series of binary splits of the input space. This is not necessarily an advantage as it returns large rulesets in terms of the number of rules. Such a case happens if there are many areas where a small perturbation of the input leads to a different prediction of the model. The decision tree needs many rules to capture all the input-output combinations.

By allowing conflicts, the argumentation framework requires, instead, a few overlapping rules with their attacks to describe the model's behaviour. The accrual of arguments determines, case by case, the most rational conclusion. In fact, the argumentation framework of this study contained 16 rules, whereas the decision tree was made by 60 rules (see Fig. 3).

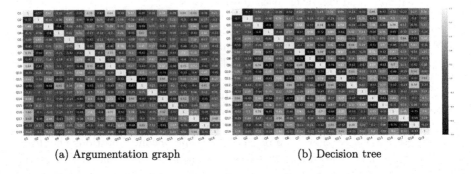

(a) Argumentation graph   (b) Decision tree

Fig. 5. Correlation matrices of the 19 Likert-scale questions assessing the degree of explainability of the (a) argument-based and (b) decision-tree XAI methods.

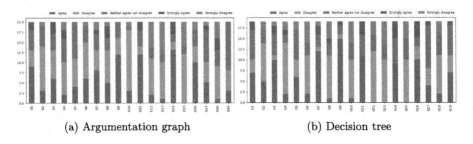

(a) Argumentation graph   (b) Decision tree

Fig. 6. Distributions of the answers of the questionnaire assessing the degree of explainability of the (a) argument-based and (b) decision-tree XAI methods.

5   Conclusions

This study proposed a novel XAI method to extract IF-THEN rules automatically from ML models and treat them as arguments in the form of premises to a conclusion. Principles from AT were exploited to create an argumentation framework employing the notions of arguments and attacks among them. A novel method to automatically generate undercutting and undermining attacks among extracted arguments was devised. The hypothesis was that this argumentation framework could improve the degree of explainability of 'black-box models', namely trained neural networks with an Airline Passenger Satisfaction dataset. Two interactive interfaces were built: one for the argumentation framework and one for a decision tree which was treated as a baseline since often deemed highly interpretable and explainable. The hypothesis was tested by designing and running a Likert-scale questionnaire of 19 questions to measure various notions related to the concept of explainability over the two interactive interfaces. Two groups of participants answered the survey after interacting with one of the two interfaces. The Mann-Whitney U test verified if the distribution of the responses related to the explainability of the argumentation framework stochastically dominated the distributions of the responses related to the explainability of the decision tree. The test did not reveal evidence to support the hypothesis of the superiority of the explainability of the argumentation-based representation over the decision tree. However, it did not also underperform the explainability of the decision trees, showing its appealing properties and characteristics for the interpretability and comprehensibility of machine-learned models. Future work will include the improvement of the internal computational mechanisms associated with the argumentation framework, particularly the definition of the valid attacks among arguments by employing gradualism, the application of other semantics for producing the dialectical status of arguments, and the strategies for their accrual in order to promote rational conclusions.

References

1. Amgoud, L., Ben-Naim, J.: Ranking-based semantics for argumentation frameworks. In: Liu, W., Subrahmanian, V.S., Wijsen, J. (eds.) SUM 2013. LNCS (LNAI), vol. 8078, pp. 134–147. Springer, Heidelberg (2013). https://doi.org/10.1007/978-3-642-40381-1_11
2. Baroni, P., Caminada, M., Giacomin, M.: An introduction to argumentation semantics. Knowl. Eng. Rev. **26**(4), 365–410 (2011)
3. Besnard, P., Hunter, A.: A logic-based theory of deductive arguments. Artif. Intell. **128**(1–2), 203–235 (2001)
4. Bryant, D., Krause, P.: A review of current defeasible reasoning implementations. Knowl. Eng. Rev. **23**(3), 227–260 (2008)
5. Choi, B.C., Pak, A.W.: Peer reviewed: a catalog of biases in questionnaires. Prevent Chronic Disease **2**(1), 1 (2005)
6. Cocarascu, O., Toni, F.: Argumentation for machine learning: a survey. In: COMMA, pp. 219–230 (2016)
7. Dam, H.K., Tran, T., Ghose, A.: Explainable software analytics. In: Proceedings of the 40th International Conference on Software Engineering: New Ideas and Emerging Results, pp. 53–56. ACM, Gothenburg, Sweden (2018)
8. Dejl, A., et al.: Argflow: a toolkit for deep argumentative explanations for neural networks. In: Proceedings of the 20th International Conference on Autonomous Agents and MultiAgent Systems, pp. 1761–1763 (2021)
9. Došilović, F.K., Brčić, M., Hlupić, N.: Explainable artificial intelligence: a survey. In: 41st International Convention on Information and Communication Technology, Electronics and Microelectronics (MIPRO), pp. 0210–0215. IEEE (2018)
10. Dung, P.M.: On the acceptability of arguments and its fundamental role in non-monotonic reasoning, logic programming and n-person games. Artif. Intell. **77**(2), 321–357 (1995)
11. Freitas, A.A.: Are we really discovering interesting knowledge from data. Expert Update (BCS-SGAI Mag.) **9**(1), 41–47 (2006)

12. Gómez, S.A., Chesnevar, C.I.: Integrating defeasible argumentation and machine learning techniques: a preliminary report. In: Proceedings of Workshop of Researchers in Computer Science, pp. 320–324 (2003)
13. Gómez, S.A., Chesnevar, C.I.: Integrating defeasible argumentation with fuzzy art neural networks for pattern classification. J. Comput. Sci. Technol. 4(1), 45–51 (2004)
14. Kriegel, H.P., Kröger, P., Sander, J., Zimek, A.: Density-based clustering. Wiley Interdisc. Rev. Data Mining Knowl. Disc. 1(3), 231–240 (2011)
15. Lakkaraju, H., Bach, S.H., Leskovec, J.: Interpretable decision sets: a joint framework for description and prediction. In: Proceedings of the 22nd ACM SIGKDD International Conference on Knowledge Discovery and Data Mining, pp. 1675–1684. ACM, San Francisco, California, USA (2016)
16. Lipton, Z.C.: The mythos of model interpretability. Commun. ACM 61(10), 36–43 (2018)
17. Longo, L.: Argumentation for knowledge representation, conflict resolution, defeasible inference and its integration with machine learning. In: Holzinger, A. (ed.) Machine Learning for Health Informatics. LNCS (LNAI), vol. 9605, pp. 183–208. Springer, Cham (2016). https://doi.org/10.1007/978-3-319-50478-0_9
18. Longo, L.: Formalising human mental workload as a defeasible computational concept. Ph.D. thesis, Technological University Dublin (2014)
19. Longo, L., Goebel, R., Lecue, F., Kieseberg, P., Holzinger, A.: Explainable artificial intelligence: concepts, applications, research challenges and visions. In: Holzinger, A., Kieseberg, P., Tjoa, A.M., Weippl, E. (eds.) CD-MAKE 2020. LNCS, vol. 12279, pp. 1–16. Springer, Cham (2020). https://doi.org/10.1007/978-3-030-57321-8_1
20. Longo, L., Rizzo, L., Dondio, P.: Examining the modelling capabilities of defeasible argumentation and non-monotonic fuzzy reasoning. Knowl. Based Syst. 211, 106514 (2021)
21. Modgil, S., Prakken, H.: The aspic+ framework for structured argumentation: a tutorial. Argum. Comput. 5(1), 31–62 (2014)
22. Modgil, S., et al.: The added value of argumentation. In: Ossowski, S. (eds) Agreement Technologies. Law, Governance and Technology Series, vol. 8, pp. 357–403. Springer, Dordrecht (2013). https://doi.org/10.1007/978-94-007-5583-3_21
23. Riveret, R., Governatori, G.: On learning attacks in probabilistic abstract argumentation. In: Proceedings of the 2016 International Conference on Autonomous Agents and Multiagent Systems, pp. 653–661 (2016)
24. Rizzo, L., Longo, L.: An empirical evaluation of the inferential capacity of defeasible argumentation, non-monotonic fuzzy reasoning and expert systems. Expert Syst. App. 147, 113220 (2020)
25. Thimm, M., Kersting, K.: Towards argumentation-based classification. In: Logical Foundations of Uncertainty and Machine Learning, IJCAI Workshop, vol. 17 (2017)
26. Vilone, G., Longo, L.: Explainable artificial intelligence: a systematic review. arXiv preprint arXiv:2006.00093 (2020)
27. Vilone, G., Longo, L.: Classification of explainable artificial intelligence methods through their output formats. Mach. Learn. Knowl. Extract. 3(3), 615–661 (2021)
28. Vilone, G., Longo, L.: Notions of explainability and evaluation approaches for explainable artificial intelligence. Inf. Fusion 76, 89–106 (2021)

An Analysis on Graph-Processing Frameworks: Neo4j and Spark GraphX

Alabbas Alhaj Ali and Doina Logofatu$^{(\boxtimes)}$

Frankfurt University of Applied Sciences, Nibelungenpl. 1,
60318 Frankfurt am Main, Germany
`logofatu@fb2.fra-uas.de`
`https://www.informatik.fb2.fh-frankfurt.de/~logofatu`

Abstract. Numerous graph algorithms have been developed to address a variety of problems in the industry, ranging from fraud detection to scheduling or even recommendation systems. Graph-processing frameworks are hence created to simplify the implementation of graph-based solutions. Nonetheless, the number of such frameworks has grown significantly over the past decades with varying benefits and drawbacks. Understanding the requirements and characteristics of each framework plays a vital role in the selection of a suitable solution to a given problem. In this work, we evaluate the performance and usability of 2 popular graph-processing frameworks Neo4j and Apache Spark GraphX by implementing a PageRank solution to solve a practical business problem derived from the Yelp dataset.

Keywords: Graph-processing frameworks · Neo4j · Apache Spark GraphX PageRank · Yelp dataset

1 Introduction

Graph algorithms have always proven to be an efficient problem-solving technique thanks to their natural ability to model real-world domains. Their applications are diverse and numerous, ranging from basic routing problems in transportation/logistic industry [12] to fraud detection in the financial world [33], from recommendation systems in user-oriented services like e-commerce [39] to social media [3], and much more. Efficient as they are, developing a graph-based solution to handle an industrial problem is no trivial task in that graph theory is among the oldest and most complex areas of mathematics and computer science [34].

Furthermore, in 2018, more than 3 billion people used the Internet, 2.5 quintillion bytes of data were produced on a daily basis, and over 90% of data in the whole world was generated in a period of two years [1]. The growth was even more impressive especially for online social networking services where graph algorithms always played a dominant role. For example, Fig. 1 illustrates the

---

Supported by the Frankfurt University of Applied Sciences.

I. Maglogiannis et al. (Eds.): AIAI 2022, IFIP AICT 646, pp. 461–470, 2022.
https://doi.org/10.1007/978-3-031-08333-4_37

dramatic growth of Facebook - a famous social network platform - between 2008 and 2019. As the data magnitude grows exponentially, developers face new challenges in using graph algorithms. It is no longer sufficient to only be capable of applying them, but we must be able to implement these algorithms efficiently. The work in [20], for instance, introduces numerous scalable variants of graph algorithms such as Minimum Spanning Tree (MST), Breadth-First Search (BFS) and Single-Source Shortest Path (SSSP) algorithms to address several challenges in large-scale classical graph problems.

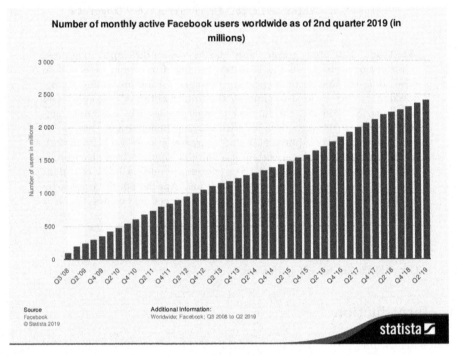

Fig. 1. Facebook users worldwide 2008–2019 [8] Please note that short captions are centered, while long ones are justified by the macro package automatically.

To bridge the gap between academic research and software development, many graph-processing frameworks are created to accelerate the design, implementation and testing of graph-based solutions and their integration into existing systems. These frameworks have grown significantly over the past decades. Each framework of this type provides functionalities either as a graph database (Neo4j [17] and OrientDB [37]) or a graph processing engine (Apache Spark GraphX [13], Pregel [25], BGL [35] and GraphBase [21]) or even both (Giraph [2]). A more thorough review of key players in this domain can be found in [29].

In this study, we conduct an experiment using 2 of the most popular graph-processing frameworks - Neo4j and Spark GraphX - to analyze the Yelp dataset

[43]. Our paper aims at providing future researchers and developers with a good reference about the usability and performance between these 2 libraries. A clear understanding of these characteristics will help them choose the best solution for a given problem.

2 Study Case

2.1 Motivation

One major challenge for all types of businesses is user acquisition. In simpler terms, companies must find a way to attract customers. There are various strategies to address this challenge, from giving coupons to placing advertisements. In this study, we focus on a more traditional method which is to invite influential people to test our services with the intention of attracting their followers. For instance, if Michael Jackson was to use the services provided by our company and put on a good word, his billions of fans would more likely follow his choice and be willing to buy the same services he used. However, those celebrities may be too expensive for small and medium businesses to afford, which leads to the question of how we can find affordable and influential customers from the general population? A similar problem can be found in [19].

With the invention of social media platforms such as Yelp [23], Facebook [36], Twitter [27] or YouTube [16], more and more ordinary people can achieve great fame overnight by creating sharing their inspiring stories. They are normal non-celebrity people who are much more affordable for businesses to invite and still have a huge population of fans. If we have access to some customer data, it is possible to search for these people. In this work, we employ the Yelp dataset for the sake of experiment.

2.2 Yelp Dataset

Yelp is an American company born with a mission to connect people with great local businesses. They create a digital platform that makes it easy for users to provide their reviews and recommendations about local restaurants, shopping or any services from their real-life experience. Yelp has published a subset of information accumulated by their platform since 2013 via their annual machine learning challenge, namely Yelp Challenge [43]. As of Round 10 of the challenge, the dataset includes 9,489,337 users and 156,639 businesses from 10 states in the North America region. There are a total of 1,005,693 tips from users about businesses, 4,736,897 reviews of businesses by users and 35,444,850 friend relationships.

2.3 Problem Description

In this research, we are only interested in users and their friends. From the original dataset, let's construct a friendship network as a graph $G = (V, E)$ with vertex set V and edge set E. Each vertex represents a user from the Yelp dataset, while each edge represents a bidirectional relationship between 2 users: friendship. Over half a million users without friends are ignored since their influence is assumed to be zero. Table 1 illustrates the scale of this friendship network where WCC stands for Weakly Connected Component [6]. The remaining task is to implement algorithms that input this graph and output the influential users we are searching for.

Table 1. Statistics of the friendship network

Nodes	Edges	WCCs	Largest WCC	
			Nodes	Edges
8,981,389	35,444,850	18,512	8,938,630	35,420,520

2.4 Approach

To search for influential people, it is of paramount importance to define a deterministic approach to measure *influence*. Measuring influence of a person by his number of friends is the most natural but naive approach. Practice has demonstrated that such a method will not provide the best candidates. For instance, imagine a network where the top 5 users have at least a million friends each. However, none of these 5 users is a friend to each other, but all of them are friends to a common user X who, strangely, has exactly 5 friends. Is it more beneficial for a business to invite all 5 users or should they invite only X instead? That is the motivation behind algorithms like PageRank [11,30] whose superiority has been proven in practice.

In our study, influential people are identified by their PageRank score. The same program will be implemented as a query in both Neo4j and Spark GraphX in that these frameworks have out-of-the-box support for PageRank. The implementations and results will be then used to assess the performance and usability of these 2 frameworks.

3   Related Works

In the work [10] the author's analyzed a seven graph processing frameworks under five design aspects including distribution policy, on-disk data organization, programming model, synchronization policy and message model. the work reveal some interesting finding that the vertex-cut method over weighs the edge-cut method on neighbor-based algorithms while leads to inefficiency for non-neighbor-based algorithms using asynchronous update can reduce the total workload by 20% to 30% however the processing time may still doubled due to fine-grained lock conflicts.

The work [31] analyse the use of Pregel-like Large Scale Graph Processing Frameworks in processing the data of Social Network. The work discussed various different methods, compared their run-times, and proved that the graph processing framework is suitable for analysis of social networks. The work concludes by providing several key observations about algorithmic design and framework flexibility.

The work [7] focus in the comparison terms of execution time between second generation frameworks and the de-facto standard Hadoop in processing large-scale graph analysis. The authors selected the k-core algorithm and its adaptation each platform. They found that from a programming paradigm point of view, a vertex centric framework is the better fit for graph related problems. They recommend one of the Pregel-inspired frameworks for graph processing as the performance of vertex-centric frameworks is not matched by Map/Reduce-based frameworks, even by improved ones, such as Stratosphere.

An intensive Analysis of distributed programming models and frameworks for large-scale graph processing has been introduced by the work of *Corbellini, A., Godoy, D., Mateos, C., Schiaffino, S. and Zunino, A.* [4], The work provide an perspective analyse for adopted programming model of popular frameworks designed to process large-scale graphs with the goal of assisting software developers/designers in choosing the most adequate tool.

4   Solution in Neo4j

4.1   Overview

Neo4j is a native graph database that is optimized for storing and processing data relationships. Distinguished from traditional databases where data is usually arranged in rows, columns and tables, Neo4j introduces a flexible structure, namely data record (or node) which stores direct pointers to all the nodes it's connected to. Because Neo4j is designed around this simple, and yet powerful optimization, it enables queries with complexity never before imagined and performance never before thought possible. Most importantly, Neo4j provides all functionalities as normal full-fledged databases and is fully compliant ACID transaction principles [28], making it suitable to use graphs for data in production scenarios.

4.2   Solution

Listing 1 presents a reference implementation for finding N influential users using PageRank in Neo4j. The language of implementation is Cypher [9] which is introduced by Neo4j to describe complex queries. As can be seen, the implementation is quite complicated, and what is more, requirement of learning Cypher may prove to be a challenge for many developers since it is not so popular as a programming language. Albeit Neoj4 offers drivers for multiple popular programming languages such as Java [14], Python [38], .NET [15] and JavaScript [40], Cypher still remains the default language of choice for the majority of Neoj4 developers.

```
CALL algo.pageRank.stream(
    ['MATCH (u:User)
    WHERE exists( (u)-[:FRIEND]-() )
    RETURN id(u) as id'],

    ['MATCH (u1:User)-[:FRIEND]-(u2:User)
    RETURN id(u1) as source, id(u2) as target'],

    {graph:['cypher']}
)

YIELD nodeId, score
    with algo.asNode(nodeId) as node, score
    order by score desc limit N

RETURN node.id, score
```

Listing 1. Cypher code for finding top N influential users using PageRank in Neo4j

5   Solution in Spark GraphX

5.1   Overview

A well-known approach to cope with large problem size is to follow the MapReduce paradigm [5] in combination with distributed systems. In other words, the graph data input could be replicated or partitioned across a number of computing nodes. The computation results accumulated across all nodes will then be reduced to one final result. However, the development of a distributed solution is itself no trivial task.

To simplify the development process, a variety of frameworks for distributed programming have been widely used in academic research as well as in industry such as Hadoop or Storm by Apache [26], BigQuery by Google [22], Disco by Nokia [18] and many more. Many, but not all of them, offer a builtin MapReduce programming model. In our experiment, we opt for a higher level programming model that can operates on top of Hadoop environment, namely Apache Spark [45]. It also comes with a dedicated module for graph processing called GraphX [42].

The core of Apache Spark lies in the resilient distributed dataset (RDD) model, a fault-tolerant collection of elements partitioned across the nodes of the cluster that can be operated in parallel [44]. RDD makes extensive use of distributed memory, enabling efficient data reuse and fault tolerance. Its key idea is to log coarse-grained transformation (map, filter, join) to build the dataset rather than the actual data.

GraphX is the graph processing framework that extends Spark data-parallel system with the a graph-parallel computation model called Pregel, without causing complex joins or excessive movements [41]. Pregel model is a message passing interface which features parallel vertex-centric computation, consisting of a sequence of iterations (or super steps) [25]. During each super step, a user-defined function that defines the behavior at vertex V and superstep S, is invoked. Pregel tackles various challenges in efficient processing of large graphs: they often exhibit irregular relationships, poor locality in data access patterns, unbalanced partitioned tasks and a varying degree of parallelism over the course of execution [24].

5.2 Solution

Listing 2 illustrates a reference implementation for finding influential users using PageRank in Spark GraphX. The language of implementation is Python which is supported by GraphX. Compared to Listing 1, this implementation is much shorter in length and simpler to read. Furthermore, Python is one of the most popular programming language widely used all around the world and well-known for its simplicity, readability and low learning curve [32]. Supporting Python out-of-the-box can be considered an advantage in using GraphX.

```
pg = g.pageRank(tol=0.0001)

sample = pg.vertices
    .orderBy("pagerank", ascending=False)
    .limit(N)
    .collect()
```

Listing 2. Python code for finding the top N influential users using PageRank and Spark GraphX

6   Experimental Results

Table 2 summarizes our experimental results and showcases the difference between Neo4j and GraphX in terms of performance. The Neo4j implementation of PageRank in finding top 10 influential users completed in 619 s. On the other hand, GraphX implementation finishes in 7911 s, which is around 12–13 times slower. The same pattern holds true when the input size is doubled to 20 where Neo4j program requires 1342 s (more than 20 min) and Spark GraphX requires 16253 s (more than 4.5 h). Last, but not least, when the input size is doubled, the computational duration increases by approximately 2 times. This tendency holds true for both Neo4j (2.17x) and GraphX (2.05x).

Table 2. PageRank Benchmark (in seconds)

N	Neo4J	GraphX
10	619	7911
20	1342	16253

7   Conclusion

This paper evaluates the performance and usability of the top 2 scalable graph processing frameworks, namely Neo4j and Apache Spark GraphX, with the help of Yelp dataset. In our tests, Neo4j outperformed Spark GraphX by a huge margin (around 12–13 times faster). However, when simplicity and usability are considered, Spark GraphX proves to be a much better choice considering that Python code is much shorter and more readable that its Cypher counterpart for writing the same query. In practice, no framework should be given preferences without considering other relevant characteristics. In fact, they could even be used in combination depending on the nature of the given problem. For example, when prototyping a solution, Spark GraphX would be favoured for the sake of code cleanliness, simplicity and Python. However, in production, a fast framework like Neo4j should be utilized and the Python prototype can be translated into Cypher code that run on Neo4j for performance gain. Last, but not least, the experimental results imply that GraphX tends to scale slightly better than Neo4j for larger input size but the current amount of data is insufficient to draw a firm conclusion. More experiments with varying input sizes will be needed to assess the scalability of these 2 frameworks, which remains a task for future research.

References

1. Marr, B.: How Much Data Do We Create Every Day? The Mind-Blowing Stats Everyone Should Read (2018). https://www.forbes.com/sites/bernardmarr/2018/05/21/how-much-data-do-we-create-every-day-the-mind-blowing-stats-everyone-should-read/
2. Ching, A.: Giraph: Production-grade graph processing infrastructure for trillion edge graphs. ATPESC, ser. ATPESC 14 (2014)
3. Ching, A., Edunov, S., Kabiljo, M., Logothetis, D., Muthukrishnan, S.: One trillion edges: graph processing at Facebook-scale. Proc. VLDB Endow. **8**(12), 1804–1815 (2015)
4. Corbellini, A., Godoy, D., Mateos, C., Schiaffino, S., Zunino, A.: An analysis of distributed programming models and frameworks for large-scale graph processing. IETE J. Res. 1–9 (2020). https://doi.org/10.1080/03772063.2020.1754139
5. Dean, J., Ghemawat, S.: Mapreduce: simplified data processing on large clusters. Commun. ACM **51**(1), 107–113 (2008)
6. Dunbar, J.E., Grossman, J.W., Hattingh, J.H., Hedetniemi, S.T., McRae, A.A.: On weakly connected domination in graphs. Discret. Math. **167**, 261–269 (1997)

7. Elser, B., Montresor, A.: An evaluation study of bigdata frameworks for graph processing. In: 2013 IEEE International Conference on Big Data, pp. 60–67 (2013). https://doi.org/10.1109/BigData.2013.6691555
8. Facebook users worldwide 2019, Statista. https://www.statista.com/statistics/264810/number-of-monthly-active-facebook-users-worldwide/
9. Francis, N., et al.: Cypher: an evolving query language for property graphs. In: Proceedings of the 2018 International Conference on Management of Data, pp. 1433–1445 (2018)
10. Gao, Y., Zhou, W., Han, J., Meng, D., Zhang, Z., Xu, Z.: An evaluation and analysis of graph processing frameworks on five key issues. In: Proceedings of the 12th ACM International Conference on Computing Frontiers, Ischia, Italy, pp. 1–8. ACM, May 2015. https://doi.org/10.1145/2742854.2742884. https://dl.acm.org/doi/10.1145/2742854.2742884
11. Gleich, D.: PageRank beyond the web. SIAM Rev. **57**(3), 321–363 (2015)
12. Golden, B.L., Raghavan, S., Wasil, E.A.: The Vehicle Routing Problem: Latest Advances and New Challenges, vol. 43. Springer, New York (2008). https://doi.org/10.1007/978-0-387-77778-8
13. Gonzalez, J.E., Xin, R.S., Dave, A., Crankshaw, D., Franklin, M.J., Stoica, I.: Graphx: graph processing in a distributed dataflow framework. In: 11th {USENIX} Symposium on Operating Systems Design and Implementation ({OSDI} 2014), pp. 599–613 (2014)
14. Gosling, J., Joy, B., Steele, G., Bracha, G.: The Java Language Specification. Addison-Wesley Professional, Boston (2000)
15. Hejlsberg, A., Wiltamuth, S.: C# language reference. Microsoft (2000)
16. Hilker, C.: Social Media für Unternehmer: Wie man Xing, Twitter. Youtube und Co. erfolgreich im Business einsetzt. Linde Verlag GmbH (2010)
17. Robinson, I., Webber, J., Eifrem, E.: Graph Databases 2e Neo4j. O'Reilly Media (2015)
18. Isojärvi, S.: Disco and nokia: experiences of disco with modeling real-time system in multiprocessor environment. In: Formal Methods Europe Industial Seminar (1997)
19. Jindal, T.: Finding local experts from yelp dataset. Ideals (2015)
20. Klauck, H., Nanongkai, D., Pandurangan, G., Robinson, P.: Distributed computation of large-scale graph problems. In: Proceedings of the Twenty-Sixth Annual ACM-SIAM Symposium on Discrete Algorithms, pp. 391–410. Society for Industrial and Applied Mathematics, December 2014
21. Knuth, D.E.: The Stanford GraphBase: A Platform for Combinatorial Computing. ACM, New York (1993)
22. Krishnan, S.P.T., Gonzalez, J.L.: Google BigQuery. In: Krishnan, S.P.T., Gonzalez, J.L. (eds.) Building Your Next Big Thing with Google Cloud Platform, pp. 235–253. Apress, Berkeley (2015). https://doi.org/10.1007/978-1-4842-1004-8_10
23. Luca, M.: Reviews, reputation, and revenue: the case of yelp. com. Com (March 15, 2016). Harvard Business School NOM Unit Working Paper **1234**(12-016) (2016)
24. Lumsdaine, A., Gregor, D.P., Hendrickson, B., Berry, J.W.: Challenges in parallel graph processing. Parallel Process. Lett. **17**, 5–20 (2007)
25. Malewicz, G., et al.: Pregel: a system for large-scale graph processing. In: Proceedings of the 2010 ACM SIGMOD International Conference on Management of Data, SIGMOD 2010. ACM, New York (2010)
26. Mera, D., Batko, M., Zezula, P.: Towards fast multimedia feature extraction: hadoop or storm. In: 2014 IEEE International Symposium on Multimedia, pp. 106–109. IEEE (2014)

27. Murthy, D.: Twitter. Polity Press, Cambridge (2018)
28. Muth, P., Rakow, T.C.: Atomic commitment for integrated database systems. In: Proceedings of Seventh International Conference on Data Engineering, pp. 296–297. IEEE Computer Society (1991)
29. Nguyen, T.: Model the relations between geospatial objects with a graph database. Master thesis, Frankfurt University of Applied Sciences (2019)
30. Page, L., Brin, S., Motwani, R., Winograd, T.: The PageRank citation ranking: bringing order to the web. Technical report, Stanford InfoLab, Stanford InfoLab (1999)
31. Quick, L., Wilkinson, P., Hardcastle, D.: Using pregel-like large scale graph processing frameworks for social network analysis. In: 2012 IEEE/ACM International Conference on Advances in Social Networks Analysis and Mining, pp. 457–463 (2012). https://doi.org/10.1109/ASONAM.2012.254
32. Ranking, P.: Pypi python modules ranking (2020). http://pypi-ranking.info/alltime
33. Sabau, A.S.: Survey of clustering based financial fraud detection research. Informatica Economica **16**(1), 110 (2012)
34. Shirinivas, S., Vetrivel, S., Elango, N.: Applications of graph theory in computer science an overview. Int. J. Eng. Sci. Technol. **2**(9), 4610–4621 (2010)
35. Siek, J.G., Lee, L.Q.: Andrew Lumsdaine: The Boost Graph Library: User Guide and Reference Manual. Addison-Wesley Longman Publishing Co. Inc, Boston (2002)
36. Simanowski, R.: Facebook-Gesellschaft. Matthes & Seitz Berlin Verlag (2016)
37. Tesoriero, C.: Getting started with orientDB. Packt Publishing Ltd (2013)
38. Van Rossum, G., Drake, F.L.: The python language reference manual. Network Theory Ltd. (2011)
39. Wang, J., Huang, P., Zhao, H., Zhang, Z., Zhao, B., Lee, D.L.: Billion-scale commodity embedding for e-commerce recommendation in Alibaba. In: Billion-Scale Commodity Embedding for E-Commerce Recommendation in Alibaba, p. 10 (2018)
40. White, A.: JavaScript Programmer's Reference. Wiley, Hoboken (2010)
41. Xin, R.S., Gonzalez, J.E., Crankshaw, D., Franklin, M.J., Dave, A., Stoica, I.: GraphX: unifying data-parallel and graph-parallel analytics. In: GraphX: Unifying Data-Parallel and Graph-Parallel Analytics (2014)
42. Xin, R.S., Gonzalez, J.E., Franklin, M.J., Stoica, I.: Graphx: a resilient distributed graph system on spark. In: First International Workshop on Graph Data Management Experiences and Systems, pp. 1–6 (2013)
43. Yelp: Yelp Dataset (2019). https://www.yelp.com/dataset
44. Zaharia, M., et al.: Resilient distributed datasets: a fault-tolerant abstraction for in-memory cluster computing. In: Resilient Distributed Datasets: A Fault-Tolerant Abstraction for In-Memory Cluster Computing (2012)
45. Zaharia, M., et al.: Apache spark: a unified engine for big data processing. Commun. ACM **59**(11), 56–65 (2016)

Application of Graph-Based Technique to Identity Resolution

Hassan Kazemian[1(✉)], Mohammad-Hossein Amirhosseini[2], and Michael Phillips[1]

[1] Intelligent Systems Research Centre, London Metropolitan University, London N7 8DB, UK
h.kazemian@londonmet.ac.uk
[2] Intelligent Systems Research Group, University of East London,
Docklands Campus, London E16 2RD, UK

Abstract. These days the ability to prove an individual identity is crucial in social, economic and legal aspects of life. Identity resolution is the process of semantic reconciliation that determines whether a single identity is the same when being described differently. The importance of identity resolution has been greatly felt these days in the world of online social networking where personal details can be fabricated or manipulated easily. In this research a new graph-based approach has been used for identity resolution, which tries to resolve an identity based on the similarity of attribute values which are related to different identities in a dataset. Graph analysis techniques such as centrality measurement and community detection have been used in this approach. Moreover, a new identity model has been used for the first time. This method has been tested on SPIRIT policing dataset, which is an anonymized dataset used in SPIRIT project funded by European Union's Horizon 2020. There are 892 identity records in this dataset and two of them are 'known' identities who are using two different names, but they are both belonging to the same person. These two identities were recognized successfully after using the presented method in this paper. This method can assist police forces in their investigation process to find criminals and those who committed a fraud. It can also be useful in other fields such as finance and banking, marketing or customer service.

Keywords: Identity resolution · Identity model · Graph analysis · Community detection · Centrality measurement

1 Introduction

1.1 Importance of Identity Resolution

Identity can be described as a set of identifiable characteristics that can distinguish one individual from another. Nowadays electronic records are replacing paper-based documents and identity records can be generated easily. Therefore, duplicate and false identity records are quite common in electronic systems and databases because of lack of sufficient verification or validation during data entry processes [1]. In this situation,

I. Maglogiannis et al. (Eds.): AIAI 2022, IFIP AICT 646, pp. 471–482, 2022.
https://doi.org/10.1007/978-3-031-08333-4_38

finding an effective solution to address this issue is extremely critical and it can facilitate fighting crime, terrorism or enforce national security. Li and Wang [1] pointed out that criminals and terrorists try to hide their true identity via using fake identities. There are some cases documented by government reports which are showing terrorists in different countries have committed different identity crimes such as falsifying passports or birth certificates to facilitate their travelling or their financial operations [2, 3]. The problem of multiple identities for an individual can mislead police and law enforcement investigators [4]. Identity resolution is a pathway to tackle problems when it becomes intensely difficult to determine if the resultant identity is same when criminals describe it differently.

1.2 Identity Model

There should be a clear identity model before starting identity resolution process. Based on the identity theories from the social science literature, an individual's identity is considered to have two basic components, namely a personal identity and a social identity. A personal identity is one's self-perception as an individual, whereas a social identity is one's biographical history that builds up over time [5]. These two aspects of identity have been considered by researchers for identity resolution. But the previous identity models have been suffering from some limitations which can affect on the accuracy of the results. In fact, individuals are not isolated but interconnected to each another in a society. The social context associated with an individual can be clues that reveal his or her undeniable identity. Recognizing the limitations of personal attributes, many recent studies have started exploiting social context information for identity resolution.

For instance, Ananthakrishna et al. [6] introduced a method that eliminates duplicates in data warehouses using a dimensional hierarchy over the link relations. This method can improve the performance of the matching technique by only comparing those attribute values that have the same foreign key dependency. For instance, the similarity of two identity will be analyzed only when both of them live in the same city. Afterwards, Kalashnikov et al. [7] combined co-affiliation and co-authorship relationships and created a new resolution model for reference disambiguation. In another research, Köpcke and Rahm [8] categorized entity resolution methods into context matchers and attribute value matchers. They explain that attribute value matchers rely on descriptive attributes, while context matchers consider information inferred from social interactions which is represented as linkages in a graph.

A new identity model for identity resolution has been used in this research. In addition to physical and social aspects of an identity, this new identity model is considering two more aspects of an identity which results in considering more attributes and can improve the accuracy and reliability of the identity resolution. This will be explained in methodology section.

1.3 Identity Resolution Methods

Existing identity resolution methods can be categorized into two groups which are (1) rule-based and (2) machine learning methods. Most of the rule-based identity resolution methods have been developed based on the matching rules. As an example, for a simple rule, two identity records match only if their first name, surname, and date of birth values are identical [9]. Li and Wang [1] explained that matching rules try to have high precision, but they usually suffer from low sensitivity in detecting true matches. This is because of data quality issues such as missing data, entry error and deceptions. They also discussed that the most important challenge for a rule-based method can be creation of the rule set because creating an effective and comprehensive rule set can be very complicated and time consuming and the rules may not be portable and applicable across different contexts.

Creating a comprehensive rule sets can be highly time consuming and expensive. Another issue might be portability as some of rules could be dependent to a specific domain and not portable across different domains. In this situation, machine learning can be considered as an alternative approach to manual rule coding because it can automatically recognize patterns in training data with matching pairs. This will help to build a resolution model for new identity records. Li and Wang [1] explained that when there is a pair of identity records, distance measures can be defined for different descriptive attributes and then they can be combined into an overall score. The overall distance score will be compared to a pre-defined threshold and the pair should be considered as a match if this score is below or above the threshold.

One of the first identity resolution methods was a data association method for linking criminal records that possibly refer to the same suspect [10]. This method was comparing two different records and calculating an overall distance measure as a weighted sum of the distance measures of all corresponding feature values. In another attempt, Wang et al. [11] proposed a record linkage method which was detecting misleading identities by comparing four attributes and combining them into an overall distance score. These attributes were (1) name, (2) date of birth, (3) social security number, and (4) address. They used a supervised learning method to determine a threshold for match decisions. This was done via using a set of identity pairs which were labelled by an expert. Wang et al. [12] discussed that these methods perform based on a limited number of descriptive attributes and the most important issue in this case is that they tend to fail if one or more of considered attributes contains missing values.

In another study, a graph-based method for entity resolution was proposed by Bhattacharya and Getoor [13]. This new method defined a distance measure that combined graph-based relational similarity with corresponding attribute similarities between each entity reference pair. They extended this approach later and proposed a collective entity resolution method. As a result, instead of simply making pair-wise entity comparisons, they could derive new social information and incorporate it into further resolution process repeatedly.

There were some other researchers tackled the issue of one person having several profiles on different social media platforms and some techniques for matching user profiles have been developed. For instance, a CRF-based approach was proposed by Bartunov et al. [14]. They used two user graphs which were created using both user profile attributes and social linkages and then they combined these two graphs. These researchers have successfully demonstrated that social information can help to improve the performance of identity resolution, when incorporated in matching algorithms.

2 Methodology

2.1 SPIRIT Policing Dataset

SPIRIT policing dataset is an anonymized dataset which has been used in SPIRIT project funded by European Union's Horizon 2020. This dataset includes 891 identities, and each identity has 30 different attributes. Eight of these attributes will be considered in this research which are (1) postcode, (2) date of birth, (3) town, (4) offence, (5) gender, (6) street name, (7) district, and (8) ethnicity. There are two 'known' identities in this dataset who are using two different names 'Billy Smith' and 'Mariet Snehh' but they are both belonging to the same person.

2.2 Identity Model

Identity refers to those attributes that enable us to recognize an individual from others. A new identity model has been used in this research for the first time, which includes four categories of attributes. The first category is physical identity which includes characteristics which an object or person is definitely recognizable or known by. The second category is official identity which is the identity that carries a legal status, usually issued by governments to their citizens. The third category is virtual identity which is the identity created by human user that acts as an interface between physical person and virtual person that other users see on their computer screen. It is a model for self expression, and tools for virtual interaction and a representation of a user in a virtual world. Finally, the fourth category is social identity which is a set of behavioral or personal characteristics by which an individual is recognizable as a member of a group.

2.3 Graph Creation

Eight graphs will be created after selecting 8 highly valued attributes which were mentioned in the previous section. In this case, for instance if 4 identities have the same postcode, the graph shows that these 4 identities are connected to each other. In these graphs, the nodes will be presenting a person with his/her first name and surname, and each edge will be showing that there is a similarity between two nodes (person).

2.4 Community Detection Algorithm

After graph creation step, the Louvain algorithm will be used for community detection based on the selected attributes. This method is a very efficient method for identifying communities in large networks. Blondel et al. [15] mentioned that the Louvain method has been used successfully for analyzing different type of networks and for sizes up to 100 million nodes and billions of links. They also pointed out that the analysis of a typical network of 2 million nodes takes 2 min on a standard PC. In fact, this method is a greedy optimization method which tries to optimize the modularity of a partition of the network [15]. Modularity is a metric that can be used to quantify the quality of an assignment of nodes to communities. In other words, modularity can be defined as a value between − 1 and 1 that measures the density of links inside communities compared to links between communities [16]. For a weighted graph, modularity is defined as:

$$M = \frac{1}{2k} \sum_{xy} \left[Q_{xy} - \frac{p_x p_y}{2k} \right] \delta(n_x, n_y) \tag{1}$$

In this equation, Q_{xy} represents the edge weight between nodes x and y. p_x and p_y are the sum of the weights of the edges attached to nodes x and y. k is the sum of all of the edge weights in the graph. n_x and n_y are the communities of the nodes and δ is a Kronecker delta which is a function of tow variables. It is 1 if the variables are equal and it is 0 if the variables are not equal. Equation 2 explains this.

$$\delta_{wt} \begin{cases} 0 \, xf \, w \neq t \\ 1 \, xf \, w = t \end{cases} \tag{2}$$

In the Louvain algorithm, optimization will be performed in two steps. In the first step, small communities will be found by optimizing modularity locally. Then in the second step, the nodes which are belonging to the same community will be cumulated and a new network will be built where its nodes are the communities. These steps will be repeated until a maximum of modularity is achieved and a hierarchy of communities is produced [15]. In other words, in the first step, each node in the network will be assigned to its own community. Then for each node x, the change in modularity will be calculated for removing node x from its own community and moving it into the community of each neighbor y of x. Equation (3) explains the process of inserting x to the community of y.

$$\Delta M = \left[\frac{\sum_{in} + 2p_{x,in}}{2k} - \left(\frac{\sum_{tot} + p_x}{2k} \right)^2 \right] - \left[\frac{\sum_{in}}{2k} - \left(\frac{\sum_{tot}}{2k} \right)^2 - \left(\frac{p_x}{2k} \right)^2 \right] \tag{3}$$

In this equation, $\sum_{in}$ is the sum of all the weights of the links inside the community that node x is moving into. $\sum_{tot}$ is the sum of all the weights of the links to nodes in the community that node x is moving into. Moreover, the weighted degree of node x is represented by p_x and the sum of the weights of the links between node x and other nodes in the community that x is moving into, is represented by $p_{x,in}$. Finally, k is the sum of the weights of all links in the network. Table 1 shows some of the most important studies used Louvain method for community detection.

2.5 Investigating Potential Targets

One of the most important things in network analysis is finding the most important nodes in a graph. Newman [17] explained that 'centrality' is a term that can be used to describe importance of individual nodes in a graph and 'degree of a node' is the number of edges that it has. The nodes with more connections are more influential and important in a network. As a result, the person with more friends in a social graph, is the one that is more central. Thus, in the next step of our method, eight different lists of names will be provided based on the measurement of centrality and the degree of nodes in each graph. Top 20 nodes based on their degree (number of connections that they have) will be recorded in each list. Then these lists will be compared with each other to find the similar identities. If any identity is repeated in at least five lists, it will be recorded in a new list as a potential target. Following this step, a new list of all related identities to the potential targets will be provided.

Table 1. Louvain method for community detection

Project	Number of nodes	Source
Twitter social network	2.4M	Divide and conquer: partitioning online social networks [18]
Mobile phone networks	4M	Tracking the evolution of communities in dynamic social networks [19]
Flickr	1.8M	Real world routing using virtual world information [20]
LiveJournal	5.3M	
YouTube	1.1M	
Citation network	6M	Subject clustering analysis based on ISI category classification [21]
LinkedIn social network	21M	Mapping search relevance to social networks [22]

2.6 Phonetic Algorithms

In the next step, a cascading method will be used for applying three phonetic algorithms on the potential targets and their relevant identities in order to detect any possible human errors during data entry or wrong information given by the person. Three phonetic algorithms have been implemented for indexing names by sound. They are (1) Soundex, (2) Metaphone, and (3) Jaro-Winkler that will be applied following each other on the potential targets and their relevant identities. This means that in the first cycle, Soundex method will be applied. Then in the second cycle Metaphone will be applied on the results of Soundex method. Finally, in the third cycle the Jaro-Winkler method will be applied on the results of Metaphone method. Thus, we narrow down the results to get the best output. As a result, all similar first names and surnames to the potential target identities and their relevant identities, with a potential of being manipulated will be detected to be considered in the next step.

2.7 Comparison Process

After applying Soundex, Metaphone and Jaro-Winkler algorithms using a cascading method, all potential targets and their relevant identities as well as similar identities with a potential of using manipulated forenames and surnames will be added to a new dataset for comparison purpose. All attributes of the potential targets and their relevant identities in the new dataset will be compared separately and similarity will be scored. This means that all 30 attributes for each one of these identities in SPIRIT policing dataset will be considered for comparison and scoring process. The same identities will be investigated based on the similarity scores.

3   Results and Discussion

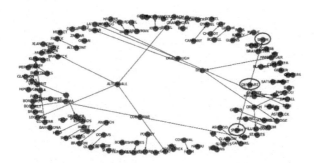

Fig. 1. Graph based on the same postcode

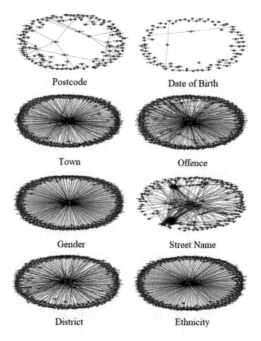

Postcode   Date of Birth

Town   Offence

Gender   Street Name

District   Ethnicity

Fig. 2. Graphs for eight selected attributes

As it was explained in the methodology, eight attributes in SPIRIT policing dataset were selected and they are including (1) postcode, (2) date of birth, (3) town, (4) offence, (5) gender, (6) street name, (7) district, and (8) ethnicity. As a result, in the first step 8 graphs were created. Figure 1 shows one of these graphs, which was created based on the same postcodes and it shows that Billy Smith, Lorret Denhart and Mariet Snehh have been using the same postcode. Moreover, Fig. 2 shows all eight created graphs.

In the second step, the Louvain algorithm was used for community detection based on the 8 selected attributes. Figure 3 shows the community detection graphs.

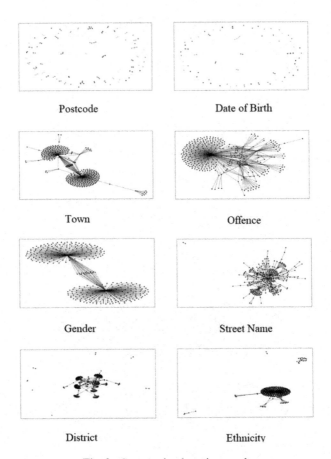

Fig. 3. Community detection graphs

Following this step, centrality and the degree of nodes in each graph were measured, and top 20 nodes in each graph were recorded in eight different lists. These lists were compared, and those identities which were repeated in at least 5 lists were recorded in a new list for potential targets. Table 3 shows the surnames which were repeated in at least five lists.

According to Table 2, three surnames including Smith, Snehh and Bordleon were existed in at least five lists for top 20 nodes. These lists are related to (1) postcode graph, (2) town graph, (3) date of birth graph, (4) offence graph, and (5) street name graph.

Table 2. Surnames which were repeated at least in 5 lists.

Top 20 nodes in				
postcode graph	town graph	date of birth graph	offence graph	street name graph
ALTUNDALL	AINSBURY	**SMITH**	AINSBURY	BESSER
DROACH	ADRE	VELLOIRS	ALTUNDALL	ADRE
FIEL	ARTHURS	BOWLES	AMENT	GLAASOW
GROTHER	BATISTE	DENHART	ALOKS	DICIANI
BECKFOREST	**BORDELON**	GLAASOW	VELLOIRS	BALOW
BESSER	BOSSERMAN	KER	ADRE	**SMITH**
BLAESER	DENHART	MERRET	**SNEHH**	CRECO
BORDELON	GAYROR	ANCHORRS	ASTFALCK	**SNEHH**
DICIANI	VELLOIRS	ASTFALCK	BECKFOREST	FETTES
DORCUS	**SMITH**	**SNEHH**	BALOW	BRAHMS
DRAWBAUGH	**SNEHH**	BARCELONA	**BORDELON**	CRECO
GAYROR	BECH	BECH	ALOI	DORCUS
GELTZ	GROTHER	BECKFOREST	CRECO	FAHREN
GETEL	FETTES	BERROW	FAHREN	KER
JUNCALL	BHOTT	BHOTT	KER	**BORDELON**
KER	BUTLAND	BLAESER	**SMITH**	GETEL
SNEHH	'CORSA	BLATZ	GOSNEL	JUNCALL
KNIISIS	DEGNER	**BORDELON**	BARCELONA	GAYROR
POOZEY	DORCUS	BRADWICK	GAYROR	KNIISIS
SMITH	FONES	BRAHMS	FILLINGHAM	SATVINGRER
		BROWEL		

The relevant surnames to these surnames were detected in the next step based on their connections in different graphs and they were added to a new dataset after applying the phonetic algorithms. Table 3 shows these identities.

Table 3. Potential target names and their identities

Loret Denhart
Billy Smith
Nizie Bordelon
Mariet Snehh
Jasmalinne Beckforest
Kemp Bech

This new dataset was included all 30 attributes for each identity. These 30 attributes were mentioned in section A of the methodology. Figure 4 shows a screenshot from a part of the new dataset, which is created after applying Soundex, Metaphone and Jaro-Winkler algorithms.

As Fig. 4 shows, some of the names in this dataset were repeated. The reason is that some of the values of their different attributes are different. For instance, there are two rows for Kemp Bech. This is because there are two different postcodes related to this name and this person was committed two different offences. As a result, there are two rows related to this person with different values for two attributes including postcode and offence. Finally, every single row of this dataset was compared with other rows and based on the number of attributes which had the same value, a score was assigned to show the similarity between each two identities. After comparing these scores, it was realized that two identities including Billy Smith and Mariet Snehh have the most similarity. As it was explained in section A of the methodology, these two were 'known' identities in SPIRIT policing dataset who had two different names, but they were both belonging to the same person. Thus, the system was successful in resolve their identities.

Surname	Forename	Datae_of_birth	Postcode	Town	Offence
BECH	KEMP	25/02/2003 00:00	B35 6DE	CARSINGTON	THEFT FROM MOTOR VEHICLE
BECH	KEMP	25/02/2003 00:00	B23 6PU	CARSINGTON	BURGLARY OTHER BUILDING
BECH	LGAH	18/03/1945 00:00	B75 7EN	TURNBURY	ATTEMPT BURGLARY DWELLING
BECKFOREST	JASMALINNE	29/03/1989 00:00	B44 0TD	CARSINGTON	CRIMINAL DAMAGE TO DWELLING
BECKFOREST	JASMALINNE	29/03/1989 00:00	B44 0TD	CARSINGTON	CRIMINAL DAMAGE TO DWELLING
BORDELON	NIZIE	01/01/1989 00:00	B44 0TD	CARSINGTON	ASSAULT OCCASION ABH
BORDELON	NIZIE	01/01/1989 00:00	B44 0TD	CARSINGTON	COMMON ASSAULT
BORDELON	NIZIE	01/01/1989 00:00	B23 7UP	CARSINGTON	HARASSMENT
BORDELON	NIZIE	01/01/1989 00:00	B23 7UP	CARSINGTON	HARASSMENT
BORDELON	NIZIE	01/01/1989 00:00	B23 7UP	CARSINGTON	PUTTING PEOPLE IN FEAR OF VIOLENCE
BORDELON	NIZIE	01/01/1989 00:00	B23 7UP	CARSINGTON	HARASSMENT
BORDELON	NIZIE	01/01/1989 00:00	B23 7UP	CARSINGTON	HARASSMENT
BORDELON	NIZIE	01/01/1989 00:00	B44 0TD	CARSINGTON	CRIMINAL DAMAGE TO DWELLING
BORDELON	NIZIE	01/01/1989 00:00	B44 0TD	CARSINGTON	COMMON ASSAULT
BORDELON	NIZIE	01/01/1989 00:00	B44 0TD	CARSINGTON	CRIMINAL DAMAGE TO DWELLING
BORDELON	NIZIE	01/01/1989 00:00	B44 0TD	CARSINGTON	OTHER CRIMINAL DAMAGE
BORDELON	NIZIE	01/01/1989 00:00	B44 0TD	CARSINGTON	BURGLARY DWELLING
BORDELON	NIZIE	01/01/1989 00:00	B44 0TD	CARSINGTON	THEFT DWELLING NOT MACHINE/METER
BORDELON	NIZIE	01/01/1989 00:00	B44 0TD	CARSINGTON	OTHER CRIMINAL DAMAGE
BORDELON	NIZIE	01/01/1989 00:00	B44 0TD	CARSINGTON	CRIMINAL DAMAGE TO DWELLING
BORDELON	NIZIE	01/01/1989 00:00	B43 7BX	YARNFORTH	CRIMINAL DAMAGE TO DWELLING
BORDELON	NIZIE	01/01/1989 00:00	B44 0TD	CARSINGTON	CRIMINAL DAMAGE TO DWELLING
BORDELON	NIZIE	01/01/1989 00:00	B44 0TD	CARSINGTON	BURGLARY DWELLING
BORDELON	NIZIE	01/01/1989 00:00	B43 7BW	YARNFORTH	BURGLARY DWELLING
DENHART	LORRET	01/06/1994 00:00	SF19 9NF	CAERLEON	BURGLARY DWELLING
DENHART	LORRET	01/06/1994 00:00	SF19 9NF	CAERLEON	BURGLARY DWELLING
DENHART	LORRET	01/06/1994 00:00	B18 4AS	CARSINGTON	BURGLARY DWELLING

Fig. 4. New dataset including all potential targets and their relevant identities to be used for comparison process.

4 Conclusion

This research introduces a new graph-based approach for identity resolution. In this approach, graph analysis techniques such as community detection and centrality measurement have been used. Furthermore, this research introduces a new identity model which represents four different types of attributes including (1) physical attributes, (2) social attributes, (3) official attributes, and (4) virtual attributes. SPIRIT policing dataset was used for testing this method. This dataset is an anonymized dataset which has been used in SPIRIT project funded by European Union's Horizon 2020 and includes 892 identity records. Two of these identities are 'known' identities which both are belonging to the same person, but they are using two different names. The methodology presented in this paper successfully recognized these two identities in SPIRIT policing dataset and the expected results were exactly the same as actual results. This identity resolution approach can effectively facilitate the investigation process for police forces and assist them to find criminals and individuals who committed a fraud. It can also be useful for other similar datasets which are containing identity records related to other fields such as finance and banking, customer service or marketing.

Acknowledgement. This research was supported by European Union's Horizon 2020, grant no: 786993. We thank our colleagues from SPIRIT project consortium who provided insight and expertise that greatly assisted the research.

References

1. Li, J., Wang, A.G.: A framework of identity resolution: evaluating identity attributes and matching algorithms. Secur. Inf. **4**(6), (2015). https://doi.org/10.1186/s13388-015-0021-0
2. Kean, T.H., et al.: The 9/11 Commission Report (2004). http://govinfo.library.unt.edu/911/report/index.htm
3. U.S. Department of State: Country Reports on Terrorism (2006). http://www.state.gov/j/ct/rls/crt/2006/
4. Li, J., Wang, G.A., Chen, H.: Identity matching using personal and social identity features. Inf. Syst. Front. **13**, 101–113 (2010)
5. Cheek, J.M., Briggs, S.R.: Self-consciousness and aspects of identity. J. Res. Pers. **16**, 401–408 (1982)
6. Ananthakrishna, R., Chaudhuri, S., Ganti, V.: Eliminating fuzzy duplicates in data warehouses. In: Procceeding of 28th International Conference on Very Large Data Bases, Hong Kong, China, pp. 586–597 (2002)
7. Kalashnikov, D.V., Mehrotra, S., Chen, Z.: Exploiting relationships for domain-independent data cleaning. In: Proceeding of 2005 SIAM International Conference on Data Mining, pp. 262–273. Newport Beach, CA (2005)
8. Köpcke, H., Rahm, E.: Frameworks for entity matching: a comparison. Data Knowl. Eng. **69**, 197–210 (2010)
9. Marshall, B., Kaza, S., Xu, J., Atabakhsh, H., Petersen, T., Violette, C., Chen, H.: Cross-jurisdictional criminal activity networks to support border and transportation security. In: Proceedings 7th Int IEEE Conference Intelligent Transportation Systems, Washington, D.C., pp. 100–105 (2004)
10. Brown, D.E., Hagen, S.C.: Data association methods with applications to law enforcement. Decis. Support Syst. **34**, 369–378 (2003)
11. Wang, G.A., Chen, H., Atabakhsh, H.: Automatically detecting deceptive criminal identities. Commun. ACM **47**, 70–76 (2004)
12. Wang, G.A., Chen, H.C., Xu, J.J., Atabakhsh, H.: Automatically detecting criminal identity deception: an adaptive detection algorithm. IEEE Trans. Syst. Man Cybern. Part A: Syst. Humans **36**, 988–999 (2006)
13. Bhattacharya, I., Getoor, L.: Entity Resolution in Graphs, in Min Graph Data. Wiley-Blackwell, Hoboken (2006)
14. Bartunov, S., Korshunov, A., Park, S., Ryu, W., Lee, H.: Joint link-attribute user identity resolution in online social networks. In: Proceeding of the 6th International Conference on Knowledge Discovery and Data Mining, Workshop on Social Network Mining and Analysis, Beijing, China (2012)
15. Blondel, V.D., Guillaume, J.L., Lambiotte, R., Lefebvre, E.: Fast unfolding of communities in large networks. J. Statist. Mech. Theory. Exp. **10**, P10008 (2008)
16. Hua, F., Fang, Z., Qiu, T.: Modeling ethylene cracking process by learning convolutional neural networks. Comput. Aided Chem. Eng. **44**, 841–846 (2018)
17. Newman, M.: Networks: An Introduction, Chapter 7: Measures and Metrics, pp. 168–234. Oxford University Press, Oxford (2010)
18. Pujol, J.M., Erramilli, V., Rodriguez, P.: Divide and Conquer: Partitioning Online Social Networks (2010)
19. Greene, D., Doyle, D., Cunningham, P.: Tracking the evolution of communities in dynamic social networks. In: International Conference on Advances in Social Networks Analysis and Mining (2010)
20. Hui, P., Sastry, N.R.: Real world routing using virtual world information. In: International Conference on Computational Science and Engineering (2009)

21. Zhang, L., Liu, X., Janssens, F., Liang, L., Glänzel, W.: Subject clustering analysis based on ISI category classification. J. Inform. **4**(2), 185–193 (2010)
22. Haynes, J., Perisic, I.: Mapping search relevance to social networks. In: Proceedings of the 3rd Workshop on Social Network Mining and Analysis (2010)

Knowledge Engineering and Ontology for Crime Investigation

Wilmuth Müller[1]([✉]), Dirk Mühlenberg[1], Dirk Pallmer[1], Uwe Zeltmann[1], Christian Ellmauer[1], and Konstantinos Demestichas[2]

[1] Fraunhofer IOSB, Fraunhoferstr. 1, 76131 Karlsruhe, Germany
wilmuth.mueller@iosb.fraunhofer.de
[2] Institute of Communication and Computer Systems, Iroon Polytechneiou 9, 15773 Zografou, Greece
cdemest@cn.ntua.gr

Abstract. Building upon the possibilities of technologies like ontology engineering, knowledge representational models, and semantic reasoning, our work presented in this paper, which has been performed within the collaborative research project PREVISION (Prediction and Visual Intelligence for Security Information), co-funded by the European Commission within Horizon 2020 programme, is going to support Law Enforcement Agencies (LEAs) in their critical need to exploit all available resources, and handling the large amount of diversified media modalities to effectively carry out criminal investigation.

A series of tools have been developed within PREVISION which provide LEAs with the capabilities of analyzing and exploiting multiple massive data streams coming from social networks, the open web, the Darknet, traffic and financial data sources, etc. and to semantically integrate these into dynamic knowledge graphs that capture the structure, interrelations and trends of terrorist groups and individuals and Organized Crime Groups (OCG).

The paper at hand focuses on the developed ontology, the tool for Semantic Reasoning and the knowledge base and knowledge visualization.

Keywords: Ontology · Knowledge base · Semantic reasoning · Knowledge visualisation

1 Introduction

Organised Crime Groups (OCGs) quickly adopt and integrate new technologies into their 'modi operandi' or build brand-new business models around them (such as CaaS) [1]. More than 5,000 OCGs operating on an international level are currently under investigation in the EU, whereas document fraud, money laundering and the online trade in illicit goods and services are recognised as the engines of organised crime. Notably, goods and services offered on the Darknet are available to anyone, be it an individual user, an OCG or terrorist organization [2].

© IFIP International Federation for Information Processing 2022
Published by Springer Nature Switzerland AG 2022
I. Maglogiannis et al. (Eds.): AIAI 2022, IFIP AICT 646, pp. 483–494, 2022.
https://doi.org/10.1007/978-3-031-08333-4_39

This calls for new tools that allow Law Enforcement Agencies (LEAs) to understand the structure, complexity, dynamics and interrelations within and across OCGs or terrorist organisations. It is important to provide LEAs advanced Big Data capabilities and appropriate Information and Communication Technology (ICT) tools that analyse social networks, utilising advanced linguistic models and semantic technologies.

The EU funded project PREVISION developed a series of tools which provide LEAs with the capabilities of analysing and exploiting multiple massive data streams. These are coming from social networks, the open web, the Darknet, traffic and financial data sources, etc. These tools semantically integrate the acquired data into dynamic knowledge graphs that capture the structure, interrelations and trends of terrorist groups and individuals and OCGs. The tools have been integrated into and interconnected in a platform, providing LEAs a common access to them. Figure 1 presents an overview of the architecture of the developed platform. The platform has been described in [3].

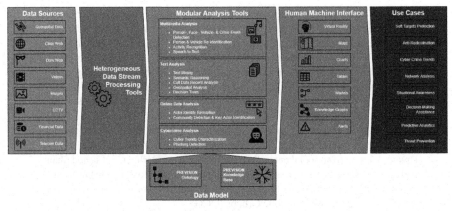

Fig. 1. Overview of the PREVISION platform architecture

This paper focuses on the developed ontology, the semantic reasoning tool, the knowledge base and knowledge visualization tools.

The rest of the paper is structured as follows: Sect. 2 describes related work, especially other EU funded projects addressing the topic of technologies improving the knowledge of investigators when fighting crime and terrorism. Section 3 introduces the PREVISION ontology, which is the core of the PREVISION platform. Section 4 describes how the knowledge base has been implemented. In Sect. 5 semantic reasoning tools, which operate on the knowledge base and produce new entries in it are provided. Section 6 presents how the knowledge is visualized. The paper concludes with a conclusion and the acknowledgment.

2   Related Work

In order to foster the fight against organized crime and terrorism, the European Union funded a series of research projects to develop tools needed by LEAs. These projects are similar to PREVISION, each of it focusing on specific aspects regarding the investigation of criminal and terrorist activities.

The ANITA (Advanced tools for fighting online illegal trafficking) project [4] focused on the design and development of a knowledge-based user-centered investigation system for analyzing heterogeneous (text, audio, video, image) online (surface web, deep web, DarkNet) and offline content for fighting financing terrorism, illegal trafficking of drugs, counterfeit medicines, and firearms.

The COPKIT project [5] has developed data-driven policing technologies to support Law Enforcement Agencies in analysing, investigating, mitigating and preventing the use of new information and communication technologies by organized crime and terrorist groups. It developed a toolkit for knowledge production and exploitation in investigative and strategic analysis work to support the Early Warning /Early Action paradigm for both strategic and operational levels.

The AIDA (Artificial Intelligence and Advanced Data Analytics for Law Enforcement Agencies) project [6] is developing a Big Data Analysis and Analytics framework equipped with a complete set of automated data mining and analytics solutions to deal with standardised investigative workflows, extensive content acquisition, information extraction and fusion, knowledge management and enrichment through applications of Big Data processing, Machine Learning, AI and predictive and visual analytics. It is focusing on cybercrime and terrorism by approaching specific issues and challenges related to LEAs' investigation using machine learning and artificial intelligence methods.

The ASGARD (Analysis System for Gathered Raw Data) project [7] developed a best-of-class tool set for the extraction, fusion, exchange and analysis of Big Data, including cyber-offense data for forensic investigation.

The INSPECTr (Intelligence Network & Secure Platform for Evidence Correlation and Transfer) project [8] develops a shared intelligent platform and a process for gathering, analysing, prioritizing, and presenting key data to help in the prediction, detection and management of crime in support of multiple agencies at local, national and international level. Using both structured and unstructured data as input the developed platform facilitates the ingestion and homogenisation of this data with increased levels of automation, allowing for interoperability between multiple data formats.

The TENSOR (Retrieval and Analysis of Heterogeneous Online Content for Terrorist Activity Recognition) project [9] developed a unified semantic infrastructure for information fusion of terrorism-related content and threat detection on the Web. The TENSOR framework consists of an ontology and an adaptable semantic reasoning mechanism.

In literature there are several attempts to model terrorism-related concepts as ontologies, with the work by Mannes and Golbeck being one of the first attempts [10, 11]. In their work the authors present an ontology for representing terrorist activity, mostly focusing on the description of sequences of events and the representation of social networks underpinning terrorist organizations.

3   Ontology

One of the first steps in the development of the PREVISION toolset has been the design of an ontology capturing the relevant concepts used in criminal investigations.

The model has been defined using the semantic web technology Resource Description Framework (RDF) for describing an ontology. Ontologies are a formal way to describe taxonomies and classification networks, essentially defining the structure of knowledge for various domains. The World Wide Web Consortium (W3C) defines the Web Ontology Language (OWL) as a knowledge representation language for authoring ontologies.

The PREVISION ontology is based on the so-called intelligence pentagram (Fig. 2) that is widely used in the field of intelligence analysis [12]: The pentagram connects the following main concepts:

- Event: A description of an incident or occurrence of some significance that happens during a defined time period. Examples of important PREVISION-specific event types are special crime types, actions in the preparation or execution of a crime, watching a crime by witnesses/testimonies and police counter-crime measures.
- Equipment: Any item of material used to equip a person, organization or place to fulfil its role.
- Organization: An organizational entity or grouping which has a common purpose and which may have a recognizable hierarchical structure.
- Place: Represents all spatial areas, which may be relevant in the context of a crime. A place may be a natural or a man-made feature, an area or a geospatial reference point.
- Person: A description of the physical characteristics and of the private and professional attributes of an individual. This will consist of, amongst other matters, details of the identification, relationships to other persons and digital identities and individual behavior patterns of the person.

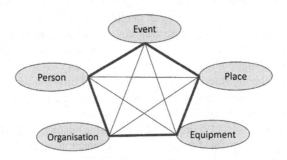

Fig. 2. Main ontology concepts

In order to support information integration and cyber situational awareness in cyber-security systems, the PREVISION ontology has been enhanced by integrating the Unified Cybersecurity Ontology (UCO). The ontology incorporates and integrates heterogeneous data and knowledge schemas from different cybersecurity systems and most commonly used cybersecurity standards for information sharing and exchange [13].

Significant effort has also been placed on identifying complementary underlying concepts via a data-driven process, by further analyzing the knowledge generated by PREVISION data sources. One of these data sources have been datasets acquired by the Dark Web crawler (see Fig. 1, left part). The analysis of these datasets revealed new concepts related to online marketplace advertisements, user profiles in forums, marketplaces, forum posts and digital currency addresses (e.g. Bitcoin addresses). The concepts have been integrated in the ontology, thus enlarging its coverage of criminal acts.

The PREVISION ontology is compatible with the Universal Message Format (UMF), a standard or agreement on what the structure of the most important law enforcement concepts when they are exchanged across borders should be. UMF is a set of concepts (building blocks) to construct standard data exchanges for interconnecting dispersed law enforcement systems [14].

Based on the PREVISON ontology, a message format for the information exchange between analysis tools has been developed. Messages are formulated in the widely used JSON format, where keys and values of JSON objects are governed by the PREVISION ontology. This approach opens up the possibility to standardize the interfaces for message exchange within the platform and even the platform and external systems in order to establish a modularized, open architecture.

4 Knowledge Base

The output of several tools for data mining, data stream processing, and information extraction is fused in a common knowledge graph. It is represented as a set of triples of the form "subject" – "predicate" – "object" according to the RDF standard and can be queried with the SPARQL Protocol and RDF Query Language (SPARQL). Besides this kind of information which we call "semantic data", also other kinds of data like text, image, and video files are produced and stored.

As an implementation of the semantic data base, the Apache Jena Fuseki server has been chosen, while binary data is stored in an Apache Hadoop Distributed File System (HDFS) and MongoDB is used as a document-oriented data base. Furthermore, an API encapsulating the Fuseki server has been developed which serves several purposes:

Data consistency: Write operations on the knowledge base are only accepted if the inserted data is consistent with the PREVISION ontology. In particular, the class and property hierarchy as well as domain and range specifications are respected.

Data provenance: The RDF format allows the partition of a knowledge graph into named subgraphs. In the PREVISION knowledge base, the name of a subgraph is an OWL individual itself, which is assigned information to by a set of triples about the system component or user which has inserted the triples in the subgraph. In this way transparency about data provenance is assured. In theory, it would also be possible to encode the point in time in this way, when a triple has been created in the knowledge base. However, in PREVISION this option has not been used.

REST API: The PREVISION knowledge base provides a Representational State Transfer (REST) API which is accessible over the HTTP as well as Advanced Message Queuing Protocol (AMQP) protocols. As an implementation for the latter, PREVISION makes use of the message broker RabbitMQ[1].

---

[1] https://www.rabbitmq.com/.

Several functions are included in the API:

SPARQL Read Access: For read access, the knowledge base exposes a SPARQL 1.1 Protocol compliant SPARQL endpoint.

Nested JSON Object Interpretation: Data insertions can be made in the form of nested JSON structures, which the API internally translates into sets of RDF triples. Keys and values of objects within these structures are checked to be compliant with the PREVISION ontology.

As an example, the JSON object

```
{  "a": "EmailAccount",
   "isAccountOf": {
            "a": "Person",
            "hasPersonSurname": "Smith"}
   }
```

resolves in the four RDF triples

```
pv:ie_3 a pv:EmailAccount
pv:ie_3 pv:isAccountOf pv:ie_4
pv:ie_4 a pv:Person
pv:ie_4 pv:hasPersonSurname "Smith"
```

where "pv:" denotes the PREVISION namespace prefix and pv:ie_3 and pv:ie_4 are automatically generated IRIs. To identify several automatically created IRIs, objects can be assigned temporary names to by key/value pairs of the form "TAG": "temporary name". Multiple values for properties can be listed as JSON arrays, and inverse properties can be expressed with the syntax "inverse(property_name)".

Graph Node and Property Value Access: Furthermore, the knowledge base API includes a service providing an overview as well as editing facilities of information directly related to a user selected node in the knowledge graph. For a selected entity, all RDF triples in the knowledge graph adjacent to it can be returned. Moreover, in case of the entity being an individual, properties, of which the given individual is an element of the domain or range, together with possibly empty value lists are included in the output. The names of the graphs containing the returned information as well as some technical annotations required by the knowledge base GUI described in Sect. 6.2 are included in the result, too.

In addition, ontology compliant editing options of individuals and their property values, and according write access to create, add, or delete individuals and values of properties is implemented as well.

Case Management: PREVISION separates information belonging to independent crime cases from each other. In this context, the knowledge base provides functions to create, delete and clear case data sets.

5 Semantic Reasoning

PREVISION's semantic reasoning toolset consists of a logic reasoning tool and a probabilistic reasoning tool. The logic Reasoning Tool is based on Semantic Web Rule Language (SWRL). It extracts information from the knowledge base focused on specific SPARQL requests using Fuseki's inbuilt reasoner to apply the ontology-inherent rules resulting from the taxonomy of classes. The results are displayed in tabular or graphical node-network presentation. The various queries include the following aspects:

- Persons and attributes. i.e. vehicle owner/holders, residence, guns/weapons
- Vehicles (route planning)
- Events
- Crisis Event

The probabilistic reasoning tool uses a semantic reasoning technique for extending existing information with new knowledge by adding additional relations between persons, events, places or objects in the knowledgebase. It is based on the so-called Markov Logic Networks (MLN) [15], which enables probabilistic reasoning by combining a probabilistic graphical model with first-order logic.

An MLN represents a first-order knowledge base, i.e. a set of formulas expressed in first-order logic. MLNs have been introduced in 2006 by M. Richardson and P. Domingos, see [15]. Since then they have been an active area of research and were widely applied in different scenarios, e.g. ontology matching, statistical learning and probabilistic inference, see [16–18]. The advantage of probabilistic reasoning is the capability to deal with uncertainties in the knowledge and the rules that the reasoning is applied on.

An MLN is a first-order knowledge base, i.e. a set of formulas $\{F_i \mid i \in I\}$ stated in first-order logic (FOL), where every formula is equipped with a corresponding weight $\omega_i \in \mathbb{R}$. The weight assigned to each formula expresses the degree of believe that the formula is correct. These formulas serve as the base of a procedure yielding a Markov network, which then can be used to assign probabilities to possible states of instances of the underlying ontology.

The set of formulas consists of the evidence retrieved from the knowledge base and the rules that have to be developed in cooperation with law enforcement agencies. The advantage of the probabilistic reasoning is the ability to cope with rules that have uncertainties, meaning they may not hold in every case, but in most cases. So, the confidence in a rule is expressed in a weight factor. As a result, the new evidence inferred has a weight that may be seen as a measure for the probability that it is correct.

The probabilistic reasoning module in PREVISION is based on the open-source implementation of the MLN reasoner Tuffy, developed by Stanford University, which achieves a better scalability than other MLN implementations (see [19]).

In [20] the MLN implementation Tuffy has been integrated into an information fusion component for fusing information acquired by a distributed surveillance system with prior information contained in intelligence databases. Information given in the form of an OWL ontology, such as a taxonomy of defined concepts as well as relations, have proven to be easily convertible into FOL formulas and integrable into an MLN model.

The MAGNETO project [21] developed an MLN based reasoning module for generating new knowledge from witness statements that may contain unreliable information [22].

An adapter has been developed to integrate the MLN reasoner into the PREVISION framework. The adapter connects to the knowledge stored in the Fuseki RDF Triple Store for input and output (see Fig. 3).

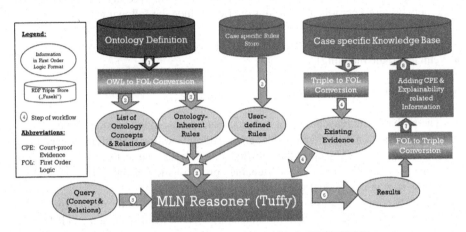

Fig. 3. Workflow of the MLN reasoning in PREVISION

6   Visualisation of Knowledge

Tools in the PREVISION platform like the text mining tool produce results on a high information density level, which corresponds to the information density in the source data. But this data density is not appropriate for an investigator, who is interested in certain indicators related to the case he is in charge of. A central aspect during a criminal investigation is evidence discovery to support some of the hypothesis the investigator has in mind.

To gain condensed and problem-oriented information, PREVISION has developed a web-based graphical user interface providing several visualization tools to give a comprehensive view on the evidence gathered in the knowledge base by various tools and users. These visualization tools are incorporated in the Knowledge Base Inspector, a web-based graphical user interface (GUI) as part of the overall PREVISION GUI.

6.1   Table View

The Table View of the Knowledge Base Inspector allows the user to run custom SPARQL queries as well as to choose predefined SPARQL query patterns for frequently performed query tasks (see Fig. 4). Also, for each OWL entity stored in the knowledge base, it is possible to list all triples adjacent to it in tabular form.

The display of OWL entities is implemented as web-links in the Table View, which allows the user to browse through the knowledge graph. Also type-specific editing options are provided to create, insert and delete data, while consistency with the ontology is assured.

The Table View further provides the option to display text, image or video files stored in Hadoop which are associated via a dedicated OWL property with the individuals stored in the knowledge base. Also, context menus associated with entities provide the option to run several context specific analysis processes or data visualization tools.

Browse	Query						
Persons	Social Network Posts	Emails	Activities	Face Matches	Telephone Calls	Individuals	
Display Query Result					Display Query Pattern		

dateTimeStamp	eventClass	latitude	longitude
2020-03-04T10:12:14Z	Movement	38.062e0	23.5363e0
2020-03-04T10:15:12Z	Movement	38.0605e0	23.5444e0
	TelephoneCall	38.086e0	23.107e0

Fig. 4. Results of a SPARQL-query for geo- and time-referenced data. By clicking on the events Movement or TelephoneCall, these could be further investigated.

6.2 Graph View

The Knowledge Graph Visualizer is a data visualization tool incorporated into the Knowledge Base Inspector offering a graphical view on the linked data of the knowledge base. The tool is designed as a REST[2]-API. It combines the power of SPARQL queries via the Knowledge Base API with state-of-the-art software packages for working with RDF data like RDFLib [23] and Networkx [24], providing algorithms for graph-analysis and manipulation.

Based on a selection of classes and individuals or by providing a list of search terms, the RDF-triples (subject, predicate and object) of their instances are queried. The subjects and objects result in nodes of a directed graph, connected via predicates representing the edges. Subjects and objects which are instances of a certain class are depicted in blue whereas literal objects are depicted in yellow. To further simplify the view on the linked data, technical details which are not relevant to the end user are removed from the view.

A more comprehensive view on the requested data provides a so-called ego-graph where the result entity is used as a center node, surrounded by a number of nodes containing associated data. These depend on a radius to be specified, which defines the distance in nodes to be displayed around the center-node.

The following excerpt depicts the nodes and edges from an ego-graph with a radius of three around "TelephoneCall", "Person", and "Movement" instances in the knowledge

---

[2] Representational State Transfer.

base (Fig. 5). The instances are the same as the one displayed via the Table View and Map-based View.

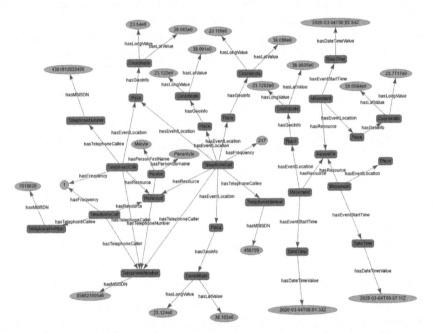

Fig. 5. Graph-based view on the knowledge base data.

6.3   Map-Based View

Events that have a geo and an optional time reference may be displayed in an interactive map that the user can explore. Different visualization types will help an investigator to get an overview of the event-locations which can be either displayed as simple markers on a map or as heatmaps in order to get an impression of the data distribution. Depending on the zoom-level and density of markers, they are clustered into marker-clusters representing a number of events in a certain area.

With an additional time-component, events may be sorted in chronological order and connected with each other with arrows to form trajectories. Connection maps show the locations of two simultaneous events connected by a line, for example the locations of two persons involved in a telephone call.

Finally, a timeseries analysis provides the ability to analyze a sequence of events collected over a specific recording duration where the events are then aggregated over a set period of time (e.g. hourly, daily, etc.) in order to present a specific heatmap or marker cluster for each period of the whole recording duration as an animation. An example may be to analyze the development of monthly burglaries over a recording duration of ten years.

The following illustration shows a heatmap and marker cluster of the knowledge base containing a "Person" instance who produced some geo-referenced "TelephoneCall" and additionally timestamped "Movement" events resulting in a trajectory (Fig. 6).

Fig. 6. Map-based view on the knowledge base data.

7 Conclusion

In this paper, a semantic framework for knowledge management is presented to support LEAs by improving their situation awareness in criminal investigation.

Various analysis tools have been developed to extract information from heterogenous data. The output of the information extraction components is used to populate a knowledge base structured by an ontology, which has been developed specifically for crime investigation purposes.

The consequent usage of the PREVISION ontology as the basis for an exchange format of messages between platform components, which can themselves be interpreted and persisted as parts of a knowledge graph, turned out to be a promising approach for a platform architecture in the domain of criminal investigation.

The visualization of the knowledge base empowers the investigators to gain an enhanced overview and situation awareness of the case under investigation. The paper presented three different views on the same data set in the knowledge-base.

The PREVISION ontology has been asked by and offered to other research projects funded by the European Union in the domain of fight against organized crime and terrorism.

Acknowledgments. This work has been performed under the H2020 833115 project PREVISION, which has received funding from the European Union's Horizon 2020 Programme. This paper reflects only the authors' view, and the European Commission is not liable to any use that may be made of the information contained therein.

References

1. Europol. Serious and Organised Crime Threat Assessment (SOCTA) (2017)
2. Europol. Internet Organised Crime Threat Assessment (IOCTA) (2017)
3. Demestichas, K., et al.: Prediction and visual intelligence platform for detection of irregularities and abnormal behaviour. In: Detection Machine Learning for Trend and Weak Signal Detection in Social Networks and Social Media, vol. 2606, no. paper 4, pp. 25–30. CEUR (2020)

4. ANITA project. https://www.anita-project.eu/
5. COPKIT project. https://copkit.eu/
6. AIDA project. https://www.project-aida.eu
7. ASGARD project. https://www.asgard-project.eu
8. INSPECTr project. https://inspectr-project.eu
9. TENSOR project. https://tensor-project.eu
10. Mannes, A., Golbeck, J.: Building a terrorism ontology. In: ISWC Workshop on Ontology Patterns for the Semantic Web, vol. 36 (2005)
11. Mannes, A., Golbeck, J.: Ontology building: a terrorism specialist's perspective. In: Aerospace Conference, 2007 IEEE, pp. 1–5. IEEE (2007)
12. Dragos, V.: Developing a core ontology to improve military intelligence analysis. Int. J. Knowl.-Based Intell. Eng. Syst. **17**, 29–36 (2013). https://doi.org/10.3233/KES-130253
13. Syed, Z., Padia, A., Finin, T., Mathews, L., Joshi, A.: UCO: a unified cybersecurity ontology. In: AAAI Workshop on Artificial Intelligence for Cyber Security 2016. AAAI Press (2016). https://doi.org/10.13016/M2862BG1V
14. Europol. Universal Message Format: faster, cheaper, better. Publications Office of the European Union. https://op.europa.eu/en/publication-detail/-/publication/3b2cc49f-72bb-419f-8742-eb21cd15e35c
15. Richardson, M., Domingos, P.: Markov logic networks. Mach. Learn. **62**(1–2), 107–136 (2006). https://homes.cs.washington.edu/~pedrod/mln.pdf
16. Niepert, M., Meilicke, C., Stuckenschmidt, H.: A probabilistic-logical framework for ontology matching. In: AAAI (2010)
17. Chen, H., et al.: Scaling up Markov logic probabilistic inference for social graphs. IEEE Trans. Knowl. Data Eng. **29**(2), 433–445 (2017)
18. Wittek, P., Gogolin, C.: Quantum enhanced inference in Markov logic networks. Sci. Rep. **7**, 45672 (2017)
19. Niu, et al.: Tuffy: scaling up statistical inference in Markov logic networks using an RDBMS. Proc. VLDB Endow. **4**(6), 373–384 (2011)
20. Kuwertz, A., Mühlenberg, D., Sander, J., Müller, W.: Applying knowledge-based reasoning for information fusion in intelligence, surveillance, and reconnaissance. In: Lee, S., Ko, H., Oh, S. (eds.) MFI 2017. LNEE, vol. 501, pp. 119–139. Springer, Cham (2018). https://doi.org/10.1007/978-3-319-90509-9_7
21. MAGNETO homepage. http://www.magneto-h2020.eu/. Accessed 09 Feb 2022
22. Müller, W., et al.: Reasoning with small data samples for organised crime. In: Artificial Intelligence and Machine Learning for Multi-Domain Operations Applications II, (S. 21) (2020). https://doi.org/10.1117/12.2557543
23. RDFLib software package. https://rdflib.readthedocs.io/. Accessed 11 Feb 2022
24. NetworkX software package. https://networkx.org/. Accessed 11 Feb 2022

Quantum Approach for Vertex Separator Problem in Directed Graphs

Ahmed Zaiou[1,2,3]([✉]), Younès Bennani[2,3], Mohamed Hibti[1],
and Basarab Matei[2,3]

[1] EDF R&D, Palaiseau, France
{ahmed.zaiou,mohamed.hibti}@sorbonne-paris-nord.fr
[2] LIPN - CNRS UMR 7030, Université Sorbonne Paris Nord, Villetaneuse, France
{younes.bennani,basarab.matei}@sorbonne-paris-nord.fr
[3] LaMSN - La Maison des Sciences Numériques, Saint-Denis, France

Abstract. The Vertex Separator Problem of a directed graph consists in finding all combinations of vertices which can disconnect the source and the terminal of the graph, these combinations are minimal if they contain only the minimal number of vertices. In this paper, we introduce a new quantum algorithm based on a movement strategy to find these separators in a quantum superposition with linear complexity. Our algorithm has been tested on small directed graphs using a real Quantum Computer made by IBM.

Keywords: Quantum computation · Vertex separators · Minimal cuts · Directed graphs

1 Introduction

Quantum computing [24] has attracted enormous interest in recent years and attracted many researchers in different disciplines. This excitement followed the two main revolutionary algorithms introduced by Grover and Shor. The first algorithm introduced by Grover [10], manages to reduce the complexity of finding an element in an unstructured dataset of size N to $O(\sqrt{N})$, the second by Shor [28], which can break the RSA code in a polynomial time. One of the main goals of this new research area is to solve problems that can't be solved in the classical framework and to break the computational complexity of many hard problems and sometimes find good shortcuts and new approaches to solve them. In 2012, John Preskill introduced the term "quantum supremacy", a concept to describe that quantum computers can do some things that classical computers can't [26]. Various algorithms were then proposed to achieve this goal (sycamore [25], chinese [29]). Others have shown significant acceleration compared to the best results of classical computers. In graph theory, we can mention Quantum Max-Flow/Min-cut [5] by Shawn et al., which demonstrates that, unlike the classical case, the conjecture max-flow/min-cut quantum is not true in general. Under certain conditions, for example, when the capacity of each edge is a power

© IFIP International Federation for Information Processing 2022
Published by Springer Nature Switzerland AG 2022
I. Maglogiannis et al. (Eds.): AIAI 2022, IFIP AICT 646, pp. 495–506, 2022.
https://doi.org/10.1007/978-3-031-08333-4_40

of a fixed integer, it is proved that the quantum max-flow is equal to the quantum min-cut. Also, they found connections of the quantum max-flow/min-cut with entanglement entropy and the quantum satisfiability problem. Also, the paper [14] gives a new upper bound on the quantum complexity of queries for deciding st-connectivity on some classes of planar graphs, and shows that this bound is sometimes exponential and also that the evaluation of Boolean formulas reduces to deciding connectivity on such a class of graphs. This paper gives for some classes of boolean formulas a quadratic acceleration with respect to the classical complexity. Kazuya and Ryuhei [27] provided an exponential-time quantum algorithm to calculate the chromatic number, and there are several other works published in these fields like [7] for the graph walk problems, which shows results that improve the best classical algorithms for Eulerian or Hamiltonian circuit problems, the traveling salesman problem and project scheduling. [23] provides two quantum algorithms to find a triangle in an undirected graph or to reject it if the graph is without triangle. The first algorithm uses combinatorial ideas with Grover Search and the second algorithm based on a concept of Ambainis [1]. In addition, we cite the following papers [2,8].

In this paper, we address the problem of vertex partitioning of a directed graph that has not been solved yet by an accurate quantum algorithm. We provide a quantum algorithm to solve this problem and we also show that this algorithm is easily applicable in the existing frameworks of graph partitioning and that it is also computationally feasible. To show this, we make a study case where we use a small graph as an example, then we explain each iteration of our algorithm by indicating the results found in the quantum computer after each iteration.

This paper is organized as follows: In the next section, we give a formal description of the vertex separator problem. In Sect. 3 we discuss our contribution and we define movement oracles and describe our algorithm and its complexity. In Sect. 4, we perform a comparative analysis on qualitative grounds and on the basis of some test cases. The paper is finally concluded in Sect. 5.

2 Problem Statement and State of the Art

We model our problem by directed graphs (networks). In graph theory, the Vertex Separator Problem (VSP) consists of finding a subset of vertices (called a vertex separator) that allows the set of vertices in the graph to be divided into two related components. The VSP is NP-hard [4]. There are a number of algorithms that can find these vertex separators. We mention [15], which presents a heuristic method for partitioning arbitrary graphs that is both efficient in finding optimal partitions and fast enough to be practical in solving large problems. The paper [9] presents a linear time heuristic method for improving network partitions. Both papers [9,15] are adapted by [3,13] to generalize the methods and improve the runtime. According to [11], the vertex separator problem can be formulated by a bilinear quadratic programming problem. And, recently, several works [6,12,17] and [19] have combined the traditional combinatorial method and the optimization-based method to improve the performance and quality of the separator. We mention the result of [18] who introduced a new hybrid algorithm for computing vertex separators in arbitrary graphs using computational optimization.

In the classical approach of the vertex separator problem for a planar graph with n vertices, Lipton and Tarjan [21] provided a polynomial time algorithm for finding a single vertex separator. This algorithm was improved in [22] for other families of graphs such as fixed genus graphs. These families of graphs include trees, 3D grids, and meshes that have small spacers. To obtain all minimal vertex separator of a graph, Kloks and Kratsch [16] provided an efficient algorithm listing all minimal vertex separator of an undirected graph. The algorithm requires a polynomial time for each single separator found. In this paper, we are interested in the vertex separator problem (VSP) in a directed graph that has a source s and a bound t, we search in this graph for all vertex separator that separate the source s and the bound t. In order to do this, let us first define a directed graph and a vertex separator:

Definition 1. *A directed graph or network is a graph in which the edges are oriented. More precisely, a directed graph is an ordered pair (V, E) including: (i) V a set of vertices and (ii) $E \subset \{(x, y) | (x, y) \in V \times V, x \neq y\}$ a set of oriented edges or arcs that are ordered and distinct pairs of vertices.*

Definition 2. *A vertex separator $s - t$ noted (S, C, T) is a partition of V such that $s \in S$ and $t \in T$. Then the $s - t$-cut for us is a division of the vertices of the graph into three independent subsets S, C and T, with the source s in the subset S, the terminal t in T and the subset C representing the vertex separator (the cut). The cut C is minimal, it means that the number of vertices existing in C is minimal, that is to say, if we remove only one vertex from C the remainder is not sufficient for a cut.*

For a single directed graph, we can find several minimal cuts between the source and the terminal. In the rest of this paper, we propose our quantum algorithm to determine all the minimal cuts of a directed graph.

3   Our Contribution

In this section, we will describe our quantum algorithm for finding all the minimal cuts that can stop the flow between the source and the terminal of a directed graph. This algorithm is based on a movement strategy that uses movement oracles to construct a quantum superposition that contains all these minimal cuts. The first question that arrives here is how to represent all the sets of vertices with quantum qubits? For a graph with n vertices, we will find 2^n different subsets of these vertices. In the quantum framework, with n qubits, we can represent 2^n possible states (we cite this book for the basics of quantum computing [20]). In both cases with n elements we have 2^n possibilities, so we represent the subsets by the quantum states of these n qubits. To do this, we use for each vertex of the graph a qubit, and each state of these qubits represents a subset of the vertices.

Before starting explaining the functioning of our algorithm, we start with the definition of a movement in a graph and how these movements are applied by quantum circuits.

Definition 3. *Let $G = (V, E)$, a directed graph, the movement of a vertex $v \in V$ corresponds to the move from v to its successors $Succ(v)$.*

$$Mov(v) = Succ(v) \tag{1}$$

The movement of a vertex $v \in \theta$ where $\theta \subset V$ is the substitution of v by its successors $Succ(v)$ in the set θ.

$$Mov_\theta(v) = \{\theta \setminus v\} \cup Succ(v) \tag{2}$$

In the quantum setting, to apply these moves, we use quantum oracles called movement oracles. Each vertex has a movement oracle, which allows to apply the movement if the vertex of the movement exists in the input subset and provide in the output the input and also the subsets after the movement.

For a vertex v and a given subset of vertices θ, such that $v \in \theta$. We assume that the subset θ is represented by the quantum state $|\psi_\theta\rangle$. To apply the movement of v, we give the quantum state $|\psi_\theta\rangle$ to the oracle as an input, and in the output of the oracle we find a superposition which contains two states $|\psi_\theta\rangle$ and the state $|\psi_{\theta'}\rangle$, with $\theta' = (\theta \setminus v) \cup Succ(v)$.

More generally, suppose that the input set is the union of two subsets $\theta = \theta_1 \cup \theta_2$ represented by the quantum superposition $|\psi_\theta\rangle = \alpha_1 |\theta_1\rangle + \alpha_2 |\theta_2\rangle$ where the state $|\theta_1\rangle$ represents the subset θ_1 and the state $|\theta_2\rangle$ represents the subset θ_2. Consider a vertex $w \in \theta_1$ and $w \notin \theta_2$. The output of the movement oracle of $w \in \theta$ is $|\psi_{out}\rangle = \frac{\alpha_1}{\sqrt{2}} |\theta_1\rangle + \alpha_2 |\theta_2\rangle + \frac{\alpha_1}{\sqrt{2}} |\theta_3\rangle$, where the state $|\theta_3\rangle$ represents the subset $\theta_3 = Mov_{\theta_1}(w) = \{\theta_1 \setminus w\} \cup Succ(w)$.

To provide a general formula for a movement oracle, let $v \in V$ be a vertex, O_v be the movement oracle of v and $|\psi_\theta\rangle = \sum_i \beta_i \psi_{\theta_i}$, $i = 1, \ldots, N$ is a quantum superposition which represents N subsets of vertices $\{i = 1, \ldots, N\}$. The general formula for the movement oracle of a vertex v is:

$$|\psi'_\theta\rangle = O_v |\psi_\theta\rangle = \sum \alpha_e f_v(e) |\psi_{\theta_e}\rangle \tag{3}$$

$$f_v(e) = \begin{cases} 1 & \text{if } \theta_e \in \{\theta_i\}_{i=1,\ldots,N} \\ 1 & \text{if } \theta_e \in \{Mov_{\theta_i}(v)\}_{i=1,\ldots,N} \\ 0 & \text{else} \end{cases} \quad \text{and} \quad \begin{cases} \alpha_e = 0 & \text{if } f_v(e) = 0 \\ \sum_e \alpha_e = 1 \end{cases}$$

In order to represent an oracle with a simple quantum circuit, we need to add two additional control qubits $|c_0\rangle$ and $|c_1\rangle$. The qubit $|c_0\rangle$ is used to check if the vertex of the movement exists in the input set and it will be in the state $|1\rangle$, if it exists in the input set, and in $|0\rangle$ otherwise. For this, we use the C-X gate with the qubit corresponding to the vertex of the movement as control and the $|c_0\rangle$ qubit as target. If the vertex is in the input set, we add another set to the collection of cuts. In other words, if the vertex qubit is in the $|1\rangle$ state, we add a new state to the input superposition. To do this, we use the C-H gate with the qubit $|c_0\rangle$ as control and the qubit of the vertex of the movement as target. Then, we use a C-X gate to apply the movement to the new set. To add all the successors of the movement vertex to the new set, we use the circuit of the Fig. 1 which allows to flip the qubit of the successor into the state $|1\rangle$ if it is in the state $|0\rangle$ and to do nothing if it is in the state $|1\rangle$.

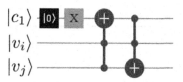

Fig. 1. The movement circuit from v_i to v_j, this circuit uses three qubits: $|v_i\rangle$, $|v_j\rangle$ the movement vertex and the successor respectively and $|c_1\rangle$ for the control.

3.1 Algorithm Description

Let $G = (V, E)$ be a directed graph, with V being the set of vertices such that $|V| = n$ and E the set of edges, the source of the graph is the vertex s and the terminal is the vertex t. The first step of the algorithm consists in preparing the necessary number of qubits to represent all the possible subsets of vertices of the graph. The graph has n vertices, so we use n quits. These n qubits are initialised in the state $|0\rangle$, so the quantum state it initialized to $|\psi\rangle = |0\ldots0\rangle$. With the first qubit corresponding to the source vertex s, the second qubit for the second vertex, until the last qubit for the last vertex (the sink vertex t). There are only zeros in the state $|\psi\rangle$, which means all the vertices are absent in the cut represented by $|\psi\rangle$.

$$|\psi\rangle = |tv_n \ldots v_1 s\rangle = |00\ldots00\rangle \iff \psi = \{\} \tag{4}$$

To start with a set ψ containing only the input vertex s, we apply the **not gate** on the first qubit, which gives us $|\psi\rangle = |0\ldots01\rangle$ as a result, with the qubit $|s\rangle$ is in the state $|1\rangle$.

In the second step, for each vertex, we have an oracle of movement, so we call all these oracles of movement. The first oracle corresponding to the movement of the vertex s to its successors:

$$|\psi_1\rangle = O_1 |\psi\rangle = \alpha_1 |\psi\rangle + \alpha_2 |Mov_\psi(s)\rangle \tag{5a}$$
$$= \alpha_1 |\psi\rangle + \alpha_2 |Succ(s)\rangle \tag{5b}$$

After this iteration, the oracle O_1 adds to the superposition the state $|Succ(s)\rangle$ which represent the first cut of the graph. After that, we apply all the remaining oracles:

$$|\psi_{fin}\rangle = O_n O_{n-1} \ldots O_2 |\psi\rangle \tag{6}$$

Each one of these oracles adds a number of states to the superposition, which means its adds a number of cuts to the set of cuts represented by the superposition.

$$|\psi_{fin}\rangle = \alpha_1 |cut_1\rangle + \cdots + \alpha_k |cut_k\rangle \tag{7}$$

After the n oracles, in the output superposition $|\psi_{fin}\rangle = \sum_i \alpha_i |cut_i\rangle$, we find all the possible minimal cuts represented by the states $|cut_i\rangle$. Finally, we use a simple classical filter to eliminate non-minimal cuts. The Algorithm 1 represents the steps to generate the quantum circuit to find all the possible minimal cuts.

Algorithm 1: All Minimum cuts sets

Input   : Graph $G = (V, E)$, with $n = |V|$ is the number of vertices of the graph, source vertex s, sink vertex t

Output: Min-cuts Cs

Start:

Initialized n qubits,

$$|\psi_0\rangle = |0\ldots0\rangle$$

Apply the not gate X in the first qubit which represents the source s

$$|\psi_1\rangle = |0\ldots01\rangle$$

Make the movement of s we apply the oracle O_s

$$|\psi_2\rangle = O_s |\psi_1\rangle$$

for *each $v \in V$ and $v \mathrel{!=} s$ and t is not a successor of v* **do**

$$\quad |\psi_{i+1}\rangle = O_v |\psi_i\rangle$$

Cs = measured $|\psi_{n-1}\rangle$ and eliminate non-minimal cuts.

return Cs

3.2   Complexity Analysis

Suppose that we have a graph $G = (V, E)$, with V the set of vertices and E the set of edges such that $|V| = n$ and $|E| = m$. To build the circuit, we need n qubits to represent all the possible states of the graph and 2 auxiliary qubits for the control. For n oracles of movements we need n gates C-H, $2n - 2$ gates C-X, $m + 2$ gates X and $2m$ gates CC-X. Therefore, our algorithm has a linear complexity either in terms of memory (number of qubits used), or in terms of computation (n oracles of movements).

4   Case Study

In this section, we present the detailed version of the case study of our algorithm. For that, let us take the graph $G = (V, E)$ represented in the Fig. 2, where V is the set of vertices of size 9 ($n = |V| = 9$), which is labeled from v_0 to v_8 as follows: $V = \{v_0, v_1, v_2, v_3, v_4, v_5, v_6, v_7, v_8\}$. And the set of edges between these vertices is noted E and is presented like the following: $E = \{(v_0, v_1), (v_0, v_2), (v_1, v_5), (v_1, v_7), (v_2, v_3), (v_2, v_4), (v_3, v_5), (v_4, v_6), (v_4, v_8), (v_5, v_6), (v_6, v_7), (v_7, v_8)\}$. We have also fixed the source s in the vertex v_0 and the terminal t in the vertex v_8.

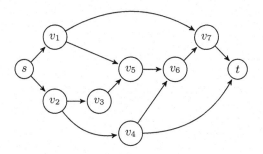

Fig. 2. Directed graph of 9 vertices

Visually, we can identify the set of vertex separators defining the minimal cuts: $Cs = \{C_1 = \{v_1, v_2\}, C_2 = \{v_2, v_7\}, C_3 = \{v_4, v_7\}, C_4 = \{v_1, v_4, v_5\}, C_5 = \{v_1, v_3, v_4\}, C_6 = \{v_1, v_4, v_6\}\}$, with each subset $C_i, i = 1, \ldots, 6$ is a vertex separators of the graph with a minimal number of vertices. In the following, we want to find this set of minimal cuts Cs by our quantum algorithm. To do this, we use IBM's quantum simulator to show the intermediate results of our algorithm. In the graph G we have $n = 9$ vertices, to represent all the possible combinations of these vertices we use 9 qubits. The source s is represented by the first qubit $|v_0\rangle$ and each vertex $v_i, i = 1, \ldots, 7$ is associated to the qubit $|v_i\rangle, i = 1, \ldots, 7$ and the sink t is associated to the last qubit $|v_8\rangle$. These 9 qubits $|v_i\rangle, i = 0, \ldots, i = 9$ can represent 2^9 possibles states, therefore, these qubits can represent the superposition $|v_8 v_7 v_6 v_5 v_4 v_3 v_2 v_1 v_0\rangle = \sum_{i=0}^{2^9 - 1} \alpha_i |C_i\rangle$, which represent the all possible subsets of vertices of the graph G. Each state $|C_i\rangle$ in the superposition $|v_8 v_7 v_6 v_5 v_4 v_3 v_2 v_1 v_0\rangle$ represent a single vertex separator, we say the vertex v_i belongs to the vertex separator $|C_i\rangle$ (or the minimal cuts $|C_i\rangle$) if the corresponding qubit $|v_i\rangle$ in the state $|C_i\rangle$ is in the state $|1\rangle$. For example, the vertex separator $C = \{v_1, v_2\}$ can be encoded by the quantum state $|000000110\rangle$.

Suppose now that all the successors of the source $s = v_0$ are down, then there is no other way to go to the next vertices, so the subset of the successors of the vertex $s = v_0$ is a vertex separator, in addition, if one of these successors is in good condition, we will find a way to go to the next vertices. Therefore, the subset of successors of $s = v_0$ is a vertex separator with a minimal number of vertices, in other words a minimal cut. Then, to find this first minimal cut, we apply the first oracle of the movement O_S on the state $|\psi_0\rangle$. That is to say that we take $|\psi_0\rangle$ as the input state and we apply the movement of the vertex $v_0 = s$ to its successors v_1 and v_2, which gives us the output state $|\psi_1\rangle = |000000110\rangle$. The graph of the movement of the oracle s and the result in output are represented in the Fig. 3.

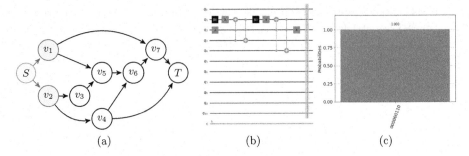

(a)   (b)   (c)

Fig. 3. The movement of s towards the two successors v_1 and v_2 represented in (a) can be managed by the oracle (b). (c) The result of the execution gives the state $|000000110\rangle$ which represents the first cut $\{v_1, v_2\}$.

Now, suppose that one of the successors v_1 and v_2 is in a good condition, then there is a way to go to the following vertices. For example, if vertex v_1 is in a good condition we can find a path to the terminal through the successors of v_1. If these successors of v_1 are out of order, we cannot find a path to the terminal. Therefore, the subset $Succ(v_1) \cup C_1 \setminus \{v_1\}$ is a cut. So, if we apply the movement of v_1 in the state $|\psi_1\rangle$, we find a new minimal cut containing the successors of v_1 and the vertex v_2. Here, the oracle uses the Hadamard gate to keep the first cut and add the new state corresponding to the new cut. The Fig. 4 presents the circuit with the second oracle and the execution results in the simulator. At step k, we apply the oracle O_k on the output superposition of step $k-1$, therefore, we apply the movement of the vertex v_k corresponding to the oracle O_k, which adds new states in the superposition $|\psi_k\rangle$, if the qubit corresponding to the vertex v_k is in the state $|1\rangle$ for each state of the superposition $|\psi_{k-1}\rangle$.

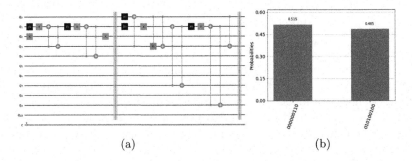

(a)   (b)

Fig. 4. (a) The second oracle starts after the first barrier in the circuit. (b) The result of the run gives two states: $|000000110\rangle$ represents the input and $|010100100\rangle$ represents the new cut after the movement. Note that the second oracle in (a) uses the Hadamard gate to add the new state into the superposition.

$$|\psi_k\rangle = O_k |\psi_{k-1}\rangle$$
$$= O_k \sum_j \alpha_j |C_j\rangle = \sum_j \alpha_j O_k |C_j\rangle$$
$$= \sum_j \beta_j |C_j\rangle + \sum_j \beta_j Mov_{v_k}(|C_j\rangle)$$

with $\sum_j \alpha_j = 1$ and $\sum_j \beta_j = 1$.

After all the possible movements, we found the superposition $|\psi_{final}\rangle$.

$$|\psi_{final}\rangle = \sum_i \alpha_i |v_i\rangle = \sum_i \alpha_i |v_{i_8} v_{i_7} v_{i_6} v_{i_5} v_{i_4} v_{i_3} v_{i_2} v_{i_1} v_{i_0}\rangle \tag{9}$$

where $\sum_i \alpha_i = 1$ and each state $|i\rangle = |v_{i8}v_{i7}v_{i6}v_{i5}v_{i4}v_{i3}v_{i2}v_{i1}v_{i0}c_{i_1}c_{i_0}\rangle$ of the state $|\psi_{final}\rangle$ represents a cut, with $|v_{ij}\rangle = |1\rangle$ if the vertex j is in the cut i and $|v_{ij}\rangle = |0\rangle$ in the otherwise.

In our graph example, after the execution of the circuit Fig. 5 in IBM's simulator and the quantum computer IBM Q 16 Melbourne, we present the results in the Fig. 6. Finally, we remove the non minimal cuts. For this, for each (i, j) we eliminate the cut C_j if $C_i \in C_j$. To verify the results, we visualized each state of the superposition Fig. 6 in an independent graph, with red color if the vertex qubit in the state $|1\rangle$ (present in the minimal cut) and black if it's in the state $|0\rangle$.

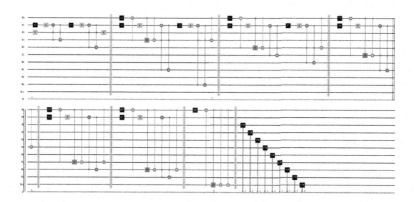

Fig. 5. The circuit uses 11 qubits: 9 to represent all possible subsets of vertices, 2 for the control. And also it uses 7 movement oracles separated by vertical separators. Each oracle represents the movement of a vertex. At the end of the circuit, we measure the 9 qubits to find the superposition which represents all the minimal cuts.

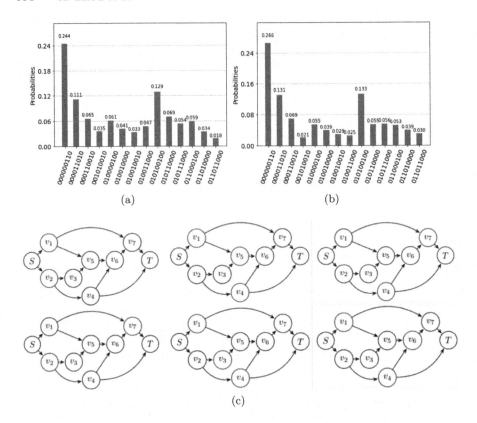

Fig. 6. The histograms represent the superposition of output $|\psi_{final}\rangle$. (a) The results of the execution in IBM's Qasm simulator. (b) The results of the execution in IBM Q 16 Melbourne quantum computer. (C) Results in the graph with red color represent the cuts.

5   Conclusion

We have proposed a quantum algorithm to find all the minimal cuts of a directed graph. More precisely, we propose a quantum algorithm that uses movement oracles to generate as output a superposition of all states that represent the minimal cuts. In this paper, cuts are represented by a set of vertices, which can separate the source and the terminal of the graph, and they are minimal if they contain just the minimal number of vertices to represent a cut. Also, the complexity of our algorithm is linear, because: it uses only $n + 2$ qubits, n to represent all the possible combinations of vertices and 2 for the counter, and it uses n oracles of movements, n being the number of vertices of the graph.

Acknowledgements. This research work was partially funded by the European project NExt ApplicationS of Quantum Computing (NEASQC), supported by the Horizon 2020-FETFLAG (Grant Agreement 951821).

References

1. Ambainis, A.: Quantum walk algorithm for element distinctness. SIAM J. Comput. **37**(1), 210–239 (2007)
2. Apers, S., Lee, T.: Quantum complexity of minimum cut. arXiv preprint arXiv:2011.09823 (2020)
3. Ashcraft, C., Liu, J.W.H.: A partition improvement algorithm for generalized nested dissection. Boeing Computer Services, Seattle, WA, Technical report, BCSTECH-94-020 (1994)
4. Bui, T.N., Jones, C.: Finding good approximate vertex and edge partitions is NP-hard. Inf. Process. Lett. **42**(3), 153–159 (1992)
5. Cui, S.X., Freedman, M.H., Sattath, O., Stong, R., Minton, G.: Quantum max-flow/min-cut. J. Math. Phys. **57**(6), 062206 (2016)
6. Davis, T.A., Hager, W.W., Kolodziej, S.P., Yeralan, S.N.: Algorithm 1003: mongoose, a graph coarsening and partitioning library. ACM Trans. Math. Softw. **46**(1), 1–18 (2019)
7. Dörn, S.: Quantum algorithms for graph traversals and related problems. In: Proceedings of CIE, vol. 7, pp. 123–131. Citeseer (2007)
8. Eldredge, Z., et al.: Entanglement bounds on the performance of quantum computing architectures. Phys. Rev. Res. **2**(3), 033316 (2020)
9. Fiduccia, C.M., Mattheyses, R.M.: A linear-time heuristic for improving network partitions. In: 19th Design Automation Conference, pp. 175–181. IEEE (1982)
10. Grover, L.K.: A fast quantum mechanical algorithm for database search. In: Proceedings of the Twenty-Eighth Annual ACM Symposium on Theory of Computing, pp. 212–219 (1996)
11. Hager, W.W., Hungerford, J.T.: Continuous quadratic programming formulations of optimization problems on graphs. Eur. J. Oper. Res. **240**(2), 328–337 (2015)
12. Hager, W.W., Hungerford, J.T., Safro, I.: A multilevel bilinear programming algorithm for the vertex separator problem. Comput. Optim. Appl. **69**(1), 189–223 (2017). https://doi.org/10.1007/s10589-017-9945-2
13. Hendrickson, B., Rothberg, E.: Improving the run time and quality of nested dissection ordering. SIAM J. Sci. Comput. **20**(2), 468–489 (1998)
14. Jeffery, S., Kimmel, S.: Quantum algorithms for graph connectivity and formula evaluation. Quantum **1**, 26 (2017)
15. Kernighan, B.W., Lin, S.: An efficient heuristic procedure for partitioning graphs. Bell Syst. Tech. J. **49**(2), 291–307 (1970)
16. Kloks, T., Kratsch, D.: Listing all minimal separators of a graph. SIAM J. Comput. **27**(3), 605–613 (1998)
17. Kolodziej, S., Davis, T.: Vertex separators with mixed-integer linear optimization. In: 17th SIAM Conference on Parallel Processing for Scientific Computing (2016)
18. Kolodziej, S.P., Davis, T.A.: Generalized gains for hybrid vertex separator algorithms. In: 2020 Proceedings of the SIAM Workshop on Combinatorial Scientific Computing, pp. 96–105. SIAM (2020)
19. Kolodziej, S.P.: Computational optimization techniques for graph partitioning. Ph.D. thesis (2019)
20. Bellac, M.L.: Introduction à l'information quantique. Belin (2005)
21. Lipton, R.J., Tarjan, R.E.: A separator theorem for planar graphs. SIAM J. Appl. Math. **36**(2), 177–189 (1979)
22. Lipton, R.J., Tarjan, R.E.: Applications of a planar separator theorem. SIAM J. Comput. **9**(3), 615–627 (1980)

23. Magniez, F., Santha, M., Szegedy, M.: Quantum algorithms for the triangle problem. SIAM J. Comput. **37**(2), 413–424 (2007)
24. Nielsen, M.A., Chuang, I.: Quantum computation and quantum information (2002)
25. Pednault, E., Gunnels, J.A., Nannicini, G., Horesh, L., Wisnieff, R.: Leveraging secondary storage to simulate deep 54-qubit sycamore circuits. arXiv preprint arXiv:1910.09534 (2019)
26. Preskill, J.: Quantum computing and the entanglement frontier. arXiv preprint arXiv:1203.5813 (2012)
27. Shimizu, K., Mori, R.: Exponential-time quantum algorithms for graph coloring problems. In: Kohayakawa, Y., Miyazawa, F.K. (eds.) LATIN 2021. LNCS, vol. 12118, pp. 387–398. Springer, Cham (2020). https://doi.org/10.1007/978-3-030-61792-9_31
28. Shor, P.W.: Polynomial-time algorithms for prime factorization and discrete logarithms on a quantum computer. SIAM Rev. **41**(2), 303–332 (1999)
29. Zhong, H.-S., et al.: Quantum computational advantage using photons. Science **370**(6523), 1460–1463 (2020)

Unsupervised Multi-sensor Anomaly Localization with Explainable AI

Mina Ameli[1,2(✉)] [ID], Viktor Pfanschilling[3] [ID], Anar Amirli[1,2] [ID],
Wolfgang Maaß[1,2] [ID], and Kristian Kersting[3] [ID]

[1] Saarland University, Saarbrücken, Germany
[2] German Research Center for Artificial Intelligence (DFKI), Saarbrücken, Germany
{mina.ameli,anar.amirli,wolfgang.maass}@dfki.de
[3] TU Darmstadt, Darmstadt, Germany
{viktor.pfanschilling,kersting}@cs.tu-darmstadt.de

Abstract. Multivariate and Multi-sensor data acquisition for the purpose of device monitoring had a significant impact on recent research in Anomaly Detection. Despite the wide range of anomaly detection approaches, localization of detected anomalies in multivariate and Multi-sensor time-series data remains a challenge. Interpretation and anomaly attribution is critical and could improve the analysis and decision-making for many applications. With anomaly attribution, explanations can be leveraged to understand, on a per-anomaly basis, which sensors cause the root of anomaly and which features are the most important in causing an anomaly. To this end, we propose using saliency-based Explainable-AI approaches to localize the essential sensors responsible for anomalies in an unsupervised manner. While most Explainable AI methods are considered as interpreters of AI models, we show for the first time that Saliency Explainable AI can be utilized in Multi-sensor Anomaly localization applications. Our approach is demonstrated for localizing the detected anomalies in an unsupervised multi-sensor setup, and the experiments show promising results. We evaluate and compare different classes of saliency explainable AI approach on the Server Machine Data (SMD) Dataset and compared the results with the state-of-the-art OmniAnomaly Localization approach. The results of our empirical analysis demonstrate a promising performance.

Keywords: Anomaly localization · Explainable artificial intelligence · Unsupervised anomaly detection · Multivariate time-series · Multi-sensor data

1 Introduction

Anomaly detection has been an active topic in diverse research communities. There is a wide range of existing approaches to this end. With the increasing amount of Multivariate data generated in many monitoring applications and domains such as process industry, medical diagnosis, computer networks,

© IFIP International Federation for Information Processing 2022
Published by Springer Nature Switzerland AG 2022
I. Maglogiannis et al. (Eds.): AIAI 2022, IFIP AICT 646, pp. 507–519, 2022.
https://doi.org/10.1007/978-3-031-08333-4_41

etc., unsupervised anomaly detection on multivariate data is of great importance. While many solutions focus on the accuracy of the anomaly detection approaches, localizing the root cause of anomaly for decision-making, analysis, and interpretability of the proposed solutions are critical. To this end, anomaly detection can be considered as a pre-processing step for anomaly localization. Anomaly detection in multi-sensor setup refers to identification of rare events in specific time and anomaly localization refers to identification of the sensors which caused a particular anomaly. There have been several studies that, in particular, focused on the interpretability of predictions in multivariate time-series, including [6,14,23]. For instance, [15] presents the series saliency framework for temporal interpretation for multivariate time-series forecasting. Some other studies focus on the interpretability and trust-worthiness of classifiers [19], or other AI models like Autoencoders [17]. However, there is presently a lack of approaches for multi-sensor and multivariate time-series data anomaly localization. Currently, most approaches in this scheme focus on anomaly detection, and the few that handle in the wild scenarios do not focus on anomaly localization. Localizing the anomalous sensors in a wide number of sensors can assist reliable decision making in monitoring systems. Furthermore, with the explainability of AI solutions attracting more the attention of researchers and being used for different purposes, there is the opportunity to not only interpret the models with this tool but to use it as an additional application in solution pipelines. This paper, proposes using Saliency Explainable AI approaches to localize anomalies in multivariate time-series, and our main contribution can be summarized as follows:

- A novel method for unsupervised Multi-sensor Anomaly Localization.
- A novel application of saliency Explainable AI methods.
- Literature review over available multivariate anomaly localization solutions.
- Evaluation the performance of different Explainable AI methods for anomaly location on multi-sensor and multivariate data.
- A generalized Anomaly Localization solution for different kinds of Anomaly Detection models.
- Proposing future focus of studying on the impact of explanations on bridging the gap between AI practitioners and domain experts.

The remainder of the paper is organized as follows. In Sect. 2, we outline the related work. The Background is explained in Sect. 3. The proposed solution is addressed in Sect. 4. Experimental results are presented in Sect. 5. In Sect. 6, the results are discussed. And Sect. 7 concludes the paper.

2 Related Work

Usage of Anomaly Detection and solutions to address this subject in different multivariate data applications have a long history such as TadGAN [7], LSTM [8], DAGMM [28], and OmniAnomaly [20], but the focus of literature review in this paper is anomaly localization. In this section, we introduce different kinds of anomaly localization that already were investigated in multivariate data in the relevant literature. Feature importance, feature attributions, root cause analysis, and some other terminologies could be found in the literature to address the anomaly localization of multi-sensor, multivariate datasets, and data streams:

[9] proposes sparse PCA methods to perform anomaly detection and localization for network data streams. They identify a sparse low dimensional space that captures the abnormal events in data streams to localize anomalies.

[3] proposed a feature importance evaluation approach which is designed for Isolation Forests. [13] performs this task by examining the contribution of each dimension individually to the decision statistics.

[18] uses ARCANA, an autoencoder-based anomaly root cause analysis. It describes the process of reconstruction as an optimization problem that aims to remove anomalous properties from an anomalous instance.

The anomaly interpretation solution from [20] is to annotate the detected entity rare-event with the top few univariate time-series ranked by their reconstruction probabilities. Recently, [1] extends Shapley Additive Explanation (Shap) to explain anomalies detected by an autoencoder.

[24] proposed a novel anomaly attribution approach for multivariate temporal and spatio-temporal data based on the counterfactual replacements of variables within the anomalous intervals. This counterfactual replacement determines whether the anomaly still has occurred if a subset of variables is more similar to the data outside of that interval.

[4] transform multivariate time-series into the 2D images and with point-wise convolution in a series of images ensures to encode temporal information of each time-series data as well as the correlation between each variable. As a result, an anomaly can be detected and localized by conducting a residual image and an anomaly score function.

Our Anomaly localization method differs from any of the mentioned approaches. While most state-of-the-art anomaly localization approaches are either depending on the anomaly detection pipeline or describe the probability of features contributions by statistical study, we show for the first time that Saliency Explainable AI can be utilized in multi-sensor time-series Anomaly localization applications.

3   Background

In this section, we describe the details of our proposed Multi-Sensor Anomaly Localization with Explainable AI in an unsupervised setup. The overall architecture is shown in Fig. 2. In the following sections, we briefly introduce all the associated fields.

3.1   LSTM Autoencoder

Reconstructions based on LSTM Autoencoders are commonly utilized for unsupervised multivariate anomaly detection and have shown to be effective [11].

As a result, in the anomaly detection pipeline, we used this family of algorithms as the fundamental training architecture. Autoencoders are technically
unsupervised learning methods, as they do not require labelled data. For the
purpose of anomaly detection, a part of the data which is assumed as normal
data and doesn't contain anomalous samples is considered for training, therefore,
the method is a semi-supervised method in the context of anomaly detection. An
LSTM Autoencoder uses an Encoder-Decoder LSTM architecture to construct
an autoencoder for sequential data. In the architecture shown in Fig. 1, a LSTM
Autoencoder model reads the sequential data input step-by-step. The hidden
state or output represents an internal learned representation of the entire input
as a fixed-length vector. The decoder uses this vector as an input and interprets
it as each step in the output. Unsupervised autoencoder-based Anomaly Detection techniques use the reconstruction error computed by generated output as
key anomaly score identifier. The reconstruction error we use in this paper is the
Mean Absolute Error (MAE).

$$MAE = \frac{\sum_{i=1}^{n} |y_i - x_i|}{n} \tag{1}$$

where y_i is prediction, x_i is true value, and n is the total number of data points.

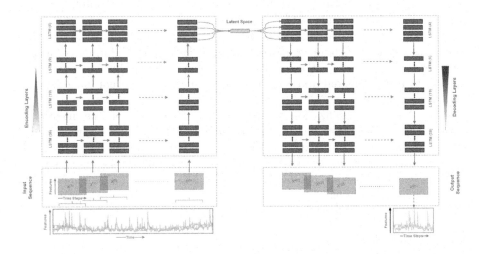

Fig. 1. Architecture of the LSTM Autoencoder used in the experiments.

3.2   Explainable AI Methods

In this section, the different available Explainable AI methods applicable to
Time-Series data are described.

Additive Feature-Based. Shapley Value Sampling [10] is an additive feature attribution method based on Shapley Values. Shapley Values originate from cooperative game theory and calculate the unique and fair attribution of each feature to the output. Fair feature attribution is achieved by computing the weighted average contribution of the given features by comparing the attribution score between when the feature is present and when the feature is absent over all the possible feature subsets of each case which have an explanatory model as a linear function of binary variables:

$$g(z') = \varphi_0 + \sum \varphi_i z_i' \tag{2}$$

where $z' \in \{0,1\}^M$, M is the number of simplified input features, and $\varphi_i \in \mathbb{R}$. However, the exact computation of Shapley Values is computationally challenging for a large number of features. To that extent, Shapley Value Sampling is used to estimate the Shapley values by choosing a new random permutation of the input feature.

Perturbation-Based. Feature perturbation methods are applied to find the minimum subset of features that are enough to provide a good prediction performance by perturbing some of the original input features with some noise values. The assumption here is that if a feature is irrelevant, it can be expected to have little impact on the model performance. Thus, ablating the irrelevant features, permutation methods find a minimum subset of features that are significant for the model to issue a prediction. Feature Ablation is a method that replaces each input feature with a reference value and computes the difference in feature attribution. Similar to the Feature Ablation [2], Feature Occlusion [22] compares the group of contiguous features with reference values [12]. [16] provides a detailed study about Occlusion-based explanations in deep recurrent models for biomedical signals. Another method is Feature Permutation [2] which involves comparing the difference between individual permutation of features within a batch with the shuffled outputs of that batch.

Gradient-Based. Gradient-based methods are formulated around the similar assumption used in perturbation-based methods. The main difference is that salient features are found through propagating activation differences with respect to local variability of the features along the path from a different reference value to input. In order to capture the information flow through the network better, several approaches have been proposed with different ways to compute gradients that propagate more quantitative information than direct gradients. The Integrated Gradient is one of the prevalent methods which computes feature importance by approximating the integral of gradients of the model's output using Riemann summation [21]. The integrated gradient along the ith dimension for an input x and reference value x_i is defined as follows.

$$IG_i(x) := (x_i - x_i') \times \int_{\alpha=0}^{1} \frac{\partial F(x' + \alpha \times (x - x'))}{\partial x_i} \tag{3}$$

The other method we use is Gradient Shap [10]. Gradient Shap adds Gaussian noise to select a random point along the path from reference data to input and then computes the expectation of gradient of model's prediction with respect to the randomly selected point through the additive composition of features.

Attention-Based. By adding an attention layer into the neural network architecture, we can compute the importance of features explicitly as part of training [5]. We applied the above-mentioned approaches from saliency methods on LSTM Autoencoder. The details of our experiments, as well as the methodology used, will be discussed in the following sections.

4   Proposed Solution

While most state-of-the-art anomaly localization approaches are either depending on the anomaly detection pipeline or describe the probability of features contributions by statistical study, we show for the first time that Saliency Explainable AI can be utilized in multivariate time-series Anomaly localization applications. An overview of proposed Multi-sensor Anomaly Localization Pipeline is shown in Fig. 2.

In this study, we experimentally evaluate Anomaly Localization by Saliency Explainable-AI approaches. Saliency methods were originally utilized in image classification, and there have been few attentions of using these approaches in time-series studies [5]. In our experiments, we use the Mean Absolute Error Eq. 1 in the wrapper function. To that extent, we focus on features contributing to the reconstruction error rather than reducing it. In this work we are utilizing the notion of interpretabilty of Explainable AI based on the categorizations in [26] and the numerical output [25] is accounted for in the design and execution of the experiments.

The approach to verify an explanation method is implemented in three main phases: training the model, defining ta wrapper function to interface with Explainable AI (XAI) methods, and evaluating the output of XAI approaches. In the first step, we train a black-box model on temporal data of any dimension to represent the normal behaviour of the data. Next, the trained model is used to generate new samples from test inputs. Later we construct a wrapper to integrate an autoencoder into saliency Explainable AI methods.

The purpose of the saliency methods is to determine the features or sensors that contribute to the prediction issued by a model. However, autoencoder methods learn and reconstruct the normal behaviour of the temporal data. Hence, unlike other autoencoder settings (e.g., image segmentation), there is no direct accuracy score attributed to the output in rare-event detection. For that, we trace the input to the reconstructed features via the reconstruction loss so that the explanation model signifies the features that impact the reconstruction error. Lastly, we compare features with positive contribution values with the ground truth features over the whole anomalous regions to verify how accurate the explanation methods signify the sensor localization.

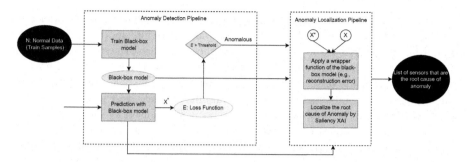

Fig. 2. Overview of the proposed Multi-sensor Anomaly Localization Pipeline.

5   Experiments

This section applies the explanation methods described in Sect. 3 to a black-box model and evaluates the quality of the feature attribution for each method on temporal anomalies. We inspect the quality of the XAI methods on local anomalous regions by comparing the most relevant sensors with the annotated sensors. This is achieved by calculating the average feature attribution score over the true anomaly regions, and comparing features sorted by attribution scores with the true anomalous sensors.

5.1   Dataset

In the experiments we used Server Machine Dataset (SMD) which is collected by [20]. SMD is a 5-week-long multivariate dataset collected from a large Internet company. It is comprised of data from 28 subsets, each being collected from different machines. For each subset, the dataset is divided into two parts of equal length of training and testing datasets. Each subset has 38 features such as CPU load, network usage, memory usage, etc. In addition to anomalies being labeled, features contributing to the anomaly at each anomalous region are also annotated, making it possible to evaluate feature attributions. The number and indices of features inducing anomalies vary upon each anomalous region, and the annotated features do not contain feature attribution values.

5.2   Experiment Setting

Explainable AI methods for the purpose of anomaly localization could be utilized to interpret any black-box model, the validation technique is model-agnostic and can be implemented using any model that is desired for multivariate temporal data analysis, such as TadGAN [7], LSTM [8], DAGMM [28], and OmniAnomaly [20]. Nevertheless, it is important to mention that the performance of any explanation model for computing the feature attribution depends on the quality of the black-box model.

In our experiments, we utilize a simple bottleneck LSTM autoencoder consisting of a two-layer encoder and decoder as a baseline model. Training the model is unsupervised and we considered the first part of the data as normal data. Firstly, features are encoded and then the latent feature representation is reversed in the same order in the decoder part to reconstruct the initial data. The increase in reconstruction error for anomalous data will lead us to detect anomalies. During the preprocessing, the data is normalized by min-max scaling, and then it is segmented into sequences through a sliding window of length 50.

We use the ADAM optimizer and stochastic gradient descent with a learning rate of 10^{-3} with a mini-batch size of 64 to train the model. We train the model with an early stopping technique on the validation data back from 20% of the training. Furthermore, to deal with the gradient overflow and prevent the exploding gradients, we incorporate a gradient clipping of norm with 5.0 as a limit.

5.3   Evaluation Metrics

Since the attribution value of true salient features is unknown, we measure how most relevant features are represented in the true saliency list for the given anomalous regions. To calculate this, we use Intersection over Union (Jaccard) similarity, Sørensen–Dice (Dice) similarity, and simple Accuracy coefficients to compute the relevance between the annotated features with size n and features with positive attribution score, ordered by their anomaly contributions. The Sørensen–Dice similarity metric is the same as the F1 score and for better representation, we use F1 Score terminology. For a ground truth y and positive attribution set y', ordered by their anomaly contributions, where K is the number of the true anomalous features, the IoU, F1, and Acc similarity coefficients are given as follows:

$$IoU\,(y',y) = \frac{1}{K} \sum \left(\frac{|\{y' \wedge y\}|}{|\{y' \vee y\}|} \right) \tag{4}$$

$$F_1\,(y',y) = \frac{1}{K} \sum \left(\frac{2 \times |\{y' \wedge y\}|}{|\{y' \vee y\}| + |\{y' \wedge y\}|} \right) \tag{5}$$

$$Acc\,(y',y) = \frac{1}{K} \sum \left(\frac{|\{y' \wedge y\}|}{|y'|} \right) \tag{6}$$

For example, for a 7-dimensional observation x_t, a feature attribution score FA_t of {"3":1.5, "1":0.3, "7":0.23, "6":0.2, "4":0.1, "5":−0.3, "2":−0.35} and ground truth GT_t of {"1", "2", "6", "7"}, the evaluation results are $IoU = 0.5$, $F1 = 0.66$, and $Acc = 0.75$.

In some cases, the number of explained features with a positive attribution scores may be larger than the number of true annotated features and sometimes vice-versa as the number of features with the reducing impact on the anomaly is more. The latter happens when only a few numbers of features show enough deviation to propagate through the network and perturb all the outputs that result in high reconstruction error for the given model. The performance of the suggested evaluation metrics depends on the number of elements picked out from the predicted attribution list. Hence, the way in which we combine the attribution result with the ground truth data affects the overall assessment.

To evaluate the interpretability of anomalous regions, we compare real anomalous features data with that of predicted anomalous features. For instance, one of the direct ways to determine which fraction of the attributed futures to use for the comparison is to pick the top n features with the highest attribution score. The number n here is the number of ground truth feature that account for the anomaly. However, this method alone fails to give us sensible reasoning about the capability of the explanation methods. Therefore, we conducted slightly different experiments motivated by the top-k hit ratio which is applied for the recommendation systems [27] to achieve a more extensive and robust evaluation of the performance of the explanation methods. Hence, we employ three different ways to pick out the different numbers of top-k relevant features from the feature attribution list for comparison with the annotated features. The first approach is GT@%120, where instead of selecting the top n features with the highest positive attribution score from the attribution list, we choose the top $n * 120\%$ features.

The purpose is to give the above-mentioned evaluation metrics more flexibility as sometimes some features located close to the top n features in the attribution list are also found in the ground truth list. In the second experiment, FA@%80, we only single out the features that account for 80% of the overall attribution score to understand how well the features with the largest attribution score are represented in the ground truth list. With FA@5, we only use the top 5 features from the calculated attribution list to examine the relevance of the explanation methods regarding human reasoning, as humans inherently are only able to make reasoning about small chunks of information.

6   Results

Finally, we test the saliency Explanation AI methods by connecting them to the reconstruction loss using the wrapper function. We report in Table 1 the localization performance of different saliency Explainable AI approaches over the wrapper of reconstruction error of the LSTM Autoencoder. Moreover, to examine whether the proposed explanation methods are effective, we conduct a baseline evaluation for the LSTM Autoencoder model. In this baseline experiment, we compare the annotated features directly to that of individual reconstruction, scores ordered by their reconstruction error, using the same evaluation metrics motioned in Sect. 5.3. Furthermore, we examined OmniAnomaly [20] localization, which provides interpretations based on the reconstruction probabilities of its constituent univariate time-series with our evaluation metrics to conduct a comparison.

The overall findings in our experiment setting show that all the explanation methods, especially Occlusion, Kernel Shap, and Integrated Gradients methods

Table 1. Localization performance of different saliency Explainable AI approaches over the wrapper of reconstruction error of LSTM Autoencoder.

Approach	GT@120%			AT@80%			AT@5		
	IoU	F1	Acc	IoU	F1	Acc	IoU	F1	Acc
Baseline	43.66	52.45	50.92	32.76	43.24	45.72	37.67	46.84	57.5
OmniAnomaly	44.96	59.77	62.5	42.45	58.17	**70.75**	35.19	50.68	48.22
Occlusion	**64.39**	**76.66**	**73.66**	**62.44**	**75.44**	66.01	**47.04**	**59.18**	**72.5**
Kernel Shap	55.71 ± 0.64	66.50 ± 0.68	64.60 ± 0.76	39.07 ± 0.39	50.04 ± 0.54	66.87 ± 0.51	42.06	53.09	65.0
Shapley Val. Samp.	50.27 ± 1.29	59.68 ± 1.51	60.80 ± 1.61	39.16 ± 0.62	49.73 ± 0.83	46.61 ± 0.97	38.41 ± 1.36	47.87 ± 1.94	48.40 ± 1.53
Gradient Shap.	51.92 ± 2.41	60.18 ± 1.51	60.57 ± 1.51	30.46 ± 0.52	41.37 ± 0.68	60.63 ± 0.66	38.16	47.61	57.5
Integrated Grad.	55.61	65.65	64.26	38.54	49.52	66.25	42.06	53.09	65.0

perform significantly better than the baseline experiment, which supports the positive effect of the explanation methods for anomalous feature localization. We can see that the methods based on the Shapley value estimation yield very similar results in feature explanation. Kernel Shap method, which uses a more elaborate weighted linear regression to estimate the Shapley value, performs better than the rest of the Shapley-based solutions used in the experiment. Nevertheless, these methods indicate some variation that might induce lower stability in practice. This is caused as Kernel Shap, Shapley Value Sampling, and Gradient Shap methods use different estimation techniques to approximate the Shapley values rather than directly calculating them. The same variation is not observed in Ablation and Integrated Gradient methods as the direct solutions are possible for both.

Furthermore, explanation methods based on Ablation, particularly Occlusion, are more robust in inducing anomalous features in multivariate time-series as it outperforms all the other methods significantly for our test case. Though the Occlusion method is not the as sophisticated a method as the remaining ones, the reason that it yields better results might be due to the simple and direct connection between the occluded values (based on good reference values from good training data without any unknown anomaly) and the wrapper function.

We can observe that this result holds the same across all the different top-k ratio experiments. Though the results of the AT@%80 are less relevant than that of GT@%120, the gap between is being not too wide suggests that the features that account for 80% or more fraction of the overall attribution score are mainly rare-event inducing features. The result of *Acc* metric in FA@5, which uses only the attributed feature list as a denominator, demonstrates that the explanation methods such as Occlusion, Integrated Gradient, and Kernel Shap still manage to show significant interpretation ability compared to the baseline method when an only small fraction of feature attribution list is selected. This proves that some of the explanation methods can give considerably interpretation for domain experts in practice when a small number of features with the highest attribution score are selected for self reasoning.

The second baseline method we use is OmniAnomaly localization [20]. Although OmniAnomaly feature localization based on the reconstruction values outperforms the result of that of the baseline based on reconstruction values

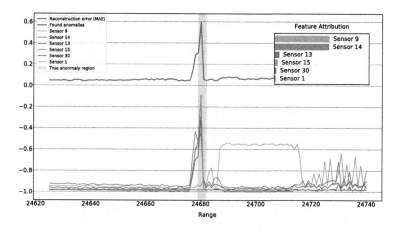

Fig. 3. An example of multi-sensor anomaly detection and localization for the given range between 24675 and 24691. The list of sensors depicted in the figure accounts for 99% of the total attribution score estimated by the Kernel Shap method for the selected range. The sensor attribution result is given in the top-right corner of the figure. The actual salient sensors for that range are 9, 13, 14, and 15th.

from LSTM Autoencoder, it does perform poorer than XAI methods in most of the experiments. This proposes that the explanation methods improve the quality of feature interpretation to a greater extent than the baseline performance conducted even with a better autoencoder architecture.

In Fig. 3, an example of Multi-sensor anomaly detection and Localization for the given range between 24675 and 24691 is demonstrated. The list of sensors depicted in the figure accounts for 99% of the total attribution score estimated by the Kernel Shap method for the selected range. Note that the values of these features are not in their original state as a representation of their scaled values. The sensor attribution result is given in the top-right corner of the figure. The actual salient sensors for that range are 9, 13, 14, and 15 which are the root cause of anomaly in this specific detected anomaly.

7   Conclusion

In this work, we addressed the issue of anomaly localization in an unsupervised multivariate setup. In particular, we focused on the interpretability of LSTM Autoencoders which is one of the state-of-the-art algorithms in Multivariate time-series anomaly detection. To this end, we have applied saliency Explained AI approaches. These approaches could be applied over different families of networks for anomaly detection. As a baseline, we tested these approaches on LSTM Autoencoder and SMD datasets. The explanation could be utilized in unsupervised multivariate anomaly localization. Previous work in Explainable AI has often looked at how to interpret different AI models and contrast their results.

Going forward, we think it is crucial to also investigate applications of Explainable AI. This might include studying the impact of explanations on trusting AI solutions and bridging the gap between AI practitioners and domain experts.

Acknowledgments. Resources used in preparing this research have received funding by the Federal Ministry for Economic Affairs and Climate Action (BMWK) in the research project SPAICER. The collaboration is among partners of the project: German Research Center for Artificial Intelligence (DFKI) and TU Darmstadt. The proposed approach is going to be part of Smart Resilience Services.

References

1. Antwarg, L., Miller, R.M., Shapira, B., Rokach, L.: Explaining anomalies detected by autoencoders using shapley additive explanations. Expert Syst. Appl. **186**, 115736 (2021)
2. Breiman, L.: Random forests. Mach. Learn. **45**(1), 5–32 (2001). https://doi.org/10.1023/A:1010933404324
3. Carletti, M., Masiero, C., Beghi, A., Susto, G.A.: Explainable machine learning in industry 4.0: evaluating feature importance in anomaly detection to enable root cause analysis. In: 2019 IEEE International Conference on Systems, Man and Cybernetics (SMC), pp. 21–26 (2019)
4. Choi, Y., Lim, H., Choi, H., Kim, I.J.: Gan-based anomaly detection and localization of multivariate time series data for power plant. In: 2020 IEEE International Conference on Big Data and Smart Computing (BigComp), pp. 71–74 (2020)
5. Crabbe, J., van der Schaar, M.: Explaining time series predictions with dynamic masks. In: ICML (2021)
6. Fisher, A.J., Rudin, C., Dominici, F.: All models are wrong, but many are useful: learning a variable's importance by studying an entire class of prediction models simultaneously. J. Mach. Learn. Res. JMLR **20**, 1–81 (2019)
7. Geiger, A., Liu, D., Alnegheimish, S., Cuesta-Infante, A., Veeramachaneni, K.: Tadgan: time series anomaly detection using generative adversarial networks. In: 2020 IEEE International Conference on Big Data (Big Data), pp. 33–43 (2020)
8. Hundman, K., Constantinou, V., Laporte, C., Colwell, I., Söderström, T.: Detecting spacecraft anomalies using LSTMS and nonparametric dynamic thresholding. In: Proceedings of the 24th ACM SIGKDD International Conference on Knowledge Discovery and Data Mining (2018)
9. Jiang, R., Fei, H., Huan, J.: Anomaly localization for network data streams with graph joint sparse PCA. In: KDD (2011)
10. Lundberg, S.M., Lee, S.I.: A unified approach to interpreting model predictions. arXiv arXiv:abs/1705.07874 (2017)
11. Malhotra, P., Ramakrishnan, A., Anand, G., Vig, L., Agarwal, P., Shroff, G.: LSTM-based encoder-decoder for multi-sensor anomaly detection. arXiv preprint arXiv:1607.00148 (2016)
12. Meyes, R., Lu, M., de Puiseau, C.W., Meisen, T.: Ablation studies in artificial neural networks. arXiv:abs/1901.08644 (2019)
13. Mozaffari, M., Yılmaz, Y.: Multivariate and online anomaly detection and localization for high-dimensional systems (2019)
14. Mujkanovic, F., Doskoc, V., Schirneck, M., Schäfer, P., Friedrich, T.: Timexplain - a framework for explaining the predictions of time series classifiers. arXiv:abs/2007.07606 (2020)

15. Pan, Q., Hu, W., Zhu, J.: Series saliency: temporal interpretation for multivariate time series forecasting. arXiv abs/2012.09324 (2020)
16. Resta, M., Monreale, A., Bacciu, D.: Occlusion-based explanations in deep recurrent models for biomedical signals. Entropy **23**, 1064 (2021)
17. Ribeiro, M.T., Singh, S., Guestrin, C.: "Why should i trust you?": explaining the predictions of any classifier. In: Proceedings of the 22nd ACM SIGKDD International Conference on Knowledge Discovery and Data Mining (2016)
18. Roelofs, C.M., Lutz, M.A., Faulstich, S., Vogt, S.: Autoencoder-based anomaly root cause analysis for wind turbines (2021)
19. Shankaranarayana, S.M., Runje, D.: Alime: autoencoder based approach for local interpretability. arXiv:abs/1909.02437 (2019)
20. Su, Y., Zhao, Y., Niu, C., Liu, R., Sun, W., Pei, D.: Robust anomaly detection for multivariate time series through stochastic recurrent neural network. In: Proceedings of the 25th ACM SIGKDD International Conference on Knowledge Discovery and Data Mining (2019)
21. Sundararajan, M., Taly, A., Yan, Q.: Axiomatic attribution for deep networks. arXiv:abs/1703.01365 (2017)
22. Suresh, H., Hunt, N., Johnson, A.E.W., Celi, L.A., Szolovits, P., Ghassemi, M.: Clinical intervention prediction and understanding with deep neural networks. In: MLHC (2017)
23. Tonekaboni, S., Joshi, S., Campbell, K., Duvenaud, D.K., Goldenberg, A.: What went wrong and when? Instance-wise feature importance for time-series black-box models. In: NeurIPS (2020)
24. Trifunov, V.T., Shadaydeh, M., Barz, B., Denzler, J.: Anomaly attribution of multivariate time series using counterfactual reasoning. In: 2021 20th IEEE International Conference on Machine Learning and Applications (ICMLA), pp. 166–172 (2021)
25. Vilone, G., Longo, L.: Classification of explainable artificial intelligence methods through their output formats. Mach. Learn. Knowl. Extr. **3**(3), 615–661 (2021)
26. Vilone, G., Longo, L.: Notions of explainability and evaluation approaches for explainable artificial intelligence. Inf. Fusion **76**, 89–106 (2021)
27. Yang, X., Steck, H., Guo, Y., Liu, Y.: On top-k recommendation using social networks. In: Proceedings of the Sixth ACM Conference on Recommender Systems, RecSys 2012, pp. 67–74. Association for Computing Machinery, New York (2012). https://doi.org/10.1145/2365952.2365969
28. Zong, B., et al.: Deep autoencoding gaussian mixture model for unsupervised anomaly detection. In: ICLR (2018)

Author Index

Printed in the United States
by Baker & Taylor Publisher Services